The Descendants of Edmond Reaves (1775 – 1855)

Volume 1 – Register Report of Robert Ryves, Dorset, England

Researched, Compiled and Written by

Reeves Alan Daves

AlanDavesPublishing

Virginia Beach, Virginia, 23464

Contact: AlanDavesPublishing@cox.net

Library of Congress Control Number: 2011909330

ISBN: 0615495524

ISBN-13: 978-0615495521 (AlanDavesPublishing)

Foreword

This first effort at putting my genealogy interest into book form lays the groundwork for future volumes. The book is available in an eBook format as well as this printed version. This book provided an easy and inexpensive way to expand my genealogy hobby and to share some of what I have learned with family and friends. If you learn something from this book or it provides enjoyment in finding out about our ancestors then my goal has been met. The book will be divided into multiple volumes: Volume I contains the Register Report of Robert Ryves and Volume II will contain the detailed genealogy of the ancestors and descendants of William Clemens Reeves.

The release of Volume II will follow this release of Volume I by a few months. I wanted to get this info out as soon as I could to those who have been waiting to read about the Reeves/Reaves genealogy.

There may be missing information or mistakes. If there are mistakes, they are solely my own. You may contact AlanDavesPublishing to correct any information or provide additional information if you desire. Updated information will be available via updated Register Reports and future volumes.

There is a private website for the descendants of Edmond Reaves to share information and access the full information here including the images of the references via Ancestry.com. There is no cost associated with joining this website; however, it is private and you must request access or be invited. The website is: http://www.myfamily.com/group/reevesfamily/. Normally to view family trees on Ancestry.com, you must be a member. The fee for the myfamily.com website is paid by the author to allow family members to access the information, including census images, for the tree on ancestry.com; however, for privacy purposes, you must be a family member to gain access.

Dedication and Acknowledgements

This book is dedicated to my fantastic wife and my three wonderful children.

My wife is very supportive, providing editing assistance and suggestions. I owe her more than just a dedication or thanks, especially for all of the nights when my head was buried in the computer. Thank you!

I also want to take the time to acknowledge those who helped over the last few months. I especially want to thank the members of my extended family who have assisted with portions of the research. The family members who have helped are too many to name but I want to provide a special thank you to a few who were always willing to take the time to help: Lynda Cardwell, Brenda Barnes Huff, and Wendy Reeves Gray.

It has been a joy to get to know many members of my extended family that I never knew or grew up with and did not realize were family. I believe I am already able to count many of those long lost relations as friends.

Reeves Alan Daves, May 2011

"In every conceivable manner, the family is link to our past, bridge to our future."
Alex Haley - American Author

Table of Contents

Preface

Volume I - Register Report of Robert Ryves is a stand-alone document constructed in the recognized standard format for genealogical reports. The report provides basic genealogical facts and details the sources that support those facts. In addition to providing the detailed ancestry of Robert Ryves, the report also provides the factual references that will be used in Volume II - The Ancestors and Descendants of William Clemens Reeves of Etowah County, Alabama.

The Register Report details the direct ancestors of Edmond Reaves back to the earliest known ancestor, Robert Ryves of Dorset, England; however, it provides information on more people than will be discussed in Volume II. Some of the information, beyond the scope of Volume II, has not yet been verified.

This book does not include or discuss any siblings or children that are not in the direct line down to Edmond Reaves (1775 – 1855). Edmond Reaves immigrated with much of his family to Alabama in the early 19th century and is the ancestor of interest to many of the REEVES and REAVES families of Alabama. Volume II will focus on Edmond Reaves' great grandson William Clemens Reeves, William's immediate family and descendants. A more complete discussion of other descendants of Edmond will be included in a future book after Volume II.

As demonstrated in the book, the surname, which started out as RYVES in England, became RIVES in America. In America, the name also changed through the generations. In some cases it changed to REAVES and then to REEVES and in other cases it stayed as RIVES or REAVES. In one case, three sons changed their name to Reaves but their half siblings maintained the Rives spelling. Today the surname that started as Ryves in England is now Rives, Reaves, or Reeves in America.

While this volume is basically a reference book, Volume II will tell a story…a story of the pioneer family of Robert Ryves, that left 16th century France because of religious persecution and established a family seat in Dorset, England. Years later, descendants of Robert Ryves traveled to the American colony of Virginia to escape the political and religious climate in 17th century England. In the 18th century, some members traveled south from Virginia, looking for opportunities opening in North Carolina and some members of the Rives/Reaves family fought in the American Revolution.

Robert Ryves' seventh great grandson Edmond Reaves and much of his family continued their southern migration by moving into Georgia in the early 19th century and settling in Alabama by the middle of that century. Much of the family remained in Alabama as pioneers in the northeastern Alabama Territory and then the new state of Alabama. The Reaves/Reeves family was part of the founding of many towns, communities and churches throughout the new state. Toward the end of the 19th century, many Reaves/Reeves men continued the tradition of service to their community by fighting in the Civil War in Alabama Regiments.

While some family members continued to the western frontier in the 19th century, many of Robert Ryves' descendants settled in modern day Etowah and Calhoun Counties in Alabama, making the area the seat of the modern Reaves/Reeves family. The area of Hokes Bluff, Alabama was where Edmond's son, Nathan Reaves, Nathan's son, John S. Reeves, and grandson, William Clemens Reeves, lived in the 19th and 20th centuries and where, in the 21st century, many of William Clemens Reeves' descendants still remain.

Since the genealogical research continues, the genealogical information is constantly being updated. You may receive an updated electronic copy of the Register Report at no additional cost, by contacting AlanDavesPublishing and providing your date of purchase.

Notes:

1. This Register Report provides the individual reference numbers subsequently used in later volumes. For example, "Robert Ryves (1)" or "(1) Robert Ryves" shows Robert Ryves with the individual reference number 1. The numbering is computer generated for reference purposes only and is not always logical. The "Principal Members of Each Generation" section lists, by generation, family members and their reference numbers.

2. A Principal Member is generally someone who has children discussed in the report.

3. If a name is surrounded by question marks, the name represents a best guess but without documented evidence. Most often the information is from other researchers who also do not have a documented source but may have personal knowledge.

4. Many names appear to be misspelled; however, the spelling represents the transcriptionists best interpretation. If oral or written histories were available, the name was corrected to match the best information available.

5. For privacy purposes, some information, including publically available information, has been deleted. For example, only birth years are given, even when the birth day is readily available in a public records search.

St Peter and St Paul Parish Church

St Peter and St Paul Parish Church, Blandford Forum, Dorset, England

This church was the Parish church of the earliest known ancestor of the Reeves/Reaves family in Alabama – Robert Ryves. The Ryves family played a large role in this Parish Church as indicated by being one of only two families granted a crypt in the church. The Ryves Crypt is under the floor on the north side of the church.

REGISTER REPORT FOR ROBERT RYVES

Generation 1

1.   *Robert Ryves*-1 was born about 1490 in England. He was employed as a Merchant Clothier in 1549 in Dorset, England. He died on 11 Feb 1551 in Blandford Forum, Dorset County, England. Joan (unknown maiden name) was born before 1500. She died on 12 Dec 1560 in Dorset, England. Robert Ryves and Joan (unknown maiden name) were married before 1514. They had the following children:

   i.   (2) John Ryves [1, 2] was born about 1514 in Dorset, England.

Generation 2

2.   *John Ryves*-2 (Robert-1) [1, 2] was born about 1514 in Dorset, England. He died about 1549 in Dorset, England. **Amye Harvey** daughter of John Harvey was born in 1515 in Dorset, England [3]. She died in May 1577 in Dorset, England. John Ryves and Amye Harvey married and had the following children:

   i.   (3) Richard Ryves [4, 1] was born about 1547 in Damory Court, Dorset County, England [5].

Generation 3

3.   *Richard Ryves*-3 (John-2, Robert-1) [4, 1] was born about 1547 in Damory Court, Dorset County, England [5]. He died after 1588. Richard Ryves and Unknown were married in 1577. They had the following children:

   i.   (4) Timothy Ryves [6] was born in Sep 1588 in Oxford, Oxfordshire, England (Parish of St. Mary Magdalen) [6].

Generation 4

4.   *Timothy Ryves*-4 (Richard-3, John-2, Robert-1) [6] was born in Sep 1588 in Oxford, Oxfordshire, England (Parish of St. Mary Magdalen) [6]. He was employed as a Steward of Oxford in 1625 in Oxford, Oxfordshire, England [9]. He died on 30 Sep 1643 in Oxford, Oxfordshire, England [8]. Timothy Ryves and Mary (unknown maiden name) were married before 29 Jul 1615 in Oxford, Oxfordshire, England (St. Mary Magdalen Parish Church) [19]. She died on 08 Nov 1629 in Oxford, Oxfordshire, England [18]. They had the following children:

   i.   Timothy Ryves was born in 1625 in Oxfordshire, England. He died between 1687-1695 in Charles City, Virginia.

Timothy Ryves and Elizabeth (unknown maiden name) were married after 1629 [7]. She died in Aug 1643 in Oxfordshire, England [10]. They had the following children:

i.   (5) William Ryves [11, 12, 13, 14, 15, 16] was born in 1636 in Oxfordshire, England [16].

Generation 5

5.   *William Ryves*-5 (Timothy-4, Richard-3, John-2, Robert-1) [11, 12, 13, 14, 15, 16] was born in 1636 in Oxfordshire, England [16]. He was employed as a Ship Captain, working with cousin Brune Ryves before 1684 in Virginia [20]. He died after 1695 in Virginia [15]. He lived in Virginia [11]. William Ryves and Indian Maiden of the Powhatan Tribe were married after 1652 in Jamestown, Virginia (probably arrived around 1652 as a seaman apprentice.) [17]. They had the following children:

i.   (6) John Rives [21, 22, 23, 24, 25, 26] was born in 1665 in Surry, Virginia [21, 22, 23, 24, 25].

Generation 6

6.   *John Rives*-6 (William-5, Timothy-4, Richard-3, John-2, Robert-1) [21, 22, 23, 24, 25, 26] was born in 1665 in Surry, Virginia [21, 22, 23, 24, 25]. He died in 1720 in Surry, Virginia [22]. **Grace (unknown maiden name) [21]** was born in 1665 in Surrey, Virginia [21]. She died after 1720 in Surry, Virginia [27]. John Rives and Grace (unknown maiden name) married and had the following children:

i.   (7) Richard Rives [28, 29, 30] was born in 1690 in Surry, Virginia [31].

Generation 7

7.   *Richard Rives*-7 (John-6, William-5, Timothy-4, Richard-3, John-2, Robert-1) [28, 29, 30] was born in 1690 in Surry, Virginia [31]. He lived in Pitt, North Carolina in 1761 [28]. He died after 1762 in Pitt, North Carolina [31]. **Dorothy (unknown maiden name)** was born about 1690 in Surry, Virginia. She died in 1748 in Surry, Virginia [31]. Richard Rives and Dorothy (unknown maiden name) were married before 1715 in Surry [32]. They had the following children:

i.   (8) William Rives [33, 34, 35] was born in 1715 in Surry, Virginia [36].

Generation 8

8.   *William Rives*-8 (Richard-7, John-6, William-5, Timothy-4, Richard-3, John-2, Robert-1) [33, 34, 35] was born in 1715 in Surry, Virginia [36]. He lived in Bute, North Carolina about 1767 [36]. He died in 1778 in Bute County, North Carolina, USA [36]. **Frances (unknown maiden name)** was born in 1715 in Surrey County, Virginia. She died on 13 Apr 1751 in Virginia [37]. William Rives and Frances (unknown maiden name) were married in 1738 [36]. They had the following children:

i.   (9) William Rives [38, 39, 40, 41, 42, 43, 33, 44, 45, 46] was born on 01 Jul 1748 in Surry, Virginia [40].

Eleanor (unknown maiden name) was born in 1730. She died after 1778. William Rives and Eleanor (unknown maiden name) were married in 1751 in Virginia [36].

Generation 9

9.   ***William Rives*-9** (William-8, Richard-7, John-6, William-5, Timothy-4, Richard-3, John-2, Robert-1) [38, 39, 40, 41, 42, 43, 33, 44, 45, 46] was born on 01 Jul 1748 in Surry (Sussex), Virginia (Sussex County was named for the English county, and was formed from Surry County in 1753.) [40]. He lived in North Carolina, USA in 1783 [38]. He died on 06 Oct 1828 in Iredell, North Carolina, USA [36]. **Anna ?Smith?** was born in 1750 in Virginia, USA. She died in 1778 in North Carolina, USA. William Rives and Anna ?Smith? were married in 1771 in Virginia. They had the following children:

    i.   Rebecca Rives was born on 04 Jul 1772 in Virginia. She died in 1800 in North Carolina, USA.

    ii.   Smith Rives was born on 22 Sep 1774 in Virginia. He died in 1784 in North Carolina, USA.

    iii.   (10) Eli Rives [47, 48] was born in 1775 in Virginia. He married Maury Lowery on 01 Jan 1817 in Clarke, Alabama, USA [48].

    iv.   (28) Edmond Reaves [49, 50, 51, 52, 53, 54, 55, 56] was born in 1776 in Bute, North Carolina, USA [51].

    v.   (12) Nathan Reaves [58, 59] was born in 1778 in North Carolina, USA.

William Rives and Rebecca Freeman were married after 1790 in Franklin, North Carolina, USA [36].

Generation 10

10.   ***Eli Rives*-10** (William-9, William-8, Richard-7, John-6, William-5, Timothy-4, Richard-3, John-2, Robert-1) [47, 48] was born in 1775 in Virginia. He died on 09 Jan 1850 in Grove Hill, Clarke, Alabama, USA. **Maury Lowery** [48] was born in 1779. She died in 1850 in Grove Hill, Clarke, Alabama, USA. Eli Rives and Maury Lowery were married on 01 Jan 1817 in Clarke, Alabama, USA [48]. They had the following children:

    i.   Stephen Rives was born in 1818 in Grove Hill, Clarke, Alabama, USA.

    ii.   Elbert Rives was born in 1819 in Alabama, USA.

    iii.   J. Rives was born in 1819.

    iv.   (11) William Rives [60] was born on 02 May 1819 in Grove Hill, Clarke, Alabama, USA.

    v.   Mary Rives was born in 1824 in Grove Hill, Clarke, Alabama, USA.

    vi.   Martha Rives was born on 05 Sep 1826 in Grove Hill, Clarke, Alabama, USA. She died on 11 May 1913 in Wayne, Mississippi, USA.

12.   ***Nathan Reaves*-10** (William-9, William-8, Richard-7, John-6, William-5, Timothy-4, Richard-3, John-2, Robert-1) [58, 59] was born in 1778 in North

Carolina, USA. He lived in Marion, Tennessee, USA in 1840 [58]. He died in 1845 in Tennessee, USA. Nathan Reaves and unknown spouse married and had the following children:

    i.   (13) Susan Jane Reaves [61, 62, 63, 64] was born in 1808 in Georgia, USA [61, 62, 63, 64].

28.   *Edmond Reaves*-10 (William-9, William-8, Richard-7, John-6, William-5, Timothy-4, Richard-3, John-2, Robert-1) [49, 50, 51, 52, 53, 54, 55, 56] was born in 1776 in Bute, North Carolina, USA [51]. He lived in Greene, Georgia, USA in May 1802 [65]. He died in 1855 in Benton, Alabama, USA. **Unknown ?Ransom?** [54, 66] was born in 1780 in North Carolina, USA [66]. She died on 05 Jan 1841 in Alabama, USA. She lived in Subdivision 29, Benton, Alabama in 1850 [66]. Edmond Reaves and Unknown ?Ransom? were married on 24 Feb 1798 in North Carolina, USA [54]. They had the following children:

    i.   (29) William Emery Reaves [67, 68, 69, 70, 71, 72, 73] was born in Dec 1798 in North Carolina, USA [67, 68, 69].

    ii.   (133) Ransom Columbus Reaves [74, 75] was born in 1800 in Franklin, North Carolina, USA.

    iii.   (121) Nancy Reaves [76, 77, 78, 79, 80, 81] was born about 1802 in Georgia, USA [76, 77, 78, 79].

    iv.   (150) Nathan Reaves [83, 84, 85, 86, 87, 88, 89, 90, 91, 92, 93, 94, 95, 96, 97, 98, 99] was born in 1808 in Georgia, USA [95, 96, 97, 98].

    v.   (146) Richmond Reaves [100, 101, 102, 103, 104, 105] was born about 1814 in Georgia, USA [100, 101, 102].

    vi.   (145) Emory G. Reaves [107, 108, 109] was born about 1817 in Georgia, USA [107, 108, 109].

    vii.   Unknown Reaves was born about 1820 in Georgia, USA.

Nancy Fisher [66, 57] was born about 1805 in North Carolina, USA [66]. She lived in Subdivision 29, Benton, Alabama, USA in 1850 [66]. Edmond Reaves and Nancy Fisher were married on 07 Dec 1848 in Calhoun, Alabama, USA [56, 57]. They had no children.

Generation 11

11.   *William Rives*-11 (Eli-10, William-9, William-8, Richard-7, John-6, William-5, Timothy-4, Richard-3, John-2, Robert-1) [60] was born on 02 May 1819 in Grove Hill, Clarke, Alabama, USA. He died on 23 Oct 1925. William Rives and unknown spouse married and had the following children:

    i.   ?Susannah? Rives.

    ii.   ?Thomas? Rives.

13.   *Susan Jane Reaves*-11 (Nathan-10, William-9, William-8, Richard-7, John-6, William-5, Timothy-4, Richard-3, John-2, Robert-1) [61, 62, 63, 64] was born in 1808 in Georgia, USA [61, 62, 63, 64]. She lived in Cherokee, Alabama, USA in 1870 [64]. She died on 13 Jul 1889 in Cherokee, Colbert, Alabama, USA.

James Wade Farrar son of John Sanders Farrar and Dorcas Barnett [110, 111, 112, 113, 114, 115, 116] was born about 1805 in Georgia, USA [110, 111, 115, 116]. He lived in Cherokee, Alabama, USA in 1870 [116]. He died on 28 Jun 1894 in Cherokee, Alabama. James Wade Farrar and Susan Jane Reaves married and had the following children:

    i.   Matilda Farrar was born about 1827 in Campbell, Georgia.

    ii.   Mahala Farrar was born on 30 May 1830 in Campbell, Georgia, USA. She died on 14 Jul 1896 in Etowah, Alabama, USA. She married James Young and was the great-great grandmother of Carolyn Jo Young who married Gary Wendell Reeves (63) and the mother of John Thomas Young who married Rebecca Reeves (151).

    iii.   (14) Elizabeth Anna Farrar [117, 118] was born in 1831 in Georgia, USA [117].

    iv.   Kizza Emmaline Farrar was born in 1838 in Campbell, Georgia, USA

    v.   (19) John Thomas Farrar [119, 120, 121] was born in 1839 in Benton County, Alabama, USA [119, 120, 121].

    vi.   James H. Farrar was born in 1842 in Benton County, Alabama, USA.

    vii.   William F. Farrar was born in Feb 1845 in Benton County, Alabama, USA. He died in 1900 in Texas, USA.

    viii.   (27) Winfield Scott Farrar [122, 123, 124, 125, 126, 127] was born in 1847 in Benton County, Alabama, USA [122, 123, 124, 125, 126].

    ix.   (21) Susan Jane Farrar [128, 129, 130, 131, 132] was born on 27 Jun 1851 in Benton County, Alabama, USA [128, 129, 130, 131, 132].

29.   ***William Emery Reaves*-11** (Edmond-10, William-9, William-8, Richard-7, John-6, William-5, Timothy-4, Richard-3, John-2, Robert-1) [67, 68, 69, 70, 71, 72, 73] was born in Dec 1798 in North Carolina, USA [67, 68, 69]. He lived in Subdivision 29, Benton, Alabama in 1850 [69]. He died on 04 Nov 1884 in Calhoun, Alabama, USA. Narcissa Cissy (Polly) Chandler daughter of John Chandler and Elizabeth Camp [134, 135, 136] was born in 1804 in Greenville, Greenville, South Carolina, USA [134, 135, 136]. She lived in Calhoun, Alabama, USA in 1860 [136]. She died in 1860 in Alabama, USA. William Emery Reaves and Narcissa Cissy (Polly) Chandler were married in 1820 in Georgia, USA. They had the following children:

    i.   (30) Elizabeth Reaves [137] was born on 13 Jul 1820 in Walton, Georgia, USA.

    ii.   (82) Caroline Temple Reaves [138, 139, 140] was born on 08 Feb 1823 in Georgia, USA [138, 139, 140].

    iii.   (54) Carter Hill Reaves [141, 142, 143, 144, 145, 146, 147, 148] was born on 26 Sep 1825 in Gwinnett, Georgia, USA [141, 142, 143, 144, 145].

    iv.   (31) William McGuire Reaves [149, 150, 151, 152] was born on 28 Nov 1828 in Gwinnett, Georgia, USA [149, 150, 151].

v.   (88) Emory G. Reaves [153, 154, 155, 156, 157] was born on 29 Jan 1831 in Gwinnett, Georgia, USA [153, 154].

vi.   (87) John Harrison Reaves [158, 159, 160, 161] was born on 15 Jan 1832 in Georgia, USA [158, 159, 160].

vii.   (104) James Washington Reaves [162, 163] was born on 25 Sep 1835 in Benton, Alabama, USA [162].

viii.   (102) David R. Reaves [164, 165, 166, 167, 168] was born on 19 Feb 1837 in Benton, Alabama, USA [164, 165].

ix.   (91) Sarah Ann Marinda Reaves [169, 170, 171, 172, 173, 174, 175] was born on 07 Mar 1839 in Benton, Alabama, USA [171, 172, 173, 174, 175].

x.   Mary Francis Reaves [176] was born on 15 Mar 1841 in Benton, Alabama, USA. She died on 25 Feb 1891 in Calhoun, Alabama, USA.

xi.   (105) Ira Jackson Reaves [177, 178, 179, 180, 181, 182, 183] was born on 26 Jul 1843 in Benton, Alabama, USA [177, 178, 179, 180, 181, 182].

xii.   Tilda Permealie Reaves was born on 16 Jul 1845 in Benton County, Alabama, USA. She died in 1855 in Alabama, USA.

121.   Nancy Reaves-11 (Edmond-10, William-9, William-8, Richard-7, John-6, William-5, Timothy-4, Richard-3, John-2, Robert-1) [76, 77, 78, 79, 80, 81] was born about 1802 in Georgia, USA [76, 77, 78, 79]. She lived in Clanton, Chilton, Alabama, USA in 1880 [79]. She died on 22 Jun 1885 in Alabama, USA. **Caleb Moncrief** son of Caleb Moncrief and Mary Daniel [185, 186, 82] was born in 1792 in Columbia, Georgia, USA. He lived in Montgomery, Alabama, USA in 1835 [186]. He died on 01 Apr 1835 in Montgomery, Alabama, USA [187]. Caleb Moncrief and Nancy Reaves were married on 04 Jul 1820 in Jones, Georgia, USA [82]. They had the following children:

i.   Georgiana Moncrief was born on 01 Jan 1821 in Macon, Bibb, Georgia, USA. She died on 15 Dec 1883 in Clanton, Chilton, Alabama, USA.

ii.   (123) Caleb Jackson Moncrief [188, 189, 190, 191] was born in Mar 1821 in Georgia, USA [188, 189, 190, 191].

iii.   (122) William Moncrief [192, 193] was born on 08 Apr 1829 in Montgomery, Alabama, USA [192, 193].

iv.   Mariah L. Moncrief [194] was born about 1832 in Alabama, USA [194]. She lived in Montgomery, Alabama, USA in 1850 [194].

v.   (131) Mary Missouri Moncrief [195, 196, 197, 198, 199, 200, 201, 202] was born in Aug 1834 in Alabama, USA [195, 196, 197, 198, 199].

133.   Ransom Columbus Reaves-11 (Edmond-10, William-9, William-8, Richard-7, John-6, William-5, Timothy-4, Richard-3, John-2, Robert-1) [74, 75] was born in 1800 in Franklin, North Carolina, USA. He died on 04 Sep 1859 in Pontotoc, Mississippi, USA. **Martha Ann Farrar** daughter of John Sanders Farrar and Dorcas Barnett was born in 1800 in Georgia, USA. She died in 1860. Ransom Columbus Reaves and Martha Ann Farrar were married in 1821 in Walton, Georgia, USA. They had the following children:

i.   (134) John Anderson Reaves [204, 205] was born on 01 Jan 1823 in Gwinnett, Georgia, USA [204].

ii.   Burton William Reaves was born in 1826 in Walton, Georgia, USA. He died on 02 Oct 1872 in Mississippi, USA.

iii.   (141) Cassinda Ann Reaves [206, 207, 208] was born in 1827 in Walton, Georgia, USA [206, 207].

iv.   Susan Arminda Reaves was born in 1827 in Walton, Georgia, USA. She died after Dec 1882.

v.   (140) Edmond Young Reaves [210, 211] was born on 22 Nov 1830 in Campbell, Georgia, USA [211].

vi.   Dorcas Reaves was born in 1834 in Carroll, Georgia, USA.

vii.   James Buchanan Reaves was born in 1835 in Carroll, Georgia, USA. He died on 17 Mar 1888 in California, USA.

viii.   (144) Henry Green Reaves [212, 213] was born on 01 Jan 1837 in Carroll, Georgia, USA [212, 213].

ix.   Wesley Davis Reaves [214] was born on 25 Oct 1838 in Benton County, Alabama, USA [214]. He lived in Pontotoc, Mississippi, USA in 1860 [214]. He died in Mar 1899 in White, Arkansas, USA.

x.   Temperance Jane Reaves was born in 1843 in Benton County, Alabama, USA. She died in 1895 in Wynnewood, Garvin, Oklahoma, USA.

145. ***Emory G. Reaves***-11 (Edmond-10, William-9, William-8, Richard-7, John-6, William-5, Timothy-4, Richard-3, John-2, Robert-1) [107, 108, 109] was born about 1817 in Georgia, USA [107, 108, 109]. He lived in Calhoun, Alabama, USA in 1870 [109]. He died after 1870. **Elizabeth C. (unknown maiden name)** [218, 219] was born about 1821 in Georgia, USA [218, 219]. She lived in Calhoun, Alabama, USA in 1860 [219]. She died between 1860-1869 in Calhoun, Alabama, USA. Emory G. Reaves and Elizabeth C. (unknown maiden name) were married in 1842 in Georgia, USA. They had the following children:

i.   Washington Reaves [220, 221, 222] was born in 1843 in Georgia, USA [220, 221, 222]. He lived in Subdivision 29, Benton, Alabama, USA in 1850 [222].

ii.   Martha Reaves [223, 224] was born in 1848 in Benton County, Alabama, USA [223, 224]. She lived in St Francis, Arkansas, USA in 1870 [223].

iii.   Marion Reaves [225, 226, 227] was born in 1849 in Benton County, Alabama, USA [226, 227]. He lived in Alabama, USA [225].

iv.   Edmond Reaves [228, 229] was born in 1851 in Benton County, Alabama, USA [228, 229]. He lived in Calhoun, Alabama, USA in 1870 [229].

v.   Sarah E. Reaves [230, 231] was born in 1855 in Benton County, Alabama, USA [230, 231]. She lived in Calhoun, Alabama, USA in 1870 [230].

vi.   Andrew Jackson Reaves [232, 233, 234] was born in 1858 in Calhoun, Alabama, USA [232, 233, 234]. He lived in Calhoun, Alabama, USA in 1870 [234].

Sarah Owens [215, 216, 217] was born in 1845 in Alabama, USA [215, 216, 217]. She lived in Calhoun, Alabama, USA in 1870 [215]. Emory G. Reaves and Sarah Owens were married on 02 Nov 1869 in Calhoun, Alabama, USA.

146. ***Richmond Reaves***-11 (Edmond-10, William-9, William-8, Richard-7, John-6, William-5, Timothy-4, Richard-3, John-2, Robert-1) [100, 101, 102, 103, 104, 105] was born about 1814 in Georgia, USA [100, 101, 102]. **Marinda Chandler** daughter of David Chandler and Susan Gunnell [235, 236, 106] was born in 1817 in South Carolina, USA [235, 236]. She lived in Etowah, Alabama, USA in 1870 [236]. She died in 1880. Richmond Reaves and Marinda Chandler were married on 29 Jan 1837 in Benton, Alabama, USA [106, 105]. They had the following children:

    i.   Edmond G. Reaves was born in 1838 in Benton, Alabama.

    ii.   (147) Benjamin W. Reaves [237, 238, 239, 240] was born about 1841 in Calhoun, Alabama, USA [237, 238, 239, 240].

    iii.   Thomas C. Reaves was born in 1846 in Benton, Alabama, USA.

    iv.   Ellen C. (Elizabeth) Reaves was born in 1849.

    v.   William P. Reaves was born in 1849. He died before Oct 1890 in Alabama, USA.

    vi.   (149) Francis M. Reaves [241, 242, 243, 244, 245, 246, 247] was born on 14 Nov 1853 in Alabama, USA [241, 242, 243, 244, 245].

    vii.   John W. Reaves.

150. ***Nathan Reaves***-11 (Edmond-10, William-9, William-8, Richard-7, John-6, William-5, Timothy-4, Richard-3, John-2, Robert-1) [83, 84, 85, 86, 87, 88, 89, 90, 91, 92, 93, 94, 95, 96, 97, 98, 99] was born in 1808 in Georgia, USA [95, 96, 97, 98]. He lived in Hokes Bluff, Etowah, Alabama, USA in 1880 [98]. He died on 03 Mar 1891 in Hokes Bluff, Etowah, Alabama, USA. **Elizabeth A. ?Davis?** was born in 1813 in Georgia, USA. She died on 03 Mar 1881 in Hokes Bluff, Etowah, Alabama, USA. Nathan Reaves and Elizabeth A. ?Davis? were married in 1830 in Georgia, USA. They had the following children:

    i.   (154) John S. Reeves [248, 249, 250, 251, 252, 253, 254, 255, 256, 257] was born about 1828 in Georgia, USA [251, 254].

    ii.   Adam Reeves [258] was born in 1832 in Georgia, USA [258]. He lived in Cherokee, Alabama, USA in 1850 [258].

    iii.   George Reeves [259] was born in 1833 in Georgia, USA [259]. He lived in Cherokee, Alabama, USA in 1850 [259]. He died in Arkansas, USA.

    iv.   Dorcas Reeves was born in 1834.

    v.   Wylie Reeves was born in 1835 in Alabama, USA.

    vi.   (256) Sarah A. Reeves [260] was born in 1838 in Benton County, Alabama, USA [260].

    vii.   (255) Betsy Green Reeves [261, 262] was born in 1840 in Benton, Alabama, USA [261, 262].

viii.	(153) Nancy Ann Reaves [263, 264] was born on 10 Feb 1841 in Alabama, USA [263, 264].
ix.	(151) Rebecca Reeves [265, 266, 267] was born in 1843 in Cherokee, Alabama, USA [265, 266].
x.	Adaline Reeves was born in 1846 in Alabama, USA.
xi.	Dorcas Reeves was born in 1848 in Alabama, USA.
xii.	Robert Vestel Reeves was born in 1850 in Alabama, USA.
xiii.	Cassenda Reeves was born in 1851.
xiv.	Martha K Reeves [268] was born in 1854 in Alabama, USA.

Generation 12

14. *Elizabeth Anna Farrar*-12 (Susan ?Jane?-11, Nathan-10, William-9, William-8, Richard-7, John-6, William-5, Timothy-4, Richard-3, John-2, Robert-1) [117, 118] was born in 1831 in Georgia, USA [117]. She lived in Etowah, Alabama, USA in 1870 [117]. She died after 1870 in Etowah, Alabama, USA. **Joseph Baylis Earle McCollum** [118, 269, 270] was born in 1827 in South Carolina, USA [269, 270]. He lived in Calhoun, Alabama, USA in 1860 [270]. He died on 01 Nov 1862 in Knoxville, Knox, Tennessee, USA. Joseph Baylis Earle McCollum and Elizabeth Anna Farrar were married on 13 Jan 1850 in Benton County, Alabama, USA [118]. They had the following children:

i.	Green Baylis McCollum [271] was born in 1852 in Mississippi, USA [271]. He lived in Calhoun, Alabama, USA in 1860 [271].
ii.	Baylis Earle McCollum was born in Dec 1853 in Benton County, Alabama, USA. He died on 04 May 1912 in Texas, USA.
iii.	Mary A. McCollum was born in Sep 1855 in Benton County, Alabama, USA.
iv.	Irby Wade McCollum [272, 273, 274] was born on 18 Aug 1859 in Calhoun, Alabama, USA [272, 273, 274]. He married Charlsie A. Brannon in 1881 [274]. He lived in Grayson, Texas, USA in 1900 [274]. He died on 30 Oct 1936.
v.	(15) Samantha Alice McCollum [275, 276, 277, 278, 279] was born on 05 Sep 1861 in Calhoun, Alabama, USA [275, 276, 277, 278].

19. *John Thomas Farrar*-12 (Susan ?Jane?-11, Nathan-10, William-9, William-8, Richard-7, John-6, William-5, Timothy-4, Richard-3, John-2, Robert-1) [119, 120, 121] was born in 1839 in Benton County, Alabama, USA [119, 120, 121]. He lived in Calhoun, Alabama, USA in 1860 [121]. He died in Alabama, USA. **Betsy Green Reeves (255)** daughter of Nathan Reaves and Elizabeth A. ?Davis? [261, 262] was born in 1840 in Benton, Alabama, USA [261, 262]. She lived in Gadsden, Etowah, Alabama, USA in 1880 [262]. She died before 1910. John Thomas Farrar and Betsy Green Reeves married and had the following children:

i. Sarah Elizabeth Farrar [281] was born on 15 Nov 1858 in Gadsden, Etowah, Alabama, USA [281]. She lived in Gadsden, Etowah, Alabama, USA in 1880 [281]. She died on 04 Jun 1943 in Van Alstyne, Grayson, Texas, USA.

ii. (20) Frank Joel Farrar [282, 283, 284] was born about 1860 in Centre, Cherokee, Alabama, USA [282, 283].

iii. James T. Farrar [285] was born about 1864 in Alabama, USA [285]. He lived in Gadsden, Etowah, Alabama, USA in 1880 [285].

iv. John M. Farrar [286] was born about 1866 in Alabama, USA [286]. He lived in Gadsden, Etowah, Alabama, USA in 1880 [286].

v. Jefferson W. Farrar was born about 1868 in Alabama, USA. He lived in Gadsden, Etowah, Alabama, USA in 1880 [287]. He died in 1943.

vi. Laura J. Farrar [288] was born about 1872 in Alabama, USA [288]. She lived in Gadsden, Etowah, Alabama, USA in 1880 [288].

21. *Susan Jane Farrar*-12 (Susan ?Jane?-11, Nathan-10, William-9, William-8, Richard-7, John-6, William-5, Timothy-4, Richard-3, John-2, Robert-1) [128, 129, 130, 131, 132] was born on 27 Jun 1851 in Benton County, Alabama, USA [128, 129, 130, 131, 132]. She lived in Piedmont, Calhoun, Alabama, USA in 1910 [132]. She died on 07 Apr 1919 in Cherokee, Alabama, USA. **James Stuely Parker** son of Thomas S. Parker and Mary Sara McFarland [133, 289, 290, 291] was born on 03 Apr 1851 in Alabama, USA [133, 289, 290, 291]. He lived in Cherokee, Alabama, USA in 1870 [291]. He died on 06 Aug 1903 in Cherokee, Alabama, USA. James Stuely Parker and Susan Jane Farrar were married in 1870 in Alabama, USA [133]. They had the following children:

i. Ira Columbus Parker [292, 293] was born on 06 Oct 1870 in Alabama, USA [292, 293]. He lived in Coloma, Cherokee, Alabama, USA in 1900 [293]. He died on 22 Sep 1922 in Alabama, USA.

ii. (22) Alice Parker [294, 295, 296, 297] was born on 16 Apr 1873 in Cherokee, Alabama, USA [294, 295, 296, 297].

iii. Ella Parker was born on 09 Feb 1875 in Cherokee, Alabama, USA. She died on 06 Aug 1903 in Cherokee, Alabama, USA.

iv. Fannie Parker was born on 14 Dec 1875 in Cherokee, Alabama, USA. She died on 05 Feb 1956 in Amarillo, Potter, Texas, USA.

v. (26) Lela Parker [298, 299, 300, 301] was born on 20 Jan 1878 in Cherokee, Alabama, USA [298, 299, 300].

vi. Ada Bell Parker [302, 303] was born on 14 Feb 1880 in Alabama, USA [302, 303]. She lived in Coloma, Cherokee, Alabama, USA in 1900 [303].

vii. Robert E. Parker [304] was born in Oct 1882 in Alabama, USA [304]. He lived in Coloma, Cherokee, Alabama, USA in 1900 [304].

viii. Robert Parker was born on 11 Oct 1884 in Cherokee, Alabama, USA. He died on 11 Oct 1884 in Cherokee, Alabama, USA.

ix. Vallie Pearl Parker [305, 306] was born in Apr 1885 in Alabama, USA [305, 306]. She lived in Piedmont, Calhoun, Alabama, USA in 1910 [306]. She died on 26 Nov 1967 in Cherokee, Alabama, USA.

x. James Vernie Parker [307, 308] was born on 25 Mar 1888 in Alabama, USA [307, 308]. He lived in Piedmont, Calhoun, Alabama, USA in 1910 [308]. He died on 01 Nov 1971 in Cherokee, Alabama, USA.

xi. Abbie Inez Parker [309, 310] was born on 25 Sep 1890 in Alabama, USA [309, 310]. She lived in Piedmont, Calhoun, Alabama, USA in 1910 [310]. She died on 17 Jan 1971 in Cherokee, Alabama, USA.

xii. Corinna Parker was born on 05 Sep 1893 in Cherokee, Alabama, USA. She died in Jun 1923 in Alabama, USA.

27. *Winfield Scott Farrar*-12 (Susan ?Jane?-11, Nathan-10, William-9, William-8, Richard-7, John-6, William-5, Timothy-4, Richard-3, John-2, Robert-1) [122, 123, 124, 125, 126, 127] was born in 1847 in Benton County, Alabama, USA [122, 123, 124, 125, 126]. He lived in Cherokee, Alabama, USA in 1870 [126]. He died on 18 Mar 1922 in Cherokee, Alabama, USA [127]. **Nancy Ann Reaves (153)** daughter of Nathan Reaves and Elizabeth A. ?Davis? [263, 264] was born on 10 Feb 1841 in Alabama, USA [263, 264]. She lived in Ball Play, Cherokee, Alabama, USA in 1900 [264]. She died on 04 Jun 1902 in Cherokee, Alabama, USA. Winfield Scott Farrar (27) and Nancy Ann Reaves were married on 15 Aug 1866 in Calhoun, Alabama, USA [122]. They had the following children:

i. James W. Farrar [311] was born in 1868 in Alabama, USA [311]. He lived in Cherokee, Alabama, USA in 1880 [311].

ii. Cynthia R. Farrar was born on 17 Jun 1870.

iii. Sarah E. Farrar [312] was born on 25 Sep 1878 in Alabama, USA [312]. She lived in Cherokee, Alabama, USA in 1880 [312].

iv. Willis Alexander Farrar was born on 05 Jun 1882 in Cherokee, Alabama, USA. He died on 31 Dec 1950 in Cherokee, Alabama, USA.

v. Isaac Newton Farrar was born on 25 May 1885 in Cherokee, Alabama, USA. He died on 11 Nov 1964 in Cherokee, Alabama, USA.

30. *Elizabeth Reaves*-12 (William Emery-11, Edmond-10, William-9, William-8, Richard-7, John-6, William-5, Timothy-4, Richard-3, John-2, Robert-1) [137] was born on 13 Jul 1820 in Walton, Georgia, USA. She died in 1896 in Jefferson, Alabama, USA. **James C. Sides** was born in 1818 in Benton County, Alabama, USA. He died in 1850. James C. Sides and Elizabeth Reaves were married on 19 Dec 1837 in Benton County, Alabama, USA. They had the following children:

i. Charles Sides was born in 1838.

ii. William Sides was born in 1840 in Georgia, USA.

iii. Narcissa Sides was born in 1842 in Georgia, USA.

iv. James Sides was born in 1843 in Alabama, USA.

v. John D. Sides was born in 1844 in Alabama, USA.

vi. Lucinda Sides was born in 1847 in Arkansas, USA.

vii. Patrick Lord Sides was born on 13 Aug 1851 in Hempstead, Arkansas, USA.

viii.   Dicie Mae Sides was born in 1855 in Arkansas, USA.

ix.   Ozias Denton Sides was born in 1857 in Arkansas, USA.

x.   Sarah Sides was born in 1860 in Hempstead, Arkansas, USA.

31.   ***William McGuire Reaves***-12 (William Emery-11, Edmond-10, William-9, William-8, Richard-7, John-6, William-5, Timothy-4, Richard-3, John-2, Robert-1) [149, 150, 151, 152] was born on 28 Nov 1828 in Gwinnett, Georgia, USA [149, 150, 151]. He lived in Talladega, Alabama, USA in 1870 [151]. He died on 09 Aug 1872 in Calhoun, Alabama, USA [149]. **Margaret Ann Bonds** daughter of Andrew B. Bonds and Lucinda Chandler [313, 314] was born about 1830 in Gwinnett, Georgia, USA [313, 314]. She lived in Talladega, Alabama, USA in 1870 [314]. She died on 23 Mar 1896 in Calhoun, Alabama, USA. William McGuire Reaves and Margaret Ann Bonds were married on 05 Dec 1847 in Benton County, Alabama, USA. They had the following children:

i.   Lucinda J. Reaves was born about 1849.

ii.   (33) Elizabeth Marinda Reaves [315, 316, 317, 318] was born about 1851 in Benton, Alabama, United States [315, 316, 317].

iii.   (32) Pollyann Reaves [319, 320, 321] was born about 1853 in Alabama, USA [319, 320, 321].

iv.   David M. Reaves was born about 1854.

v.   Kizziah Reaves [322, 323] was born about 1855 in Alabama, USA [322, 323]. She died in 1868. She lived in Talladega, Alabama, USA in 1870 [322].

vi.   (38) William Patrick Reaves [324, 325, 326, 327, 328, 329, 330] was born on 19 May 1857 in Calhoun, Alabama, USA [324, 325, 326, 327, 328, 329, 330].

vii.   (48) Andrew Jackson Reaves [331, 332, 232, 333] was born on 19 Sep 1859 in Benton, Alabama, USA [331, 332, 232, 333].

viii.   (47) James Ashley Reaves [334, 335, 336] was born on 15 Nov 1862 in Alabama, USA [334, 335].

ix.   Allie Rosella Reaves [337] was born about 1866 in Alabama, USA [337]. She lived in Talladega, Alabama, USA in 1870 [337].

x.   Caldmon Reaves was born in 1868.

xi.   (53) John Silvanous Reaves [338, 339, 340] was born on 16 Sep 1869 in Talladega, Alabama, USA [338, 339, 340].

xii.   Narcissa E. Reaves was born in Apr 1872.

54.   ***Carter Hill Reaves***-12 (William Emery-11, Edmond-10, William-9, William-8, Richard-7, John-6, William-5, Timothy-4, Richard-3, John-2, Robert-1) [141, 142, 143, 144, 145, 146, 147, 148] was born on 26 Sep 1825 in Gwinnett, Georgia, USA [141, 142, 143, 144, 145]. He lived in Greens Schoolhouse, Calhoun, Alabama, USA in 1900 [145]. He died on 03 Mar 1902 in Calhoun County, Alabama, USA [141]. **Barbra Dale** daughter of George Dale and Barbara Ikard [341, 342, 343] was born in May 1827 in North Carolina, USA [341, 342, 343]. She lived in Greens Schoolhouse, Calhoun, Alabama, USA in 1900

[343]. She died in 1900 in Calhoun, Alabama, USA. Carter Hill Reaves and Barbra Dale were married on 16 Oct 1845 in Benton County, Alabama, USA [145]. They had the following children:

i. Mary Ann Reaves was born in 1847 in Benton County, Alabama, USA. She died in 1929.

ii. (77) William Carey Reaves [344, 345, 346] was born on 02 May 1849 in Benton County, Alabama, USA [344, 345, 346].

iii. (78) George M. D. Reaves [347, 348, 349, 350, 351, 352] was born on 03 May 1849 in Jacksonville, Calhoun, Alabama, USA [347, 348, 349, 350, 351].

iv. Barbara J. Reaves was born about 1851 in Alabama, USA. She died in 1878 in Calhoun, Alabama, USA.

v. (55) Narcissa Reaves [353] was born in Jun 1852 in Benton County, Alabama, USA [353].

vi. Margaret C. Reaves was born about 1855 in Benton County, Alabama, USA.

vii. John L. Reaves was born on 20 Mar 1856 in Benton County, Alabama, USA. He died on 20 Sep 1887.

viii. (58) James Martin Reeves [354, 355, 356, 357, 358, 359, 360, 361] was born on 03 Apr 1857 in Jacksonville, Calhoun, Alabama, USA [354, 355, 356, 357, 358, 359, 360].

ix. Joe Reaves [362] was born in 1858 in Alabama, USA [362]. He lived in Calhoun, Alabama, USA in 1880 [362].

x. Rosina Reaves was born about 1863 in Calhoun, Alabama, USA.

xi. Moses Reaves [363, 364] was born about 1865 in Alabama, USA [363, 364]. He lived in Calhoun, Alabama, USA in 1870 [364].

xii. (73) Belzona Reaves was born in Jul 1867 in Calhoun, Alabama, USA.

xiii. (75) Alice Louisa Reaves [365, 366, 367, 368] was born on 21 Jun 1868 in Calhoun, Alabama, USA [365, 366, 367, 368].

xiv. Jonisa Reaves [370] was born about 1868 in Alabama, USA [370]. She lived in Calhoun, Alabama, USA in 1880 [370].

82. *Caroline Temple Reaves*-12 (William Emery-11, Edmond-10, William-9, William-8, Richard-7, John-6, William-5, Timothy-4, Richard-3, John-2, Robert-1) [138, 139, 140] was born on 08 Feb 1823 in Georgia, USA [138, 139, 140]. She lived in Calhoun, Alabama, USA in 1880 [138]. She died in 1896 in Jefferson, Alabama, USA. **William Frederick Henley** [371] was born in 1820 in Georgia, USA [371]. He lived in Subdivision 29, Benton, Alabama, USA in 1850 [371]. He died about 1855 in Benton County, Alabama, USA. William Frederick Henley and Caroline Temple Reaves were married on 09 Jul 1840 in Benton County, Alabama, USA. They had the following children:

i. (84) Sarah D. Henley [372] was born in 1842 in Alabama, USA [372]. She married ?Henry J. Lambert? in 1858 in Benton, Alabama, USA.

ii. Mary A. Henley [373] was born in 1845 in Alabama, USA [373]. She lived in Calhoun, Alabama, USA in 1860 [373].

13

iii. William G. Henley [374] was born in 1847 in Alabama, USA [374]. He lived in Calhoun, Alabama, USA in 1860 [374].

iv. (85) Tabitha C. Henley [375] was born in 1849 in Alabama, USA [375].

v. Narcissa H. Henley was born in 1852 in Alabama, USA.

vi. (86) James Carter Henley was born in 1854 in Calhoun, Alabama, USA.

John Thomas Kay [376, 377] was born in Dec 1831 in Abbeville County, South Carolina, USA [376, 377]. He lived in Calhoun, Alabama, USA in 1880 [376]. John Thomas Kay and Caroline Temple Reaves were married on 07 Feb 1856 in Benton County, Alabama. They had the following children:

i. James M. Kay [378] was born about 1851 in Alabama, USA [378]. He lived in Calhoun, Alabama, USA in 1880 [378].

ii. Marion T. Kay [379] was born about 1852 in Alabama, USA [379]. He lived in Calhoun, Alabama, USA in 1880 [379].

iii. Rita E. Kay [380] was born in 1858 in Calhoun, Alabama, USA [380]. She lived in Calhoun, Alabama, USA in 1880 [380].

iv. Frances C. Kay [381] was born between 1859-1863 in Calhoun, Alabama, USA [381]. She lived in Calhoun, Alabama, USA in 1880 [381].

v. (83) John G. Kay [382, 383] was born in Mar 1864 in Calhoun, Alabama, USA [382, 383].

87. *John Harrison Reaves*-12 (William Emery-11, Edmond-10, William-9, William-8, Richard-7, John-6, William-5, Timothy-4, Richard-3, John-2, Robert-1) [158, 159, 160, 161] was born on 15 Jan 1832 in Georgia, USA [158, 159, 160]. He lived in Calhoun, Alabama, USA in 1870 [158]. He died on 19 Feb 1906 in Weaver, Calhoun, Alabama, USA. **Elizabeth McCullars** daughter of George David McCullars and Anna Pace was born on 06 Aug 1828 in Franklin, Tennessee, USA. She died on 15 Sep 1906 in Calhoun, Alabama, USA. John Harrison Reaves and Elizabeth McCullars married and had the following children:

i. J. M. L. Reaves was born about 1857.

ii. Theodocia Reaves was born about 1861.

iii. Dordelia Reaves [384] was born about 1867 in Alabama, USA [384, 385]. She lived in Calhoun, Alabama, USA in 1870 [385].

iv. John Reaves was born about 1868.

88. *Emory G. Reaves*-12 (William Emery-11, Edmond-10, William-9, William-8, Richard-7, John-6, William-5, Timothy-4, Richard-3, John-2, Robert-1) [153, 154, 155, 156, 157] was born on 29 Jan 1831 in Gwinnett, Georgia, USA [153, 154]. He lived in Calhoun, Alabama, USA in 1880 [153]. He died on 15 Jun 1892 in Anniston, Calhoun, Alabama, USA. **Elizabeth Ann Davis** daughter of ?Enoch Davis?[389, 390] was born in 1831 in Alabama, USA [389]. She lived in Calhoun, Alabama, USA in 1880 [389]. She died in 1880 in Calhoun, Alabama, USA. Emory G. Reaves and Elizabeth Ann Davis were married on 12 Jan 1848 in Calhoun, Alabama, USA [390]. They had the following children:

i.   Emaline America Reaves was born on 09 Nov 1849 in Alabama, USA.

ii.   William Pinkney Reaves was born on 23 Jun 1850 in Alabama, USA. He died in 1897 in Arkansas, USA.

iii.   Amanda Jane Reaves was born in 1853 in Alabama, USA.

iv.   John Thompson Reaves was born in 1855 in Benton County, Alabama, USA. He died in 1910 in Alabama, USA.

v.   (89) George W. Reaves [391, 392, 393] was born in Aug 1857 in Calhoun, Alabama, USA [391, 392].

vi.   Nancy Ann Reaves [394] was born in 1858 in Alabama, USA [394]. She lived in Calhoun, Alabama, USA in 1880 [394].

vii.   Sarah Elizabeth (Sallie) Reaves [395] was born in 1862 in Alabama, USA [395]. She lived in Calhoun, Alabama, USA in 1880 [395].

viii.   Ira Jackson John Reaves [396] was born in Mar 1866 in Alabama, USA [396]. He lived in Calhoun, Alabama, USA in 1880 [396]. He died in 1911 in Alabama, USA.

ix.   Narcissa C. Reaves was born in 1869 in Calhoun, Alabama, USA. She died on 04 Jul 1927 in Arkansas, USA.

x.   (90) Thomas Edward Reaves [397, 398, 399, 400] was born on 01 Mar 1872 in Alabama, USA [397, 398, 399, 400].

xi.   David Benjamin Reaves [401, 402] was born on 27 Oct 1873 in Alabama, USA [401]. He died on 12 Sep 1953 in Anniston, Calhoun, Alabama, USA [402]. He lived in Calhoun, Alabama, USA [401].

Emory G. Reaves and Susanna Foster were married in Dec 1880 in Calhoun, Alabama, USA. They had the following children:

i.   Lillie Reaves was born in 1881 in Calhoun, Alabama, USA.

ii.   Josie Reaves was born in 1882.

iii.   Zacariah Franklin Reaves [387, 388] was born on 10 Aug 1888 in Alabama, USA [388]. He died on 24 Jun 1954 in Jefferson, Alabama, USA [387]. He lived in Calhoun, Alabama, USA [388].

91.   *Sarah Ann Marinda Reaves*-12 (William Emery-11, Edmond-10, William-9, William-8, Richard-7, John-6, William-5, Timothy-4, Richard-3, John-2, Robert-1) [169, 170, 171, 172, 173, 174, 175] was born on 07 Mar 1839 in Benton, Alabama, USA [171, 172, 173, 174, 175]. She lived in Calhoun, Alabama, USA in 1870 [175]. She died on 14 Jan 1920 in Lincoln, Talladega, Alabama, USA. **James Osburne McCullars** son of George David McCullars and Anna Pace [403, 404, 405, 169, 170] was born on 05 May 1830 in Franklin, Tennessee, USA [403, 404, 405]. He lived in Screven, Georgia, USA in 1870. He died on 12 Apr 1900 in Lincoln, Talladega, Alabama, USA. James Osburne McCullars and Sarah Ann Marinda Reaves married and had the following children:

i.   (97) Mary E. McCullars [406, 407] was born in Jul 1855 in Calhoun, Alabama, USA [406, 407].

ii. (92) David Jackson McCullars [408, 409, 410, 411, 412, 413, 414, 415] was born on 27 Aug 1857 in Weaver, Calhoun, Alabama, USA [408, 409, 410, 411, 412, 413, 414].

iii. J. O. McCullars [416] was born about 1865 in Alabama, USA [416]. He lived in Calhoun, Alabama, USA in 1880 [416].

iv. Ann McCullars [417] was born about 1867 in Alabama, USA [417]. She lived in Calhoun, Alabama, USA in 1880 [417].

v. (100) Samuel M. McCullars [418, 419] was born on 02 Mar 1869 in Calhoun, Alabama, USA [418, 419].

vi. J. M. McCullars [420] was born about 1871 in Alabama, USA [420]. He lived in Calhoun, Alabama, USA in 1880 [420].

vii. M. L. McCullars [421] was born about 1873 in Alabama, USA [421]. She lived in Calhoun, Alabama, USA in 1880 [421].

viii. T. B. McCullars [422] was born about 1875 in Alabama, USA [422]. She lived in Calhoun, Alabama, USA in 1880 [422].

ix. A. T. McCullars [423] was born about 1877 in Alabama, USA [423]. She lived in Calhoun, Alabama, USA in 1880 [423].

x. (101) Josie F. McCullars [424, 425] was born in Jan 1880 in Alabama, USA [424, 425].

102. *David R. Reaves*-12 (William Emery-11, Edmond-10, William-9, William-8, Richard-7, John-6, William-5, Timothy-4, Richard-3, John-2, Robert-1) [164, 165, 166, 167, 168] was born on 19 Feb 1837 in Benton, Alabama, USA [164, 165]. He lived in Calhoun, Alabama, USA in 1880 [165]. He died on 04 Mar 1888 in Calhoun, Alabama, USA [164]. **Charlotte J. "Lottie" Reidinger** daughter of Joseph Reidinger and Emaline Turner was born in 1834 in Calhoun, Alabama, USA. She died about 1875. David R. Reaves and Charlotte J. "Lottie" Reidinger were married on 16 Jan 1856 in Benton, Alabama, USA. They had the following children:

i. James Joseph Reaves was born in 1858 in Calhoun, Alabama, USA.

ii. William A. Reaves was born in 1860 in Alabama, USA. He died before 1870 in Calhoun, Alabama, USA.

iii. N. E. (Sally) Reaves was born in 1862 in Calhoun, Alabama, USA.

iv. Sarah Jane E. Reaves was born in 1866 in Calhoun, Alabama, USA. She died about 1899 in Calhoun, Alabama, USA.

v. David Benjamin Reaves was born on 06 Jan 1870 in Anniston, Calhoun, Alabama, USA. He died in 1930 in Alabama, USA.

vi. Fannie Jane Reaves.

vii. Nancy Matilda Reaves.

viii. Richard McDaniel Reaves.

ix. (103) Mary Ann Reaves [428] was born on 08 Mar 1861 in Calhoun, Alabama, USA [428].

x.   Sarah E. Reaves was born in 1866. She died about 1899 in Talladega, Alabama, USA.

xi.   Caroline Louise Reaves was born in 1872 in Calhoun, Alabama, USA. She died about 1902 in Alabama, USA.

Nancy Matilda Broadway Sullivan [426] was born in 1836 in Alabama, USA [426]. She lived in Calhoun, Alabama, USA in 1880 [426]. David R. Reaves and Nancy Matilda Broadway Sullivan were married on 05 Nov 1875 in Calhoun, Alabama, USA. They had the following children:

i.   Richard McDaniel Reaves [427] was born about 1878 in Calhoun, Alabama, USA [427]. He lived in Calhoun, Alabama, USA in 1880 [427].

104. *James Washington Reaves*-12 (William Emery-11, Edmond-10, William-9, William-8, Richard-7, John-6, William-5, Timothy-4, Richard-3, John-2, Robert-1) [162, 163] was born on 25 Sep 1835 in Benton County, Alabama, USA [162]. He lived in Cherokee, Alabama, USA in 1880 [162]. He died in 1886 in Alabama, USA. **Sarah A. Reeves** (256) daughter of Nathan Reaves and Elizabeth A. ?Davis? [260] was born in 1838 in Benton County, Alabama, USA [260]. She lived in Cherokee, Alabama, USA in 1880 [260]. James Washington Reaves and Sarah A. Reeves married and had the following children:

i.   Marion Reaves [429] was born about 1863 in Alabama, USA [429]. He lived in Cherokee, Alabama, USA in 1880 [429].

ii.   Nancy Reaves [430] was born about 1866 in Alabama, USA [430]. She lived in Cherokee, Alabama, USA in 1880 [430].

iii.   Lucinda Reaves [431] was born about 1869 in Alabama, USA [431]. She lived in Cherokee, Alabama, USA in 1880 [431].

iv.   William Reaves [432] was born about 1872 in Alabama, USA [432]. He lived in Cherokee, Alabama, USA in 1880 [432].

v.   Roda N. Reaves [433] was born about 1875 in Alabama, USA [433]. She lived in Cherokee, Alabama, USA in 1880 [433].

vi.   Beda N. Reaves [434] was born about 1879 in Alabama, USA [434]. She lived in Cherokee, Alabama, USA in 1880 [434].

105. *Ira Jackson Reaves*-12 (William Emery-11, Edmond-10, William-9, William-8, Richard-7, John-6, William-5, Timothy-4, Richard-3, John-2, Robert-1) [177, 178, 179, 180, 181, 182, 183] was born on 26 Jul 1843 in Benton, Alabama, USA [177, 178, 179, 180, 181, 182]. He lived in Talladega, Alabama, USA in 1910 [177]. He died on 17 Feb 1914 in Talladega, Alabama, USA [178]. **Sarah McCullars** daughter of George David McCullars and Anna Pace [183, 435, 436, 437, 438] was born on 28 Jul 1845 in Benton, Alabama, USA [435, 436, 437]. She lived in Subdivision 29, Benton, Alabama, USA in 1850 [435]. She died on 20 Jan 1910 in Calhoun, Alabama, USA. Ira Jackson Reaves and Sarah McCullars were married on 24 Oct 1860 in Calhoun County, Alabama, United States. They had the following children:

i.   (106) Bunyon Rubin Britton Reaves [439, 440, 441, 442, 443, 444] was born on 09 Jun 1866 in Calhoun, Alabama, USA [439, 440, 441, 443, 444].

ii. (112) William David Reaves [445, 446, 447, 448, 449, 450] was born on 17 Jun 1868 in Oxford, Calhoun, Alabama, USA [445, 446, 447, 448].

iii. (111) Sarah Malissa Caroline Reaves [451, 452] was born in Aug 1871 in Alabama, USA [451, 452].

iv. (110) Ellen Marcilea Elizabeth Reaves [454, 455, 456, 457] was born on 09 Mar 1874 in Alabama, USA [454, 455, 456, 457].

v. (118) Amy Kentucky Reaves [458, 459, 460, 461, 462] was born on 09 Mar 1876 in Alabama, USA [458, 459, 460, 461].

vi. Ira Jackson Reaves Jr was born on 26 Aug 1877 in Alabama, USA.

vii. Annice R. Reaves [464] was born on 04 Apr 1880 in Alabama, USA [464]. She lived in Calhoun, Alabama, USA in 1880 [464].

viii. (120) Cynthia Bitty Lugene Reaves was born on 01 Jun 1882 in Alabama, USA.

ix. (119) John Perry Osburne Reaves [465, 466, 467, 468, 469, 470] was born on 29 Mar 1885 in Alabama, USA [465, 466, 467, 468, 469].

Ira Jackson Reaves and Cynthia (unknown maiden name) were married in 1910 [184]. They had no children.

122. *William Moncrief*-12 (Nancy-11, Edmond-10, William-9, William-8, Richard-7, John-6, William-5, Timothy-4, Richard-3, John-2, Robert-1) [192, 193] was born on 08 Apr 1829 in Montgomery, Alabama, USA [192, 193]. He lived in Bibb, Alabama, USA in 1860 [193]. He died about 1875 in Montgomery, Alabama, USA. **Elizabeth Ann Dimon** was born on 06 Jan 1837 in Georgia, USA. She died on 10 May 1896 in Montgomery, Alabama, USA. William Moncrief and Elizabeth Ann Dimon were married on 29 Mar 1866 in Salem, Lee, Alabama, USA. They had the following children:

i. Caleb Moncrief was born on 02 Jun 1868 in Montgomery, Alabama, USA. He died on 30 Sep 1926 in Montgomery, Alabama, USA.

ii. George Marshall Moncrief was born on 24 Jun 1869 in Montgomery, Alabama, USA. He died after 1920.

iii. Mae Nancy Moncrief was born on 17 Jun 1871 in Montgomery, Alabama, USA. She died on 17 Apr 1947 in Washington City, District Of Columbia, USA.

iv. Richard Ellick Moncrief was born on 07 Jun 1873 in Montgomery, Alabama, USA. He died on 07 Jun 1873 in Montgomery, Alabama, USA.

123. *Caleb Jackson Moncrief*-12 (Nancy-11, Edmond-10, William-9, William-8, Richard-7, John-6, William-5, Timothy-4, Richard-3, John-2, Robert-1) [188, 189, 190, 191] was born in Mar 1821 in Georgia, USA [188, 189, 190, 191]. He lived in Claiborne, Louisiana, USA in 1900 [189]. He died on 19 Sep 1909 in Louisiana, USA. **Mary A. ?Knight?** [485] was born about 1828 in Georgia, USA [485]. She lived in Meriwether, Georgia, USA in 1850 [485]. She died about 1852. Caleb Jackson Moncrief and Mary A. ?Knight? were married before 1845. They had the following children:

i. (128) John M. Moncrief [486, 487, 488, 489] was born in Oct 1845 in Georgia, USA [486, 487, 488, 489, 490].

ii. (126) Georgia Ann Moncrief [491, 492] was born about 1847 in Georgia, USA [491, 492].

iii. (124) Mary Jane Moncrief [493, 494] was born on 15 Jan 1848 in Georgia, USA [493, 494].

iv. (129) Henry Alexander Moncrief [496, 497, 498, 499, 500, 501, 502, 503] was born on 20 Jun 1849 in Georgia, USA [496, 497, 498, 499, 500, 501, 502, 503].

Mary A. ?Jones? [471, 472, 473, 474] was born in Aug 1836 in Louisiana, USA [471, 472, 473, 474]. She lived in Union, Louisiana, USA in 1910 [474]. Caleb Jackson Moncrief and Mary A. ?Jones? were married in 1854 [189]. They had the following children:

i. Rebecca E. Moncrief [475] was born about 1856 in Georgia, USA [475]. She lived in Lincoln, Louisiana, USA in 1880 [475].

ii. Sarah F. Moncrief [476] was born about 1858 in Georgia, USA [476]. She lived in Lincoln, Louisiana, USA in 1880 [476].

iii. Della Moncrief [477] was born about 1863 in Arkansas, USA [477]. She lived in Lincoln, Louisiana, USA in 1880 [477].

iv. William F. Moncrief [478] was born about 1866 in Louisiana, USA [478]. He lived in Lincoln, Louisiana, USA in 1880 [478].

v. Annette Moncrief [479] was born about 1868 in Louisiana, USA [479]. She lived in Lincoln, Louisiana, USA in 1880 [479].

vi. Eliza A. Moncrief [480] was born about 1870 in Louisiana, USA [480]. She lived in Lincoln, Louisiana, USA in 1880 [480].

vii. Augustus C. Moncrief [481, 482] was born in Jan 1873 in Louisiana, USA [481, 482]. He lived in Claiborne, Louisiana, USA in 1900 [482].

viii. Josaphine Moncrief [483] was born about 1874 in Louisiana, USA [483]. She lived in Lincoln, Louisiana, USA in 1880 [483].

ix. Claudius O. Moncrief [484] was born about 1879 in Louisiana, USA [484]. He lived in Lincoln, Louisiana, USA in 1880 [484].

131. *Mary Missouri Moncrief*-12 (Nancy-11, Edmond-10, William-9, William-8, Richard-7, John-6, William-5, Timothy-4, Richard-3, John-2, Robert-1) [195, 196, 197, 198, 199, 200, 201, 202] was born in Aug 1834 in Alabama, USA [195, 196, 197, 198, 199]. She lived in Montgomery, Alabama, USA in 1870 [199]. **John Grant** [504, 203, 505] was born on 19 Sep 1826 in New Harmony, Posey, Indiana, USA [504, 203, 505]. He lived in Montgomery, Alabama, USA in 1860 [505]. He died on 09 Nov 1900 in Chilton, Alabama, USA. John Grant and Mary Missouri Moncrief were married on 08 Jun 1854 in Montgomery, Alabama, USA [201, 202, 203]. They had the following children:

i. John D. Grant [506, 507, 508] was born in Aug 1855 in Alabama, USA [506, 507, 508]. He lived in Montgomery, Alabama, USA in 1860 [508].

ii.   (132) Mariah Louise Grant [509, 510, 511] was born on 15 Jul 1857 in Clanton, Chilton, Alabama, USA [509, 510, 511].

iii. William R. Grant [512] was born on 05 Jan 1861 in Alabama, USA [512]. He lived in Clanton, Chilton, Alabama, USA in 1880 [512]. He died on 15 Jul 1896 in the USA.

iv.   Hectorina Kennedy Grant [513, 514] was born on 23 Nov 1870 in Alabama, USA [514]. She lived in Clanton, Chilton, Alabama, USA in 1900 [513].

134.   *John Anderson Reaves*-12 (Ransom Columbus-11, Edmond-10, William-9, William-8, Richard-7, John-6, William-5, Timothy-4, Richard-3, John-2, Robert-1) [204, 205] was born on 01 Jan 1823 in Gwinnett, Georgia, USA [204]. He lived in Pontotoc, Mississippi, USA in 1860 [204]. He died on 16 Oct 1916 in Tippah, Mississippi, USA. **Frances Emily Spencer** was born on 06 Feb 1840. She died on 06 Feb 1912. John Anderson Reaves and Frances Emily Spencer married and had the following children:

i.   Julia Alice Reaves was born on 20 Jan 1865. She died in 1870.

ii.   (138) John Anderson Reaves Jr [515, 516, 517] was born on 18 Sep 1869 in Mississippi, USA [515, 516, 517].

iii. Mary Jane (Janie) Verlie Reaves [518] was born on 03 Sep 1874 [518]. She died on 11 Nov 1975 in Memphis, Shelby, Tennessee, USA.

iv.   (135) Dorothy Reaves [519, 520] was born on 18 Oct 1876 in Monroe, Mississippi, USA [519]. She married Allen Pugh in 1899 [521]. She died in Apr 1983 in Germantown, Shelby, Tennessee, USA [520].

140.   *Edmond Young Reaves*-12 (Ransom Columbus-11, Edmond-10, William-9, William-8, Richard-7, John-6, William-5, Timothy-4, Richard-3, John-2, Robert-1) [210, 211] was born on 22 Nov 1830 in Campbell, Georgia, USA [211]. He lived in Union, Mississippi, USA in 1880 [211]. He died on 02 May 1907 in New Albany, Union, Mississippi, USA. **Lucinda Jane Pitts** daughter of Hiram Pitts and Clarissa Calhoun [522, 523, 210] was born on 10 Jul 1831 in Laurens, South Carolina, USA [522, 523]. She lived in Pontotoc, Mississippi, USA in 1860 [523]. She died on 27 Jul 1911 in New Albany, Union, Mississippi, USA. Edmond Young Reaves and Lucinda Jane Pitts were married on 19 Oct 1850 in Pontotoc, Mississippi, USA [210]. They had the following children:

i.   Joel L. Reeves was born on 01 Nov 1852 in Mississippi, USA.

ii.   John Henry Reeves was born on 12 Nov 1852 in Mississippi, USA. He died on 26 Feb 1900 in Texas, USA.

iii. William Franklin Reaves [524, 525, 526] was born on 11 Dec 1853 in Mississippi, USA [524, 525, 526]. He lived in New Albany, Union, Mississippi, USA in 1920 [526].

iv.   Sarah Elizabeth Reaves [527] was born on 31 Aug 1855 in Mississippi, USA [527]. She died on 24 Nov 1856 in Mississippi, USA. She lived in Tippah, Mississippi, USA in 1860 [527].

v.   Nancy Jane Reaves [528] was born about 1858 in Mississippi, USA [528]. She lived in Union, Mississippi, USA in 1880 [528].

vi. Martha Ann Reeves was born on 16 Jul 1859 in New Albany, Union, Mississippi, USA. She died on 25 Jan 1940 in Mississippi, USA.

vii. James Reuben Reaves [529] was born about 1862 in Mississippi, USA [529]. He lived in Union, Mississippi, USA in 1880 [529].

viii. Druory J. Reaves [530] was born about 1864 in Mississippi, USA [530]. He lived in Union, Mississippi, USA in 1880 [530].

ix. Chester Young Reaves [531] was born about 1868 in Mississippi, USA [531]. He lived in Union, Mississippi, USA in 1880 [531]. He died on 16 Jun 1949 in New Albany, Union, Mississippi, USA.

x. Emma Katherine Reaves [532] was born on 08 Mar 1869 in Mississippi, USA [532]. She lived in Union, Mississippi, USA in 1880 [532]. She died on 05 Sep 1911 in Mississippi, USA.

141. *Cassinda Ann Reaves*-12 (Ransom Columbus-11, Edmond-10, William-9, William-8, Richard-7, John-6, William-5, Timothy-4, Richard-3, John-2, Robert-1) [206, 207, 208] was born in 1827 in Walton, Georgia, USA [206, 207]. She lived in Hopkins, Texas, USA in 1900 [207]. She died in 1905 in Hopkins, Texas, USA. **Elijah Baker Jr** son of Elijah Baker Sr and Mary Wiley [208, 209] was born in 1813 in North Carolina, USA. He died in Texas, USA. Elijah Baker Jr and Cassinda Ann Reaves were married on 21 Jul 1840 in Calhoun, Alabama, USA [209]. They had the following children:

i. Edmund Wiley Baker was born in 1849 in Mississippi, USA. He died on 08 Jun 1919 in Cardwell, Dunklin, Missouri, USA.

ii. Eli W. Baker was born in 1851 in Mississippi, USA. He died on 03 Feb 1938 in Clay, Missouri, USA.

iii. John Baker.

iv. Sarah Amanda Baker [533, 534] was born in 1843 in Cherokee, Alabama, USA [533]. She lived in Red River, Texas, USA in 1870 [533]. She died In 1881 in Hopkins, Texas, USA.

v. (142) Elijah Baker [535, 536, 537] was born on 09 Dec 1853 in Pontotoc, Mississippi, USA [535, 536, 537].

vi. James Mathew Baker was born on 13 Dec 1854 in Pontotoc, Mississippi, USA. He died on 07 Nov 1923 in Hopkins, Texas, USA.

vii. Martha J. Baker was born in 1857 in Pontotoc, Pontotoc, Mississippi, USA. She died on 28 Feb 1938 in Greene, Arkansas, USA.

viii. (143) Texas Lucy Baker [538, 539, 540, 541] was born in Oct 1862 in Mississippi, USA [538, 539, 540, 541].

144. *Henry Green Reaves*-12 (Ransom Columbus-11, Edmond-10, William-9, William-8, Richard-7, John-6, William-5, Timothy-4, Richard-3, John-2, Robert-1) [212, 213] was born on 01 Jan 1837 in Carroll, Georgia, USA [212, 213]. He lived in Dyer, Tennessee, USA in 1880 [212]. He died in Dyer, Tennessee, USA. **Virginia (unknown maiden name)** was born about 1843 in Pontotoc, Mississippi, USA [543]. She lived in Dyer, Tennessee, USA in 1880 [543]. Henry

Green Reaves and Virginia (unknown maiden name) married and had the following children:

    i.   Ellen Reaves [544] was born about 1866 in Tennessee, USA [544]. She lived in Dyer, Tennessee, USA in 1880 [544].

    ii.   Thomas Reaves [545] was born about 1872 in Tennessee, USA [545]. He lived in Dyer, Tennessee, USA in 1880 [545].

    iii.   William Reaves [546] was born about 1874 in Tennessee, USA [546]. He lived in Dyer, Tennessee, USA in 1880 [546].

147. Benjamin W. Reaves-12 (Richmond-11, Edmond-10, William-9, William-8, Richard-7, John-6, William-5, Timothy-4, Richard-3, John-2, Robert-1) [237, 238, 239, 240] was born about 1841 in Calhoun, Alabama, USA [237, 238, 239, 240]. He lived in Ball Play, Etowah, Alabama, USA in 1880 [237]. He died in 1905 in Alabama, USA. **Phoebia Ann Ship** [547] was born about 1843 in Tennessee, USA [547]. She lived in Ball Play, Etowah, Alabama, USA in 1880 [547]. She died in Alabama, USA. Benjamin W. Reaves and Phoebia Ann Ship were married in 1863. They had the following children:

    i.   John Hamilton Reeves [548] was born in 1861 in Alabama, USA [548]. He lived in Ball Play, Etowah, Alabama, USA in 1880 [548].

    ii.   David Reeves [549] was born in Apr 1864 in Alabama, USA [549]. He lived in Ball Play, Etowah, Alabama, USA in 1880 [549].

    iii.   Hamilton Reeves [548] was born about 1866 in Alabama, USA [548]. He lived in Ball Play, Etowah, Alabama, USA in 1880 [548].

    iv.   Ellen Clementine Reeves [550] was born in 1869. She lived in Ball Play, Etowah, Alabama, USA in 1880 [550].

    v.   Judge D. Reeves [551, 552] was born in 1870 in Alabama, USA [551, 552]. He lived in Ball Play, Etowah, Alabama, USA in 1880 [551].

    vi.   (148) James Franklin Reeves [553, 554, 555, 556] was born on 04 Oct 1874 in Attalla, Etowah, Alabama, USA [553, 554, 555, 556]. He died on 30 Aug 1941 in Etowah, Alabama, USA.

    vii.   Sarah F. Reeves [557] was born in 1876 in Alabama, USA [557]. She lived in Ball Play, Etowah, Alabama, USA in 1880 [557].

    viii.   Narcissus Reeves [558, 559] was born in Dec 1876 in Alabama, USA [558, 559]. She lived in Hokes Bluff, Etowah, Alabama, USA in 1900 [559].

    ix.   Fannie B. Reeves [560] was born in Oct 1883 in Alabama, USA [560]. She lived in Hokes Bluff, Etowah, Alabama, USA in 1900 [560]. She died in 1923 in Alabama, USA.

149. Francis M. Reaves-12 (Richmond-11, Edmond-10, William-9, William-8, Richard-7, John-6, William-5, Timothy-4, Richard-3, John-2, Robert-1) [241, 242, 243, 244, 245, 246, 247] was born on 14 Nov 1853 in Alabama, USA [241, 242, 243, 244, 245]. He lived in Camp, Texas, USA in 1920 [245]. He died on 15 Sep 1933 in Camp, Texas, USA [247]. **Margaret Chappell** [571] was born about 1855 in Alabama, USA [571]. She lived in Etowah, Alabama, USA in 1880 [571].

Francis M. Reaves and Margaret (unknown maiden name) married and had the following children:

   i.   Calvin John Reaves [572, 573] was born in Jan 1877 in Alabama, USA [572, 573]. He lived in Camp, Texas, USA in 1900 [573].

   ii.   Marietta Reaves [574] was born about 1878 in Alabama, USA [574]. She lived in Etowah, Alabama, USA in 1880 [574].

   iii. Josie Reaves [575] was born about 1880 in Alabama, USA [575]. He lived in Etowah, Alabama, USA in 1880 [575]. He lived in Camp, Texas, USA in 1900 [564].

   iv.   Arthur Reeves [564] was born in Oct 1881 in Alabama, USA [564]. He lived in Camp, Texas, USA in 1900 [564].

   v.   Ida Reeves [565] was born in Sep 1883 in Alabama, USA [565]. She lived in Camp, Texas, USA in 1900 [565].

   vi.   Ernest Reeves [566] was born in Feb 1887 in Alabama, USA [566]. He lived in Camp, Texas, USA in 1900 [566].

   vii. Esland Reeves [567] was born in Dec 1888 in Alabama, USA [567]. She lived in Camp, Texas, USA in 1900 [567].

   viii. Eva Reeves [568] was born in Aug 1891 in Alabama, USA [568]. She lived in Camp, Texas, USA in 1900 [568].

   ix.   Ada Reeves [569] was born in Dec 1893 in Alabama, USA [569]. She lived in Camp, Texas, USA in 1900 [569].

   x.   Alma Reeves [570] was born in Oct 1896 in Alabama, USA [570]. She lived in Camp, Texas, USA in 1900 [570].

151. *Rebecca Reeves*-12 (Nathan-11, Edmond-10, William-9, William-8, Richard-7, John-6, William-5, Timothy-4, Richard-3, John-2, Robert-1) [265, 266, 267] was born in 1843 in Cherokee, Alabama, USA [265, 266]. She lived in Hokes Bluff, Etowah, Alabama, USA in 1920 [265]. She died on 29 Jan 1921 in Etowah, Alabama, USA [267]. **John Thomas Young** [577] was born on 13 Feb 1848 in Alabama, USA [577], son of Mahala Farrar and James Young. He lived in Cherokee, Alabama, USA in 1880 [577]. He died on 13 May 1902. John Thomas Young and Rebecca Reeves were married on 26 Jul 1863 in Alabama, USA. They had the following children:

   i.   James N. Young [578, 579, 580, 581] was born on 09 Apr 1865 in Alabama, USA [578, 579, 580, 581]. He married Emily F. (Unknown maiden name) in 1897 [580]. He lived in Hokes Bluff, Etowah, Alabama, USA in 1930 [581]. He died in Somme, Picardie, France.

   ii.   Lucinda J. Young [582] was born on 26 Feb 1868 in Alabama, USA [582]. She lived in Cherokee, Alabama, USA in 1880 [582].

   iii. Canzadia Young [583, 576] was born on 14 Jan 1871 in Alabama, USA [583, 576]. She lived in Hokes Bluff, Etowah, Alabama, USA in 1920 [576]. She died on 19 Feb 1920.

   iv.   Joseph Lapolian Young was born on 10 Jul 1873 in Alabama, USA. He died on 24 Mar 1900.

23

v.   Fannie Florence Young [584] was born on 19 Oct 1876 in Alabama, USA [584]. She lived in Cherokee, Alabama, USA in 1880 [584]. She died in 1961.

vi.   (152) Sarah Irene Young [585, 586, 587] was born on 14 Jan 1882 in Cherokee, Alabama, USA [585, 586].

153.   *Nancy Ann Reaves*-12 (Nathan-11, Edmond-10, William-9, William-8, Richard-7, John-6, William-5, Timothy-4, Richard-3, John-2, Robert-1) [263, 264] was born on 10 Feb 1841 in Alabama, USA [263, 264]. She lived in Ball Play, Cherokee, Alabama, USA in 1900 [264]. She died on 04 Jun 1902 in Cherokee, Alabama, USA. **Winfield Scott Farrar (27)** son of James Wade Farrar and Susan Jane Reaves [122, 123, 124, 125, 126, 127] was born in 1847 in Benton County, Alabama, USA [122, 123, 124, 125, 126]. He lived in Cherokee, Alabama, USA in 1870 [126]. He died on 18 Mar 1922 in Cherokee, Alabama, USA [127]. Winfield Scott Farrar and Nancy Ann Reaves were married on 15 Aug 1866 in Calhoun, Alabama, USA [122]. They had the following children:

i.   James W. Farrar [311] was born in 1868 in Alabama, USA [311]. He lived in Cherokee, Alabama, USA in 1880 [311].

ii.   Cynthia R. Farrar was born on 17 Jun 1870.

iii.   Sarah E. Farrar [312] was born on 25 Sep 1878 in Alabama, USA [312]. She lived in Cherokee, Alabama, USA in 1880 [312].

iv.   Willis Alexander Farrar was born on 05 Jun 1882 in Cherokee, Alabama, USA. He died on 31 Dec 1950 in Cherokee, Alabama, USA.

v.   Isaac Newton Farrar was born on 25 May 1885 in Cherokee, Alabama, USA. He died on 11 Nov 1964 in Cherokee, Alabama, USA.

154.   *John S. Reeves*-12 (Nathan-11, Edmond-10, William-9, William-8, Richard-7, John-6, William-5, Timothy-4, Richard-3, John-2, Robert-1) [248, 249, 250, 251, 252, 253, 254, 255, 256, 257] was born about 1828 in Georgia, USA [251, 254]. He died before Mar 1863 (in the service of the Confederate States of America). He lived in Alabama, USA [248]. **Rhoda Shaw** [250, 588, 589, 590, 591] was born on 19 Oct 1831 in Georgia, USA [588, 589, 590, 591]. She lived in Hokes Bluff, Etowah, Alabama, USA in 1900 [591]. She died on 13 Nov 1907 in Etowah, Alabama, USA. John S. Reeves and Rhoda Shaw were married on 25 Apr 1847 in Benton County, Alabama [249, 250]. They had the following children:

i.   (155) Irena D. Reeves [592, 593, 594, 595, 596, 597] was born in Feb 1847 in Alabama, USA [592, 593, 594, 595].

ii.   (250) Lucinda Jane Reeves [598, 599, 600, 601, 602, 603, 604, 605] was born on 05 Oct 1848 in Alabama, USA [598, 599, 600, 601, 602, 603, 604].

iii.   (249) John H. Reeves [606, 607, 608, 609] was born about 1849 in Alabama, USA [606, 607, 608, 609].

iv.   (158) William Clemens Reeves [610, 611, 612, 613, 614, 615] was born on 25 Feb 1853 in Etowah, Alabama, USA [611, 612, 614, 615].

v.   (251) Nathan C. Reeves [617, 618, 619, 620, 621, 622, 623] was born on 10 Mar 1857 in Alabama, USA [619, 620, 621].

vi.   C. B. Lafayette Reeves [626, 627] was born about 1860. He died in Jan 1926 in Calhoun, Alabama, USA [626].

vii.   (254) James H. Reeves [628] was born about 1863 in Alabama, USA [628].

255. *Betsy Green Reeves*-12 (Nathan-11, Edmond-10, William-9, William-8, Richard-7, John-6, William-5, Timothy-4, Richard-3, John-2, Robert-1) [261, 262] was born in 1840 in Benton County, Alabama, USA [261, 262]. She lived in Gadsden, Etowah, Alabama, USA in 1880 [262]. She died before 1910. **John Thomas Farrar (19)** son of James Wade Farrar and Susan Jane Reaves [119, 120, 121] was born in 1839 in Benton County, Alabama, USA [119, 120, 121]. He lived in Calhoun, Alabama, USA in 1860 [121]. He died in Alabama, USA. John Thomas Farrar and Betsy Green Reeves married and had the following children:

i.   Sarah Elizabeth Farrar [281] was born on 15 Nov 1858 in Gadsden, Etowah, Alabama, USA [281].

ii.   (20) Frank Joel Farrar [282, 283, 284] was born about 1860 in Centre, Cherokee, Alabama, USA [282, 283].

iii.   James T. Farrar [285] was born about 1864 in Alabama, USA [285]. He lived in Gadsden, Etowah, Alabama, USA in 1880 [285].

iv.   John M. Farrar [286] was born about 1866 in Alabama, USA [286]. He lived in Gadsden, Etowah, Alabama, USA in 1880 [286].

v.   Jefferson W. Farrar was born about 1868 in Alabama, USA. He lived in Gadsden, Etowah, Alabama, USA in 1880 [287].He died in 1943.

vi.   Laura J. Farrar [288] was born about 1872 in Alabama, USA [288]. She lived in Gadsden, Etowah, Alabama, USA in 1880 [288].

256. *Sarah A. Reeves*-12 (Nathan-11, Edmond-10, William-9, William-8, Richard-7, John-6, William-5, Timothy-4, Richard-3, John-2, Robert-1) [260] was born in 1838 in Benton County, Alabama, USA [260]. She lived in Cherokee, Alabama, USA in 1880 [260]. **James Washington Reaves** son of William Emery Reaves and Narcissa Cissy (Polly) Chandler [162, 163] was born on 25 Sep 1835 in Benton County, Alabama, USA [162]. He lived in Cherokee, Alabama, USA in 1880 [162]. He died in 1886 in Alabama, USA. James Washington Reaves and Sarah A. Reeves married and had the following children:

i.   Marion Reaves [429] was born about 1863 in Alabama, USA [429]. He lived in Cherokee, Alabama, USA in 1880 [429].

ii.   Nancy Reaves [430] was born about 1866 in Alabama, USA [430]. She lived in Cherokee, Alabama, USA in 1880 [430].

iii.   Lucinda Reaves [431] was born about 1869 in Alabama, USA [431]. She lived in Cherokee, Alabama, USA in 1880 [431].

iv.   William Reaves [432] was born about 1872 in Alabama, USA [432]. He lived in Cherokee, Alabama, USA in 1880 [432].

v.   Roda N. Reaves [433] was born about 1875 in Alabama, USA [433]. She lived in Cherokee, Alabama, USA in 1880 [433].

vi.   Beda N. Reaves [434] was born about 1879 in Alabama, USA [434]. She lived in Cherokee, Alabama, USA in 1880 [434].

Generation 13

15.   *Samantha Alice McCollum*-13 (Elizabeth Anna-12, Susan ?Jane?-11, Nathan-10, William-9, William-8, Richard-7, John-6, William-5, Timothy-4, Richard-3, John-2, Robert-1) [275, 276, 277, 278, 279] was born on 05 Sep 1861 in Calhoun, Alabama, USA [275, 276, 277, 278]. She lived in Piedmont, Calhoun, Alabama, USA in 1910 [278]. She died on 15 Apr 1926 in Spring Garden, Cherokee, Alabama, USA [279]. **William Riley Batey** [280, 629, 630, 631, 632, 633] was born on 21 Jul 1861 in Paulding, Georgia, USA [280, 629, 630, 631, 632]. He lived in Greens Schoolhouse, Calhoun, Alabama, USA in 1930 [632]. He died on 10 Jan 1939 in Spring Garden, Cherokee, Alabama, USA [633]. William Riley Batey and Samantha Alice McCollum were married on 17 Jan 1884 in Cherokee, Alabama, USA [280]. They had the following children:

i.   (16) Winfield Frank Batey [634, 635, 636] was born in Mar 1885 in Cherokee, Alabama, USA [634, 635, 636].

ii.   (17) Shelby Alloway Batey [637, 638, 639, 640, 641, 642] was born on 12 Nov 1886 in Alabama, USA [637, 638, 639, 640, 641].

iii.   Shaley Batey [637] was born in 1887 in Alabama, USA [637]. He lived in Piedmont, Calhoun, Alabama, USA in 1910 [637].

iv.   George W. Batey [643, 644] was born in Feb 1889 in Cherokee, Alabama, USA [643, 644]. He lived in Piedmont, Calhoun, Alabama, USA in 1910 [644]. He died on 04 May 1956 in Alabama, USA.

v.   Anna (Annie) Alistra Celestra Batey was born on 10 Nov 1890 in Cherokee, Alabama, USA. She lived in Coloma, Cherokee, Alabama, USA in 1900 [645].

vi.   Harry B. Batey [646] was born in Jan 1893 in Alabama, USA [646]. He lived in Coloma, Cherokee, Alabama, USA in 1900 [646].

vii.   (18) Lela Ruth Batey [647, 648, 649, 650, 651] was born on 22 Mar 1896 in Cherokee, Alabama, USA [647, 648, 649, 650, 651].

viii.   Thomas Kaiser Batey [652] was born in Apr 1899 in Cherokee, Alabama, USA [652]. He lived in Coloma, Cherokee, Alabama, USA in 1900 [652]. He died on 06 Jun 1979 in Anniston, Calhoun, Alabama, USA.

20.   *Frank Joel Farrar*-13 (John Thomas-12, Susan Jane-11, Nathan-10, William-9, William-8, Richard-7, John-6, William-5, Timothy-4, Richard-3, John-2, Robert-1) [282, 283, 284] was born about 1860 in Centre, Cherokee, Alabama, USA [282, 283]. He lived in Gadsden, Etowah, Alabama, USA in 1930 [283]. He died on 19 Jan 1935 in Gadsden, Etowah, Alabama, USA. **Eula Farrar** [653, 654] was born about 1871 in Georgia, USA [653, 654]. She lived in Gadsden, Etowah, Alabama, USA in 1930 [654]. Frank Joel Farrar and Eula Farrar married and had the following children:

i.   Guthrie Farrar [655] was born about 1899 in Alabama, USA [655]. He lived in Gadsden, Etowah, Alabama, USA in 1920 [655].

ii. Edna Farrar [656, 657] was born about 1907 in Alabama, USA [656, 657]. She lived in Gadsden, Etowah, Alabama, USA in 1930 [657].

22. Alice Parker-13 (Susan Jane-12, Susan ?Jane?-11, Nathan-10, William-9, William-8, Richard-7, John-6, William-5, Timothy-4, Richard-3, John-2, Robert-1) [294, 295, 296, 297] was born on 16 Apr 1873 in Cherokee, Alabama, USA [294, 295, 296, 297]. She lived in Borger, Hutchinson, Texas, USA in 1930 [297]. She died on 04 Nov 1953 in Hobbs, Lea, New Mexico, USA. **Marcus Houston Smith** [658, 659, 660, 661, 662] was born on 13 Feb 1868 in Cherokee, Alabama, USA [658, 659, 660, 661, 662]. He lived in Cherokee, Alabama, USA in 1880 [662]. He died on 18 Jan 1941 in Hobbs, Lea, New Mexico, USA. Marcus Houston Smith and Alice Parker were married on 22 Mar 1891 in Cherokee, Alabama, USA. They had the following children:

i. (23) Vernie Leroy Smith [663, 664, 665, 666, 667] was born on 31 May 1893 in Denton, Denton, Texas, USA [663, 664, 665, 666, 667]. He died on 23 Nov 1979 in Henryetta, Okmulgee, Oklahoma, USA [663].

ii. Lilla Zina Smith was born on 22 Nov 1894 in Denton, Denton, Texas, USA. She lived in Coalgate, Coal, Oklahoma, USA in 1910 [668]. She died on 02 May 1913 in Coalgate, Coal, Oklahoma, USA.

iii. (24) Gertrude Vashti Smith [669, 670, 671, 672] was born on 19 May 1896 in Conroe, Montgomery, Texas, USA [669, 670, 671, 672].

iv. (25) James Harrison Smith [673, 674, 675, 676, 677] was born on 09 Nov 1899 in Gainesville, Cooke, Texas, USA [673, 674, 675, 676, 677].

v. Lola Mae Smith [678, 679] was born on 08 Sep 1903 in Henryetta, Okmulgee, Oklahoma, USA [678, 679]. She lived in Henry, Okmulgee, Oklahoma, USA in 1920 [679]. She died on 04 Jan 1991 in Richmond, Virginia, USA.

vi. Robert Bryan Smith [680, 681, 682, 683] was born on 29 May 1906 in Coalgate, Coal, Oklahoma, USA [680, 681, 682, 683]. He lived in Henry, Okmulgee, Oklahoma, USA in 1920 [683]. He died on 03 Feb 1984 in Lee, Florida, USA [681, 682].

vii. Robert L. Smith [680] was born in 1907 in Oklahoma [680]. He lived in Coalgate, Coal, Oklahoma, USA in 1910 [680].

viii. Marcus Houston "Dusty" Smith, Jr [684, 685, 686] was born on 07 Feb 1909 in Coalgate, Coal, Oklahoma, USA [684, 685, 686]. He lived in Borger, Hutchinson, Texas, USA in 1930 [686]. He died in Mar 1973 in Denver, Denver, Colorado, USA.

ix. Lerette Smith [687] was born about 1914 in Oklahoma, USA [687]. She lived in Henry, Okmulgee, Oklahoma, USA in 1920 [687].

x. Ausburn Gordon Smith was born on 08 Dec 1915 in Henryetta, Okmulgee, Oklahoma, USA [688]. He lived in Henry, Okmulgee, Oklahoma, USA in 1920 [688]. He died on 29 Jul 1963 in Moffat, Colorado, USA.

26. Lela Parker-13 (Susan Jane-12, Susan Jane-11, Nathan-10, William-9, William-8, Richard-7, John-6, William-5, Timothy-4, Richard-3, John-2, Robert-1) [298, 299, 300, 301] was born on 20 Jan 1878 in Cherokee, Alabama, USA [298,

299, 300]. She lived in Cherokee, Alabama, USA in 1880 [300]. She died in Jul 1976 in Birmingham, Jefferson, Alabama, USA [298]. **John Patterson Rankin** [689] was born in 1879 in Alabama, USA [689]. He lived in Coloma, Cherokee, Alabama, USA in 1910 [689]. John Patterson Rankin and Lela Parker married and had the following children:

    i.   Cordia J. Rankin [690] was born in 1902 in Alabama, USA [690]. She lived in Coloma, Cherokee, Alabama, USA in 1910 [690].

    ii.   Lillian E. Rankin [691] was born in 1904 in Alabama, USA [691]. She lived in Coloma, Cherokee, Alabama, USA in 1910 [691].

    iii.   Melvin J. Rankin [692] was born in 1906 in Alabama, USA [692]. He lived in Coloma, Cherokee, Alabama, USA in 1910 [692].

    iv.   Olian M. Rankin [693] was born about 1910 in Alabama, USA [693]. He lived in Coloma, Cherokee, Alabama, USA in 1910 [693].

32.   ***Pollyann Reaves***-13 (William McGuire-12, William Emery-11, Edmond-10, William-9, William-8, Richard-7, John-6, William-5, Timothy-4, Richard-3, John-2, Robert-1) [319, 320, 321] was born about 1853 in Alabama, USA [319, 320, 321]. She lived in Calhoun, Alabama, USA in 1880 [319]. She died on 13 Feb 1882 in Anniston, Calhoun, Alabama, USA. **William F. Wells** [694] was born about 1840 in North Carolina, USA [694]. He lived in Calhoun, Alabama, USA in 1880 [694]. William F. Wells and Pollyann Reaves married and had the following children:

    i.   Edward Wells [695] was born about 1872 in Alabama, USA [695]. He lived in Calhoun, Alabama, USA in 1880 [695].

    ii.   William Wells [696] was born about 1874 in Alabama, USA [696]. He lived in Calhoun, Alabama, USA in 1880 [696].

    iii.   Wyly G. Wells [697] was born about 1876 in Alabama, USA [697]. He lived in Calhoun, Alabama, USA in 1880 [697].

    iv.   Ellen Wells [698] was born about 1878 in Alabama, USA [698]. She lived in Calhoun, Alabama, USA in 1880 [698].

33.   ***Elizabeth Marinda Reaves***-13 (William McGuire-12, William Emery-11, Edmond-10, William-9, William-8, Richard-7, John-6, William-5, Timothy-4, Richard-3, John-2, Robert-1) [315, 316, 317, 318] was born about 1851 in Benton, Alabama, United States [315, 316, 317]. She lived in Renfroe, Talladega, Alabama, USA in 1920 [317]. She died on 26 Feb 1925 in Talladega, Alabama, USA [318]. **Winford B. Henley** son of Jefferson Henley and Pernesia Bonds [699] was born on 08 Dec 1851 in Alabama, USA [700, 699]. He lived in Talladega, Alabama, USA in 1870 [700]. He died on 18 Nov 1933 in Talladega, Talladega, Alabama, USA. Winford B. Henley and Elizabeth Marinda Reaves married and had the following children:

    i.   Linley Henley was born on 06 Nov 1870 in the USA. He died in the USA.

    ii.   (34) William Monroe Henley [701, 702, 703, 704] was born on 12 Mar 1872 in Alabama, USA [701, 702, 703].

iii. Maggie Henley was born on 14 Mar 1874 in the USA. She died on 15 Nov 1902 in Talladega, Talladega, Alabama, USA.

iv. Mary Lou Henley was born on 24 Jun 1876. She died on 27 Oct 1958.

v. (37) Porter Wallace Henley [705, 706, 707] was born on 22 Apr 1878 in Alabama, USA [705, 706].

vi. Ida Henley was born on 23 Nov 1880 in the USA. She died on 04 Oct 1910 in the USA.

vii. Minnie Mae Henley was born on 13 May 1885 in the USA. She died on 23 Sep 1901 in Talladega, Talladega, Alabama, USA.

viii. Winford Clyde Henley was born on 03 May 1892. He died in the USA.

38. **_William Patrick Reaves_**-13 (William McGuire-12, William Emery-11, Edmond-10, William-9, William-8, Richard-7, John-6, William-5, Timothy-4, Richard-3, John-2, Robert-1) [324, 325, 326, 327, 328, 329, 330] was born on 19 May 1857 in Calhoun, Alabama, USA [324, 325, 326, 327, 328, 329, 330]. He lived in Munford, Talladega, Alabama, USA in 1920 [330]. He died on 04 Dec 1929 in Anniston, Calhoun, Alabama, USA. **Mary Ann Reaves** daughter of David R. Reaves and Charlotte J. "Lottie" Reidinger [428] was born on 08 Mar 1861 in Calhoun, Alabama, USA [428]. She lived in Calhoun, Alabama, USA in 1880 [428]. She died on 05 Jan 1891 in Calhoun, Alabama, USA. William Patrick Reaves and Mary Ann Reaves married and had the following children:

i. (39) Sylvester Reaves [729, 730, 731, 732, 733, 734] was born on 25 Aug1878 in Anniston, Calhoun, Alabama, USA [729, 730, 731, 732, 733].

ii. Mary Jane (Jenny) Reaves was born on 02 Jul 1880 in Anniston, Calhoun, Alabama, USA. She died on 30 Sep 1953 in Anniston, Calhoun, Alabama, USA.

iii. (41) William Monroe Reaves [735, 736] was born in Jun 1882 in Alabama, USA [735, 736].

iv. (40) Margie Belle Reaves [737] was born on 23 Jan 1884 in Alabama, USA [737].

v. Henry Walker Reaves was born on 05 Feb 1886 in Anniston, Calhoun, Alabama, USA. He died in Jun 1888 in Anniston, Calhoun, Alabama, USA.

vi. Rosa Annie Reaves [738] was born on 13 Nov 1887 in Alabama, USA [738]. She lived in Calhoun, Alabama, USA in 1900 [738]. She died on 15 Jul 1910.

vii. (42) Lula Merendia Reaves [739] was born on 15 Jan 1890 in Alabama, USA [739].

Cicilia (Sisly) Ida Bice daughter of William Richard Bice and Millie Bertha Beaty [708] was born on 04 Feb 1876 in Anniston, Calhoun, Alabama, USA [708, 709]. She lived in Anniston, Calhoun, Alabama, USA in 1910 [708]. She died on 29 Oct 1917 in Anniston, Calhoun, Alabama, USA. William Patrick Reaves and Cicilia (Sisly) Ida Bice were married about 1891 [327]. They had the following children:

i. Lillie Etta Reaves [710] was born in Feb 1893 in Alabama, USA [710]. She lived in Calhoun, Alabama, USA in 1900 [710].

ii. (44) Ida Lee Reaves [711, 712, 713] was born on 20 Dec 1894 in Alabama, USA [711, 712, 713].

iii. (43) Minnie Mae Reaves [714, 715, 716, 717, 718] was born on 07 Dec 1896 in Alabama, USA [714, 715, 716, 717, 718].

iv. (46) Richard Patrick Reaves [719, 720, 721] was born on 23 Jun 1899 in Alabama, USA [719, 720, 721].

v. Era Betha Reaves [722] was born about 1902 in Alabama, USA [722]. She lived in Anniston, Calhoun, Alabama, USA in 1910 [722].

vi. (45) Josie Elva Reaves [723, 724] was born on 31 Aug 1903 in Alabama, USA [723, 724].

vii. Robert Jackson Reaves [725, 726, 727] was born about 1906 in Alabama, USA [725, 726, 727]. He lived in Chattahoochee, Georgia, USA in 1930 [725]. He died on 31 May 1975 in Gadsden, Etowah, Alabama, USA.

viii. Flora Ocile Reaves [728] was born about 1909 in Alabama, USA [728]. She lived in Anniston, Calhoun, Alabama, USA in 1910 [728].

ix. Allie Nerine Reaves was born on 02 Jul 1911 in Anniston, Calhoun, Alabama, USA. She died on 12 May 1996 in San Diego, California, USA.

47. **James Ashley Reaves**-13 (William McGuire-12, William Emery-11, Edmond-10, William-9, William-8, Richard-7, John-6, William-5, Timothy-4, Richard-3, John-2, Robert-1) was born on 15 Nov 1862 in Alabama, USA. He lived in Anniston, Calhoun, Alabama, USA in 1920. He died on 20 Dec 1943 in Calhoun, Alabama, USA. **Sarah Elizabeth Reaves** daughter of David R. Reaves and Charlotte J. "Lottie" Reidinger was born in 1866 in Alabama, USA. She lived in Calhoun, Alabama, USA in 1880. She died about 1899 in Talladega, Alabama, USA. James Ashley Reaves and Sarah Elizabeth Reaves were married on 04 Aug 1883 in Calhoun, Alabama, USA. They had the following children:

i. Anna Reaves was born on 07 May 1891 in Calhoun, Alabama, USA. She died on 16 Dec 1961 in Calhoun, Alabama, USA.

ii. William Forest Reaves was born on 17 May 1894. He died in 1971 in Birmingham, Jefferson, Alabama, USA.

iii. James Porter Reaves was born on 08 May 1897 in Talladega, Alabama, USA. He married Lula or Lola Dutton on 24 Apr 1920 in Calhoun, Alabama, USA. He died on 25 Aug 1951 in Calhoun, Alabama, USA.

Louiza ?Crawford? was born about 1876 in Alabama, USA. She lived in Anniston, Calhoun, Alabama, USA in 1920. James Ashley Reaves and Louiza ?Crawford? married. They had the following children:

i. Grady Reaves was born about 1899 in Alabama, USA. He lived in Anniston, Calhoun, Alabama, USA in 1920.

ii. Mary Lou Reaves was born about 1910 in Alabama, USA. She lived in Anniston, Calhoun, Alabama, USA in 1920.

48. **Andrew Jackson Reaves**-13 (William McGuire-12, William Emery-11, Edmond-10, William-9, William-8, Richard-7, John-6, William-5, Timothy-4, Richard-3, John-2, Robert-1) [331, 332, 232, 333] was born on 19 Sep 1859 in Calhoun County, Alabama, USA [331, 332, 232, 333]. He lived in Redland,

Hempstead, Arkansas, USA in 1910 [331]. He died on 20 Feb 1918 in Hempstead, Arkansas, USA. **Margaret (Maggie) Horton** was born in 1868 in Talladega, Alabama, USA. She died in 1896 in Hempstead, Arkansas, USA. Andrew Jackson Reaves and Margaret (Maggie) Horton married and had the following children:

    i.   (51) Margaret Elizabeth (Lizzie) Reaves [744, 745] was born on 05 Mar 1884 in Alabama, USA [744, 745].

    ii. (50) Andrew Walter Reaves [746, 747, 748, 749] was born on 17 Aug 1887 in Calhoun, Alabama, USA [746, 747, 748, 749].

    iii. (49) Sydney Jackson Reaves [750, 751, 752, 753, 754, 755] was born on 08 Jul 1890 in Alabama, USA [750, 751, 752, 753, 754].

Nora Hall daughter of Mary E. (unknown maiden name) [756, 757, 758, 759] was born on 11 Oct 1879 in Indiana, USA [756, 757, 758]. She lived in Redland, Hempstead, Arkansas, USA in 1910 [756]. She died on 15 Mar 1970 in McCaskill, Hempstead, Arkansas, USA [758]. Andrew Jackson Reaves and Nora Hall married and had the following children:

    i.   Flosie B. Reeves [760] was born in 1900 in Arkansas, USA [760]. She lived in Redland, Hempstead, Arkansas, USA in 1910 [760].

    ii. Clifford O. Reeves [761, 762] was born in 1904 in Arkansas, USA [761, 762]. He lived in Hope, Hempstead, Arkansas, USA in 1930 [761].

    iii. (52) Otha Lee Reeves [763, 764, 765] was born on 05 Feb 1906 in Hempstead, Arkansas, USA [763, 764, 766, 767]. He married Lucille E. Borsenberger on 07 Feb 1926. He died on 20 Jul 1981 in McCaskill, Hempstead, Arkansas, USA [763].

    iv. Vaughnie N. Reeves [768] was born in 1909 in Arkansas, USA [768]. He lived in Redland, Hempstead, Arkansas, USA in 1910 [768].

53.   *John Silvanous Reaves*-13 (William McGuire-12, William Emery-11, Edmond-10, William-9, William-8, Richard-7, John-6, William-5, Timothy-4, Richard-3, John-2, Robert-1) [338, 339, 340] was born on 16 Sep 1869 in Talladega, Alabama, USA [338, 339, 340]. He lived in Talladega, Alabama, USA in 1870 [338]. He died on 16 Jul 1929 in Anniston, Calhoun, Alabama, USA. **Rena H. (unknown maiden name)** [769, 770] was born in Feb 1870 in Alabama, USA [769, 770]. She lived in Anniston, Calhoun, Alabama, USA in 1910 [769]. John Silvanous Reaves and Rena H. (unknown maiden name) were married in 1888 [339]. They had the following children:

    i.   Sidney J. Reaves [771] [772] was born in Sep 1893 in Alabama, USA [771]. He lived in Anniston, Calhoun, Alabama, USA in 1900 [771]. He lived in Anniston, Calhoun, Alabama, USA in 1910 [772].

55.   *Narcissa Reaves*-13 (Carter Hill-12, William Emery-11, Edmond-10, William-9, William-8, Richard-7, John-6, William-5, Timothy-4, Richard-3, John-2, Robert-1) [353] was born in Jun 1852 in Benton County, Alabama, USA [353]. She lived in Greens Schoolhouse, Calhoun, Alabama, USA in 1910 [353]. She died after 1910 in Calhoun, Alabama, USA. **Cephas Andrew Ledbetter** was born on 02 Nov 1850 in Anderson, South Carolina, USA. He died in 1891 in Jacksonville, Calhoun, Alabama, USA. Cephas Andrew Ledbetter and Narcissa Reaves were married on 16 Dec 1873 in Calhoun, Alabama, USA. They had the following children:

<ol type="i">
<li>Albert Monroe Ledbetter was born on 15 Oct 1875 in Jacksonville, Calhoun, Alabama, USA. He died on 02 Jun 1929 in Miami, Dade, Florida, USA.</li>
<li>Andrew Harrison Ledbetter was born in Feb 1878 in Jacksonville, Calhoun, Alabama, USA. He died in 1936 in Miami, Dade, Florida, USA.</li>
<li>Lee Ronie Rosie Rosetta Ledbetter was born on 07 Apr 1881 in Jacksonville, Calhoun, Alabama, USA. She died on 18 Mar 1918.</li>
<li>(57) James Wesley Ledbetter [773, 774] was born on 10 Nov 1883 in Jacksonville, Calhoun, Alabama, USA [773, 774].</li>
<li>(56) Collie Peyton Ledbetter was born on 10 May 1886 in Jacksonville, Calhoun, Alabama, USA [775, 776, 777].</li>
<li>Luther Gaston Ledbetter was born on 01 Aug 1887 in Jacksonville, Calhoun, Alabama, USA. He died on 19 Nov 1945 in Atlanta, Fulton, Georgia, USA.</li>
<li>Lucy Jane Ledbetter was born on 12 Aug 1889 in Jacksonville, Calhoun, Alabama, USA. She died on 26 Sep 1947 in Piedmont, Calhoun, Alabama, USA.</li>
<li>Turner Hill Ledbetter was born on 11 Jun 1891 in Jacksonville, Calhoun, Alabama, USA. He died on 15 Feb 1937 in Birmingham, Jefferson, Alabama, USA.</li>
</ol>

58.   *James Martin Reeves*-13 (Carter Hill-12, William Emery-11, Edmond-10, William-9, William-8, Richard-7, John-6, William-5, Timothy-4, Richard-3, John-2, Robert-1) [354, 355, 356, 357, 358, 359, 360, 361] was born on 03 Apr 1857 in Jacksonville, Calhoun, Alabama, USA [354, 355, 356, 357, 358, 359, 360]. He lived in Greens Schoolhouse, Calhoun, Alabama, USA in 1910 [360]. He died on 07 Jul 1940 in Calhoun, Alabama, USA [361]. **Mary E. Holder** daughter of Green Berry Holder and Mary Ann Rhodes [780, 781, 782, 783] was born on 10 Mar 1852 in Georgia, USA [781, 782, 783, 784]. She lived in Greens Schoolhouse, Calhoun, Alabama, USA in 1900 [781]. She died on 23 Mar 1916 in Calhoun, Alabama, USA [780]. James Martin Reeves and Mary E. Holder were married in 1875 in Calhoun, Alabama, USA [358]. They had the following children:

<ol type="i">
<li>Mittie E. Reeves [785] was born about 1873 in Georgia, USA [785]. She lived in Webster, Georgia, USA in 1880 [785].</li>
<li>(66) Robert Joseph Reaves [786] was born on 23 Nov 1875 in Calhoun, Alabama, USA [786]. He died on 24 Jan 1949 in Calhoun, Alabama, USA.</li>
<li>Conealia Z. Reeves [787] was born about 1875 in Georgia, USA [787]. She lived in Webster, Georgia, USA in 1880 [787].</li>
<li>(59) Barbara Mary Ann Reaves [788, 789, 790] was born on 30 May 1877 in Calhoun, Alabama, USA [788, 789, 790].</li>
<li>(68) Walter Thomas Reaves [792, 793, 794] was born on 26 Feb 1879 in Jacksonville, Calhoun, Alabama, USA [792, 793, 794].</li>
</ol>

vi.   (67) Frances Elizabeth Reaves [795, 796] was born on 11 Mar 1880 in Alabama, USA [795, 796].

vii.   Lillie Mae Reaves [798] was born on 19 Mar 1881 in Alabama, USA [798]. She lived in Greens Schoolhouse, Calhoun, Alabama, USA in 1900 [798]. She died on 30 Jun 1990 in Harris, Texas, USA.

viii.   Benjamin Franklin Reaves [799, 800] was born on 12 Feb 1883 in Calhoun, Alabama, USA [800]. He lived in Greens Schoolhouse, Calhoun, Alabama, USA in 1900 [800]. He married Alabama Dempsey on 22 Jan 1908. He died on 17 Mar 1934 in Calhoun, Alabama, USA [799].

ix.   Greene B. Reaves was born on 22 Nov 1885 in Jacksonville, Calhoun, Alabama, USA. He died on 09 Aug 1886 in Jacksonville, Calhoun, Alabama, USA.

x.   Lilla Reaves [798] was born in Mar 1887 in Alabama, USA [798]. She lived in Greens Schoolhouse, Calhoun, Alabama, USA in 1900 [798].

xi.   Daughter Reaves was born on 01 Nov 1887 in Jacksonville, Calhoun, Alabama, USA. She died on 04 Dec 1887 in Jacksonville, Calhoun, Alabama, USA.

xii.   (71) Samuel George Reaves [801, 802, 803, 804] was born on 04 Nov 1889 in Alabama, USA [801, 802, 803].

xiii.   Ella Matt Reaves [805] was born in Jan 1892 in Alabama, USA [805]. She lived in Greens Schoolhouse, Calhoun, Alabama, USA in 1900 [805]. She died on 23 Nov 1981.

xiv.   John Nathaniel Reaves [806, 807, 808] was born on 07 Jan 1892 in Jacksonville, Calhoun, Alabama, USA [806, 807, 808]. He lived in Greens Schoolhouse, Calhoun, Alabama, USA in 1910 [806]. He married ?Mary Elizabeth McKee? about 1919. He died on 24 Oct 1961 in Gadsden, Etowah, Alabama, USA.

xv.   (72) Levi Hilton Reaves [809, 810, 811, 812] was born on 04 Mar 1894 in Jacksonville, Calhoun, Alabama, USA [809, 810, 811, 812].

Mary Willie Hendrix [779] was born on 17 Oct 1889 in Alabama, USA [779]. She lived in Greens Schoolhouse, Calhoun, Alabama, USA in 1920 [779]. She died on 08 Sep 1930. James Martin Reeves and Mary Willie Hendrix were married after 1916. They had the following children:

i.   James Oscar Reaves was born on 27 Dec 1921 in Alabama, USA. He died on 20 Jul 1927 in Alabama, USA.

73.   *Belzona Reaves*-13 (Carter Hill-12, William Emery-11, Edmond-10, William-9, William-8, Richard-7, John-6, William-5, Timothy-4, Richard-3, John-2, Robert-1) was born in Jul 1867 in Calhoun, Alabama, USA. She died in Dec 1938 in Calhoun, Alabama, USA. **Henry L. Couch** son of John S. Couch and Jamima Demeris Woolf was born about 1858 in Alabama, USA. He died before 1910. Henry L. Couch and Belzona Reaves were married on 27 Jul 1879 in Calhoun, Alabama, USA. They had the following children:

i.   Rosa Lee Couch was born in 1880 in Calhoun, Alabama, USA. She died in 1922 in Anniston, Calhoun, Alabama, USA.

ii.   May A. Couch was born on 02 May 1883 in Calhoun, Alabama, USA. She died on 19 Jul 1949 in Calhoun, Alabama, USA.

iii. (74) Malvin L. Couch [813, 814, 815] was born on 21 May 1885 in Calhoun, Alabama, USA [813, 814, 815, 816].

iv.   Mary Frances Couch was born on 28 Jan 1887 in Calhoun, Alabama, USA. She died on 19 Aug 1965 in Calhoun, Alabama, USA.

v.   Oma Mandy Couch was born on 29 Oct 1891 in Calhoun, Alabama, USA. She died on 26 Sep 1935 in Calhoun, Alabama, USA.

vi.   Pearl Couch was born in Jun 1892 in Alabama, USA.

75.   ***Alice Louisa Reaves*-13** (Carter Hill-12, William Emery-11, Edmond-10, William-9, William-8, Richard-7, John-6, William-5, Timothy-4, Richard-3, John-2, Robert-1) [365, 366, 367, 368] was born on 21 Jun 1868 in Calhoun, Alabama, USA [365, 366, 367, 368]. She lived in Hollingsworth, Calhoun, Alabama, USA in 1930 [368]. She died on 19 Jan 1946 in Calhoun, Alabama, USA. **Levi Brickenridge Dempsey** [817, 818, 819, 820, 369, 821] was born on 15 May 1864 in Alabama, USA [817, 818, 819, 820]. He lived in Hollingsworth, Calhoun, Alabama, USA in 1930 [820]. He died on 25 Aug 1944 in Calhoun, Alabama, USA. Levi Brickenridge Dempsey and Alice Louisa Reaves were married on 12 Sep 1885 in Calhoun, Alabama, USA [369]. They had the following children:

i.   Arthur W. Dempsey [822] was born in Apr 1887 in Alabama, USA [822]. He lived in Anniston, Calhoun, Alabama, USA in 1900 [822]. He died on 19 Mar 1956 in Calhoun, Alabama, USA.

ii.   Thomas Milton Dempsey [823, 824] was born on 29 Apr 1888 in Alabama, USA [823, 824]. He lived in Ball Play, Etowah, Alabama, USA in 1910 [824]. He died on 04 May 1953 in Piedmont, Calhoun, Alabama, USA.

iii. (76) Lucy Dempsey [825, 826, 827, 828, 829] was born on 01 Jul 1889 in Alabama, USA [825, 826, 827, 828]. She died on 15 Sep 1948 in Calhoun, Alabama, USA [829].

iv.   Alabama Dempsey [830] was born in Jan 1892 in Alabama, USA [830]. She lived in Anniston, Calhoun, Alabama, USA in 1900 [830]. She married Benjamin Franklin Reaves on 22 Jan 1908. She died on 26 Mar 1985 in Calhoun, Alabama, USA.

v.   John Dempsey [831, 832] was born in May 1892 in Alabama, USA [831, 832]. He lived in Ball Play, Etowah, Alabama, USA in 1910 [832].

vi.   Lee R. Dempsey [833, 834] was born in Aug 1893 in Alabama, USA [833, 834]. He lived in Ball Play, Etowah, Alabama, USA in 1910 [834]. He died on 18 Aug 1964.

vii. Etta Dempsey [835, 836] was born in Aug 1896 in Alabama, USA [835]. She lived in Ball Play, Etowah, Alabama, USA in 1910 [835].

viii. Florence Dempsey [837, 838] was born on 12 Aug 1899 in Alabama, USA [837]. She lived in Ball Play, Etowah, Alabama, USA in 1910 [837]. She died on 17 Aug 1978 in Patterson, Putnam, New York, USA.

ix. Lou Ollie Dempsey [839, 840] was born about 1900 in Alabama, USA [839, 840]. She lived in Hollingsworth, Calhoun, Alabama, USA in 1930 [840].

x. Ola M. Dempsey [841, 842] was born about 1904 in Alabama, USA [841, 842]. She lived in Ball Play, Etowah, Alabama, USA in 1910 [842].

77. ***William Carey Reaves**-13 (Carter Hill-12, William Emery-11, Edmond-10, William-9, William-8, Richard-7, John-6, William-5, Timothy-4, Richard-3, John-2, Robert-1) [344, 345, 346] was born on 02 May 1849 in Benton County, Alabama, USA [344, 345, 346]. He lived in Silver Run, Talladega, Alabama, USA in 1920 [346]. He died on 23 Oct 1925 in Calhoun, Alabama, USA. **Mary Ann Elizabeth (Polly Ann) Dale** daughter of George Dale and Mary Mahala Bonds was born on 17 Sep 1849 in Alabama, USA. She lived in Calhoun, Alabama, USA in 1880. She died on 21 Jan 1921 in Oxford, Calhoun, Alabama, USA. William Carey Reaves and Mary Ann Elizabeth (Polly Ann) Dale were married in 1869. They had the following children:

i. Louisa Jane Reaves was born on 11 Feb 1872 in Calhoun, Alabama, USA. She married Joe D. Humphries in 1890. She died on 26 Apr 1932 in Calhoun, Alabama, USA.

ii. William Jackson Reaves was born in Dec 1872 in Alabama, USA. He lived in Calhoun, Alabama, USA in 1880. He died on 20 Aug 1958.

iii. Alfred Mark Reaves was born on 09 Oct 1873 in Calhoun, Alabama, USA. He married Ada Lelia Reaves on 12 Jan 1896 in Calhoun, Alabama, USA. He died on 04 Apr 1948 in Calhoun, Alabama, USA.

iv. Mary Emma Reaves was born on 01 Mar 1875 in Calhoun, Alabama, USA. She lived in Calhoun, Alabama, USA in 1880. She died on 15 Jul 1959 in Calhoun, Alabama, USA.

v. Emily Reaves was born about 1877 in Alabama, USA. She lived in Calhoun, Alabama, USA in 1880. She died before 20 Aug 1958.

vi. Clem Park Reaves was born on 23 Mar 1879 in Calhoun, Alabama, USA. He lived in Calhoun, Alabama, USA in 1880. He died on 15 Nov 1956 in Ragland, St Clair, Alabama, USA.

vii. Sara Ann Reaves was born in Dec 1879 in Alabama, USA. She died on 20 Aug 1958 in Eastaboga, Calhoun, Alabama, USA.

viii. John Lawyer Reaves was born on 12 Aug 1885 in Alabama, USA. He married Jewel Iwilda Edwards on 27 Nov 1912 in Calhoun, Alabama, USA. He died on 21 Nov 1958 in Calhoun, Alabama, USA.

ix. Carrie Caroline Reaves was born on 01 May 1887 in Alabama, USA. She married David Robert Gamble about 1905 in Alabama, USA. She died on 01 Nov 1958 in Calhoun, Alabama, USA.

x. Benjamin Harrison Reaves was born in Aug 1890 in Alabama, USA. He lived in Calhoun, Alabama, USA in 1900.

78. ***George M. D. Reaves**-13 (Carter Hill-12, William Emery-11, Edmond-10, William-9, William-8, Richard-7, John-6, William-5, Timothy-4, Richard-3, John-2, Robert-1) [347, 348, 349, 350, 351, 352] was born on 03 May 1849 in

Jacksonville, Calhoun, Alabama, USA [347, 348, 349, 350, 351]. He lived in Oxford, Calhoun, Alabama, USA in 1930 [351]. He died on 27 May 1935 in Calhoun, Alabama, USA [352]. **Amrilla Vestula Gamble** was born on 24 Sep 1858 in Bowdon, Carroll, Georgia, USA. She died on 17 Sep 1951 in Oxford, Calhoun, Alabama, USA. George M. D. Reaves and Amrilla Vestula Gamble were married on 01 Aug 1876 in Calhoun, Alabama, USA. They had the following children:

    i.   (79) Huston R. Reaves [854] was born on 27 Jul 1877 in Alabama, USA [855, 854].

    ii.   (80) Rufus Alexander Reaves [856, 857, 858, 859, 860] was born on 17 Nov 1878 in Alabama, USA [856, 857, 858, 859, 860].

    iii.   Daniel C. Reaves [861] was born on 11 Nov 1884 in Alabama, USA [861]. He lived in Calhoun, Alabama, USA in 1900 [861]. He died on 05 Jul 1964 in Calhoun, Alabama, USA.

    iv.   Willie S. Reaves [853] was born in Jul 1887 in Alabama, USA [853]. He lived in Calhoun, Alabama, USA in 1900 [853].

    v.   Oscar Burton Reaves [862, 863] was born on 15 Oct 1891 in Alabama, USA [862, 863]. He died on 10 Jan 1919. He lived in Calhoun, Alabama, USA [863].

    vi.   Ollie Vestula Reaves [864] was born on 25 Apr 1895 in Calhoun, Alabama, USA [864]. She lived in Calhoun, Alabama, USA in 1900 [864]. She died on 21 Jul 1989 in Calhoun, Alabama, USA.

    vii.   Hermon Belton Reaves [865, 866, 867, 868] was born on 10 Jun 1898 in Calhoun, Alabama, USA [865, 866, 867, 868]. He lived in Oxford, Calhoun, Alabama, USA in 1910 [868]. He died on 01 Jun 1964 in Anniston, Calhoun, Alabama, USA [867].

    viii.   (81) Alma Irene Reaves [869, 870, 871] was born about 1901 in Alabama, USA [869, 870, 871].

    ix.   Ola Vesta Reaves [872] was born about 1904 in Alabama, USA [872]. She lived in Oxford, Calhoun, Alabama, USA in 1920 [872]. She died on 04 Mar 1994 in Calhoun, Alabama, USA.

83.   *John G. Kay*-13 (Caroline Temple-12, William Emery-11, Edmond-10, William-9, William-8, Richard-7, John-6, William-5, Timothy-4, Richard-3, John-2, Robert-1) [382, 383] was born in Mar 1864 in Calhoun, Alabama, USA [382, 383]. He lived in Calhoun, Alabama, USA in 1880 [382]. He died in 1902 in Calhoun, Alabama, USA. **Emma ?Trammell?** [873] was born in Nov 1866 in Crenshaw, Alabama, USA [873]. She lived in Talladega, Alabama, USA in 1900 [873]. John G. Kay and Emma ?Trammell? were married in 1885 [383]. They had the following children:

    i.   Aaron Kay [874] was born in Mar 1886 in Crenshaw, Alabama, USA [874]. He lived in Talladega, Alabama, USA in 1900 [874].

    ii.   Ira Kay [875] was born in Jan 1888 in Alabama, USA [875]. He lived in Talladega, Alabama, USA in 1900 [875]. He died on 23 Feb 1960 in Ragland, St Clair, Alabama, USA.

iii. Emma Etta Imogene Caroline Kay [876] was born in Apr 1890 in Alabama, USA [876]. She lived in Talladega, Alabama, USA in 1900 [876]. She died on 26 Jun 1965 in Gadsden, Etowah, Alabama, USA.

iv. Oney Kay [877] was born in May 1892 in Alabama, USA [877]. He lived in Talladega, Alabama, USA in 1900 [877].

v. Macy Kay [878] was born in Jun 1893 in Crenshaw, Alabama, USA [878]. He lived in Talladega, Alabama, USA in 1900 [878].

vi. Archie Kay [879] was born in Nov 1897 in Alabama, USA [879]. He lived in Talladega, Alabama, USA in 1900 [879]. He died on 25 May 1929.

vii. Nathan Kay was born in 1900 in Crenshaw, Alabama, USA. He died in 1910.

84. **Sarah D. Henley**-13 (Caroline Temple-12, William Emery-11, Edmond-10, William-9, William-8, Richard-7, John-6, William-5, Timothy-4, Richard-3, John-2, Robert-1) [372] was born in 1842 in Alabama, USA [372]. She lived in Subdivision 29, Benton, Alabama, USA in 1850 [372]. **?Henry J. Lambert?** was born in 1840 in Georgia, USA. He died on 26 Jun 1862 in Calhoun, Alabama, USA. ?Henry J. Lambert? and Sarah D. Henley were married in 1858 in Benton, Alabama, USA. They had the following children:

i. John M. Lambert was born in 1859 in Calhoun, Alabama, USA.

85. **Tabitha C. Henley**-13 (Caroline Temple-12, William Emery-11, Edmond-10, William-9, William-8, Richard-7, John-6, William-5, Timothy-4, Richard-3, John-2, Robert-1) [375] was born in 1849 in Alabama, USA [375]. She lived in Subdivision 29, Benton, Alabama, USA in 1850 [375]. She died on 24 Oct 1871 in Alabama, USA. **John Benjamin Garrett** was born in 1852 in Georgia, USA. John Benjamin Garrett and Tabitha C. Henley were married on 06 Oct 1869 in Calhoun, Alabama, USA. They had the following children:

i. John Thomas Garrett was born in 1872 in Alabama, USA. He died on 17 Dec 1928 in Calhoun, Alabama, USA.

ii. Rosalea Garrett was born in 1874 in Alabama, USA.

iii. Carrie Garrett was born in 1876 in Alabama, USA. She died on 08 May 1942.

iv. Noah Benjamin Garrett was born in 1879 in Alabama, USA. He died on 05 Dec 1918.

86. **James Carter Henley**-13 (Caroline Temple-12, William Emery-11, Edmond-10, William-9, William-8, Richard-7, John-6, William-5, Timothy-4, Richard-3, John-2, Robert-1) was born in 1854 in Calhoun, Alabama, USA. He died on 31 Jul 1920 in Ruston, Lincoln, Louisiana, USA. **Rebecca Ann Garrett** was born in 1859 in Calhoun, Alabama, USA. She died in 1907 in Ruston, Lincoln, Louisiana, USA. James Carter Henley and Rebecca Ann Garrett were married on 19 Sep 1875 in Calhoun County, Alabama, USA. They had the following children:

i. Leola Henley was born in 1879 in Calhoun, Alabama, USA.

ii. Marion Hughes Henley [880] was born on 06 Sep 1880 [880]. He lived in Lincoln, Louisiana, USA [880].

37

    iii.   James Oscar Henley [881] was born in Nov 1883 in Alabama, USA [881]. He died on 14 Aug 1918 in Louisiana, USA [881].

    iv.   Henry Charles Henley Sr [882] was born on 15 Mar 1885 in Iron City, Calhoun, Alabama, USA [882]. He died on 20 Oct 1967 in Shreveport, Caddo, Louisiana, USA [882].

    v.   Maude Henley was born in Jul 1887.

    vi.   Josie Henley was born in Apr 1893.

89. *George W. Reaves*-13 (Emory G.-12, William Emery-11, Edmond-10, William-9, William-8, Richard-7, John-6, William-5, Timothy-4, Richard-3, John-2, Robert-1) [391, 392, 393] was born in Aug 1857 in Calhoun, Alabama, USA [391, 392]. He lived in Jackson, Alabama, USA in 1870 [391]. He died in Aug 1929 in Calhoun, Alabama, USA [393]. **Addie (unknown maiden name)** [883] was born in May 1860 in Alabama, USA [883]. She lived in Talladega, Talladega, Alabama, USA in 1900 [883]. George W. Reaves and Addie (unknown maiden name) were married and they had the following children:

    i.   Mary L. Reaves [884] was born in Jun 1881 in Alabama, USA [884]. She lived in Talladega, Talladega, Alabama, USA in 1900 [884].

    ii.   Emma Reaves [885] was born in Jun 1883 in Alabama, USA [885]. She lived in Talladega, Talladega, Alabama, USA in 1900 [885].

    iii.   Magie Reaves [886] was born in May 1886 in Alabama, USA [886]. She lived in Talladega, Talladega, Alabama, USA in 1900 [886].

    iv.   Hosie Reaves [887] was born in Apr 1888 in Alabama, USA [887]. He lived in Talladega, Talladega, Alabama, USA in 1900 [887].

    v.   Joeanna L. Reaves [888] was born in Dec 1891 in Alabama, USA [888]. She lived in Talladega, Talladega, Alabama, USA in 1900 [888].

    vi.   Claudie Reaves [889] was born in Jun 1897 in Alabama, USA [889]. He lived in Talladega, Talladega, Alabama, USA in 1900 [889].

Annie Ellen Campbell daughter of Thomas Campbell and Julia Ann Harden was born on 26 Mar 1864 in Alabama, USA. She lived in Tallapoosa, Alabama, USA in 1870. She died in 1918 in Alabama, USA. George W Reaves and Annie Ellen Campbell were married on 07 Aug 1902 in Talladega, Talladega, Alabama, USA. They had the following children:

    i.   Flora Lillie Reaves was born on 15 Jan 1905 in Alabama, USA. She died on 20 Dec 1914 in Calhoun, Alabama, USA.

    ii.   Ira Vernon Reaves was born on 30 Oct 1906 in Alabama, USA. He died on 18 Jan 1914.

90. *Thomas Edward Reaves*-13 (Emory G.-12, William Emery-11, Edmond-10, William-9, William-8, Richard-7, John-6, William-5, Timothy-4, Richard-3, John-2, Robert-1) [397, 398, 399, 400] was born on 01 Mar 1872 in Alabama, USA [397, 398, 399, 400]. He lived in Munford, Talladega, Alabama, USA in 1900 [397]. He died on 30 Jan 1926 in Alabama, USA. **Julia ?Hill?** [890, 891, 892] was born about 1879 in Alabama, USA [890, 891, 892]. She lived in

38

Munford, Talladega, Alabama, USA in 1900 [890]. Thomas Edward Reaves and Julia Hill? were married in 1899 [397]. They had the following children:

i.   Una Reaves [893] was born about 1902 in Alabama, USA [893]. She lived in Oxford, Calhoun, Alabama, USA in 1920 [893].

ii.   Arvel Reaves [894] was born about 1902 in Arkansas, USA [894]. He lived in Oxford, Calhoun, Alabama, USA in 1920 [894].

iii.   Raymond Reaves [895] was born about 1906 in Arkansas, USA [895]. He lived in Oxford, Calhoun, Alabama, USA in 1920 [895].

iv.   Eugene Reaves [896] was born about 1908 in Arkansas, USA [896]. He lived in Oxford, Calhoun, Alabama, USA in 1920 [896].

v.   George B. Reaves [897, 898] was born about 1910 in Arkansas, USA [897, 898]. He lived in Alexandria, Calhoun, Alabama, USA in 1930 [898].

vi.   Orrine Reaves [899] was born about 1911 in Arkansas, USA [899]. She lived in Oxford, Calhoun, Alabama, USA in 1920 [899].

vii.   Fred Reaves [900, 901] was born about 1914 in Arkansas, USA [900, 901]. He lived in Alexandria, Calhoun, Alabama, USA in 1930 [901].

viii.   Louise Reaves [902] was born about 1916 [902]. She lived in Alexandria, Calhoun, Alabama, USA in 1930 [902].

ix.   Charles Edward Reaves [903, 904] was born about 1920 in Alabama, USA [903, 904]. He lived in Alexandria, Calhoun, Alabama, USA in 1930 [904].

92. ***David Jackson McCullars*-13** (Sarah Ann Marinda-12, William Emery-11, Edmond-10, William-9, William-8, Richard-7, John-6, William-5, Timothy-4, Richard-3, John-2, Robert-1) [408, 409, 410, 411, 412, 413, 414, 415] was born on 27 Aug 1857 in Weaver, Calhoun, Alabama, USA [408, 409, 410, 411, 412, 413, 414]. He lived in Weaver, Calhoun, Alabama, USA in 1900 [408]. He died on 21 Dec 1936 in Anniston, Calhoun, Alabama, USA. **Lou Rena Nancy Young** daughter of David Young and Permelia A. Ford [905, 906, 907, 908, 909, 910, 911] was born on 21 Jun 1861 in Alabama, USA [905, 906, 907, 908, 909, 910]. She lived in Weaver, Calhoun, Alabama, USA in 1900 [905]. She died on 24 Nov 1933 in Anniston, Calhoun, Alabama, USA [911]. David Jackson McCullars and Lou Rena Nancy Young were married on 24 Jan 1879 in Calhoun, Alabama, USA [408]. They had the following children:

i.   (93) Della McCullars [912, 913, 914, 915, 916, 917, 918] was born on 24 Nov 1879 in Weaver, Calhoun, Alabama, USA [912, 913, 914, 915, 916, 917, 918].

ii.   (94) Minnie Sara Amelia McCullars [920, 921] was born on 04 Sep 1881 in Calhoun, Alabama, USA [921].

iii.   William Oscar McCullars [922] was born on 28 Oct 1883 in Weaver, Calhoun, Alabama, USA [922]. He lived in Weaver, Calhoun, Alabama, USA in 1900 [922]. He died on 02 Jan 1971 in Westminster, Collin, Texas, USA.

iv.   Minnie McCullars [920] was born on 16 Jan 1885 in Weaver, Calhoun, Alabama, USA [920]. She lived in Weaver, Calhoun, Alabama, USA in 1900 [920]. She died on 15 Jun 1969.

v.   (95) Monroe Jackson McCullars [923, 924, 925, 926] was born on 23 Mar 1886 in Calhoun, Alabama, USA [923, 924, 925, 926].

vi.   Mary E. McCullars [927] was born in Mar 1889 in Calhoun, Alabama, USA [927]. She lived in Weaver, Calhoun, Alabama, USA in 1900 [927]. She died on 15 Apr 1976 in Anniston, Calhoun, Alabama, USA.

vii.   James Albert McCullars [928, 929, 930] was born on 23 Dec 1890 in Weaver, Calhoun, Alabama, USA [928, 929, 930]. He lived in Weaver, Calhoun, Alabama, USA in 1900 [930]. He died on 22 Dec 1963 in Gadsden, Etowah, Alabama, USA [928].

viii.   (96) Mollie McCullars [927, 931] was born about 1891 in Alabama, USA [927, 931].

ix.   William J. Bryan McCullars [932, 933] was born in May 1896 in Alabama, USA [932, 933]. He lived in Weaver, Calhoun, Alabama, USA in 1900 [933]. He died on 18 May 1960 in Calhoun, Alabama, USA.

x.   Samuel Lee McCullars [934] was born on 21 May 1896 in Calhoun, Alabama, USA [934]. He lived in Weaver, Calhoun, Alabama, USA in 1910 [934]. He died on 07 Apr 1946 in Calhoun, Alabama, USA.

xi.   Bryan McCullars [932, 933] was born on 12 Sep 1898 in Calhoun, Alabama, USA [932, 933]. He lived in Weaver, Calhoun, Alabama, USA in 1900 [933]. He died on 18 May 1960 in Calhoun, Alabama, USA.

97.   Mary E. McCullars-13 (Sarah Ann Marinda-12, William Emery-11, Edmond-10, William-9, William-8, Richard-7, John-6, William-5, Timothy-4, Richard-3, John-2, Robert-1) [406, 407] was born in Jul 1855 in Calhoun, Alabama, USA [406, 407]. She lived in Calhoun, Alabama, USA in 1860 [406]. She died on 14 May 1904 in Calhoun, Alabama, USA. **George Washington Doss** son of William Beauchamp Doss and Mary Lee McCollum [935, 936, 937, 938, 939] was born in Mar 1854 in Alabama, USA [935, 936, 938, 939]. He lived in Polkville, Calhoun, Alabama, USA in 1920 [939]. He died in Feb 1926 in Calhoun, Alabama, USA [937]. George Washington Doss and Mary E. McCullars were married on 11 Oct 1871. They had the following children:

i.   (98) William Marion Doss [940, 941, 942, 943] was born on 11 Aug 1873 in Calhoun, Alabama, USA [940, 941, 942].

ii.   M. T. Doss was born in 1877 in Alabama, USA.

iii.   Paralee Doss was born on 15 May 1877. She died on 24 Jul 1950 in Calhoun, Alabama, USA.

iv.   Mary Frances Doss was born in 1880 in Alabama, USA.

v.   Fannie E. Doss [944] was born in Apr 1880 in Alabama, USA [944]. She lived in Polkville, Calhoun, Alabama, USA in 1900 [944].

vi.   Georgia A. Doss [945] was born on 04 Jun 1882 in Alabama, USA [945]. She lived in Polkville, Calhoun, Alabama, USA in 1900 [945]. She died on 09 Mar 1902.

vii.   John Leroy Doss [946, 947] was born on 06 Feb 1884 in Calhoun, Alabama, USA [946, 947]. He lived in Polkville, Calhoun, Alabama, USA in 1900 [947]. He died on 12 Mar 1964 in Alabama, USA [946].

viii.   James O. Doss [948] was born on 29 Oct 1886 in Alabama, USA [948]. He lived in Polkville, Calhoun, Alabama, USA in 1900 [948]. He died on 11 Jul 1966.

ix.   (99) Monroe Jackson Doss [949, 950, 951, 952, 953] was born on 22 Aug 1888 in Calhoun, Alabama, USA [949, 950, 951, 952].

100.   _Samuel M. McCullars_-13 (Sarah Ann Marinda-12, William Emery-11, Edmond-10, William-9, William-8, Richard-7, John-6, William-5, Timothy-4, Richard-3, John-2, Robert-1) [418, 419] was born on 02 Mar 1869 in Calhoun, Alabama, USA [418, 419]. He lived in Talladega, Alabama, USA in 1900 [419]. He died on 19 Jun 1913 in Lincoln, Talladega, Alabama, USA. Samuel M. McCullars and ?Jane Castleberry? married and had the following children:

i.   James O. McCullars was born on 13 Dec 1893 in Talladega, Alabama, USA. He died on 25 Nov 1957 in Anniston, Calhoun, Alabama, USA.

Martha Elizabeth Crow was born on 10 Feb 1881. She died on 05 Apr 1965 in Talladega, Alabama, USA. Samuel M. McCullars and Martha Elizabeth Crow were married on 21 Aug 1904 in Talladega, Alabama, USA. They had the following children:

i.   Samuel Carlye McCullars was born on 22 Jun 1905. He died on 19 May 1979 in Lincoln, Madison, Alabama, USA.

ii.   Maybelle McCullars was born on 11 Dec 1907. She died in Feb 1923 in Lincoln, Madison, Alabama, USA.

iii.   James C. McCullars was born on 12 Jan 1909 in Lincoln, Madison, Alabama, USA. He died on 01 Jul 1995 in Birmingham, Jefferson, Alabama, USA.

iv.   M. C. McCullars was born on 02 Feb 1911. He died on 21 Jun 1991.

101.   _Josie F. McCullars_-13 (Sarah Ann Marinda-12, William Emery-11, Edmond-10, William-9, William-8, Richard-7, John-6, William-5, Timothy-4, Richard-3, John-2, Robert-1) [424, 425] was born in Jan 1880 in Alabama, USA [424, 425]. She lived in Talladega, Alabama, USA in 1900 [424]. She died in 1911. **Zachirrah Reese Bunn** and Josie F. McCullars were married on 21 Aug 1904 in Talladega, Alabama, USA. They had the following children:

i.   Johnny L. Bunn was born on 02 Jun 1905. He died on 21 Sep 1978 in Weaver, Calhoun, Alabama, USA.

ii.   Willie B. Bunn was born on 10 Aug 1906. He died in 1963.

103.   _Mary Ann Reaves_-13 (David R-12, William Emery-11, Edmond-10, William-9, William-8, Richard-7, John-6, William-5, Timothy-4, Richard-3, John-2, Robert-1) [428] was born on 08 Mar 1861 in Calhoun, Alabama, USA [428]. She lived in Calhoun, Alabama, USA in 1880 [428]. She died on 05 Jan 1891 in Calhoun, Alabama, USA. **William Patrick Reaves** son of William McGuire Reaves and Margaret Ann Bonds [324, 325, 326, 327, 328, 329, 330] was born on 19 May 1857 in Calhoun, Alabama, USA [324, 325, 326, 327, 328, 329, 330]. He lived in Munford, Talladega, Alabama, USA in 1920 [330]. He died on 04 Dec 1929 in Anniston, Calhoun, Alabama, USA. William Patrick Reaves and Mary Ann Reaves married and had the following children:

    i.   (39) Sylvester Reaves [729, 730, 731, 732, 733, 734] was born on 25 Aug 1878 in Anniston, Calhoun, Alabama, USA [729, 730, 731, 732, 733].

    ii.   Mary Jane (Jenny) Reaves was born on 02 Jul 1880 in Anniston, Calhoun, Alabama, USA. She died on 30 Sep 1953 in Anniston, Calhoun, Alabama, USA.

    iii.   (41) William Monroe Reaves [735, 736] was born in Jun 1882 in Alabama, USA [735, 736].

    iv.   (40) Margie Belle Reaves [737] was born on 23 Jan 1884 in Alabama, USA [737].

    v.   Henry Walker Reaves was born on 05 Feb 1886 in Anniston, Calhoun, Alabama, USA. He died in Jun 1888 in Anniston, Calhoun, Alabama, USA.

    vi.   Rosa Annie Reaves [738] was born on 13 Nov 1887 in Alabama, USA [738]. She lived in Calhoun, Alabama, USA in 1900 [738]. She died on 15 Jul 1910.

    vii.   (42) Lula Merendia Reaves [739] was born on 15 Jan 1890 in Alabama, USA [739].

106. ***Bunyon Rubin Britton Reaves*-13** (Ira Jackson-12, William Emery-11, Edmond-10, William-9, William-8, Richard-7, John-6, William-5, Timothy-4, Richard-3, John-2, Robert-1) [439, 440, 441, 442, 443, 444] was born on 09 Jun 1866 in Calhoun, Alabama, USA [439, 440, 441, 443, 444]. He lived in Albertville, Marshall, Alabama, USA in 1930 [444]. He died on 23 Sep 1942 in Marshall, Alabama, USA [442]. **Mimie Trammell** [954, 955, 956, 957, 958] was born on 16 Mar 1874 in Alabama, USA [954, 955, 956, 957]. She lived in Albertville, Marshall, Alabama, USA in 1910 [954]. She died on 24 Oct 1958 in Marshall, Alabama, USA [958]. Bunyon Rubin Britton Reaves and Mimie Trammell were married on 17 May 1891 in Calhoun, Alabama, USA [440]. They had the following children:

    i.   (109) Lela Mae Reaves [959, 960, 961] was born on 27 Jul 1892 in Alabama, USA [959, 960, 961].

    ii.   (108) Claude Fredrick Reaves [962, 963, 964, 965, 966, 967] was born on 08 Dec 1893 in Alabama, USA [962, 963, 964, 966, 967].

    iii.   Boman Reaves [968] was born on 22 Feb 1895 in Alabama, USA [968]. He died in 1898. He lived in Rock Spring, Marshall, Alabama, USA in 1900 [968].

    iv.   Albert Jackson Reaves [969] was born on 30 Dec 1896 in Alabama, USA. He died on 06 Jul 1910 in Calhoun, Alabama, USA [969].

    v.   Pearl Idell Reaves [970, 971, 972, 973] was born on 13 Oct 1899 in Alabama, USA [970, 971, 972, 973]. She lived in Albertville, Marshall, Alabama, USA in 1930 [973]. She died in Sep 1994.

vi. Charles Sanford Reaves [974, 975, 976] was born on 07 Aug 1902 in Alabama, USA [975, 976]. He lived in Albertville, Marshall, Alabama, USA in 1920 [976]. He died in Marshall, Alabama, USA [974].

vii. Irene Reaves [977, 978] was born on 23 Dec 1903 in Marshall, Alabama, USA [977, 978]. She lived in Albertville, Marshall, Alabama, USA in 1910 [977]. She died on 29 Dec 1977 in Albertville, Marshall, Alabama, USA [978].

viii. Archie Cleve Reaves [979, 980, 981, 982] was born on 19 Oct 1905 in Alabama, USA [979, 980, 981, 982]. He lived in Albertville, Marshall, Alabama, USA in 1930 [982]. He died on 23 Jan 1972 in Albertville, Marshall, Alabama, USA [979].

ix. (107) Mary Etta Reaves [983, 984, 985] was born on 16 Jul 1909 in Alabama, USA [983, 984, 985].

x. Minnie Pauline Reaves [986, 987, 988] was born on 08 Dec 1911 in Alabama, USA [986, 987, 988]. She lived in Albertville, Marshall, Alabama, USA in 1930 [988]. She died on 15 Jun 2001 in Albertville, Marshall, Alabama, USA [986].

xi. Roy Bunyon Reaves [989] was born on 12 May 1913 in Alabama, USA. He died on 14 Jan 1915 in Marshall, Alabama, USA [989].

110. *Ellen Marcilea Elizabeth Reaves*-13 (Ira Jackson-12, William Emery-11, Edmond-10, William-9, William-8, Richard-7, John-6, William-5, Timothy-4, Richard-3, John-2, Robert-1) [454, 455, 456, 457] was born on 09 Mar 1874 in Alabama, USA [454, 455, 456, 457]. She lived in Albertville, Marshall, Alabama, USA in 1920 [457]. She died on 17 Feb 1945. **William Francis Russell** [990, 991, 992] was born in Dec 1847 in Tennessee, USA [991, 992]. He lived in Albertville, Marshall, Alabama, USA in 1920 [992]. He died on 30 Aug 1935 in Marshall, Alabama, USA [990]. William Francis Russell and Ellen Marcilea Elizabeth Reaves were married about 1909 in Calhoun, Alabama, USA. They had the following children:

i. Marla Russell [993] was born about 1902 in Alabama, USA [993]. She lived in Albertville, Marshall, Alabama, USA in 1920 [993].

ii. Neoma Russell [994] was born about 1905 in Alabama, USA [994]. She lived in Etowah, Alabama, USA in 1910 [994]. She lived in Albertville, Marshall, Alabama, USA in 1920 [995].

iii. Walter H. Russell was born in 1909 in Alabama, USA.

111. *Sarah Malissa Caroline Reaves*-13 (Ira Jackson-12, William Emery-11, Edmond-10, William-9, William-8, Richard-7, John-6, William-5, Timothy-4, Richard-3, John-2, Robert-1) [451, 452] was born in Aug 1871 in Alabama, USA [451, 452]. She lived in Calhoun, Alabama, USA in 1880 [451]. She died on 24 Apr 1908 in Marshall, Alabama, USA. **William Francis Russell** [453] was born in Dec 1847 in Tennessee, USA [453]. He lived in Friendship, Marshall, Alabama, USA in 1900 [453]. William F. Russell and Sarah Malissa Caroline Reaves were married in 1889 [453]. They had the following children:

i. Sallie C. Russell [996] was born in Dec 1878 in Georgia, USA [996]. She lived in Friendship, Marshall, Alabama, USA in 1900 [996].

ii.	Homer B. Russell [997] was born in Feb 1881 in Georgia, USA [997]. He lived in Friendship, Marshall, Alabama, USA in 1900 [997].

iii.	Houston W. Russell [998] was born in Dec 1883 in Texas, USA [998]. He lived in Friendship, Marshall, Alabama, USA in 1900 [998].

iv.	Emmett H. Russell [999] was born in Nov 1893 in Alabama, USA [999]. He lived in Friendship, Marshall, Alabama, USA in 1900 [999].

v.	Fannie Russell [1000] was born in Apr 1895 in Alabama, USA [1000]. She lived in Friendship, Marshall, Alabama, USA in 1900 [1000].

112. *William David Reaves*-13 (Ira Jackson-12, William Emery-11, Edmond-10, William-9, William-8, Richard-7, John-6, William-5, Timothy-4, Richard-3, John-2, Robert-1) [445, 446, 447, 448, 449, 450] was born on 17 Jun 1868 in Oxford, Calhoun, Alabama, USA [445, 446, 447, 448]. He lived in Weaver, Calhoun, Alabama, USA in 1920 [447]. He died on 08 Apr 1949 in Anniston, Calhoun, Alabama, USA [449]. **Margaret Arena Pruett** daughter of Charles Rossen Green Pruett and Margaret Katherine Dudley [1001, 1002, 1003, 1004, 1005] was born on 10 Apr 1876 in Weaver, Calhoun, Alabama, USA [1001, 1004, 1005]. She lived in Weaver, Calhoun, Alabama, USA in 1920 [1001]. She died on 18 Sep 1945 in Anniston, Calhoun, Alabama, USA [1003, 1006]. William David Reaves and Margaret Arena Pruett were married on 26 Jul 1892 in Calhoun, Alabama, USA (At the home of Sally's parents in Weaver, Alabama by Rev. Tom Weaver) [445]. They had the following children:

i.	(113) Maggie Lee Reaves [1007, 1008, 1009, 1010, 1011] was born on 25 May 1894 in Weaver, Calhoun, Alabama, USA [1007, 1008, 1009, 1010, 1011].

ii.	Pearl Idell Reaves was born on 28 Nov 1897 in Anniston, Calhoun, Alabama, USA. She died on 01 Apr 1899 in Anniston, Calhoun, Alabama, USA.

iii.	Griffin Ira Reaves was born on 02 May 1899 in Anniston, Calhoun, Alabama, USA. He died on 07 Jun 1899 in Anniston, Calhoun, Alabama, USA.

iv.	Grady Dewey Reaves [1012, 1013, 1014] was born on 05 Jun 1900 in Anniston, Calhoun, Alabama, USA [1012, 1013, 1014]. He lived in Weaver, Calhoun, Alabama, USA in 1920 [1012]. He died on 12 Feb 1975 in Birmingham, Jefferson, Alabama, USA.

v.	(115) Luna Emma Reaves [1015, 1016, 1017, 1018] was born on 03 Oct 1902 in Anniston, Calhoun, Alabama, USA [1015, 1016].

vi.	Willie Mae Reaves [1019, 1020, 1021] was born on 10 May 1904 in Anniston, Calhoun, Alabama, USA [1019, 1020, 1021]. She lived in Weaver, Calhoun, Alabama, USA in 1920 [1021]. She died on 06 Jul 1984 in Anniston, Calhoun, Alabama, USA [1019].

vii.	Albert David Reaves [969, 1022] was born on 25 Sep 1905 in Anniston, Calhoun, Alabama, USA [1022]. He lived in Weaver, Calhoun, Alabama, USA in 1910 [1022]. He died on 13 Jul 1910 in Anniston, Calhoun, Alabama, USA.

viii.	(116) Sallie Irene Reaves [1023, 1024, 1025] was born on 15 Jul 1907 in Anniston, Calhoun, Alabama, USA [1023, 1024, 1025].

ix.   Rena I. Reaves [1023, 1025] was born about 1907 in Alabama, USA [1023, 1025]. She lived in Weaver, Calhoun, Alabama, USA in 1920 [1023].

x.   (117) Wilma Lee Reaves [1026] was born on 13 Oct 1910 in Anniston, Calhoun, Alabama, USA [1026].

xi.   Wilmer Reaves [1027] was born about 1911 in Alabama, USA [1027]. She lived in Weaver, Calhoun, Alabama, USA in 1920 [1027].

xii. Arthur Thomas Reaves [1028, 1029] was born on 09 Nov 1914 in Anniston, Calhoun, Alabama, USA [1028, 1029]. He lived in Weaver, Calhoun, Alabama, USA in 1920 [1029]. He died on 05 Sep 1995 in Anniston, Calhoun, Alabama, USA [1028].

xiii. Evelyn Hilda Reaves [1030] was born on 15 Sep 1917 in Anniston, Calhoun, Alabama, USA [1030]. She lived in Weaver, Calhoun, Alabama, USA in 1920 [1030]. She married John Thurman Johnson in 1933. She died on 19 Jul 1992 in Anniston, Calhoun, Alabama, USA.

xiv. Evline H. Reaves [1030] was born about 1917 in Alabama, USA [1030]. She lived in Weaver, Calhoun, Alabama, USA in 1920 [1030].

118. **_Amy Kentucky Reaves_**-13 (Ira Jackson-12, William Emery-11, Edmond-10, William-9, William-8, Richard-7, John-6, William-5, Timothy-4, Richard-3, John-2, Robert-1) [458, 459, 460, 461, 462] was born on 09 Mar 1876 in Alabama, USA [458, 459, 460, 461]. She lived in Weaver, Calhoun, Alabama, USA in 1910 [458]. She died on 24 Mar 1947 in Calhoun, Alabama, USA [462]. **Lee Ander VanBuren Pettus** [1031, 463, 1032] was born on 27 Apr 1869 in Clay, Alabama, USA [1031, 463, 1032]. He lived in Weaver, Calhoun, Alabama, USA in 1910 [1032]. He died on 19 Feb 1942 in Alabama, USA. Lee Ander VanBuren Pettus and Amy Kentucky Reaves were married on 25 Oct 1891 in Calhoun, Alabama, USA [463]. They had the following children:

i.   William Jackson Pettus [1033, 1034] was born on 19 Jul 1892 in Calhoun, Alabama, USA [1033, 1034]. He lived in Weaver, Calhoun, Alabama, USA in 1910 [1034]. He died on 23 Jan 1926 in Calhoun, Alabama, USA.

ii.   Walter Lee Pettus [1035, 1036] was born on 07 Jan 1894 in Calhoun, Alabama, USA [1035, 1036]. He lived in Weaver, Calhoun, Alabama, USA in 1910 [1035]. He died on 29 Apr 1944.

iii. James Buyan Pettus [1037] was born on 26 Feb 1896 in Calhoun, Alabama, USA [1037]. He lived in Weaver, Calhoun, Alabama, USA in 1900 [1037]. He died on 09 Mar 1967 in Calhoun, Alabama, USA.

iv.   John Adolphus Pettus was born on 12 Nov 1897. He died on 12 Nov 1897 in Calhoun, Alabama, USA.

v.   Annie Elinor Pettus was born in Jan 1899 in Calhoun, Alabama, USA. She died on 09 Jan 1899 in Calhoun, Alabama, USA.

vi.   Avie Lu Jean Pettus was born on 25 Nov 1900. She died on 04 May 1974 in Calhoun, Alabama, USA.

vii. Wester Meharg Pettus [1038, 1039] was born about 1901 in Alabama, USA [1038, 1039]. He lived in Weaver, Calhoun, Alabama, USA in 1910 [1039].

viii.	Avy Pettus [1040] was born in 1903 in Alabama, USA [1040]. He lived in Weaver, Calhoun, Alabama, USA in 1910 [1040].
ix.	Annie L. Pettus [1041] was born about 1903 in Alabama, USA [1041]. She lived in Weaver, Calhoun, Alabama, USA in 1920 [1041].
x.	Unnamed son Pettus was born on 27 Feb 1906 in Calhoun, Alabama, USA. He died on 27 Feb 1906 in Calhoun, Alabama, USA.
xi.	John Dawson Pettus [1042] was born on 06 May 1909 in Calhoun, Alabama, USA [1042]. He lived in Weaver, Calhoun, Alabama, USA in 1920 [1042]. He died on 18 Mar 1976 in Heflin, Cleburne, Alabama, USA.
xii.	Ira Howard Pettus [1043] was born on 09 Jun 1910 in Calhoun, Alabama, USA [1043]. He lived in Weaver, Calhoun, Alabama, USA in 1920 [1043]. He died on 07 May 1967 in Calhoun, Alabama, USA.
xiii.	Elsie Winnie Pettus [1044] was born on 19 Mar 1912 in Calhoun, Alabama, USA [1044]. She lived in Weaver, Calhoun, Alabama, USA in 1920 [1044]. She died in New York, USA.
xiv.	Elbert Edwin Pettus [1045] was born on 19 Mar 1916 in Calhoun, Alabama, USA [1045]. He lived in Weaver, Calhoun, Alabama, USA in 1920 [1045]. He died on 27 Dec 1978.

119. *John Perry Osburne Reaves*-13 (Ira Jackson-12, William Emery-11, Edmond-10, William-9, William-8, Richard-7, John-6, William-5, Timothy-4, Richard-3, John-2, Robert-1) [465, 466, 467, 468, 469, 470] was born on 29 Mar 1885 in Alabama, USA [465, 466, 467, 468, 469]. He lived in Jay Bird, Marshall, Alabama, USA in 1930 [465]. He died on 08 Feb 1955 in Marshall, Alabama, USA [470]. **Millie (unknown maiden name)** [1051] was born about 1892 in Alabama, USA [1051]. She lived in Lincoln, Talladega, Alabama, USA in 1920 [1051]. John Perry Osburne Reaves and Millie (unknown maiden name) married and had the following children:

i.	Leola Inez Reaves [1052, 1053] was born about 1916 in Alabama, USA [1052, 1053]. She lived in Jay Bird, Marshall, Alabama, USA in 1930 [1052].
ii.	Leslie F. Reaves [1054, 1055] was born about 1918 in Alabama, USA [1054, 1055]. He lived in Jay Bird, Marshall, Alabama, USA in 1930 [1055].
iii.	Thelma Reaves [1056] was born about 1920 in Alabama, USA [1056]. She lived in Lincoln, Talladega, Alabama, USA in 1920 [1056].

John Perry Osburne Reaves and unknown spouse married and had the following children:

i.	Gladys L. Reaves [1046] was born about 1922 [1046]. She lived in Jay Bird, Marshall, Alabama, USA in 1930 [1046].
ii.	Leonard P. Reaves [1047] was born about 1924 [1047]. He lived in Jay Bird, Marshall, Alabama, USA in 1930 [1047].
iii.	Mary F. Reaves [1048] was born about 1926 [1048]. She lived in Jay Bird, Marshall, Alabama, USA in 1930 [1048].
iv.	Minnie B. Reaves [1049] was born about 1928 [1049]. She lived in Jay Bird, Marshall, Alabama, USA in 1930 [1049].

v.   William E. Reaves [1050] was born about 1928 [1050]. He lived in Jay Bird, Marshall, Alabama, USA in 1930 [1050].

120. *Cynthia Bitty Lugene Reaves*-13 (Ira Jackson-12, William Emery-11, Edmond-10, William-9, William-8, Richard-7, John-6, William-5, Timothy-4, Richard-3, John-2, Robert-1) was born on 01 Jun 1882 in Alabama, USA. She died on 23 May 1919 in Marshall, Alabama, USA. **?Rauda A. West?** and Cynthia Bitty Lugene Reaves were married on 23 Jan 1900 in Douglas, Marshall, Alabama, USA. They had the following children:

i.   Homer Britton West was born on 01 Dec 1903.

ii.   Earl West. He died on 04 Dec 1980 in Marshall, Alabama, USA.

124. *Mary Jane Moncrief*-13 (Caleb Jackson-12, Nancy-11, Edmond-10, William-9, William-8, Richard-7, John-6, William-5, Timothy-4, Richard-3, John-2, Robert-1) [493, 494] was born on 15 Jan 1848 in Georgia, USA [493, 494]. She lived in Moss, Columbia, Arkansas, USA in 1860 [494]. She died on 22 Jun 1888. **Charles Henry Autrey** son of Absalom Autrey and Elizabeth Norris [1057, 1058, 1059, 1060, 495] was born on 04 Apr 1850 in Dubach, Lincoln, Louisiana, USA [1057, 1058, 1059, 1060]. He lived in Lincoln, Louisiana, USA in 1910 [1060]. He died on 02 Nov 1917 in Lincoln, Louisiana, USA [1058]. Charles Henry Autrey and Mary Jane Moncrief were married on 23 Nov 1873 in Lincoln, Louisiana, USA [495]. They had the following children:

i.   (125) James Robert Autrey [1061] was born on 07 Aug 1874 in Dubach, Lincoln, Louisiana, USA [1061].

ii.   Laura Alice Autrey was born on 15 Feb 1876 in Lincoln, Louisiana, USA. She died on 14 Oct 1958 in Lincoln, Louisiana, USA.

iii.   Elizabeth Bush Autrey was born on 03 Nov 1877 in Dubach, Lincoln, Louisiana, USA. She died on 10 Jan 1949 in Harlingen, Cameron, Texas, USA.

iv.   Mary Pearl Autrey [1062] was born on 30 Nov 1884 in Lincoln, Louisiana, USA [1062]. She lived in Lincoln, Louisiana, USA in 1900 [1062]. She died on 04 Apr 1964 in Dubach, Lincoln, Louisiana, USA.

126. *Georgia Ann Moncrief*-13 (Caleb Jackson-12, Nancy-11, Edmond-10, William-9, William-8, Richard-7, John-6, William-5, Timothy-4, Richard-3, John-2, Robert-1) [491, 492] was born about 1847 in Georgia, USA [491, 492]. She lived in Moss, Columbia, Arkansas, USA in 1860 [492]. **Bird Griffin Autrey** son of Absalom Autrey and Elizabeth Norris [1063, 1064, 1065, 1066] was born on 27 May 1847 in Perry, Alabama, USA [1063, 1064, 1065]. He lived in Gatesville, Coryell, Texas, USA in 1920 [1065]. He died on 04 Mar 1922 in Waco, McLennan, Texas, USA [1066]. Bird Griffin Autrey and Georgia Ann Moncrief married and had the following children:

i.   David J. Autrey was born in Jul 1869 in Union, Louisiana, USA. He died in Union, Louisiana, USA.

ii.   Absalom W. Autrey was born in Apr 1872 in Union, Louisiana, USA.

iii.   (127) Mary Lucinda Autrey [1067, 1068, 1069, 1070, 1071] was born in Aug 1874 in Lincoln, Louisiana, USA [1067, 1068, 1069, 1070].

iv.   Malcomb L. Autrey was born in 1877 in Lincoln, Louisiana, USA.

v.   Cora L. Autrey was born in Dec 1879 in Lincoln, Louisiana, USA.

128.   _John M. Moncrief_-13 (Caleb Jackson-12, Nancy-11, Edmond-10, William-9, William-8, Richard-7, John-6, William-5, Timothy-4, Richard-3, John-2, Robert-1) [486, 487, 488, 489] was born in Oct 1845 in Georgia, USA [486, 487, 488, 489, 490]. He lived in Moss, Columbia, Arkansas, USA in 1860 [490]. **Nancy Nolen** [1072, 1073, 1074] was born in Apr 1838 in Louisiana, USA [1072, 1073, 1074]. She lived in Union, Louisiana, USA in 1910 [1074]. John M. Moncrief and Nancy Nolen were married in 1870 [488]. They had the following children:

i.   J. W. Moncrief [1075] was born about 1870 in Louisiana, USA [1075]. He lived in Union, Louisiana, USA in 1880 [1075].

ii.   Nancy E. Moncrief [1076] was born about 1872 in Louisiana, USA [1076]. She lived in Union, Louisiana, USA in 1880 [1076].

iii.   Malend F. Moncrief [1077, 1078] was born in Aug 1875 in Louisiana, USA [1077, 1078]. She lived in Union, Louisiana, USA in 1900 [1078].

iv.   William Caleb Moncrief [1079] was born in Oct 1878 in Louisiana, USA [1079]. He lived in Union, Louisiana, USA in 1900 [1079].

129.   _Henry Alexander Moncrief_-13 (Caleb Jackson-12, Nancy-11, Edmond-10, William-9, William-8, Richard-7, John-6, William-5, Timothy-4, Richard-3, John-2, Robert-1) [496, 497, 498, 499, 500, 501, 502, 503] was born on 20 Jun 1849 in Georgia, USA [496, 497, 498, 499, 500, 501, 502, 503]. He lived in Claiborne, Louisiana, USA in 1920 [503]. He died on 11 Mar 1921 in Louisiana, USA [499]. [1080, 1081, 1082, 1083, 1084] was born in May 1853 in Louisiana, USA [1080, 1081, 1082, 1083]. She lived in Claiborne, Louisiana, USA in 1920 [1083]. She died on 15 Jun 1920 in Claiborne, Louisiana, USA [1084]. Henry Alexander Moncrief and **Julia Ann ?Jones?** were married in 1869 [498]. They had the following children:

i.   (130) Thomas James Moncrief [1085, 1086, 1087] was born about 1871 in Louisiana, USA [1085, 1086].

ii.   Nancy Moncrief [1088, 1089] was born in Sep 1872 in Louisiana, USA [1088, 1089]. She lived in Claiborne, Louisiana, USA in 1880 [1089].

iii.   Elizabeth Moncrief [1090] was born about 1873 in Louisiana, USA [1090]. She lived in Claiborne, Louisiana, USA in 1910 [1090].

iv.   Carrie Ella Moncrief [1091] was born in Jan 1874 in Louisiana, USA [1091]. She lived in Claiborne, Louisiana, USA in 1900 [1091].

v.   Mary Moncrief [1092] was born in 1877 in Louisiana, USA [1092]. She lived in Claiborne, Louisiana, USA in 1880 [1092].

vi.   Cora Moncrief [1093] was born in Feb 1880 in Louisiana, USA [1093]. She lived in Claiborne, Louisiana, USA in 1900 [1093].

vii. Malissa Moncrief [1094] was born in Apr 1882 in Louisiana, USA [1094]. She lived in Claiborne, Louisiana, USA in 1900 [1094].

viii. Mittie Moncrief [1095] was born in Sep 1884 in Louisiana, USA [1095]. She lived in Claiborne, Louisiana, USA in 1900 [1095].

ix. John Henry Moncrief [1096, 1097] was born on 08 Mar 1887 in Louisiana, USA [1096, 1097]. He lived in Claiborne, Louisiana, USA in 1910 [1097]. He died in Nov 1962 in Claiborne, Louisiana, USA.

x. Janettie Moncrief [1098] was born in Feb 1889 in Louisiana, USA [1098]. She lived in Claiborne, Louisiana, USA in 1900 [1098].

xi. William David Moncrief was born on 31 Mar 1889 in Union, Louisiana, USA. He died on 28 Aug 1889 in Union, Louisiana, USA.

xii. Georgia Moncrief [1099, 1100] was born in Jun 1892 in Louisiana, USA [1099, 1100]. She lived in Claiborne, Louisiana, USA in 1910 [1100].

132. *Mariah Louise Grant*-13 (Mary Missouri-12, Nancy-11, Edmond-10, William-9, William-8, Richard-7, John-6, William-5, Timothy-4, Richard-3, John-2, Robert-1) [509, 510, 511] was born on 15 Jul 1857 in Clanton, Chilton, Alabama, USA [509, 510, 511]. She lived in Montgomery, Alabama, USA in 1870 [511]. She died in 1930 in Clanton, Chilton, Alabama, USA. **James F. Frasier** [1101] was born about 1877 in Alabama, USA [1101]. He lived in Chilton, Alabama, USA in 1910 [1101]. James F. Frasier and Mariah Louise Grant married and had the following children:

i. Clara E. Frasier [1102] was born about 1889 in Alabama, USA [1102]. She lived in Chilton, Alabama, USA in 1910 [1102].

ii. Alex A. Frasier [1103] was born about 1892 in Alabama, USA [1103]. He lived in Chilton, Alabama, USA in 1910 [1103].

iii. Bessie E. Frasier [1104] was born about 1894 in Alabama, USA [1104]. She lived in Chilton, Alabama, USA in 1910 [1104].

iv. Ella N. Frasier [1105] was born about 1906 in Alabama, USA [1105]. She lived in Chilton, Alabama, USA in 1910 [1105].

135. *Dorothy Reaves*-13 (John Anderson-12, Ransom Columbus-11, Edmond-10, William-9, William-8, Richard-7, John-6, William-5, Timothy-4, Richard-3, John-2, Robert-1) [519, 520] was born on 18 Oct 1876 in Monroe, Mississippi, USA [519]. She lived in Quitman, Clarke, Mississippi, USA in 1900 [519]. She died in Apr 1983 in Germantown, Shelby, Tennessee, USA [520]. **Allen Pugh** [521] was born in Nov 1872 in Alabama, USA [521]. He lived in Quitman, Clarke, Mississippi, USA in 1900 [521]. Allen Pugh and Dorothy Reaves were married in 1899 [521]. They had the following children:

i. Coy Hilda Pugh was born on 15 Jul 1913. She died on 26 Feb 1914.

John Anthony Randolph [1106] was born on 16 Mar 1858 in McNairy, Tennessee, USA. He died on 14 Jun 1928 in Nashville, Davidson, Tennessee, USA [1106]. John Anthony Randolph and Dorothy Reaves married and had the following children:

i. (137) Melba Marie Reaves [1107, 1108, 1109] was born on 16 Dec 1895 in Mississippi, USA [1107, 1108, 1109].

ii. (138) John Mark Reaves [1110, 1111, 1112, 1113] was born on 18 Feb 1898 in Ripley, Tippah, Mississippi, USA [1110, 1111, 1112, 1113].

138. *John Anderson Reaves Jr* -13 (John Anderson-12, Ransom Columbus-11, Edmond-10, William-9, William-8, Richard-7, John-6, William-5, Timothy-4, Richard-3, John-2, Robert-1) [515, 516, 517] was born on 18 Sep 1869 in Mississippi, USA [515, 516, 517]. He lived in Tippah, Mississippi, USA in 1900 [515]. **Zora Pinkney Ashley** daughter of James Pinkney Shaw Ashley and Margaret (Mag) Ann Jernigan [1114] was born on 11 Aug 1864 in Ripley, Tippah, Mississippi, USA [1114, 1115]. She lived in Tippah, Mississippi, USA in 1900 [1114]. John Anderson Reaves Jr and Zora Pinkney Ashley were married in 1889 [515]. They had the following children:

i. Roy D. Reaves [1116, 1117] was born in Dec 1889 in Mississippi, USA [1116, 1117]. He lived in Tippah, Mississippi, USA in 1900 [1116].

ii. Hue Bert Reaves [1118] was born in Feb 1891 in Mississippi, USA [1118, 1119]. He lived in Tippah, Mississippi, USA in 1900 [1118].

iii. (139) Florence Gracie Reaves [1120, 1121] was born on 03 Mar 1896 in Tippah, Mississippi, USA [1120, 1121].

iv. Lee Alvis Reaves [1122, 1123] was born on 05 Dec 1897 in Mississippi, USA [1122, 1123]. He lived in Tippah, Mississippi, USA in 1900 [1123]. He died on 18 May 1992.

v. Lilian Ollie Reaves [1124, 1125] was born in Feb 1900 in Mississippi, USA [1124, 1125]. She lived in Tippah, Mississippi, USA in 1900 [1124].

vi. Ellis Reaves [1126] was born on 05 Dec 1908 in Mississippi, USA [1127, 1126]. He lived in Halls, Lauderdale, Tennessee, USA in 1920 [1127]. He died in Feb 1954 [1126].

vii. Charlie Reaves [1128, 1129] was born about 1908 in Mississippi, USA [1128, 1129]. He lived in Halls, Lauderdale, Tennessee, USA in 1920 [1128].

viii. Willard Reaves.

ix. Francis E. A. Reaves [1130, 1131] was born about 1910 in Mississippi, USA [1130, 1131]. She lived in Halls, Lauderdale, Tennessee, USA in 1920 [1131].

142. *Elijah Baker*-13 (Cassinda Ann-12, Ransom Columbus-11, Edmond-10, William-9, William-8, Richard-7, John-6, William-5, Timothy-4, Richard-3, John-2, Robert-1) [535, 536, 537] was born on 09 Dec 1853 in Pontotoc, Mississippi, USA [535, 536, 537]. He lived in Pontotoc, Mississippi, USA in 1860 [537]. He died on 03 Feb 1938 in Dunklin, Missouri, USA [535]. **Frances M. (unknown maiden name)** [1132] was born in Dec 1860 in Missouri, USA [1132]. She lived in Clay, Dunklin, Missouri, USA in 1900 [1132]. Elijah Baker and Frances M. (unknown maiden name) were married in 1876 [536]. They had the following children:

i. Willie L. Baker [1133] was born in Dec 1881 in Missouri, USA [1133]. She lived in Clay, Dunklin, Missouri, USA in 1900 [1133].

ii. Martha E. Baker [1134] was born in Aug 1890 in Missouri, USA [1134]. She lived in Clay, Dunklin, Missouri, USA in 1900 [1134].

iii. Charles Baker [1135] was born in May 1894 in Missouri, USA [1135]. He lived in Clay, Dunklin, Missouri, USA in 1900 [1135].

143. *Texas Lucy Baker*-13 (Cassinda Ann-12, Ransom Columbus-11, Edmond-10, William-9, William-8, Richard-7, John-6, William-5, Timothy-4, Richard-3, John-2, Robert-1) [538, 539, 540, 541] was born in Oct 1862 in Mississippi, USA [538, 539, 540, 541]. She lived in Hopkins, Texas, USA in 1880 [538]. She died in 1933 in Pickton, Hopkins, Texas, USA. **Thomas J. Jackson** [1136, 542, 1137, 1138] was born in Jun 1858 in Texas, USA [1136, 542, 1137, 1138]. He lived in Hopkins, Texas, USA in 1880 [1136]. Thomas J. Jackson and Texas Lucy Baker were married in 1879 [542]. They had the following children:

i. Jasper C. Jackson [1139] was born in May 1880 in Texas, USA [1139]. He lived in Hopkins, Texas, USA in 1900 [1139].

ii. Cora B. Jackson [1140] was born in Sep 1881 in Texas, USA [1140]. She lived in Hopkins, Texas, USA in 1900 [1140].

iii. Manda C. Jackson [1141] was born in Feb 1884 in Texas, USA [1141]. She lived in Hopkins, Texas, USA in 1900 [1141].

iv. Aldine Jackson [1142] was born in Sep 1886 in Texas, USA [1142]. He lived in Hopkins, Texas, USA in 1900 [1142].

v. John H. Jackson [1143] was born in Dec 1891 in Texas, USA [1143]. He lived in Hopkins, Texas, USA in 1900 [1143].

vi. Annie J. Jackson [1144] was born in Sep 1896 in Texas, USA [1144]. She lived in Hopkins, Texas, USA in 1900 [1144]. She lived in Hopkins, Texas, USA in 1920 [1145].

148. *James Franklin Reeves*-13 (Benjamin W-12, Richmond-11, Edmond-10, William-9, William-8, Richard-7, John-6, William-5, Timothy-4, Richard-3, John-2, Robert-1) [553, 554, 555, 556] was born on 04 Oct 1874 in Attalla, Etowah, Alabama, USA [553, 554, 555, 556]. He lived in Ball Play, Etowah, Alabama, USA in 1880 [553]. He died on 30 Aug 1941 in Etowah, Alabama, USA. **Katie Lee (unknown maiden name)** [1146, 1147] was born about 1885 in Alabama, USA [1146, 1147]. She lived in Cox, Etowah, Alabama, USA in 1930 [1147]. James Franklin Reeves and Katie Lee (unknown maiden name) married and had the following children:

i. Ethel F. Reaves [1148] was born about 1906 in Alabama, USA [1148]. She lived in Cox, Etowah, Alabama, USA in 1910 [1148].

ii. Ester L. Reaves [1149] was born about 1908 in Alabama, USA [1149]. She lived in Cox, Etowah, Alabama, USA in 1910 [1149].

iii. Vester Reeves [1150] was born about 1911 [1150]. She lived in Cox, Etowah, Alabama, USA in 1930 [1150].

iv. Chester Reeves [1151] was born about 1916 [1151]. He lived in Cox, Etowah, Alabama, USA in 1930 [1151].

v.   A. B. Reeves [1152] was born about 1919 [1152]. He lived in Cox, Etowah, Alabama, USA in 1930 [1152].

152.   *Sarah Irene Young*-13 (Rebecca-12, Nathan-11, Edmond-10, William-9, William-8, Richard-7, John-6, William-5, Timothy-4, Richard-3, John-2, Robert-1) [585, 586, 587] was born on 14 Jan 1882 in Cherokee, Alabama, USA [585, 586]. She lived in Greens Schoolhouse, Calhoun, Alabama, USA in 1910 [586]. She died on 25 Apr 1957 in Etowah, Alabama, USA [587]. **Rastus Lone Bullock** [1153, 1154] was born on 08 Jun 1881 in Walton, Georgia, USA [1153, 1154]. He lived in Greens Schoolhouse, Calhoun, Alabama, USA in 1910 [1154]. He died on 18 Jun 1947 in Calhoun, Alabama, USA. Rastus Lone Bullock and Sarah Irene Young were married on 03 Jun 1902 in Cherokee, Alabama, USA. They had the following children:

i.   Infant Bullock was born on 01 Jul 1903 in Calhoun, Alabama, USA. She died in 1903 in Calhoun, Alabama, USA.

ii.   Ollivett Houston Bullock [1155, 1156, 1157] was born on 02 Sep 1904 in Alabama, USA [1155, 1156, 1157]. He lived in Greens Schoolhouse, Calhoun, Alabama, USA in 1910 [1157]. He died on 09 Dec 1979 in Gadsden, Etowah, Alabama, USA [1156].

iii.   James Tollie Bullock [1158, 1159, 1160, 1161] was born on 17 Mar 1909 in Calhoun, Alabama, USA [1158, 1159, 1160, 1161]. He lived in Greens Schoolhouse, Calhoun, Alabama, USA in 1920 [1158]. He died in Dec 1980 in Etowah, Alabama, USA [1161].

iv.   Zada Gertrude Bullock [1162] was born on 09 Sep 1911 in Alabama, USA [1162]. She lived in Greens Schoolhouse, Calhoun, Alabama, USA in 1920 [1162]. She died on 25 Feb 2002 in Hokes Bluff, Etowah, Alabama, USA.

v.   John Murman Bullock [1158] was born on 16 May 1914 in Calhoun, Alabama, USA [1158]. He lived in Greens Schoolhouse, Calhoun, Alabama, USA in 1920 [1158]. He died on 07 Aug 1997 in Etowah, Alabama, USA.

vi.   Gracey Rebecca Bullock [1163, 1164] was born on 04 Nov 1916 in Alabama, USA [1163, 1164]. She lived in Greens Schoolhouse, Calhoun, Alabama, USA in 1930 [1164]. She died on 25 Feb 2002 in Shelby, Alabama, USA.

vii.   Bernice Etna Bullock [1165] was born on 23 Oct 1919 in Calhoun, Alabama, USA [1165]. She lived in Greens Schoolhouse, Calhoun, Alabama, USA in 1920 [1165]. She died on 13 Feb 1998 in Jefferson, Alabama, USA.

155.   *Irena D. Reeves*-13 (John S.-12, Nathan-11, Edmond-10, William-9, William-8, Richard-7, John-6, William-5, Timothy-4, Richard-3, John-2, Robert-1) [592, 593, 594, 595, 596, 597] was born in Feb 1847 in Alabama, USA [592, 593, 594, 595]. She lived in Corinth, Dekalb, Alabama, USA in 1910 [592]. She died after 1920. **Joseph S. Absher [**1166, 1167, 1168, 1169, 1170, 1171] was born in Feb 1847 in Georgia, USA [1166, 1167, 1168, 1169, 1170]. He lived in Van Buren, Dekalb, Alabama, USA in 1900 [1170]. He died on 17 Feb 1922 in Dekalb, Alabama, USA [1171]. Joseph S. Absher and Irena D. Reeves married and had the following children:

i. Neina M. Absher [1172] was born in Nov 1880 in Alabama, USA [1172]. She lived in Van Buren, Dekalb, Alabama, USA in 1900 [1172].

ii. Ethel Absher [1173, 1174] was born about 1888 in Alabama, USA [1174]. She lived in Corinth, Dekalb, Alabama, USA in 1910 [1174]. She died on 30 Apr 1914 in Dekalb, Alabama, USA [1173].

iii. Lillian P. Absher [1175] was born in Apr 1892 in Alabama, USA [1175]. She lived in Van Buren, Dekalb, Alabama, USA in 1900 [1175].

iv. (156) Carrie G. Absher [1176, 1177, 1178, 1179, 1180, 1181] was born on 15 Jun 1896 in Alabama, USA [1176, 1177, 1178, 1179, 1180].

v. (157) Joseph Himond Absher [1183, 1184, 1185, 1186, 1187, 1188, 1189] was born on 04 Jul 1898 in Alabama, USA [1183, 1184, 1185, 1186, 1187, 1188, 1189].

158. William Clemens Reeves-13 (John S.-12, Nathan-11, Edmond-10, William-9, William-8, Richard-7, John-6, William-5, Timothy-4, Richard-3, John-2, Robert-1) [610, 611, 612, 613, 614, 615] was born on 25 Feb 1853 in Etowah, Alabama, USA [611, 612, 614, 615]. He died on 31 Jan 1908 in Ball Play, Etowah, Alabama, USA. He was employed as a Farmer in Hokes Bluff, Etowah, Alabama, USA. He lived in USA [610]. **Sarah J. Gaddis** daughter of Archibald Gaddis and Lou Sinthia Hunt [1190, 1191, 1192, 616] was born in 1852 in Cherokee, Alabama, USA [1190, 1191, 1192]. She lived in Cherokee, Alabama, USA in 1860 [1192]. She died on 23 May 1900 in Ball Play, Etowah, Alabama, USA. William Clemens Reeves and Sarah J. Gaddis were married on 21 Nov 1875 in Etowah, Alabama, USA [613, 616]. They had the following children:

i. (191) Euclid Reeves [1193, 1194, 1195, 1196, 1197, 1198, 1199] was born on 14 Oct 1876 in Alabama, USA [1194, 1195, 1196, 1197, 1198].

ii. (159) Luther Reeves [1202, 1203, 1204, 1205, 1206, 1207] was born on 27 Dec 1879 in Hokes Bluff, Etowah, Alabama, USA [1202, 1203, 1204, 1205, 1206].

iii. (220) Liller Reeves was born on 07 Jul 1882 in Alabama, USA [1208, 1209, 1210].

iv. (217) Riller Reeves was born on 07 Jul 1882 in Gadsden, Etowah, Alabama, USA [1215, 1216, 1217, 1218].

v. (247) Claudie Reeves [1221, 1222, 1223, 1224] was born on 16 Jun 1889 in Alabama, USA [1221, 1222, 1223, 1224].

249. John H. Reeves-13 (John S.-12, Nathan-11, Edmond-10, William-9, William-8, Richard-7, John-6, William-5, Timothy-4, Richard-3, John-2, Robert-1) [606, 607, 608, 609] was born about 1849 in Alabama, USA [606, 607, 608, 609]. He lived in Etowah, Alabama, USA in 1880 [606]. **Susan (unknown maiden name)** [1225] was born about 1851 in Alabama, USA [1225]. She lived in Etowah, Alabama, USA in 1880 [1225]. John H. Reeves and Susan (unknown maiden name) married and had the following children:

i. J. H. Reaves [1226] was born about 1874 in Alabama, USA [1226]. He lived in Etowah, Alabama, USA in 1880 [1226].

ii.   Darthla Reaves [1227] was born about 1874 in Alabama, USA [1227]. She lived in Etowah, Alabama, USA in 1880 [1227].

iii. Walter Reaves [1228] was born about 1879 in Alabama, USA [1228]. He lived in Etowah, Alabama, USA in 1880 [1228].

250.   *Lucinda Jane Reeves*-13 (John S.-12, Nathan-11, Edmond-10, William-9, William-8, Richard-7, John-6, William-5, Timothy-4, Richard-3, John-2, Robert-1) [598, 599, 600, 601, 602, 603, 604, 605] was born on 05 Oct 1848 in Alabama, USA [598, 599, 600, 601, 602, 603, 604]. She lived in Warren, Mississippi, USA in 1880 [601]. She died on 25 Feb 1926 in Louisiana, USA [603]. **William B. Davis [**1229, 1230, 1231] was born in Mar 1841 in Alabama, USA [1229, 1230, 1231]. He lived in Warren, Mississippi, USA in 1880 [1230]. He died in 1902 in Mississippi, USA. William B. Davis and Lucinda Jane Reeves were married on 17 Jan 1865 in Jacksonville, Calhoun, Alabama, USA. They had the following children:

i.   George Washington Davis [1232, 1233] was born on 12 Nov 1865 in Alabama, USA [1232, 1233]. He lived in Warren, Mississippi, USA in 1880 [1232]. He died on 28 Mar 1903 in Mississippi, USA.

ii.   William Mack Davis [1234] was born about 1867 in Alabama, USA [1234]. He lived in Warren, Mississippi, USA in 1880 [1234]. He died in 1950 in Mississippi, USA.

iii. Robert Jackson Davis [1235] was born on 15 Mar 1869 in Alabama, USA [1235]. He lived in Warren, Mississippi, USA in 1880 [1235]. He died on 10 Mar 1905.

iv.   R Jasper Davis [1236, 1237] was born in Jan 1873 in Alabama, USA [1236, 1237]. He lived in Warren, Mississippi, USA in 1880 [1237]. He died in 1900.

v.   Richmond Peeler Davis [1238, 1239, 1240] was born on 02 Feb 1875 in Louisiana, USA [1238, 1239, 1240]. He lived in Warren, Mississippi, USA in 1880 [1238]. He died on 27 Jun 1931 in Baton Rouge, East Baton Rouge, Louisiana, USA [1240].

vi.   Davis Davis [1241] was born about 1875 in Mississippi, USA [1241]. He lived in Warren, Mississippi, USA in 1880 [1241].

vii. Ben F. Davis was born on 31 Mar 1877.

viii. Ralph Valintine Davis [1242] was born on 15 Feb 1879 in Mississippi, USA [1242]. He lived in Warren, Mississippi, USA in 1880 [1242]. He died in 1926 in Texas, USA.

ix.   Sarah Margaret Ann (Annie) Davis [1243] was born on 17 Nov 1882 in Mississippi, USA [1243]. She lived in Warren, Mississippi, USA in 1900 [1243]. She died on 30 Aug 1926 in Baton Rouge, East Baton Rouge, Louisiana, USA.

x.   Olivia Davis [1244] was born in Oct 1891 in Mississippi, USA [1244]. She lived in Warren, Mississippi, USA in 1900 [1244].

251.   *Nathan C. Reeves*-13 (John S.-12, Nathan-11, Edmond-10, William-9, William-8, Richard-7, John-6, William-5, Timothy-4, Richard-3, John-2, Robert-1)

[617, 618, 619, 620, 621, 622, 623] was born on 10 Mar 1857 in Alabama, USA [619, 620, 621]. He died on 24 Jan 1909 in Hokes Bluff, Etowah, Alabama, USA [621]. He lived in USA [622]. **Sarah Ellen Pike** daughter of Joseph Mortermer Baltimore Pike and Martha Allsup [617, 1245, 1246, 1247, 1248, 624] was born on 03 Feb 1861 in Hokes Bluff, Etowah, Alabama, USA [1245, 1246, 1247]. She lived in Hokes Bluff, Etowah, Alabama, USA in 1910 [1245]. She died on 22 May 1953 in Etowah, Alabama, USA [1248]. Nathan C. Reeves and Sarah Ellen Pike were married on 10 Apr 1879 in Etowah, Alabama, USA [617, 618, 620, 624, 625]. They had the following children:

i.   Lula A. Reeves [1249] was born in Jan 1880 in Alabama, USA [1249]. She lived in Turkeytown, Etowah, Alabama, USA in 1900 [1249].

ii. (253) Arthur Columbus Reeves [1250, 1251, 1252, 1253, 1254] was born on 10 Sep 1881 in Alabama, USA [1251, 1252, 1253, 1254]. He died in May 1933 in Etowah, Alabama, USA [1250].

iii. (252) Marion Frank Reeves [1255, 1256, 1257, 1258, 1259, 1260] was born on 12 Nov 1884 in Alabama, USA [1255, 1256, 1257, 1258, 1259]. He died in Jan 1971 in Gadsden, Etowah, Alabama, USA [1260].

iv. Hattie B. Reeves [1261] was born in Aug 1886 in Alabama, USA [1261]. She lived in Turkeytown, Etowah, Alabama, USA in 1900 [1261].

v.   Mamie R. Reeves [1262] was born in Apr 1889 in Alabama, USA [1262]. She lived in Turkeytown, Etowah, Alabama, USA in 1900 [1262].

vi. Joseph N. Reeves [1263] was born in Mar 1892 in Alabama, USA [1263]. He lived in Turkeytown, Etowah, Alabama, USA in 1900 [1263].

vii. Gertrude Reeves [1264, 1265] was born in Feb 1895 in Alabama, USA [1264, 1265]. She lived in Hokes Bluff, Etowah, Alabama, USA in 1910 [1264].

254. James H. Reeves-13 (John S.-12, Nathan-11, Edmond-10, William-9, William-8, Richard-7, John-6, William-5, Timothy-4, Richard-3, John-2, Robert-1) [628] was born about 1863 in Alabama, USA [628]. He lived in Etowah, Alabama, USA in 1870 [628]. **Mattie C. Lowry** [1266, 1267, 1268] was born about 1866 in Alabama, USA [1266, 1267, 1269, 1268]. She lived in Butler, Alabama, USA in 1870 [1266]. James H. Reeves and Mattie C. Lowry married and had the following children:

i.   Maylla V. Reeves [1270] was born about 1901 in Texas, USA [1270]. She lived in Hagerman, Chaves, New Mexico, USA in 1910 [1270].

Generation 14

16. Winfield Frank Batey-14 (Samantha Alice-13, Elizabeth Anna-12, Susan ?Jane?-11, Nathan-10, William-9, William-8, Richard-7, John-6, William-5, Timothy-4, Richard-3, John-2, Robert-1) [634, 635, 636] was born in Mar 1885 in Cherokee, Alabama, USA [634, 635, 636]. He lived in Greens Schoolhouse, Calhoun, Alabama, USA in 1920 [636]. He died on 17 May 1964 in Alabama, USA. **Willie (unknown maiden name)** [1271] was born about 1896 in Georgia, USA [1271]. She lived in Greens Schoolhouse, Calhoun, Alabama, USA in 1920

[1271]. Winfield Frank Batey and Willie (unknown maiden name) married and had the following children:

    i.   Lola E. Batey [1272] was born about 1911 in Alabama, USA [1272]. She lived in Greens Schoolhouse, Calhoun, Alabama, USA in 1920 [1272].

    ii.   Trudie Pearl Batey [1273] was born about 1913 in Alabama, USA [1273]. She lived in Greens Schoolhouse, Calhoun, Alabama, USA in 1920 [1273].

    iii.   William O. Batey [1274] was born about 1916 in Alabama, USA [1274]. He lived in Greens Schoolhouse, Calhoun, Alabama, USA in 1920 [1274].

17.   *Shelby Alloway Batey*-14 (Samantha Alice-13, Elizabeth Anna-12, Susan ?Jane?-11, Nathan-10, William-9, William-8, Richard-7, John-6, William-5, Timothy-4, Richard-3, John-2, Robert-1) [637, 638, 639, 640, 641, 642] was born on 12 Nov 1886 in Alabama, USA [637, 638, 639, 640, 641]. He lived in Snows, Calhoun, Alabama, USA in 1930 [641]. He died on 02 Feb 1935 in Calhoun, Alabama, USA [642]. **Ida B. (unknown maiden name)** [1275, 1276] was born about 1891 in Alabama, USA [1275, 1276]. She lived in Snows, Calhoun, Alabama, USA in 1930 [1276]. Shelby Alloway Batey and Ida B. (unknown maiden name) married and had the following children:

    i.   Clarence S. Batey [1277, 1278] was born about 1913 in Alabama, USA [1277, 1278]. He lived in Snows, Calhoun, Alabama, USA in 1930 [1278].

    ii.   Lucile Batey [1279, 1280] was born about 1916 in Alabama, USA [1279, 1280]. She lived in Snows, Calhoun, Alabama, USA in 1930 [1280].

    iii.   Hugh L. Batey [1281, 1282] was born about 1918 in Alabama, USA [1281, 1282]. He lived in Snows, Calhoun, Alabama, USA in 1930 [1282].

    iv.   Vera Mae Batey [1283] was born about 1920 [1283]. She lived in Snows, Calhoun, Alabama, USA in 1930 [1283].

    v.   Sherman Batey [1284] was born about 1925 [1284]. He lived in Snows, Calhoun, Alabama, USA in 1930 [1284].

    vi.   Herbert Batey [1285] was born about 1928 [1285]. He lived in Snows, Calhoun, Alabama, USA in 1930 [1285].

18.   *Lela Ruth Batey*-14 (Samantha Alice-13, Elizabeth Anna-12, Susan ?Jane?-11, Nathan-10, William-9, William-8, Richard-7, John-6, William-5, Timothy-4, Richard-3, John-2, Robert-1) [647, 648, 649, 650, 651] was born on 22 Mar 1896 in Cherokee, Alabama, USA [647, 648, 649, 650, 651]. She lived in Chattanooga, Hamilton, Tennessee, USA in 1930 [651]. She died on 23 Mar 1978 in Anniston, Calhoun, Alabama, USA [650]. **Frank Marlow**'s birth date is unknown. He died before 1920. Frank Marlow and Lela Ruth Batey married and had the following children:

    i.   Lewis Dewitt Marlow [1286, 1287] was born on 28 Aug 1913 in Calhoun, Alabama, USA [1286, 1288, 1287]. He lived in Chattanooga, Hamilton, Tennessee, USA in 1930 [1287]. He died on 29 Mar 1980 in Anniston, Calhoun, Alabama, USA [1288].

ii. Frances Virginia Marlow [1289, 1290] was born in Jan 1915 in Calhoun, Alabama, USA [1289, 1290]. She lived in Chattanooga, Hamilton, Tennessee, USA in 1930 [1290]. She died on 03 Nov 1990.

23. *Vernie Leroy Smith*-14 (Alice-13, Susan Jane-12, Susan ?Jane?-11, Nathan-10, William-9, William-8, Richard-7, John-6, William-5, Timothy-4, Richard-3, John-2, Robert-1) [663, 664, 665, 666, 667] was born on 31 May 1893 in Denton, Denton, Texas, USA [663, 664, 665, 666, 667]. He lived in Coalgate, Coal, Oklahoma, USA in 1910 [665]. He died on 23 Nov 1979 in Henryetta, Okmulgee, Oklahoma, USA [663]. **Beatrice (unknown maiden name)** [1291, 1292] was born about 1897 in Texas, USA [1291, 1292]. She lived in Henryetta, Okmulgee, Oklahoma, USA in 1930 [1292]. Vernie Leroy Smith and Beatrice (unknown maiden name) married and had the following children:

i. Wanza Smith [1293, 1294] was born about 1917 in Oklahoma, USA [1293, 1294]. She lived in Henryetta, Okmulgee, Oklahoma, USA in 1930 [1294].

ii. Lavern Smith [1295] was born about 1922 [1295]. She lived in Henryetta, Okmulgee, Oklahoma, USA in 1930 [1295].

24. *Gertrude Vashti Smith*-14 (Alice-13, Susan Jane-12, Susan ?Jane?-11, Nathan-10, William-9, William-8, Richard-7, John-6, William-5, Timothy-4, Richard-3, John-2, Robert-1) [669, 670, 671, 672] was born on 19 May 1896 in Conroe, Montgomery, Texas, USA [669, 670, 671, 672]. She lived in Hobbs, Lea, New Mexico, USA in 1930 [672]. She died on 22 Aug 1990 in Tempe, Maricopa, Arizona, USA [671]. **George T. Harris** [1296, 1297] was born about 1895 in Texas, USA [1296, 1297]. He lived in Hobbs, Lea, New Mexico, USA in 1930 [1297]. George T. Harris and Gertrude Vashti Smith married and had the following children:

i. G. T. Harris [1298] was born about 1923 [1298]. He lived in Hobbs, Lea, New Mexico, USA in 1930 [1298].

ii. Glen R. Harris [1299] was born about 1925 [1299]. He lived in Hobbs, Lea, New Mexico, USA in 1930 [1299].

iii. Gladys L. Harris [1300] was born about 1927 [1300]. She lived in Hobbs, Lea, New Mexico, USA in 1930 [1300].

25. *James Harrison Smith*-14 (Alice-13, Susan Jane-12, Susan ?Jane?-11, Nathan-10, William-9, William-8, Richard-7, John-6, William-5, Timothy-4, Richard-3, John-2, Robert-1) [673, 674, 675, 676, 677] was born on 09 Nov 1899 in Gainesville, Cooke, Texas, USA [673, 674, 675, 676, 677]. He lived in Henryetta, Okmulgee, Oklahoma, USA in 1920 [677]. He died on 21 Jun 1974 in Raton, Colfax, New Mexico, USA [675]. **Callie (unknown maiden name)** [1301, 1302] was born about 1902 in Oklahoma, USA [1301, 1302]. She lived in Henryetta, Okmulgee, Oklahoma, USA in 1920 [1302]. James Harrison Smith and Callie (unknown maiden name) married and had the following children:

i. Gilbert L. Smith [1303] was born about 1921 [1303]. He lived in Borger, Hutchinson, Texas, USA in 1930 [1303].

ii. Allen R. Smith [1304] was born about 1927 [1304]. He lived in Borger, Hutchinson, Texas, USA in 1930 [1304].

34. *William Monroe Henley*-14 (Elizabeth Marinda-13, William McGuire-12, William Emery-11, Edmond-10, William-9, William-8, Richard-7, John-6, William-5, Timothy-4, Richard-3, John-2, Robert-1) [701, 702, 703, 704] was born on 12 Mar 1872 in Alabama, USA [701, 702, 703]. He lived in Renfroe, Talladega, Alabama, USA in 1930 [701]. He died on 14 Dec 1933 in Renfroe, Talladega, Alabama, USA [704]. **Minnie Lee Jones** daughter of Charles Thomas Jones and Margarette Matilda Green [1305, 1306, 1307, 1308] was born on 31 Dec 1879 in Alabama, USA [1305, 1306, 1307, 1308]. She lived in Wicker, Clay, Alabama, USA in 1900 [1305]. She died on 29 Jul 1961 in Renfroe, Talladega, Alabama, USA. William Monroe Henley and Minnie Lee Jones were married on 12 Dec 1894 [703]. They had the following children:

 i. Willie B. Henley [1309, 1310] was born on 06 Feb 1896 in Alabama, USA [1309, 1310]. She married Unknown before 1917. She died on 02 Apr 1968 in the USA. She lived in Covington, Alabama, USA [1309].

 ii. (35) Arthur Finis Henley [1311, 1312, 1313, 1314, 1315] was born on 31 Jul 1898 in Alabama, USA [1311, 1312, 1313, 1314, 1315]. He died on 07 Oct 1972 in Talladega, Talladega, Alabama, USA [1313].

 iii. (36) Winford Carl Henley [1316, 1317, 1318, 1319, 1320] was born on 13 Aug 1900 in Alabama, USA [1316, 1317, 1318, 1319, 1320]. He died on 11 May 1992 in Panama City, Bay, Florida, USA [1318, 1320].

 iv. Lelas Henley was born on 15 Sep 1902 in Talladega, Talladega, Alabama, USA. He died on 15 Feb 1903 in the USA.

 v. Cecil Monroe Henley [1321, 1322, 1323] was born on 15 Feb 1903 in Alabama, USA [1321, 1322, 1323]. He lived in Renfroe, Talladega, Alabama, USA in 1930 [1323]. He died on 03 Sep 1982 in Talladega, Talladega, Alabama, USA [1321].

 vi. Pauline Henley [1324, 1325] was born on 07 Jun 1906 in Alabama, USA [1324, 1325]. She lived in Renfroe, Talladega, Alabama, USA in 1930 [1325]. She died on 06 Aug 1962 in the USA.

 vii. Vesey O. Henley [1326, 1327, 1328] was born on 28 Oct 1908 in Alabama, USA [1326, 1327, 1328]. He lived in Renfroe, Talladega, Alabama, USA in 1930 [1327]. He married Mildred Mosley on 06 Sep 1940. He died on 24 Nov 1975 in Talladega, Talladega, Alabama, USA [1328].

 viii. Mozell Henley [1329, 1330] was born on 31 Dec 1910 in Talladega, Talladega, Alabama, USA [1329, 1330]. She lived in Renfroe, Talladega, Alabama, USA in 1930 [1330]. She died on 22 Jan 2001 in Birmingham, Jefferson, Alabama, USA.

 ix. Agnes Henley [1331, 1332] was born on 02 Mar 1913 in Talladega, Talladega, Alabama, USA [1331, 1332]. She lived in Renfroe, Talladega, Alabama, USA in 1930 [1332]. She died in the USA.

 x. David Patrick Henley [1333, 1334, 1335] was born on 12 Oct 1916 in Alabama, USA [1333, 1334, 1335]. He lived in Renfroe, Talladega, Alabama, USA in 1930 [1335]. He died on 21 Jan 1998 in Birmingham, Jefferson, Alabama, USA [1333].

xi.   Minnie Lue Henley [1336, 1337] was born on 21 Dec 1918 in Alabama, USA [1336, 1337]. She lived in Renfroe, Talladega, Alabama, USA in 1930 [1337]. She died in the USA.

xii.   Clara Lee Henley [1338] was born on 07 Oct 1921 in USA [1338]. She lived in Renfroe, Talladega, Alabama, USA in 1930 [1338]. She died in the USA.

37.   *Porter Wallace Henley*-14 (Elizabeth Marinda-13, William McGuire-12, William Emery-11, Edmond-10, William-9, William-8, Richard-7, John-6, William-5, Timothy-4, Richard-3, John-2, Robert-1) [705, 706, 707] was born on 22 Apr 1878 in Alabama, USA [705, 706]. He lived in Talladega, Talladega, Alabama, USA in 1930 [705]. He died on 11 Mar 1945 in Talladega, Talladega, Alabama, USA [707]. **Nonnie B. (unknown maiden name)** [1339] was born about 1886 [1339]. She lived in Talladega, Talladega, Alabama, USA in 1930 [1339]. Porter Wallace Henley and Nonnie B. (unknown maiden name) married and had the following children:

i.   Wallace B. Henley [1340] was born about 1909 [1340]. He lived in Talladega, Talladega, Alabama, USA in 1930 [1340].

ii.   Julian Henley [1341] was born about 1915 [1341]. He lived in Talladega, Talladega, Alabama, USA in 1930 [1341].

iii.   Thurston Henley [1342] was born about 1916 [1342]. He lived in Talladega, Talladega, Alabama, USA in 1930 [1342].

iv.   Mattie M. Henley [1343] was born about 1918 [1343]. She lived in Talladega, Talladega, Alabama, USA in 1930 [1343].

v.   James R. Henley [1344] was born about 1926 [1344]. He lived in Talladega, Talladega, Alabama, USA in 1930 [1344].

vi.   Walter W. Henley [1345] was born about 1926 [1345]. He lived in Talladega, Talladega, Alabama, USA in 1930 [1345].

39.   *Sylvester Reaves*-14 (William Patrick-13, William McGuire-12, William Emery-11, Edmond-10, William-9, William-8, Richard-7, John-6, William-5, Timothy-4, Richard-3, John-2, Robert-1) [729, 730, 731, 732, 733, 734] was born on 25 Aug 1878 in Anniston, Calhoun, Alabama, USA [729, 730, 731, 732, 733]. He lived in Anniston, Calhoun, Alabama, USA in 1930 [733]. He died on 17 Aug 1932 in Anniston, Calhoun, Alabama, USA. **Minnie Lillian Farrell** [1365] was born on 05 Aug 1880 in Anniston, Calhoun, Alabama, USA [1365]. She lived in Anniston, Calhoun, Alabama, USA in 1910 [1365]. She died on 08 Oct 1918 in Anniston, Calhoun, Alabama, USA. Sylvester Reaves and Minnie Lillian Farrell were married on 30 Dec 1900 in Anniston, Calhoun, Alabama, USA. They had the following children:

i.   Archer Ledur Reaves was born on 23 Mar 1902 in Anniston, Calhoun, Alabama, USA [1366]. He lived in Anniston, Calhoun, Alabama, USA in 1910 [1366]. He died on 15 Apr 1963 in Anniston, Calhoun, Alabama, USA.

ii.   Dallas Marie Reaves [1352] was born about 1904 in Alabama, USA [1352]. He lived in Anniston, Calhoun, Alabama, USA in 1920 [1352]. He died on 19 Apr 1960 in Lincoln, Talladega, Alabama, USA.

iii. Hayden Elonzo Reaves [1353] was born on 06 Apr 1905 in Alabama, USA [1353]. He lived in Anniston, Calhoun, Alabama, USA in 1920 [1353]. He died on 04 Jan 1944 in Calhoun, Alabama, USA.

iv. Annie Lois Reaves [1354, 1355] was born on 03 Apr 1907 in Anniston, Calhoun, Alabama, USA [1354, 1355]. She lived in Anniston, Calhoun, Alabama, USA in 1920 [1355]. She died on 30 Sep 1952.

v. Lois H. Reaves [1354, 1355] was born about 1908 in Alabama, USA [1354, 1355]. She lived in Anniston, Calhoun, Alabama, USA in 1910 [1354].

vi. William Claude Reaves [1356, 1367] was born on 03 Mar 1910 in Anniston, Calhoun, Alabama, USA [1356, 1367]. He lived in Anniston, Calhoun, Alabama, USA in 1910 [1367].

vii. James Clinton Reaves [1358, 1359] was born on 03 Mar 1910 in Anniston, Calhoun, Alabama, USA [1358, 1359]. He lived in Anniston, Calhoun, Alabama, USA in 1910 [1359]. He lived in Anniston, Calhoun, Alabama, USA in 1920 [1358]. He died on 11 Nov 1924 in Calhoun, Alabama, USA.

viii. Sylvester M. Reaves [1360] was born about 1913 in Alabama, USA [1360]. He lived in Anniston, Calhoun, Alabama, USA in 1920 [1360].

ix. Clemmie G. Reaves [1361] was born about 1915 in Alabama, USA [1361]. She lived in Anniston, Calhoun, Alabama, USA in 1920 [1361].

Cassie Floyd daughter of Cora Floyd [1348, 1349, 1350, 1351] was born on 07 Feb 1890 in Georgia, USA [1348, 1349, 1350]. She lived in Keysburg, Etowah, Alabama, USA in 1900 [1350]. She died on 02 Apr 1946 in Anniston, Calhoun, Alabama, USA. Sylvester Reaves and Cassie Floyd were married in 1919 in Calhoun, Alabama, USA. They had the following children:

i. Floyd Monroe Reaves [1362] was born on 28 Apr 1920 in Calhoun, Alabama, USA [1362]. He lived in Anniston, Calhoun, Alabama, USA in 1930 [1362]. He died on 29 Apr 1972 in Calhoun, Alabama, USA.

ii. Margaret Blanche Reaves [1363] was born on 16 Oct 1921 (lived in Florida in 1974) [1363]. She lived in Anniston, Calhoun, Alabama, USA in 1930 [1363]. She died in 1989.

iii. Bennie O'Donell Reaves [1364] was born on 23 Sep 1923 in Calhoun, Alabama, USA [1364]. He lived in Anniston, Calhoun, Alabama, USA in 1930 [1364]. He died on 02 Oct 1974 in Calhoun, Alabama, USA.

iv. Clemmie Reaves [1346] was born about 1925 [1346]. She lived in Anniston, Calhoun, Alabama, USA in 1930 [1346].

v. Charlestte Reaves [1347] was born about 1928 [1347]. She lived in Anniston, Calhoun, Alabama, USA in 1930 [1347].

40. *Margie Belle Reaves*-14 (William Patrick-13, William McGuire-12, William Emery-11, Edmond-10, William-9, William-8, Richard-7, John-6, William-5, Timothy-4, Richard-3, John-2, Robert-1) [737] was born on 23 Jan 1884 in Alabama, USA [737]. She lived in Calhoun, Alabama, USA in 1900 [737]. She died in Anniston, Calhoun, Alabama, USA. **Arthur William Locke** was born on 17 May 1884 in Willmar, Kandiyohi, Minnesota, USA. He died on 16 Apr 1959 in

Birmingham, Jefferson, Alabama, USA. Arthur William Locke and Margie Belle Reaves married and had the following children:

 i. Annie Belle Locke was born on 26 Sep 1906 in Anniston, Calhoun, Alabama, USA. She died on 14 Apr 1986 in Pasadena, Los Angeles, California, USA.

 ii. Arthur Craig Locke was born on 25 Apr 1909 in Calhoun, Alabama, USA. He died on 07 Dec 1909 in Calhoun, Alabama, USA.

 iii. Claude Chason Locke was born on 18 Jul 1911 in Alabama, USA. He died on 26 May 1969.

 iv. Wilmar Patrick Locke was born on 28 Apr 1915 in Calhoun, Alabama, USA. He died on 11 Dec 1986.

 v. Margaret Grace Locke was born on 09 Feb 1919 in Calhoun, Alabama, USA. She died on 15 Mar 1996 in Clermont, Hall, Georgia, USA.

41. *William Monroe Reaves*-14 (William Patrick-13, William McGuire-12, William Emery-11, Edmond-10, William-9, William-8, Richard-7, John-6, William-5, Timothy-4, Richard-3, John-2, Robert-1) [735, 736] was born in Jun 1882 in Alabama, USA [735, 736]. He lived in Mobile, Alabama, USA in 1910 [736]. He died on 19 Apr 1916 in Mobile, Alabama, USA. **Amy Jane Burgess [**1368] was born about 1885 in Tuscaloosa, Tuscaloosa, Alabama, USA [1368]. She lived in Mobile, Alabama, USA in 1910 [1368]. William Monroe Reaves and Amy Jane Burgess married and had the following children:

 i. Celeste M. Reaves [1369] was born about 1905 in Mobile, Alabama, USA [1369]. She lived in Mobile, Alabama, USA in 1910 [1369].

 ii. Leo W. Reaves [1370] was born about 1909 in Mobile, Alabama, USA [1370]. He lived in Mobile, Alabama, USA in 1910 [1370].

42. *Lula Merendia Reaves*-14 (William Patrick-13, William McGuire-12, William Emery-11, Edmond-10, William-9, William-8, Richard-7, John-6, William-5, Timothy-4, Richard-3, John-2, Robert-1) [739] was born on 15 Jan 1890 in Alabama, USA [739]. She lived in Calhoun, Alabama, USA in 1900 [739]. She died on 27 May 1957 in Calhoun, Alabama, USA. **William Leroy Parker** was born on 07 Feb 1890 in Gadsden, Etowah, Alabama, USA. He died on 17 Jan 1974 in Birmingham, Jefferson, Alabama, USA. William Leroy Parker and Lula Merendia Reaves were married on 15 Dec 1912. They had the following children:

 i. William Leroy Parker Jr. was born on 07 Feb 1915 in Anniston, Calhoun, Alabama, USA. He died on 17 Jan 1974 in Birmingham, Jefferson, Alabama, USA.

 ii. Mary Agnes Parker was born in Mar 1920. She died on 28 May 1921.

43. *Minnie Mae Reaves*-14 (William Patrick-13, William McGuire-12, William Emery-11, Edmond-10, William-9, William-8, Richard-7, John-6, William-5, Timothy-4, Richard-3, John-2, Robert-1) [714, 715, 716, 717, 718] was born on 07 Dec 1896 in Alabama, USA [714, 715, 716, 717, 718]. She lived in Radford, Virginia, USA in 1920 [718]. She died on 16 Mar 1983 in Plant City, Hillsborough, Florida, USA [716, 717]. **David Walker Sutphin** son of Lee Sutphin and Jane or Jennie (unknown maiden name) [1371, 1372, 1373, 1374, 1375, 1376] was born on 22 Aug 1893 in Radford, Montgomery, Virginia, USA [1371, 1372, 1373, 1374, 1375, 1376]. He lived in Radford, Virginia, USA in 1920 [1372]. He died on 06 Jun 1974 in St Petersburg, Pinellas, Florida, USA [1373, 1374]. David Walker Sutphin and Minnie Mae Reaves were married on 15 Nov 1916 in Calhoun, Alabama, USA. They had the following children:

    i.   William David Sutphin was born on 20 Aug 1917 in Montgomery, Virginia, USA. He died on 20 May 2008 in Reynoldsburg, Franklin, Ohio, USA.

    ii.   Darold Kirby Sutphin was born on 29 May 1921. He died after 1993.

44. *Ida Lee Reaves*-14 (William Patrick-13, William McGuire-12, William Emery-11, Edmond-10, William-9, William-8, Richard-7, John-6, William-5, Timothy-4, Richard-3, John-2, Robert-1) [711, 712, 713] was born on 20 Dec 1894 in Alabama, USA [711, 712, 713]. She lived in Anniston, Calhoun, Alabama, USA in 1910 [713]. She died on 09 Mar 1964 in Dayton, Greene, Ohio, USA. **John Sherman McClintock** was born on 30 Aug 1885. He died in Union City, Adams, Indiana, USA. John Sherman McClintock and Ida Lee Reaves were married on 29 Apr 1919 in Calhoun, Alabama, USA. They had the following children:

    i.   Truel Reaves McClintock was born on 29 May 1921 in Union City, Ashland, Ohio, USA. He died in Union City, Ashland, Ohio, USA.

45. *Josie Elva Reaves*-14 (William Patrick-13, William McGuire-12, William Emery-11, Edmond-10, William-9, William-8, Richard-7, John-6, William-5, Timothy-4, Richard-3, John-2, Robert-1) [723, 724] was born on 31 Aug 1903 in Alabama, USA [723, 724]. She lived in Anniston, Calhoun, Alabama, USA in 1910 [723]. She died on 22 Dec 1987 in San Joaquin, California, USA [724]. **John Alvie Henry** was born on 01 Jan 1889 in Birmingham, Jefferson, Alabama, USA. He died on 31 Mar 1955 in Cowpens, Spartanburg, South Carolina, USA. John Alvie Henry and Josie Elva Reaves were married on 20 Jul 1919. They had the following children:

    i.   William Richard Henry was born on 26 Jul 1928 in Birmingham, Jefferson, Alabama, USA. He died on 04 Dec 1929 in Roswell, Chaves, New Mexico, USA.

Michael Lenal Nelson was born on 23 Mar 1901 in Norway. He died in Fresno, Fresno, California, USA. Michael Lenal Nelson and Josie Elva Reaves were married on 21 Feb 1943. They had no children.

46. *Richard Patrick Reaves*-14 (William Patrick-13, William McGuire-12, William Emery-11, Edmond-10, William-9, William-8, Richard-7, John-6, William-5, Timothy-4, Richard-3, John-2, Robert-1) [719, 720, 721] was born on 23 Jun 1899 in Alabama, USA [719, 720, 721]. He died on 06 Mar 1977 in Birmingham, Jefferson, Alabama, USA. He lived in Calhoun, Alabama, USA [721]. **Annie Kerr Pearce** was born on 18 Apr 1901 in Huntsville, Madison, Alabama, USA. She died on 04 May 1976. Richard Patrick Reaves and Annie Kerr Pearce were married on 08 Sep 1925. They had the following children:

i.   Dorothy Alleen Reaves was born on 08 Oct 1926. She died on 15 Aug 1997 in Huntsville, Madison, Alabama, USA.

ii. Richard Franklin Reaves was born on 31 Aug 1929. He died on 03 Aug 1977 in Calhoun, Alabama, USA.

49.   *Sydney Jackson Reaves*-14 (Andrew Jackson-13, William McGuire-12, William Emery-11, Edmond-10, William-9, William-8, Richard-7, John-6, William-5, Timothy-4, Richard-3, John-2, Robert-1) [750, 751, 752, 753, 754, 755] was born on 08 Jul 1890 in Alabama, USA [750, 751, 752, 753, 754]. He lived in La Grange, Troup, Georgia, USA in 1920 [754]. He died in Mar 1965 in Gadsden, Florida, USA [751, 755]. **Jimmie Lou Johns** daughter of James Elijah Johns and Mary Emily "Mamie" Claxton [1377, 1378, 1379, 1380] was born in Mar 1891 in Georgia, USA [1377, 1378, 1380]. She lived in La Grange, Troup, Georgia, USA in 1920 [1378]. She died on 01 Feb 1942 in Calhoun, Alabama, USA [1379]. Sydney Jackson Reaves and Jimmie Lou Johns married and had the following children:

i.   Julia Winnelle Reaves [1381, 1382, 1383, 1384, 1385, 1386, 1387] was born on 22 Oct 1914 in Anniston, Calhoun, Alabama, USA [1381, 1382, 1383, 1384, 1385, 1386, 1387]. She lived in La Grange, Troup, Georgia, USA in 1920 [1386]. She died on 26 Jun 1978 in Panama City, Bay, Florida, USA [1383, 1387].

50.   *Andrew Walter Reaves*-14 (Andrew Jackson-13, William McGuire-12, William Emery-11, Edmond-10, William-9, William-8, Richard-7, John-6, William-5, Timothy-4, Richard-3, John-2, Robert-1) [746, 747, 748, 749] was born on 17 Aug 1887 in Calhoun, Alabama, USA [746, 747, 748, 749]. He was employed as a Baptist Minister in 1917 in Anniston, Calhoun, Alabama, USA [1388]. He lived in Tarrant, Texas, USA in 1920 [746]. **Julia Eunice Powell** [1389, 1390, 1391] was born about 1891 in Alabama, USA [1389, 1390, 1391]. She lived in Tarrant, Texas, USA in 1920 [1391]. She died in Dec 1973 in Tatum, Rusk, Texas, USA [1389]. Andrew Walter Reaves and Julia Eunice Powell married and had the following children:

i.   Virginia L. Reeves [1392, 1393] was born about 1913 in Alabama, USA [1392, 1393]. She lived in Tarrant, Texas, USA in 1920 [1392].

ii. Katherine Reaves [1394] was born about 1916 in Alabama, USA [1395, 1394]. She lived in Tarrant, Texas, USA in 1920 [1395].

iii. Margaret Reaves [1396] was born about 1923 [1396]. She lived in Jonesboro, Craighead, Arkansas, USA in 1930 [1396].

51.   *Margaret Elizabeth (Lizzie) Reaves*-14 (Andrew Jackson-13, William McGuire-12, William Emery-11, Edmond-10, William-9, William-8, Richard-7, John-6, William-5, Timothy-4, Richard-3, John-2, Robert-1) [744, 745] was born on 05 Mar 1884 in Alabama, USA [744, 745]. She lived in Redland, Hempstead, Arkansas, USA in 1920 [745]. She died on 30 Oct 1976 in McCaskill, Hempstead, Arkansas, USA. **John Sobeski Bittick** [1397] was born on 19 Aug 1878 in Arkansas, USA [1397]. He lived in Redland, Hempstead, Arkansas, USA in 1920 [1397]. He died on 01 May 1975. John Sobeski Bittick and Margaret

Elizabeth (Lizzie) Reaves were married on 27 Jan 1902 in Hope, Hempstead, Arkansas, USA. They had the following children:

    i.   Beatrice Jewel Bittick [1398] was born on 23 Jun 1912 in McCaskill, Hempstead, Arkansas, USA [1398]. She lived in Redland, Hempstead, Arkansas, USA in 1920 [1398]. She died in 1995.

    ii.   Cloid S. Bittick [1399] was born about 1915 in Arkansas, USA [1399]. He lived in Redland, Hempstead, Arkansas, USA in 1920 [1399].

52. ***Otha Lee Reaves*-14** (Andrew Jackson-13, William McGuire-12, William Emery-11, Edmond-10, William-9, William-8, Richard-7, John-6, William-5, Timothy-4, Richard-3, John-2, Robert-1) [763, 764, 765] was born on 05 Feb 1906 in Hempstead, Arkansas, USA [763, 764, 766, 767]. He lived in Redland, Hempstead, Arkansas, USA in 1920 [764]. He died on 20 Jul 1981 in McCaskill, Hempstead, Arkansas, USA [763]. **Lucille E. Borsenberger** daughter of John Albert Borsenberger and Susie Letitia Williams [1400, 1401, 1402, 1403] was born on 10 Aug 1908 in Delight, Pike, Arkansas, USA [1400, 1401, 1402, 1403]. She lived in Redland, Hempstead, Arkansas, USA in 1920 [1400]. She died on 14 Jun 1988 in Prescott, Nevada, Arkansas, USA [1402]. Otha Lee Reaves and Lucille E. Borsenberger were married on 07 Feb 1926. They had the following children:

    i.   Halton Harold Reaves [1404, 1405, 1406, 1407] was born on 04 Mar 1928 in Hempstead, Arkansas, USA [1404, 1405, 1407, 1408]. He lived in Arkansas, USA in 1946 [1407]. He died on 14 Jan 1976 in Harris, Texas, USA [1404, 1405, 1406].

    ii.   Travis Darwin Reaves [1409, 1410, 1411] was born on 14 Dec 1931 in Hempstead, Arkansas, USA [1409, 1411]. He died on 21 Mar 1997 in Highland, Bexar, Texas, USA [1409, 1410, 1411].

56. ***Collie Peyton Ledbetter*-14** (Narcissa-13, Carter Hill-12, William Emery-11, Edmond-10, William-9, William-8, Richard-7, John-6, William-5, Timothy-4, Richard-3, John-2, Robert-1) was born on 10 May 1886 in Jacksonville, Calhoun, Alabama, USA [775, 776, 777]. He lived in Greens Schoolhouse, Calhoun, Alabama, USA in 1930 [777]. He died on 14 Jul 1951 in Piedmont, Calhoun, Alabama, USA. **Lucy Dempsey** daughter of Levi Brickenridge Dempsey and Alice Louisa Reaves [825, 826, 827, 828, 829] was born on 01 Jul 1889 in Alabama, USA [825, 826, 827, 828]. She lived in Greens Schoolhouse, Calhoun, Alabama, USA in 1930 [828]. She died on 15 Sep 1948 in Calhoun, Alabama, USA [829]. Collie Peyton Ledbetter and Lucy Dempsey married and had the following children:

    i.   Talbert J. Ledbetter [1412] was born about 1908 in Alabama, USA [1412]. He lived in Greens Schoolhouse, Calhoun, Alabama, USA in 1920 [1412].

    ii.   Julius O. Ledbetter [1413] was born in 1909 in Alabama, USA [1413]. He lived in Ball Play, Etowah, Alabama, USA in 1910 [1413].

    iii.   Buddie O. Ledbetter [1414] was born about 1910 in Alabama, USA [1414]. He lived in Greens Schoolhouse, Calhoun, Alabama, USA in 1920 [1414].

iv. Lola L. Ledbetter [1415] was born about 1912 in Alabama, USA [1415]. She lived in Greens Schoolhouse, Calhoun, Alabama, USA in 1920 [1415].

v. Alvin T. Ledbetter [1416, 1417] was born about 1914 in Alabama, USA [1416, 1417]. He lived in Greens Schoolhouse, Calhoun, Alabama, USA in 1930 [1417].

vi. Dovvie Lala Ledbetter [1418, 1419] was born about 1915 in Alabama, USA [1418, 1419]. She lived in Greens Schoolhouse, Calhoun, Alabama, USA in 1930 [1419].

vii. Eva P. Ledbetter [1420, 1421] was born about 1917 in Alabama, USA [1420, 1421]. She lived in Greens Schoolhouse, Calhoun, Alabama, USA in 1930 [1421].

viii. Lennard S. Ledbetter [1422] was born about 1919 in Alabama, USA [1422]. He lived in Greens Schoolhouse, Calhoun, Alabama, USA in 1920 [1422].

ix. Elmon Ledbetter [1423] was born about 1919 [1423]. He lived in Greens Schoolhouse, Calhoun, Alabama, USA in 1930 [1423].

x. Ivy Ledbetter [1424] was born about 1922 [1424]. He lived in Greens Schoolhouse, Calhoun, Alabama, USA in 1930 [1424].

xi. Margaret Ledbetter [1425] was born about 1924 [1425]. She lived in Greens Schoolhouse, Calhoun, Alabama, USA in 1930 [1425].

xii. Coleman Ledbetter [1426] was born about 1925 [1426]. He lived in Greens Schoolhouse, Calhoun, Alabama, USA in 1930 [1426].

57. *James Wesley Ledbetter*-14 (Narcissa-13, Carter Hill-12, William Emery-11, Edmond-10, William-9, William-8, Richard-7, John-6, William-5, Timothy-4, Richard-3, John-2, Robert-1) [773, 774] was born on 10 Nov 1883 in Jacksonville, Calhoun, Alabama, USA [773, 774]. He lived in Anniston, Calhoun, Alabama, USA in 1930 [774]. He died on 18 Mar 1956 in Anniston, Calhoun, Alabama, USA. **Maggie E. (unknown maiden name)** [1430] was born about 1886 in Alabama, USA [1430]. She lived in Greens Schoolhouse, Calhoun, Alabama, USA in 1920 [1430]. James Wesley Ledbetter and Maggie E. (unknown maiden name) married and had the following children:

i. Oscar L. Ledbetter [1431] was born about 1904 in Alabama, USA [1431]. He lived in Greens Schoolhouse, Calhoun, Alabama, USA in 1920 [1431].

ii. Benes M. Ledbetter [1432] was born about 1910 in Alabama, USA [1432]. She lived in Greens Schoolhouse, Calhoun, Alabama, USA in 1920 [1432].

iii. Cecil S. Ledbetter [1433, 1434] was born about 1912 in Alabama, USA [1433, 1434]. He lived in Anniston, Calhoun, Alabama, USA in 1930 [1434].

iv. Bernet F. Ledbetter [1435] was born about 1920 in Alabama, USA [1435]. She lived in Greens Schoolhouse, Calhoun, Alabama, USA in 1920 [1435].

59. *Barbara Mary Ann Reaves*-14 (James Martin-13, Carter Hill-12, William Emery-11, Edmond-10, William-9, William-8, Richard-7, John-6, William-5, Timothy-4, Richard-3, John-2, Robert-1) [788, 789, 790] was born on 30 May 1877 in Calhoun, Alabama, USA [788, 789, 790]. She lived in Gum Springs, Etowah, Alabama, USA in 1920 [788]. She died on 23 Nov 1960 in Calhoun,

Alabama, USA. **Jason Daniel Couch** son of John S. Couch and Jamima Demeris Woolf [1436, 1437, 791, 1438] was born on 10 Sep 1870 in Alabama, USA [1436, 1437, 791, 1438]. He lived in Gum Springs, Etowah, Alabama, USA in 1920 [1437]. He died on 02 Oct 1929 in Calhoun, Alabama, USA. Jason Daniel Couch and Barbara Mary Ann Reaves were married on 16 Aug 1891 in Calhoun, Alabama, USA [791]. They had the following children:

i. James Robert Couch [1439] was born on 18 Jun 1892 in Calhoun, Alabama, USA [1439]. He lived in Greens Schoolhouse, Calhoun, Alabama, USA in 1900 [1439]. He died on 12 Oct 1950 in Calhoun, Alabama, USA.

ii. Mandy Emma Couch was born on 01 Sep 1893. She died on 19 Nov 1893.

iii. Ada Couch [1440] was born in Aug 1895 in Alabama, USA [1440]. She lived in Greens Schoolhouse, Calhoun, Alabama, USA in 1900 [1440]. She died on 17 Dec 1928.

iv. Samuel Couch [1441] was born in Sep 1897 in Alabama, USA [1441]. He lived in Greens Schoolhouse, Calhoun, Alabama, USA in 1900 [1441]. He died on 12 Dec in Detroit, Wayne, Michigan, USA.

v. Fannie Couch [1442] was born in Nov 1898 in Alabama, USA [1442]. She lived in Greens Schoolhouse, Calhoun, Alabama, USA in 1900 [1442]. She died on 24 Jan 1989 in Jacksonville, Calhoun, Alabama, USA.

vi. Sula Mae Couch was born on 25 Nov 1900 in Calhoun, Alabama, USA. She died in 1986.

vii. Lamar Sargeant Couch was born on 12 Mar 1902 in Alabama, USA. He died on 12 May 1916.

viii. Paralee Couch was born on 08 Nov 1904 in Alabama, USA. She died on 12 Jun 1980.

ix. Ethel Couch [1443] was born on 26 Aug 1906 in Calhoun, Alabama, USA [1443]. She lived in Gum Springs, Etowah, Alabama, USA in 1920 [1443]. She died on 12 Jul 1960 in Anniston, Calhoun, Alabama, USA.

x. Warvel Foster Couch [1444] was born on 12 Oct 1908 in Gadsden, Etowah, Alabama, USA [1444]. He lived in Gum Springs, Etowah, Alabama, USA in 1920 [1444]. He died on 06 Oct 1992 in Jacksonville, Calhoun, Alabama, USA.

xi. Buna T. Couch [1445] was born on 01 May 1911 in Alabama, USA [1445]. She lived in Gum Springs, Etowah, Alabama, USA in 1920 [1445]. She died on 20 Jan 2000.

xii. (60) Edna Couch [1446] was born on 02 Apr 1914 in Alabama, USA [1446]. She married Hoyt Reeves on 30 Nov 1933. She died on 11 Mar 1998 in Gadsden, Etowah, Alabama, USA [1446].

66. *Robert Joseph Reaves*-14 (James Martin-13, Carter Hill-12, William Emery-11, Edmond-10, William-9, William-8, Richard-7, John-6, William-5, Timothy-4, Richard-3, John-2, Robert-1) [786] was born on 23 Nov 1875 in Calhoun, Alabama, USA [786]. He lived in Greens Schoolhouse, Calhoun, Alabama, USA in 1910 [786]. He died on 24 Jan 1949 in Calhoun, Alabama,

USA. **Theodsian K. (unknown maiden name)** [1447] was born about 1882 in Alabama, USA [1447]. She lived in Greens Schoolhouse, Calhoun, Alabama, USA in 1910 [1447]. Robert Joseph Reaves and Theodsian K (unknown maiden name) married and had the following children:

    i.   Lillie F. Reaves [1448] was born about 1904 in Alabama, USA [1448]. She lived in Greens Schoolhouse, Calhoun, Alabama, USA in 1910 [1448].

    ii.   James L. Reaves [1449] was born about 1905 in Alabama, USA [1449]. He lived in Greens Schoolhouse, Calhoun, Alabama, USA in 1910 [1449].

    iii.   Arthur Reaves [1450] was born about 1909 in Alabama, USA [1450]. He lived in Greens Schoolhouse, Calhoun, Alabama, USA in 1910 [1450].

67. *Frances Elizabeth Reaves*-14 (James Martin-13, Carter Hill-12, William Emery-11, Edmond-10, William-9, William-8, Richard-7, John-6, William-5, Timothy-4, Richard-3, John-2, Robert-1) [795, 796] was born on 11 Mar 1880 in Alabama, USA [795, 796]. She lived in Greens Schoolhouse, Calhoun, Alabama, USA in 1910 [796]. She died on 28 Dec 1918 in Calhoun, Alabama, USA. **Joseph C. Glass** [797, 1451] was born in Jul 1873 in Alabama, USA [797, 1451]. He lived in Greens Schoolhouse, Calhoun, Alabama, USA in 1910 [1451]. Joseph C. Glass and Frances Elizabeth Reaves were married in 1897 [797]. They had the following children:

    i.   James E. Glass [1452, 1453] was born in Mar 1898 in Alabama, USA [1452, 1453]. He lived in Greens Schoolhouse, Calhoun, Alabama, USA in 1910 [1453].

    ii.   Amy B. Glass [1454] was born in Jul 1899 in Alabama, USA [1454]. She lived in Greens Schoolhouse, Calhoun, Alabama, USA in 1900 [1454].

    iii.   Ammie Glass [1455] was born about 1899 in Alabama, USA [1455]. She lived in Greens Schoolhouse, Calhoun, Alabama, USA in 1910 [1455].

    iv.   Mary Glass [1456] was born about 1901 in Alabama, USA [1456]. She lived in Greens Schoolhouse, Calhoun, Alabama, USA in 1910 [1456].

    v.   Clauton Glass [1457] was born about 1903 in Alabama, USA [1457]. He lived in Greens Schoolhouse, Calhoun, Alabama, USA in 1910 [1457].

    vi.   Alice Glass [1458] was born about 1905 in Alabama, USA [1458]. She lived in Greens Schoolhouse, Calhoun, Alabama, USA in 1910 [1458].

    vii.   Eular Glass [1459] was born about 1908 in Alabama, USA [1459]. She lived in Greens Schoolhouse, Calhoun, Alabama, USA in 1910 [1459].

    viii.   Charles Glass [1460] was born about 1910 in Alabama, USA [1460]. He lived in Greens Schoolhouse, Calhoun, Alabama, USA in 1910 [1460].

68. *Walter Thomas Reaves*-14 (James Martin-13, Carter Hill-12, William Emery-11, Edmond-10, William-9, William-8, Richard-7, John-6, William-5, Timothy-4, Richard-3, John-2, Robert-1) [792, 793, 794] was born on 26 Feb 1879 in Jacksonville, Calhoun, Alabama, USA [792, 793, 794]. He lived in Oxford, Calhoun, Alabama, USA in 1920 [794]. He died on 30 Jul 1961 in Weaver, Calhoun, Alabama, USA. **Malvin L. Couch** daughter of Henry L. Couch and Belzona Reaves [813, 814, 815] was born on 21 May 1885 in Calhoun,

Alabama, USA [813, 814, 815, 816]. She lived in Oxford, Calhoun, Alabama, USA in 1920 [814]. She died on 25 Feb 1978 in Weaver, Calhoun, Alabama, USA [815]. Walter Thomas Reaves and Malvin L. Couch were married on 30 Jun 1901 in Calhoun, Alabama, USA. They had the following children:

  i. (70) Samuel Lee Roy Reaves [1461, 1462, 1463] was born on 20 May 1902 in Alabama, USA [1461, 1462, 1463]. He died on 12 Feb 1984 in Calhoun, Alabama, USA.

  ii. (69) Rona Mae Reaves [1464, 1465, 1466, 1467] was born on 23 Jan 1904 in Alabama, USA [1464, 1465, 1466, 1467]. She died on 04 Jan 1984 in Alexandria, Calhoun, Alabama, USA [1465].

  iii. Bessie Mae Reaves [1468] was born on 02 Apr 1906 in Alabama, USA [1468]. She lived in Greens Schoolhouse, Calhoun, Alabama, USA in 1910 [1468]. She died on 03 Nov 1910 in Calhoun, Alabama, USA.

  iv. Ester Reaves [1469] was born on 11 Apr 1911 in Calhoun, Alabama, USA [1469]. She lived in Oxford, Calhoun, Alabama, USA in 1920 [1469].

  v. Opal Reaves [1470, 1471] was born on 13 Sep 1914 in Calhoun, Alabama, USA [1470, 1471]. She lived in Oxford, Calhoun, Alabama, USA in 1920 [1470]. She died on 16 Jun 1990 in Oswego, Oswego, New York, USA [1471].

  vi. Elizabeth E. Reaves was born on 04 Jul 1923 in Calhoun, Alabama, USA. She died on 02 Apr 2005 in Jacksonville, Calhoun, Alabama, USA.

  vii. Gaynell Reaves was born on 30 Sep 1926 in Calhoun, Alabama, USA. She died in Jul 1985 in Carrollton, Carroll, Georgia, USA.

71. *Samuel George Reaves*-14 (James Martin-13, Carter Hill-12, William Emery-11, Edmond-10, William-9, William-8, Richard-7, John-6, William-5, Timothy-4, Richard-3, John-2, Robert-1) [801, 802, 803, 804] was born on 04 Nov 1889 in Alabama, USA [801, 802, 803]. He lived in Ball Play, Etowah, Alabama, USA in 1920 [803]. He died on 09 Jun 1980. **Annie May Mildred McKee** [1472] was born about 1898 in Alabama, USA [1472]. She lived in Ball Play, Etowah, Alabama, USA in 1920 [1472]. Samuel George Reaves and Annie May Mildred McKee were married about 1916 in Alabama, USA. They had the following children:

  i. Grady Lewis Reaves [1473] was born on 27 Sep 1916 in Alabama, USA [1473]. He lived in Ball Play, Etowah, Alabama, USA in 1920 [1473]. He died on 12 Apr 1978 in Gadsden, Etowah, Alabama, USA.

  ii. John Earl Reaves [1474] was born on 21 May 1918 in Alabama, USA [1474]. He lived in Ball Play, Etowah, Alabama, USA in 1920 [1474]. He died on 16 Jul 1984.

  iii. Earl Reaves [1474] was born about 1919 in Alabama, USA [1474]. He lived in Ball Play, Etowah, Alabama, USA in 1920 [1474].

  iv. Mary Mildred Reaves was born on 21 Mar 1920 in Alabama, USA. She died on 27 Sep 1921.

v.   Charles Samuel Reaves was born on 04 Apr 1922 in Alabama, USA. He died on 16 Feb 1981.

vi. James Hersteen Reaves was born on 17 Sep 1927 in Etowah, Alabama, USA. He died on 27 Feb 1998 in Etowah, Alabama, USA.

vii. Wilmer Dale Reaves was born on 07 Apr 1932 in Alabama, USA. He died on 27 Jul 1975.

72.   ***Levi Hilton Reaves*-14** (James Martin-13, Carter Hill-12, William Emery-11, Edmond-10, William-9, William-8, Richard-7, John-6, William-5, Timothy-4, Richard-3, John-2, Robert-1) [809, 810, 811, 812] was born on 04 Mar 1894 in Jacksonville, Calhoun, Alabama, USA [809, 810, 811, 812]. He lived in Greens Schoolhouse, Calhoun, Alabama, USA in 1930 [812]. He died on 03 Jul 1962 in Anniston, Calhoun, Alabama, USA. **Flettie (unknown maiden name)** [1475] was born about 1899 in North Carolina, USA [1476, 1475]. She lived in Greens Schoolhouse, Calhoun, Alabama, USA in 1930 [1475]. Levi Hilton Reaves and Flettie (unknown maiden name) married and had the following children:

i.   William J. Reaves [1477, 1478] was born about 1919 in Alabama, USA [1477, 1478]. He lived in Greens Schoolhouse, Calhoun, Alabama, USA in 1930 [1478].

ii.   Eunice Reaves [1479] was born about 1920 [1479]. She lived in Greens Schoolhouse, Calhoun, Alabama, USA in 1930 [1479].

iii. Dorthy Reaves [1480] was born about 1922 [1480]. She lived in Greens Schoolhouse, Calhoun, Alabama, USA in 1930 [1480].

iv.   Flora Reaves [1481] was born about 1924 [1481]. She lived in Greens Schoolhouse, Calhoun, Alabama, USA in 1930 [1481].

v.   Edward Reaves [1482] was born about 1928 [1482]. He lived in Greens Schoolhouse, Calhoun, Alabama, USA in 1930 [1482].

74.   ***Malvin L. Couch*-14** (Belzona-13, Carter Hill-12, William Emery-11, Edmond-10, William-9, William-8, Richard-7, John-6, William-5, Timothy-4, Richard-3, John-2, Robert-1) [813, 814, 815] was born on 21 May 1885 in Calhoun, Alabama, USA [813, 814, 815, 816]. She lived in Oxford, Calhoun, Alabama, USA in 1920 [814]. She died on 25 Feb 1978 in Weaver, Calhoun, Alabama, USA [815]. **Walter Thomas Reaves** son of James Martin Reeves and Mary E. Holder [792, 793, 794] was born on 26 Feb 1879 in Jacksonville, Calhoun, Alabama, USA [792, 793, 794]. He lived in Oxford, Calhoun, Alabama, USA in 1920 [794]. He died on 30 Jul 1961 in Weaver, Calhoun, Alabama, USA. Walter Thomas Reaves and Malvin L. Couch were married on 30 Jun 1901 in Calhoun, Alabama, USA. They had the following children:

i.   (70) Samuel Lee Roy Reaves [1461, 1462, 1463] was born on 20 May 1902 in Alabama, USA [1461, 1462, 1463]. He died on 12 Feb 1984 in Calhoun, Alabama, USA.

ii.   (69) Rona Mae Reaves [1464, 1465, 1466, 1467] was born on 23 Jan 1904 in Alabama, USA [1464, 1465, 1466, 1467]. She died on 04 Jan 1984 in Alexandria, Calhoun, Alabama, USA [1465].

iii. Bessie Mae Reaves [1468] was born on 02 Apr 1906 in Alabama, USA [1468]. She lived in Greens Schoolhouse, Calhoun, Alabama, USA in 1910 [1468]. She died on 03 Nov 1910 in Calhoun, Alabama, USA.

iv. Ester Reaves [1469] was born on 11 Apr 1911 in Calhoun, Alabama, USA [1469]. She lived in Oxford, Calhoun, Alabama, USA in 1920 [1469].

v. Opal Reaves [1470, 1471] was born on 13 Sep 1914 in Calhoun, Alabama, USA [1470, 1471]. She lived in Oxford, Calhoun, Alabama, USA in 1920 [1470]. She died on 16 Jun 1990 in Oswego, Oswego, New York, USA [1471].

vi. Elizabeth E. Reaves was born on 04 Jul 1923 in Calhoun, Alabama, USA. She died on 02 Apr 2005 in Jacksonville, Calhoun, Alabama, USA.

vii. Gaynell Reaves was born on 30 Sep 1926 in Calhoun, Alabama, USA. She died in Jul 1985 in Carrollton, Carroll, Georgia, USA.

76. *Lucy Dempsey*-14 (Alice Louisa-13, Carter Hill-12, William Emery-11, Edmond-10, William-9, William-8, Richard-7, John-6, William-5, Timothy-4, Richard-3, John-2, Robert-1) [825, 826, 827, 828, 829] was born on 01 Jul 1889 in Alabama, USA [825, 826, 827, 828]. She lived in Greens Schoolhouse, Calhoun, Alabama, USA in 1930 [828]. She died on 15 Sep 1948 in Calhoun, Alabama, USA [829]. **Collie Peyton Ledbetter** son of Cephas Andrew Ledbetter and Narcissa Reaves was born on 10 May 1886 in Jacksonville, Calhoun, Alabama, USA [775, 776, 777]. He lived in Greens Schoolhouse, Calhoun, Alabama, USA in 1930 [777]. He died on 14 Jul 1951 in Piedmont, Calhoun, Alabama, USA. Collie Peyton Ledbetter and Lucy Dempsey married before 1908. They had the following children:

i. Talbert J. Ledbetter [1412] was born about 1908 in Alabama, USA [1412]. He lived in Greens Schoolhouse, Calhoun, Alabama, USA in 1920 [1412].

ii. Julius O. Ledbetter [1413] was born in 1909 in Alabama, USA [1413]. He lived in Ball Play, Etowah, Alabama, USA in 1910 [1413].

iii. Buddie O. Ledbetter [1414] was born about 1910 in Alabama, USA [1414]. He lived in Greens Schoolhouse, Calhoun, Alabama, USA in 1920 [1414].

iv. Lola L. Ledbetter [1415] was born about 1912 in Alabama, USA [1415]. She lived in Greens Schoolhouse, Calhoun, Alabama, USA in 1920 [1415].

v. Alvin T. Ledetter [1416, 1417] was born about 1914 in Alabama, USA [1416, 1417]. He lived in Greens Schoolhouse, Calhoun, Alabama, USA in 1930 [1417].

vi. Dovvie Lala Ledbetter [1418, 1419] was born about 1915 in Alabama, USA [1418, 1419]. She lived in Greens Schoolhouse, Calhoun, Alabama, USA in 1930 [1419].

vii. Eva P. Ledbetter [1420, 1421] was born about 1917 in Alabama, USA [1420, 1421]. She lived in Greens Schoolhouse, Calhoun, Alabama, USA in 1930 [1421].

viii. Lennard S. Ledbetter [1422] was born about 1919 in Alabama, USA [1422]. He lived in Greens Schoolhouse, Calhoun, Alabama, USA in 1920 [1422].

ix. Elmon Ledbetter [1423] was born about 1919 [1423]. He lived in Greens Schoolhouse, Calhoun, Alabama, USA in 1930 [1423].

x. Ivy Ledbetter [1424] was born about 1922 [1424]. He lived in Greens Schoolhouse, Calhoun, Alabama, USA in 1930 [1424].

xi. Margaret Ledbetter [1425] was born about 1924 [1425]. She lived in Greens Schoolhouse, Calhoun, Alabama, USA in 1930 [1425].

xii. Coleman Ledbetter [1426] was born about 1925 [1426]. He lived in Greens Schoolhouse, Calhoun, Alabama, USA in 1930 [1426].

79. *Huston R. Reaves*-14 (George M. D.-13, Carter Hill-12, William Emery-11, Edmond-10, William-9, William-8, Richard-7, John-6, William-5, Timothy-4, Richard-3, John-2, Robert-1) [854] was born on 27 Jul 1877 in Alabama, USA [855, 854]. He lived in Calhoun, Alabama, USA in 1900 [854]. He died on 01 Sep 1900 in Calhoun, Alabama, USA. **Jo Anna (Joan) Blaylock** daughter of Unknown Blaylock and Almeta M. (unknown maiden name) [1483, 1484, 1485, 1486] was born on 25 Dec 1871 in Alabama, USA [1483, 1484, 1485]. She lived in Oxford, Calhoun, Alabama, USA in 1920 [1485]. She died on 21 Jun 1951 in Calhoun, Alabama, USA [1486]. Huston R. Reaves and Jo Anna (Joan) Blaylock were married in 1899 in Calhoun, Alabama, USA [854]. They had the following children:

i. Agnes Alberta Reaves [1487, 1488] was born on 24 Oct 1899 in Calhoun, Alabama, USA [1487, 1488]. She lived in Oxford, Calhoun, Alabama, USA in 1910 [1488]. She married ?Thomas Luther Wadell? on 02 Sep 1925 in Calhoun, Alabama, USA. She died on 16 Dec 1972.

80. *Rufus Alexander Reaves*-14 (George M. D.-13, Carter Hill-12, William Emery-11, Edmond-10, William-9, William-8, Richard-7, John-6, William-5, Timothy-4, Richard-3, John-2, Robert-1) [856, 857, 858, 859, 860] was born on 17 Nov 1878 in Alabama, USA [856, 857, 858, 859, 860]. He lived in Oxford, Calhoun, Alabama, USA in 1930 [860]. He died on 02 May 1955 in Calhoun, Alabama, USA. **Della (unknown maiden name)** [1489, 1490] was born about 1883 in Georgia, USA [1489, 1490]. She lived in Oxford, Calhoun, Alabama, USA in 1920 [1490]. Rufus Alexander Reaves and Della (unknown maiden name) married and had the following children:

i. Annie Reaves [1491] was born about 1902 in Alabama, USA [1491]. She lived in Oxford, Calhoun, Alabama, USA in 1910 [1491].

ii. Herman Reaves [1492] was born about 1903 in Alabama, USA [1492]. He lived in Oxford, Calhoun, Alabama, USA in 1910 [1492].

iii. Anice Reaves [1493] was born about 1903 in Alabama, USA [1493]. She lived in Oxford, Calhoun, Alabama, USA in 1920 [1493].

iv. Herman Reaves [1494] was born about 1905 in Alabama, USA [1494]. He lived in Oxford, Calhoun, Alabama, USA in 1920 [1494].

v. Gladys Reaves [1495] was born about 1906 in Alabama, USA [1495]. She lived in Oxford, Calhoun, Alabama, USA in 1910 [1495].

vi.   Vera Reaves [1496, 1497, 1498] was born about 1909 in Alabama, USA [1496, 1497, 1498]. She lived in Oxford, Calhoun, Alabama, USA in 1930 [1498].

vii.   Suzie Reaves [1499] was born about 1915 in Alabama, USA [1499]. She lived in Oxford, Calhoun, Alabama, USA in 1920 [1499].

viii.   Carl Reaves [1500, 1501] was born about 1917 in Alabama, USA [1500, 1501]. He lived in Oxford, Calhoun, Alabama, USA in 1930 [1501].

ix.   Frances Reaves [1502, 1503] was born about 1920 in Alabama, USA [1502, 1503]. She lived in Oxford, Calhoun, Alabama, USA in 1930 [1503].

81. *Alma Irene Reaves*-14 (George M. D.-13, Carter Hill-12, William Emery-11, Edmond-10, William-9, William-8, Richard-7, John-6, William-5, Timothy-4, Richard-3, John-2, Robert-1) [869, 870, 871] was born about 1901 in Alabama, USA [869, 870, 871]. She lived in Oxford, Calhoun, Alabama, USA in 1910 [871]. She died on 06 Aug 1989 in Calhoun, Alabama, USA. **Henry Miller** [1504] was born about 1899 in Alabama, USA [1504]. He lived in Oxford, Calhoun, Alabama, USA in 1930 [1504]. Henry Miller and Alma Irene Reaves married and had the following children:

i.   Henry T. Miller was born in Nov 1928.

93. *Della McCullars*-14 (David Jackson-13, Sarah Ann Marinda-12, William Emery-11, Edmond-10, William-9, William-8, Richard-7, John-6, William-5, Timothy-4, Richard-3, John-2, Robert-1) [912, 913, 914, 915, 916, 917, 918] was born on 24 Nov 1879 in Weaver, Calhoun, Alabama, USA [912, 913, 914, 915, 916, 917, 918]. She lived in Weaver, Calhoun, Alabama, USA in 1930 [912]. She died on 07 Jan 1975 in Homestead, Dade, Florida, USA [913, 916]. **William E. Fleming** [1505, 1506] was born in Nov 1875 in Alabama, USA [1505, 1506, 919]. He lived in Weaver, Calhoun, Alabama, USA in 1910 [1505]. William E. Fleming and Della McCullars were married in 1899 [919]. They had the following children:

i.   Minnie Lee Fleming [1507, 1508, 1509] was born about 1901 in Alabama, USA [1507, 1508, 1509]. She lived in Weaver, Calhoun, Alabama, USA in 1910 [1507].

ii.   Willie Fleming [1510] was born about 1902 in Alabama, USA [1510]. He lived in Weaver, Calhoun, Alabama, USA in 1910 [1510].

iii.   Harry Fleming [1511, 1512] was born about 1905 in Alabama, USA [1511, 1512]. He lived in Weaver, Calhoun, Alabama, USA in 1910 [1511].

iv.   Irene H. Fleming [1513, 1514] was born about 1907 in Alabama, USA [1513, 1514]. She lived in Weaver, Calhoun, Alabama, USA in 1910 [1513].

v.   Graham Fleming [1515, 1516, 1517] was born about 1910 in Alabama, USA [1515, 1516, 1517]. He lived in Weaver, Calhoun, Alabama, USA in 1930 [1515].

vi.   Woodrow W. Fleming [1518, 1519] was born about 1913 in Alabama, USA [1518, 1519]. He lived in Weaver, Calhoun, Alabama, USA in 1930 [1518].

vii.   John S. Fleming [1520] was born about 1920 [1520]. He lived in Weaver, Calhoun, Alabama, USA in 1930 [1520].

94. *Minnie Sara Amelia McCullars*-14 (David Jackson-13, Sarah Ann Marinda-12, William Emery-11, Edmond-10, William-9, William-8, Richard-7, John-6, William-5, Timothy-4, Richard-3, John-2, Robert-1) [920, 921] was born on 04 Sep 1881 in Calhoun, Alabama, USA [921]. She lived in Weaver, Calhoun, Alabama, USA in 1900 [920]. She died on 28 Dec 1964 in Calhoun, Alabama, USA. **Richard Medders** [1521] was born about 1879 in Alabama, USA [1521]. He lived in Weaver, Calhoun, Alabama, USA in 1910 [1521]. Richard Medders and Minnie Sara Amelia McCullars married and had the following children:

    i.   Bula Medders [1522] was born about 1906 in Alabama, USA [1522]. She lived in Weaver, Calhoun, Alabama, USA in 1910 [1522].

    ii.   Oscar Medders [1523] was born about 1907 in Alabama, USA [1523]. He lived in Weaver, Calhoun, Alabama, USA in 1910 [1523].

    iii.   Jack Medders [1524] was born about 1908 in Alabama, USA [1524]. He lived in Weaver, Calhoun, Alabama, USA in 1910 [1524].

    iv.   Carl Medders [1525] was born about 1909 in Alabama, USA [1525]. He lived in Weaver, Calhoun, Alabama, USA in 1910 [1525].

95. *Monroe Jackson McCullars*-14 (David Jackson-13, Sarah Ann Marinda-12, William Emery-11, Edmond-10, William-9, William-8, Richard-7, John-6, William-5, Timothy-4, Richard-3, John-2, Robert-1) [923, 924, 925, 926] was born on 23 Mar 1886 in Calhoun, Alabama, USA [923, 924, 925, 926]. He lived in Menlo, Chattooga, Georgia, USA in 1920 [923]. He died on 02 Jan 1960 in Troup, Georgia, USA [925]. **Ethel Mary Jane ?Woods?** [1526, 1527, 1528, 1529] was born about 1887 in Georgia, USA [1526, 1527, 1528, 1529]. She died on 21 May 1956 in Floyd, Georgia, USA [1526]. She lived in Floyd, Georgia, USA [1526]. Monroe Jackson McCullars and Ethel Mary Jane ?Woods? married and had the following children:

    i.   Marena Ovell McCullars [1530, 1531, 1532, 1533, 1534] was born on 22 Mar 1909 in Alabama, USA [1530, 1531, 1532, 1533, 1534]. She died on 17 Oct 1993 in Troup, Georgia, USA [1533, 1534]. She lived in Troup, Georgia, USA [1534].

    ii.   Ovelle McCullars [1530] was born about 1911 [1530]. She lived in Rome, Floyd, Georgia, USA in 1930 [1530].

    iii.   Catherine E. McCullars [1535] was born about 1912 in Alabama, USA [1535]. She lived in Menlo, Chattooga, Georgia, USA in 1920 [1535].

    iv.   Kathleen McCullars [1536] was born about 1913[1536]. She lived in Rome, Floyd, Georgia, USA in 1930 [1536].

    v.   Owen McCullars [1537, 1538] was born about 1915 in Alabama, USA [1537, 1538]. He lived in Menlo, Chattooga, Georgia, USA in 1920 [1537].

    vi.   D J. McCullars [1539, 1540] was born about 1916 in Texas, USA [1539, 1540]. He lived in Menlo, Chattooga, Georgia, USA in 1920 [1539].

    vii.   Hal L. McCullars [1541, 1542] was born about 1918 in Georgia, USA [1541, 1542]. He lived in Menlo, Chattooga, Georgia, USA in 1920 [1541].

viii. Gurnelle McCullars [1543] was born about 1921 [1543]. She lived in Rome, Floyd, Georgia, USA in 1930 [1543].

ix. Glenn A. McCullars [1544] was born about 1923 [1544]. He lived in Rome, Floyd, Georgia, USA in 1930 [1544].

96. *Mollie McCullars*-14 (David Jackson-13, Sarah Ann Marinda-12, William Emery-11, Edmond-10, William-9, William-8, Richard-7, John-6, William-5, Timothy-4, Richard-3, John-2, Robert-1) [927, 931] was born about 1891 in Alabama, USA [927, 931]. She lived in Weaver, Calhoun, Alabama, USA in 1900 [927]. She died on 15 Apr 1976 in Anniston, Calhoun, Alabama, USA. **Edward Lee Hubbard** was born on 14 Apr 1871 in Alabama, USA. He died on 23 May 1921 in Anniston, Calhoun, Alabama, USA. Edward Lee Hubbard and Mollie McCullars were married on 14 Apr 1912 in Calhoun, Alabama, USA. They had the following children:

i. Edward L. Hubbard was born on 16 Aug 1913 in Alexandria, Calhoun, Alabama, USA. He died on 21 Mar 1993 in Birmingham, Jefferson, Alabama, USA.

ii. John Mac Hubbard was born on 23 Sep 1916 in Calhoun, Alabama, USA. He died on 27 May 2000 in Birmingham, Jefferson, Alabama, USA.

98. *William Marion Doss*-14 (Mary E-13, Sarah Ann Marinda-12, William Emery-11, Edmond-10, William-9, William-8, Richard-7, John-6, William-5, Timothy-4, Richard-3, John-2, Robert-1) [940, 941, 942, 943] was born on 11 Aug 1873 in Calhoun, Alabama, USA [940, 941, 942]. He lived in Polkville, Calhoun, Alabama, USA in 1920 [940]. He died on 07 Oct 1938 in Calhoun, Alabama, USA [943]. **Minnie G. (unknown maiden name)** [1545, 1546] was born in Jun 1875 in Alabama, USA [1545, 1546]. She lived in Polkville, Calhoun, Alabama, USA in 1910 [1546]. She died before 1920. William Marion Doss and Minnie G. (unknown maiden name) were married in 1896 [941]. They had the following children:

i. Lillie B. Doss [1547, 1548, 1549] was born in Mar 1897 in Alabama, USA [1547, 1548, 1549]. She lived in Polkville, Calhoun, Alabama, USA in 1920 [1547].

ii. Annie F. Doss [1550, 1551] was born in May 1898 in Alabama, USA [1550, 1551]. She lived in Polkville, Calhoun, Alabama, USA in 1910 [1551].

iii. George William Doss [1552, 1553] was born in Oct 1899 in Alabama, USA [1552, 1553]. He lived in Polkville, Calhoun, Alabama, USA in 1910 [1553].

iv. James L. Doss [1554] was born about 1902 in Alabama, USA [1554]. He lived in Polkville, Calhoun, Alabama, USA in 1910 [1554].

v. Owens Doss [1555] was born about 1904 in Alabama, USA [1555]. He lived in Polkville, Calhoun, Alabama, USA in 1910 [1555].

vi. Walter M. Doss [1556] was born about 1906 in Alabama, USA [1556]. He lived in Polkville, Calhoun, Alabama, USA in 1910 [1556].

vii. Amon D. Doss [1557] was born about 1908 in Alabama, USA [1557]. He lived in Polkville, Calhoun, Alabama, USA in 1910 [1557].

viii. Hubert M. Doss [1558, 1559] was born about 1910 in Alabama, USA [1558, 1559]. He lived in Polkville, Calhoun, Alabama, USA in 1930 [1559]. He married Minnie L. (unknown maiden name) after 1930.

99. *Monroe Jackson Doss*-14 (Mary E-13, Sarah Ann Marinda-12, William Emery-11, Edmond-10, William-9, William-8, Richard-7, John-6, William-5, Timothy-4, Richard-3, John-2, Robert-1) [949, 950, 951, 952, 953] was born on 22 Aug 1888 in Calhoun, Alabama, USA [949, 950, 951, 952]. He lived in Polkville, Calhoun, Alabama, USA in 1920 [949]. He died on 01 Nov 1925 in Calhoun, Alabama, USA [953]. **Allice T. (unknown maiden name)** [1560] was born about 1889 in Alabama, USA [1560]. She lived in Polkville, Calhoun, Alabama, USA in 1920 [1560]. Monroe Jackson Doss and Allice T. (unknown maiden name) married and had the following children:

i. Mary Achelia Doss [1561] was born about 1912 in Alabama, USA [1561]. She lived in Polkville, Calhoun, Alabama, USA in 1920 [1561].

ii. Harold J. Doss [1562] was born about 1913 in Alabama, USA [1562]. He lived in Polkville, Calhoun, Alabama, USA in 1920 [1562].

iii. Thomas Edwin Doss [1563] was born about 1915 in Alabama, USA [1563]. He lived in Polkville, Calhoun, Alabama, USA in 1920 [1563].

107. *Mary Etta Reaves*-14 (Bunyon Rubin Britton-13, Ira Jackson-12, William Emery-11, Edmond-10, William-9, William-8, Richard-7, John-6, William-5, Timothy-4, Richard-3, John-2, Robert-1) [983, 984, 985] was born on 16 Jul 1909 in Alabama, USA [983, 984, 985]. She lived in Turkey Creek, Stone, Arkansas, USA in 1930 [985]. She died on 17 Oct 1985 in Wedowee, Randolph, Alabama, USA [984]. **Charles V. Deason** [1564] was born about 1910 in Arkansas, USA [1564]. He lived in Turkey Creek, Stone, Arkansas, USA in 1930 [1564]. Charles V. Deason and Mary Etta Reaves married and had the following children:

i. Bonnle R. Deason [1565] was born about 1929 [1565]. She lived in Turkey Creek, Stone, Arkansas, USA in 1930 [1565].

108. *Claude Fredrick Reaves*-14 (Bunyon Rubin Britton-13, Ira Jackson-12, William Emery-11, Edmond-10, William-9, William-8, Richard-7, John-6, William-5, Timothy-4, Richard-3, John-2, Robert-1) [962, 963, 964, 965, 966, 967] was born on 08 Dec 1893 in Alabama, USA [962, 963, 964, 966, 967]. He lived in Albertville, Marshall, Alabama, USA in 1920 [966]. He died on 15 Feb 1959 in Marshall, Alabama, USA [965]. **Esther Mae Mitchell** daughter of William A. Mitchell and Eliza P. (unknown maiden name) [1566, 1567, 1568, 1569, 1570] was born on 20 Jan 1893 in Alabama, USA [1566, 1567, 1568, 1569]. She lived in Friendship, Marshall, Alabama, USA in 1900 [1569]. She died on 16 Jul 1954 in Albertville, Marshall, Alabama, USA [1570]. Claude Fredrick Reaves and Esther Mae Mitchell were married on 05 Apr 1913 in Marshall, Alabama, USA. They had the following children:

i. Caesar Fredrick Reaves [1571, 1572] was born on 08 Jan 1914 in Marshall, Alabama, USA [1571, 1572]. He lived in Albertville, Marshall, Alabama, USA in 1920 [1571]. He died on 21 Mar 1988 in Lynchburg, Campbell, Virginia, USA [1572].

ii. Norman Mitchell Reaves [1573, 1574] was born on 23 Sep 1915 in Marshall, Alabama, USA [1573, 1574]. He lived in Albertville, Marshall, Alabama, USA in 1920 [1573]. He died on 05 Mar 1994 in Albertville, Marshall, Alabama, USA [1574].

iii. Catharine Reeves [1575] was born about 1919 in Alabama, USA [1575]. She lived in Albertville, Marshall, Alabama, USA in 1920 [1575].

iv. Frank E. Reeves [1576] was born about 1921 [1576]. He lived in Albertville, Marshall, Alabama, USA in 1930 [1576].

v. Jack Luis Reaves [1577, 1578] was born on 14 Sep 1923 in Marshall, Alabama, USA [1577, 1578]. He lived in Albertville, Marshall, Alabama, USA in 1930 [1577]. He died on 27 Nov 1990 in Arab, Marshall, Alabama, USA [1578].

vi. Dora E. Reeves [1579] was born about 1926 [1579]. She lived in Albertville, Marshall, Alabama, USA in 1930 [1579].

vii. Ted Reeves [1580] was born about 1928 [1580]. He lived in Albertville, Marshall, Alabama, USA in 1930 [1580].

109. *Lela Mae Reaves*-14 (Bunyon Rubin Britton-13, Ira Jackson-12, William Emery-11, Edmond-10, William-9, William-8, Richard-7, John-6, William-5, Timothy-4, Richard-3, John-2, Robert-1) [959, 960, 961] was born on 27 Jul 1892 in Alabama, USA [959, 960, 961]. She lived in Albertville, Marshall, Alabama, USA in 1920 [961]. She died on 25 May 1963. **Arthur Buchannon** [1581] was born about 1894 in Alabama, USA [1581]. He lived in Albertville, Marshall, Alabama, USA in 1920 [1581]. Arthur Buchannon and Lela Mae Reaves married and had the following children:

i. Lola Buchannon [1582] was born about 1916 in Alabama, USA [1582]. She lived in Albertville, Marshall, Alabama, USA in 1920 [1582].

ii. Ira B. Buchannon [1583] was born about 1919 in Alabama, USA [1583]. He lived in Albertville, Marshall, Alabama, USA in 1920 [1583].

113. *Maggie Lee Reaves*-14 (William David-13, Ira Jackson-12, William Emery-11, Edmond-10, William-9, William-8, Richard-7, John-6, William-5, Timothy-4, Richard-3, John-2, Robert-1) [1007, 1008, 1009, 1010, 1011] was born on 25 May 1894 in Weaver, Calhoun, Alabama, USA [1007, 1008, 1009, 1010, 1011]. She lived in Weaver, Calhoun, Alabama, USA in 1910 [1009]. She died on 05 Jun 1970 in Heflin, Cleburne, Alabama, USA. **Alexander Larkin (Lark) Williamson** son of James Marion Williamson and Margaret Ann Moore [1584, 1585, 1586, 1587] was born on 21 Jan 1895 in Cleburne, Alabama, USA [1588, 1584, 1585, 1586]. He lived in Burns Cross Roads, Calhoun, Alabama, USA in 1930 [1586]. He died on 10 May 1956 in Anniston, Calhoun, Alabama, USA [1587]. Alexander Larkin (Lark) Williamson and Maggie Lee Reaves married and had the following children:

i. Ullman Lee Williamson [1589, 1590, 1591, 1592] was born on 01 Jun 1916 in Calhoun, Alabama, USA [1589, 1590, 1591]. He lived in Crumley, Dekalb, Alabama, USA in 1920 [1590]. He died on 28 Sep 2002 in Leavenworth, Kansas, USA [1589].

ii. (114) Joseph Lark Williamson [1593, 1594, 1595, 1596] was born on 05 Jul 1918 in Calhoun, Alabama, USA [1593, 1594, 1595, 1596]. He married Carrie Mae Brown on 01 Jul 1950 in Rome, Floyd, Georgia, USA. He died on 23 Apr 1983 in Anniston, Calhoun, Alabama, USA [1593, 1594].

iii. Earl Williamson.

iv. William Williamson [1591] was born about 1918 [1591]. He lived in Burns Cross Roads, Calhoun, Alabama, USA in 1930 [1591].

v. Margaret Nell Williamson [1597, 1598] was born on 17 Sep 1921 in Anniston, Calhoun, Alabama, USA [1597, 1598]. She lived in Burns Cross Roads, Calhoun, Alabama, USA in 1930 [1598]. She died on 03 Sep 1993 in Piedmont, Calhoun, Alabama, USA [1597].

vi. Odelle Williamson [1599] was born about 1925 [1599]. She lived in Burns Cross Roads, Calhoun, Alabama, USA in 1930 [1599].

vii. Howard Oliver Williamson [1600, 1601] was born on 29 Mar 1926 in Calhoun, Alabama, USA [1600, 1601]. He lived in Burns Cross Roads, Calhoun, Alabama, USA in 1930 [1601]. He died on 17 Oct 1995 in Centre, Cherokee, Alabama, USA [1600].

viii. Pearl Dean Williamson [1602] was born on 31 Mar 1931 in Calhoun, Alabama, USA. She died on 02 Feb 1932 in Calhoun, Alabama, USA [1602].

115. *Luna Emma Reaves*-14 (William David-13, Ira Jackson-12, William Emery-11, Edmond-10, William-9, William-8, Richard-7, John-6, William-5, Timothy-4, Richard-3, John-2, Robert-1) [1015, 1016, 1017, 1018] was born on 03 Oct 1902 in Anniston, Calhoun, Alabama, USA [1015, 1016]. She lived in Weaver, Calhoun, Alabama, USA in 1910 [1015]. She died on 17 Nov 1992 in Ohatchee, Calhoun, Alabama, USA [1016]. **John Vester Timmons** son of Jefferson Davis Timmons and Mary Addie Weatherly [1603, 1604, 1605, 1606] was born on 11 Jan 1889 in Alabama, USA [1604, 1605]. He lived in Alexandria, Calhoun, Alabama, USA in 1900 [1605]. He died on 12 Aug 1941 in Calhoun, Alabama, USA [1603]. John Vester Timmons and Luna Emma Reaves were married after 1917 (Single on draft registration card on June 5, 1917). They had the following children:

i. Gerald Mark Timmons [1607] was born before 1941.

116. *Sallie Irene Reaves*-14 (William David-13, Ira Jackson-12, William Emery-11, Edmond-10, William-9, William-8, Richard-7, John-6, William-5, Timothy-4, Richard-3, John-2, Robert-1) [1023, 1024, 1025] was born on 15 Jul 1907 in Anniston, Calhoun, Alabama, USA [1023, 1024, 1025]. She lived in Weaver, Calhoun, Alabama, USA in 1920 [1023]. She died on 27 Jun 1993 in Gadsden, Etowah, Alabama, USA. **Glenn Augustus Swinford Sr** son of Henry Augustus Swinford and Katie McLeod [1608, 1609, 1610, 1611] was born on 21 Mar 1904 in Calhoun, Alabama, USA [1608, 1609, 1610, 1611]. He lived in Gadsden, Etowah, Alabama, USA in 1930 [1608]. He died in May 1981 in Gadsden, Etowah, Alabama, USA [1609]. Glenn Augustus Swinford Sr and Sallie Irene Reaves were married on 05 Apr 1924 in Calhoun, Alabama, USA. They had the following children:

i.   Catherine Swinford [1612] was born about 1925 [1612]. She lived in Gadsden, Etowah, Alabama, USA in 1930 [1612].

ii.   Glenn Augustus Swinford Jr [1613, 1614, 1615] was born on 13 Nov 1927 in Alabama, USA [1613, 1615]. He lived in Gadsden, Etowah, Alabama, USA in 1930 [1613]. He married Betty Carolyn Head on 21 Jun 1953 in Etowah, Alabama, USA [1614]. He died on 04 Feb 1998 in Gadsden, Etowah, Alabama, USA [1615].

iii.   Bettie L. Swinford [1616] was born about 1930 [1616]. She lived in Gadsden, Etowah, Alabama, USA in 1930 [1616].

117.   *Wilma Lee Reaves*-14 (William David-13, Ira Jackson-12, William Emery-11, Edmond-10, William-9, William-8, Richard-7, John-6, William-5, Timothy-4, Richard-3, John-2, Robert-1) [1026] was born on 13 Oct 1910 in Anniston, Calhoun, Alabama, USA [1026]. She died on 21 Feb 1991 in Anniston, Calhoun, Alabama, USA [1026]. **George Homer Laney** son of George A. Laney and Rosa E. ?Heath?[1617, 1618] was born on 12 Nov 1906 in Eulaton, Calhoun, Alabama, USA [1617, 1618]. He lived in Calhoun, Alabama, USA in 1920 [1617]. He died in May 1983 in Anniston, Calhoun, Alabama, USA [1618]. George Homer Laney and Wilma Lee Reaves were married on 24 Jan 1931 in Anniston, Calhoun, Alabama, USA. They had the following children:

i.   Marion Laney.

125.   *James Robert Autrey*-14 (Mary Jane-13, Caleb Jackson-12, Nancy-11, Edmond-10, William-9, William-8, Richard-7, John-6, William-5, Timothy-4, Richard-3, John-2, Robert-1) [1061] was born on 07 Aug 1874 in Dubach, Lincoln, Louisiana, USA [1061]. He lived in Lincoln, Louisiana, USA in 1900 [1061]. He died on 28 Jul 1903 in Lincoln, Louisiana, USA. **Jessie A. (unknown maiden name)** [1619] was born in Jun 1876 in Georgia, USA [1619]. She lived in Lincoln, Louisiana, USA in 1900 [1619]. James Robert Autrey and Jessie A. (unknown maiden name) were married in 1892 [1061]. They had the following children:

i.   Daughter Autrey [1620] was born in Apr 1899 in Louisiana, USA [1620]. She lived in Lincoln, Louisiana, USA in 1900 [1620].

127.   *Mary Lucinda Autrey*-14 (Georgia Ann-13, Caleb Jackson-12, Nancy-11, Edmond-10, William-9, William-8, Richard-7, John-6, William-5, Timothy-4, Richard-3, John-2, Robert-1) [1067, 1068, 1069, 1070, 1071] was born in Aug 1874 in Lincoln, Louisiana, USA [1067, 1068, 1069, 1070]. She lived in Martin, Texas, USA in 1930 [1070]. She died on 24 May 1968 in Midland, Midland, Texas, USA [1071]. **Unknown Tabor** was born in Arkansas, USA. He died before 1900. Unknown Tabor and Mary Lucinda Autrey were married about 1896. They had the following children:

i.   George G. Tabor [1621, 1622] was born in May 1897 in Texas, USA [1621, 1622]. He lived in Purcell, McClain, Oklahoma, USA in 1920 [1622].

Obediah Culp [1623, 1624, 1625, 1626] was born in Jun 1869 in Texas, USA [1623, 1624, 1625, 1626]. He lived in Martin, Texas, USA in 1930 [1626]. He died in Nov 1963 in Texas, USA. Obediah Culp and Mary Lucinda Autrey were married in 1903 in Texas, USA. They had the following children:

i. Hugh B. Culp [1627] was born about 1902 in Texas, USA [1627]. He lived in Purcell, McClain, Oklahoma, USA in 1920 [1627].

ii. Georgian Culp [1628] was born about 1906 in Texas, USA [1628]. He lived in Coryell, Texas, USA in 1910 [1628].

iii. Henry Culp [1629] was born about 1906 in Texas, USA [1629]. He lived in Purcell, McClain, Oklahoma, USA in 1920 [1629].

iv. Velma Culp [1630] was born about 1907 in Texas, USA [1630]. She lived in Purcell, McClain, Oklahoma, USA in 1920 [1630].

v. Raby Vernon Culp [1631, 1632] was born on 17 Oct 1908 in Texas, USA [1631, 1632]. He lived in Purcell, McClain, Oklahoma, USA in 1920 [1632]. He died on 03 Mar 1981 in Los Angeles, Los Angeles, California, USA [1631].

vi. Ruben Samuel Culp [1633, 1634, 1635, 1636] was born on 22 Sep 1910 in Texas, USA [1633, 1634, 1635]. He lived in Purcell, McClain, Oklahoma, USA in 1920 [1635]. He died on 11 Jan 1989 in Midland, Midland, Texas, USA [1634, 1636].

vii. Reb N. Culp [1637, 1638, 1639] was born on 09 Jan 1912 in Texas, USA [1637, 1638, 1639]. He lived in Martin, Texas, USA in 1930 [1639]. He died in Dec 1974 in Maurice, Vermillion, Louisiana, USA [1638].

viii. Larene Culp [1640] was born about 1914 in Texas, USA [1640]. She lived in Purcell, McClain, Oklahoma, USA in 1920 [1640].

130. **Thomas James Moncrief**-14 (Henry Alexander-13, Caleb Jackson-12, Nancy-11, Edmond-10, William-9, William-8, Richard-7, John-6, William-5, Timothy-4, Richard-3, John-2, Robert-1) [1085, 1086, 1087] was born about 1871 in Louisiana, USA [1085, 1086]. He lived in Union, Louisiana, USA in 1920 [1086]. He died on 19 Dec 1950 in Lincoln, Louisiana, USA. **Ida M. (unknown maiden name)** [1642] was born in 1878 in Louisiana, USA [1642]. She lived in Lincoln, Louisiana, USA in 1910 [1642]. Thomas James Moncrief and Ida M. (unknown maiden name) married and had the following children:

i. Pearl Moncrief [1643] was born in 1896 in Louisiana, USA [1643]. She lived in Lincoln, Louisiana, USA in 1910 [1643].

ii. Charence Moncrief [1644] was born in 1897 in Louisiana, USA [1644]. He lived in Lincoln, Louisiana, USA in 1910 [1644].

iii. Melvin Moncrief [1645, 1646] was born in 1906 in Louisiana, USA [1645, 1646]. He lived in Union, Louisiana, USA in 1920 [1646].

iv. Eula L. Moncrief [1641] was born about 1914 in Louisiana, USA [1641]. She lived in Union, Louisiana, USA in 1920 [1641].

136. **John Mark Reaves**-14 (Dorothy-13, John Anderson-12, Ransom Columbus-11, Edmond-10, William-9, William-8, Richard-7, John-6, William-5, Timothy-4, Richard-3, John-2, Robert-1) [1110, 1111, 1112, 1113] was born on 18 Feb 1898 in Ripley, Tippah, Mississippi, USA [1110, 1111, 1112, 1113]. He died on 11 Jan 1973 in Memphis, Shelby, Tennessee, USA [1110]. He lived in

Memphis, Shelby, Tennessee, USA [1113]. **Ethel D. Parker** daughter of Ira Baxter Parker and ?Margaret Lorena Akin? [1647, 1648, 1649] was born on 29 Jul 1896 in Tennessee, USA [1647, 1648, 1649]. She lived in Hickman, Tennessee, USA in 1900 [1647]. She died on 01 Sep 1988 in Memphis, Shelby, Tennessee, USA [1649]. John Mark Reaves and Ethel D. Parker married and had the following children:

    i.   Mark J. Reaves [1650] was born about 1920 in Tennessee, USA [1650]. He lived in Shelby, Tennessee, USA in 1920 [1650].

137. *Melba Marie Reaves*-14 (Dorothy-13, John Anderson-12, Ransom Columbus-11, Edmond-10, William-9, William-8, Richard-7, John-6, William-5, Timothy-4, Richard-3, John-2, Robert-1) [1107, 1108, 1109] was born on 16 Dec 1895 in Mississippi, USA [1107, 1108, 1109]. She lived in Tippah, Mississippi, USA in 1930 [1107]. She died on 23 Apr 1981 in Memphis, Shelby, Tennessee, USA [1108]. **Owen Thomas Booker** son of Joe M. Booker and Margaret Booker [1651, 1652, 1653, 1654, 1655, 1656, 1657] was born on 10 Jun 1892 in Ripley, Tippah, Mississippi, USA [1651, 1653, 1654, 1655, 1656, 1657]. He lived in Ripley, Tippah, Mississippi, USA in 1900 [1657]. He died on 10 Jun 1982 in Buckholts, Milam, Texas, USA [1651, 1652]. Owen Thomas Booker and Melba Marie Reaves were married on 28 Aug 1911 in Ripley, Tippah, Mississippi, USA. They had the following children:

    i.   Fairy Lucille Booker [1658] was born about 1914 in Mississippi, USA [1658, 1659]. She lived in Tippah, Mississippi, USA in 1930 [1658]. She died on 24 Jul 1995 in Oxford, Lafayette, Mississippi, USA.

    ii.   Edith M. Booker [1660, 1661] was born about 1917 in Mississippi, USA [1660, 1661]. She lived in Tippah, Mississippi, USA in 1930 [1660].

    iii.   Owen Rachel Booker [1662] was born about 1922 [1662]. She lived in Tippah, Mississippi, USA in 1930 [1662].

    iv.   David E. Booker [1663, 1664] was born on 06 May 1927 in Ripley, Tippah, Mississippi, USA [1663, 1664]. He lived in Tippah, Mississippi, USA in 1930 [1663]. He died on 03 Nov 2008 in Millington, Shelby, Tennessee, USA [1664].

139. *Florence Gracie Reaves*-14 (John Anderson-13, John Anderson-12, Ransom Columbus-11, Edmond-10, William-9, William-8, Richard-7, John-6, William-5, Timothy-4, Richard-3, John-2, Robert-1) [1120, 1121] was born on 03 Mar 1896 in Tippah, Mississippi, USA [1120, 1121]. She lived in Tippah, Mississippi, USA in 1900 [1120]. She died on 10 Jul 1974 in Genesee, Michigan, USA. **Clifton Pascal Akins** [1665, 1666] was born on 13 Jun 1891 in Union, Mississippi, USA [1665, 1666]. He died on 17 Jul 1955 in Memphis, Shelby, Tennessee, USA. He lived in Tippah, Mississippi, USA [1665]. Clifton Pascal Akins and Florence Gracie Reaves were married on 22 Aug 1911 in Tippah, Mississippi, USA. They had the following children:

    i.   Paul E. Akins was born on 03 Aug 1912 in Mississippi, USA. He died on 05 Oct 1927 in Memphis, Shelby, Tennessee, USA.

ii.   Harold Pascal Akins [1667] was born on 14 Jan 1926 in Mississippi, USA [1667]. He died on 06 Oct 1996 in Flint, Genesee, Michigan, USA [1667].

156.   Carrie G. Absher-14 (Irena D-13, John S.-12, Nathan-11, Edmond-10, William-9, William-8, Richard-7, John-6, William-5, Timothy-4, Richard-3, John-2, Robert-1) [1176, 1177, 1178, 1179, 1180, 1181] was born on 15 Jun 1896 in Alabama, USA [1176, 1177, 1178, 1179, 1180]. She lived in Wrights, Marshall, Alabama, USA in 1930 [1179]. She died in Jan 1985 in Collinsville, Dekalb, Alabama, USA [1180]. **Silas N. Black** [1668] was born about 1892 in Alabama, USA [1668]. He lived in Jackson, Alabama, USA in 1920 [1668]. Silas N. Black and Carrie G. Absher were married on 09 Apr 1911 in Dekalb, Alabama, USA [1182]. They had the following children:

i.   Oval A. Black [1669, 1670] was born about 1915 in Alabama, USA [1669, 1670]. He lived in Wrights, Marshall, Alabama, USA in 1930 [1669].

ii.   Ola I. Black [1671] was born about 1917 in Alabama, USA [1671]. She lived in Jackson, Alabama, USA in 1920 [1671].

iii.   Dilmous Black [1672] was born about 1919 in Alabama, USA [1672]. He lived in Jackson, Alabama, USA in 1920 [1672].

iv.   Homer Black [1673] was born about 1922 [1673]. He lived in Wrights, Marshall, Alabama, USA in 1930 [1673].

v.   Lillian Black [1674] was born about 1923[1674]. She lived in Wrights, Marshall, Alabama, USA in 1930 [1674].

vi.   Mildred Black [1675] was born about 1926 [1675]. She lived in Wrights, Marshall, Alabama, USA in 1930 [1675].

vii.   Winford Black [1676] was born about 1929 [1676]. He lived in Wrights, Marshall, Alabama, USA in 1930 [1676].

157.   Joseph Himond Absher-14 (Irena D-13, John S.-12, Nathan-11, Edmond-10, William-9, William-8, Richard-7, John-6, William-5, Timothy-4, Richard-3, John-2, Robert-1) [1183, 1184, 1185, 1186, 1187, 1188, 1189] was born on 04 Jul 1898 in Alabama, USA [1183, 1184, 1185, 1186, 1187, 1188, 1189]. He lived in Van Buren, Dekalb, Alabama, USA in 1900 [1189]. He died in Feb 1978 in Fyffe, Dekalb, Alabama, USA [1188]. **Elsie N. Absher** [1677] was born about 1904 [1677]. She lived in Corinth, Dekalb, Alabama, USA in 1930 [1677]. Joseph Himond Absher and Elsie N. Absher married and had the following children:

i.   Ilene N. Absher [1678, 1679] was born about 1923 [1678]. She lived in Corinth, Dekalb, Alabama, USA in 1930 [1678].

ii.   Sarah F. Absher [1680] was born about 1926 [1680]. She lived in Corinth, Dekalb, Alabama, USA in 1930 [1680].

iii.   Nellie F. Absher [1681, 1682] was born about 1929 [1681]. She lived in Corinth, Dekalb, Alabama, USA in 1930 [1681].

159.   Luther Reeves-14 (William Clemens-13, John S.-12, Nathan-11, Edmond-10, William-9, William-8, Richard-7, John-6, William-5, Timothy-4, Richard-3, John-2, Robert-1) [1202, 1203, 1204, 1205, 1206, 1207] was born on

27 Dec 1879 in Hokes Bluff, Etowah, Alabama, USA [1202, 1203, 1204, 1205, 1206]. He was employed as a Farmer in 1920 in Hokes Bluff, Etowah, Alabama, USA. He died on 12 Apr 1941 in Etowah, Alabama, USA [1207]. He lived in Etowah, Alabama, USA [1206]. **Nora Rae Anna "Nonie" Rutledge** daughter of Alford Greenberry Rutledge and Rhoda A. Powell [1683, 1684, 1685, 1686, 1687] was born on 10 Oct 1881 in Calhoun, Alabama, USA [1683, 1684, 1685, 1686]. She lived in Reaves, Etowah, Alabama, USA in 1900 [1686]. She died on 09 Jan 1957 in Etowah, Alabama, USA [1687]. Luther Reeves and Nora Rae Anna "Nonie" Rutledge were married on 10 Feb 1901. They had the following children:

    i.   (160) Floyd Leon Reeves [1688, 1689, 1690, 1691] was born on 12 Feb 1902 in Alabama, USA [1689, 1690, 1691].

    ii.   (182) Neva Reeves [1693, 1694, 1695, 1696, 1697, 1688] was born on 10 Jul 1905 in Alabama, USA [1693, 1694, 1695, 1696, 1697].

    iii.   (168) Crate Funis Reeves [1698, 1699, 1700, 1701] was born on 07 Dec 1907 in Hokes Bluff, Etowah, Alabama, USA [1698, 1699, 1700, 1701].

    iv.   (190) May Reeves [1702, 1703] was born on 01 May 1915 in Alabama, USA [1702, 1704, 1705].

    v.   Etoyle Reeves [1708] was born on 08 Dec 1924 [1708, 1709]. She lived in Gadsden, Etowah, Alabama, USA in 1930 [1709]. She died in Sep 1973 in Birmingham, Jefferson, Alabama, USA [1708]. She married Ralph E. Whitt in 1960. Ralph E. Whitt died in 1967.

191. *Euclid Reeves*-14 (William Clemens-13, John S.-12, Nathan-11, Edmond-10, William-9, William-8, Richard-7, John-6, William-5, Timothy-4, Richard-3, John-2, Robert-1) [1193, 1194, 1195, 1196, 1197, 1198, 1199] was born on 14 Oct 1876 in Alabama, USA [1194, 1195, 1196, 1197, 1198]. He lived in Hokes Bluff, Etowah, Alabama, USA in 1930 [1194]. He died on 14 Jul 1945 in Etowah, Alabama, USA [1193]. He was employed as a Farmer in Hokes Bluff, Etowah, Alabama, USA. **Buena Love McMurtrey** daughter of Martin L. McMurtrey and Viola Jane Clementine Blerchet [1710, 1711, 1712, 1200, 1201] was born in Feb 1879 in Alabama, USA [1710, 1711]. She lived in Hokes Bluff, Etowah, Alabama, USA in 1920 [1711]. She died on 18 Feb 1951 in Hokes Bluff, Etowah, Alabama, USA [1712]. Euclid Reeves and Buena Love McMurtrey were married on 02 Jan 1898 in Etowah, Alabama, USA [1200, 1201, 1196, 1199]. They had the following children:

    i.   Roy Reeves [1713, 1714] was born on 28 Jul 1899 in Alabama, USA [1713]. He lived in Hokes Bluff, Etowah, Alabama, USA in 1900 [1713]. He died on 02 Jun 1918 in Etowah, Alabama, USA.

    ii.   (192) Doyle Reeves [1715, 1716, 1717] was born on 14 Feb 1902 in Alabama, USA [1715, 1716, 1717].

    iii.   Avie Reeves [1718, 1719, 1720] was born on 01 Mar 1905 in Alabama, USA [1718, 1719, 1720]. She lived in Hokes Bluff, Etowah, Alabama, USA in 1930 [1720]. She died on 15 Feb 1982 in Gadsden, Etowah, Alabama, USA [1718].

iv. (193) Hoyt Reeves [1721, 1722, 1723] was born on 05 Nov 1907 in Alabama, USA [1721, 1722, 1723].

v. (211) Cresful Reeves [1724, 1725, 1726, 1727, 1728] was born on 10 May 1912 in Etowah, Alabama, USA [1724, 1725, 1726, 1727, 1728].

vi. (196) Troy Reeves [1730, 1731, 1732] was born on 18 Dec 1914 in Glencoe, Etowah, Alabama, USA [1730, 1731, 1732].

vii. (194) H. K. Reeves [1733, 1734, 1735, 1736, 1737, 1738, 1739] was born on 04 Dec 1918 in Alabama, USA [1734, 1735, 1736, 1737].

217. *Riller Reeves*-14 (William Clemens-13, John S.-12, Nathan-11, Edmond-10, William-9, William-8, Richard-7, John-6, William-5, Timothy-4, Richard-3, John-2, Robert-1) was born on 07 Jul 1882 in Gadsden, Etowah, Alabama, USA [1215, 1216, 1217, 1218]. She lived in Keysburg, Etowah, Alabama, USA in 1930 [1215]. She died on 08 Mar 1959 in Birmingham, Jefferson, Alabama, USA [1220]. **Walter Eugene Lumpkin** son of Adoniram Judson Lumpkin and Nancy Mary Smith [1740, 1741, 1742, 1743, 1219, 1744] was born on 30 Aug 1876 in Gadsden, Etowah, Alabama, USA [1740, 1741, 1742, 1743, 1219]. He was employed as a Repair Man at Shoe Shop in 1930. He lived in Keysburg, Etowah, Alabama, USA in 1930 [1740]. He died on 27 Apr 1942 in Limestone, Alabama, USA [1744]. Walter Eugene Lumpkin and Riller Reeves were married in 1899 [1219]. They had the following children:

i. Ivaline Beatrice Lumpkin [1745, 1746, 1747] was born about 1902 in Alabama, USA [1745, 1746]. She lived in Anniston, Calhoun, Alabama, USA in 1920 [1746]. She married Ted Jordan Jr on 30 Mar 1945 in Etowah, Alabama, USA [1748].

ii. (218) Clarence Eugene Lumpkin [1749, 1750, 1751, 1752, 1753] was born on 13 Oct 1903 in Alabama, USA [1749, 1750, 1751, 1752, 1753].

iii. Pluma Viola Lumpkin [1754, 1755] was born about 1906 in Alabama, USA [1754, 1755]. She lived in Anniston, Calhoun, Alabama, USA in 1920 [1755].

iv. (219) Judson Clemens (J.C.) Lumpkin[1756, 1757, 1758, 1759, 1760] was born on 21 May 1908 in Etowah, Alabama, USA [1756, 1757, 1758, 1759, 1760].

v. Pearl Allene Lumpkin [1761, 1762, 1763, 1764, 1765] was born on 20 Feb 1911 in Etowah, Alabama, USA [1761, 1762, 1764]. She lived in Keysburg, Etowah, Alabama, USA in 1930 [1762]. She died in Mar 1980 in Huntsville, Madison, Alabama, USA [1764].

vi. Frank Weaver Lumpkin [1766, 1767, 1768, 1769, 1770] was born on 28 Jul 1921 [1767, 1768, 1769, 1770]. He died on 03 Jun 1995 in Memphis, Shelby, Tennessee, USA [1770]. He lived in Tennessee, USA [1766].

vii. Walter E. Lumpkin [1771, 1772] was born about 1925 [1772]. He lived in Keysburg, Etowah, Alabama, USA in 1930 [1772]. He died in Jun 1930 in Etowah, Alabama, USA [1771].

220. *Liller Reeves*-14 (William Clemens-13, John S.-12, Nathan-11, Edmond-10, William-9, William-8, Richard-7, John-6, William-5, Timothy-4, Richard-3, John-2, Robert-1) was born on 07 Jul 1882 in Alabama, USA [1208, 1209, 1210].

She lived in Hokes Bluff, Etowah, Alabama, USA in 1920 [1208]. She died on 23 Mar 1964 in Alabama, USA. **John Walter McMahan** son of John McMahan and Louisa (unknown maiden name) [1773, 1774, 1213, 1775, 1776, 1214, 1777, 1778] was born on 28 Jul 1879 in Alabama, USA [1774, 1213, 1775, 1776, 1777, 1778]. He lived in Hokes Bluff, Etowah, Alabama, USA in 1920 [1775]. He died on 30 Dec 1957 in Alabama, USA [1773]. John Walter McMahan and Liller Reeves were married on 01 Jan 1899 in Etowah, Alabama, USA [1211, 1212, 1213, 1214]. They had the following children:

    i.   Lloyd McMahan [1779] was born on 19 Oct 1899 in Alabama, USA [1780, 1781, 1782, 1783, 1784]. He died in Jun 1974 in Gadsden, Etowah, Alabama, USA [1783]. He lived in Gadsden, Etowah, Alabama, USA [1779].

    ii.   (229) Slaught M. McMahan [1785, 1786, 1787, 1788] was born on 02 Jun 1902 in Alabama, USA [1785, 1786, 1787, 1788].

    iii.   (221) Jewel McMahan [1789, 1790, 1791] was born on 20 Sep 1908 in Alabama, USA [1789, 1790, 1791].

    iv.   (236) Lola Matril McMahan [1792, 1793] was born on 14 Apr 1915 in Alabama, USA [1792, 1793].

    v.   (232) Doyce McMahan [1794, 1795, 1796, 1797] was born on 28 Sep 1918 in Alabama, USA [1794, 1795, 1796, 1797].

    vi.   (244) Curtis Udell McMahan [1798, 1799, 1800, 1801, 1802, 1803] was born on 16 Aug 1922 [1798, 1799, 1800].

247. Claudie Reeves-14 (William Clemens-13, John S.-12, Nathan-11, Edmond-10, William-9, William-8, Richard-7, John-6, William-5, Timothy-4, Richard-3, John-2, Robert-1) [1221, 1222, 1223, 1224] was born on 16 Jun 1889 in Alabama, USA [1221, 1222, 1223, 1224]. She lived in Hokes Bluff, Etowah, Alabama, USA in 1910 [1224]. She died on 24 May 1963 in Alabama, USA. **William Alfred McMahan** son of John McMahan and Louisa (unknown maiden name) [1804, 1805, 1806, 1807, 1808, 1809] was born on 28 Aug 1885 in Alabama, USA [1804, 1805, 1806, 1807, 1808]. He died on 05 Jun 1954 in Etowah, Alabama, USA [1809]. He lived in Etowah, Alabama, USA [1804]. William Alfred McMahan and Claudie Reeves were married before 1910. They had the following children:

    i.   (248) Verna McMahan [1810, 1811, 1812, 1813] was born on 03 Aug 1910 in Alabama, USA [1811, 1812, 1813].

252. Marion Frank Reeves-14 (Nathan C.-13, John S.-12, Nathan-11, Edmond-10, William-9, William-8, Richard-7, John-6, William-5, Timothy-4, Richard-3, John-2, Robert-1) [1255, 1256, 1257, 1258, 1259, 1260] was born on 12 Nov 1884 in Alabama, USA [1255, 1256, 1257, 1258, 1259]. He was employed as a County Jail Warden in 1910 in Gadsden, Etowah, Alabama, USA. He lived in Gadsden, Etowah, Alabama, USA in 1920 [1255]. He died in Jan 1971 in Gadsden, Etowah, Alabama, USA [1260]. **Maude Gertrude (unknown maiden name)** [1814, 1815] was born on 12 Sep 1880 in Alabama, USA [1815]. She lived in Gadsden, Etowah, Alabama, USA in 1910 [1815]. She died on 18

Apr 1920 in Etowah, Alabama, USA [1814]. Marion Frank Reeves and Maude Gertrude (unknown maiden name) married and had the following children:

i. Thelma Reaves [1816, 1817] was born about 1911 in Alabama, USA [1816]. She lived in Gadsden, Etowah, Alabama, USA in 1920 [1816].

ii. Francis Reeves [1818, 1819] was born about 1913 in Alabama, USA [1818, 1819]. She lived in Gadsden, Etowah, Alabama, USA in 1920 [1818].

253. Arthur Columbus Reeves-14 (Nathan C.-13, John S.-12, Nathan-11, Edmond-10, William-9, William-8, Richard-7, John-6, William-5, Timothy-4, Richard-3, John-2, Robert-1) [1250, 1251, 1252, 1253, 1254] was born on 10 Sep 1881 in Alabama, USA [1251, 1252, 1253, 1254]. He lived in Fairview, Etowah, Alabama, USA in 1930 [1254]. He died in May 1933 in Etowah, Alabama, USA [1250]. **Margaret E. Lafallet** daughter of William J. Lafallet [1820, 1821] was born about 1887 in Alabama, USA [1820, 1821]. She lived in Fairview, Etowah, Alabama, USA in 1930 [1820]. Arthur Columbus Reeves and Margaret E. Lafallet married and had the following children:

i. Harvey F. Reeves [1822, 1823] was born about 1906 in Alabama, USA [1822, 1823]. He lived in Fairview, Etowah, Alabama, USA in 1930 [1822].

ii. Otto C. Reeves [1824, 1825] was born about 1910 in Alabama, USA [1824, 1825]. He lived in Fairview, Etowah, Alabama, USA in 1930 [1824].

iii. Vera Inez Reeves [1826, 1827] was born about 1917 in Alabama, USA [1826, 1827]. She lived in Fairview, Etowah, Alabama, USA in 1930 [1827].

iv. Mary B. Reeves [1828] was born about 1922 [1828]. She lived in Fairview, Etowah, Alabama, USA in 1930 [1828].

v. Grace M. Reeves [1829] was born about 1926 [1829]. She lived in Fairview, Etowah, Alabama, USA in 1930 [1829].

Generation 15

35. Arthur Finis Henley-15 (William Monroe-14, Elizabeth Marinda-13, William McGuire-12, William Emery-11, Edmond-10, William-9, William-8, Richard-7, John-6, William-5, Timothy-4, Richard-3, John-2, Robert-1) [1311, 1312, 1313, 1314, 1315] was born on 31 Jul 1898 in Alabama, USA [1311, 1312, 1313, 1314, 1315]. He lived in Renfroe, Talladega, Alabama, USA in 1930 [1311]. He died on 07 Oct 1972 in Talladega, Talladega, Alabama, USA [1313]. **Jane Blanch Hallman** [1830, 1831] was born about 1899 in Alabama, USA [1830, 1831]. She lived in Renfroe, Talladega, Alabama, USA in 1930 [1830]. Arthur Finis Henley and Jane Blanch Hallman married and had the following children:

i. Kathleen Henley [1832, 1833] was born about 1920 in Alabama, USA [1832, 1833]. She lived in Renfroe, Talladega, Alabama, USA in 1930 [1833].

ii. Arther F. Henley [1834] was born about 1922 [1834]. He lived in Renfroe, Talladega, Alabama, USA in 1930 [1834].

iii. Nell Henley [1835] was born about 1925 [1835]. She lived in Renfroe, Talladega, Alabama, USA in 1930 [1835].

iv. Anna R. Henley [1836] was born about 1928 [1836]. She lived in Renfroe, Talladega, Alabama, USA in 1930 [1836].

36. *Winford Carl Henley*-15 (William Monroe-14, Elizabeth Marinda-13, William McGuire-12, William Emery-11, Edmond-10, William-9, William-8, Richard-7, John-6, William-5, Timothy-4, Richard-3, John-2, Robert-1) [1316, 1317, 1318, 1319, 1320] was born on 13 Aug 1900 in Alabama, USA [1316, 1317, 1318, 1319, 1320]. He lived in Pell City, St Clair, Alabama, USA in 1930 [1316]. He died on 11 May 1992 in Panama City, Bay, Florida, USA [1318, 1320]. **Laura L. (unknown maiden name)** [1837] was born about 1909 [1837]. She lived in Pell City, St Clair, Alabama, USA in 1930 [1837]. Winford Carl Henley and Laura L. (unknown maiden name) married and had the following children:

i. Dorthy L. Henley [1838] was born about 1927 [1838]. She lived in Pell City, St Clair, Alabama, USA in 1930 [1838].

60. *Edna Couch*-15 (Barbara Mary Ann-14, James Martin-13, Carter Hill-12, William Emery-11, Edmond-10, William-9, William-8, Richard-7, John-6, William-5, Timothy-4, Richard-3, John-2, Robert-1) [1446] was born on 02 Apr 1914 in Alabama, USA [1446]. She died on 11 Mar 1998 in Gadsden, Etowah, Alabama, USA [1446]. **Hoyt Reeves (193)** son of Euclid Reeves and Buena Love McMurtrey [1721, 1722, 1723] was born on 05 Nov 1907 in Alabama, USA [1721, 1722, 1723]. He lived in Hokes Bluff, Etowah, Alabama, USA in 1930 [1722]. He died on 30 Nov 1983 in Gadsden, Etowah, Alabama, USA [1723]. Hoyt Reeves and Edna Couch were married on 30 Nov 1933. They had the following children:

i. (63) Gary Wendell Reeves [1839] was born in 1940.

ii. (61) Debra Ann Reeves [1840] was born in 1951.

69. *Rona Mae Reaves*-15 (Walter Thomas-14, James Martin-13, Carter Hill-12, William Emery-11, Edmond-10, William-9, William-8, Richard-7, John-6, William-5, Timothy-4, Richard-3, John-2, Robert-1) [1464, 1465, 1466, 1467] was born on 23 Jan 1904 in Alabama, USA [1464, 1465, 1466, 1467]. She lived in Oxford, Calhoun, Alabama, USA in 1920 [1467]. She died on 04 Jan 1984 in Alexandria, Calhoun, Alabama, USA [1465]. **Jesse C. Walker** [1842] was born about 1905 in Alabama, USA [1842]. He lived in Oxford, Calhoun, Alabama, USA in 1930 [1842]. Jesse C. Walker and Rona Mae Reaves married and had the following children:

i. Mildred Walker [1843] was born about 1925 [1843]. She lived in Oxford, Calhoun, Alabama, USA in 1930 [1843].

ii. Pauline Walker [1844] was born about 1928 [1844]. She lived in Oxford, Calhoun, Alabama, USA in 1930 [1844].

70. *Samuel Lee Roy Reaves*-15 (Walter Thomas-14, James Martin-13, Carter Hill-12, William Emery-11, Edmond-10, William-9, William-8, Richard-7, John-6, William-5, Timothy-4, Richard-3, John-2, Robert-1) [1461, 1462, 1463] was born on 20 May 1902 in Alabama, USA [1461, 1462, 1463]. He lived in Oxford, Calhoun, Alabama, USA in 1920 [1461]. He died on 12 Feb 1984 in Calhoun, Alabama, USA. **Gertrude (unknown maiden name)** [1845] was born about 1906 [1845]. She lived in Oxford, Calhoun, Alabama, USA in 1930 [1845]. Samuel Lee Roy Reaves and Gertrude (unknown maiden name) married and had the following children:

    i.   Forrest Reaves [1846] was born about 1928 [1846]. He lived in Oxford, Calhoun, Alabama, USA in 1930 [1846].

114. *Joseph Lark Williamson*-15 (Maggie Lee-14, William David-13, Ira Jackson-12, William Emery-11, Edmond-10, William-9, William-8, Richard-7, John-6, William-5, Timothy-4, Richard-3, John-2, Robert-1) [1593, 1594, 1595, 1596] was born on 05 Jul 1918 in Calhoun, Alabama, USA [1593, 1594, 1595, 1596]. He lived in Burns Cross Roads, Calhoun, Alabama, USA in 1930 [1596]. He died on 23 Apr 1983 in Anniston, Calhoun, Alabama, USA [1593, 1594]. **Carrie Mae Brown** was born on 16 Mar 1931 in Cherokee, Alabama, USA. She died on 26 Oct 2006 in Jacksonville, Calhoun, Alabama, USA. Joseph Lark Williamson and Carrie Mae Brown were married on 01 Jul 1950 in Rome, Floyd, Georgia, USA. They had the following children:

    i.   Debbie Williamson.

    ii.   Linda Williamson.

160. *Floyd Leon Reeves*-15 (Luther-14, William Clemens-13, John S.-12, Nathan-11, Edmond-10, William-9, William-8, Richard-7, John-6, William-5, Timothy-4, Richard-3, John-2, Robert-1) [1688, 1689, 1690, 1691] was born on 12 Feb 1902 in Alabama, USA [1689, 1690, 1691]. He lived in Gadsden, Etowah, Alabama, USA in 1930 [1691]. He died on 25 May 1964 in Anniston, Calhoun, Alabama, USA [1692]. **Mabel Clairelta Sewell** [1847, 1848] was born on 02 Aug 1903 in Alabama, USA [1847, 1848]. She lived in Gadsden, Etowah, Alabama, USA in 1930 [1847]. She died in Dec 1982 in Gadsden, Etowah, Alabama, USA [1848]. Floyd Leon Reeves and Mabel Clairelta Sewell were married on 08 Jul 1925. They had the following children:

    i.   (164) Maurice Leon Reeves [1849, 1850, 1851, 1852, 1853, 1854, 1855, 1856] was born in 1927 [1849].

    ii.   (161) Malline Louise Reeves [1857, 1858] was born in 1928 [1858]. She married Arthur Joe Watford on 14 Jun 1952 in Etowah, Alabama, USA [1859, 1860].

168. *Crate Funis Reeves*-15 (Luther-14, William Clemens-13, John S.-12, Nathan-11, Edmond-10, William-9, William-8, Richard-7, John-6, William-5, Timothy-4, Richard-3, John-2, Robert-1) [1698, 1699, 1700, 1701] was born on 07 Dec 1907 in Hokes Bluff, Etowah, Alabama, USA [1698, 1699, 1700, 1701]. He lived in Gadsden, Etowah, Alabama, USA in 1930 [1698]. He died on 12 Sep 1960 in Gadsden, Etowah, Alabama, USA [1701]. **Earline Ester Hamilton** daughter of Earley L. Hamilton and Eva Goodman [1861, 1862, 1863, 1864] was born on 23 Jul 1908 in Tennessee, USA [1861, 1862]. She lived in Gadsden, Etowah, Alabama, USA in 1920 [1861]. She died on 02 Jan 1970 in Gadsden, Etowah, Alabama, USA [1863]. Crate Funis Reeves and Earline Ester Hamilton were married before 1930. They had the following children:

i.   (174) Martha Evenette Reeves [1865] was born in 1933.

ii. (170) Marilyn Yvonne Reeves [1867, 1868, 1869, 1870] was born in 1935 [1867].

iii. (169) Jerry Lamar Reeves [1872, 1873, 1874, 1875] was born in 1936 [1872,1873].

iv. (180) Sherry Frances Reeves [1877, 1878] was born in 1939 [1877].

182. *Neva Reeves*-15 (Luther-14, William Clemens-13, John S.-12, Nathan-11, Edmond-10, William-9, William-8, Richard-7, John-6, William-5, Timothy-4, Richard-3, John-2, Robert-1) [1693, 1694, 1695, 1696, 1697, 1688] was born on 10 Jul 1905 in Alabama, USA [1693, 1694, 1695, 1696, 1697]. She lived in Decatur, Dekalb, Georgia, USA in 1964 [1879]. She died on 29 Mar 1998 in Douglasville, Douglas, Georgia, USA [1695, 1696]. **Charles David Barnes** son of Newton Eldridge Barnes and Mary Elizabeth Blair [1880, 1881, 1882, 1883, 1884] was born on 01 Jan 1904 in Alabama, USA [1880, 1881, 1882, 1883, 1884]. He lived in Gadsden, Etowah, Alabama, USA in 1910 [1884]. He died on 13 Oct 1984 in Decatur, Dekalb, Georgia, USA [1882, 1883]. Charles David Barnes and Neva Reeves were married before 1930. They had the following children:

i.   (183) Bobby Leland Barnes was born in 1931.

ii. Luther Boyce Barnes was born in 1933. He lived in Carrollton, Carroll, Georgia, USA in 2011.

iii. (187) Brenda Barnes was born in 1939.

190. *May Reeves*-15 (Luther-14, William Clemens-13, John S.-12, Nathan-11, Edmond-10, William-9, William-8, Richard-7, John-6, William-5, Timothy-4, Richard-3, John-2, Robert-1) [1702, 1703] was born on 01 May 1915 in Alabama, USA [1702, 1704, 1705]. She lived in Birmingham, Jefferson, Alabama, USA in 1987 [1702]. She died on 31 Aug 1992 in Fairfield, Jefferson, Alabama, USA [1707]. **Francis M. Houghton Jr.** son of Francis M. Houghton and Lula Elizabeth ?Appling? [1890, 1891, 1892, 1893, 1894, 1895] was born on 10 Sep 1909 in Alabama, USA [1890, 1891, 1892, 1893, 1894]. He died on 11 Jun 1997 in Birmingham, Jefferson, Alabama, USA [1893]. Francis M. Houghton Jr. and May Reeves were married after 1930. They had the following children:

i.   Francis M., III "Scotty" Houghton was born in 1935 in Etowah County, Alabama, USA.

ii. Larry Houghton was born about 1938 in Etowah County, Alabama, USA.

Otis K. Lawson son of Kyle Lawson and Flora B. Lawson [1703, 1885, 1886, 1887, 1888, 1889] was born on 22 Oct 1907 in Alabama, USA [1885, 1886, 1887]. He lived in Birmingham, Jefferson, Alabama, USA in 1993 [1889]. He died on 25 Jan 1994 in Birmingham, Jefferson, Alabama, USA [1887]. Otis K. Lawson and May Reeves were married on 14 Apr 1944 in Jefferson, Alabama, USA [1706]. They had no children.

192. *Doyle Reeves*-15 (Euclid-14, William Clemens-13, John S.-12, Nathan-11, Edmond-10, William-9, William-8, Richard-7, John-6, William-5, Timothy-4, Richard-3, John-2, Robert-1) [1715, 1716, 1717] was born on 14 Feb 1902 in Alabama, USA [1715, 1716, 1717]. He lived in Hokes Bluff, Etowah, Alabama, USA in 1930 [1717]. He died in Apr 1974 in Gadsden, Etowah, Alabama, USA [1716]. **Myrtie D. Morris** daughter of Nathan Davis Morris and Sula Floy Ford [1896, 1897, 1898, 1899] was born on 15 Oct 1908 in Alabama, USA [1896, 1897, 1898, 1899]. She lived in Hokes Bluff, Etowah, Alabama, USA in 1930 [1896]. She died on 16 Jun 2000 in Gadsden, Etowah, Alabama, USA [1897]. Doyle Reeves and Myrtie D. Morris were married before 1930. They had the following children:

    i.   John Dewey Reeves was born in 1936. He married Clarissa (unknown maiden name) in 1960.

    ii.   Mary Marlene Reeves was born on 22 January 1933. She married Donald Morgan in 1954.

    iii.   Wilma Faye Reeves [1900, 1901, 1902] was born in 1929 [1900, 1901]. She married Billy F. Lancaster on 28 Feb 1948 in Etowah, Alabama, USA [1903]. She lived in Gadsden, Etowah, Alabama, USA in 1995 [1901].

    iv.   Bobby Dale Reeves was born on 25 Jun 1933. He died in 2005.

    v.   Billy Kay Reeves was born in 1943.

193. *Hoyt Reeves*-15 (Euclid-14, William Clemens-13, John S.-12, Nathan-11, Edmond-10, William-9, William-8, Richard-7, John-6, William-5, Timothy-4, Richard-3, John-2, Robert-1) [1721, 1722, 1723] was born on 05 Nov 1907 in Alabama, USA [1721, 1722, 1723]. He lived in Hokes Bluff, Etowah, Alabama, USA in 1930 [1722]. He died on 30 Nov 1983 in Gadsden, Etowah, Alabama, USA [1723]. **Edna Couch (60)** daughter of Jason Daniel Couch and Barbara Mary Ann Reaves [1446] was born on 02 Apr 1914 in Alabama, USA [1446]. She died on 11 Mar 1998 in Gadsden, Etowah, Alabama, USA [1446]. Hoyt Reeves and Edna Couch were married on 30 Nov 1933. They had the following children:

    i.   (63) Gary Wendell Reeves [1839] was born in 1940.

    ii.   (61) Debra Ann Reeves [1840] was born in 1951.

194. *H. K. Reeves*-15 (Euclid-14, William Clemens-13, John S.-12, Nathan-11, Edmond-10, William-9, William-8, Richard-7, John-6, William-5, Timothy-4, Richard-3, John-2, Robert-1) [1733, 1734, 1735, 1736, 1737, 1738, 1739] was born on 04 Dec 1918 in Alabama, USA [1734, 1735, 1736, 1737]. He died on 27 Jan 1953 in Etowah, Alabama, USA [1737, 1738]. He lived in Gadsden, Etowah, Alabama, USA [1733]. **Francis Day** daughter of George E. Day and Mamie Day [1739, 1904] was born about 1924 [1904]. She lived in Hokes Bluff, Etowah, Alabama, USA in 1930 [1904]. H. K. Reeves and Francis Day married in 1942 and later divorced. They had the following children:

    i.   (195) Terry Gene Reeves [1905, 1906, 1907] was born in 1942 [1907].

196. *Troy Reeves*-15 (Euclid-14, William Clemens-13, John S.-12, Nathan-11, Edmond-10, William-9, William-8, Richard-7, John-6, William-5, Timothy-4,

Richard-3, John-2, Robert-1) [1730, 1731, 1732] was born on 18 Dec 1914 in Glencoe, Etowah, Alabama, USA [1730, 1731, 1732]. He lived in Hokes Bluff, Etowah, Alabama, USA in 1930 [1732]. He died on 21 May 1991 in Gadsden, Etowah, Alabama, USA [1730]. **Martha Louise Boyd** daughter of Gurley Rise Boyd and Jesse Ruth Morgan [1909, 1910] was born on 18 Oct 1916 in Southside, Etowah, Alabama, USA [1909, 1910]. She lived in Gadsden, Etowah, Alabama, USA in 1920 [1910]. She died on 23 Apr 1986 in Gadsden, Etowah, Alabama, USA [1909]. Troy Reeves and Martha Louise Boyd were married before 1936. They had the following children:

i.   (197) Troy Reeves Jr [1911, 1912] was born in 1936 (Born at home) [1911].

ii. (208) Glenda Janice Reeves [1913, 1914, 1915, 1916] was born in 1937 in Etowah, Alabama, USA (Born at home) [1913].

iii. (205) Boyd McMurtrey Reeves [1918] was born in 1939.

iv. (202) Haralson Kerr Reeves [1919] was born in 1943.

211.   *Cresful Reeves*-15 (Euclid-14, William Clemens-13, John S.-12, Nathan-11, Edmond-10, William-9, William-8, Richard-7, John-6, William-5, Timothy-4, Richard-3, John-2, Robert-1) [1724, 1725, 1726, 1727, 1728] was born on 10 May 1912 in Etowah, Alabama, USA [1724, 1725, 1726, 1727, 1728]. He died on 28 Feb 2004 in Gadsden, Etowah, Alabama, USA [1726]. **Peggy Lee Ables** daughter of Arthur Lee Ables and Pauline N. Davis [1921, 1922] was born on 27 Mar 1924 in Gadsden, Etowah, Alabama, USA [1923]. She lived in Gadsden, Etowah, Alabama, USA in 1930 [1923]. She died on 11 Jul 1957 in Gadsden, Etowah, Alabama, USA [1921]. Cresful Reeves and Peggy Lee Ables were married on 17 Sep 1949 in Etowah, Alabama, USA [1729]. They had the following children:

i.   (216) Cresful Reeves Jr [1924] was born in 1950 [1924].

ii. (213) William Patrick Reeves was born in 1954.

iii. (212) Peggy Maria Reeves [1925] was born in 1957 [1925].

Cresful married Margaret Rutledge (b. March 23, 1929) around 1984. They had no children. Margaret died on March 21, 1997.

218.   *Clarence Eugene Lumpkin*-15 (Riller-14, William Clemens-13, John S.-12, Nathan-11, Edmond-10, William-9, William-8, Richard-7, John-6, William-5, Timothy-4, Richard-3, John-2, Robert-1) [1749, 1750, 1751, 1752, 1753] was born on 13 Oct 1903 in Alabama, USA [1749, 1750, 1751, 1752, 1753]. He was employed as a Shoemakers and shoe repairmen, not in factory in 1941 in Alabama, USA [1926]. He died in Jan 1971 [1753]. He lived in Alabama, USA [1749]. **Margaret Evelyn Robinette** daughter of Lonnie Polk Robinette and Donnie Odessa Humphries [1927, 1928] was born on 13 Dec 1905 in Anniston, Calhoun, Alabama, USA [1927, 1928]. She lived in Anniston, Calhoun, Alabama, USA in 1920 [1928]. She died on 21 Oct 1950 in Athens, Limestone, Alabama, USA. Clarence Eugene Lumpkin and were married on 13 Jan 1922. They had the following children:

i. Rubye Dean Lumpkin [1929, 1930, 1931, 1932, 1933, 1934, 1935] was born on 12 Jan 1923 in Anniston, Calhoun, Alabama, USA [1930, 1931, 1932]. She lived in Anniston, Calhoun, Alabama, USA in 1930 [1932]. She married Edward Ganderson on 02 May 1952 in Calhoun, Alabama, USA [1936]. She died on 06 Nov 2010 in Pasadena, Harris, Texas, USA [1930].

ii. C. Robert Lumpkin [1937, 1938, 1939, 1940, 1941, 1942, 1943, 1944, 1945, 1946] was born on 20 Jun 1925 in Alabama, USA [1937, 1938, 1939, 1940, 1942]. He lived in Fayetteville, Cumberland, North Carolina, USA between 1993-1994 [1945]. He died on 31 Jan 2003 in Fayetteville, Cumberland, North Carolina, USA [1938, 1939, 1940].

iii. Eleanor Virginia Lumpkin [1947, 1948, 1949] was born in 1926 in Anniston, Calhoun, Alabama, USA [1947]. She lived in Anniston, Calhoun, Alabama, USA in 1930 [1947]. She died on 07 Dec 1955.

iv. Betty L. Lumpkin [1950] was born about 1929 [1950]. She lived in Anniston, Calhoun, Alabama, USA in 1930 [1950].

219. *Judson Clemens (J.C.) Lumpkin*-15 (Riller-14, William Clemens-13, John S.-12, Nathan-11, Edmond-10, William-9, William-8, Richard-7, John-6, William-5, Timothy-4, Richard-3, John-2, Robert-1) [1756, 1757, 1758, 1759, 1760] was born on 21 May 1908 in Etowah, Alabama, USA [1756, 1757, 1758, 1759, 1760]. He died on 22 Jan 1976 in Gadsden, Etowah, Alabama, USA [1759]. **Pearl Pauline Smith** daughter of H. J. Smith and Rhoda (unknown maiden name) [1951, 1952, 1953] was born on 01 Jan 1907 in Etowah, Alabama, USA [1951, 1952, 1953]. She lived in Gadsden, Etowah, Alabama, USA in 1920 [1951]. She died on 27 May 1988 in Gadsden, Etowah, Alabama, USA [1953]. Judson Clemens (J.C.) Lumpkin and Pearl Pauline Smith were married on 04 Jan 1930 in Gadsden, Etowah, Alabama, USA. They had the following children:

i. Joseph Eugene Lumpkin [1954] was born on 06 Dec 1932 [1954]. He died on 18 Feb 1965 in Gadsden, Etowah, Alabama, USA [1954].

ii. Shirley Ann Lumpkin [1955, 1956] was born on 16 Sep 1935 in Gadsden, Etowah, Alabama, USA [1955]. She died on 24 Dec 1987 in Gadsden, Etowah, Alabama, USA [1955].

221. *Jewel McMahan*-15 (Liller-14, William Clemens-13, John S.-12, Nathan-11, Edmond-10, William-9, William-8, Richard-7, John-6, William-5, Timothy-4, Richard-3, John-2, Robert-1) [1789, 1790, 1791] was born on 20 Sep 1908 in Alabama, USA [1789, 1790, 1791]. She lived in Hokes Bluff, Etowah, Alabama, USA in 1930 [1790]. She died on 19 Feb 1990 in Gadsden, Etowah, Alabama, USA [1791]. **Grady M. Marbut** son of John C. Marbut and Joicie A. (unknown maiden name) [1957, 1958, 1959] was born on 17 Jun 1905 in Alabama, USA [1957, 1958, 1959]. He lived in Reaves, Etowah, Alabama, USA in 1920 [1959]. He died in Jun 1987 in Gadsden, Etowah, Alabama, USA [1958]. Grady M. Marbut and Jewel McMahan were married about 1925. They had the following children:

i. (226) Ennis Marbut [1960, 1961, 1962, 1963, 1964] was in 1926 [1960, 1961].

ii.   (222) Donnie Marbut [1965, 1966] was born on 20 Jun 1932 [1965].

iii.   (227) Leva Wylene Marbut [1967, 1968, 1969] was born in 1939 [1967].

229.   *Slaught M. McMahan*-15 (Liller-14, William Clemens-13, John S.-12, Nathan-11, Edmond-10, William-9, William-8, Richard-7, John-6, William-5, Timothy-4, Richard-3, John-2, Robert-1) [1785, 1786, 1787, 1788] was born on 02 Jun 1902 in Alabama, USA [1785, 1786, 1787, 1788]. He lived in Hokes Bluff, Etowah, Alabama, USA in 1930 [1788]. He died in Dec 1971 in Gadsden, Etowah, Alabama, USA [1786]. **Nellie Mae Marbut** daughter of James Luther Marbut and Susan Elizabeth Ford [1970, 1971, 1972] was born on 16 Apr 1905 in Alabama, USA [1970, 1971, 1972]. She lived in Hokes Bluff, Etowah, Alabama, USA in 1920 [1972]. She died on 01 Dec 1988 in Gadsden, Etowah, Alabama, USA [1971]. Slaught M. McMahan and Nellie Mae Marbut were married about 1925. They had the following children:

i.   Aldridge McMahan [1973, 1974, 1975] was born in 1926 [1973, 1974, 1975]. He lived in Jacksonville, St Johns, Florida, USA in 1993[1975].

ii.   (230) Edwina McMahan [1976, 1977, 1978] was born in 1929 [1976, 1977].

232.   *Doyce McMahan*-15 (Liller-14, William Clemens-13, John S.-12, Nathan-11, Edmond-10, William-9, William-8, Richard-7, John-6, William-5, Timothy-4, Richard-3, John-2, Robert-1) [1794, 1795, 1796, 1797] was born on 28 Sep 1918 in Alabama, USA [1794, 1795, 1796, 1797]. He lived in Hokes Bluff, Etowah, Alabama, USA in 1920 [1794]. He died on 30 May 2003 in Gadsden, Etowah, Alabama, USA [1796]. **Agatha (Nanny) Turner** daughter of Marvin Turner and Mollie (unknown maiden name) [1979, 1980, 1981, 1982, 1983] was born on 12 Oct 1918 [1979, 1980, 1981]. She lived in Hokes Bluff, Etowah, Alabama, USA in 1930 [1981]. She died on 27 Dec 2009 in Gadsden, Etowah, Alabama, USA [1979, 1982, 1983]. Doyce McMahan and Agatha (Nanny) Turner were married about 1940. They had the following children:

i.   (233) Royce McMahan [1984, 1985] was born in 1944 in Etowah, Alabama, USA [1984].

236.   *Lola Matril McMahan*-15 (Liller-14, William Clemens-13, John S.-12, Nathan-11, Edmond-10, William-9, William-8, Richard-7, John-6, William-5, Timothy-4, Richard-3, John-2, Robert-1) [1792, 1793] was born on 14 Apr 1915 in Alabama, USA [1792, 1793]. She lived in Hokes Bluff, Etowah, Alabama, USA in 1920 [1793]. She died on 04 Jan 1979 in Alabama, USA. **William Comer Shields** son of William David Shields and Eva Gidley [1986, 1987, 1988] was born on 20 Jul 1914 in Alabama, USA [1986, 1987, 1988]. He lived in Hokes Bluff, Etowah, Alabama, USA in 1920 [1988]. He died on 28 Oct 1994 in Gadsden, Etowah, Alabama, USA [1986]. William Comer Shields and Lola Matril McMahan married and had the following children:

i.   (240) Billy Mack Shields [1989] was born on 22 May 1935.

ii.   (237) Murrell Brack Shields [1990, 1991] was born on 07 Sep 1942 in Gadsden, Etowah, Alabama, USA [1990].

244.   *Curtis Udell McMahan*-15 (Liller-14, William Clemens-13, John S.-12, Nathan-11, Edmond-10, William-9, William-8, Richard-7, John-6, William-5, Timothy-4, Richard-3, John-2, Robert-1) [1798, 1799, 1800, 1801, 1802, 1803] was born on 16 Aug 1922 [1798, 1799, 1800]. He lived in Gadsden, Etowah, Alabama, USA in 1981 [1802]. He died on 06 Feb 1992 [1798]. **Mary Frances (Bet) Moore** daughter of John Waymon Moore and Ella Vesta Blankenship [1992] was born on 22 Nov 1920 [1992]. She lived in Gadsden, Etowah, Alabama, USA in 1981 [1992]. Curtis Udell McMahan and Mary Frances (Bet) Moore married and had the following children:

    i.   (246) C. Wayne McMahan [1993, 1994] was born in 1946 [1994].

    ii.   (245) Elizabeth Ann McMahan.

248.   *Verna McMahan*-15 (Claudie-14, William Clemens-13, John S.-12, Nathan-11, Edmond-10, William-9, William-8, Richard-7, John-6, William-5, Timothy-4, Richard-3, John-2, Robert-1) [1810, 1811, 1812, 1813] was born on 03 Aug 1910 in Alabama, USA [1811, 1812, 1813]. She lived in Hokes Bluff, Etowah, Alabama, USA in 1930 [1812]. She died in Jul 1978 in Gadsden, Etowah, Alabama, USA [1813]. **Hugh Hamilton Collins** son of John H. Collins and Laura Bell West [1995, 1996, 1997, 1810] was born on 11 Sep 1910 in Alabama, USA [1995, 1996, 1997]. He lived in Hokes Bluff, Etowah, Alabama, USA in 1920 [1997]. He died on 24 Aug 1977 in Gadsden, Etowah, Alabama, USA [1995]. Hugh Hamilton Collins and Verna McMahan married and had the following children:

    i.   Glenda Gail Collins [1998] was born in 1944 [1998]. She lived in Gadsden, Etowah, Alabama, USA in 1986 [1998].

Generation 16

61.   *Debra Ann Reeves*-16 (Edna-15, Barbara Mary Ann-14, James Martin-13, Carter Hill-12, William Emery-11, Edmond-10, William-9, William-8, Richard-7, John-6, William-5, Timothy-4, Richard-3, John-2, Robert-1) [1840] was in 1951. Dennis Ray Jones and Debra Ann Reeves were married in Dec 1969 in Etowah, Alabama, USA [1840, 1841]. They had the following children:

    i.   (62) Crystal Nicole Jones was born in 1973.

63.   *Gary Wendell Reeves*-16 (Edna-15, Barbara Mary Ann-14, James Martin-13, Carter Hill-12, William Emery-11, Edmond-10, William-9, William-8, Richard-7, John-6, William-5, Timothy-4, Richard-3, John-2, Robert-1) [1839] was born in 1940. Gary Wendell Reeves and **Carolyn Jo Young** married and had the following children:

    i.   (64) Gary Scott Reeves [2000] was born in 1965 [2000].

    ii.   Steven Mark Reeves [2001] was born in 1966 [2001]. He married Paula Ann Blake in 1990. He lived in Etowah County, Alabama, USA in 1994 [2001].

    iii. (65) Wendy Carol Reeves [2002] was born in 1973 [2002].

161.   *Malline Louise Reeves*-16 (Floyd Leon-15, Luther-14, William Clemens-13, John S.-12, Nathan-11, Edmond-10, William-9, William-8, Richard-7, John-6,

William-5, Timothy-4, Richard-3, John-2, Robert-1) [1857, 1858] was born in 1928 [1858]. She lived in Gadsden, Etowah, Alabama, USA in 1994 [1857]. **Arthur Joe Watford** son of Troy E. Watford and Josephine Blevins [2003, 2004, 2005, 2006, 1860] was born on 18 Feb 1927 [2003, 2004, 2006]. He died on 14 Sep 1974 in Gadsden, Etowah, Alabama, USA [2006]. Arthur Joe Watford and Malline Louise Reeves were married on 14 Jun 1952 in Etowah, Alabama, USA [1859, 1860]. They had the following children:

    i.   (162) Leon Ellis (Skipper) Watford [2007, 2008] was born in 1953 [2008]. He married Tina Renee Patterson before 1979.

    ii.   (163) Arthur Joseph (Art) Watford II [2009] was born in 1956 [2009]. He married Debra Allyson Dial in 1982.

Malline Louise Reeves Watford married Don Wright before 1982. They had no children.

164.   *Maurice Leon Reeves*-16 (Floyd Leon-15, Luther-14, William Clemens-13, John S.-12, Nathan-11, Edmond-10, William-9, William-8, Richard-7, John-6, William-5, Timothy-4, Richard-3, John-2, Robert-1) [1849, 1850, 1851, 1852, 1853, 1854, 1855, 1856] was born in 1927 [1849]. He lived in Anniston, Calhoun, Alabama, USA between 1998-2002 [1855]. **Lela Frances Nelson** daughter of Crawford Nelson and Addie I. Dickines [2010] was born in 1926. Maurice Leon Reeves and Lela Frances Nelson married and had the following children:

    i.   (165) Cathy Marilyn Reeves [2011, 2012, 2013, 2014, 2015] was born in 1950.

169.   *Jerry Lamar Reeves*-16 (Crate Funis-15, Luther-14, William Clemens-13, John S.-12, Nathan-11, Edmond-10, William-9, William-8, Richard-7, John-6, William-5, Timothy-4, Richard-3, John-2, Robert-1) [1872, 1873, 1874, 1875] was born in 1936 [1872, 1873]. He lived in Birmingham, Jefferson, Alabama, USA between 1995-1999 [1874]. Jerry Lamar Reeves married Bernice Blevins and adopted her son:

    i.   Brian Reeves was born in 1966.

170.   *Marilyn Yvonne Reeves*-16 (Crate Funis-15, Luther-14, William Clemens-13, John S.-12, Nathan-11, Edmond-10, William-9, William-8, Richard-7, John-6, William-5, Timothy-4, Richard-3, John-2, Robert-1) [1867, 1868, 1869, 1870] was born in 1935 [1867]. She lived in Gadsden, Etowah, Alabama, USA between 1998-2002 [1869]. **Tim Auston Gentry Jr** son of Tim Auston Gentry [2017, 2018, 1871, 2019, 2020, 2021] was born on 07 May 1930 [2017, 2018]. He lived in Gadsden, Etowah, Alabama, USA in 1992 [2017]. He died on 15 Dec 1998 in Gadsden, Etowah, Alabama, USA [2018]. Tim Auston Gentry Jr. and Marilyn Yvonne Reeves were married in May 1954 in Etowah, Alabama, USA [1870, 1871]. They had the following children:

    i.   (172) Alan Gentry [2022] was born in 1957 [2022].

    ii.   (171) Jennifer Lynn Gentry [2023, 2024] was born in 1961 [2023, 2024].

174. *Martha Evenette Reeves*-16 (Crate Funis-15, Luther-14, William Clemens-13, John S.-12, Nathan-11, Edmond-10, William-9, William-8, Richard-7, John-6, William-5, Timothy-4, Richard-3, John-2, Robert-1) [1865] was born in 1933. **James Spearman Johnson** [1866] was born on 15 May 1929. He died on 23 Feb 2011. James Spearman Johnson and Martha Evenette Reeves were married on 02 Jun 1951 in Etowah, Alabama, USA [1866, 1865]. They had the following children:

- i.   (178) James Spearman (Jim or Jet) Johnson Jr was born in 1952.
- ii.   (177) Karla Eve Johnson [2025] was born in 1954 [2025].
- iii. (175) Kerry Lee Johnson was born in 1955.
- iv.   (179) Kyle Reeves Johnson was born in 1962.

180.   *Sherry Frances Reeves*-16 (Crate Funis-15, Luther-14, William Clemens-13, John S.-12, Nathan-11, Edmond-10, William-9, William-8, Richard-7, John-6, William-5, Timothy-4, Richard-3, John-2, Robert-1) [1877, 1878] was born in 1939 [1877]. She lived in Hokes Bluff, Etowah, Alabama, USA in 1985 [1877]. **Kelly Nyle Cardwell** [2026] was born on 07 Jun 1930 [2026]. He died on 29 Apr 1993. Kelly Nyle Cardwell and Sherry Frances Reeves married and had the following children:

- i.   (181) Mark Craig Cardwell was born in 1959.
- ii.   Lynda Lee Cardwell [2027] was born in 1961 [2027]. She lived in Birmingham, Jefferson, Alabama, USA in 1995 [2027].

183.   *Bobby Leland Barnes*-16 (Neva-15, Luther-14, William Clemens-13, John S.-12, Nathan-11, Edmond-10, William-9, William-8, Richard-7, John-6, William-5, Timothy-4, Richard-3, John-2, Robert-1) was born in 1931. **Mary Elizabeth Williams** was born in 1936. Bobby Leland Barnes and Mary Elizabeth Williams were married in 1956. They had the following children:

- i.   (184) James David Barnes was born in 1959 in Duluth, Gwinnett, Georgia, USA.
- ii.   (186) Gena Lynn Barnes [2028] was born in 1963 in Atlanta, Dekalb, Georgia, USA [2028].
- iii. (185) Andrea Jo (Jo-Jo) Barnes was born in 1964 in Atlanta, Dekalb, Georgia, USA.

187.   *Brenda Barnes*-16 (Neva-15, Luther-14, William Clemens-13, John S.-12, Nathan-11, Edmond-10, William-9, William-8, Richard-7, John-6, William-5, Timothy-4, Richard-3, John-2, Robert-1) was born in 1939. **Melvin Leon Huff** was born in 1937. Melvin Leon Huff and Brenda Barnes were married in Nov 1964 in Decatur, Georgia, USA (Decatur Baptist Church). They had the following children:

- i.   Kenneth Melvin Huff was born in 1965. He married Coleen Elizabeth Coyle in 2005.
- ii.   (188) Kevin Leon Huff was born in 1967.

iii.   (189) Kristina Huff was born in 1970.

195. *Terry Gene Reeves*-16 (H. K.-15, Euclid-14, William Clemens-13, John S.-12, Nathan-11, Edmond-10, William-9, William-8, Richard-7, John-6, William-5, Timothy-4, Richard-3, John-2, Robert-1) [1905, 1906, 1907] was born in 1942 [1907]. He lived in Leicester, Buncombe, North Carolina, USA between 1999-2002 [1905]. **Shirley I. Spinks [**1908] was born about 1942. Terry Gene Reeves and Shirley I. Spinks were married in Apr 1963 in Etowah, Alabama, USA [1908]. They had the following children:

i.   ?John? Reeves [2029, 2030] was born about 1963. He lived in Gadsden, Etowah, Alabama, USA in 1994 [2029].

197. *Troy Reeves Jr*-16 (Troy-15, Euclid-14, William Clemens-13, John S.-12, Nathan-11, Edmond-10, William-9, William-8, Richard-7, John-6, William-5, Timothy-4, Richard-3, John-2, Robert-1) [1911, 1912] was born in 1936 (Born at home) [1911]. He lived in Gadsden, Etowah, Alabama, USA in 1993 [1911]. Troy Reeves Jr and Manara Jane Posey were married in Jul 1953 in Etowah, Alabama, USA [2043]. They had the following children:

i.   Troy Reeves III [2036] was born in 1960 [2036]. He lived in Vidalia, Montgomery, Georgia, USA in 1986 [2036].

ii.   Jena Louise Reeves [2039] was born in 1961 [2039]. She lived in Birmingham, Jefferson, Alabama, USA in 1993 [2039].

iii.   (198) Kim Renèe Reeves was born in 1963 in Paris, Île-de-France, France.

Roberta Esther Hartel [2031, 2032, 2033] was born in 1941 [2031, 2032, 2033]. She lived in Gadsden, Etowah, Alabama, USA in 1990 [2032]. Troy Reeves Jr and Roberta Esther Hartel were married in 1972. Roberta brought Troy four step-children to the marriage:

i.   Joseph Patrick Couillard [2034, 2035] was born in 1960 in Hennepin, Minnesota, USA [2034, 2035]. He lived in Minneapolis, Anoka, Minnesota, USA in 1989 [2034].

ii.   (199) Jacqueline Anne Couillard [2037, 2038] was born in 1961 in Hennepin, Minnesota, USA [2037, 2038].

iii.   (200) Jill Annette Couillard [2040] was born in 1962 in Hennepin, Minnesota, USA [2040].

iv.   (201) Jennifer Marie Couillard [2041, 2042] was born in 1964 in Hennepin, Minnesota, USA [2041, 2042].

202. *Haralson Kerr (Cootie) Reeves*-16 (Troy-15, Euclid-14, William Clemens-13, John S.-12, Nathan-11, Edmond-10, William-9, William-8, Richard-7, John-6, William-5, Timothy-4, Richard-3, John-2, Robert-1) [1919] was born in 1943. Haralson Kerr Reeves and Sharon L. Sims were married in 1962 in Etowah, Alabama, USA [1920]. They had the following children:

i.   (204) Haralson Kerr Reeves Jr was born in 1967.

ii.   (203) Traci Lynn Reeves [2044] was born in 1973 [2044].

205. Boyd McMurtrey (Mac) Reeves-16 (Troy-15, Euclid-14, William Clemens-13, John S.-12, Nathan-11, Edmond-10, William-9, William-8, Richard-7, John-6, William-5, Timothy-4, Richard-3, John-2, Robert-1) [1918] was born in 1939. Boyd McMurtrey Reeves and Charlotte Patterson were married in 1960 in Etowah, Alabama, USA [1918]. They had the following children:

    i.   (207) Jana Elizabeth Reeves [2045, 2046, 2047] was born in 1963 [2045, 2046, 2047].

    ii.   Martha Charlene Reeves was born in 1965.

    iii. (206) Jason Mack Reeves [2048, 2049] was born in 1974 [2049].

208. Glenda Janice Reeves-16 (Troy-15, Euclid-14, William Clemens-13, John S.-12, Nathan-11, Edmond-10, William-9, William-8, Richard-7, John-6, William-5, Timothy-4, Richard-3, John-2, Robert-1) [1913, 1914, 1915, 1916] was born in 1937 in Etowah, Alabama, USA (Born at home.) [1913]. She lived in Gadsden, Etowah, Alabama, USA in 1993 [1913]. **Hugh Alan Daves** son of Samuel Alexander Daves and Vera Myrtle Gilbert [2050] was born in 1933 in Etowah, Alabama, USA. Hugh Alan Daves and Glenda Janice Reeves were married on in 1962 in Etowah, Alabama, USA [1917]. Glenda Janice brought a daughter to the marriage which Hugh subsequently adopted. They had the following children:

    i.   (210) Susan Yvonne Daves was born in 1957.

    ii.   (209) Reeves Alan Daves [2051, 2052, 2053, 2054, 2055] was born in 1965 in Gadsden, Etowah, Alabama, USA [2051, 2052, 2053, 2054].

212. Peggy Maria (Peree) Reeves-16 (Cresful-15, Euclid-14, William Clemens-13, John S.-12, Nathan-11, Edmond-10, William-9, William-8, Richard-7, John-6, William-5, Timothy-4, Richard-3, John-2, Robert-1) [1925] was born in 1957 [1925]. She lived in Rome, Floyd, Georgia, USA in 1987 [1925]. **Lynn Collier** and Peggy Maria Reeves married and had the following children:

    i.   Bertram Reeves Collier was born about 1985. He married Anna Claire Williamson (b. 1987) in 2010.

    ii.   Elizabeth Knight Collier was born in 1986. She married Justin Bruce in 2010.

    iii. Patrick Lynn Collier was born in 1989.

213. William Patrick (Pat) Reeves-16 (Cresful-15, Euclid-14, William Clemens-13, John S.-12, Nathan-11, Edmond-10, William-9, William-8, Richard-7, John-6, William-5, Timothy-4, Richard-3, John-2, Robert-1) was born in 1954. **Fran Griffith** was born in 1953. William Patrick Reeves and Fran Griffith were married in 1976. They had the following children:

    i.   Sally Reeves was born in 1985.

    ii.   (214) Abby Lane Reeves was born in 1982.

    iii. (215) Katie Pauline Reeves was born in 1980.

216. Cresful (Corky) Reeves Jr-16 (Cresful-15, Euclid-14, William Clemens-13, John S.-12, Nathan-11, Edmond-10, William-9, William-8, Richard-7, John-6, William-5, Timothy-4, Richard-3, John-2, Robert-1) [1924] was born in 1950

[1924]. He lived in Athens, Clarke, Georgia, USA in 1995 [1924]. Cresful Reeves Jr and Lisa Malaine Willis married and had the following children:

    i.   Amber Malaine Reeves was born in 1984.

222. ***Donnie Marbut*-16** (Jewel-15, Liller-14, William Clemens-13, John S.-12, Nathan-11, Edmond-10, William-9, William-8, Richard-7, John-6, William-5, Timothy-4, Richard-3, John-2, Robert-1) [1965, 1966] was born on 20 Jun 1932 [1965]. He died in Jun 1982 [1965]. **Catherine A. Shields** daughter of William David Shields and Eva Gidley [2061, 2062, 2063] was born in 1932 [2061]. She lived in Gadsden, Etowah, Alabama, USA in 1993 [2062]. Donnie Marbut and Catherine A. Shields married and had the following children:

    i.   (223) Terry Marbut [2064] was born in 1961 [2064].

    ii.   Cathy Ann Marbut was born about 1964.

226. *Ennis Marbut*-16 (Jewel-15, Liller-14, William Clemens-13, John S.-12, Nathan-11, Edmond-10, William-9, William-8, Richard-7, John-6, William-5, Timothy-4, Richard-3, John-2, Robert-1) [1960, 1961, 1962, 1963, 1964] was born in 1926 [1960, 1961]. He lived in Hokes Bluff, Etowah, Alabama, USA between 1998-2002 [1963]. **Tommie Donaleen Shields** daughter of William David Shields and Eva Gidley [2065, 2066, 2067] was born in 1930 [2065, 2066]. She lived in Hokes Bluff, Etowah, Alabama, USA in 1930 [2066]. Ennis Marbut and Tommie Donaleen Shields married and had the following children:

    i.   Daryl Marbut [2068, 2069, 2070] was born in 1958 in Etowah, Alabama, USA [2068]. He lived in Hokes Bluff, Etowah, Alabama, USA in 1993 [2068]. He married Shirley Bobbitt in 1987.

227. *Leva Wylene Marbut*-16 (Jewel-15, Liller-14, William Clemens-13, John S.-12, Nathan-11, Edmond-10, William-9, William-8, Richard-7, John-6, William-5, Timothy-4, Richard-3, John-2, Robert-1) [1967, 1968, 1969] was born in 1939 [1967]. She lived in Hokes Bluff, Etowah, Alabama, USA in 1996 [1968]. **Herbert Ray McGinnis** [2071, 2072, 2073, 2074] was born on 14 Jul 1937 [2071, 2073]. He lived in Hokes Bluff, Etowah, Alabama, USA between 1995-1997 [2072]. He died on 06 Nov 2005 in Gadsden, Etowah, Alabama, USA [2073]. Herbert Ray McGinnis and Leva Wylene Marbut married and had the following children:

    i.   (258) Tim McGinnis [2075] was born in 1960 in Etowah, Alabama, USA [2075]. He lived in Glencoe, Etowah, Alabama, USA in 1994 [2075].

    ii.   (257) Christopher Alan McGinnis [2076] was born in 1973 in Etowah, Alabama, USA [2076]. He lived in Birmingham, Jefferson, Alabama, USA in 1993 [2076].

    iii.   (228) Todd Landon McGinnis [2077] was born in 1964 in Etowah, Alabama, USA [2077].

230. *Edwina McMahan*-16 (Slaught M-15, Liller-14, William Clemens-13, John S.-12, Nathan-11, Edmond-10, William-9, William-8, Richard-7, John-6, William-5, Timothy-4, Richard-3, John-2, Robert-1) [1976, 1977, 1978] was born in 1929 [1976, 1977]. She lived in Gadsden, Etowah, Alabama, USA in 1989 [1977]. **Jerry C. Kangelos** [2078, 2079, 2080, 2081, 2082, 2083, 2084] was born on 04

May 1927 [2078, 2079, 2080, 2081, 2082]. He died on 18 Dec 2006 in Union City, Obion, Tennessee, USA [2081]. Jerry C. Kangelos and Edwina McMahan married and had the following children:

    i.   (231) John Slaught Kangelos was born in 1959.

233. *Royce McMahan*-16 (Doyce-15, Liller-14, William Clemens-13, John S.-12, Nathan-11, Edmond-10, William-9, William-8, Richard-7, John-6, William-5, Timothy-4, Richard-3, John-2, Robert-1) [1984, 1985] was born in 1944 in Etowah, Alabama, USA [1984]. He lived in Hokes Bluff, Etowah, Alabama, USA in 1995 [1984]. **Mary Sue Nix** [2086] was born about 1945. Royce McMahan and Mary Sue Nix were married in Apr 1964 in Etowah, Alabama, USA [2086]. They were divorced before 1972. They had the following children:

    i.   Kelley McMahan was born about 1965 in Etowah, Alabama, USA. Kelley married Lynn Norris.

    ii.   Kevin Royce McMahan[2087] was born in 1969 in Southside, Etowah, Alabama, USA [2087]. He lived in Southside, Etowah, Alabama, USA in 1994 [2087].

Pat Bearden [2085] was born in 1950 in Etowah, Alabama, USA [2085]. She lived in Gadsden, Etowah, Alabama, USA in 1993 [2085]. Royce McMahan and Pat Bearden were married in 1972 in Etowah, Alabama, USA. Royce adopted Pat's children:

    i.   (235) Sharron McMahan was born about 1966 in Etowah, Alabama, USA.

    ii.   Alan McMahan was born in 1969.

    iii.   (234) Kelli McMahan was born about 1970.

237. *Murrell Brack Shields*-16 (Lola Matril-15, Liller-14, William Clemens-13, John S.-12, Nathan-11, Edmond-10, William-9, William-8, Richard-7, John-6, William-5, Timothy-4, Richard-3, John-2, Robert-1) [1990, 1991] was born on 07 Sep 1942 in Gadsden, Etowah, Alabama, USA [1990]. He died in March 1985 in Gadsden, Etowah, Alabama, USA [1990]. **Loretta Bullock** daughter of Ollivett Houston Bullock and Minnie Bertie Sewell was born in 1945 in Etowah, Alabama, USA. Ollivett Houston Bullock is the son of Sarah Irene Young (152). Murrell Brack Shields and Loretta Bullock married in 1963. They had the following children:

    i.   (238) Jeffrey Brack Shields was born in 1964 in Etowah, Alabama, USA.

    ii.   (261) Jana Matril Shields was born about 1977.

    iii.   (260) Jay Anthony Shields was born in 1967.

    iv.   (239) Jason Lamar Shields was born about 1969.

240. *Billy Mack Shields*-16 (Lola Matril-15, Liller-14, William Clemens-13, John S.-12, Nathan-11, Edmond-10, William-9, William-8, Richard-7, John-6, William-5, Timothy-4, Richard-3, John-2, Robert-1) [1989] was born on 22 May 1935. He died on 19 April 1985 in Gadsden, Etowah, Alabama, USA [1989].

Shirley Griffith was born about 1939. Billy Mack Shields and Shirley Griffith married and had the following children:

    i.   (242) Steve Shields was born in 1958.

    ii.   Kathy Shields was born in 1963. She married Andrew (Dickie) Jackson about 1995.

    iii.   (241) Scott Shields was born in 1967.

245. Elizabeth Ann McMahan-16 (Curtis Udell-15, Liller-14, William Clemens-13, John S.-12, Nathan-11, Edmond-10, William-9, William-8, Richard-7, John-6, William-5, Timothy-4, Richard-3, John-2, Robert-1). Ann McMahan and Tim Perry married and divorced. They had the following children:

    i.   Elizabeth Perry. Elizabeth married Richard Knecht in 2010.

246. C. Wayne McMahan-16 (Curtis Udell-15, Liller-14, William Clemens-13, John S.-12, Nathan-11, Edmond-10, William-9, William-8, Richard-7, John-6, William-5, Timothy-4, Richard-3, John-2, Robert-1) [1993, 1994] was born in 1946 [1994]. He lived in Montgomery, Alabama, USA between 1996-2002 [1993]. **Patricia Hudgins** was born on 19 Mar 1948. She died on 11 Sep 1987 in Montgomery, Alabama, USA. C. Wayne McMahan and Pat Hudgins married and had the following children:

    i.   Kurt Moore McMahan was born in 1983.

Sue Anne Chalker [2088, 2089] was born in 1954 [2088]. She lived in Montgomery, Alabama, USA in 1989 [2088]. C. Wayne McMahan and Sue Anne Chalker married and had the following children:

    i.   Brannen McMahan was born in 1993.

Generation 17

62. Crystal Nicole (Nikki) Jones-17 (Debra A-16, Edna-15, Barbara Mary Ann-14, James Martin-13, Carter Hill-12, William Emery-11, Edmond-10, William-9, William-8, Richard-7, John-6, William-5, Timothy-4, Richard-3, John-2, Robert-1) was born in 1973. **Christopher Marker** and Crystal Nicole Jones were married in 1994. They had the following children:

    i.   Anna Catherine Marker was born in 1998.

    ii.   Jacob Christopher Marker was born in 2007.

64. Gary Scott Reeves-17 (Gary Wendell-16, Edna-15, Barbara Mary Ann-14, James Martin-13, Carter Hill-12, William Emery-11, Edmond-10, William-9, William-8, Richard-7, John-6, William-5, Timothy-4, Richard-3, John-2, Robert-1) [2000] was born in 1965 [2000]. He lived in Gadsden, Etowah, Alabama, USA in 1990 [2000]. Gary Scott Reeves and **Stacy Ann Mason** were married in 1989. They had the following children:

    i.   Michael Drey Reeves was born in 1988.

    ii.   Gary Andrew Reeves was born in 1992.

65. *Wendy Carol Reeves*-17 (Gary Wendell-16, Edna-15, Barbara Mary Ann-14, James Martin-13, Carter Hill-12, William Emery-11, Edmond-10, William-9, William-8, Richard-7, John-6, William-5, Timothy-4, Richard-3, John-2, Robert-1) [2002] was born in 1973 [2002]. She lived in Gadsden, Etowah, Alabama, USA in 1993 [2002]. **Ronald Keith Gray** and Wendy Carol Reeves were married in 1996. They had the following children:

    i.   Brylie Carol Gray was born in 2005.

162. *Leon Ellis (Skipper) Watford*-17 (Malline Louise-16, Floyd Leon-15, Luther-14, William Clemens-13, John S.-12, Nathan-11, Edmond-10, William-9, William-8, Richard-7, John-6, William-5, Timothy-4, Richard-3, John-2, Robert-1) [2007, 2008] was born in 1953v[2008]. He lived in Rainbow City, Etowah, Alabama, USA between 1998-2002 [2007]. **Tina Renee Patterson** [2090] was born in 1955 [2090]. She lived in Rainbow City, Etowah, Alabama, USA in 1993 [2090]. Leon Ellis (Skipper) Watford and Tina Renee Patterson were married before 1979. They had the following children:

    i.   Amanda Renee Watford was born in 1979. She married Benjamin Green in 2004. They have one daughter, Emily Renee Green, born 2008.

    ii.   Alyson Leigh Watford was born in 1980. She married Erick Anderton in 2006.

163. *Arthur Joseph (Art) Watford II*-17 (Malline Louise-16, Floyd Leon-15, Luther-14, William Clemens-13, John S.-12, Nathan-11, Edmond-10, William-9, William-8, Richard-7, John-6, William-5, Timothy-4, Richard-3, John-2, Robert-1) [2009] was born in 1956 [2009]. He lived in Gadsden, Etowah, Alabama, USA in 1989 [2009]. **Debra Allyson Dial** was born in 1959. Debra Allyson Dial and Arthur Joe (Art) Watford II married had the following children:

    i.   Kacy Waits Watford was born in 1983.

    ii.   Katie Beth Watford was born in 1986.

Christa Luann Usry was born about 1957. Arthur Watford and Christa Luann Usry married. They had no children.

165. *Cathy Marilyn Reeves*-17 (Maurice Leon-16, Floyd Leon-15, Luther-14, William Clemens-13, John S.-12, Nathan-11, Edmond-10, William-9, William-8, Richard-7, John-6, William-5, Timothy-4, Richard-3, John-2, Robert-1) [2011, 2012, 2013, 2014, 2015] was born in 1950. **Dale Miller Roberts** son of William Wallace Roberts [2091] was born in 1945 in Calhoun, Alabama, USA. He lived in Anniston, Calhoun, Alabama, USA in 1996 [2091]. Dale Miller Roberts and Cathy Marilyn Reeves were married in 1970 in Anniston, Calhoun, Alabama, USA [2016]. They had the following children:

    i.   (166) Kyle Cameron Roberts was born in 1972.

    ii.   (167) Bianca Melissa Roberts [2092] was born in 1975 [2092].

171. *Jennifer Lynn Gentry*-17 (Marilyn Yvonne-16, Crate Funis-15, Luther-14, William Clemens-13, John S.-12, Nathan-11, Edmond-10, William-9, William-8, Richard-7, John-6, William-5, Timothy-4, Richard-3, John-2, Robert-1) [2023, 2024] was born in 1961 [2023, 2024]. She lived in Midland, Muscogee, Georgia,

USA in 1986 [2023]. **Jeff Whitehorn** and Jennifer Lynn Gentry were married before 1986. They had the following children:

    i.   Ashleigh Whitehorn was born in 1995.

    ii.   Emily Whitehorn was born in 2000.

***172. Alan Gentry*-17** (Marilyn Yvonne-16, Crate Funis-15, Luther-14, William Clemens-13, John S.-12, Nathan-11, Edmond-10, William-9, William-8, Richard-7, John-6, William-5, Timothy-4, Richard-3, John-2, Robert-1) [2022] was born in 1957 [2022]. He lived in Gadsden, Etowah, Alabama, USA in 1982 [2022]. **Ann Garrett** was born in 1952. Alan Gentry and Ann Garrett married and had the following children:

    i.   (173) Erin Gentry was born in 1981.

    ii.   Mark Gentry was born in 1993.

***175. Kerry Lee Johnson*-17** (Martha Evenette-16, Crate Funis-15, Luther-14, William Clemens-13, John S.-12, Nathan-11, Edmond-10, William-9, William-8, Richard-7, John-6, William-5, Timothy-4, Richard-3, John-2, Robert-1) was born in 1955. **Jennifer Sims** was born in 1957. Kerry Lee Johnson and Jennifer Sims married and divorced. They had the following children:

    i.   (176) Eric Lee Johnson was born in 1980.

    ii.   Evan Allen Johnson was born in1988.

***177. Karla Eve Johnson*-17** (Martha Evenette-16, Crate Funis-15, Luther-14, William Clemens-13, John S.-12, Nathan-11, Edmond-10, William-9, William-8, Richard-7, John-6, William-5, Timothy-4, Richard-3, John-2, Robert-1) [2025] was born in 1954 [2025]. She lived in Gadsden, Etowah, Alabama, USA in 1995 [2025]. Daniel James Little and Karla Eve Johnson married in 1970. They had the following children:

    i.   Daniel James Little Jr was born in 1971. He has one son, Zachery Daniel Little, born in 1999.

Garry Wayne Blevins and Karla Eve Johnson married in 1976. They had the following children:

    i.   (262) Sherri Evonne Blevins [2093, 2094] was born in 1978 [2093, 2094].

***178. James Spearman (Jim or Jet) Johnson Jr*-17** (Martha Evenette-16, Crate Funis-15, Luther-14, William Clemens-13, John S.-12, Nathan-11, Edmond-10, William-9, William-8, Richard-7, John-6, William-5, Timothy-4, Richard-3, John-2, Robert-1) was born in 1952. Jet Johnson and Marguerite Walker married and divorced. They had the following children:

    i.   Dustin Edward Johnson was born in1981.

Gail Archer daughter of Dan Archer was born on 24 Mar 1949. She died on 19 Jul 2006 in Gadsden, Etowah, Alabama, USA. James Spearman (Jim or Jet) Johnson Jr and Gail Archer were married after 2000. They had no children.

179. *Kyle Reeves Johnson*-17 (Martha Evenette-16, Crate Funis-15, Luther-14, William Clemens-13, John S.-12, Nathan-11, Edmond-10, William-9, William-8, Richard-7, John-6, William-5, Timothy-4, Richard-3, John-2, Robert-1) was born in 1962. Kyle Reeves Johnson and Dana Musick married and had the following children:

    i.   Rachel Diane Johnson was born in 1990. She married John Head in 2011.

    ii.   Nathan Kyle Johnson was born in 1995.

    iii.   Heather Johnson was born in 1995.

181. *Mark Craig Cardwell*-17 (Sherry Frances-16, Crate Funis-15, Luther-14, William Clemens-13, John S.-12, Nathan-11, Edmond-10, William-9, William-8, Richard-7, John-6, William-5, Timothy-4, Richard-3, John-2, Robert-1) was born in 1959. **Nancy Lou Whorton** was born in 1959. Mark Craig Cardwell and Nancy Lou Whorton married in 1984. They had the following children:

    i.   Alex Craig Cardwell was born in 1991.

    ii.   Caroline Grace Cardwell was born in 1995.

    iii.   Olivia Marie Cardwell was born in 2000.

184. *James David Barnes*-17 (Bobby Leland-16, Neva-15, Luther-14, William Clemens-13, John S.-12, Nathan-11, Edmond-10, William-9, William-8, Richard-7, John-6, William-5, Timothy-4, Richard-3, John-2, Robert-1) was born in 1959 in Duluth, Gwinnett, Georgia, USA. **Sheryl Lynn Singleton** was born in 1960. James David Barnes and Sheryl Lynn Singleton were married in 1982. They had the following children:

    i.   Danielle Lauren Barnes was born in 1988 in Atlanta, Georgia, USA.

    ii.   Cynthia Gabrielle Barnes was born in 1993 in Atlanta, Georgia, USA.

185. *Andrea Jo (Jo-Jo) Barnes*-17 (Bobby Leland-16, Neva-15, Luther-14, William Clemens-13, John S.-12, Nathan-11, Edmond-10, William-9, William-8, Richard-7, John-6, William-5, Timothy-4, Richard-3, John-2, Robert-1) was born in 1964 in Atlanta, Dekalb, Georgia, USA. **Terry Carroll** was born in 1962. Terry Carroll and Andrea Jo (Jo-Jo) Barnes were married in 1984. They were divorced about 2006. They had the following children:

    i.   Somer Nicole Carroll was born in 1988 in Marietta, Cobb, Georgia, USA.

    ii.   Audrey Brooke Carroll was born in 1994 in Marietta, Cobb, Georgia, USA.

Anthony (Tony) Allen was born in 1962. Anthony (Tony) Allen and Andrea Jo (Jo-Jo) Barnes were married about 2010 in South Carolina, USA. They had no children.

186. *Gena Lynn Barnes*-17 (Bobby Leland-16, Neva-15, Luther-14, William Clemens-13, John S.-12, Nathan-11, Edmond-10, William-9, William-8, Richard-7, John-6, William-5, Timothy-4, Richard-3, John-2, Robert-1) [2028] was born in 1963 in Atlanta, Dekalb, Georgia, USA [2028]. **Jeff DelGreco** and Gena Lynn Barnes were married in 1984. They were divorced in 1986. They had no children.

Darryl Eugene Chappell was born in 1962 in Cobb, Georgia, USA. Darryl Eugene Chappell and Gena Lynn Barnes were married in 1988. They were divorced in 1994. They had the following children:

    i.   Kristen Elizabeth Chappell was born in 1991 in Cobb, Georgia, USA.

    ii.   Eric Mitchell Chappell was born in 1993 in Cobb, Georgia, USA.

Christopher Snowden and Gena Lynn Barnes were married in 1997. They were divorced in 1999. They had no children.

Lance Odom and Gena Lynn Barnes were married in 2010. They have no children.

188. ***Kevin Leon Huff***-17 (Brenda-16, Neva-15, Luther-14, William Clemens-13, John S.-12, Nathan-11, Edmond-10, William-9, William-8, Richard-7, John-6, William-5, Timothy-4, Richard-3, John-2, Robert-1) was born in 1967. **Courtney Macklin Ezell** was born in 1972. Kevin Leon Huff and Courtney Macklin Ezell were married in 2000. They had the following children:

    i.   Tyler Landon Huff was born in 2003.

    ii.   Addison Melanie Huff was born in 2006.

189. ***Kristina Huff***-17 (Brenda-16, Neva-15, Luther-14, William Clemens-13, John S.-12, Nathan-11, Edmond-10, William-9, William-8, Richard-7, John-6, William-5, Timothy-4, Richard-3, John-2, Robert-1) was born in 1970. **Raymond Joe Gomez** was born in 1964. Raymond Joe Gomez and Kristina Huff were married in 1990. They had the following children:

    i.   Samantha Jo Gomez was born in 1995.

198. ***Kim Renèe Reeves***-17 (Troy-16, Troy-15, Euclid-14, William Clemens-13, John S.-12, Nathan-11, Edmond-10, William-9, William-8, Richard-7, John-6, William-5, Timothy-4, Richard-3, John-2, Robert-1) was born on 31 Jul 1963 in Paris, Paris, Île-de-France, France. **Jeff Graham** and Kim Renèe Reeves were married and divorced. They had the following children:

    i.   Gavin Graham was born in 1990.

199. ***Jacqueline Anne Couillard***-17 (Troy-16, Troy-15, Euclid-14, William Clemens-13, John S.-12, Nathan-11, Edmond-10, William-9, William-8, Richard-7, John-6, William-5, Timothy-4, Richard-3, John-2, Robert-1) [2037, 2038] was born in 1961 in Hennepin, Minnesota, USA [2037, 2038]. She lived in Dothan, Dale, Alabama, USA in 1996 [2037]. **John Joseph Ferry** was born in 1960. John Joseph Ferry and Jacqueline Anne Couillard were married in 1984. They had the following children:

    i.   Megan Kayleigh Ferry was born in 1989.

    ii.   Joseph Ryan Ferry was born on in 1991.

200. ***Jill Annette Couillard***-17 (Troy-16, Troy-15, Euclid-14, William Clemens-13, John S.-12, Nathan-11, Edmond-10, William-9, William-8, Richard-7, John-6, William-5, Timothy-4, Richard-3, John-2, Robert-1) [2040] was born in 1962 in Hennepin, Minnesota, USA [2040]. **Wayne D. Martin** [2095, 2096] was born in

1960 [2095, 2096]. Wayne D. Martin and Jill Annette Couillard married and had the following children:

    i.   Jessica Lynn Martin was born in 1990.

    ii.   Jeremy Martin was born in 1992.

201. Jennifer Marie Couillard-17 (Troy-16, Troy-15, Euclid-14, William Clemens-13, John S.-12, Nathan-11, Edmond-10, William-9, William-8, Richard-7, John-6, William-5, Timothy-4, Richard-3, John-2, Robert-1) [2041, 2042] was born in 1964 in Hennepin, Minnesota, USA [2041, 2042]. Robert L. Tucker and Jennifer Marie Couillard married and had the following children:

    i.   Allison Tucker was born in 1996.

    ii.   Harrison Tucker was born in 1999.

203. Traci Lynn Reeves-17 (Haralson Kerr-16, Troy-15, Euclid-14, William Clemens-13, John S.-12, Nathan-11, Edmond-10, William-9, William-8, Richard-7, John-6, William-5, Timothy-4, Richard-3, John-2, Robert-1) [2044] was born in 1973 [2044]. She lived in Gadsden, Etowah, Alabama, USA in 1995 [2044]. **Jason Jones** and Traci Lynn Reeves married in 1998 and divorced in 2007. They had the following children:

    i.   Parker Jones was born in 2001.

    ii.   Carter Jones was born in 2003.

204. Haralson Kerr (Chip) Reeves Jr-17 (Haralson Kerr-16, Troy-15, Euclid-14, William Clemens-13, John S.-12, Nathan-11, Edmond-10, William-9, William-8, Richard-7, John-6, William-5, Timothy-4, Richard-3, John-2, Robert-1) was born in 1967. **Kelley Leigh Starling** [2097] was born in 1967 [2097]. Haralson Kerr Reeves Jr and Kelley Leigh Starling were married in 1987. They had the following children:

    i.   Haralson Kerr (Trey) Reeves III as born in 1990.

    ii.   Abigail Reeves was born in 1999.

    iii.   Hayden Reeves was born in 2001.

206. Jason Mack Reeves-17 (Boyd McMurtrey-16, Troy-15, Euclid-14, William Clemens-13, John S.-12, Nathan-11, Edmond-10, William-9, William-8, Richard-7, John-6, William-5, Timothy-4, Richard-3, John-2, Robert-1) [2048, 2049] was born in 1974 [2049]. He lived in Birmingham, Jefferson, Alabama, USA in 2002 [2048]. **Lesli Day** [2098] was born in 1973 [2098]. She lived in Ashville, Pike, Alabama, USA in 1993 [2098]. Jason Mack Reeves and Lesli Day were married in 1998. They had the following children:

    i.   Cassidy Reeves was born in 2005.

    ii.   Tyler Reeves was born in 2007.

207. Jana Elizabeth Reeves-17 (Boyd McMurtrey-16, Troy-15, Euclid-14, William Clemens-13, John S.-12, Nathan-11, Edmond-10, William-9, William-8, Richard-7, John-6, William-5, Timothy-4, Richard-3, John-2, Robert-1) [2045,

2046, 2047] was born in 1963[2045, 2046, 2047]. She lived in Birmingham, Jefferson, Alabama, USA in 1984 [2045]. David Cagle and Jana Elizabeth Reeves married and divorced. They had the following children:

    i.   Tristen Cagle was born in 1995.

209. ***Reeves Alan Daves***-17 (Glenda Janice-16, Troy-15, Euclid-14, William Clemens-13, John S.-12, Nathan-11, Edmond-10, William-9, William-8, Richard-7, John-6, William-5, Timothy-4, Richard-3, John-2, Robert-1) [2051, 2052, 2053, 2054, 2055] was born in 1965 in Gadsden, Etowah, Alabama, USA [2051, 2052, 2053, 2054]. **Michelle Lee Williams** daughter of Melvin Lomax Williams and Priscilla Irene Brock [2099, 2100, 2101, 2102, 2103] was born in 1965 in Fulton, Georgia, USA [2099, 2100, 2101]. Reeves Alan Daves and Michelle Lee Williams were married in 1988 in Gadsden, Etowah, Alabama, USA (Goodyear Heights Baptist Church). They had the following children:

    i.   Jessica Michelle Daves was born in 1989 in Orlando, Florida, USA.

    ii.   Christopher Alan Daves was born in 1992 in Hampton, Virginia, USA.

    iii.   Katherine Elizabeth Daves was born in 1995 in Opelika, Alabama, USA.

210. ***Susan Yvonne Daves***-17 (Glenda Janice-16, Troy-15, Euclid-14, William Clemens-13, John S.-12, Nathan-11, Edmond-10, William-9, William-8, Richard-7, John-6, William-5, Timothy-4, Richard-3, John-2, Robert-1) was born in 1957. **Glenn Ashley Bryan** [2104] was born in 1955 [2104]. Glenn Ashley Bryan and Susan Yvonne Daves were married in 1976. They had the following children:

    i.   Nathan Ashley Bryan was born in 1984 in Birmingham, Jefferson, Alabama, USA.

    ii.   Kyle Bryan was born in 1991.

214. ***Abby Lane Reeves***-17 (William Patrick-16, Cresful-15, Euclid-14, William Clemens-13, John S.-12, Nathan-11, Edmond-10, William-9, William-8, Richard-7, John-6, William-5, Timothy-4, Richard-3, John-2, Robert-1) was born in 1982. **Justin Doss** (b. about 1980) and Abby Lane Reeves married in 2006. They had the following children:

    i.   Emma Claire Doss was born in 2007.

    ii.   Ellie Cate Doss was born in 2010.

215. ***Katie Pauline Reeves***-17 (William Patrick-16, Cresful-15, Euclid-14, William Clemens-13, John S.-12, Nathan-11, Edmond-10, William-9, William-8, Richard-7, John-6, William-5, Timothy-4, Richard-3, John-2, Robert-1) was born in 1980. **Dustin Gillihan** and Katie Pauline Reeves married in 2007. They had the following children:

    i.   William David Gillihan (Will) was born in 2008.

223. ***Terry Marbut***-17 (Donnie-16, Jewel-15, Liller-14, William Clemens-13, John S.-12, Nathan-11, Edmond-10, William-9, William-8, Richard-7, John-6, William-5, Timothy-4, Richard-3, John-2, Robert-1) [2064] was born in 1961 [2064]. He lived in Hokes Bluff, Etowah, Alabama, USA in 1977 [2064]. **Andrea**

Jolley was born in 1960. Terry Marbut and Andrea Jolley married and had the following children:

    i.   Stephanie Marbut was born in 1985.

    ii.   (225) Shayanna Marbut was born about 1986.

    iii. (224) Sierra Marbut was born in 1988.

228. *Todd Landon McGinnis*-17 (Leva Wylene-16, Jewel-15, Liller-14, William Clemens-13, John S.-12, Nathan-11, Edmond-10, William-9, William-8, Richard-7, John-6, William-5, Timothy-4, Richard-3, John-2, Robert-1) [2077] was born in 1964 in Etowah, Alabama, USA [2077]. He lived in Hokes Bluff, Etowah, Alabama, USA in 1994 [2077]. **Cindy Johnson** was born in 1966. Todd Landon McGinnis and Cindy Johnson married and had the following children:

    i.   Brittani McGinnis was born in 1989. She married Jarrod Handley in 2007.

    ii.   Brooke Danielle McGinnis was born in 1997.

    iii. Baylee McGinnis was born in 1999.

231. *John Slaught Kangelos*-17 (Edwina-16, Slaught M-15, Liller-14, William Clemens-13, John S.-12, Nathan-11, Edmond-10, William-9, William-8, Richard-7, John-6, William-5, Timothy-4, Richard-3, John-2, Robert-1) was born in 1959. John Slaught Kangelos and Pam (unknown maiden name) married and had the following children:

    i.   Aury Kangelos was born about 1986.

    ii.   Erin Kangelos was born about 1989. She married Daniel Keith Maybe in 2010.

234. *Kelli McMahan*-17 (Royce-16, Doyce-15, Liller-14, William Clemens-13, John S.-12, Nathan-11, Edmond-10, William-9, William-8, Richard-7, John-6, William-5, Timothy-4, Richard-3, John-2, Robert-1) was born about 1970. Unknown Brown and Kelli McMahan married and had the following children:

    i.   Jordan Brown was born in 1994.

Joe Trull and Kelli McMahan married and had the following children:

    i.   Jody Trull was born in 1990.

235. *Sharron McMahan*-17 (Royce-16, Doyce-15, Liller-14, William Clemens-13, John S.-12, Nathan-11, Edmond-10, William-9, William-8, Richard-7, John-6, William-5, Timothy-4, Richard-3, John-2, Robert-1) was born about 1966 in Etowah, Alabama, USA. Sharron McMahan and **Mark Hargrove** married and had the following children:

    i.   Tyler Hargrove was born in 1990.

Mark Hargrove died in 1997. **Mike Bullock** and Sharron McMahan married and had the following children:

    i.   Tayler Bullock was born in 1999.

Mike and Sharron divorced and she married **Johnny Nash**. They have the following children:

    i.   Braxton Nash was born in 2008.

238. ***Jeffrey Brack Shields***-17 (Murrell Brack-16, Lola Matril-15, Liller-14, William Clemens-13, John S.-12, Nathan-11, Edmond-10, William-9, William-8, Richard-7, John-6, William-5, Timothy-4, Richard-3, John-2, Robert-1) was born in 1964 in Etowah, Alabama, USA. **Paula Croft** was born in 1967. Jeffrey Brack Shields and Paula Croft married about 1985. They had the following children:

    i.   Cody Brack Shields was born in 1991.

    ii.   Courtney Shields was born about 1994.

239. ***Jason Lamar Shields***-17 (Murrell Brack-16, Lola Matril-15, Liller-14, William Clemens-13, John S.-12, Nathan-11, Edmond-10, William-9, William-8, Richard-7, John-6, William-5, Timothy-4, Richard-3, John-2, Robert-1) was born about 1969. **Cassie Duncan** was born in 1970. Jason Lamar Shields and Cassie Duncan married in 1993. They had the following children:

    i.   Carlie Madison Shields was born about 1995.

    ii.   Brack Murrell Shields was born about 1997.

    iii. Kristen Shields was born about 2001.

241. ***Scott Shields***-17 (Billy Mack-16, Lola Matril-15, Liller-14, William Clemens-13, John S.-12, Nathan-11, Edmond-10, William-9, William-8, Richard-7, John-6, William-5, Timothy-4, Richard-3, John-2, Robert-1) was born in 1967. Scott Shields and **Melissa Small** (b. 1968) married in 1990. They had the following children:

    i.   Kaitlyn Alexandra Shields was born in 1993.

    ii.   Ashlyn Nicole Shields was born in 1994.

242. ***Steve Shields***-17 (Billy Mack-16, Lola Matril-15, Liller-14, William Clemens-13, John S.-12, Nathan-11, Edmond-10, William-9, William-8, Richard-7, John-6, William-5, Timothy-4, Richard-3, John-2, Robert-1) was born in 1958. **Patti Brittain** was born in 1958. Steve Shields and Patti Brittain married in 1977. They had the following children:

    i.   (243) Tyler Shields.

    ii.   Brett Shields was born about 1988.

257. ***Christopher Alan McGinnis***-17 (Leva Wylene-16, Jewel-15, Liller-14, William Clemens-13, John S.-12, Nathan-11, Edmond-10, William-9, William-8, Richard-7, John-6, William-5, Timothy-4, Richard-3, John-2, Robert-1) [2096] was born in 1973. Christopher Alan McGinnis and **Kelley Kimmons** married. Kelley brought a son to the marriage. They have the following children:

    i.   Matthew Qualls was born in 1997.

    ii.   Caleb McGinnis was born in 2003.

258.   Tim McGinnis-17 (Leva Wylene-16, Jewel-15, Liller-14, William Clemens-13, John S.-12, Nathan-11, Edmond-10, William-9, William-8, Richard-7, John-6, William-5, Timothy-4, Richard-3, John-2, Robert-1) was born in 1960. **Dianne Dowdy** was born in 1960. Tim McGinnis and Dianne Dowdy married in 1981. They had the following children:

  i.   (259) Timothy Adam McGinnis was born in 1983.

  ii.   Laura McGinnis was born in 1986.

  iii.   Mallory McGinnis was born in 1992.

260.   Jay Anthony Shields-17 (Murrell Brack-16, Lola Matril-15, Liller-14, William Clemens-13, John S.-12, Nathan-11, Edmond-10, William-9, William-8, Richard-7, John-6, William-5, Timothy-4, Richard-3, John-2, Robert-1) was born in 1967. **Christie Colegrove** was born about 1968. Christie Colegrove and Jay Anthony Shields married and had the following children:

  i.   Taylor Shields was born in 1992. He has a daughter Ella Kate Shields (b. about 2008).
  ii.   Tanner Shields was born in 1994.

261.   Jana Matril Shields-17 (Murrell Brack-16, Lola Matril-15, Liller-14, William Clemens-13, John S.-12, Nathan-11, Edmond-10, William-9, William-8, Richard-7, John-6, William-5, Timothy-4, Richard-3, John-2, Robert-1) was born about 1977. **Ryan Lloyd Smith** and Jana Matril Shields married in 2001. They had the following children:

  i.   Maddie Smith
  ii.   Colby Smith

Generation 18

166.   Kyle Cameron Roberts-18 (Cathy Marilyn-17, Maurice Leon-16, Floyd Leon-15, Luther-14, William Clemens-13, John S.-12, Nathan-11, Edmond-10, William-9, William-8, Richard-7, John-6, William-5, Timothy-4, Richard-3, John-2, Robert-1) was born in 1972. **Meghan Perkins** was born in 1977. Kyle Cameron Roberts and Meghan Perkins were married in 2005. They had the following children:

  i.   Taylor Caroline Roberts was born in 2009.

167.   Bianca Melissa Roberts-18 (Cathy Marilyn-17, Maurice Leon-16, Floyd Leon-15, Luther-14, William Clemens-13, John S.-12, Nathan-11, Edmond-10, William-9, William-8, Richard-7, John-6, William-5, Timothy-4, Richard-3, John-2, Robert-1) [2092] was born in 1975 [2092]. She lived in Atlanta, Dekalb, Georgia, USA [2092]. **Michael Tairon Cofer** was born in 1971. Michael Tairon Cofer and Bianca Melissa Roberts were married in 2002. They had the following children:

  i.   Gabriel Wynn Cofer was born in 2007.

  ii.   Maura Teagon Cofer was born in 2009.

  iii.   Seley Cay Cofer was born in 2011.

173. *Erin Gentry*-18 (Alan-17, Marilyn Yvonne-16, Crate Funis-15, Luther-14, William Clemens-13, John S.-12, Nathan-11, Edmond-10, William-9, William-8, Richard-7, John-6, William-5, Timothy-4, Richard-3, John-2, Robert-1) was born in 1981. Erin has the following children:

    i.   Austin Gentry was born in 2008.

176. *Eric Lee Johnson*-18 (Kerry Lee-17, Martha Evenette-16, Crate Funis-15, Luther-14, William Clemens-13, John S.-12, Nathan-11, Edmond-10, William-9, William-8, Richard-7, John-6, William-5, Timothy-4, Richard-3, John-2, Robert-1) was born in 1980. **Shea Mann** was born in 1982. Eric Lee Johnson and Shea Mann married and had the following children:

    i.   Naomie Elizabeth Johnson was born in 2010.

224. *Sierra Marbut*-18 (Terry-17, Donnie-16, Jewel-15, Liller-14, William Clemens-13, John S.-12, Nathan-11, Edmond-10, William-9, William-8, Richard-7, John-6, William-5, Timothy-4, Richard-3, John-2, Robert-1) was born in 1988. **B. J. Sewell** and Sierra Marbut were married in 2009. They had the following children:

    i.   Lillie Catherine Sewell was born in 2010.

225. *Shayanna Marbut*-18 (Terry-17, Donnie-16, Jewel-15, Liller-14, William Clemens-13, John S.-12, Nathan-11, Edmond-10, William-9, William-8, Richard-7, John-6, William-5, Timothy-4, Richard-3, John-2, Robert-1) was born about 1986. Shayanna Marbut has the following children:

    i.   Riley

    ii.   Sadie

243. *Tyler Shields*-18 (Steve-17, Billy Mack-16, Lola Matril-15, Liller-14, William Clemens-13, John S.-12, Nathan-11, Edmond-10, William-9, William-8, Richard-7, John-6, William-5, Timothy-4, Richard-3, John-2, Robert-1). Tyler Shields and **Brook Doss** married and had the following children:

    i.   Colten Shields was born in 2007.

    ii.   Ethan Tyler Shields was born in 2010.

259. *Timothy Adam McGinnis*-18 (Tim-17, Leva Wylene-16, Jewel-15, Liller-14, William Clemens-13, John S.-12, Nathan-11, Edmond-10, William-9, William-8, Richard-7, John-6, William-5, Timothy-4, Richard-3, John-2, Robert-1) was born in 1983. Jasmine Colvin was born in 1984. Timothy Adam McGinnis and **Jasmine Colvin** were married in 2007. They had the following children:

    i.   Coleman McGinnis was born in 2005.

    ii.   Ethan Bryant Patterson McGinnis was born in 2006.

    iii. Mila McGinnis was born in 2009.

262. *Sherri Evonne Blevins*-18 (Karla Eve-17, Martha Evenette-16, Crate Funis-15, Luther-14, William Clemens-13, John S.-12, Nathan-11, Edmond-10, William-9, William-8, Richard-7, John-6, William-5, Timothy-4, Richard-3, John-2,

Robert-1) was born in 1978[2094]. She lived in Rossville, Walker, Georgia, USA [2094]. She married **Craig Womack** in 2002. They have the following children:

    i.   Riley Scott Womack (b. 2007)

    ii.   Wyatt Womack (b. 2009)

SOURCES FOR REGISTER REPORT OF ROBERT RYVES

1   Ancestry.com, Landed Gentry of Great Britain and Ireland (Online publication - Provo, UT, USA: The Generations Network, Inc., 2002. Original data - Sir Bernard Burke. A Genealogical and Heraldic Dictionary of the Landed Gentry of Great Britain and Ireland. London, England: Hurst and Blackett, 1855. Original data: S), Ancestry.com, http://www.Ancestry.com, Residence date: 1855Residence place:.

2   Ancestry.com, Peerage of the United Kingdom and Ireland, Volumes I-IV (Online publication - Provo, UT, USA: Ancestry.com Operations Inc, 2002. Original data - Cokayne, George Edward. The Complete Peerage of England Scotland Ireland Great Britain and the United Kingdom. London, England: The St. Catherine Press Ltd., 1910-1916. O), Ancestry.com, http://www.Ancestry.com.

3   Ancestry.com, Reliques of the Rives (Ryves) : being historical and genealogical notes of the ancient family Ryves of County Dorset and of the (Online publication - Provo, UT: The Generations Network, Inc., 2005. Original data - Childs, J. Rives. Reliques of the Rives (Ryves) : being historical and genealogical notes of the ancient family Ryves of County Dorset and of the Rives of Virginia, an essay), Ancestry.com, http://www.Ancestry.com, Refers to marriage of John Ryves to Amye Harvey.

4   Ancestry.com, General Armory of England, Scotland, Ireland and Wales (Online publication - Provo, UT, USA: The Generations Network, Inc., 2002. Original data - Sir Bernard Burke. The General Armory of England, Scotland, Wales; Comprising A Registry of Armorial Bearings From the Earliest To the Present Time. London, England: H), Ancestry.com, http://www.Ancestry.com.

5   W. Patrick Reaves, The Ryves-Rives-Reaves Families of Europe and America (A. H. Cather Publishing Co.), Personal Library of Alan Daves, Virginia Beach, Virginia, Birth date information.

6   Yates Publishing, U.S. and International Marriage Records, 1560-1900 (Online publication - Provo, UT, USA: Ancestry.com Operations Inc, 2004. Original data - This unique collection of records was extracted from a variety of sources including family group sheets and electronic databases. Originally, the information was derived), Ancestry.com, http://www.Ancestry.com, Source number: 68.000; Source type: Electronic Database; Number of Pages: 1; Submitter Code: SBA. Birth date: 1588 Birth place:.

7   Yates Publishing, U.S. and International Marriage Records, 1560-1900 (Online publication - Provo, UT, USA: Ancestry.com Operations Inc, 2004. Original data - This unique collection of records was extracted from a variety of sources including family group sheets and electronic databases. Originally, the information was derived), Ancestry.com, http://www.Ancestry.com, List birth year and spouse name.

8   W. Patrick Reaves

9   W. Patrick Reaves

10   W. Patrick Reaves

11   Ancestry.com, Reliques of the Rives (Ryves) : being historical and genealogical notes of the ancient family Ryves of County Dorset and of the (Online publication - Provo, UT: The Generations Network, Inc., 2005. Original data - Childs, J. Rives. Reliques of the Rives (Ryves) : being historical and genealogical notes of the ancient family Ryves of County Dorset and of the Rives of Virginia, an essay), Ancestry.com, http://www.Ancestry.com, Residence date: Residence place: USA.

12   Gale Research, Passenger and Immigration Lists Index, 1500s-1900s (Online publication - Provo, UT, USA: Ancestry.com Operations Inc, 2009. Original data - Filby, P. William, ed.. Passenger and Immigration Lists Index, 1500s-1900s. Farmington Hills, MI, USA: Gale Research, 2009. Original data: Filby, P. William, ed.. Passenger), Ancestry.com, http://www.Ancestry.com, Place: Virginia; Year: 1655; Page Number: 324. Arrival date: 1655 Arrival place: Virginia.

13   Gale Research, Passenger and Immigration Lists Index, 1500s-1900s (Online publication - Provo, UT, USA: Ancestry.com Operations Inc, 2009. Original data - Filby, P. William, ed.. Passenger and Immigration Lists Index, 1500s-1900s. Farmington Hills, MI, USA: Gale Research, 2009. Original data: Filby, P. William, ed.. Passenger), Ancestry.com, http://www.Ancestry.com, Place: Virginia; Year: 1652; Page Number: 288. Arrival date: 1652 Arrival place: Virginia.

14   Gale Research, Passenger and Immigration Lists Index, 1500s-1900s (Online publication - Provo, UT, USA: Ancestry.com Operations Inc, 2009. Original data - Filby, P. William, ed.. Passenger and Immigration Lists Index, 1500s-1900s. Farmington Hills, MI, USA: Gale Research, 2009. Original data: Filby, P. William, ed.. Passenger), Ancestry.com, http://www.Ancestry.com, Place: Virginia; Year: 1652; Page Number: 274. Arrival date: 1652 Arrival place: Virginia.

15   Edmund West, comp., Family Data Collection - Deaths (Online publication - Provo, UT, USA: The Generations Network, Inc., 2001.), Ancestry.com, http://www.Ancestry.com, Death date: 1695 Death place: VA, USA.

16   Edmund West, comp., Family Data Collection - Births (Online publication - Provo, UT, USA: The Generations Network, Inc., 2001.), Ancestry.com, http://www.Ancestry.com, Birth date: 1636 Birth place: Woodstock.

17   W. Patrick Reaves

18   W. Patrick Reaves

19   W. Patrick Reaves

20   W. Patrick Reaves

21   Yates Publishing, U.S. and International Marriage Records, 1560-1900 (Online publication - Provo, UT, USA: Ancestry.com Operations Inc, 2004. Original data - This unique collection of records was extracted from a variety of sources including family group sheets and electronic databases. Originally, the information was derived), Ancestry.com, http://www.Ancestry.com, Source number: 50.000; Source type: Electronic Database; Number of Pages: 1; Submitter Code: BR1. Birth date: 1665 Birth place: VA Marriage date: Marriage place: VA.

22   Edmund West, comp., Family Data Collection - Individual Records (Online publication - Provo, UT, USA: Ancestry.com Operations Inc, 2000.), Ancestry.com, http://www.Ancestry.com, Birth year: 1665; Birth city: Surry Co; Birth state: VA. Birth date: 1665 Birth place: Surry Co, VA Death date: 1701 Death place: Marriage date: 1696 Marriage place: VA.

23   Edmund West, comp., Family Data Collection - Individual Records (Online publication - Provo, UT, USA: Ancestry.com Operations Inc, 2000.), Ancestry.com, http://www.Ancestry.com, Birth year: 1665; Birth city: Surry; Birth state: VA. Birth date: 1665 Birth place: Surry, VA.

24   Edmund West, comp., Family Data Collection - Individual Records (Online publication - Provo, UT, USA: Ancestry.com Operations Inc, 2000.), Ancestry.com, http://www.Ancestry.com, Birth year: 1665; Birth city: ; Birth state: VA. Birth date: 1665 Birth place: Surry, VA.

25   Edmund West, comp., Family Data Collection - Births (Online publication - Provo, UT, USA: The Generations Network, Inc., 2001.), Ancestry.com, http://www.Ancestry.com, Birth date: 1665 Birth place: Surry, VA, USA.

26   Ancestry.com, Reliques of the Rives (Ryves) : being historical and genealogical notes of the ancient family Ryves of County Dorset and of the (Online publication - Provo, UT: The Generations Network, Inc., 2005. Original data - Childs, J. Rives. Reliques of the Rives (Ryves) : being historical and genealogical notes of the ancient family Ryves of County Dorset and of the Rives of Virginia, an essay), Ancestry.com, http://www.Ancestry.com, Residence date: Residence place: USA.

27   W. Patrick Reaves

28   Jackson, Ron V., Accelerated Indexing Systems, comp., North Carolina Census, 1790-1890 (Online publication - Provo, UT, USA: Ancestry.com Operations Inc, 1999. Original data - Compiled and digitized by Mr. Jackson and AIS from microfilmed schedules of the U.S. Federal Decennial Census, territorial/state censuses, and/or census substitutes. Original), Ancestry.com, http://www.Ancestry.com, Residence date: 1761 Residence place: Pitt County, NC.

29   Historical Southern Families. Volume XX, Ancestry.com, http://www.Ancestry.com.

30   Ancestry.com, North Carolina Taxpayers, 1679-1790. Vol. 2 (Online publication - Provo, UT, USA: The Generations Network, Inc., 2006. Original data - Ratcliff, Clarence E. North Carolina Taxpayers, 1679-1790. Baltimore, MD, USA: Genealogical Publishing Co., 2003. Original data: Ratcliff, Clarence E. North Carolina Ta), Ancestry.com, http://www.Ancestry.com.

31   W. Patrick Reaves

32   W. Patrick Reaves

33   Ancestry.com, Reliques of the Rives (Ryves) : being historical and genealogical notes of the ancient family Ryves of County Dorset and of the (Online publication - Provo, UT: The Generations Network, Inc., 2005. Original data - Childs, J. Rives. Reliques of the Rives (Ryves) : being historical and genealogical notes of the ancient family Ryves of County Dorset and of the Rives of Virginia, an essay), Ancestry.com, http://www.Ancestry.com, Residence date: Residence place: USA.

34   Ancestry.com, Reliques of the Rives (Ryves) : being historical and genealogical notes of the ancient family Ryves of County Dorset and of the (Online publication - Provo, UT: The Generations Network, Inc., 2005. Original data - Childs, J. Rives. Reliques of the Rives (Ryves) : being historical and genealogical notes of the ancient family Ryves of County Dorset and of the Rives of Virginia, an essay), Ancestry.com, http://www.Ancestry.com, Residence date: Residence place: USA.

35   Ancestry.com, Bute County, North Carolina: Minutes of the Court of Pleas and Quarter Sessions, 1767-1779 (Online publication - Provo, UT, USA: Ancestry.com Operations Inc, 2006. Original data - Holcomb, Brent H. Bute County, North Carolina: Minutes of the Court of Pleas and Quarter Sessions, 1767-1779. Baltimore, MD, USA: Genealogical Publishing Co., 1988. Origi), Ancestry.com, http://www.Ancestry.com.

36   W. Patrick Reaves

37   W. Patrick Reaves

38   Ancestry.com, Roster of soldiers from North Carolina in the American Revolution : with an appendix containing a collection of miscellaneous R. (Online publication - Provo, UT: Ancestry.com Operations Inc, 2005. Original data -

Roster of soldiers from North Carolina in the American Revolution : with an appendix containing a collection of miscellaneous records.. unknown: The D.A.R., 1932. Original data), Ancestry.com, http://www.Ancestry.com, Residence date: 1783-1932Residence place: North Carolina, USA.

39   Ancestry.com, 1790 United States Federal Census (Online publication - Provo, UT, USA: Ancestry.com Operations, Inc., 2010. Images reproduced by FamilySearch. Original data - First Census of the United States, 1790 (NARA microfilm publication M637, 12 rolls). Records of the Bureau of the Census, Record Group), Ancestry.com, http://www.Ancestry.com, Year: 1790; Census Place: , Wake, North Carolina; Roll: ; Image:. Residence date: 1790 Residence place: Wake, North Carolina, United States.

40   Godfrey Memorial Library, comp., American Genealogical-Biographical Index (AGBI) (Online publication - Provo, UT, USA: Ancestry.com Operations Inc, 1999. Original data - Godfrey Memorial Library. American Genealogical-Biographical Index. Middletown, CT, USA: Godfrey Memorial Library. Original data: Godfrey Memorial Library. American Genea), Ancestry.com, http://www.Ancestry.com, Birth date: 1750 Birth place: North Carolina.

41   Ancestry.com, 1790 United States Federal Census (Online publication - Provo, UT, USA: Ancestry.com Operations, Inc., 2010. Images reproduced by FamilySearch. Original data - First Census of the United States, 1790 (NARA microfilm publication M637, 12 rolls). Records of the Bureau of the Census, Record Group), Ancestry.com, http://www.Ancestry.com, Year: 1790; Census Place: , Franklin, North Carolina; Roll: ; Image:. Residence date: 1790 Residence place: Franklin, North Carolina, United States.

42   Ancestry.com, 1800 United States Federal Census (Online publication - Provo, UT, USA: Ancestry.com Operations Inc, 2010. Images reproduced by FamilySearch. Original data - Second Census of the United States, 1800. (NARA microfilm publication M32, 52 rolls). Records of the Bureau of the Census, Record Group), Ancestry.com, http://www.Ancestry.com, Year: 1800; Census Place: Louisburg, Franklin, North Carolina; Roll: ; Page: ; Image:. Residence date: 1800 Residence place: Louisburg, Franklin, North Carolina.

43   Ancestry.com, 1820 United States Federal Census (Online publication - Provo, UT, USA: Ancestry.com Operations, Inc., 2010. Images reproduced by FamilySearch. Original data - Fourth Census of the United States, 1820. (NARA microfilm publication M33, 142 rolls). Records of the Bureau of the Census, Record G), Ancestry.com, http://www.Ancestry.com, Year: 1820; Census Place: , Iredell, North Carolina; Roll: M33_80; Page: ; Image:. Residence date: 1820 Residence place: Iredell, North Carolina, United States.

44   Ancestry.com, Reliques of the Rives (Ryves) : being historical and genealogical notes of the ancient family Ryves of County Dorset and of the (Online publication - Provo, UT: The Generations Network, Inc., 2005. Original data - Childs, J. Rives. Reliques of the Rives (Ryves) : being historical and genealogical notes of the ancient family Ryves of County Dorset and of the Rives of Virginia, an essay), Ancestry.com, http://www.Ancestry.com, Residence date: Residence place: USA.

45   Revolutionary War Records: Virginia, Ancestry.com, http://www.Ancestry.com.

46   Ancestry.com, U.S. Revolutionary War Rolls, 1775-1783 (Online publication - Provo, UT, USA: Ancestry.com Operations Inc, 2007. Original data - Revolutionary War Rolls, 1775-1783; (National Archives Microfilm Publication M246, 138 rolls); War Department Collection of Revolutionary War Records, Record Group 93; N), Ancestry.com, http://www.Ancestry.com, Residence date: Residence place: United States.

47   Ancestry.com, Alabama Marriage Collection, 1800-1969 (Online publication - Provo, UT, USA: Ancestry.com Operations Inc, 2006. Original data - Alabama Center for Health Statistics. Alabama Marriage Index, 1936-1969. Alabama Center for Health Statistics, Montgomery, Alabama. Dodd, Jordan R., et. al. Early America), Ancestry.com, http://www.Ancestry.com, Marriage date: 1 Jan 1817 Marriage place: Clarke, Alabama.

48   Ancestry.com, Alabama Marriage Collection, 1800-1969 (Online publication - Provo, UT, USA: Ancestry.com Operations Inc, 2006. Original data - Alabama Center for Health Statistics. Alabama Marriage Index, 1936-1969. Alabama Center for Health Statistics, Montgomery, Alabama. Dodd, Jordan R., et. al. Early America), Ancestry.com, http://www.Ancestry.com, Marriage date: 1 Jan 1817 Marriage place: Clarke, Alabama.

49   Ancestry.com, 1840 United States Federal Census (Online publication - Provo, UT, USA: Ancestry.com Operations, Inc., 2010. Images reproduced by FamilySearch. Original data - Sixth Census of the United States, 1840. (NARA microfilm publication M704, 580 rolls). Records of the Bureau of the Census, Record G), Ancestry.com, http://www.Ancestry.com, Year: 1840; Census Place: , Benton, Alabama; Roll: ; Page:. Residence date: 1840 Residence place: Benton, Alabama, United States.

50   Ancestry.com, Marriages of Bute and Warren Counties, North Carolina 1764-1868 (Online publication - Provo, UT, USA: Ancestry.com Operations Inc, 2006. Original data - Holcomb, Brent H. Marriages of Bute and Warren Counties, North Carolina 1764-1868. Baltimore, MD, USA: Genealogical Publishing Co., 2004. Original data: Holcomb, Brent H.), Ancestry.com, http://www.Ancestry.com.

51   Ancestry.com, 1850 United States Federal Census (Online publication - Provo, UT, USA: Ancestry.com Operations, Inc., 2009. Images reproduced by FamilySearch. Original data - Seventh Census of the United States, 1850; (National Archives Microfilm Publication M432, 1009 rolls); Records of the Bureau of the), Ancestry.com, http://www.Ancestry.com, Year: 1850; Census Place: Subdivision 29, Benton, Alabama; Roll: M432_1; Page: 334A; Image:. Birth date: about 1776 Birth place: North Carolina Residence date: 1850 Residence place: Subdivision 29, Benton, Alabama.

52   Ancestry.com, 1830 United States Federal Census (Online publication - Provo, UT, USA: Ancestry.com Operations, Inc., 2010. Images reproduced by FamilySearch. Original data - Fifth Census of the United States, 1830. (NARA microfilm publication M19, 201 rolls). Records of the Bureau of the Census, Record Gr), Ancestry.com, http://www.Ancestry.com, Year: 1830; Census Place: , Campbell, Georgia; Roll: ; Page:. Residence date: 1830 Residence place: Campbell, Georgia, United States.

53   Ancestry.com, 1820 United States Federal Census (Online publication - Provo, UT, USA: Ancestry.com Operations, Inc., 2010. Images reproduced by FamilySearch. Original data - Fourth Census of the United States, 1820. (NARA microfilm publication M33, 142 rolls). Records of the Bureau of the Census, Record G), Ancestry.com, http://www.Ancestry.com, Year: 1820; Census Place: , Walton, Georgia; Roll: M33_10; Page: ; Image:. Residence date: 1820 Residence place: Walton, Georgia, United States.

54   Ancestry.com, North Carolina Marriage Collection, 1741-2004 (Online publication - Provo, UT, USA: Ancestry.com Operations Inc, 2007. Original data - Dodd, Jordan, Liahona Research, comp. (P. O. Box 740, Orem, Utah 84059) from county marriage records on microfilm located at the Family History Library in Salt Lake City,), Ancestry.com, http://www.Ancestry.com, Data Source: County Court Records - FHL # 0432251 - 0432254). Marriage date: 24 Feb 1798 Marriage place: Warren, North Carolina.

55   Ancestry.com, 1790 United States Federal Census (Online publication - Provo, UT, USA: Ancestry.com Operations, Inc., 2010. Images reproduced by FamilySearch. Original data - First Census of the United States, 1790 (NARA microfilm publication M637, 12 rolls). Records of the Bureau of the Census, Record Group), Ancestry.com, http://www.Ancestry.com, Year: 1790; Census Place: , Iredell, North Carolina; Roll: ; Image:. Residence date: 1790 Residence place: Iredell, North Carolina, United States.

56   Ancestry.com, Alabama Marriage Collection, 1800-1969 (Online publication - Provo, UT, USA: Ancestry.com Operations Inc, 2006. Original data - Alabama Center for Health Statistics. Alabama Marriage Index, 1936-1969. Alabama Center for Health Statistics, Montgomery, Alabama. Dodd, Jordan R., et. al. Early America), Ancestry.com, http://www.Ancestry.com, Marriage date: 7 Dec 1848 Marriage place: Calhoun, Alabama.

57   Ancestry.com, Alabama Marriage Collection, 1800-1969 (Online publication - Provo, UT, USA: Ancestry.com Operations Inc, 2006. Original data - Alabama Center for Health Statistics. Alabama Marriage Index, 1936-1969. Alabama Center for Health Statistics, Montgomery, Alabama. Dodd, Jordan R., et. al. Early America), Ancestry.com, http://www.Ancestry.com, Marriage date: 7 Dec 1848 Marriage place: Calhoun, Alabama.

58   Ancestry.com, 1840 United States Federal Census (Online publication - Provo, UT, USA: Ancestry.com Operations, Inc., 2010. Images reproduced by FamilySearch. Original data - Sixth Census of the United States, 1840. (NARA microfilm publication M704, 580 rolls). Records of the Bureau of the Census, Record G), Ancestry.com, http://www.Ancestry.com, Year: 1840; Census Place: , Marion, Tennessee; Roll: ; Page:. Residence date: 1840 Residence place: Marion, Tennessee, United States.

59   Ancestry.com, 1830 United States Federal Census (Online publication - Provo, UT, USA: Ancestry.com Operations, Inc., 2010. Images reproduced by FamilySearch. Original data - Fifth Census of the United States, 1830. (NARA microfilm publication M19, 201 rolls). Records of the Bureau of the Census, Record Gr), Ancestry.com, http://www.Ancestry.com, Year: 1830; Census Place: , Marion, Tennessee; Roll: ; Page:. Residence date: 1830 Residence place: Marion, Tennessee, United States.

60   Ancestry.com, U.S. Southern Claims Commission, Allowed Claims, 1871-1880 (Online publication - Provo, UT, USA: Ancestry.com Operations Inc, 2008. Original data - Southern Claims Commission Approved Claims, 1871-1880: Georgia; (National Archives Microfilm Publication M1658, 761 fiche); Records of the Accounting Officers of the Dep), Ancestry.com, http://www.Ancestry.com, Residence date: Residence place: USA.

61   Ancestry.com and The Church of Jesus Christ of Latter-day Saints, 1880 United States Federal Census (Online publication - Provo, UT, USA: Ancestry.com Operations Inc, 2010. 1880 U.S. Census Index provided by The Church of Jesus Christ of Latter-day Saints © Copyright 1999 Intellectual Reserve, Inc. All rights reserved. All use is subject to the limited), Ancestry.com, http://www.Ancestry.com, Year: 1880; Census Place: , Cherokee, Alabama; Roll: 6; Family History Film: 1254006; Page: 396D; Enumeration District: 27; Image:. Birth date: about 1812 Birth place: Georgia Residence date: 1880 Residence place: Cherokee, Alabama, United States.

62   Ancestry.com, 1850 United States Federal Census (Online publication - Provo, UT, USA: Ancestry.com Operations, Inc., 2009. Images reproduced by FamilySearch. Original data - Seventh Census of the United States, 1850; (National Archives Microfilm Publication M432, 1009 rolls); Records of the Bureau of the), Ancestry.com, http://www.Ancestry.com, Year: 1850; Census Place: Subdivision 29, Benton, Alabama; Roll: M432_1; Page: 334A; Image:. Birth date: about 1812 Birth place: Georgia Residence date: 1850 Residence place: Subdivision 29, Benton, Alabama.

63   Ancestry.com, 1860 United States Federal Census (Online publication - Provo, UT, USA: Ancestry.com Operations, Inc., 2009. Images reproduced by FamilySearch. Original data - 1860 U.S. census, population schedule. NARA microfilm publication M653, 1,438 rolls. Washington, D.C.: National Archives and Records), Ancestry.com, http://www.Ancestry.com, Year: 1860; Census Place: Division 1, Cherokee, Alabama; Roll: ; Page: 266; Image: 272. Birth date: about 1811 Birth place: Georgia Residence date: 1860 Residence place: Division 1, Cherokee, Alabama, United States.

64   Ancestry.com, 1870 United States Federal Census (Online publication - Provo, UT, USA: Ancestry.com Operations, Inc., 2009. Images reproduced by FamilySearch. Original data - 1870 U.S. census, population schedules.

NARA microfilm publication M593, 1,761 rolls. Washington, D.C.: National Archives and Record), Ancestry.com, http://www.Ancestry.com, Year: 1870; Census Place: Township 12 Range 9, Cherokee, Alabama; Roll: M593_; Page: ; Image:. Birth date: about 1810 Birth place: Georgia Residence date: 1870 Residence place: Township 12 Range 9, Cherokee, Alabama, United States.

65   Paul K Graham, 1805 Georgia Land Lottery - Fortunate Drawers and Grantees (The Genealogy Company, Decatur, Georgia), Personal Library of Alan Daves, Virginia Beach, Virginia, Identifies Edmond as a resident of Green County. Land lottery Act of May 1803 required all participants to be a resident from 1 year prior to the act (May 1802).

66   Ancestry.com, 1850 United States Federal Census (Online publication - Provo, UT, USA: Ancestry.com Operations, Inc., 2009. Images reproduced by FamilySearch. Original data - Seventh Census of the United States, 1850; (National Archives Microfilm Publication M432, 1009 rolls); Records of the Bureau of the), Ancestry.com, http://www.Ancestry.com, Year: 1850; Census Place: Subdivision 29, Benton, Alabama; Roll: M432_1; Page: 334A; Image:. Birth date: about 1805 Birth place: North Carolina Residence date: 1850 Residence place: Subdivision 29, Benton, Alabama.

67   Yates Publishing, U.S. and International Marriage Records, 1560-1900 (Online publication - Provo, UT, USA: Ancestry.com Operations Inc, 2004. Original data - This unique collection of records was extracted from a variety of sources including family group sheets and electronic databases. Originally, the information was derived), Ancestry.com, http://www.Ancestry.com, Source number: 2730.025; Source type: Family group sheet, FGSE, listed as parents; Number of Pages: 1; Submitter Code:. Birth date: 1798 Birth place: NC.

68   Yates Publishing, U.S. and International Marriage Records, 1560-1900 (Online publication - Provo, UT, USA: Ancestry.com Operations Inc, 2004. Original data - This unique collection of records was extracted from a variety of sources including family group sheets and electronic databases. Originally, the information was derived), Ancestry.com, http://www.Ancestry.com, Source number: 35.000; Source type: Electronic Database; Number of Pages: 1; Submitter Code: WBF. Birth date: 1798 Birth place: NC.

69   Ancestry.com, 1850 United States Federal Census (Online publication - Provo, UT, USA: Ancestry.com Operations, Inc., 2009. Images reproduced by FamilySearch. Original data - Seventh Census of the United States, 1850; (National Archives Microfilm Publication M432, 1009 rolls); Records of the Bureau of the), Ancestry.com, http://www.Ancestry.com, Year: 1850; Census Place: Subdivision 29, Benton, Alabama; Roll: M432_1; Page: 360A; Image:. Birth date: about 1798 Birth place: North Carolina Residence date: 1850 Residence place: Subdivision 29, Benton, Alabama.

70   Ancestry.com, 1820 United States Federal Census (Online publication - Provo, UT, USA: Ancestry.com Operations, Inc., 2010. Images reproduced by FamilySearch. Original data - Fourth Census of the United States, 1820. (NARA microfilm publication M33, 142 rolls). Records of the Bureau of the Census, Record G), Ancestry.com, http://www.Ancestry.com, Year: 1820; Census Place: , Walton, Georgia; Roll: M33_10; Page: ; Image:. Residence date: 1820 Residence place: Walton, Georgia, United States.

71   Ancestry.com, 1840 United States Federal Census (Online publication - Provo, UT, USA: Ancestry.com Operations, Inc., 2010. Images reproduced by FamilySearch. Original data - Sixth Census of the United States, 1840. (NARA microfilm publication M704, 580 rolls). Records of the Bureau of the Census, Record G), Ancestry.com, http://www.Ancestry.com, Year: 1840; Census Place: , Benton, Alabama; Roll: ; Page:. Residence date: 1840 Residence place: Benton, Alabama, United States.

72   Ancestry.com, U.S. General Land Office Records, 1796-1907 (Online publication - Provo, UT, USA: Ancestry.com Operations Inc, 2008. Original data - United States. Bureau of Land Management, General Land Office Records. Automated Records Project; Federal Land Patents, State Volumes. Springfield, Virginia: Bureau of L), Ancestry.com, http://www.Ancestry.com, Residence date: Residence place: United States.

73   United States, Bureau of Land Management, Alabama Land Records (Online publication - Provo, UT, USA: Ancestry.com Operations Inc, 1997. Original data - United States. Bureau of Land Management. Alabama Pre-1908 Homestead and Cash Entry Patent and Cadastral Survey Plat Index. General Land Office Automated Records Project), Ancestry.com, http://www.Ancestry.com.

74   Historical Data Systems, comp., American Civil War Soldiers (Online publication - Provo, UT, USA: Ancestry.com Operations Inc, 1999. Original data - Data compiled by Historical Data Systems of Kingston, MA form the following list of works. Copyright 1997-2000 Historical Data Systems, Inc. PO Box 35 Duxbury. Original), Ancestry.com, http://www.Ancestry.com, Side served: Confederacy; State served: Mississippi; Enlistment date:.

75   National Park Service, U.S. Civil War Soldiers, 1861-1865 (Online publication - Provo, UT, USA: Ancestry.com Operations Inc, 2007. Original data - National Park Service, Civil War Soldiers and Sailors System, online, http://www.itd.nps.gov/cwss/, acquired 2007. Original data: National Park Service, Civil War), Ancestry.com, http://www.Ancestry.com.

76   Ancestry.com, 1850 United States Federal Census (Online publication - Provo, UT, USA: Ancestry.com Operations, Inc., 2009. Images reproduced by FamilySearch. Original data - Seventh Census of the United States, 1850; (National Archives Microfilm Publication M432, 1009 rolls); Records of the Bureau of the), Ancestry.com, http://www.Ancestry.com, Year: 1850; Census Place: Montgomery Ward 3, Montgomery, Alabama; Roll: M432_12; Page: 145A; Image:. Birth date: about 1802 Birth place: Georgia Residence date: 1850 Residence place: Montgomery Ward 3, Montgomery, Alabama.

77   Ancestry.com, 1860 United States Federal Census (Online publication - Provo, UT, USA: Ancestry.com Operations, Inc., 2009. Images reproduced by FamilySearch. Original data - 1860 U.S. census, population schedule. NARA microfilm publication M653, 1,438 rolls. Washington, D.C.: National Archives and Records), Ancestry.com, http://www.Ancestry.com, Year: 1860; Census Place: Division 1, Montgomery, Alabama; Roll: ; Page: 217; Image: 217. Birth date: about 1804 Birth place: Georgia Residence date: 1860 Residence place: Division 1, Montgomery, Alabama, United States.

78   Ancestry.com, 1870 United States Federal Census (Online publication - Provo, UT, USA: Ancestry.com Operations, Inc., 2009. Images reproduced by FamilySearch. Original data - 1870 U.S. census, population schedules. NARA microfilm publication M593, 1,761 rolls. Washington, D.C.: National Archives and Record), Ancestry.com, http://www.Ancestry.com, Year: 1870; Census Place: Montgomery Ward 5, Montgomery, Alabama; Roll: M593_; Page: ; Image:. Birth date: about 1802 Birth place: Georgia Residence date: 1870 Residence place: Montgomery Ward 5, Montgomery, Alabama, United States.

79   Ancestry.com and The Church of Jesus Christ of Latter-day Saints, 1880 United States Federal Census (Online publication - Provo, UT, USA: Ancestry.com Operations Inc, 2010. 1880 U.S. Census Index provided by The Church of Jesus Christ of Latter-day Saints © Copyright 1999 Intellectual Reserve, Inc. All rights reserved. All use is subject to the limited), Ancestry.com, http://www.Ancestry.com, Year: 1880; Census Place: Clanton, Chilton, Alabama; Roll: 6; Family History Film: 1254006; Page: 74A; Enumeration District: 29; Image: 0595. Birth date: about 1802 Birth place: Georgia Residence date: 1880 Residence place: Clanton, Chilton, Alabama, United States.

80   Dodd, Jordan, Georgia Marriages to 1850 (Online publication - Provo, UT, USA: Ancestry.com Operations Inc, 1997. Original data - Electronic transcription of marriage records held by the individual counties in Georgia. Original data: Electronic transcription of marriage records held by the individual), Ancestry.com, http://www.Ancestry.com, Marriage date: 4 Jul 1820 Marriage place: Jones, Georgia.

81   Ancestry.com, 1840 United States Federal Census (Online publication - Provo, UT, USA: Ancestry.com Operations, Inc., 2010. Images reproduced by FamilySearch. Original data - Sixth Census of the United States, 1840. (NARA microfilm publication M704, 580 rolls). Records of the Bureau of the Census, Record G), Ancestry.com, http://www.Ancestry.com, Year: 1840; Census Place: Montgomery, Montgomery, Alabama; Roll: ; Page:. Residence date: 1840 Residence place: Montgomery, Alabama, United States.

82   Hunting For Bears, comp., Georgia Marriages, 1699-1944 (Online publication - Provo, UT, USA: Ancestry.com Operations Inc, 2004. Original data - Georgia marriage information taken from county courthouse records. Many of these records were extracted from copies of the original records in microfilm, microfiche, or), Ancestry.com, http://www.Ancestry.com, Marriage date: 4 Jul 1820 Marriage place: Jones, Georgia.

83   Ancestry.com, U.S. General Land Office Records, 1796-1907 (Online publication - Provo, UT, USA: Ancestry.com Operations Inc, 2008. Original data - United States. Bureau of Land Management, General Land Office Records. Automated Records Project; Federal Land Patents, State Volumes. Springfield, Virginia: Bureau of L), Ancestry.com, http://www.Ancestry.com, Residence date: Residence place: United States.

84   Ancestry.com, U.S. General Land Office Records, 1796-1907 (Online publication - Provo, UT, USA: Ancestry.com Operations Inc, 2008. Original data - United States. Bureau of Land Management, General Land Office Records. Automated Records Project; Federal Land Patents, State Volumes. Springfield, Virginia: Bureau of L), Ancestry.com, http://www.Ancestry.com, Residence date: Residence place: United States.

85   Ancestry.com, U.S. General Land Office Records, 1796-1907 (Online publication - Provo, UT, USA: Ancestry.com Operations Inc, 2008. Original data - United States. Bureau of Land Management, General Land Office Records. Automated Records Project; Federal Land Patents, State Volumes. Springfield, Virginia: Bureau of L), Ancestry.com, http://www.Ancestry.com, Residence date: Residence place: United States.

86   United States, Bureau of Land Management, Alabama Land Records (Online publication - Provo, UT, USA: Ancestry.com Operations Inc, 1997. Original data - United States. Bureau of Land Management. Alabama Pre-1908 Homestead and Cash Entry Patent and Cadastral Survey Plat Index. General Land Office Automated Records Project), Ancestry.com, http://www.Ancestry.com.

87   United States, Bureau of Land Management, Alabama Land Records (Online publication - Provo, UT, USA: Ancestry.com Operations Inc, 1997. Original data - United States. Bureau of Land Management. Alabama Pre-1908 Homestead and Cash Entry Patent and Cadastral Survey Plat Index. General Land Office Automated Records Project), Ancestry.com, http://www.Ancestry.com.

88   United States, Bureau of Land Management, Alabama Land Records (Online publication - Provo, UT, USA: Ancestry.com Operations Inc, 1997. Original data - United States. Bureau of Land Management. Alabama Pre-1908 Homestead and Cash Entry Patent and Cadastral Survey Plat Index. General Land Office Automated Records Project), Ancestry.com, http://www.Ancestry.com.

89   United States, Bureau of Land Management, Alabama Land Records (Online publication - Provo, UT, USA: Ancestry.com Operations Inc, 1997. Original data - United States. Bureau of Land Management. Alabama Pre-1908 Homestead and Cash Entry Patent and Cadastral Survey Plat Index. General Land Office Automated Records Project), Ancestry.com, http://www.Ancestry.com.

90   Ancestry.com, 1830 United States Federal Census (Online publication - Provo, UT, USA: Ancestry.com Operations, Inc., 2010. Images reproduced by FamilySearch. Original data - Fifth Census of the United States, 1830.

(NARA microfilm publication M19, 201 rolls). Records of the Bureau of the Census, Record Gr), Ancestry.com, http://www.Ancestry.com, Year: 1830; Census Place: , Campbell, Georgia; Roll: ; Page:. Residence date: 1830 Residence place: Campbell, Georgia, United States.

91   Ancestry.com, U.S. General Land Office Records, 1796-1907 (Online publication - Provo, UT, USA: Ancestry.com Operations Inc, 2008. Original data - United States. Bureau of Land Management, General Land Office Records. Automated Records Project; Federal Land Patents, State Volumes. Springfield, Virginia: Bureau of L), Ancestry.com, http://www.Ancestry.com, Residence date: Residence place: United States.

92   Ancestry.com, Alabama State Census, 1820-1866 (Online publication - Provo, UT, USA: Ancestry.com Operations Inc, 2010. This collection was indexed by Ancestry.com World Archives Project contributors. Original data - Alabama State Census, 1820, 1850, 1855 and 1866. Montgomery, Alabama: Alabama Department), Ancestry.com, http://www.Ancestry.com, Residence date: 1850 Residence place: Cherokee, Alabama.

93   Ancestry.com, Alabama State Census, 1820-1866 (Online publication - Provo, UT, USA: Ancestry.com Operations Inc, 2010. This collection was indexed by Ancestry.com World Archives Project contributors. Original data - Alabama State Census, 1820, 1850, 1855 and 1866. Montgomery, Alabama: Alabama Department), Ancestry.com, http://www.Ancestry.com, Residence date: 1866Residence place: Cherokee, Alabama.

94   Ancestry.com, 1840 United States Federal Census (Online publication - Provo, UT, USA: Ancestry.com Operations, Inc., 2010. Images reproduced by FamilySearch. Original data - Sixth Census of the United States, 1840. (NARA microfilm publication M704, 580 rolls). Records of the Bureau of the Census, Record G), Ancestry.com, http://www.Ancestry.com, Year: 1840; Census Place: , Benton, Alabama; Roll: ; Page:. Residence date: 1840 Residence place: Benton, Alabama, United States.

95   Ancestry.com, 1850 United States Federal Census (Online publication - Provo, UT, USA: Ancestry.com Operations, Inc., 2009. Images reproduced by FamilySearch. Original data - Seventh Census of the United States, 1850; (National Archives Microfilm Publication M432, 1009 rolls); Records of the Bureau of the), Ancestry.com, http://www.Ancestry.com, Year: 1850; Census Place: District 27, Cherokee, Alabama; Roll: M432_3; Page: 84B; Image:. Birth date: about 1805 Birth place: Georgia Residence date: 1850 Residence place: District 27, Cherokee, Alabama.

96   Ancestry.com, 1860 United States Federal Census (Online publication - Provo, UT, USA: Ancestry.com Operations, Inc., 2009. Images reproduced by FamilySearch. Original data - 1860 U.S. census, population schedule. NARA microfilm publication M653, 1,438 rolls. Washington, D.C.: National Archives and Records), Ancestry.com, http://www.Ancestry.com, Year: 1860; Census Place: Ranges 8 and 9, Calhoun, Alabama; Roll: ; Page: 417; Image: 137. Birth date: about 1808 Birth place: Georgia Residence date: 1860 Residence place: Ranges 8 and 9, Calhoun, Alabama, United States.

97   Ancestry.com, 1870 United States Federal Census (Online publication - Provo, UT, USA: Ancestry.com Operations, Inc., 2009. Images reproduced by FamilySearch. Original data - 1870 U.S. census, population schedules. NARA microfilm publication M593, 1,761 rolls. Washington, D.C.: National Archives and Record), Ancestry.com, http://www.Ancestry.com, Year: 1870; Census Place: Township 12 Range 7, Etowah, Alabama; Roll: M593_; Page: ; Image:. Birth date: about 1807 Birth place: Georgia Residence date: 1870 Residence place: Township 12 Range 7, Etowah, Alabama, United States.

98   Ancestry.com and The Church of Jesus Christ of Latter-day Saints, 1880 United States Federal Census (Online publication - Provo, UT, USA: Ancestry.com Operations Inc, 2010. 1880 U.S. Census Index provided by The Church of Jesus Christ of Latter-day Saints © Copyright 1999 Intellectual Reserve, Inc. All rights reserved. All use is subject to the limited), Ancestry.com, http://www.Ancestry.com, Year: 1880; Census Place: Hokes Bluff, Etowah, Alabama; Roll: 13; Family History Film: 1254013; Page: 330B; Enumeration District: 67; Image: 0168. Birth date: about 1808 Birth place: Georgia Residence date: 1880 Residence place: Hokes Bluff, Etowah, Alabama, United States.

99   Ancestry.com, Cemetery survey, Etowah County, Alabama (Online publication - Provo, UT: Ancestry.com Operations Inc, 2005. Original data - Cemetery survey, Etowah County, Alabama. Gadsden, Ala.: Church of Jesus Christ of Latter-day Saints, 1963. Original data: Cemetery survey, Etowah County, Alabama. Gadsden, Ala), Ancestry.com, http://www.Ancestry.com, Residence date: 1700-1963Residence place: Etowah, Alabama, USA.

100   Ancestry.com, 1850 United States Federal Census (Online publication - Provo, UT, USA: Ancestry.com Operations, Inc., 2009. Images reproduced by FamilySearch. Original data - Seventh Census of the United States, 1850; (National Archives Microfilm Publication M432, 1009 rolls); Records of the Bureau of the), Ancestry.com, http://www.Ancestry.com, Year: 1850; Census Place: Subdivision 29, Benton, Alabama; Roll: M432_1; Page: 334A; Image:. Birth date: about 1814 Birth place: Georgia Residence date: 1850 Residence place: Subdivision 29, Benton, Alabama.

101   Ancestry.com, 1860 United States Federal Census (Online publication - Provo, UT, USA: Ancestry.com Operations, Inc., 2009. Images reproduced by FamilySearch. Original data - 1860 U.S. census, population schedule. NARA microfilm publication M653, 1,438 rolls. Washington, D.C.: National Archives and Records), Ancestry.com, http://www.Ancestry.com, Year: 1860; Census Place: Division 1, Cherokee, Alabama; Roll: ; Page: 265; Image: 271. Birth date: about 1814 Birth place: Georgia Residence date: 1860 Residence place: Division 1, Cherokee, Alabama, United States.

102   Ancestry.com, 1870 United States Federal Census (Online publication - Provo, UT, USA: Ancestry.com Operations, Inc., 2009. Images reproduced by FamilySearch. Original data - 1870 U.S. census, population schedules. NARA microfilm publication M593, 1,761 rolls. Washington, D.C.: National Archives and Record), Ancestry.com,

http://www.Ancestry.com, Year: 1870; Census Place: Township 12 Range 7, Etowah, Alabama; Roll: M593_; Page: ; Image:. Birth date: about 1813 Birth place: Georgia Residence date: 1870 Residence place: Township 12 Range 7, Etowah, Alabama, United States.

103   Ancestry.com, U.S. General Land Office Records, 1796-1907 (Online publication - Provo, UT, USA: Ancestry.com Operations Inc, 2008. Original data - United States. Bureau of Land Management, General Land Office Records. Automated Records Project; Federal Land Patents, State Volumes. Springfield, Virginia: Bureau of L), Ancestry.com, http://www.Ancestry.com, Residence date: Residence place: United States.

104   United States, Bureau of Land Management, Alabama Land Records (Online publication - Provo, UT, USA: Ancestry.com Operations Inc, 1997. Original data - United States. Bureau of Land Management. Alabama Pre-1908 Homestead and Cash Entry Patent and Cadastral Survey Plat Index. General Land Office Automated Records Project), Ancestry.com, http://www.Ancestry.com.

105   Ancestry.com, Alabama Marriage Collection, 1800-1969 (Online publication - Provo, UT, USA: Ancestry.com Operations Inc, 2006. Original data - Alabama Center for Health Statistics. Alabama Marriage Index, 1936-1969. Alabama Center for Health Statistics, Montgomery, Alabama. Dodd, Jordan R., et. al. Early America), Ancestry.com, http://www.Ancestry.com, Marriage date: 29 Jan 1837 Marriage place: Calhoun, Alabama.

106   Ancestry.com, Alabama Marriage Collection, 1800-1969 (Online publication - Provo, UT, USA: Ancestry.com Operations Inc, 2006. Original data - Alabama Center for Health Statistics. Alabama Marriage Index, 1936-1969. Alabama Center for Health Statistics, Montgomery, Alabama. Dodd, Jordan R., et. al. Early America), Ancestry.com, http://www.Ancestry.com, Marriage date: 29 Jan 1837 Marriage place: Calhoun, Alabama.

107   Ancestry.com, 1850 United States Federal Census (Online publication - Provo, UT, USA: Ancestry.com Operations, Inc., 2009. Images reproduced by FamilySearch. Original data - Seventh Census of the United States, 1850; (National Archives Microfilm Publication M432, 1009 rolls); Records of the Bureau of the), Ancestry.com, http://www.Ancestry.com, Year: 1850; Census Place: Subdivision 29, Benton, Alabama; Roll: M432_1; Page: 334A; Image:. Birth date: about 1817 Birth place: Georgia Residence date: 1850 Residence place: Subdivision 29, Benton, Alabama.

108   Ancestry.com, 1860 United States Federal Census (Online publication - Provo, UT, USA: Ancestry.com Operations, Inc., 2009. Images reproduced by FamilySearch. Original data - 1860 U.S. census, population schedule. NARA microfilm publication M653, 1,438 rolls. Washington, D.C.: National Archives and Records), Ancestry.com, http://www.Ancestry.com, Year: 1860; Census Place: Ranges 8 and 9, Calhoun, Alabama; Roll: ; Page: 330; Image: 46. Birth date: about 1816 Birth place: Georgia Residence date: 1860 Residence place: Ranges 8 and 9, Calhoun, Alabama, United States.

109   Ancestry.com, 1870 United States Federal Census (Online publication - Provo, UT, USA: Ancestry.com Operations, Inc., 2009. Images reproduced by FamilySearch. Original data - 1870 U.S. census, population schedules. NARA microfilm publication M593, 1,761 rolls. Washington, D.C.: National Archives and Record), Ancestry.com, http://www.Ancestry.com, Year: 1870; Census Place: Township 15, Calhoun, Alabama; Roll: M593_; Page: ; Image:. Birth date: about 1817 Birth place: Georgia Residence date: 1870 Residence place: Township 15, Calhoun, Alabama, United States.

110   Ancestry.com, 1850 United States Federal Census (Online publication - Provo, UT, USA: Ancestry.com Operations, Inc., 2009. Images reproduced by FamilySearch. Original data - Seventh Census of the United States, 1850; (National Archives Microfilm Publication M432, 1009 rolls); Records of the Bureau of the), Ancestry.com, http://www.Ancestry.com, Year: 1850; Census Place: Subdivision 29, Benton, Alabama; Roll: M432_1; Page: 334A; Image:. Birth date: about 1805 Birth place: Georgia Residence date: 1850 Residence place: Subdivision 29, Benton, Alabama.

111   Ancestry.com and The Church of Jesus Christ of Latter-day Saints, 1880 United States Federal Census (Online publication - Provo, UT, USA: Ancestry.com Operations Inc, 2010. 1880 U.S. Census Index provided by The Church of Jesus Christ of Latter-day Saints © Copyright 1999 Intellectual Reserve, Inc. All rights reserved. All use is subject to the limited), Ancestry.com, http://www.Ancestry.com, Year: 1880; Census Place: , Cherokee, Alabama; Roll: 6; Family History Film: 1254006; Page: 396D; Enumeration District: 27; Image:. Birth date: about 1805 Birth place: Georgia Residence date: 1880 Residence place: Cherokee, Alabama, United States.

112   United States, Bureau of Land Management, Alabama Land Records (Online publication - Provo, UT, USA: Ancestry.com Operations Inc, 1997. Original data - United States. Bureau of Land Management. Alabama Pre-1908 Homestead and Cash Entry Patent and Cadastral Survey Plat Index. General Land Office Automated Records Project), Ancestry.com, http://www.Ancestry.com.

113   Ancestry.com, 1830 United States Federal Census (Online publication - Provo, UT, USA: Ancestry.com Operations, Inc., 2010. Images reproduced by FamilySearch. Original data - Fifth Census of the United States, 1830. (NARA microfilm publication M19, 201 rolls). Records of the Bureau of the Census, Record Gr), Ancestry.com, http://www.Ancestry.com, Year: 1830; Census Place: , Campbell, Georgia; Roll: ; Page:. Residence date: 1830 Residence place: Campbell, Georgia, United States.

114   Ancestry.com, 1840 United States Federal Census (Online publication - Provo, UT, USA: Ancestry.com Operations, Inc., 2010. Images reproduced by FamilySearch. Original data - Sixth Census of the United States, 1840. (NARA microfilm publication M704, 580 rolls). Records of the Bureau of the Census, Record G), Ancestry.com,

http://www.Ancestry.com, Year: 1840; Census Place: , Benton, Alabama; Roll: ; Page:. Residence date: 1840 Residence place: Benton, Alabama, United States.

115   Ancestry.com, 1860 United States Federal Census (Online publication - Provo, UT, USA: Ancestry.com Operations, Inc., 2009. Images reproduced by FamilySearch. Original data - 1860 U.S. census, population schedule. NARA microfilm publication M653, 1,438 rolls. Washington, D.C.: National Archives and Records), Ancestry.com, http://www.Ancestry.com, Year: 1860; Census Place: Division 1, Cherokee, Alabama; Roll: ; Page: 266; Image: 272. Birth date: about 1806 Birth place: Georgia Residence date: 1860 Residence place: Division 1, Cherokee, Alabama, United States.

116   Ancestry.com, 1870 United States Federal Census (Online publication - Provo, UT, USA: Ancestry.com Operations, Inc., 2009. Images reproduced by FamilySearch. Original data - 1870 U.S. census, population schedules. NARA microfilm publication M593, 1,761 rolls. Washington, D.C.: National Archives and Record), Ancestry.com, http://www.Ancestry.com, Year: 1870; Census Place: Township 12 Range 9, Cherokee, Alabama; Roll: M593_; Page: ; Image:. Birth date: about 1803 Birth place: Georgia Residence date: 1870 Residence place: Township 12 Range 9, Cherokee, Alabama, United States.

117   Ancestry.com, 1870 United States Federal Census (Online publication - Provo, UT, USA: Ancestry.com Operations, Inc., 2009. Images reproduced by FamilySearch. Original data - 1870 U.S. census, population schedules. NARA microfilm publication M593, 1,761 rolls. Washington, D.C.: National Archives and Record), Ancestry.com, http://www.Ancestry.com, Year: 1870; Census Place: Township 13 Range 6, Etowah, Alabama; Roll: M593_; Page: ; Image:. Birth date: about 1831 Birth place: Georgia Residence date: 1870 Residence place: Township 13 Range 6, Etowah, Alabama, United States.

118   Ancestry.com, Alabama Marriage Collection, 1800-1969 (Online publication - Provo, UT, USA: Ancestry.com Operations Inc, 2006. Original data - Alabama Center for Health Statistics. Alabama Marriage Index, 1936-1969. Alabama Center for Health Statistics, Montgomery, Alabama. Dodd, Jordan R., et. al. Early America), Ancestry.com, http://www.Ancestry.com, Marriage date: 13 Jan 1850 Marriage place: Calhoun, Alabama.

119   Ancestry.com and The Church of Jesus Christ of Latter-day Saints, 1880 United States Federal Census (Online publication - Provo, UT, USA: Ancestry.com Operations Inc, 2010. 1880 U.S. Census Index provided by The Church of Jesus Christ of Latter-day Saints © Copyright 1999 Intellectual Reserve, Inc. All rights reserved. All use is subject to the limited), Ancestry.com, http://www.Ancestry.com, Year: 1880; Census Place: Gadsden, Etowah, Alabama; Roll: 13; Family History Film: 1254013; Page: 375C; Enumeration District: 70; Image: 0257. Birth date: about 1840 Birth place: Alabama Residence date: 1880 Residence place: Gadsden, Etowah, Alabama, United States.

120   Ancestry.com, 1850 United States Federal Census (Online publication - Provo, UT, USA: Ancestry.com Operations, Inc., 2009. Images reproduced by FamilySearch. Original data - Seventh Census of the United States, 1850; (National Archives Microfilm Publication M432, 1009 rolls); Records of the Bureau of the), Ancestry.com, http://www.Ancestry.com, Year: 1850; Census Place: Subdivision 29, Benton, Alabama; Roll: M432_1; Page: 334A; Image:. Birth date: about 1839 Birth place: Alabama Residence date: 1850 Residence place: Subdivision 29, Benton, Alabama.

121   Ancestry.com, 1860 United States Federal Census (Online publication - Provo, UT, USA: Ancestry.com Operations, Inc., 2009. Images reproduced by FamilySearch. Original data - 1860 U.S. census, population schedule. NARA microfilm publication M653, 1,438 rolls. Washington, D.C.: National Archives and Records), Ancestry.com, http://www.Ancestry.com, Year: 1860; Census Place: Ranges 8 and 9, Calhoun, Alabama; Roll: ; Page: 411; Image: 131. Birth date: about 1840 Birth place: Alabama Residence date: 1860 Residence place: Ranges 8 and 9, Calhoun, Alabama, United States.

122   Ancestry.com, 1900 United States Federal Census (Online publication - Provo, UT, USA: Ancestry.com Operations Inc, 2004. Original data - United States of America, Bureau of the Census. Twelfth Census of the United States, 1900. Washington, D.C.: National Archives and Records Administration, 1900. T623, 18), Ancestry.com, http://www.Ancestry.com, Year: 1900; Census Place: Ball Play, Cherokee, Alabama; Roll: T623_6; Page: 7A; Enumeration District: 123. Birth date: Apr 1847 Birth place: Alabama Marriage date: 1868 Marriage place: Residence date: 1900 Residence place: Precinct 8 Ballplay, Cherokee, Alabama.

123   Ancestry.com and The Church of Jesus Christ of Latter-day Saints, 1880 United States Federal Census (Online publication - Provo, UT, USA: Ancestry.com Operations Inc, 2010. 1880 U.S. Census Index provided by The Church of Jesus Christ of Latter-day Saints © Copyright 1999 Intellectual Reserve, Inc. All rights reserved. All use is subject to the limited), Ancestry.com, http://www.Ancestry.com, Year: 1880; Census Place: , Cherokee, Alabama; Roll: 6; Family History Film: 1254006; Page: 396D; Enumeration District: 27; Image:. Birth date: about 1847 Birth place: Alabama Residence date: 1880 Residence place: Cherokee, Alabama, United States.

124   Ancestry.com, 1850 United States Federal Census (Online publication - Provo, UT, USA: Ancestry.com Operations, Inc., 2009. Images reproduced by FamilySearch. Original data - Seventh Census of the United States, 1850; (National Archives Microfilm Publication M432, 1009 rolls); Records of the Bureau of the), Ancestry.com, http://www.Ancestry.com, Year: 1850; Census Place: Subdivision 29, Benton, Alabama; Roll: M432_1; Page: 334A; Image:. Birth date: about 1847 Birth place: Alabama Residence date: 1850 Residence place: Subdivision 29, Benton, Alabama.

125   Ancestry.com, 1860 United States Federal Census (Online publication - Provo, UT, USA: Ancestry.com Operations, Inc., 2009. Images reproduced by FamilySearch. Original data - 1860 U.S. census, population schedule. NARA microfilm publication M653, 1,438 rolls. Washington, D.C.: National Archives and Records), Ancestry.com,

http://www.Ancestry.com, Year: 1860; Census Place: Division 1, Cherokee, Alabama; Roll: ; Page: 266; Image: 272. Birth date: about 1848 Birth place: Alabama Residence date: 1860 Residence place: Division 1, Cherokee, Alabama, United States.

126   Ancestry.com, 1870 United States Federal Census (Online publication - Provo, UT, USA: Ancestry.com Operations, Inc., 2009. Images reproduced by FamilySearch. Original data - 1870 U.S. census, population schedules. NARA microfilm publication M593, 1,761 rolls. Washington, D.C.: National Archives and Record), Ancestry.com, http://www.Ancestry.com, Year: 1870; Census Place: Township 12 Range 9, Cherokee, Alabama; Roll: M593_; Page: ; Image:. Birth date: about 1847 Birth place: Alabama Residence date: 1870 Residence place: Township 12 Range 9, Cherokee, Alabama, United States.

127   Ancestry.com, Alabama Deaths, 1908-59 (Online publication - Provo, UT, USA: Ancestry.com Operations Inc, 2000. Original data - State of Alabama. Index of Vital Records for Alabama: Deaths, 1908-1959. Montgomery, AL, USA: State of Alabama Center for Health Statistics, Record Services Division. Original), Ancestry.com, http://www.Ancestry.com, Death date: 18 Mar? 1922 Death place: Cherokee.

128   Ancestry.com, 1860 United States Federal Census (Online publication - Provo, UT, USA: Ancestry.com Operations, Inc., 2009. Images reproduced by FamilySearch. Original data - 1860 U.S. census, population schedule. NARA microfilm publication M653, 1,438 rolls. Washington, D.C.: National Archives and Records), Ancestry.com, http://www.Ancestry.com, Year: 1860; Census Place: Division 1, Cherokee, Alabama; Roll: ; Page: 266; Image: 272. Birth date: about 1851 Birth place: Alabama Residence date: 1860 Residence place: Division 1, Cherokee, Alabama, United States.

129   Ancestry.com, 1870 United States Federal Census (Online publication - Provo, UT, USA: Ancestry.com Operations, Inc., 2009. Images reproduced by FamilySearch. Original data - 1870 U.S. census, population schedules. NARA microfilm publication M593, 1,761 rolls. Washington, D.C.: National Archives and Record), Ancestry.com, http://www.Ancestry.com, Year: 1870; Census Place: Township 12 Range 9, Cherokee, Alabama; Roll: M593_; Page: ; Image:. Birth date: about 1851 Birth place: Alabama Residence date: 1870 Residence place: Township 12 Range 9, Cherokee, Alabama, United States.

130   Ancestry.com and The Church of Jesus Christ of Latter-day Saints, 1880 United States Federal Census (Online publication - Provo, UT, USA: Ancestry.com Operations Inc, 2010. 1880 U.S. Census Index provided by The Church of Jesus Christ of Latter-day Saints © Copyright 1999 Intellectual Reserve, Inc. All rights reserved. All use is subject to the limited), Ancestry.com, http://www.Ancestry.com, Year: 1880; Census Place: , Cherokee, Alabama; Roll: 6; Family History Film: 1254006; Page: 437D; Enumeration District: 30; Image:. Birth date: about 1851 Birth place: Alabama Residence date: 1880 Residence place: Cherokee, Alabama, United States.

131   Ancestry.com, 1900 United States Federal Census (Online publication - Provo, UT, USA: Ancestry.com Operations Inc, 2004. Original data - United States of America, Bureau of the Census. Twelfth Census of the United States, 1900. Washington, D.C.: National Archives and Records Administration, 1900. T623, 18), Ancestry.com, http://www.Ancestry.com, Year: 1900; Census Place: Coloma, Cherokee, Alabama; Roll: T623_6; Page: 2B; Enumeration District: 122. Birth date: Jul 1851 Birth place: Alabama Marriage date: 1870 Marriage place: Residence date: 1900 Residence place: Precinct 7 Coloma, Cherokee, Alabama.

132   Ancestry.com, 1910 United States Federal Census (Online publication - Provo, UT, USA: Ancestry.com Operations Inc, 2006. Original data - Thirteenth Census of the United States, 1910 (NARA microfilm publication T624, 1,178 rolls). Records of the Bureau of the Census, Record Group 29. National Archives, Washington), Ancestry.com, http://www.Ancestry.com, Year: 1910; Census Place: Piedmont, Calhoun, Alabama; Roll: ; Page: ; Enumeration District: ; Image:. Birth date: 1851 Birth place: Alabama Residence date: 1910 Residence place: Piedmont, Calhoun, Alabama.

133   Ancestry.com, 1900 United States Federal Census (Online publication - Provo, UT, USA: Ancestry.com Operations Inc, 2004. Original data - United States of America, Bureau of the Census. Twelfth Census of the United States, 1900. Washington, D.C.: National Archives and Records Administration, 1900. T623, 18), Ancestry.com, http://www.Ancestry.com, Year: 1900; Census Place: Coloma, Cherokee, Alabama; Roll: T623_6; Page: 2B; Enumeration District: 122. Birth date: Apr 1851 Birth place: Alabama Marriage date: 1870 Marriage place: Residence date: 1900 Residence place: Precinct 7 Coloma, Cherokee, Alabama.

134   Ancestry.com, 1850 United States Federal Census (Online publication - Provo, UT, USA: Ancestry.com Operations, Inc., 2009. Images reproduced by FamilySearch. Original data - Seventh Census of the United States, 1850; (National Archives Microfilm Publication M432, 1009 rolls); Records of the Bureau of the), Ancestry.com, http://www.Ancestry.com, Year: 1850; Census Place: Subdivision 29, Benton, Alabama; Roll: M432_1; Page: 360B; Image:. Birth date: about 1804 Birth place: South Carolina Residence date: 1850 Residence place: Subdivision 29, Benton, Alabama.

135   Yates Publishing, U.S. and International Marriage Records, 1560-1900 (Online publication - Provo, UT, USA: Ancestry.com Operations Inc, 2004. Original data - This unique collection of records was extracted from a variety of sources including family group sheets and electronic databases. Originally, the information was derived), Ancestry.com, http://www.Ancestry.com, Source number: 35.000; Source type: Electronic Database; Number of Pages: 1; Submitter Code: WBF. Birth date: 1804 Birth place: NC.

136   Ancestry.com, 1860 United States Federal Census (Online publication - Provo, UT, USA: Ancestry.com Operations, Inc., 2009. Images reproduced by FamilySearch. Original data - 1860 U.S. census, population schedule. NARA microfilm publication M653, 1,438 rolls. Washington, D.C.: National Archives and Records), Ancestry.com, http://www.Ancestry.com, Year: 1860; Census Place: Ranges 8 and 9, Calhoun, Alabama; Roll: ; Page: 327; Image: 43.

Birth date: about 1805 Birth place: South Carolina Residence date: 1860 Residence place: Ranges 8 and 9, Calhoun, Alabama, United States.

137   Ancestry.com, Alabama Marriage Collection, 1800-1969 (Online publication - Provo, UT, USA: Ancestry.com Operations Inc, 2006. Original data - Alabama Center for Health Statistics. Alabama Marriage Index, 1936-1969. Alabama Center for Health Statistics, Montgomery, Alabama. Dodd, Jordan R., et. al. Early America), Ancestry.com, http://www.Ancestry.com, Marriage date: 19 Dec 1837 Marriage place: Calhoun, Alabama.

138   Ancestry.com and The Church of Jesus Christ of Latter-day Saints, 1880 United States Federal Census (Online publication - Provo, UT, USA: Ancestry.com Operations Inc, 2010. 1880 U.S. Census Index provided by The Church of Jesus Christ of Latter-day Saints © Copyright 1999 Intellectual Reserve, Inc. All rights reserved. All use is subject to the limited), Ancestry.com, http://www.Ancestry.com, Year: 1880; Census Place: Davisville, Calhoun, Alabama; Roll: 5; Family History Film: 1254005; Page: 682B; Enumeration District: 13; Image: 0106. Birth date: about 1826 Birth place: Georgia Residence date: 1880 Residence place: Davisville, Calhoun, Alabama, United States.

139   Ancestry.com, 1850 United States Federal Census (Online publication - Provo, UT, USA: Ancestry.com Operations, Inc., 2009. Images reproduced by FamilySearch. Original data - Seventh Census of the United States, 1850; (National Archives Microfilm Publication M432, 1009 rolls); Records of the Bureau of the), Ancestry.com, http://www.Ancestry.com, Year: 1850; Census Place: Subdivision 29, Benton, Alabama; Roll: M432_1; Page: 344A; Image:. Birth date: about 1823 Birth place: Georgia Residence date: 1850 Residence place: Subdivision 29, Benton, Alabama.

140   Ancestry.com, 1860 United States Federal Census (Online publication - Provo, UT, USA: Ancestry.com Operations, Inc., 2009. Images reproduced by FamilySearch. Original data - 1860 U.S. census, population schedule. NARA microfilm publication M653, 1,438 rolls. Washington, D.C.: National Archives and Records), Ancestry.com, http://www.Ancestry.com, Year: 1860; Census Place: Ranges 8 and 9, Calhoun, Alabama; Roll: ; Page: 327; Image: 43. Birth date: about 1823 Birth place: Georgia Residence date: 1860 Residence place: Ranges 8 and 9, Calhoun, Alabama, United States.

141   National Cemetery Administration, U.S. Veterans Gravesites, ca.1775-2006 (Online publication - Provo, UT, USA: Ancestry.com Operations Inc, 2006. Original data - National Cemetery Administration. Nationwide Gravesite Locator. Original data: National Cemetery Administration. Nationwide Gravesite Locator), Ancestry.com, http://www.Ancestry.com, Birth date: 09/25/1825 Birth place: Death date: 03/03/1902 Death place: AL.

142   Yates Publishing, U.S. and International Marriage Records, 1560-1900 (Online publication - Provo, UT, USA: Ancestry.com Operations Inc, 2004. Original data - This unique collection of records was extracted from a variety of sources including family group sheets and electronic databases. Originally, the information was derived), Ancestry.com, http://www.Ancestry.com, Source number: 33.000; Source type: Electronic Database; Number of Pages: 1; Submitter Code: WBF. Birth date: 1825 Birth place: GA Marriage date: 1845 Marriage place: AL.

143   Ancestry.com and The Church of Jesus Christ of Latter-day Saints, 1880 United States Federal Census (Online publication - Provo, UT, USA: Ancestry.com Operations Inc, 2010. 1880 U.S. Census Index provided by The Church of Jesus Christ of Latter-day Saints © Copyright 1999 Intellectual Reserve, Inc. All rights reserved. All use is subject to the limited), Ancestry.com, http://www.Ancestry.com, Year: 1880; Census Place: Allens, Calhoun, Alabama; Roll: 5; Family History Film: 1254005; Page: 645A; Enumeration District: 10; Image: 0031. Birth date: about 1827 Birth place: Georgia Residence date: 1880 Residence place: Allens, Calhoun, Alabama, United States.

144   Ancestry.com, 1870 United States Federal Census (Online publication - Provo, UT, USA: Ancestry.com Operations, Inc., 2009. Images reproduced by FamilySearch. Original data - 1870 U.S. census, population schedules. NARA microfilm publication M593, 1,761 rolls. Washington, D.C.: National Archives and Record), Ancestry.com, http://www.Ancestry.com, Year: 1870; Census Place: Precinct 8, Calhoun, Alabama; Roll: M593_; Page: ; Image:. Birth date: about 1827 Birth place: Georgia Residence date: 1870 Residence place: Precinct 8, Calhoun, Alabama, United States.

145   Ancestry.com, 1900 United States Federal Census (Online publication - Provo, UT, USA: Ancestry.com Operations Inc, 2004. Original data - United States of America, Bureau of the Census. Twelfth Census of the United States, 1900. Washington, D.C.: National Archives and Records Administration, 1900. T623, 18), Ancestry.com, http://www.Ancestry.com, Year: 1900; Census Place: Allen, Calhoun, Alabama; Roll: T623_5; Page: 1B; Enumeration District: 32. Birth date: Sep 1826 Birth place: Georgia Marriage date: 1846 Marriage place: Residence date: 1900 Residence place: Precinct 8 Green's Schoolhouse, Calhoun, Alabama.

146   National Park Service, U.S. Civil War Soldiers, 1861-1865 (Online publication - Provo, UT, USA: Ancestry.com Operations Inc, 2007. Original data - National Park Service, Civil War Soldiers and Sailors System, online, http://www.itd.nps.gov/cwss/, acquired 2007. Original data: National Park Service, Civil War), Ancestry.com, http://www.Ancestry.com.

147   Historical Data Systems, comp., American Civil War Soldiers (Online publication - Provo, UT, USA: Ancestry.com Operations Inc, 1999. Original data - Data compiled by Historical Data Systems of Kingston, MA form the following list of works. Copyright 1997-2000 Historical Data Systems, Inc. PO Box 35 Duxbury. Original), Ancestry.com, http://www.Ancestry.com, Side served: Confederacy; State served: Alabama; Enlistment date:.

148   Ancestry.com, Alabama Marriage Collection, 1800-1969 (Online publication - Provo, UT, USA: Ancestry.com Operations Inc, 2006. Original data - Alabama Center for Health Statistics. Alabama Marriage Index, 1936-1969. Alabama

Center for Health Statistics, Montgomery, Alabama. Dodd, Jordan R., et. al. Early America), Ancestry.com, http://www.Ancestry.com, Marriage date: 16 Oct 1845 Marriage place: Calhoun, Alabama.

149   National Cemetery Administration, U.S. Veterans Gravesites, ca.1775-2006 (Online publication - Provo, UT, USA: Ancestry.com Operations Inc, 2006. Original data - National Cemetery Administration. Nationwide Gravesite Locator. Original data: National Cemetery Administration. Nationwide Gravesite Locator), Ancestry.com, http://www.Ancestry.com, Birth date: 11/28/1828 Birth place: Death date: 08/09/1872 Death place: AL.

150   Ancestry.com, 1860 United States Federal Census (Online publication - Provo, UT, USA: Ancestry.com Operations, Inc., 2009. Images reproduced by FamilySearch. Original data - 1860 U.S. census, population schedule. NARA microfilm publication M653, 1,438 rolls. Washington, D.C.: National Archives and Records), Ancestry.com, http://www.Ancestry.com, Year: 1860; Census Place: Ranges 8 and 9, Calhoun, Alabama; Roll: ; Page: 313; Image: 29. Birth date: about 1829 Birth place: Georgia Residence date: 1860 Residence place: Ranges 8 and 9, Calhoun, Alabama, United States.

151   Ancestry.com, 1870 United States Federal Census (Online publication - Provo, UT, USA: Ancestry.com Operations, Inc., 2009. Images reproduced by FamilySearch. Original data - 1870 U.S. census, population schedules. NARA microfilm publication M593, 1,761 rolls. Washington, D.C.: National Archives and Record), Ancestry.com, http://www.Ancestry.com, Year: 1870; Census Place: Township 19 Range 4, Talladega, Alabama; Roll: M593_; Page: ; Image:. Birth date: about 1830 Birth place: Georgia Residence date: 1870 Residence place: Township 19 Range 4, Talladega, Alabama, United States.

152   Ancestry.com, Alabama Marriage Collection, 1800-1969 (Online publication - Provo, UT, USA: Ancestry.com Operations Inc, 2006. Original data - Alabama Center for Health Statistics. Alabama Marriage Index, 1936-1969. Alabama Center for Health Statistics, Montgomery, Alabama. Dodd, Jordan R., et. al. Early America), Ancestry.com, http://www.Ancestry.com, Marriage date: 5 Dec 1847 Marriage place: Calhoun, Alabama.

153   Ancestry.com and The Church of Jesus Christ of Latter-day Saints, 1880 United States Federal Census (Online publication - Provo, UT, USA: Ancestry.com Operations Inc, 2010. 1880 U.S. Census Index provided by The Church of Jesus Christ of Latter-day Saints © Copyright 1999 Intellectual Reserve, Inc. All rights reserved. All use is subject to the limited), Ancestry.com, http://www.Ancestry.com, Year: 1880; Census Place: June Bug, Calhoun, Alabama; Roll: 4; Family History Film: 1254004; Page: 538D; Enumeration District: 6; Image: 0637. Birth date: about 1832 Birth place: Alabama Residence date: 1880 Residence place: June Bug, Calhoun, Alabama, United States.

154   National Cemetery Administration, U.S. Veterans Gravesites, ca.1775-2006 (Online publication - Provo, UT, USA: Ancestry.com Operations Inc, 2006. Original data - National Cemetery Administration. Nationwide Gravesite Locator. Original data: National Cemetery Administration. Nationwide Gravesite Locator), Ancestry.com, http://www.Ancestry.com, Birth date: 01/29/1831 Birth place: Death date: 06/18/1892 Death place: AL.

155   National Park Service, U.S. Civil War Soldiers, 1861-1865 (Online publication - Provo, UT, USA: Ancestry.com Operations Inc, 2007. Original data - National Park Service, Civil War Soldiers and Sailors System, online, http://www.itd.nps.gov/cwss/, acquired 2007. Original data: National Park Service, Civil War), Ancestry.com, http://www.Ancestry.com.

156   Historical Data Systems, comp., American Civil War Soldiers (Online publication - Provo, UT, USA: Ancestry.com Operations Inc, 1999. Original data - Data compiled by Historical Data Systems of Kingston, MA form the following list of works. Copyright 1997-2000 Historical Data Systems, Inc. PO Box 35 Duxbury. Original), Ancestry.com, http://www.Ancestry.com, Side served: Confederacy; State served: Alabama; Enlistment date:.

157   Ancestry.com, Alabama Marriage Collection, 1800-1969 (Online publication - Provo, UT, USA: Ancestry.com Operations Inc, 2006. Original data - Alabama Center for Health Statistics. Alabama Marriage Index, 1936-1969. Alabama Center for Health Statistics, Montgomery, Alabama. Dodd, Jordan R., et. al. Early America), Ancestry.com, http://www.Ancestry.com, Marriage date: 12 Jan 1848 Marriage place: Calhoun, Alabama.

158   Ancestry.com, 1870 United States Federal Census (Online publication - Provo, UT, USA: Ancestry.com Operations, Inc., 2009. Images reproduced by FamilySearch. Original data - 1870 U.S. census, population schedules. NARA microfilm publication M593, 1,761 rolls. Washington, D.C.: National Archives and Record), Ancestry.com, http://www.Ancestry.com, Year: 1870; Census Place: Precinct 4, Calhoun, Alabama; Roll: M593_; Page: ; Image:. Birth date: about 1833 Birth place: Georgia Residence date: 1870 Residence place: Precinct 4, Calhoun, Alabama, United States.

159   Ancestry.com and The Church of Jesus Christ of Latter-day Saints, 1880 United States Federal Census (Online publication - Provo, UT, USA: Ancestry.com Operations Inc, 2010. 1880 U.S. Census Index provided by The Church of Jesus Christ of Latter-day Saints © Copyright 1999 Intellectual Reserve, Inc. All rights reserved. All use is subject to the limited), Ancestry.com, http://www.Ancestry.com, Year: 1880; Census Place: June Bug, Calhoun, Alabama; Roll: 4; Family History Film: 1254004; Page: 531B; Enumeration District: 6; Image: 0623. Birth date: about 1833 Birth place: Georgia Residence date: 1880 Residence place: June Bug, Calhoun, Alabama, United States.

160   Ancestry.com, 1850 United States Federal Census (Online publication - Provo, UT, USA: Ancestry.com Operations, Inc., 2009. Images reproduced by FamilySearch. Original data - Seventh Census of the United States, 1850; (National Archives Microfilm Publication M432, 1009 rolls); Records of the Bureau of the), Ancestry.com, http://www.Ancestry.com, Year: 1850; Census Place: Subdivision 29, Benton, Alabama; Roll: M432_1; Page: 360B; Image:. Birth date: about 1831 Birth place: Georgia Residence date: 1850 Residence place: Subdivision 29, Benton, Alabama.

161   Ancestry.com, Alabama Marriage Collection, 1800-1969 (Online publication - Provo, UT, USA: Ancestry.com Operations Inc, 2006. Original data - Alabama Center for Health Statistics. Alabama Marriage Index, 1936-1969. Alabama Center for Health Statistics, Montgomery, Alabama. Dodd, Jordan R., et. al. Early America), Ancestry.com, http://www.Ancestry.com, Marriage date: 16 Oct 1855 Marriage place: Calhoun, Alabama.

162   Ancestry.com and The Church of Jesus Christ of Latter-day Saints, 1880 United States Federal Census (Online publication - Provo, UT, USA: Ancestry.com Operations Inc, 2010. 1880 U.S. Census Index provided by The Church of Jesus Christ of Latter-day Saints © Copyright 1999 Intellectual Reserve, Inc. All rights reserved. All use is subject to the limited), Ancestry.com, http://www.Ancestry.com, Year: 1880; Census Place: , Cherokee, Alabama; Roll: 6; Family History Film: 1254006; Page: 394D; Enumeration District: 27; Image:. Birth date: about 1835 Birth place: Alabama Residence date: 1880 Residence place: Cherokee, Alabama, United States.

163   Ancestry.com, Alabama Marriage Collection, 1800-1969 (Online publication - Provo, UT, USA: Ancestry.com Operations Inc, 2006. Original data - Alabama Center for Health Statistics. Alabama Marriage Index, 1936-1969. Alabama Center for Health Statistics, Montgomery, Alabama. Dodd, Jordan R., et. al. Early America), Ancestry.com, http://www.Ancestry.com, Marriage date: 2 Dec 1856 Marriage place: Calhoun, Alabama.

164   National Cemetery Administration, U.S. Veterans Gravesites, ca.1775-2006 (Online publication - Provo, UT, USA: Ancestry.com Operations Inc, 2006. Original data - National Cemetery Administration. Nationwide Gravesite Locator. Original data: National Cemetery Administration. Nationwide Gravesite Locator), Ancestry.com, http://www.Ancestry.com, Birth date: 02/19/1837 Birth place: Death date: 03/04/1888 Death place: AL.

165   Ancestry.com and The Church of Jesus Christ of Latter-day Saints, 1880 United States Federal Census (Online publication - Provo, UT, USA: Ancestry.com Operations Inc, 2010. 1880 U.S. Census Index provided by The Church of Jesus Christ of Latter-day Saints © Copyright 1999 Intellectual Reserve, Inc. All rights reserved. All use is subject to the limited), Ancestry.com, http://www.Ancestry.com, Year: 1880; Census Place: June Bug, Calhoun, Alabama; Roll: 4; Family History Film: 1254004; Page: 535A; Enumeration District: 6; Image: 0630. Birth date: about 1836 Birth place: Alabama Residence date: 1880 Residence place: June Bug, Calhoun, Alabama, United States.

166   Ancestry.com, Alabama Marriage Collection, 1800-1969 (Online publication - Provo, UT, USA: Ancestry.com Operations Inc, 2006. Original data - Alabama Center for Health Statistics. Alabama Marriage Index, 1936-1969. Alabama Center for Health Statistics, Montgomery, Alabama. Dodd, Jordan R., et. al. Early America), Ancestry.com, http://www.Ancestry.com, Marriage date: 16 Jan 1856 Marriage place: Calhoun, Alabama.

167   Ancestry.com, Alabama Civil War Muster Rolls, 1861-1865 (Online publication - Provo, UT, USA: Ancestry.com Operations, Inc., 2010. Original data - Alabama Dept. of Archives and History. Muster rolls of Alabama Civil War units, SG025006-25100. Alabama Department of Archives and History, Montgomery, AL. Original data), Ancestry.com, http://www.Ancestry.com, Residence date: Residence place: Alabama, United States.

168   National Park Service, U.S. Civil War Soldiers, 1861-1865 (Online publication - Provo, UT, USA: Ancestry.com Operations Inc, 2007. Original data - National Park Service, Civil War Soldiers and Sailors System, online, http://www.itd.nps.gov/cwss/, acquired 2007. Original data: National Park Service, Civil War), Ancestry.com, http://www.Ancestry.com.

169   Ancestry.com, Alabama Marriage Collection, 1800-1969 (Online publication - Provo, UT, USA: Ancestry.com Operations Inc, 2006. Original data - Alabama Center for Health Statistics. Alabama Marriage Index, 1936-1969. Alabama Center for Health Statistics, Montgomery, Alabama. Dodd, Jordan R., et. al. Early America), Ancestry.com, http://www.Ancestry.com, Marriage date: 8 Sep 1853 Marriage place: Calhoun, Alabama.

170   Ancestry.com, Alabama Marriage Collection, 1800-1969 (Online publication - Provo, UT, USA: Ancestry.com Operations Inc, 2006. Original data - Alabama Center for Health Statistics. Alabama Marriage Index, 1936-1969. Alabama Center for Health Statistics, Montgomery, Alabama. Dodd, Jordan R., et. al. Early America), Ancestry.com, http://www.Ancestry.com, Marriage date: 8 Sep 1853 Marriage place: Calhoun, Alabama.

171   Ancestry.com and The Church of Jesus Christ of Latter-day Saints, 1880 United States Federal Census (Online publication - Provo, UT, USA: Ancestry.com Operations Inc, 2010. 1880 U.S. Census Index provided by The Church of Jesus Christ of Latter-day Saints © Copyright 1999 Intellectual Reserve, Inc. All rights reserved. All use is subject to the limited), Ancestry.com, http://www.Ancestry.com, Year: 1880; Census Place: June Bug, Calhoun, Alabama; Roll: 4; Family History Film: 1254004; Page: 534D; Enumeration District: 6; Image: 0629. Birth date: about 1839 Birth place: Alabama Residence date: 1880 Residence place: June Bug, Calhoun, Alabama, United States.

172   Ancestry.com, 1900 United States Federal Census (Online publication - Provo, UT, USA: Ancestry.com Operations Inc, 2004. Original data - United States of America, Bureau of the Census. Twelfth Census of the United States, 1900. Washington, D.C.: National Archives and Records Administration, 1900. T623, 18), Ancestry.com, http://www.Ancestry.com, Year: 1900; Census Place: Bluff Eye, Talladega, Alabama; Roll: T623_40; Page: 9A; Enumeration District: 84. Birth date: Mar 1839 Birth place: Alabama Residence date: 1900 Residence place: Bluff Eye, Talladega, Alabama.

173   Ancestry.com, 1850 United States Federal Census (Online publication - Provo, UT, USA: Ancestry.com Operations, Inc., 2009. Images reproduced by FamilySearch. Original data - Seventh Census of the United States, 1850; (National Archives Microfilm Publication M432, 1009 rolls); Records of the Bureau of the), Ancestry.com, http://www.Ancestry.com, Year: 1850; Census Place: Subdivision 29, Benton, Alabama; Roll: M432_1; Page: 360B; Image:. Birth date: about 1840 Birth place: Alabama Residence date: 1850 Residence place: Subdivision 29, Benton, Alabama.

125

174   Ancestry.com, 1860 United States Federal Census (Online publication - Provo, UT, USA: Ancestry.com Operations, Inc., 2009. Images reproduced by FamilySearch. Original data - 1860 U.S. census, population schedule. NARA microfilm publication M653, 1,438 rolls. Washington, D.C.: National Archives and Records), Ancestry.com, http://www.Ancestry.com, Year: 1860; Census Place: Ranges 8 and 9, Calhoun, Alabama; Roll: ; Page: 328; Image: 44. Birth date: about 1840 Birth place: Alabama Residence date: 1860 Residence place: Ranges 8 and 9, Calhoun, Alabama, United States.

175   Ancestry.com, 1870 United States Federal Census (Online publication - Provo, UT, USA: Ancestry.com Operations, Inc., 2009. Images reproduced by FamilySearch. Original data - 1870 U.S. census, population schedules. NARA microfilm publication M593, 1,761 rolls. Washington, D.C.: National Archives and Record), Ancestry.com, http://www.Ancestry.com, Year: 1870; Census Place: Township 15, Calhoun, Alabama; Roll: M593_; Page: ; Image:. Birth date: about 1838 Birth place: Alabama Residence date: 1870 Residence place: Township 15, Calhoun, Alabama, United States.

176   Ancestry.com, Alabama Marriage Collection, 1800-1969 (Online publication - Provo, UT, USA: Ancestry.com Operations Inc, 2006. Original data - Alabama Center for Health Statistics. Alabama Marriage Index, 1936-1969. Alabama Center for Health Statistics, Montgomery, Alabama. Dodd, Jordan R., et. al. Early America), Ancestry.com, http://www.Ancestry.com, Marriage date: 27 Aug 1857 Marriage place: Calhoun, Alabama.

177   Ancestry.com, 1910 United States Federal Census (Online publication - Provo, UT, USA: Ancestry.com Operations Inc, 2006. Original data - Thirteenth Census of the United States, 1910 (NARA microfilm publication T624, 1,178 rolls). Records of the Bureau of the Census, Record Group 29. National Archives, Washington), Ancestry.com, http://www.Ancestry.com, Year: 1910; Census Place: Precinct 1, Talladega, Alabama; Roll: ; Page: ; Enumeration District: ; Image:. Birth date: about 1844 Birth place: Alabama Residence date: 1910 Residence place: Precinct 1, Talladega, Alabama.

178   National Cemetery Administration, U.S. Veterans Gravesites, ca.1775-2006 (Online publication - Provo, UT, USA: Ancestry.com Operations Inc, 2006. Original data - National Cemetery Administration. Nationwide Gravesite Locator. Original data: National Cemetery Administration. Nationwide Gravesite Locator), Ancestry.com, http://www.Ancestry.com, Birth date: 07/26/1843 Birth place: Death date: 02/17/1914 Death place: AL.

179   Ancestry.com and The Church of Jesus Christ of Latter-day Saints, 1880 United States Federal Census (Online publication - Provo, UT, USA: Ancestry.com Operations Inc, 2010. 1880 U.S. Census Index provided by The Church of Jesus Christ of Latter-day Saints © Copyright 1999 Intellectual Reserve, Inc. All rights reserved. All use is subject to the limited), Ancestry.com, http://www.Ancestry.com, Year: 1880; Census Place: June Bug, Calhoun, Alabama; Roll: 4; Family History Film: 1254004; Page: 534D; Enumeration District: 6; Image: 0629. Birth date: about 1844 Birth place: Alabama Residence date: 1880 Residence place: June Bug, Calhoun, Alabama, United States.

180   Ancestry.com, 1850 United States Federal Census (Online publication - Provo, UT, USA: Ancestry.com Operations, Inc., 2009. Images reproduced by FamilySearch. Original data - Seventh Census of the United States, 1850; (National Archives Microfilm Publication M432, 1009 rolls); Records of the Bureau of the), Ancestry.com, http://www.Ancestry.com, Year: 1850; Census Place: Subdivision 29, Benton, Alabama; Roll: M432_1; Page: 360B; Image:. Birth date: about 1844 Birth place: Alabama Residence date: 1850 Residence place: Subdivision 29, Benton, Alabama.

181   Ancestry.com, 1900 United States Federal Census (Online publication - Provo, UT, USA: Ancestry.com Operations Inc, 2004. Original data - United States of America, Bureau of the Census. Twelfth Census of the United States, 1900. Washington, D.C.: National Archives and Records Administration, 1900. T623, 18), Ancestry.com, http://www.Ancestry.com, Year: 1900; Census Place: Reed Brake, Marshall, Alabama; Roll: T623_30; Page: 8A; Enumeration District: 97. Birth date: Jul 1843 Birth place: Alabama Marriage date: 1870 Marriage place: Residence date: 1900 Residence place: Reed Brake, Marshall, Alabama.

182   Ancestry.com, 1860 United States Federal Census (Online publication - Provo, UT, USA: Ancestry.com Operations, Inc., 2009. Images reproduced by FamilySearch. Original data - 1860 U.S. census, population schedule. NARA microfilm publication M653, 1,438 rolls. Washington, D.C.: National Archives and Records), Ancestry.com, http://www.Ancestry.com, Year: 1860; Census Place: Ranges 8 and 9, Calhoun, Alabama; Roll: ; Page: 327; Image: 43. Birth date: about 1843 Birth place: Alabama Residence date: 1860 Residence place: Ranges 8 and 9, Calhoun, Alabama, United States.

183   Ancestry.com, Alabama Marriage Collection, 1800-1969 (Online publication - Provo, UT, USA: Ancestry.com Operations Inc, 2006. Original data - Alabama Center for Health Statistics. Alabama Marriage Index, 1936-1969. Alabama Center for Health Statistics, Montgomery, Alabama. Dodd, Jordan R., et. al. Early America), Ancestry.com, http://www.Ancestry.com, Marriage date: 24 Oct 1860 Marriage place: Calhoun, Alabama.

184   Ancestry.com, 1910 United States Federal Census (Online publication - Provo, UT, USA: Ancestry.com Operations Inc, 2006. Original data - Thirteenth Census of the United States, 1910 (NARA microfilm publication T624, 1,178 rolls). Records of the Bureau of the Census, Record Group 29. National Archives, Washington), Ancestry.com, http://www.Ancestry.com, Identifies spouse and less than 1 year of marriage.

185   Ancestry.com, 1830 United States Federal Census (Online publication - Provo, UT, USA: Ancestry.com Operations, Inc., 2010. Images reproduced by FamilySearch. Original data - Fifth Census of the United States, 1830. (NARA microfilm publication M19, 201 rolls). Records of the Bureau of the Census, Record Gr), Ancestry.com, http://www.Ancestry.com, Year: 1830; Census Place: , Montgomery, Alabama; Roll: ; Page:. Residence date: 1830 Residence place: Montgomery, Alabama, United States.

126

186   Ancestry.com, City directory and history of Montgomery, Alabama (Online publication - Provo, UT: The Generations Network, Inc., 2004. Original data - Beale, Jesse D.. City directory and history of Montgomery, Alabama : with a summary of events in that history, calendarically arranged, besides other valuable and useful in), Ancestry.com, http://www.Ancestry.com, Residence date: 1818-1878Residence place: Montgomery, Alabama, USA.

187   Ancestry.com, City directory and history of Montgomery, Alabama (Online publication - Provo, UT: The Generations Network, Inc., 2004. Original data - Beale, Jesse D.. City directory and history of Montgomery, Alabama : with a summary of events in that history, calendarically arranged, besides other valuable and useful in), Ancestry.com, http://www.Ancestry.com, Cites death of Caleb Moncrief.

188   Ancestry.com, 1850 United States Federal Census (Online publication - Provo, UT, USA: Ancestry.com Operations, Inc., 2009. Images reproduced by FamilySearch. Original data - Seventh Census of the United States, 1850; (National Archives Microfilm Publication M432, 1009 rolls); Records of the Bureau of the), Ancestry.com, http://www.Ancestry.com, Year: 1850; Census Place: Division 59, Meriwether, Georgia; Roll: M432_77; Page: 335B; Image:. Birth date: about 1821 Birth place: Georgia Residence date: 1850 Residence place: Division 59, Meriwether, Georgia.

189   Ancestry.com, 1900 United States Federal Census (Online publication - Provo, UT, USA: Ancestry.com Operations Inc, 2004. Original data - United States of America, Bureau of the Census. Twelfth Census of the United States, 1900. Washington, D.C.: National Archives and Records Administration, 1900. T623, 18), Ancestry.com, http://www.Ancestry.com, Year: 1900; Census Place: Police Jury Ward 8, Claiborne, Louisiana; Roll: T623_562; Page: 11A; Enumeration District: 27. Birth date: Mar 1821 Birth place: Georgia Marriage date: 1854 Marriage place: Residence date: 1900 Residence place: Ward 8 (South Half), Claiborne, Louisiana.

190   Ancestry.com and The Church of Jesus Christ of Latter-day Saints, 1880 United States Federal Census (Online publication - Provo, UT, USA: Ancestry.com Operations Inc, 2010. 1880 U.S. Census Index provided by The Church of Jesus Christ of Latter-day Saints © Copyright 1999 Intellectual Reserve, Inc. All rights reserved. All use is subject to the limited), Ancestry.com, http://www.Ancestry.com, Year: 1880; Census Place: 6th Ward, Lincoln, Louisiana; Roll: 456; Family History Film: 1254456; Page: 28C; Enumeration District: 38; Image: 0058. Birth date: about 1821 Birth place: Georgia Residence date: 1880 Residence place: 6th Ward, Lincoln, Louisiana, United States.

191   Ancestry.com, 1860 United States Federal Census (Online publication - Provo, UT, USA: Ancestry.com Operations, Inc., 2009. Images reproduced by FamilySearch. Original data - 1860 U.S. census, population schedule. NARA microfilm publication M653, 1,438 rolls. Washington, D.C.: National Archives and Records), Ancestry.com, http://www.Ancestry.com, Year: 1860; Census Place: Moss, Columbia, Arkansas; Roll: ; Page: 309; Image: 311. Birth date: about 1821 Birth place: Georgia Residence date: 1860 Residence place: Moss, Columbia, Arkansas, United States.

192   Ancestry.com, 1850 United States Federal Census (Online publication - Provo, UT, USA: Ancestry.com Operations, Inc., 2009. Images reproduced by FamilySearch. Original data - Seventh Census of the United States, 1850; (National Archives Microfilm Publication M432, 1009 rolls); Records of the Bureau of the), Ancestry.com, http://www.Ancestry.com, Year: 1850; Census Place: Montgomery Ward 3, Montgomery, Alabama; Roll: M432_12; Page: 145A; Image:. Birth date: about 1829 Birth place: Alabama Residence date: 1850 Residence place: Montgomery Ward 3, Montgomery, Alabama.

193   Ancestry.com, 1860 United States Federal Census (Online publication - Provo, UT, USA: Ancestry.com Operations, Inc., 2009. Images reproduced by FamilySearch. Original data - 1860 U.S. census, population schedule. NARA microfilm publication M653, 1,438 rolls. Washington, D.C.: National Archives and Records), Ancestry.com, http://www.Ancestry.com, Year: 1860; Census Place: East Side Cahaba River, Bibb, Alabama; Roll: ; Page: 839; Image: 193. Birth date: about 1829 Birth place: Alabama Residence date: 1860 Residence place: East Side Cahaba River, Bibb, Alabama, United States.

194   Ancestry.com, 1850 United States Federal Census (Online publication - Provo, UT, USA: Ancestry.com Operations, Inc., 2009. Images reproduced by FamilySearch. Original data - Seventh Census of the United States, 1850; (National Archives Microfilm Publication M432, 1009 rolls); Records of the Bureau of the), Ancestry.com, http://www.Ancestry.com, Year: 1850; Census Place: Montgomery Ward 3, Montgomery, Alabama; Roll: M432_12; Page: 145A; Image:. Birth date: about 1832 Birth place: Alabama Residence date: 1850 Residence place: Montgomery Ward 3, Montgomery, Alabama.

195   Ancestry.com, 1850 United States Federal Census (Online publication - Provo, UT, USA: Ancestry.com Operations, Inc., 2009. Images reproduced by FamilySearch. Original data - Seventh Census of the United States, 1850; (National Archives Microfilm Publication M432, 1009 rolls); Records of the Bureau of the), Ancestry.com, http://www.Ancestry.com, Year: 1850; Census Place: Montgomery Ward 3, Montgomery, Alabama; Roll: M432_12; Page: 145A; Image:. Birth date: about 1834 Birth place: Alabama Residence date: 1850 Residence place: Montgomery Ward 3, Montgomery, Alabama.

196   Ancestry.com, 1860 United States Federal Census (Online publication - Provo, UT, USA: Ancestry.com Operations, Inc., 2009. Images reproduced by FamilySearch. Original data - 1860 U.S. census, population schedule. NARA microfilm publication M653, 1,438 rolls. Washington, D.C.: National Archives and Records), Ancestry.com, http://www.Ancestry.com, Year: 1860; Census Place: Division 1, Montgomery, Alabama; Roll: ; Page: 217; Image: 217. Birth date: about 1836 Birth place: Alabama Residence date: 1860 Residence place: Division 1, Montgomery, Alabama, United States.

197   Ancestry.com, 1900 United States Federal Census (Online publication - Provo, UT, USA: Ancestry.com Operations Inc, 2004. Original data - United States of America, Bureau of the Census. Twelfth Census of the United

States, 1900. Washington, D.C.: National Archives and Records Administration, 1900. T623, 18), Ancestry.com, http://www.Ancestry.com, Year: 1900; Census Place: Clanton, Chilton, Alabama; Roll: T623_7; Page: 20A; Enumeration District: 27. Birth date: Aug 1834 Birth place: Alabama Marriage date: 1855 Marriage place: Residence date: 1900 Residence place: Clanton Town, Chilton, Alabama.

198   Ancestry.com, 1910 United States Federal Census (Online publication - Provo, UT, USA: Ancestry.com Operations Inc, 2006. Original data - Thirteenth Census of the United States, 1910 (NARA microfilm publication T624, 1,178 rolls). Records of the Bureau of the Census, Record Group 29. National Archives, Washington), Ancestry.com, http://www.Ancestry.com, Year: 1910; Census Place: Precinct 4, Chilton, Alabama; Roll: ; Page: ; Enumeration District: ; Image:. Birth date: about 1834 Birth place: Alabama Residence date: 1910 Residence place: Precinct 4, Chilton, Alabama.

199   Ancestry.com, 1870 United States Federal Census (Online publication - Provo, UT, USA: Ancestry.com Operations, Inc., 2009. Images reproduced by FamilySearch. Original data - 1870 U.S. census, population schedules. NARA microfilm publication M593, 1,761 rolls. Washington, D.C.: National Archives and Record), Ancestry.com, http://www.Ancestry.com, Year: 1870; Census Place: Montgomery Ward 5, Montgomery, Alabama; Roll: M593_; Page: ; Image:. Birth date: about 1834 Birth place: Alabama Residence date: 1870 Residence place: Montgomery Ward 5, Montgomery, Alabama, United States.

200   Ancestry.com and The Church of Jesus Christ of Latter-day Saints, 1880 United States Federal Census (Online publication - Provo, UT, USA: Ancestry.com Operations Inc, 2010. 1880 U.S. Census Index provided by The Church of Jesus Christ of Latter-day Saints © Copyright 1999 Intellectual Reserve, Inc. All rights reserved. All use is subject to the limited), Ancestry.com, http://www.Ancestry.com, Year: 1880; Census Place: Clanton, Chilton, Alabama; Roll: 6; Family History Film: 1254006; Page: 74A; Enumeration District: 29; Image: 0595. Birth date: about 1835 Birth place: Georgia Residence date: 1880 Residence place: Clanton, Chilton, Alabama, United States.

201   Ancestry.com, Alabama Marriage Collection, 1800-1969 (Online publication - Provo, UT, USA: Ancestry.com Operations Inc, 2006. Original data - Alabama Center for Health Statistics. Alabama Marriage Index, 1936-1969. Alabama Center for Health Statistics, Montgomery, Alabama. Dodd, Jordan R., et. al. Early America), Ancestry.com, http://www.Ancestry.com, Marriage date: 8 Jun 1854 Marriage place: Montgomery, Alabama.

202   Dodd, Jordan R., comp., Alabama Marriages, 1809-1920 (Selected Counties) (Online publication - Provo, UT, USA: The Generations Network, Inc., 1999. Original data - Early American Marriages: Alabama, 1800 to 1920. Original data: Early American Marriages: Alabama, 1800 to 1920), Ancestry.com, http://www.Ancestry.com, Marriage date: 08 Jun 1854 Marriage place: Montgomery.

203   Ancestry.com, 1900 United States Federal Census (Online publication - Provo, UT, USA: Ancestry.com Operations Inc, 2004. Original data - United States of America, Bureau of the Census. Twelfth Census of the United States, 1900. Washington, D.C.: National Archives and Records Administration, 1900. T623, 18), Ancestry.com, http://www.Ancestry.com, Year: 1900; Census Place: Clanton, Chilton, Alabama; Roll: T623_7; Page: 20A; Enumeration District: 27. Birth date: Sep 1826 Birth place: Indiana Marriage date: 1855 Marriage place: Residence date: 1900 Residence place: Clanton Town, Chilton, Alabama.

204   Ancestry.com, 1860 United States Federal Census (Online publication - Provo, UT, USA: Ancestry.com Operations, Inc., 2009. Images reproduced by FamilySearch. Original data - 1860 U.S. census, population schedule. NARA microfilm publication M653, 1,438 rolls. Washington, D.C.: National Archives and Records), Ancestry.com, http://www.Ancestry.com, Year: 1860; Census Place: , Pontotoc, Mississippi; Roll: ; Page: 844; Image: 366. Birth date: about 1823 Birth place: Georgia Residence date: 1860 Residence place: Pontotoc, Mississippi, United States.

205   National Park Service, U.S. Civil War Soldiers, 1861-1865 (Online publication - Provo, UT, USA: Ancestry.com Operations Inc, 2007. Original data - National Park Service, Civil War Soldiers and Sailors System, online, http://www.itd.nps.gov/cwss/, acquired 2007. Original data: National Park Service, Civil War), Ancestry.com, http://www.Ancestry.com.

206   Ancestry.com, 1860 United States Federal Census (Online publication - Provo, UT, USA: Ancestry.com Operations, Inc., 2009. Images reproduced by FamilySearch. Original data - 1860 U.S. census, population schedule. NARA microfilm publication M653, 1,438 rolls. Washington, D.C.: National Archives and Records), Ancestry.com, http://www.Ancestry.com, Year: 1860; Census Place: , Pontotoc, Mississippi; Roll: ; Page: 601; Image: 121. Birth date: about 1819 Birth place: Georgia Residence date: 1860 Residence place: Pontotoc, Mississippi, United States.

207   Ancestry.com, 1900 United States Federal Census (Online publication - Provo, UT, USA: Ancestry.com Operations Inc, 2004. Original data - United States of America, Bureau of the Census. Twelfth Census of the United States, 1900. Washington, D.C.: National Archives and Records Administration, 1900. T623, 18), Ancestry.com, http://www.Ancestry.com, Year: 1900; Census Place: Justice Precinct 6, Hopkins, Texas; Roll: T623_1646; Page: 3A; Enumeration District: 57. Birth date: Oct 1820 Birth place: Georgia Residence date: 1900 Residence place: Justice Precinct 6, Hopkins, Texas.

208   Ancestry.com, Alabama Marriage Collection, 1800-1969 (Online publication - Provo, UT, USA: Ancestry.com Operations Inc, 2006. Original data - Alabama Center for Health Statistics. Alabama Marriage Index, 1936-1969. Alabama Center for Health Statistics, Montgomery, Alabama. Dodd, Jordan R., et. al. Early America), Ancestry.com, http://www.Ancestry.com, Marriage date: 21 Jul 1840 Marriage place: Calhoun, Alabama.

209   Ancestry.com, Alabama Marriage Collection, 1800-1969 (Online publication - Provo, UT, USA: Ancestry.com Operations Inc, 2006. Original data - Alabama Center for Health Statistics. Alabama Marriage Index, 1936-1969. Alabama

Center for Health Statistics, Montgomery, Alabama. Dodd, Jordan R., et. al. Early America), Ancestry.com, http://www.Ancestry.com, Marriage date: 21 Jul 1840 Marriage place: Calhoun, Alabama.

210   Hunting For Bears, comp., Mississippi Marriages, 1776-1935 (Online publication - Provo, UT, USA: Ancestry.com Operations Inc, 2004. Original data - Mississippi marriage information taken from county courthouse records. Many of these records were extracted from copies of the original records in microfilm, microfiche,), Ancestry.com, http://www.Ancestry.com, Marriage date: 19 Oct 1850 Marriage place: Pontotoc, Mississippi.

211   Ancestry.com and The Church of Jesus Christ of Latter-day Saints, 1880 United States Federal Census (Online publication - Provo, UT, USA: Ancestry.com Operations Inc, 2010. 1880 U.S. Census Index provided by The Church of Jesus Christ of Latter-day Saints © Copyright 1999 Intellectual Reserve, Inc. All rights reserved. All use is subject to the limited), Ancestry.com, http://www.Ancestry.com, Year: 1880; Census Place: Albany, Union, Mississippi; Roll: 666; Family History Film: 1254666; Page: 260A; Enumeration District: 202; Image: 0660. Birth date: about 1830 Birth place: Georgia Residence date: 1880 Residence place: Albany, Union, Mississippi, United States.

212   Ancestry.com and The Church of Jesus Christ of Latter-day Saints, 1880 United States Federal Census (Online publication - Provo, UT, USA: Ancestry.com Operations Inc, 2010. 1880 U.S. Census Index provided by The Church of Jesus Christ of Latter-day Saints © Copyright 1999 Intellectual Reserve, Inc. All rights reserved. All use is subject to the limited), Ancestry.com, http://www.Ancestry.com, Year: 1880; Census Place: District 2, Dyer, Tennessee; Roll: 1253; Family History Film: 1255253; Page: 17A; Enumeration District: 5; Image:. Birth date: about 1836 Birth place: Alabama Residence date: 1880 Residence place: District 2, Dyer, Tennessee, United States.

213   Ancestry.com, 1860 United States Federal Census (Online publication - Provo, UT, USA: Ancestry.com Operations, Inc., 2009. Images reproduced by FamilySearch. Original data - 1860 U.S. census, population schedule. NARA microfilm publication M653, 1,438 rolls. Washington, D.C.: National Archives and Records), Ancestry.com, http://www.Ancestry.com, Year: 1860; Census Place: , Pontotoc, Mississippi; Roll: ; Page: 840; Image: 362. Birth date: about 1837 Birth place: Alabama Residence date: 1860 Residence place: Pontotoc, Mississippi, United States.

214   Ancestry.com, 1860 United States Federal Census (Online publication - Provo, UT, USA: Ancestry.com Operations, Inc., 2009. Images reproduced by FamilySearch. Original data - 1860 U.S. census, population schedule. NARA microfilm publication M653, 1,438 rolls. Washington, D.C.: National Archives and Records), Ancestry.com, http://www.Ancestry.com, Year: 1860; Census Place: , Pontotoc, Mississippi; Roll: ; Page: 843; Image: 365. Birth date: about 1839 Birth place: Alabama Residence date: 1860 Residence place: Pontotoc, Mississippi, United States.

215   Ancestry.com, 1870 United States Federal Census (Online publication - Provo, UT, USA: Ancestry.com Operations, Inc., 2009. Images reproduced by FamilySearch. Original data - 1870 U.S. census, population schedules. NARA microfilm publication M593, 1,761 rolls. Washington, D.C.: National Archives and Record), Ancestry.com, http://www.Ancestry.com, Year: 1870; Census Place: Township 15, Calhoun, Alabama; Roll: M593_; Page: ; Image:. Birth date: about 1845 Birth place: Alabama Residence date: 1870 Residence place: Township 15, Calhoun, Alabama, United States.

216   Ancestry.com, 1850 United States Federal Census (Online publication - Provo, UT, USA: Ancestry.com Operations, Inc., 2009. Images reproduced by FamilySearch. Original data - Seventh Census of the United States, 1850; (National Archives Microfilm Publication M432, 1009 rolls); Records of the Bureau of the), Ancestry.com, http://www.Ancestry.com, Year: 1850; Census Place: Subdivision 29, Benton, Alabama; Roll: M432_1; Page: 347A; Image:. Birth date: about 1845 Birth place: Alabama Residence date: 1850 Residence place: Subdivision 29, Benton, Alabama.

217   Ancestry.com, 1860 United States Federal Census (Online publication - Provo, UT, USA: Ancestry.com Operations, Inc., 2009. Images reproduced by FamilySearch. Original data - 1860 U.S. census, population schedule. NARA microfilm publication M653, 1,438 rolls. Washington, D.C.: National Archives and Records), Ancestry.com, http://www.Ancestry.com, Year: 1860; Census Place: Ranges 8 and 9, Calhoun, Alabama; Roll: ; Page: 305; Image: 21. Birth date: about 1846 Birth place: Alabama Residence date: 1860 Residence place: Ranges 8 and 9, Calhoun, Alabama, United States.

218   Ancestry.com, 1850 United States Federal Census (Online publication - Provo, UT, USA: Ancestry.com Operations, Inc., 2009. Images reproduced by FamilySearch. Original data - Seventh Census of the United States, 1850; (National Archives Microfilm Publication M432, 1009 rolls); Records of the Bureau of the), Ancestry.com, http://www.Ancestry.com, Year: 1850; Census Place: Subdivision 29, Benton, Alabama; Roll: M432_1; Page: 334A; Image:. Birth date: about 1821 Birth place: Georgia Residence date: 1850 Residence place: Subdivision 29, Benton, Alabama.

219   Ancestry.com, 1860 United States Federal Census (Online publication - Provo, UT, USA: Ancestry.com Operations, Inc., 2009. Images reproduced by FamilySearch. Original data - 1860 U.S. census, population schedule. NARA microfilm publication M653, 1,438 rolls. Washington, D.C.: National Archives and Records), Ancestry.com, http://www.Ancestry.com, Year: 1860; Census Place: Ranges 8 and 9, Calhoun, Alabama; Roll: ; Page: 330; Image: 46. Birth date: about 1820 Birth place: Georgia Residence date: 1860 Residence place: Ranges 8 and 9, Calhoun, Alabama, United States.

220   Ancestry.com, 1860 United States Federal Census (Online publication - Provo, UT, USA: Ancestry.com Operations, Inc., 2009. Images reproduced by FamilySearch. Original data - 1860 U.S. census, population schedule. NARA microfilm publication M653, 1,438 rolls. Washington, D.C.: National Archives and Records), Ancestry.com, http://www.Ancestry.com, Year: 1860; Census Place: Ranges 8 and 9, Calhoun, Alabama; Roll: ; Page: 330; Image: 46.

Birth date: about 1843 Birth place: Alabama Residence date: 1860 Residence place: Ranges 8 and 9, Calhoun, Alabama, United States.

221   Ancestry.com, 1870 United States Federal Census (Online publication - Provo, UT, USA: Ancestry.com Operations, Inc., 2009. Images reproduced by FamilySearch. Original data - 1870 U.S. census, population schedules. NARA microfilm publication M593, 1,761 rolls. Washington, D.C.: National Archives and Record), Ancestry.com, http://www.Ancestry.com, Year: 1870; Census Place: Township 15, Calhoun, Alabama; Roll: M593_; Page: ; Image:. Birth date: about 1844 Birth place: Alabama Residence date: 1870 Residence place: Township 15, Calhoun, Alabama, United States.

222   Ancestry.com, 1850 United States Federal Census (Online publication - Provo, UT, USA: Ancestry.com Operations, Inc., 2009. Images reproduced by FamilySearch. Original data - Seventh Census of the United States, 1850; (National Archives Microfilm Publication M432, 1009 rolls); Records of the Bureau of the), Ancestry.com, http://www.Ancestry.com, Year: 1850; Census Place: Subdivision 29, Benton, Alabama; Roll: M432_1; Page: 334A; Image:. Birth date: about 1843 Birth place: Alabama Residence date: 1850 Residence place: Subdivision 29, Benton, Alabama.

223   Ancestry.com, 1870 United States Federal Census (Online publication - Provo, UT, USA: Ancestry.com Operations, Inc., 2009. Images reproduced by FamilySearch. Original data - 1870 U.S. census, population schedules. NARA microfilm publication M593, 1,761 rolls. Washington, D.C.: National Archives and Record), Ancestry.com, http://www.Ancestry.com, Year: 1870; Census Place: Texas, St Francis, Arkansas; Roll: M593_; Page: ; Image:. Birth date: about 1848 Birth place: Alabama Residence date: 1870 Residence place: Texas, St Francis, Arkansas, United States.

224   Ancestry.com, 1860 United States Federal Census (Online publication - Provo, UT, USA: Ancestry.com Operations, Inc., 2009. Images reproduced by FamilySearch. Original data - 1860 U.S. census, population schedule. NARA microfilm publication M653, 1,438 rolls. Washington, D.C.: National Archives and Records), Ancestry.com, http://www.Ancestry.com, Year: 1860; Census Place: Ranges 8 and 9, Calhoun, Alabama; Roll: ; Page: 330; Image: 46. Birth date: about 1848 Birth place: Alabama Residence date: 1860 Residence place: Ranges 8 and 9, Calhoun, Alabama, United States.

225   Ancestry.com, Alabama Civil War Muster Rolls, 1861-1865 (Online publication - Provo, UT, USA: Ancestry.com Operations, Inc., 2010. Original data - Alabama Dept. of Archives and History. Muster rolls of Alabama Civil War units, SG025006-25100. Alabama Department of Archives and History, Montgomery, AL. Original data), Ancestry.com, http://www.Ancestry.com, Residence date: Residence place: Alabama, United States.

226   Ancestry.com, 1860 United States Federal Census (Online publication - Provo, UT, USA: Ancestry.com Operations, Inc., 2009. Images reproduced by FamilySearch. Original data - 1860 U.S. census, population schedule. NARA microfilm publication M653, 1,438 rolls. Washington, D.C.: National Archives and Records), Ancestry.com, http://www.Ancestry.com, Year: 1860; Census Place: Ranges 8 and 9, Calhoun, Alabama; Roll: ; Page: 330; Image: 46. Birth date: about 1849 Birth place: Alabama Residence date: 1860 Residence place: Ranges 8 and 9, Calhoun, Alabama, United States.

227   Ancestry.com, 1870 United States Federal Census (Online publication - Provo, UT, USA: Ancestry.com Operations, Inc., 2009. Images reproduced by FamilySearch. Original data - 1870 U.S. census, population schedules. NARA microfilm publication M593, 1,761 rolls. Washington, D.C.: National Archives and Record), Ancestry.com, http://www.Ancestry.com, Year: 1870; Census Place: Township 15, Calhoun, Alabama; Roll: M593_; Page: ; Image:. Birth date: about 1849 Birth place: Alabama Residence date: 1870 Residence place: Township 15, Calhoun, Alabama, United States.

228   Ancestry.com, 1860 United States Federal Census (Online publication - Provo, UT, USA: Ancestry.com Operations, Inc., 2009. Images reproduced by FamilySearch. Original data - 1860 U.S. census, population schedule. NARA microfilm publication M653, 1,438 rolls. Washington, D.C.: National Archives and Records), Ancestry.com, http://www.Ancestry.com, Year: 1860; Census Place: Ranges 8 and 9, Calhoun, Alabama; Roll: ; Page: 330; Image: 46. Birth date: about 1851 Birth place: Alabama Residence date: 1860 Residence place: Ranges 8 and 9, Calhoun, Alabama, United States.

229   Ancestry.com, 1870 United States Federal Census (Online publication - Provo, UT, USA: Ancestry.com Operations, Inc., 2009. Images reproduced by FamilySearch. Original data - 1870 U.S. census, population schedules. NARA microfilm publication M593, 1,761 rolls. Washington, D.C.: National Archives and Record), Ancestry.com, http://www.Ancestry.com, Year: 1870; Census Place: Township 15, Calhoun, Alabama; Roll: M593_; Page: ; Image:. Birth date: about 1852 Birth place: Alabama Residence date: 1870 Residence place: Township 15, Calhoun, Alabama, United States.

230   Ancestry.com, 1870 United States Federal Census (Online publication - Provo, UT, USA: Ancestry.com Operations, Inc., 2009. Images reproduced by FamilySearch. Original data - 1870 U.S. census, population schedules. NARA microfilm publication M593, 1,761 rolls. Washington, D.C.: National Archives and Record), Ancestry.com, http://www.Ancestry.com, Year: 1870; Census Place: Township 15, Calhoun, Alabama; Roll: M593_; Page: ; Image:. Birth date: about 1855 Birth place: Alabama Residence date: 1870 Residence place: Township 15, Calhoun, Alabama, United States.

231   Ancestry.com, 1860 United States Federal Census (Online publication - Provo, UT, USA: Ancestry.com Operations, Inc., 2009. Images reproduced by FamilySearch. Original data - 1860 U.S. census, population schedule. NARA microfilm publication M653, 1,438 rolls. Washington, D.C.: National Archives and Records), Ancestry.com,

http://www.Ancestry.com, Year: 1860; Census Place: Ranges 8 and 9, Calhoun, Alabama; Roll: ; Page: 330; Image: 46. Birth date: about 1855 Birth place: Alabama Residence date: 1860 Residence place: Ranges 8 and 9, Calhoun, Alabama, United States.

232   Ancestry.com, 1860 United States Federal Census (Online publication - Provo, UT, USA: Ancestry.com Operations, Inc., 2009. Images reproduced by FamilySearch. Original data - 1860 U.S. census, population schedule. NARA microfilm publication M653, 1,438 rolls. Washington, D.C.: National Archives and Records), Ancestry.com, http://www.Ancestry.com, Year: 1860; Census Place: Ranges 8 and 9, Calhoun, Alabama; Roll: ; Page: 313; Image: 29. Birth date: about 1859 Birth place: Alabama Residence date: 1860 Residence place: Ranges 8 and 9, Calhoun, Alabama, United States.

233   Ancestry.com, 1860 United States Federal Census (Online publication - Provo, UT, USA: Ancestry.com Operations, Inc., 2009. Images reproduced by FamilySearch. Original data - 1860 U.S. census, population schedule. NARA microfilm publication M653, 1,438 rolls. Washington, D.C.: National Archives and Records), Ancestry.com, http://www.Ancestry.com, Year: 1860; Census Place: Ranges 8 and 9, Calhoun, Alabama; Roll: ; Page: 330; Image: 46. Birth date: about 1858 Birth place: Alabama Residence date: 1860 Residence place: Ranges 8 and 9, Calhoun, Alabama, United States.

234   Ancestry.com, 1870 United States Federal Census (Online publication - Provo, UT, USA: Ancestry.com Operations, Inc., 2009. Images reproduced by FamilySearch. Original data - 1870 U.S. census, population schedules. NARA microfilm publication M593, 1,761 rolls. Washington, D.C.: National Archives and Record), Ancestry.com, http://www.Ancestry.com, Year: 1870; Census Place: Township 15, Calhoun, Alabama; Roll: M593_; Page: ; Image:. Birth date: about 1858 Birth place: Alabama Residence date: 1870 Residence place: Township 15, Calhoun, Alabama, United States.

235   Ancestry.com, 1850 United States Federal Census (Online publication - Provo, UT, USA: Ancestry.com Operations, Inc., 2009. Images reproduced by FamilySearch. Original data - Seventh Census of the United States, 1850; (National Archives Microfilm Publication M432, 1009 rolls); Records of the Bureau of the), Ancestry.com, http://www.Ancestry.com, Year: 1850; Census Place: Subdivision 29, Benton, Alabama; Roll: M432_1; Page: 334A; Image:. Birth date: about 1817 Birth place: South Carolina Residence date: 1850 Residence place: Subdivision 29, Benton, Alabama.

236   Ancestry.com, 1870 United States Federal Census (Online publication - Provo, UT, USA: Ancestry.com Operations, Inc., 2009. Images reproduced by FamilySearch. Original data - 1870 U.S. census, population schedules. NARA microfilm publication M593, 1,761 rolls. Washington, D.C.: National Archives and Record), Ancestry.com, http://www.Ancestry.com, Year: 1870; Census Place: Township 12 Range 7, Etowah, Alabama; Roll: M593_; Page: ; Image:. Birth date: about 1818 Birth place: South Carolina Residence date: 1870 Residence place: Township 12 Range 7, Etowah, Alabama, United States.

237   Ancestry.com and The Church of Jesus Christ of Latter-day Saints, 1880 United States Federal Census (Online publication - Provo, UT, USA: Ancestry.com Operations Inc, 2010. 1880 U.S. Census Index provided by The Church of Jesus Christ of Latter-day Saints © Copyright 1999 Intellectual Reserve, Inc. All rights reserved. All use is subject to the limited), Ancestry.com, http://www.Ancestry.com, Year: 1880; Census Place: Ball Play, Etowah, Alabama; Roll: 13; Family History Film: 1254013; Page: 319A; Enumeration District: 66; Image:. Birth date: about 1840 Birth place: Tennessee Residence date: 1880 Residence place: Ball Play, Etowah, Alabama, United States.

238   Ancestry.com, 1850 United States Federal Census (Online publication - Provo, UT, USA: Ancestry.com Operations, Inc., 2009. Images reproduced by FamilySearch. Original data - Seventh Census of the United States, 1850; (National Archives Microfilm Publication M432, 1009 rolls); Records of the Bureau of the), Ancestry.com, http://www.Ancestry.com, Year: 1850; Census Place: Subdivision 29, Benton, Alabama; Roll: M432_1; Page: 334A; Image:. Birth date: about 1841 Birth place: Alabama Residence date: 1850 Residence place: Subdivision 29, Benton, Alabama.

239   Ancestry.com, 1900 United States Federal Census (Online publication - Provo, UT, USA: Ancestry.com Operations Inc, 2004. Original data - United States of America, Bureau of the Census. Twelfth Census of the United States, 1900. Washington, D.C.: National Archives and Records Administration, 1900. T623, 18), Ancestry.com, http://www.Ancestry.com, Year: 1900; Census Place: Hokes Bluff, Etowah, Alabama; Roll: T623_15; Page: 14B; Enumeration District: 151. Birth date: Oct 1841 Birth place: Alabama Marriage date: 1863 Marriage place: Residence date: 1900 Residence place: Precinct 4 Hokes Bluff, Etowah, Alabama.

240   Ancestry.com, 1920 United States Federal Census (Online publication - Provo, UT, USA: Ancestry.com Operations Inc, 2010. Images reproduced by FamilySearch. Original data - Fourteenth Census of the United States, 1920. (NARA microfilm publication T625, 2076 rolls). Records of the Bureau of the Census, Record), Ancestry.com, http://www.Ancestry.com, Year: 1920; Census Place: Louisville, Barbour, Alabama; Roll: T625_3; Page: 12A; Enumeration District: 17; Image:. Birth date: about 1841 Birth place: Alabama Residence date: 1920 Residence place: Louisville, Barbour, Alabama.

241   Ancestry.com, 1870 United States Federal Census (Online publication - Provo, UT, USA: Ancestry.com Operations, Inc., 2009. Images reproduced by FamilySearch. Original data - 1870 U.S. census, population schedules. NARA microfilm publication M593, 1,761 rolls. Washington, D.C.: National Archives and Record), Ancestry.com, http://www.Ancestry.com, Year: 1870; Census Place: Township 12 Range 7, Etowah, Alabama; Roll: M593_; Page: ; Image:. Birth date: about 1852 Birth place: Alabama Residence date: 1870 Residence place: Township 12 Range 7, Etowah, Alabama, United States.

242   Ancestry.com, 1860 United States Federal Census (Online publication - Provo, UT, USA: Ancestry.com Operations, Inc., 2009. Images reproduced by FamilySearch. Original data - 1860 U.S. census, population schedule. NARA microfilm publication M653, 1,438 rolls. Washington, D.C.: National Archives and Records), Ancestry.com, http://www.Ancestry.com, Year: 1860; Census Place: Division 1, Cherokee, Alabama; Roll: ; Page: 265; Image: 271. Birth date: about 1852 Birth place: Alabama Residence date: 1860 Residence place: Division 1, Cherokee, Alabama, United States.

243   Ancestry.com and The Church of Jesus Christ of Latter-day Saints, 1880 United States Federal Census (Online publication - Provo, UT, USA: Ancestry.com Operations Inc, 2010. 1880 U.S. Census Index provided by The Church of Jesus Christ of Latter-day Saints © Copyright 1999 Intellectual Reserve, Inc. All rights reserved. All use is subject to the limited), Ancestry.com, http://www.Ancestry.com, Year: 1880; Census Place: Gadsden and Turkey Town, Etowah, Alabama; Roll: 13; Family History Film: 1254013; Page: 327B; Enumeration District: 66; Image:. Birth date: about 1854 Birth place: Alabama Residence date: 1880 Residence place: Gadsden and Turkey Town, Etowah, Alabama, United States.

244   Ancestry.com, 1900 United States Federal Census (Online publication - Provo, UT, USA: Ancestry.com Operations Inc, 2004. Original data - United States of America, Bureau of the Census. Twelfth Census of the United States, 1900. Washington, D.C.: National Archives and Records Administration, 1900. T623, 18), Ancestry.com, http://www.Ancestry.com, Year: 1900; Census Place: Justice Precinct 1, Camp, Texas; Roll: T623_1618; Page: 19A; Enumeration District: 13. Birth date: Nov 1853 Birth place: Alabama Marriage date: 1873 Marriage place: Residence date: 1900 Residence place: Justice Precinct 1 (Excl. Pittsburg Town), Camp, Texas.

245   Ancestry.com, 1920 United States Federal Census (Online publication - Provo, UT, USA: Ancestry.com Operations Inc, 2010. Images reproduced by FamilySearch. Original data - Fourteenth Census of the United States, 1920. (NARA microfilm publication T625, 2076 rolls). Records of the Bureau of the Census, Record), Ancestry.com, http://www.Ancestry.com, Year: 1920; Census Place: Justice Precinct 1, Camp, Texas; Roll: T625_1785; Page: 14A; Enumeration District: 24; Image:. Birth date: about 1854 Birth place: Alabama Residence date: 1920 Residence place: Justice Precinct 1, Camp, Texas.

246   Ancestry.com, Alabama Marriage Collection, 1800-1969 (Online publication - Provo, UT, USA: Ancestry.com Operations Inc, 2006. Original data - Alabama Center for Health Statistics. Alabama Marriage Index, 1936-1969. Alabama Center for Health Statistics, Montgomery, Alabama. Dodd, Jordan R., et. al. Early America), Ancestry.com, http://www.Ancestry.com, Marriage date: 15 Dec 1874 Marriage place: Chambers, Alabama.

247   Ancestry.com, Texas Death Index, 1903-2000 (Online publication - Provo, UT, USA: Ancestry.com Operations Inc, 2006. Original data - Texas Department of Health. Texas Death Indexes, 1903-2000. Austin, TX, USA: Texas Department of Health, State Vital Statistics Unit. Original data: Texas Department of H), Ancestry.com, http://www.Ancestry.com, Death date: 15 Sep 1933 Death place: Camp, Texas.

248   Ancestry.com, Alabama Civil War Muster Rolls, 1861-1865 (Online publication - Provo, UT, USA: Ancestry.com Operations, Inc., 2010. Original data - Alabama Dept. of Archives and History. Muster rolls of Alabama Civil War units, SG025006-25100. Alabama Department of Archives and History, Montgomery, AL. Original data), Ancestry.com, http://www.Ancestry.com, Residence date: Residence place: Alabama, United States.

249   Ancestry.com, Alabama Marriage Collection, 1800-1969 (Online publication - Provo, UT, USA: Ancestry.com Operations Inc, 2006. Original data - Alabama Center for Health Statistics. Alabama Marriage Index, 1936-1969. Alabama Center for Health Statistics, Montgomery, Alabama. Dodd, Jordan R., et. al. Early America), Ancestry.com, http://www.Ancestry.com, Marriage date: 25 Apr 1847 Marriage place: Calhoun, Alabama.

250   Ancestry.com, Alabama Marriage Collection, 1800-1969 (Online publication - Provo, UT, USA: Ancestry.com Operations Inc, 2006. Original data - Alabama Center for Health Statistics. Alabama Marriage Index, 1936-1969. Alabama Center for Health Statistics, Montgomery, Alabama. Dodd, Jordan R., et. al. Early America), Ancestry.com, http://www.Ancestry.com, Marriage date: 25 Apr 1847 Marriage place: Calhoun, Alabama.

251   Ancestry.com, 1860 United States Federal Census (Online publication - Provo, UT, USA: Ancestry.com Operations, Inc., 2009. Images reproduced by FamilySearch. Original data - 1860 U.S. census, population schedule. NARA microfilm publication M653, 1,438 rolls. Washington, D.C.: National Archives and Records), Ancestry.com, http://www.Ancestry.com, Year: 1860; Census Place: Ranges 8 and 9, Calhoun, Alabama; Roll: ; Page: 417; Image: 137. Birth date: about 1828 Birth place: Georgia Residence date: 1860 Residence place: Ranges 8 and 9, Calhoun, Alabama, United States.

252   Ancestry.com, U.S. General Land Office Records, 1796-1907 (Online publication - Provo, UT, USA: Ancestry.com Operations Inc, 2008. Original data - United States. Bureau of Land Management, General Land Office Records. Automated Records Project; Federal Land Patents, State Volumes. Springfield, Virginia: Bureau of L), Ancestry.com, http://www.Ancestry.com, Residence date: Residence place: United States.

253   Ancestry.com, U.S. General Land Office Records, 1796-1907 (Online publication - Provo, UT, USA: Ancestry.com Operations Inc, 2008. Original data - United States. Bureau of Land Management, General Land Office Records. Automated Records Project; Federal Land Patents, State Volumes. Springfield, Virginia: Bureau of L), Ancestry.com, http://www.Ancestry.com, Residence date: Residence place: United States.

254   Ancestry.com, 1850 United States Federal Census (Online publication - Provo, UT, USA: Ancestry.com Operations, Inc., 2009. Images reproduced by FamilySearch. Original data - Seventh Census of the United States, 1850; (National Archives Microfilm Publication M432, 1009 rolls); Records of the Bureau of the), Ancestry.com,

http://www.Ancestry.com, Year: 1850; Census Place: District 27, Cherokee, Alabama; Roll: M432_3; Page: 84B; Image:. Birth date: about 1828 Birth place: Nk Residence date: 1850 Residence place: District 27, Cherokee, Alabama.

255   United States, Bureau of Land Management, Alabama Land Records (Online publication - Provo, UT, USA: Ancestry.com Operations Inc, 1997. Original data - United States. Bureau of Land Management. Alabama Pre-1908 Homestead and Cash Entry Patent and Cadastral Survey Plat Index. General Land Office Automated Records Project), Ancestry.com, http://www.Ancestry.com.

256   United States, Bureau of Land Management, Alabama Land Records (Online publication - Provo, UT, USA: Ancestry.com Operations Inc, 1997. Original data - United States. Bureau of Land Management. Alabama Pre-1908 Homestead and Cash Entry Patent and Cadastral Survey Plat Index. General Land Office Automated Records Project), Ancestry.com, http://www.Ancestry.com.

257   United States, Bureau of Land Management, Alabama Land Records (Online publication - Provo, UT, USA: Ancestry.com Operations Inc, 1997. Original data - United States. Bureau of Land Management. Alabama Pre-1908 Homestead and Cash Entry Patent and Cadastral Survey Plat Index. General Land Office Automated Records Project), Ancestry.com, http://www.Ancestry.com.

258   Ancestry.com, 1850 United States Federal Census (Online publication - Provo, UT, USA: Ancestry.com Operations, Inc., 2009. Images reproduced by FamilySearch. Original data - Seventh Census of the United States, 1850; (National Archives Microfilm Publication M432, 1009 rolls); Records of the Bureau of the), Ancestry.com, http://www.Ancestry.com, Year: 1850; Census Place: District 27, Cherokee, Alabama; Roll: M432_3; Page: 84B; Image:. Birth date: about 1831 Birth place: Georgia Residence date: 1850 Residence place: District 27, Cherokee, Alabama.

259   Ancestry.com, 1850 United States Federal Census (Online publication - Provo, UT, USA: Ancestry.com Operations, Inc., 2009. Images reproduced by FamilySearch. Original data - Seventh Census of the United States, 1850; (National Archives Microfilm Publication M432, 1009 rolls); Records of the Bureau of the), Ancestry.com, http://www.Ancestry.com, Year: 1850; Census Place: District 27, Cherokee, Alabama; Roll: M432_3; Page: 84B; Image:. Birth date: about 1833 Birth place: Georgia Residence date: 1850 Residence place: District 27, Cherokee, Alabama.

260   Ancestry.com and The Church of Jesus Christ of Latter-day Saints, 1880 United States Federal Census (Online publication - Provo, UT, USA: Ancestry.com Operations Inc, 2010. 1880 U.S. Census Index provided by The Church of Jesus Christ of Latter-day Saints © Copyright 1999 Intellectual Reserve, Inc. All rights reserved. All use is subject to the limited), Ancestry.com, http://www.Ancestry.com, Year: 1880; Census Place: , Cherokee, Alabama; Roll: 6; Family History Film: 1254006; Page: 394D; Enumeration District: 27; Image:. Birth date: about 1838 Birth place: Alabama Residence date: 1880 Residence place: Cherokee, Alabama, United States.

261   Ancestry.com, 1860 United States Federal Census (Online publication - Provo, UT, USA: Ancestry.com Operations, Inc., 2009. Images reproduced by FamilySearch. Original data - 1860 U.S. census, population schedule. NARA microfilm publication M653, 1,438 rolls. Washington, D.C.: National Archives and Records), Ancestry.com, http://www.Ancestry.com, Year: 1860; Census Place: Ranges 8 and 9, Calhoun, Alabama; Roll: ; Page: 411; Image: 131. Birth date: about 1841 Birth place: Alabama Residence date: 1860 Residence place: Ranges 8 and 9, Calhoun, Alabama, United States.

262   Ancestry.com and The Church of Jesus Christ of Latter-day Saints, 1880 United States Federal Census (Online publication - Provo, UI, USA: Ancestry.com Operations Inc, 2010. 1880 U.S. Census Index provided by The Church of Jesus Christ of Latter-day Saints © Copyright 1999 Intellectual Reserve, Inc. All rights reserved. All use is subject to the limited), Ancestry.com, http://www.Ancestry.com, Year: 1880; Census Place: Gadsden, Etowah, Alabama; Roll: 13; Family History Film: 1254013; Page: 375C; Enumeration District: 70; Image: 0257. Birth date: about 1840 Birth place: Alabama Residence date: 1880 Residence place: Gadsden, Etowah, Alabama, United States.

263   Ancestry.com and The Church of Jesus Christ of Latter-day Saints, 1880 United States Federal Census (Online publication - Provo, UT, USA: Ancestry.com Operations Inc, 2010. 1880 U.S. Census Index provided by The Church of Jesus Christ of Latter-day Saints © Copyright 1999 Intellectual Reserve, Inc. All rights reserved. All use is subject to the limited), Ancestry.com, http://www.Ancestry.com, Year: 1880; Census Place: , Cherokee, Alabama; Roll: 6; Family History Film: 1254006; Page: 396D; Enumeration District: 27; Image:. Birth date: about 1843 Birth place: Alabama Residence date: 1880 Residence place: Cherokee, Alabama, United States.

264   Ancestry.com, 1900 United States Federal Census (Online publication - Provo, UT, USA: Ancestry.com Operations Inc, 2004. Original data - United States of America, Bureau of the Census. Twelfth Census of the United States, 1900. Washington, D.C.: National Archives and Records Administration, 1900. T623, 18), Ancestry.com, http://www.Ancestry.com, Year: 1900; Census Place: Ball Play, Cherokee, Alabama; Roll: T623_6; Page: 7A; Enumeration District: 123. Birth date: Feb 1843 Birth place: Alabama Marriage date: 1868 Marriage place: Residence date: 1900 Residence place: Precinct 8 Ballplay, Cherokee, Alabama.

265   Ancestry.com, 1920 United States Federal Census (Online publication - Provo, UT, USA: Ancestry.com Operations Inc, 2010. Images reproduced by FamilySearch. Original data - Fourteenth Census of the United States, 1920. (NARA microfilm publication T625, 2076 rolls). Records of the Bureau of the Census, Record), Ancestry.com, http://www.Ancestry.com, Year: 1920; Census Place: Hokes Bluff, Etowah, Alabama; Roll: T625_15; Page: 9A; Enumeration District: 99; Image:. Birth date: about 1844 Birth place: Alabama Residence date: 1920 Residence place: Hokes Bluff, Etowah, Alabama.

266   Ancestry.com and The Church of Jesus Christ of Latter-day Saints, 1880 United States Federal Census (Online publication - Provo, UT, USA: Ancestry.com Operations Inc, 2010. 1880 U.S. Census Index provided by The Church of

Jesus Christ of Latter-day Saints © Copyright 1999 Intellectual Reserve, Inc. All rights reserved. All use is subject to the limited), Ancestry.com, http://www.Ancestry.com, Year: 1880; Census Place: , Cherokee, Alabama; Roll: 6; Family History Film: 1254006; Page: 441D; Enumeration District: 30; Image:. Birth date: about 1845 Birth place: Alabama Residence date: 1880 Residence place: Cherokee, Alabama, United States.

267   Ancestry.com, Alabama Deaths, 1908-59 (Online publication - Provo, UT, USA: Ancestry.com Operations Inc, 2000. Original data - State of Alabama. Index of Vital Records for Alabama: Deaths, 1908-1959. Montgomery, AL, USA: State of Alabama Center for Health Statistics, Record Services Division. Original), Ancestry.com, http://www.Ancestry.com, Death date: 29 Jan 1921 Death place: Etowah.

268   Ancestry.com, Alabama Marriage Collection, 1800-1969 (Online publication - Provo, UT, USA: Ancestry.com Operations Inc, 2006. Original data - Alabama Center for Health Statistics. Alabama Marriage Index, 1936-1969. Alabama Center for Health Statistics, Montgomery, Alabama. Dodd, Jordan R., et. al. Early America), Ancestry.com, http://www.Ancestry.com, Marriage date: 21 Dec 1874 Marriage place: Etowah, Alabama.

269   Ancestry.com, 1850 United States Federal Census (Online publication - Provo, UT, USA: Ancestry.com Operations, Inc., 2009. Images reproduced by FamilySearch. Original data - Seventh Census of the United States, 1850; (National Archives Microfilm Publication M432, 1009 rolls); Records of the Bureau of the), Ancestry.com, http://www.Ancestry.com, Year: 1850; Census Place: Subdivision 29, Benton, Alabama; Roll: M432_1; Page: 336A; Image:. Birth date: about 1828 Birth place: South Carolina Residence date: 1850 Residence place: Subdivision 29, Benton, Alabama.

270   Ancestry.com, 1860 United States Federal Census (Online publication - Provo, UT, USA: Ancestry.com Operations, Inc., 2009. Images reproduced by FamilySearch. Original data - 1860 U.S. census, population schedule. NARA microfilm publication M653, 1,438 rolls. Washington, D.C.: National Archives and Records), Ancestry.com, http://www.Ancestry.com, Year: 1860; Census Place: Ranges 8 and 9, Calhoun, Alabama; Roll: ; Page: 406; Image: 126. Birth date: about 1827 Birth place: South Carolina Residence date: 1860 Residence place: Ranges 8 and 9, Calhoun, Alabama, United States.

271   Ancestry.com, 1860 United States Federal Census (Online publication - Provo, UT, USA: Ancestry.com Operations, Inc., 2009. Images reproduced by FamilySearch. Original data - 1860 U.S. census, population schedule. NARA microfilm publication M653, 1,438 rolls. Washington, D.C.: National Archives and Records), Ancestry.com, http://www.Ancestry.com, Year: 1860; Census Place: Ranges 8 and 9, Calhoun, Alabama; Roll: ; Page: 406; Image: 126. Birth date: about 1852 Birth place: Mississippi Residence date: 1860 Residence place: Ranges 8 and 9, Calhoun, Alabama, United States.

272   Ancestry.com and The Church of Jesus Christ of Latter-day Saints, 1880 United States Federal Census (Online publication - Provo, UT, USA: Ancestry.com Operations Inc, 2010. 1880 U.S. Census Index provided by The Church of Jesus Christ of Latter-day Saints © Copyright 1999 Intellectual Reserve, Inc. All rights reserved. All use is subject to the limited), Ancestry.com, http://www.Ancestry.com, Year: 1880; Census Place: Phillips, Etowah, Alabama; Roll: 13; Family History Film: 1254013; Page: 412B; Enumeration District: 73; Image: 0332. Birth date: about 1860 Birth place: Alabama Residence date: 1880 Residence place: Phillips, Etowah, Alabama, United States.

273   Ancestry.com, 1860 United States Federal Census (Online publication - Provo, UT, USA: Ancestry.com Operations, Inc., 2009. Images reproduced by FamilySearch. Original data - 1860 U.S. census, population schedule. NARA microfilm publication M653, 1,438 rolls. Washington, D.C.: National Archives and Records), Ancestry.com, http://www.Ancestry.com, Year: 1860; Census Place: Ranges 8 and 9, Calhoun, Alabama; Roll: ; Page: 406; Image: 126. Birth date: about 1859 Birth place: Alabama Residence date: 1860 Residence place: Ranges 8 and 9, Calhoun, Alabama, United States.

274   Ancestry.com, 1900 United States Federal Census (Online publication - Provo, UT, USA: Ancestry.com Operations Inc, 2004. Original data - United States of America, Bureau of the Census. Twelfth Census of the United States, 1900. Washington, D.C.: National Archives and Records Administration, 1900. T623, 18), Ancestry.com, http://www.Ancestry.com, Year: 1900; Census Place: Justice Precinct 3, Grayson, Texas; Roll: T623_1640; Page: 15B; Enumeration District: 104. Birth date: Aug 1859 Birth place: Alabama Marriage date: 1881 Marriage place: Residence date: 1900 Residence place: Justice Precinct 3 (South Part), Grayson, Texas.

275   Ancestry.com, 1870 United States Federal Census (Online publication - Provo, UT, USA: Ancestry.com Operations, Inc., 2009. Images reproduced by FamilySearch. Original data - 1870 U.S. census, population schedules. NARA microfilm publication M593, 1,761 rolls. Washington, D.C.: National Archives and Record), Ancestry.com, http://www.Ancestry.com, Year: 1870; Census Place: Township 13 Range 6, Etowah, Alabama; Roll: M593_; Page: ; Image:. Birth date: about 1861 Birth place: Alabama Residence date: 1870 Residence place: Township 13 Range 6, Etowah, Alabama, United States.

276   Ancestry.com and The Church of Jesus Christ of Latter-day Saints, 1880 United States Federal Census (Online publication - Provo, UT, USA: Ancestry.com Operations Inc, 2010. 1880 U.S. Census Index provided by The Church of Jesus Christ of Latter-day Saints © Copyright 1999 Intellectual Reserve, Inc. All rights reserved. All use is subject to the limited), Ancestry.com, http://www.Ancestry.com, Year: 1880; Census Place: Phillips, Etowah, Alabama; Roll: 13; Family History Film: 1254013; Page: 412B; Enumeration District: 73; Image: 0332. Birth date: about 1863 Birth place: Alabama Residence date: 1880 Residence place: Phillips, Etowah, Alabama, United States.

277   Ancestry.com, 1900 United States Federal Census (Online publication - Provo, UT, USA: Ancestry.com Operations Inc, 2004. Original data - United States of America, Bureau of the Census. Twelfth Census of the United States, 1900. Washington, D.C.: National Archives and Records Administration, 1900. T623, 18), Ancestry.com,

http://www.Ancestry.com, Year: 1900; Census Place: Coloma, Cherokee, Alabama; Roll: T623_6; Page: 1A; Enumeration District: 122. Birth date: Sep 1861 Birth place: Alabama Marriage date: 1884 Marriage place: Residence date: 1900 Residence place: Precinct 7 Coloma, Cherokee, Alabama.

278   Ancestry.com, 1910 United States Federal Census (Online publication - Provo, UT, USA: Ancestry.com Operations Inc, 2006. Original data - Thirteenth Census of the United States, 1910 (NARA microfilm publication T624, 1,178 rolls). Records of the Bureau of the Census, Record Group 29. National Archives, Washington), Ancestry.com, http://www.Ancestry.com, Year: 1910; Census Place: Piedmont, Calhoun, Alabama; Roll: ; Page: ; Enumeration District: ; Image:. Birth date: 1861 Birth place: Alabama Residence date: 1910 Residence place: Piedmont, Calhoun, Alabama.

279   Ancestry.com, Alabama Deaths, 1908-59 (Online publication - Provo, UT, USA: Ancestry.com Operations Inc, 2000. Original data - State of Alabama. Index of Vital Records for Alabama: Deaths, 1908-1959. Montgomery, AL, USA: State of Alabama Center for Health Statistics, Record Services Division. Original), Ancestry.com, http://www.Ancestry.com, Death date: Apr 1926 Death place: Calhoun.

280   Ancestry.com, 1900 United States Federal Census (Online publication - Provo, UT, USA: Ancestry.com Operations Inc, 2004. Original data - United States of America, Bureau of the Census. Twelfth Census of the United States, 1900. Washington, D.C.: National Archives and Records Administration, 1900. T623, 18), Ancestry.com, http://www.Ancestry.com, Year: 1900; Census Place: Coloma, Cherokee, Alabama; Roll: T623_6; Page: 1A; Enumeration District: 122. Birth date: Jul 1861 Birth place: Georgia Marriage date: 1884 Marriage place: Residence date: 1900 Residence place: Precinct 7 Coloma, Cherokee, Alabama.

281   Ancestry.com and The Church of Jesus Christ of Latter-day Saints, 1880 United States Federal Census (Online publication - Provo, UT, USA: Ancestry.com Operations Inc, 2010. 1880 U.S. Census Index provided by The Church of Jesus Christ of Latter-day Saints © Copyright 1999 Intellectual Reserve, Inc. All rights reserved. All use is subject to the limited), Ancestry.com, http://www.Ancestry.com, Year: 1880; Census Place: Gadsden, Etowah, Alabama; Roll: 13; Family History Film: 1254013; Page: 375D; Enumeration District: 70; Image: 0258. Birth date: about 1859 Birth place: Alabama Residence date: 1880 Residence place: Gadsden, Etowah, Alabama, United States.

282   Ancestry.com and The Church of Jesus Christ of Latter-day Saints, 1880 United States Federal Census (Online publication - Provo, UT, USA: Ancestry.com Operations Inc, 2010. 1880 U.S. Census Index provided by The Church of Jesus Christ of Latter-day Saints © Copyright 1999 Intellectual Reserve, Inc. All rights reserved. All use is subject to the limited), Ancestry.com, http://www.Ancestry.com, Year: 1880; Census Place: Gadsden, Etowah, Alabama; Roll: 13; Family History Film: 1254013; Page: 375C; Enumeration District: 70; Image: 0257. Birth date: about 1860 Birth place: Alabama Residence date: 1880 Residence place: Gadsden, Etowah, Alabama, United States.

283   Ancestry.com, 1930 United States Federal Census (Online publication - Provo, UT, USA: Ancestry.com Operations Inc, 2002. Original data - United States of America, Bureau of the Census. Fifteenth Census of the United States, 1930. Washington, D.C.: National Archives and Records Administration, 1930. T626,), Ancestry.com, http://www.Ancestry.com, Year: 1930; Census Place: Gadsden, Etowah, Alabama; Roll: 16; Page: 21B; Enumeration District: 9; Image: 420.0. Birth date: about 1860 Birth place: Florida Residence date: 1930 Residence place: Gadsden, Etowah, Alabama.

284   Ancestry.com, 1920 United States Federal Census (Online publication - Provo, UT, USA: Ancestry.com Operations Inc, 2010. Images reproduced by FamilySearch. Original data - Fourteenth Census of the United States, 1920. (NARA microfilm publication T625, 2076 rolls). Records of the Bureau of the Census, Record), Ancestry.com, http://www.Ancestry.com, Year: 1920; Census Place: Gadsden Ward 4, Etowah, Alabama; Roll: T625_15; Page: 11B; Enumeration District: 94; Image:. Birth date: about 1861 Birth place: Georgia Residence date: 1920 Residence place: Gadsden Ward 4, Etowah, Alabama.

285   Ancestry.com and The Church of Jesus Christ of Latter-day Saints, 1880 United States Federal Census (Online publication - Provo, UT, USA: Ancestry.com Operations Inc, 2010. 1880 U.S. Census Index provided by The Church of Jesus Christ of Latter-day Saints © Copyright 1999 Intellectual Reserve, Inc. All rights reserved. All use is subject to the limited), Ancestry.com, http://www.Ancestry.com, Year: 1880; Census Place: Gadsden, Etowah, Alabama; Roll: 13; Family History Film: 1254013; Page: 375C; Enumeration District: 70; Image: 0257. Birth date: about 1864 Birth place: Alabama Residence date: 1880 Residence place: Gadsden, Etowah, Alabama, United States.

286   Ancestry.com and The Church of Jesus Christ of Latter-day Saints, 1880 United States Federal Census (Online publication - Provo, UT, USA: Ancestry.com Operations Inc, 2010. 1880 U.S. Census Index provided by The Church of Jesus Christ of Latter-day Saints © Copyright 1999 Intellectual Reserve, Inc. All rights reserved. All use is subject to the limited), Ancestry.com, http://www.Ancestry.com, Year: 1880; Census Place: Gadsden, Etowah, Alabama; Roll: 13; Family History Film: 1254013; Page: 375C; Enumeration District: 70; Image: 0257. Birth date: about 1866 Birth place: Alabama Residence date: 1880 Residence place: Gadsden, Etowah, Alabama, United States.

287   Ancestry.com and The Church of Jesus Christ of Latter-day Saints, 1880 United States Federal Census (Online publication - Provo, UT, USA: Ancestry.com Operations Inc, 2010. 1880 U.S. Census Index provided by The Church of Jesus Christ of Latter-day Saints © Copyright 1999 Intellectual Reserve, Inc. All rights reserved. All use is subject to the limited), Ancestry.com, http://www.Ancestry.com, Year: 1880; Census Place: Gadsden, Etowah, Alabama; Roll: 13; Family History Film: 1254013; Page: 375D; Enumeration District: 70; Image: 0258. Birth date: about 1868 Birth place: Alabama Residence date: 1880 Residence place: Gadsden, Etowah, Alabama, United States.

288   Ancestry.com and The Church of Jesus Christ of Latter-day Saints, 1880 United States Federal Census (Online publication - Provo, UT, USA: Ancestry.com Operations Inc, 2010. 1880 U.S. Census Index provided by The Church of Jesus Christ of Latter-day Saints © Copyright 1999 Intellectual Reserve, Inc. All rights reserved. All use is subject to the

limited), Ancestry.com, http://www.Ancestry.com, Year: 1880; Census Place: Gadsden, Etowah, Alabama; Roll: 13; Family History Film: 1254013; Page: 375D; Enumeration District: 70; Image: 0258. Birth date: about 1872 Birth place: Alabama Residence date: 1880 Residence place: Gadsden, Etowah, Alabama, United States.

289   Ancestry.com and The Church of Jesus Christ of Latter-day Saints, 1880 United States Federal Census (Online publication - Provo, UT, USA: Ancestry.com Operations Inc, 2010. 1880 U.S. Census Index provided by The Church of Jesus Christ of Latter-day Saints © Copyright 1999 Intellectual Reserve, Inc. All rights reserved. All use is subject to the limited), Ancestry.com, http://www.Ancestry.com, Year: 1880; Census Place: , Cherokee, Alabama; Roll: 6; Family History Film: 1254006; Page: 437D; Enumeration District: 30; Image:. Birth date: about 1851 Birth place: Alabama Residence date: 1880 Residence place: Cherokee, Alabama, United States.

290   Ancestry.com, 1860 United States Federal Census (Online publication - Provo, UT, USA: Ancestry.com Operations, Inc., 2009. Images reproduced by FamilySearch. Original data - 1860 U.S. census, population schedule. NARA microfilm publication M653, 1,438 rolls. Washington, D.C.: National Archives and Records), Ancestry.com, http://www.Ancestry.com, Year: 1860; Census Place: Division 1, Cherokee, Alabama; Roll: ; Page: 363; Image: 369. Birth date: about 1851 Birth place: Alabama Residence date: 1860 Residence place: Division 1, Cherokee, Alabama, United States.

291   Ancestry.com, 1870 United States Federal Census (Online publication - Provo, UT, USA: Ancestry.com Operations, Inc., 2009. Images reproduced by FamilySearch. Original data - 1870 U.S. census, population schedules. NARA microfilm publication M593, 1,761 rolls. Washington, D.C.: National Archives and Record), Ancestry.com, http://www.Ancestry.com, Year: 1870; Census Place: Township 12 Range 9, Cherokee, Alabama; Roll: M593_; Page: ; Image:. Birth date: about 1851 Birth place: Alabama Residence date: 1870 Residence place: Township 12 Range 9, Cherokee, Alabama, United States.

292   Ancestry.com and The Church of Jesus Christ of Latter-day Saints, 1880 United States Federal Census (Online publication - Provo, UT, USA: Ancestry.com Operations Inc, 2010. 1880 U.S. Census Index provided by The Church of Jesus Christ of Latter-day Saints © Copyright 1999 Intellectual Reserve, Inc. All rights reserved. All use is subject to the limited), Ancestry.com, http://www.Ancestry.com, Year: 1880; Census Place: , Cherokee, Alabama; Roll: 6; Family History Film: 1254006; Page: 437D; Enumeration District: 30; Image:. Birth date: about 1870 Birth place: Alabama Residence date: 1880 Residence place: Cherokee, Alabama, United States.

293   Ancestry.com, 1900 United States Federal Census (Online publication - Provo, UT, USA: Ancestry.com Operations Inc, 2004. Original data - United States of America, Bureau of the Census. Twelfth Census of the United States, 1900. Washington, D.C.: National Archives and Records Administration, 1900. T623, 18), Ancestry.com, http://www.Ancestry.com, Year: 1900; Census Place: Coloma, Cherokee, Alabama; Roll: T623_6; Page: 2B; Enumeration District: 122. Birth date: Oct 1870 Birth place: Alabama Residence date: 1900 Residence place: Precinct 7 Coloma, Cherokee, Alabama.

294   Ancestry.com and The Church of Jesus Christ of Latter-day Saints, 1880 United States Federal Census (Online publication - Provo, UT, USA: Ancestry.com Operations Inc, 2010. 1880 U.S. Census Index provided by The Church of Jesus Christ of Latter-day Saints © Copyright 1999 Intellectual Reserve, Inc. All rights reserved. All use is subject to the limited), Ancestry.com, http://www.Ancestry.com, Year: 1880; Census Place: , Cherokee, Alabama; Roll: 6; Family History Film: 1254006; Page: 437D; Enumeration District: 30; Image:. Birth date: about 1873 Birth place: Alabama Residence date: 1880 Residence place: Cherokee, Alabama, United States.

295   Ancestry.com, 1910 United States Federal Census (Online publication - Provo, UT, USA: Ancestry.com Operations Inc, 2006. Original data - Thirteenth Census of the United States, 1910 (NARA microfilm publication T624, 1,178 rolls). Records of the Bureau of the Census, Record Group 29. National Archives, Washington), Ancestry.com, http://www.Ancestry.com, Year: 1910; Census Place: Coalgate Ward 2, Coal, Oklahoma; Roll: ; Page: ; Enumeration District: ; Image:. Birth date: 1874 Birth place: Alabama Residence date: 1910 Residence place: Coalgate Ward 2, Coal, Oklahoma.

296   Ancestry.com, 1920 United States Federal Census (Online publication - Provo, UT, USA: Ancestry.com Operations Inc, 2010. Images reproduced by FamilySearch. Original data - Fourteenth Census of the United States, 1920. (NARA microfilm publication T625, 2076 rolls). Records of the Bureau of the Census, Record), Ancestry.com, http://www.Ancestry.com, Year: 1920; Census Place: Henry, Okmulgee, Oklahoma; Roll: T625_1476; Page: 10B; Enumeration District: 113; Image:. Birth date: about 1873 Birth place: Alabama Residence date: 1920 Residence place: Henry, Okmulgee, Oklahoma.

297   Ancestry.com, 1930 United States Federal Census (Online publication - Provo, UT, USA: Ancestry.com Operations Inc, 2002. Original data - United States of America, Bureau of the Census. Fifteenth Census of the United States, 1930. Washington, D.C.: National Archives and Records Administration, 1930. T626,), Ancestry.com, http://www.Ancestry.com, Year: 1930; Census Place: Borger, Hutchinson, Texas; Roll: 2360; Page: 13B; Enumeration District: 2; Image: 551.0. Birth date: about 1874 Birth place: Residence date: 1930 Residence place: Borger, Hutchinson, Texas.

298   Ancestry.com, Social Security Death Index (Online publication - Provo, UT, USA: Ancestry.com Operations Inc, 2010. Original data - Social Security Administration. Social Security Death Index, Master File. Social Security Administration. Original data: Social Security Administration. Social Security D), Ancestry.com, http://www.Ancestry.com, Number: 420-68-5443; Issue State: Alabama; Issue Date: 1965. Birth date: 20 Jan 1878 Birth place: Death date: Jul 1976 Death place: Birmingham, Jefferson, Alabama, United States of America.

299   Ancestry.com, 1910 United States Federal Census (Online publication - Provo, UT, USA: Ancestry.com Operations Inc, 2006. Original data - Thirteenth Census of the United States, 1910 (NARA microfilm publication T624, 1,178 rolls). Records of the Bureau of the Census, Record Group 29. National Archives, Washington), Ancestry.com, http://www.Ancestry.com, Year: 1910; Census Place: Coloma, Cherokee, Alabama; Roll: ; Page: ; Enumeration District: ; Image:. Birth date: 1879 Birth place: Alabama Residence date: 1910 Residence place: Coloma, Cherokee, Alabama.

300   Ancestry.com and The Church of Jesus Christ of Latter-day Saints, 1880 United States Federal Census (Online publication - Provo, UT, USA: Ancestry.com Operations Inc, 2010. 1880 U.S. Census Index provided by The Church of Jesus Christ of Latter-day Saints © Copyright 1999 Intellectual Reserve, Inc. All rights reserved. All use is subject to the limited), Ancestry.com, http://www.Ancestry.com, Year: 1880; Census Place: , Cherokee, Alabama; Roll: 6; Family History Film: 1254006; Page: 437D; Enumeration District: 30; Image:. Birth date: about 1878 Birth place: Alabama Residence date: 1880 Residence place: Cherokee, Alabama, United States.

301   Ancestry.com, 1900 United States Federal Census (Online publication - Provo, UT, USA: Ancestry.com Operations Inc, 2004. Original data - United States of America, Bureau of the Census. Twelfth Census of the United States, 1900. Washington, D.C.: National Archives and Records Administration, 1900. T623, 18), Ancestry.com, http://www.Ancestry.com, Year: 1900; Census Place: Coloma, Cherokee, Alabama; Roll: T623_6; Page: 2B; Enumeration District: 122. Birth date: Apr 1878 Birth place: Alabama Residence date: 1900 Residence place: Precinct 7 Coloma, Cherokee, Alabama.

302   Ancestry.com and The Church of Jesus Christ of Latter-day Saints, 1880 United States Federal Census (Online publication - Provo, UT, USA: Ancestry.com Operations Inc, 2010. 1880 U.S. Census Index provided by The Church of Jesus Christ of Latter-day Saints © Copyright 1999 Intellectual Reserve, Inc. All use is subject to the limited), Ancestry.com, http://www.Ancestry.com, Year: 1880; Census Place: , Cherokee, Alabama; Roll: 6; Family History Film: 1254006; Page: 437D; Enumeration District: 30; Image:. Birth date: about 1880 Birth place: Alabama Residence date: 1880 Residence place: Cherokee, Alabama, United States.

303   Ancestry.com, 1900 United States Federal Census (Online publication - Provo, UT, USA: Ancestry.com Operations Inc, 2004. Original data - United States of America, Bureau of the Census. Twelfth Census of the United States, 1900. Washington, D.C.: National Archives and Records Administration, 1900. T623, 18), Ancestry.com, http://www.Ancestry.com, Year: 1900; Census Place: Coloma, Cherokee, Alabama; Roll: T623_6; Page: 2B; Enumeration District: 122. Birth date: Feb 1880 Birth place: Alabama Residence date: 1900 Residence place: Precinct 7 Coloma, Cherokee, Alabama.

304   Ancestry.com, 1900 United States Federal Census (Online publication - Provo, UT, USA: Ancestry.com Operations Inc, 2004. Original data - United States of America, Bureau of the Census. Twelfth Census of the United States, 1900. Washington, D.C.: National Archives and Records Administration, 1900. T623, 18), Ancestry.com, http://www.Ancestry.com, Year: 1900; Census Place: Coloma, Cherokee, Alabama; Roll: T623_6; Page: 2B; Enumeration District: 122. Birth date: Oct 1882 Birth place: Alabama Residence date: 1900 Residence place: Precinct 7 Coloma, Cherokee, Alabama.

305   Ancestry.com, 1900 United States Federal Census (Online publication - Provo, UT, USA: Ancestry.com Operations Inc, 2004. Original data - United States of America, Bureau of the Census. Twelfth Census of the United States, 1900. Washington, D.C.: National Archives and Records Administration, 1900. T623, 18), Ancestry.com, http://www.Ancestry.com, Year: 1900; Census Place: Coloma, Cherokee, Alabama; Roll: T623_6; Page: 2B; Enumeration District: 122. Birth date: Apr 1885 Birth place: Alabama Residence date: 1900 Residence place: Precinct 7 Coloma, Cherokee, Alabama.

306   Ancestry.com, 1910 United States Federal Census (Online publication - Provo, UT, USA: Ancestry.com Operations Inc, 2006. Original data - Thirteenth Census of the United States, 1910 (NARA microfilm publication T624, 1,178 rolls). Records of the Bureau of the Census, Record Group 29. National Archives, Washington), Ancestry.com, http://www.Ancestry.com, Year: 1910; Census Place: Piedmont, Calhoun, Alabama; Roll: ; Page: ; Enumeration District: ; Image:. Birth date: 1885 Birth place: Alabama Residence date: 1910 Residence place: Piedmont, Calhoun, Alabama.

307   Ancestry.com, 1900 United States Federal Census (Online publication - Provo, UT, USA: Ancestry.com Operations Inc, 2004. Original data - United States of America, Bureau of the Census. Twelfth Census of the United States, 1900. Washington, D.C.: National Archives and Records Administration, 1900. T623, 18), Ancestry.com, http://www.Ancestry.com, Year: 1900; Census Place: Coloma, Cherokee, Alabama; Roll: T623_6; Page: 2B; Enumeration District: 122. Birth date: Mar 1888 Birth place: Alabama Residence date: 1900 Residence place: Precinct 7 Coloma, Cherokee, Alabama.

308   Ancestry.com, 1910 United States Federal Census (Online publication - Provo, UT, USA: Ancestry.com Operations Inc, 2006. Original data - Thirteenth Census of the United States, 1910 (NARA microfilm publication T624, 1,178 rolls). Records of the Bureau of the Census, Record Group 29. National Archives, Washington), Ancestry.com, http://www.Ancestry.com, Year: 1910; Census Place: Piedmont, Calhoun, Alabama; Roll: ; Page: ; Enumeration District: ; Image:. Birth date: 1889 Birth place: Alabama Residence date: 1910 Residence place: Piedmont, Calhoun, Alabama.

309   Ancestry.com, 1900 United States Federal Census (Online publication - Provo, UT, USA: Ancestry.com Operations Inc, 2004. Original data - United States of America, Bureau of the Census. Twelfth Census of the United States, 1900. Washington, D.C.: National Archives and Records Administration, 1900. T623, 18), Ancestry.com, http://www.Ancestry.com, Year: 1900; Census Place: Coloma, Cherokee, Alabama; Roll: T623_6; Page: 2B; Enumeration District: 122. Birth date: Sep 1890 Birth place: Alabama Residence date: 1900 Residence place: Precinct 7 Coloma, Cherokee, Alabama.

310 Ancestry.com, 1910 United States Federal Census (Online publication - Provo, UT, USA: Ancestry.com Operations Inc, 2006. Original data - Thirteenth Census of the United States, 1910 (NARA microfilm publication T624, 1,178 rolls). Records of the Bureau of the Census, Record Group 29. National Archives, Washington), Ancestry.com, http://www.Ancestry.com, Year: 1910; Census Place: Piedmont, Calhoun, Alabama; Roll: ; Page: ; Enumeration District: ; Image:. Birth date: 1891 Birth place: Alabama Residence date: 1910 Residence place: Piedmont, Calhoun, Alabama.

311 Ancesty.com and The Church of Jesus Christ of Latter-day Saints, 1880 United States Federal Census (Online publication - Provo, UT, USA: Ancestry.com Operations Inc, 2010. 1880 U.S. Census Index provided by The Church of Jesus Christ of Latter-day Saints © Copyright 1999 Intellectual Reserve, Inc. All rights reserved. All use is subject to the limited), Ancestry.com, http://www.Ancestry.com, Year: 1880; Census Place: , Cherokee, Alabama; Roll: 6; Family History Film: 1254006; Page: 396D; Enumeration District: 27; Image:. Birth date: about 1868 Birth place: Alabama Residence date: 1880 Residence place: Cherokee, Alabama, United States.

312 Ancestry.com and The Church of Jesus Christ of Latter-day Saints, 1880 United States Federal Census (Online publication - Provo, UT, USA: Ancestry.com Operations Inc, 2010. 1880 U.S. Census Index provided by The Church of Jesus Christ of Latter-day Saints © Copyright 1999 Intellectual Reserve, Inc. All rights reserved. All use is subject to the limited), Ancestry.com, http://www.Ancestry.com, Year: 1880; Census Place: , Cherokee, Alabama; Roll: 6; Family History Film: 1254006; Page: 396D; Enumeration District: 27; Image:. Birth date: about 1878 Birth place: Alabama Residence date: 1880 Residence place: Cherokee, Alabama, United States.

313 Ancestry.com, 1860 United States Federal Census (Online publication - Provo, UT, USA: Ancestry.com Operations, Inc., 2009. Images reproduced by FamilySearch. Original data - 1860 U.S. census, population schedule. NARA microfilm publication M653, 1,438 rolls. Washington, D.C.: National Archives and Records), Ancestry.com, http://www.Ancestry.com, Year: 1860; Census Place: Ranges 8 and 9, Calhoun, Alabama; Roll: ; Page: 313; Image: 29. Birth date: about 1830 Birth place: Georgia Residence date: 1860 Residence place: Ranges 8 and 9, Calhoun, Alabama, United States.

314 Ancestry.com, 1870 United States Federal Census (Online publication - Provo, UT, USA: Ancestry.com Operations, Inc., 2009. Images reproduced by FamilySearch. Original data - 1870 U.S. census, population schedules. NARA microfilm publication M593, 1,761 rolls. Washington, D.C.: National Archives and Record), Ancestry.com, http://www.Ancestry.com, Year: 1870; Census Place: Township 19 Range 4, Talladega, Alabama; Roll: M593_; Page: ; Image:. Birth date: about 1829 Birth place: Georgia Residence date: 1870 Residence place: Township 19 Range 4, Talladega, Alabama, United States.

315 Ancestry.com, 1860 United States Federal Census (Online publication - Provo, UT, USA: Ancestry.com Operations, Inc., 2009. Images reproduced by FamilySearch. Original data - 1860 U.S. census, population schedule. NARA microfilm publication M653, 1,438 rolls. Washington, D.C.: National Archives and Records), Ancestry.com, http://www.Ancestry.com, Year: 1860; Census Place: Ranges 8 and 9, Calhoun, Alabama; Roll: ; Page: 313; Image: 29. Birth date: about 1851 Birth place: Alabama Residence date: 1860 Residence place: Ranges 8 and 9, Calhoun, Alabama, United States.

316 Ancestry.com, 1870 United States Federal Census (Online publication - Provo, UT, USA: Ancestry.com Operations, Inc., 2009. Images reproduced by FamilySearch. Original data - 1870 U.S. census, population schedules. NARA microfilm publication M593, 1,761 rolls. Washington, D.C.: National Archives and Record), Ancestry.com, http://www.Ancestry.com, Year: 1870; Census Place: Township 18, Randolph, Alabama; Roll: M593_; Page: ; Image:. Birth date: about 1849 Birth place: Alabama Residence date: 1870 Residence place: Township 18, Randolph, Alabama, United States.

317 Ancestry.com, 1920 United States Federal Census (Online publication - Provo, UT, USA: Ancestry.com Operations Inc, 2010. Images reproduced by FamilySearch. Original data - Fourteenth Census of the United States, 1920. (NARA microfilm publication T625, 2076 rolls). Records of the Bureau of the Census, Record), Ancestry.com, http://www.Ancestry.com, Year: 1920; Census Place: Renfroe, Talladega, Alabama; Roll: T625_41; Page: 7A; Enumeration District: 141; Image:. Birth date: about 1850 Birth place: Alabama Residence date: 1920 Residence place: Renfroe, Talladega, Alabama.

318 Ancestry.com, Alabama Deaths, 1908-59 (Online publication - Provo, UT, USA: Ancestry.com Operations Inc, 2000. Original data - State of Alabama. Index of Vital Records for Alabama: Deaths, 1908-1959. Montgomery, AL, USA: State of Alabama Center for Health Statistics, Record Services Division. Original), Ancestry.com, http://www.Ancestry.com, Death date: Feb 1925 Death place: Talladega.

319 Ancestry.com and The Church of Jesus Christ of Latter-day Saints, 1880 United States Federal Census (Online publication - Provo, UT, USA: Ancestry.com Operations Inc, 2010. 1880 U.S. Census Index provided by The Church of Jesus Christ of Latter-day Saints © Copyright 1999 Intellectual Reserve, Inc. All rights reserved. All use is subject to the limited), Ancestry.com, http://www.Ancestry.com, Year: 1880; Census Place: June Bug, Calhoun, Alabama; Roll: 4; Family History Film: 1254004; Page: 535A; Enumeration District: 6; Image: 0630. Birth date: about 1853 Birth place: Alabama Residence date: 1880 Residence place: June Bug, Calhoun, Alabama, United States.

320 Ancestry.com, 1860 United States Federal Census (Online publication - Provo, UT, USA: Ancestry.com Operations, Inc., 2009. Images reproduced by FamilySearch. Original data - 1860 U.S. census, population schedule. NARA microfilm publication M653, 1,438 rolls. Washington, D.C.: National Archives and Records), Ancestry.com, http://www.Ancestry.com, Year: 1860; Census Place: Ranges 8 and 9, Calhoun, Alabama; Roll: ; Page: 313; Image: 29. Birth date: about 1853 Birth place: Alabama Residence date: 1860 Residence place: Ranges 8 and 9, Calhoun, Alabama, United States.

321   Ancestry.com, 1870 United States Federal Census (Online publication - Provo, UT, USA: Ancestry.com Operations, Inc., 2009. Images reproduced by FamilySearch. Original data - 1870 U.S. census, population schedules. NARA microfilm publication M593, 1,761 rolls. Washington, D.C.: National Archives and Record), Ancestry.com, http://www.Ancestry.com, Year: 1870; Census Place: Township 19 Range 4, Talladega, Alabama; Roll: M593_; Page: ; Image:. Birth date: about 1853 Birth place: Alabama Residence date: 1870 Residence place: Township 19 Range 4, Talladega, Alabama, United States.

322   Ancestry.com, 1870 United States Federal Census (Online publication - Provo, UT, USA: Ancestry.com Operations, Inc., 2009. Images reproduced by FamilySearch. Original data - 1870 U.S. census, population schedules. NARA microfilm publication M593, 1,761 rolls. Washington, D.C.: National Archives and Record), Ancestry.com, http://www.Ancestry.com, Year: 1870; Census Place: Township 19 Range 4, Talladega, Alabama; Roll: M593_; Page: ; Image:. Birth date: about 1856 Birth place: Alabama Residence date: 1870 Residence place: Township 19 Range 4, Talladega, Alabama, United States.

323   Ancestry.com, 1860 United States Federal Census (Online publication - Provo, UT, USA: Ancestry.com Operations, Inc., 2009. Images reproduced by FamilySearch. Original data - 1860 U.S. census, population schedule. NARA microfilm publication M653, 1,438 rolls. Washington, D.C.: National Archives and Records), Ancestry.com, http://www.Ancestry.com, Year: 1860; Census Place: Ranges 8 and 9, Calhoun, Alabama; Roll: ; Page: 313; Image: 29. Birth date: about 1855 Birth place: Alabama Residence date: 1860 Residence place: Ranges 8 and 9, Calhoun, Alabama, United States.

324   Ancestry.com and The Church of Jesus Christ of Latter-day Saints, 1880 United States Federal Census (Online publication - Provo, UT, USA: Ancestry.com Operations Inc, 2010. 1880 U.S. Census Index provided by The Church of Jesus Christ of Latter-day Saints © Copyright 1999 Intellectual Reserve, Inc. All rights reserved. All use is subject to the limited), Ancestry.com, http://www.Ancestry.com, Year: 1880; Census Place: June Bug, Calhoun, Alabama; Roll: 4; Family History Film: 1254004; Page: 535A; Enumeration District: 6; Image: 0630. Birth date: about 1857 Birth place: Alabama Residence date: 1880 Residence place: June Bug, Calhoun, Alabama, United States.

325   Ancestry.com, 1860 United States Federal Census (Online publication - Provo, UT, USA: Ancestry.com Operations, Inc., 2009. Images reproduced by FamilySearch. Original data - 1860 U.S. census, population schedule. NARA microfilm publication M653, 1,438 rolls. Washington, D.C.: National Archives and Records), Ancestry.com, http://www.Ancestry.com, Year: 1860; Census Place: Ranges 8 and 9, Calhoun, Alabama; Roll: ; Page: 313; Image: 29. Birth date: about 1857 Birth place: Alabama Residence date: 1860 Residence place: Ranges 8 and 9, Calhoun, Alabama, United States.

326   Ancestry.com, 1870 United States Federal Census (Online publication - Provo, UT, USA: Ancestry.com Operations, Inc., 2009. Images reproduced by FamilySearch. Original data - 1870 U.S. census, population schedules. NARA microfilm publication M593, 1,761 rolls. Washington, D.C.: National Archives and Record), Ancestry.com, http://www.Ancestry.com, Year: 1870; Census Place: Township 19 Range 4, Talladega, Alabama; Roll: M593_; Page: ; Image:. Birth date: about 1858 Birth place: Alabama Residence date: 1870 Residence place: Township 19 Range 4, Talladega, Alabama, United States.

327   Ancestry.com, 1900 United States Federal Census (Online publication - Provo, UT, USA: Ancestry.com Operations Inc, 2004. Original data - United States of America, Bureau of the Census. Twelfth Census of the United States, 1900. Washington, D.C.: National Archives and Records Administration, 1900. T623, 18), Ancestry.com, http://www.Ancestry.com, Year: 1900; Census Place: Cold Water, Calhoun, Alabama; Roll: T623_5; Page: 2A; Enumeration District: 28. Birth date: May 1857 Birth place: Alabama Marriage date: 1891 Marriage place: Residence date: 1900 Residence place: Cold Water, Calhoun, Alabama.

328   Ancestry.com, 1910 United States Federal Census (Online publication - Provo, UT, USA: Ancestry.com Operations Inc, 2006. Original data - Thirteenth Census of the United States, 1910 (NARA microfilm publication T624, 1,178 rolls). Records of the Bureau of the Census, Record Group 29. National Archives, Washington), Ancestry.com, http://www.Ancestry.com, Year: 1910; Census Place: Anniston Ward 1, Calhoun, Alabama; Roll: ; Page: ; Enumeration District: ; Image:. Birth date: about 1858 Birth place: Alabama Residence date: 1910 Residence place: Anniston Ward 1, Calhoun, Alabama.

329   Ancestry.com, 1920 United States Federal Census (Online publication - Provo, UT, USA: Ancestry.com Operations Inc, 2010. Images reproduced by FamilySearch. Original data - Fourteenth Census of the United States, 1920. (NARA microfilm publication T625, 2076 rolls). Records of the Bureau of the Census, Record), Ancestry.com, http://www.Ancestry.com, Year: 1920; Census Place: Justice Precinct 2, San Saba, Texas; Roll: T625_1844; Page: 10B; Enumeration District: 230; Image:. Birth date: about 1856 Birth place: Alabama Residence date: 1920 Residence place: Justice Precinct 2, San Saba, Texas.

330   Ancestry.com, 1920 United States Federal Census (Online publication - Provo, UT, USA: Ancestry.com Operations Inc, 2010. Images reproduced by FamilySearch. Original data - Fourteenth Census of the United States, 1920. (NARA microfilm publication T625, 2076 rolls). Records of the Bureau of the Census, Record), Ancestry.com, http://www.Ancestry.com, Year: 1920; Census Place: Munford, Talladega, Alabama; Roll: T625_41; Page: 19A; Enumeration District: 155; Image:. Birth date: about 1855 Birth place: Alabama Residence date: 1920 Residence place: Munford, Talladega, Alabama.

331   Ancestry.com, 1910 United States Federal Census (Online publication - Provo, UT, USA: Ancestry.com Operations Inc, 2006. Original data - Thirteenth Census of the United States, 1910 (NARA microfilm publication T624, 1,178 rolls). Records of the Bureau of the Census, Record Group 29. National Archives, Washington), Ancestry.com,

http://www.Ancestry.com, Year: 1910; Census Place: Redland, Hempstead, Arkansas; Roll: ; Page: ; Enumeration District: ; Image:. Birth date: 1861 Birth place: Alabama Residence date: 1910 Residence place: Redland, Hempstead, Arkansas.

332   Ancestry.com, 1870 United States Federal Census (Online publication - Provo, UT, USA: Ancestry.com Operations, Inc., 2009. Images reproduced by FamilySearch. Original data - 1870 U.S. census, population schedules. NARA microfilm publication M593, 1,761 rolls. Washington, D.C.: National Archives and Record), Ancestry.com, http://www.Ancestry.com, Year: 1870; Census Place: Township 19 Range 4, Talladega, Alabama; Roll: M593_; Page: ; Image:. Birth date: about 1860 Birth place: Alabama Residence date: 1870 Residence place: Township 19 Range 4, Talladega, Alabama, United States.

333   Ancestry.com, 1900 United States Federal Census (Online publication - Provo, UT, USA: Ancestry.com Operations Inc, 2004. Original data - United States of America, Bureau of the Census. Twelfth Census of the United States, 1900. Washington, D.C.: National Archives and Records Administration, 1900. T623, 18), Ancestry.com, http://www.Ancestry.com, Year: 1900; Census Place: Mine Creek, Hempstead, Arkansas; Roll: T623_60; Page: 7A; Enumeration District: 46. Birth date: Sep 1859 Birth place: Alabama Residence date: 1900 Residence place: Mine Creek, Hempstead, Arkansas.

334   Ancestry.com, 1920 United States Federal Census (Online publication - Provo, UT, USA: Ancestry.com Operations Inc, 2010. Images reproduced by FamilySearch. Original data - Fourteenth Census of the United States, 1920. (NARA microfilm publication T625, 2076 rolls). Records of the Bureau of the Census, Record), Ancestry.com, http://www.Ancestry.com, Year: 1920; Census Place: Anniston Ward 2, Calhoun, Alabama; Roll: T625_5; Page: 8A; Enumeration District: 23; Image:. Birth date: about 1863 Birth place: Alabama Residence date: 1920 Residence place: Anniston Ward 2, Calhoun, Alabama.

335   Ancestry.com, 1870 United States Federal Census (Online publication - Provo, UT, USA: Ancestry.com Operations, Inc., 2009. Images reproduced by FamilySearch. Original data - 1870 U.S. census, population schedules. NARA microfilm publication M593, 1,761 rolls. Washington, D.C.: National Archives and Record), Ancestry.com, http://www.Ancestry.com, Year: 1870; Census Place: Township 19 Range 4, Talladega, Alabama; Roll: M593_; Page: ; Image:. Birth date: about 1863 Birth place: Alabama Residence date: 1870 Residence place: Township 19 Range 4, Talladega, Alabama, United States.

336   Ancestry.com, Alabama Deaths, 1908-59 (Online publication - Provo, UT, USA: Ancestry.com Operations Inc, 2000. Original data - State of Alabama. Index of Vital Records for Alabama: Deaths, 1908-1959. Montgomery, AL, USA: State of Alabama Center for Health Statistics, Record Services Division. Original), Ancestry.com, http://www.Ancestry.com, Death date: 20 Dec 1943 Death place: Calhoun.

337   Ancestry.com, 1870 United States Federal Census (Online publication - Provo, UT, USA: Ancestry.com Operations, Inc., 2009. Images reproduced by FamilySearch. Original data - 1870 U.S. census, population schedules. NARA microfilm publication M593, 1,761 rolls. Washington, D.C.: National Archives and Record), Ancestry.com, http://www.Ancestry.com, Year: 1870; Census Place: Township 19 Range 4, Talladega, Alabama; Roll: M593_; Page: ; Image:. Birth date: about 1866 Birth place: Alabama Residence date: 1870 Residence place: Township 19 Range 4, Talladega, Alabama, United States.

338   Ancestry.com, 1870 United States Federal Census (Online publication - Provo, UT, USA: Ancestry.com Operations, Inc., 2009. Images reproduced by FamilySearch. Original data - 1870 U.S. census, population schedules. NARA microfilm publication M593, 1,761 rolls. Washington, D.C.: National Archives and Record), Ancestry.com, http://www.Ancestry.com, Year: 1870; Census Place: Township 19 Range 4, Talladega, Alabama; Roll: M593_; Page: ; Image:. Birth date: about 1870 Birth place: Alabama Residence date: 1870 Residence place: Township 19 Range 4, Talladega, Alabama, United States.

339   Ancestry.com, 1900 United States Federal Census (Online publication - Provo, UT, USA: Ancestry.com Operations Inc, 2004. Original data - United States of America, Bureau of the Census. Twelfth Census of the United States, 1900. Washington, D.C.: National Archives and Records Administration, 1900. T623, 18), Ancestry.com, http://www.Ancestry.com, Year: 1900; Census Place: Anniston Ward 1, Calhoun, Alabama; Roll: T623_5; Page: 10B; Enumeration District: 42. Birth date: Sep 1869 Birth place: Alabama Marriage date: 1888 Marriage place: Residence date: 1900 Residence place: Anniston Ward 1, Calhoun, Alabama.

340   Ancestry.com, 1910 United States Federal Census (Online publication - Provo, UT, USA: Ancestry.com Operations Inc, 2006. Original data - Thirteenth Census of the United States, 1910 (NARA microfilm publication T624, 1,178 rolls). Records of the Bureau of the Census, Record Group 29. National Archives, Washington), Ancestry.com, http://www.Ancestry.com, Year: 1910; Census Place: Anniston Ward 1, Calhoun, Alabama; Roll: ; Page: ; Enumeration District: ; Image:. Birth date: about 1870 Birth place: Alabama Residence date: 1910 Residence place: Anniston Ward 1, Calhoun, Alabama.

341   Ancestry.com and The Church of Jesus Christ of Latter-day Saints, 1880 United States Federal Census (Online publication - Provo, UT, USA: Ancestry.com Operations Inc, 2010. 1880 U.S. Census Index provided by The Church of Jesus Christ of Latter-day Saints © Copyright 1999 Intellectual Reserve, Inc. All rights reserved. All use is subject to the limited), Ancestry.com, http://www.Ancestry.com, Year: 1880; Census Place: Allens, Calhoun, Alabama; Roll: 5; Family History Film: 1254005; Page: 645A; Enumeration District: 10; Image: 0031. Birth date: about 1830 Birth place: North Carolina Residence date: 1880 Residence place: Allens, Calhoun, Alabama, United States.

342   Ancestry.com, 1870 United States Federal Census (Online publication - Provo, UT, USA: Ancestry.com Operations, Inc., 2009. Images reproduced by FamilySearch. Original data - 1870 U.S. census, population schedules. NARA microfilm publication M593, 1,761 rolls. Washington, D.C.: National Archives and Record), Ancestry.com,

http://www.Ancestry.com, Year: 1870; Census Place: Precinct 8, Calhoun, Alabama; Roll: M593_; Page: ; Image:. Birth date: about 1829 Birth place: North Carolina Residence date: 1870 Residence place: Precinct 8, Calhoun, Alabama, United States.

343   Ancestry.com, 1900 United States Federal Census (Online publication - Provo, UT, USA: Ancestry.com Operations Inc, 2004. Original data - United States of America, Bureau of the Census. Twelfth Census of the United States, 1900. Washington, D.C.: National Archives and Records Administration, 1900. T623, 18), Ancestry.com, http://www.Ancestry.com, Year: 1900; Census Place: Allen, Calhoun, Alabama; Roll: T623_5; Page: 1B; Enumeration District: 32. Birth date: May 1827 Birth place: North Carolina Marriage date: 1846 Marriage place: Residence date: 1900 Residence place: Precinct 8 Green's Schoolhouse, Calhoun, Alabama.

344   Ancestry.com, 1900 United States Federal Census (Online publication - Provo, UT, USA: Ancestry.com Operations Inc, 2004. Original data - United States of America, Bureau of the Census. Twelfth Census of the United States, 1900. Washington, D.C.: National Archives and Records Administration, 1900. T623, 18), Ancestry.com, http://www.Ancestry.com, Year: 1900; Census Place: Oxford, Calhoun, Alabama; Roll: T623_5; Page: 8B; Enumeration District: 37. Birth date: May 1849 Birth place: Alabama Marriage date: 1869 Marriage place: Residence date: 1900 Residence place: Precinct 13 (Excl. Hobson & Oxford Towns), Calhoun, Alabama.

345   Ancestry.com, 1910 United States Federal Census (Online publication - Provo, UT, USA: Ancestry.com Operations Inc, 2006. Original data - Thirteenth Census of the United States, 1910 (NARA microfilm publication T624, 1,178 rolls). Records of the Bureau of the Census, Record Group 29. National Archives, Washington), Ancestry.com, http://www.Ancestry.com, Year: 1910; Census Place: Oxford, Calhoun, Alabama; Roll: ; Page: ; Enumeration District: ; Image:. Birth date: about 1849 Birth place: Alabama Residence date: 1910 Residence place: Oxford, Calhoun, Alabama.

346   Ancestry.com, 1920 United States Federal Census (Online publication - Provo, UT, USA: Ancestry.com Operations Inc, 2010. Images reproduced by FamilySearch. Original data - Fourteenth Census of the United States, 1920. (NARA microfilm publication T625, 2076 rolls). Records of the Bureau of the Census, Record), Ancestry.com, http://www.Ancestry.com, Year: 1920; Census Place: Silver Run, Talladega, Alabama; Roll: T625_41; Page: 3B; Enumeration District: 131; Image:. Birth date: about 1848 Birth place: Alabama Residence date: 1920 Residence place: Silver Run, Talladega, Alabama.

347   Ancestry.com and The Church of Jesus Christ of Latter-day Saints, 1880 United States Federal Census (Online publication - Provo, UT, USA: Ancestry.com Operations Inc, 2010. 1880 U.S. Census Index provided by The Church of Jesus Christ of Latter-day Saints © Copyright 1999 Intellectual Reserve, Inc. All rights reserved. All use is subject to the limited), Ancestry.com, http://www.Ancestry.com, Year: 1880; Census Place: Allens, Calhoun, Alabama; Roll: 5; Family History Film: 1254005; Page: 645A; Enumeration District: 10; Image: 0031. Birth date: about 1849 Birth place: Alabama Residence date: 1880 Residence place: Allens, Calhoun, Alabama, United States.

348   Ancestry.com, 1900 United States Federal Census (Online publication - Provo, UT, USA: Ancestry.com Operations Inc, 2004. Original data - United States of America, Bureau of the Census. Twelfth Census of the United States, 1900. Washington, D.C.: National Archives and Records Administration, 1900. T623, 18), Ancestry.com, http://www.Ancestry.com, Year: 1900; Census Place: Oxford, Calhoun, Alabama; Roll: T623_5; Page: 10B; Enumeration District: 37. Birth date: May 1849 Birth place: Alabama Marriage date: 1876 Marriage place: Residence date: 1900 Residence place: Precinct 13 (Excl. Hobson & Oxford Towns), Calhoun, Alabama.

349   Ancestry.com, 1910 United States Federal Census (Online publication - Provo, UT, USA: Ancestry.com Operations Inc, 2006. Original data - Thirteenth Census of the United States, 1910 (NARA microfilm publication T624, 1,178 rolls). Records of the Bureau of the Census, Record Group 29. National Archives, Washington), Ancestry.com, http://www.Ancestry.com, Year: 1910; Census Place: Oxford, Calhoun, Alabama; Roll: ; Page: ; Enumeration District: ; Image:. Birth date: about 1849 Birth place: Alabama Residence date: 1910 Residence place: Oxford, Calhoun, Alabama.

350   Ancestry.com, 1920 United States Federal Census (Online publication - Provo, UT, USA: Ancestry.com Operations Inc, 2010. Images reproduced by FamilySearch. Original data - Fourteenth Census of the United States, 1920. (NARA microfilm publication T625, 2076 rolls). Records of the Bureau of the Census, Record), Ancestry.com, http://www.Ancestry.com, Year: 1920; Census Place: Oxford, Calhoun, Alabama; Roll: T625_5; Page: 11A; Enumeration District: 16; Image:. Birth date: about 1850 Birth place: Alabama Residence date: 1920 Residence place: Oxford, Calhoun, Alabama.

351   Ancestry.com, 1930 United States Federal Census (Online publication - Provo, UT, USA: Ancestry.com Operations Inc, 2002. Original data - United States of America, Bureau of the Census. Fifteenth Census of the United States, 1930. Washington, D.C.: National Archives and Records Administration, 1930. T626,), Ancestry.com, http://www.Ancestry.com, Year: 1930; Census Place: Oxford, Calhoun, Alabama; Roll: 5; Page: 3A; Enumeration District: 20; Image: 480.0. Birth date: about 1850 Birth place: Alabama Residence date: 1930 Residence place: Oxford, Calhoun, Alabama.

352   Ancestry.com, Alabama Deaths, 1908-59 (Online publication - Provo, UT, USA: Ancestry.com Operations Inc, 2000. Original data - State of Alabama. Index of Vital Records for Alabama: Deaths, 1908-1959. Montgomery, AL, USA: State of Alabama Center for Health Statistics, Record Services Division. Original), Ancestry.com, http://www.Ancestry.com, Death date: May 1935 Death place: Calhoun.

353   Ancestry.com, 1910 United States Federal Census (Online publication - Provo, UT, USA: Ancestry.com Operations Inc, 2006. Original data - Thirteenth Census of the United States, 1910 (NARA microfilm publication T624, 1,178 rolls). Records of the Bureau of the Census, Record Group 29. National Archives, Washington), Ancestry.com, http://www.Ancestry.com, Year: 1910; Census Place: Greens Schoolhouse, Calhoun, Alabama; Roll: ; Page: ;

Enumeration District: ; Image:. Birth date: 1853 Birth place: Alabama Residence date: 1910 Residence place: Greens Schoolhouse, Calhoun, Alabama.

354   Ancestry.com, 1870 United States Federal Census (Online publication - Provo, UT, USA: Ancestry.com Operations, Inc., 2009. Images reproduced by FamilySearch. Original data - 1870 U.S. census, population schedules. NARA microfilm publication M593, 1,761 rolls. Washington, D.C.: National Archives and Record), Ancestry.com, http://www.Ancestry.com, Year: 1870; Census Place: Precinct 8, Calhoun, Alabama; Roll: M593_; Page: ; Image:. Birth date: about 1857 Birth place: Alabama Residence date: 1870 Residence place: Precinct 8, Calhoun, Alabama, United States.

355   Yates Publishing, U.S. and International Marriage Records, 1560-1900 (Online publication - Provo, UT, USA: Ancestry.com Operations Inc, 2004. Original data - This unique collection of records was extracted from a variety of sources including family group sheets and electronic databases. Originally, the information was derived), Ancestry.com, http://www.Ancestry.com, Source number: 27.000; Source type: Electronic Database; Number of Pages: 1; Submitter Code: WBF. Birth date: 1857 Birth place:.

356   Ancestry.com and The Church of Jesus Christ of Latter-day Saints, 1880 United States Federal Census (Online publication - Provo, UT, USA: Ancestry.com Operations Inc, 2010. 1880 U.S. Census Index provided by The Church of Jesus Christ of Latter-day Saints © Copyright 1999 Intellectual Reserve, Inc. All rights reserved. All use is subject to the limited), Ancestry.com, http://www.Ancestry.com, Year: 1880; Census Place: District 1105, Webster, Georgia; Roll: 171; Family History Film: 1254171; Page: 456B; Enumeration District: 86; Image: 0296. Birth date: about 1854 Birth place: Georgia Residence date: 1880 Residence place: District 1105, Webster, Georgia, United States.

357   Ancestry.com, 1870 United States Federal Census (Online publication - Provo, UT, USA: Ancestry.com Operations, Inc., 2009. Images reproduced by FamilySearch. Original data - 1870 U.S. census, population schedules. NARA microfilm publication M593, 1,761 rolls. Washington, D.C.: National Archives and Record), Ancestry.com, http://www.Ancestry.com, Year: 1870; Census Place: Precinct 4, Calhoun, Alabama; Roll: M593_; Page: ; Image:. Birth date: about 1857 Birth place: Alabama Residence date: 1870 Residence place: Precinct 4, Calhoun, Alabama, United States.

358   Ancestry.com, 1900 United States Federal Census (Online publication - Provo, UT, USA: Ancestry.com Operations Inc, 2004. Original data - United States of America, Bureau of the Census. Twelfth Census of the United States, 1900. Washington, D.C.: National Archives and Records Administration, 1900. T623, 18), Ancestry.com, http://www.Ancestry.com, Year: 1900; Census Place: Allen, Calhoun, Alabama; Roll: T623_5; Page: 1B; Enumeration District: 32. Birth date: Apr 1857 Birth place: Alabama Marriage date: 1875 Marriage place: Residence date: 1900 Residence place: Precinct 8 Green's Schoolhouse, Calhoun, Alabama.

359   Ancestry.com, 1920 United States Federal Census (Online publication - Provo, UT, USA: Ancestry.com Operations Inc, 2010. Images reproduced by FamilySearch. Original data - Fourteenth Census of the United States, 1920. (NARA microfilm publication T625, 2076 rolls). Records of the Bureau of the Census, Record), Ancestry.com, http://www.Ancestry.com, Year: 1920; Census Place: Greens Schoolhouse, Calhoun, Alabama; Roll: T625_5; Page: 3B; Enumeration District: 10; Image:. Birth date: about 1858 Birth place: Alabama Residence date: 1920 Residence place: Greens Schoolhouse, Calhoun, Alabama.

360   Ancestry.com, 1910 United States Federal Census (Online publication - Provo, UT, USA: Ancestry.com Operations Inc, 2006. Original data - Thirteenth Census of the United States, 1910 (NARA microfilm publication T624, 1,178 rolls). Records of the Bureau of the Census, Record Group 29. National Archives, Washington), Ancestry.com, http://www.Ancestry.com, Year: 1910; Census Place: Greens Schoolhouse, Calhoun, Alabama; Roll: ; Page: ; Enumeration District: ; Image:. Birth date: about 1857 Birth place: Alabama Residence date: 1910 Residence place: Greens Schoolhouse, Calhoun, Alabama.

361   Ancestry.com, Alabama Deaths, 1908-59 (Online publication - Provo, UT, USA: Ancestry.com Operations Inc, 2000. Original data - State of Alabama. Index of Vital Records for Alabama: Deaths, 1908-1959. Montgomery, AL, USA: State of Alabama Center for Health Statistics, Record Services Division. Original), Ancestry.com, http://www.Ancestry.com, Death date: 07 Jul 1940 Death place: Calhoun.

362   Ancestry.com and The Church of Jesus Christ of Latter-day Saints, 1880 United States Federal Census (Online publication - Provo, UT, USA: Ancestry.com Operations Inc, 2010. 1880 U.S. Census Index provided by The Church of Jesus Christ of Latter-day Saints © Copyright 1999 Intellectual Reserve, Inc. All rights reserved. All use is subject to the limited), Ancestry.com, http://www.Ancestry.com, Year: 1880; Census Place: Allens, Calhoun, Alabama; Roll: 5; Family History Film: 1254005; Page: 647B; Enumeration District: 10; Image: 0036. Birth date: about 1858 Birth place: Alabama Residence date: 1880 Residence place: Allens, Calhoun, Alabama, United States.

363   Ancestry.com and The Church of Jesus Christ of Latter-day Saints, 1880 United States Federal Census (Online publication - Provo, UT, USA: Ancestry.com Operations Inc, 2010. 1880 U.S. Census Index provided by The Church of Jesus Christ of Latter-day Saints © Copyright 1999 Intellectual Reserve, Inc. All rights reserved. All use is subject to the limited), Ancestry.com, http://www.Ancestry.com, Year: 1880; Census Place: Allens, Calhoun, Alabama; Roll: 5; Family History Film: 1254005; Page: 645A; Enumeration District: 10; Image: 0031. Birth date: about 1866 Birth place: Alabama Residence date: 1880 Residence place: Allens, Calhoun, Alabama, United States.

364   Ancestry.com, 1870 United States Federal Census (Online publication - Provo, UT, USA: Ancestry.com Operations, Inc., 2009. Images reproduced by FamilySearch. Original data - 1870 U.S. census, population schedules. NARA microfilm publication M593, 1,761 rolls. Washington, D.C.: National Archives and Record), Ancestry.com, http://www.Ancestry.com, Year: 1870; Census Place: Precinct 8, Calhoun, Alabama; Roll: M593_; Page: ; Image:. Birth

date: about 1865 Birth place: Alabama Residence date: 1870 Residence place: Precinct 8, Calhoun, Alabama, United States.

365   Ancestry.com, 1900 United States Federal Census (Online publication - Provo, UT, USA: Ancestry.com Operations Inc, 2004. Original data - United States of America, Bureau of the Census. Twelfth Census of the United States, 1900. Washington, D.C.: National Archives and Records Administration, 1900. T623, 18), Ancestry.com, http://www.Ancestry.com, Year: 1900; Census Place: Anniston Ward 2, Calhoun, Alabama; Roll: T623_5; Page: 1B; Enumeration District: 43. Birth date: Jan 1868 Birth place: Alabama Marriage date: 1885 Marriage place: Residence date: 1900 Residence place: Anniston City, Calhoun, Alabama.

366   Ancestry.com, 1910 United States Federal Census (Online publication - Provo, UT, USA: Ancestry.com Operations Inc, 2006. Original data - Thirteenth Census of the United States, 1910 (NARA microfilm publication T624, 1,178 rolls). Records of the Bureau of the Census, Record Group 29. National Archives, Washington), Ancestry.com, http://www.Ancestry.com, Year: 1910; Census Place: Ballplay, Etowah, Alabama; Roll: ; Page: ; Enumeration District: ; Image:. Birth date: about 1868 Birth place: Alabama Residence date: 1910 Residence place: Ballplay, Etowah, Alabama.

367   Ancestry.com, 1920 United States Federal Census (Online publication - Provo, UT, USA: Ancestry.com Operations Inc, 2010. Images reproduced by FamilySearch. Original data - Fourteenth Census of the United States, 1920. (NARA microfilm publication T625, 2076 rolls). Records of the Bureau of the Census, Record), Ancestry.com, http://www.Ancestry.com, Year: 1920; Census Place: Greens Schoolhouse, Calhoun, Alabama; Roll: T625_5; Page: 7B; Enumeration District: 10; Image:. Birth date: about 1867 Birth place: Alabama Residence date: 1920 Residence place: Greens Schoolhouse, Calhoun, Alabama.

368   Ancestry.com, 1930 United States Federal Census (Online publication - Provo, UT, USA: Ancestry.com Operations Inc, 2002. Original data - United States of America, Bureau of the Census. Fifteenth Census of the United States, 1930. Washington, D.C.: National Archives and Records Administration, 1930. T626,), Ancestry.com, http://www.Ancestry.com, Year: 1930; Census Place: Hollingsworth, Calhoun, Alabama; Roll: 5; Page: 1B; Enumeration District: 10; Image: 225.0. Birth date: about 1868 Birth place: Residence date: 1930 Residence place: Hollingsworth, Calhoun, Alabama.

369   Ancestry.com, 1900 United States Federal Census (Online publication - Provo, UT, USA: Ancestry.com Operations Inc, 2004. Original data - United States of America, Bureau of the Census. Twelfth Census of the United States, 1900. Washington, D.C.: National Archives and Records Administration, 1900. T623, 18), Ancestry.com, http://www.Ancestry.com, Year: 1900; Census Place: Anniston Ward 2, Calhoun, Alabama; Roll: T623_5; Page: 1B; Enumeration District: 43. Birth date: Mar 1862 Birth place: Alabama Marriage date: 1885 Marriage place: Residence date: 1900 Residence place: Anniston City, Calhoun, Alabama.

370   Ancestry.com and The Church of Jesus Christ of Latter-day Saints, 1880 United States Federal Census (Online publication - Provo, UT, USA: Ancestry.com Operations Inc, 2010. 1880 U.S. Census Index provided by The Church of Jesus Christ of Latter-day Saints © Copyright 1999 Intellectual Reserve, Inc. All rights reserved. All use is subject to the limited), Ancestry.com, http://www.Ancestry.com, Year: 1880; Census Place: Allens, Calhoun, Alabama; Roll: 5; Family History Film: 1254005; Page: 645A; Enumeration District: 10; Image: 0031. Birth date: about 1868 Birth place: Alabama Residence date: 1880 Residence place: Allens, Calhoun, Alabama, United States.

371   Ancestry.com, 1850 United States Federal Census (Online publication - Provo, UT, USA: Ancestry.com Operations, Inc., 2009. Images reproduced by FamilySearch. Original data - Seventh Census of the United States, 1850; (National Archives Microfilm Publication M432, 1009 rolls); Records of the Bureau of the), Ancestry.com, http://www.Ancestry.com, Year: 1850; Census Place: Subdivision 29, Benton, Alabama; Roll: M432_1; Page: 344A; Image:. Birth date: about 1820 Birth place: Georgia Residence date: 1850 Residence place: Subdivision 29, Benton, Alabama.

372   Ancestry.com, 1850 United States Federal Census (Online publication - Provo, UT, USA: Ancestry.com Operations, Inc., 2009. Images reproduced by FamilySearch. Original data - Seventh Census of the United States, 1850; (National Archives Microfilm Publication M432, 1009 rolls); Records of the Bureau of the), Ancestry.com, http://www.Ancestry.com, Year: 1850; Census Place: Subdivision 29, Benton, Alabama; Roll: M432_1; Page: 344A; Image:. Birth date: about 1842 Birth place: Alabama Residence date: 1850 Residence place: Subdivision 29, Benton, Alabama.

373   Ancestry.com, 1860 United States Federal Census (Online publication - Provo, UT, USA: Ancestry.com Operations, Inc., 2009. Images reproduced by FamilySearch. Original data - 1860 U.S. census, population schedule. NARA microfilm publication M653, 1,438 rolls. Washington, D.C.: National Archives and Records), Ancestry.com, http://www.Ancestry.com, Year: 1860; Census Place: Ranges 8 and 9, Calhoun, Alabama; Roll: ; Page: 327; Image: 43. Birth date: about 1845 Birth place: Alabama Residence date: 1860 Residence place: Ranges 8 and 9, Calhoun, Alabama, United States.

374   Ancestry.com, 1860 United States Federal Census (Online publication - Provo, UT, USA: Ancestry.com Operations, Inc., 2009. Images reproduced by FamilySearch. Original data - 1860 U.S. census, population schedule. NARA microfilm publication M653, 1,438 rolls. Washington, D.C.: National Archives and Records), Ancestry.com, http://www.Ancestry.com, Year: 1860; Census Place: Ranges 8 and 9, Calhoun, Alabama; Roll: ; Page: 327; Image: 43. Birth date: about 1847 Birth place: Alabama Residence date: 1860 Residence place: Ranges 8 and 9, Calhoun, Alabama, United States.

375   Ancestry.com, 1850 United States Federal Census (Online publication - Provo, UT, USA: Ancestry.com Operations, Inc., 2009. Images reproduced by FamilySearch. Original data - Seventh Census of the United States, 1850;

(National Archives Microfilm Publication M432, 1009 rolls); Records of the Bureau of the), Ancestry.com, http://www.Ancestry.com, Year: 1850; Census Place: Subdivision 29, Benton, Alabama; Roll: M432_1; Page: 344A; Image:. Birth date: about 1848 Birth place: Alabama Residence date: 1850 Residence place: Subdivision 29, Benton, Alabama.

376   Ancestry.com and The Church of Jesus Christ of Latter-day Saints, 1880 United States Federal Census (Online publication - Provo, UT, USA: Ancestry.com Operations Inc, 2010. 1880 U.S. Census Index provided by The Church of Jesus Christ of Latter-day Saints © Copyright 1999 Intellectual Reserve, Inc. All rights reserved. All use is subject to the limited), Ancestry.com, http://www.Ancestry.com, Year: 1880; Census Place: Davisville, Calhoun, Alabama; Roll: 5; Family History Film: 1254005; Page: 682B; Enumeration District: 13; Image: 0106. Birth date: about 1832 Birth place: South Carolina Residence date: 1880 Residence place: Davisville, Calhoun, Alabama, United States.

377   Ancestry.com, 1850 United States Federal Census (Online publication - Provo, UT, USA: Ancestry.com Operations, Inc., 2009. Images reproduced by FamilySearch. Original data - Seventh Census of the United States, 1850; (National Archives Microfilm Publication M432, 1009 rolls); Records of the Bureau of the), Ancestry.com, http://www.Ancestry.com, Year: 1850; Census Place: Subdivision 29, Benton, Alabama; Roll: M432_1; Page: 361B; Image:. Birth date: about 1831 Birth place: South Carolina Residence date: 1850 Residence place: Subdivision 29, Benton, Alabama.

378   Ancestry.com and The Church of Jesus Christ of Latter-day Saints, 1880 United States Federal Census (Online publication - Provo, UT, USA: Ancestry.com Operations Inc, 2010. 1880 U.S. Census Index provided by The Church of Jesus Christ of Latter-day Saints © Copyright 1999 Intellectual Reserve, Inc. All rights reserved. All use is subject to the limited), Ancestry.com, http://www.Ancestry.com, Year: 1880; Census Place: Davisville, Calhoun, Alabama; Roll: 5; Family History Film: 1254005; Page: 682B; Enumeration District: 13; Image: 0106. Birth date: about 1851 Birth place: Alabama Residence date: 1880 Residence place: Davisville, Calhoun, Alabama, United States.

379   Ancestry.com and The Church of Jesus Christ of Latter-day Saints, 1880 United States Federal Census (Online publication - Provo, UT, USA: Ancestry.com Operations Inc, 2010. 1880 U.S. Census Index provided by The Church of Jesus Christ of Latter-day Saints © Copyright 1999 Intellectual Reserve, Inc. All rights reserved. All use is subject to the limited), Ancestry.com, http://www.Ancestry.com, Year: 1880; Census Place: Davisville, Calhoun, Alabama; Roll: 5; Family History Film: 1254005; Page: 682B; Enumeration District: 13; Image: 0106. Birth date: about 1852 Birth place: Alabama Residence date: 1880 Residence place: Davisville, Calhoun, Alabama, United States.

380   Ancestry.com and The Church of Jesus Christ of Latter-day Saints, 1880 United States Federal Census (Online publication - Provo, UT, USA: Ancestry.com Operations Inc, 2010. 1880 U.S. Census Index provided by The Church of Jesus Christ of Latter-day Saints © Copyright 1999 Intellectual Reserve, Inc. All rights reserved. All use is subject to the limited), Ancestry.com, http://www.Ancestry.com, Year: 1880; Census Place: Davisville, Calhoun, Alabama; Roll: 5; Family History Film: 1254005; Page: 682B; Enumeration District: 13; Image: 0106. Birth date: about 1858 Birth place: Alabama Residence date: 1880 Residence place: Davisville, Calhoun, Alabama, United States.

381   Ancestry.com and The Church of Jesus Christ of Latter-day Saints, 1880 United States Federal Census (Online publication - Provo, UT, USA: Ancestry.com Operations Inc, 2010. 1880 U.S. Census Index provided by The Church of Jesus Christ of Latter-day Saints © Copyright 1999 Intellectual Reserve, Inc. All rights reserved. All use is subject to the limited), Ancestry.com, http://www.Ancestry.com, Year: 1880; Census Place: Davisville, Calhoun, Alabama; Roll: 5; Family History Film: 1254005; Page: 682B; Enumeration District: 13; Image: 0106. Birth date: about 1863 Birth place: Alabama Residence date: 1880 Residence place: Davisville, Calhoun, Alabama, United States.

382   Ancestry.com and The Church of Jesus Christ of Latter-day Saints, 1880 United States Federal Census (Online publication - Provo, UT, USA: Ancestry.com Operations Inc, 2010. 1880 U.S. Census Index provided by The Church of Jesus Christ of Latter-day Saints © Copyright 1999 Intellectual Reserve, Inc. All rights reserved. All use is subject to the limited), Ancestry.com, http://www.Ancestry.com, Year: 1880; Census Place: Davisville, Calhoun, Alabama; Roll: 5; Family History Film: 1254005; Page: 682B; Enumeration District: 13; Image: 0106. Birth date: about 1864 Birth place: Alabama Residence date: 1880 Residence place: Davisville, Calhoun, Alabama, United States.

383   Ancestry.com, 1900 United States Federal Census (Online publication - Provo, UT, USA: Ancestry.com Operations Inc, 2004. Original data - United States of America, Bureau of the Census. Twelfth Census of the United States, 1900. Washington, D.C.: National Archives and Records Administration, 1900. T623, 18), Ancestry.com, http://www.Ancestry.com, Year: 1900; Census Place: Bluff Eye, Talladega, Alabama; Roll: T623_40; Page: 10A; Enumeration District: 84. Birth date: Mar 1864 Birth place: Alabama Marriage date: 1885 Marriage place: Residence date: 1900 Residence place: Bluff Eye, Talladega, Alabama.

384   Ancestry.com and The Church of Jesus Christ of Latter-day Saints, 1880 United States Federal Census (Online publication - Provo, UT, USA: Ancestry.com Operations Inc, 2010. 1880 U.S. Census Index provided by The Church of Jesus Christ of Latter-day Saints © Copyright 1999 Intellectual Reserve, Inc. All rights reserved. All use is subject to the limited), Ancestry.com, http://www.Ancestry.com, Year: 1880; Census Place: June Bug, Calhoun, Alabama; Roll: 4; Family History Film: 1254004; Page: 531B; Enumeration District: 6; Image: 0623. Birth date: about 1867 Birth place: Alabama Residence date: 1880 Residence place: June Bug, Calhoun, Alabama, United States.

385   Ancestry.com, 1870 United States Federal Census (Online publication - Provo, UT, USA: Ancestry.com Operations, Inc., 2009. Images reproduced by FamilySearch. Original data - 1870 U.S. census, population schedules. NARA microfilm publication M593, 1,761 rolls. Washington, D.C.: National Archives and Record), Ancestry.com, http://www.Ancestry.com, Year: 1870; Census Place: Precinct 4, Calhoun, Alabama; Roll: M593_; Page: ; Image:. Birth

date: about 1866 Birth place: Alabama Residence date: 1870 Residence place: Precinct 4, Calhoun, Alabama, United States.

386   Ancestry.com and The Church of Jesus Christ of Latter-day Saints, 1880 United States Federal Census (Online publication - Provo, UT, USA: Ancestry.com Operations Inc, 2010. 1880 U.S. Census Index provided by The Church of Jesus Christ of Latter-day Saints © Copyright 1999 Intellectual Reserve, Inc. All rights reserved. All use is subject to the limited), Ancestry.com, http://www.Ancestry.com, Year: 1880; Census Place: June Bug, Calhoun, Alabama; Roll: 4; Family History Film: 1254004; Page: 531B; Enumeration District: 6; Image: 0623. Birth date: about 1872 Birth place: Alabama Residence date: 1880 Residence place: June Bug, Calhoun, Alabama, United States.

387   Ancestry.com, Alabama Deaths, 1908-59 (Online publication - Provo, UT, USA: Ancestry.com Operations Inc, 2000. Original data - State of Alabama. Index of Vital Records for Alabama: Deaths, 1908-1959. Montgomery, AL, USA: State of Alabama Center for Health Statistics, Record Services Division. Original), Ancestry.com, http://www.Ancestry.com, Death date: 24 Jun 1954 Death place: Jefferson.

388   Ancestry.com, World War I Draft Registration Cards, 1917-1918 (Online publication - Provo, UT, USA: Ancestry.com Operations Inc, 2005. Original data - United States, Selective Service System. World War I Selective Service System Draft Registration Cards, 1917-1918. Washington, D.C.: National Archives and Records Administration), Ancestry.com, http://www.Ancestry.com, Registration Location: Calhoun County, Alabama; Roll: 1509363; Draft Board: 0. Birth date: 10 Aug 1888 Birth place: Residence date: Residence place: Calhoun, Alabama.

389   Ancestry.com and The Church of Jesus Christ of Latter-day Saints, 1880 United States Federal Census (Online publication - Provo, UT, USA: Ancestry.com Operations Inc, 2010. 1880 U.S. Census Index provided by The Church of Jesus Christ of Latter-day Saints © Copyright 1999 Intellectual Reserve, Inc. All rights reserved. All use is subject to the limited), Ancestry.com, http://www.Ancestry.com, Year: 1880; Census Place: June Bug, Calhoun, Alabama; Roll: 4; Family History Film: 1254004; Page: 538D; Enumeration District: 6; Image: 0637. Birth date: about 1833 Birth place: Alabama Residence date: 1880 Residence place: June Bug, Calhoun, Alabama, United States.

390   Ancestry.com, Alabama Marriage Collection, 1800-1969 (Online publication - Provo, UT, USA: Ancestry.com Operations Inc, 2006. Original data - Alabama Center for Health Statistics. Alabama Marriage Index, 1936-1969. Alabama Center for Health Statistics, Montgomery, Alabama. Dodd, Jordan R., et. al. Early America), Ancestry.com, http://www.Ancestry.com, Marriage date: 12 Jan 1848 Marriage place: Calhoun, Alabama.

391   Ancestry.com, 1870 United States Federal Census (Online publication - Provo, UT, USA: Ancestry.com Operations, Inc., 2009. Images reproduced by FamilySearch. Original data - 1870 U.S. census, population schedules. NARA microfilm publication M593, 1,761 rolls. Washington, D.C.: National Archives and Record), Ancestry.com, http://www.Ancestry.com, Year: 1870; Census Place: District 4 Subdivision 1, Jackson, Alabama; Roll: M593_; Page: ; Image:. Birth date: about 1856 Birth place: Alabama Residence date: 1870 Residence place: District 4 Subdivision 1, Jackson, Alabama, United States.

392   Ancestry.com, 1900 United States Federal Census (Online publication - Provo, UT, USA: Ancestry.com Operations Inc, 2004. Original data - United States of America, Bureau of the Census. Twelfth Census of the United States, 1900. Washington, D.C.: National Archives and Records Administration, 1900. T623, 18), Ancestry.com, http://www.Ancestry.com, Year: 1900; Census Place: Talladega, Talladega, Alabama; Roll: T623_40; Page: 22A; Enumeration District: 90. Birth date: Aug 1857 Birth place: Alabama Marriage date: 1877 Marriage place: Residence date: 1900 Residence place: Talladega, Talladega, Alabama.

393   Ancestry.com, Alabama Deaths, 1908-59 (Online publication - Provo, UT, USA: Ancestry.com Operations Inc, 2000. Original data - State of Alabama. Index of Vital Records for Alabama: Deaths, 1908-1959. Montgomery, AL, USA: State of Alabama Center for Health Statistics, Record Services Division. Original), Ancestry.com, http://www.Ancestry.com, Death date: Aug 1929 Death place: Calhoun.

394   Ancestry.com and The Church of Jesus Christ of Latter-day Saints, 1880 United States Federal Census (Online publication - Provo, UT, USA: Ancestry.com Operations Inc, 2010. 1880 U.S. Census Index provided by The Church of Jesus Christ of Latter-day Saints © Copyright 1999 Intellectual Reserve, Inc. All rights reserved. All use is subject to the limited), Ancestry.com, http://www.Ancestry.com, Year: 1880; Census Place: June Bug, Calhoun, Alabama; Roll: 4; Family History Film: 1254004; Page: 538D; Enumeration District: 6; Image: 0637. Birth date: about 1859 Birth place: Alabama Residence date: 1880 Residence place: June Bug, Calhoun, Alabama, United States.

395   Ancestry.com and The Church of Jesus Christ of Latter-day Saints, 1880 United States Federal Census (Online publication - Provo, UT, USA: Ancestry.com Operations Inc, 2010. 1880 U.S. Census Index provided by The Church of Jesus Christ of Latter-day Saints © Copyright 1999 Intellectual Reserve, Inc. All rights reserved. All use is subject to the limited), Ancestry.com, http://www.Ancestry.com, Year: 1880; Census Place: June Bug, Calhoun, Alabama; Roll: 4; Family History Film: 1254004; Page: 538D; Enumeration District: 6; Image: 0637. Birth date: about 1862 Birth place: Alabama Residence date: 1880 Residence place: June Bug, Calhoun, Alabama, United States.

396   Ancestry.com and The Church of Jesus Christ of Latter-day Saints, 1880 United States Federal Census (Online publication - Provo, UT, USA: Ancestry.com Operations Inc, 2010. 1880 U.S. Census Index provided by The Church of Jesus Christ of Latter-day Saints © Copyright 1999 Intellectual Reserve, Inc. All rights reserved. All use is subject to the limited), Ancestry.com, http://www.Ancestry.com, Year: 1880; Census Place: June Bug, Calhoun, Alabama; Roll: 4; Family History Film: 1254004; Page: 538D; Enumeration District: 6; Image: 0637. Birth date: about 1866 Birth place: Alabama Residence date: 1880 Residence place: June Bug, Calhoun, Alabama, United States.

397   Ancestry.com, 1900 United States Federal Census (Online publication - Provo, UT, USA: Ancestry.com Operations Inc, 2004. Original data - United States of America, Bureau of the Census. Twelfth Census of the United States, 1900. Washington, D.C.: National Archives and Records Administration, 1900. T623, 18), Ancestry.com, http://www.Ancestry.com, Year: 1900; Census Place: Munford, Talladega, Alabama; Roll: T623_41; Page: 14A; Enumeration District: 100. Birth date: May 1872 Birth place: Alabama Marriage date: 1899 Marriage place: Residence date: 1900 Residence place: Munford, Talladega, Alabama.

398   Ancestry.com and The Church of Jesus Christ of Latter-day Saints, 1880 United States Federal Census (Online publication - Provo, UT, USA: Ancestry.com Operations Inc, 2010. 1880 U.S. Census Index provided by The Church of Jesus Christ of Latter-day Saints © Copyright 1999 Intellectual Reserve, Inc. All rights reserved. All use is subject to the limited), Ancestry.com, http://www.Ancestry.com, Year: 1880; Census Place: June Bug, Calhoun, Alabama; Roll: 4; Family History Film: 1254004; Page: 538D; Enumeration District: 6; Image: 0637. Birth date: about 1871 Birth place: Alabama Residence date: 1880 Residence place: June Bug, Calhoun, Alabama, United States.

399   Ancestry.com, 1920 United States Federal Census (Online publication - Provo, UT, USA: Ancestry.com Operations Inc, 2010. Images reproduced by FamilySearch. Original data - Fourteenth Census of the United States, 1920. (NARA microfilm publication T625, 2076 rolls). Records of the Bureau of the Census, Record), Ancestry.com, http://www.Ancestry.com, Year: 1920; Census Place: Oxford, Calhoun, Alabama; Roll: T625_5; Page: 10B; Enumeration District: 16; Image:. Birth date: about 1872 Birth place: Alabama Residence date: 1920 Residence place: Oxford, Calhoun, Alabama.

400   Ancestry.com, 1930 United States Federal Census (Online publication - Provo, UT, USA: Ancestry.com Operations Inc, 2002. Original data - United States of America, Bureau of the Census. Fifteenth Census of the United States, 1930. Washington, D.C.: National Archives and Records Administration, 1930. T626,), Ancestry.com, http://www.Ancestry.com, Year: 1930; Census Place: Alexandria, Calhoun, Alabama; Roll: 5; Page: 5A; Enumeration District: 4; Image: 100.0. Birth date: about 1872 Birth place: Alabama Residence date: 1930 Residence place: Alexandria, Calhoun, Alabama.

401   Ancestry.com, World War I Draft Registration Cards, 1917-1918 (Online publication - Provo, UT, USA: Ancestry.com Operations Inc, 2005. Original data - United States, Selective Service System. World War I Selective Service System Draft Registration Cards, 1917-1918. Washington, D.C.: National Archives and Records Administration), Ancestry.com, http://www.Ancestry.com, Registration Location: Calhoun County, Alabama; Roll: 1509363; Draft Board: 0. Birth date: 27 Oct 1873 Birth place: Residence date: Residence place: Calhoun, Alabama.

402   Ancestry.com, Alabama Deaths, 1908-59 (Online publication - Provo, UT, USA: Ancestry.com Operations Inc, 2000. Original data - State of Alabama. Index of Vital Records for Alabama: Deaths, 1908-1959. Montgomery, AL, USA: State of Alabama Center for Health Statistics, Record Services Division. Original), Ancestry.com, http://www.Ancestry.com, Death date: 12 Sep 1953 Death place: Calhoun.

403   Historical Data Systems, comp., U.S. Civil War Soldier Records and Profiles (Online publication - Provo, UT, USA: Ancestry.com Operations Inc, 2009. Original data - Data compiled by Historical Data Systems of Kingston, MA from the following list of works. Copyright 1997-2009Historical Data Systems, Inc. PO Box 35Duxbury, MA 02331. Original), Ancestry.com, http://www.Ancestry.com, Birth date: about 1830 Birth place: Residence date: Residence place: USA.

404   Ancestry.com and The Church of Jesus Christ of Latter-day Saints, 1880 United States Federal Census (Online publication - Provo, UT, USA: Ancestry.com Operations Inc, 2010. 1880 U.S. Census Index provided by The Church of Jesus Christ of Latter-day Saints © Copyright 1999 Intellectual Reserve, Inc. All rights reserved. All use is subject to the limited), Ancestry.com, http://www.Ancestry.com, Year: 1880; Census Place: June Bug, Calhoun, Alabama; Roll: 4; Family History Film: 1254004; Page: 534D; Enumeration District: 6; Image: 0629. Birth date: about 1830 Birth place: Tennessee Residence date: 1880 Residence place: June Bug, Calhoun, Alabama, United States.

405   Ancestry.com, 1860 United States Federal Census (Online publication - Provo, UT, USA: Ancestry.com Operations, Inc., 2009. Images reproduced by FamilySearch. Original data - 1860 U.S. census, population schedule. NARA microfilm publication M653, 1,438 rolls. Washington, D.C.: National Archives and Records), Ancestry.com, http://www.Ancestry.com, Year: 1860; Census Place: Ranges 8 and 9, Calhoun, Alabama; Roll: ; Page: 328; Image: 44. Birth date: about 1830 Birth place: Tennessee Residence date: 1860 Residence place: Ranges 8 and 9, Calhoun, Alabama, United States.

406   Ancestry.com, 1860 United States Federal Census (Online publication - Provo, UT, USA: Ancestry.com Operations, Inc., 2009. Images reproduced by FamilySearch. Original data - 1860 U.S. census, population schedule. NARA microfilm publication M653, 1,438 rolls. Washington, D.C.: National Archives and Records), Ancestry.com, http://www.Ancestry.com, Year: 1860; Census Place: Ranges 8 and 9, Calhoun, Alabama; Roll: ; Page: 328; Image: 44. Birth date: about 1854 Birth place: Alabama Residence date: 1860 Residence place: Ranges 8 and 9, Calhoun, Alabama, United States.

407   Ancestry.com, 1900 United States Federal Census (Online publication - Provo, UT, USA: Ancestry.com Operations Inc, 2004. Original data - United States of America, Bureau of the Census. Twelfth Census of the United States, 1900. Washington, D.C.: National Archives and Records Administration, 1900. T623, 18), Ancestry.com, http://www.Ancestry.com, Year: 1900; Census Place: Polkville, Calhoun, Alabama; Roll: T623_5; Page: 3B; Enumeration District: 29. Birth date: Jul 1855 Birth place: Alabama Marriage date: 1880 Marriage place: Residence date: 1900 Residence place: Polkville, Calhoun, Alabama.

408   Ancestry.com, 1900 United States Federal Census (Online publication - Provo, UT, USA: Ancestry.com Operations Inc, 2004. Original data - United States of America, Bureau of the Census. Twelfth Census of the United

States, 1900. Washington, D.C.: National Archives and Records Administration, 1900. T623, 18), Ancestry.com, http://www.Ancestry.com, Year: 1900; Census Place: Weavers, Calhoun, Alabama; Roll: T623_5; Page: 5A; Enumeration District: 27. Birth date: Aug 1857 Birth place: Alabama Marriage date: 1879 Marriage place: Residence date: 1900 Residence place: Weavers, Calhoun, Alabama.

409   Ancestry.com, 1920 United States Federal Census (Online publication - Provo, UT, USA: Ancestry.com Operations Inc, 2010. Images reproduced by FamilySearch. Original data - Fourteenth Census of the United States, 1920. (NARA microfilm publication T625, 2076 rolls). Records of the Bureau of the Census, Record), Ancestry.com, http://www.Ancestry.com, Year: 1920; Census Place: Anniston Ward 5, Calhoun, Alabama; Roll: T625_5; Page: 5A; Enumeration District: 156; Image:. Birth date: about 1859 Birth place: Alabama Residence date: 1920 Residence place: Anniston Ward 5, Calhoun, Alabama.

410   Ancestry.com, 1930 United States Federal Census (Online publication - Provo, UT, USA: Ancestry.com Operations Inc, 2002. Original data - United States of America, Bureau of the Census. Fifteenth Census of the United States, 1930. Washington, D.C.: National Archives and Records Administration, 1930. T626,), Ancestry.com, http://www.Ancestry.com, Year: 1930; Census Place: Oxford, Calhoun, Alabama; Roll: 5; Page: 7A; Enumeration District: 19; Image: 462.0. Birth date: about 1857 Birth place: Alabama Residence date: 1930 Residence place: Oxford, Calhoun, Alabama.

411   Ancestry.com, 1870 United States Federal Census (Online publication - Provo, UT, USA: Ancestry.com Operations, Inc., 2009. Images reproduced by FamilySearch. Original data - 1870 U.S. census, population schedules. NARA microfilm publication M593, 1,761 rolls. Washington, D.C.: National Archives and Record), Ancestry.com, http://www.Ancestry.com, Year: 1870; Census Place: Township 15, Calhoun, Alabama; Roll: M593_; Page: ; Image:. Birth date: about 1858 Birth place: Alabama Residence date: 1870 Residence place: Township 15, Calhoun, Alabama, United States.

412   Ancestry.com, 1860 United States Federal Census (Online publication - Provo, UT, USA: Ancestry.com Operations, Inc., 2009. Images reproduced by FamilySearch. Original data - 1860 U.S. census, population schedule. NARA microfilm publication M653, 1,438 rolls. Washington, D.C.: National Archives and Records), Ancestry.com, http://www.Ancestry.com, Year: 1860; Census Place: Ranges 8 and 9, Calhoun, Alabama; Roll: ; Page: 328; Image: 44. Birth date: about 1857 Birth place: Alabama Residence date: 1860 Residence place: Ranges 8 and 9, Calhoun, Alabama, United States.

413   Ancestry.com, 1910 United States Federal Census (Online publication - Provo, UT, USA: Ancestry.com Operations Inc, 2006. Original data - Thirteenth Census of the United States, 1910 (NARA microfilm publication T624, 1,178 rolls). Records of the Bureau of the Census, Record Group 29. National Archives, Washington), Ancestry.com, http://www.Ancestry.com, Year: 1910; Census Place: Weaver, Calhoun, Alabama; Roll: ; Page: ; Enumeration District: ; Image:. Birth date: about 1858 Birth place: Alabama Residence date: 1910 Residence place: Weaver, Calhoun, Alabama.

414   Ancestry.com and The Church of Jesus Christ of Latter-day Saints, 1880 United States Federal Census (Online publication - Provo, UT, USA: Ancestry.com Operations Inc, 2010. 1880 U.S. Census Index provided by The Church of Jesus Christ of Latter-day Saints © Copyright 1999 Intellectual Reserve, Inc. All rights reserved. All use is subject to the limited), Ancestry.com, http://www.Ancestry.com, Year: 1880; Census Place: June Bug, Calhoun, Alabama; Roll: 4; Family History Film: 1254004; Page: 533B; Enumeration District: 6; Image: 0627. Birth date: about 1856 Birth place: Alabama Residence date: 1880 Residence place: June Bug, Calhoun, Alabama, United States.

415   Ancestry.com, Alabama Deaths, 1908-59 (Online publication - Provo, UT, USA: Ancestry.com Operations Inc, 2000. Original data - State of Alabama. Index of Vital Records for Alabama: Deaths, 1908-1959. Montgomery, AL, USA: State of Alabama Center for Health Statistics, Record Services Division. Original), Ancestry.com, http://www.Ancestry.com, Death date: Dec 1935 Death place: Calhoun.

416   Ancestry.com and The Church of Jesus Christ of Latter-day Saints, 1880 United States Federal Census (Online publication - Provo, UT, USA: Ancestry.com Operations Inc, 2010. 1880 U.S. Census Index provided by The Church of Jesus Christ of Latter-day Saints © Copyright 1999 Intellectual Reserve, Inc. All rights reserved. All use is subject to the limited), Ancestry.com, http://www.Ancestry.com, Year: 1880; Census Place: June Bug, Calhoun, Alabama; Roll: 4; Family History Film: 1254004; Page: 534D; Enumeration District: 6; Image: 0629. Birth date: about 1865 Birth place: Alabama Residence date: 1880 Residence place: June Bug, Calhoun, Alabama, United States.

417   Ancestry.com and The Church of Jesus Christ of Latter-day Saints, 1880 United States Federal Census (Online publication - Provo, UT, USA: Ancestry.com Operations Inc, 2010. 1880 U.S. Census Index provided by The Church of Jesus Christ of Latter-day Saints © Copyright 1999 Intellectual Reserve, Inc. All rights reserved. All use is subject to the limited), Ancestry.com, http://www.Ancestry.com, Year: 1880; Census Place: June Bug, Calhoun, Alabama; Roll: 4; Family History Film: 1254004; Page: 534D; Enumeration District: 6; Image: 0629. Birth date: about 1867 Birth place: Alabama Residence date: 1880 Residence place: June Bug, Calhoun, Alabama, United States.

418   Ancestry.com and The Church of Jesus Christ of Latter-day Saints, 1880 United States Federal Census (Online publication - Provo, UT, USA: Ancestry.com Operations Inc, 2010. 1880 U.S. Census Index provided by The Church of Jesus Christ of Latter-day Saints © Copyright 1999 Intellectual Reserve, Inc. All rights reserved. All use is subject to the limited), Ancestry.com, http://www.Ancestry.com, Year: 1880; Census Place: June Bug, Calhoun, Alabama; Roll: 4; Family History Film: 1254004; Page: 534D; Enumeration District: 6; Image: 0629. Birth date: about 1869 Birth place: Alabama Residence date: 1880 Residence place: June Bug, Calhoun, Alabama, United States.

419   Ancestry.com, 1900 United States Federal Census (Online publication - Provo, UT, USA: Ancestry.com Operations Inc, 2004. Original data - United States of America, Bureau of the Census. Twelfth Census of the United

States, 1900. Washington, D.C.: National Archives and Records Administration, 1900. T623, 18), Ancestry.com, http://www.Ancestry.com, Year: 1900; Census Place: Bluff Eye, Talladega, Alabama; Roll: T623_40; Page: 9A; Enumeration District: 84. Birth date: Mar 1869 Birth place: Alabama Residence date: 1900 Residence place: Bluff Eye, Talladega, Alabama.

420   Ancestry.com and The Church of Jesus Christ of Latter-day Saints, 1880 United States Federal Census (Online publication - Provo, UT, USA: Ancestry.com Operations Inc, 2010. 1880 U.S. Census Index provided by The Church of Jesus Christ of Latter-day Saints © Copyright 1999 Intellectual Reserve, Inc. All rights reserved. All use is subject to the limited), Ancestry.com, http://www.Ancestry.com, Year: 1880; Census Place: June Bug, Calhoun, Alabama; Roll: 4; Family History Film: 1254004; Page: 534D; Enumeration District: 6; Image: 0629. Birth date: about 1871 Birth place: Alabama Residence date: 1880 Residence place: June Bug, Calhoun, Alabama, United States.

421   Ancestry.com and The Church of Jesus Christ of Latter-day Saints, 1880 United States Federal Census (Online publication - Provo, UT, USA: Ancestry.com Operations Inc, 2010. 1880 U.S. Census Index provided by The Church of Jesus Christ of Latter-day Saints © Copyright 1999 Intellectual Reserve, Inc. All rights reserved. All use is subject to the limited), Ancestry.com, http://www.Ancestry.com, Year: 1880; Census Place: June Bug, Calhoun, Alabama; Roll: 4; Family History Film: 1254004; Page: 534D; Enumeration District: 6; Image: 0629. Birth date: about 1873 Birth place: Alabama Residence date: 1880 Residence place: June Bug, Calhoun, Alabama, United States.

422   Ancestry.com and The Church of Jesus Christ of Latter-day Saints, 1880 United States Federal Census (Online publication - Provo, UT, USA: Ancestry.com Operations Inc, 2010. 1880 U.S. Census Index provided by The Church of Jesus Christ of Latter-day Saints © Copyright 1999 Intellectual Reserve, Inc. All rights reserved. All use is subject to the limited), Ancestry.com, http://www.Ancestry.com, Year: 1880; Census Place: June Bug, Calhoun, Alabama; Roll: 4; Family History Film: 1254004; Page: 534D; Enumeration District: 6; Image: 0629. Birth date: about 1875 Birth place: Alabama Residence date: 1880 Residence place: June Bug, Calhoun, Alabama, United States.

423   Ancestry.com and The Church of Jesus Christ of Latter-day Saints, 1880 United States Federal Census (Online publication - Provo, UT, USA: Ancestry.com Operations Inc, 2010. 1880 U.S. Census Index provided by The Church of Jesus Christ of Latter-day Saints © Copyright 1999 Intellectual Reserve, Inc. All rights reserved. All use is subject to the limited), Ancestry.com, http://www.Ancestry.com, Year: 1880; Census Place: June Bug, Calhoun, Alabama; Roll: 4; Family History Film: 1254004; Page: 534D; Enumeration District: 6; Image: 0629. Birth date: about 1877 Birth place: Alabama Residence date: 1880 Residence place: June Bug, Calhoun, Alabama, United States.

424   Ancestry.com, 1900 United States Federal Census (Online publication - Provo, UT, USA: Ancestry.com Operations Inc, 2004. Original data - United States of America, Bureau of the Census. Twelfth Census of the United States, 1900. Washington, D.C.: National Archives and Records Administration, 1900. T623, 18), Ancestry.com, http://www.Ancestry.com, Year: 1900; Census Place: Bluff Eye, Talladega, Alabama; Roll: T623_40; Page: 9A; Enumeration District: 84. Birth date: Jan 1880 Birth place: Alabama Residence date: 1900 Residence place: Bluff Eye, Talladega, Alabama.

425   Ancestry.com and The Church of Jesus Christ of Latter-day Saints, 1880 United States Federal Census (Online publication - Provo, UT, USA: Ancestry.com Operations Inc, 2010. 1880 U.S. Census Index provided by The Church of Jesus Christ of Latter-day Saints © Copyright 1999 Intellectual Reserve, Inc. All rights reserved. All use is subject to the limited), Ancestry.com, http://www.Ancestry.com, Year: 1880; Census Place: June Bug, Calhoun, Alabama; Roll: 4; Family History Film: 1254004; Page: 534D; Enumeration District: 6; Image: 0629. Birth date: about 1879 Birth place: Alabama Residence date: 1880 Residence place: June Bug, Calhoun, Alabama, United States.

426   Ancestry.com and The Church of Jesus Christ of Latter-day Saints, 1880 United States Federal Census (Online publication - Provo, UT, USA: Ancestry.com Operations Inc, 2010. 1880 U.S. Census Index provided by The Church of Jesus Christ of Latter-day Saints © Copyright 1999 Intellectual Reserve, Inc. All rights reserved. All use is subject to the limited), Ancestry.com, http://www.Ancestry.com, Year: 1880; Census Place: June Bug, Calhoun, Alabama; Roll: 4; Family History Film: 1254004; Page: 535A; Enumeration District: 6; Image: 0630. Birth date: about 1836 Birth place: Alabama Residence date: 1880 Residence place: June Bug, Calhoun, Alabama, United States.

427   Ancestry.com and The Church of Jesus Christ of Latter-day Saints, 1880 United States Federal Census (Online publication - Provo, UT, USA: Ancestry.com Operations Inc, 2010. 1880 U.S. Census Index provided by The Church of Jesus Christ of Latter-day Saints © Copyright 1999 Intellectual Reserve, Inc. All rights reserved. All use is subject to the limited), Ancestry.com, http://www.Ancestry.com, Year: 1880; Census Place: June Bug, Calhoun, Alabama; Roll: 4; Family History Film: 1254004; Page: 535A; Enumeration District: 6; Image: 0630. Birth date: about 1878 Birth place: Alabama Residence date: 1880 Residence place: June Bug, Calhoun, Alabama, United States.

428   Ancestry.com and The Church of Jesus Christ of Latter-day Saints, 1880 United States Federal Census (Online publication - Provo, UT, USA: Ancestry.com Operations Inc, 2010. 1880 U.S. Census Index provided by The Church of Jesus Christ of Latter-day Saints © Copyright 1999 Intellectual Reserve, Inc. All rights reserved. All use is subject to the limited), Ancestry.com, http://www.Ancestry.com, Year: 1880; Census Place: June Bug, Calhoun, Alabama; Roll: 4; Family History Film: 1254004; Page: 535A; Enumeration District: 6; Image: 0630. Birth date: about 1862 Birth place: Alabama Residence date: 1880 Residence place: June Bug, Calhoun, Alabama, United States.

429   Ancestry.com and The Church of Jesus Christ of Latter-day Saints, 1880 United States Federal Census (Online publication - Provo, UT, USA: Ancestry.com Operations Inc, 2010. 1880 U.S. Census Index provided by The Church of Jesus Christ of Latter-day Saints © Copyright 1999 Intellectual Reserve, Inc. All rights reserved. All use is subject to the limited), Ancestry.com, http://www.Ancestry.com, Year: 1880; Census Place: , Cherokee, Alabama; Roll: 6; Family History

148

Film: 1254006; Page: 394D; Enumeration District: 27; Image:. Birth date: about 1863 Birth place: Alabama Residence date: 1880 Residence place: Cherokee, Alabama, United States.

430	Ancestry.com and The Church of Jesus Christ of Latter-day Saints, 1880 United States Federal Census (Online publication - Provo, UT, USA: Ancestry.com Operations Inc, 2010. 1880 U.S. Census Index provided by The Church of Jesus Christ of Latter-day Saints © Copyright 1999 Intellectual Reserve, Inc. All rights reserved. All use is subject to the limited), Ancestry.com, http://www.Ancestry.com, Year: 1880; Census Place: , Cherokee, Alabama; Roll: 6; Family History Film: 1254006; Page: 394D; Enumeration District: 27; Image:. Birth date: about 1866 Birth place: Alabama Residence date: 1880 Residence place: Cherokee, Alabama, United States.

431	Ancestry.com and The Church of Jesus Christ of Latter-day Saints, 1880 United States Federal Census (Online publication - Provo, UT, USA: Ancestry.com Operations Inc, 2010. 1880 U.S. Census Index provided by The Church of Jesus Christ of Latter-day Saints © Copyright 1999 Intellectual Reserve, Inc. All rights reserved. All use is subject to the limited), Ancestry.com, http://www.Ancestry.com, Year: 1880; Census Place: , Cherokee, Alabama; Roll: 6; Family History Film: 1254006; Page: 394D; Enumeration District: 27; Image:. Birth date: about 1869 Birth place: Alabama Residence date: 1880 Residence place: Cherokee, Alabama, United States.

432	Ancestry.com and The Church of Jesus Christ of Latter-day Saints, 1880 United States Federal Census (Online publication - Provo, UT, USA: Ancestry.com Operations Inc, 2010. 1880 U.S. Census Index provided by The Church of Jesus Christ of Latter-day Saints © Copyright 1999 Intellectual Reserve, Inc. All rights reserved. All use is subject to the limited), Ancestry.com, http://www.Ancestry.com, Year: 1880; Census Place: , Cherokee, Alabama; Roll: 6; Family History Film: 1254006; Page: 395A; Enumeration District: 27; Image:. Birth date: about 1872 Birth place: Alabama Residence date: 1880 Residence place: Cherokee, Alabama, United States.

433	Ancestry.com and The Church of Jesus Christ of Latter-day Saints, 1880 United States Federal Census (Online publication - Provo, UT, USA: Ancestry.com Operations Inc, 2010. 1880 U.S. Census Index provided by The Church of Jesus Christ of Latter-day Saints © Copyright 1999 Intellectual Reserve, Inc. All rights reserved. All use is subject to the limited), Ancestry.com, http://www.Ancestry.com, Year: 1880; Census Place: , Cherokee, Alabama; Roll: 6; Family History Film: 1254006; Page: 395A; Enumeration District: 27; Image:. Birth date: about 1875 Birth place: Alabama Residence date: 1880 Residence place: Cherokee, Alabama, United States.

434	Ancestry.com and The Church of Jesus Christ of Latter-day Saints, 1880 United States Federal Census (Online publication - Provo, UT, USA: Ancestry.com Operations Inc, 2010. 1880 U.S. Census Index provided by The Church of Jesus Christ of Latter-day Saints © Copyright 1999 Intellectual Reserve, Inc. All rights reserved. All use is subject to the limited), Ancestry.com, http://www.Ancestry.com, Year: 1880; Census Place: , Cherokee, Alabama; Roll: 6; Family History Film: 1254006; Page: 395A; Enumeration District: 27; Image:. Birth date: about 1879 Birth place: Alabama Residence date: 1880 Residence place: Cherokee, Alabama, United States.

435	Ancestry.com, 1850 United States Federal Census (Online publication - Provo, UT, USA: Ancestry.com Operations, Inc., 2009. Images reproduced by FamilySearch. Original data - Seventh Census of the United States, 1850; (National Archives Microfilm Publication M432, 1009 rolls); Records of the Bureau of the), Ancestry.com, http://www.Ancestry.com, Year: 1850; Census Place: Subdivision 29, Benton, Alabama; Roll: M432_1; Page: 360B; Image:. Birth date: about 1841 Birth place: Alabama Residence date: 1850 Residence place: Subdivision 29, Benton, Alabama.

436	Ancestry.com, 1900 United States Federal Census (Online publication - Provo, UT, USA: Ancestry.com Operations Inc, 2004. Original data - United States of America, Bureau of the Census. Twelfth Census of the United States, 1900. Washington, D.C.: National Archives and Records Administration, 1900. T623, 18), Ancestry.com, http://www.Ancestry.com, Year: 1900; Census Place: Reed Brake, Marshall, Alabama; Roll: T623_30; Page: 8A; Enumeration District: 97. Birth date: Jul 1841 Birth place: Alabama Marriage date: 1870 Marriage place: Residence date: 1900 Residence place: Reed Brake, Marshall, Alabama.

437	Ancestry.com and The Church of Jesus Christ of Latter-day Saints, 1880 United States Federal Census (Online publication - Provo, UT, USA: Ancestry.com Operations Inc, 2010. 1880 U.S. Census Index provided by The Church of Jesus Christ of Latter-day Saints © Copyright 1999 Intellectual Reserve, Inc. All rights reserved. All use is subject to the limited), Ancestry.com, http://www.Ancestry.com, Year: 1880; Census Place: June Bug, Calhoun, Alabama; Roll: 4; Family History Film: 1254004; Page: 534D; Enumeration District: 6; Image: 0629. Birth date: about 1843 Birth place: Alabama Residence date: 1880 Residence place: June Bug, Calhoun, Alabama, United States.

438	Ancestry.com, 1860 United States Federal Census (Online publication - Provo, UT, USA: Ancestry.com Operations, Inc., 2009. Images reproduced by FamilySearch. Original data - 1860 U.S. census, population schedule. NARA microfilm publication M653, 1,438 rolls. Washington, D.C.: National Archives and Records), Ancestry.com, http://www.Ancestry.com, Year: 1860; Census Place: Ranges 8 and 9, Calhoun, Alabama; Roll: ; Page: 328; Image: 44. Birth date: about 1842 Birth place: Alabama Residence date: 1860 Residence place: Ranges 8 and 9, Calhoun, Alabama, United States.

439	Ancestry.com and The Church of Jesus Christ of Latter-day Saints, 1880 United States Federal Census (Online publication - Provo, UT, USA: Ancestry.com Operations Inc, 2010. 1880 U.S. Census Index provided by The Church of Jesus Christ of Latter-day Saints © Copyright 1999 Intellectual Reserve, Inc. All rights reserved. All use is subject to the limited), Ancestry.com, http://www.Ancestry.com, Year: 1880; Census Place: June Bug, Calhoun, Alabama; Roll: 4; Family History Film: 1254004; Page: 534D; Enumeration District: 6; Image: 0629. Birth date: about 1866 Birth place: Alabama Residence date: 1880 Residence place: June Bug, Calhoun, Alabama, United States.

440		Ancestry.com, 1900 United States Federal Census (Online publication - Provo, UT, USA: Ancestry.com Operations Inc, 2004. Original data - United States of America, Bureau of the Census. Twelfth Census of the United States, 1900. Washington, D.C.: National Archives and Records Administration, 1900. T623, 18), Ancestry.com, http://www.Ancestry.com, Year: 1900; Census Place: Rock Spring, Marshall, Alabama; Roll: T623_30; Page: 5A; Enumeration District: 90. Birth date: Jun 1866 Birth place: Alabama Marriage date: 1891 Marriage place: Residence date: 1900 Residence place: Rock Spring, Marshall, Alabama.

441		Ancestry.com, 1910 United States Federal Census (Online publication - Provo, UT, USA: Ancestry.com Operations Inc, 2006. Original data - Thirteenth Census of the United States, 1910 (NARA microfilm publication T624, 1,178 rolls). Records of the Bureau of the Census, Record Group 29. National Archives, Washington), Ancestry.com, http://www.Ancestry.com, Year: 1910; Census Place: Albertville, Marshall, Alabama; Roll: ; Page: ; Enumeration District: ; Image:. Birth date: about 1866 Birth place: Alabama Residence date: 1910 Residence place: Albertville, Marshall, Alabama.

442		Ancestry.com, Alabama Deaths, 1908-59 (Online publication - Provo, UT, USA: Ancestry.com Operations Inc, 2000. Original data - State of Alabama. Index of Vital Records for Alabama: Deaths, 1908-1959. Montgomery, AL, USA: State of Alabama Center for Health Statistics, Record Services Division. Original), Ancestry.com, http://www.Ancestry.com, Death date: 23 Sep 1942 Death place: Marshall.

443		Ancestry.com, 1920 United States Federal Census (Online publication - Provo, UT, USA: Ancestry.com Operations Inc, 2010. Images reproduced by FamilySearch. Original data - Fourteenth Census of the United States, 1920. (NARA microfilm publication T625, 2076 rolls). Records of the Bureau of the Census, Record), Ancestry.com, http://www.Ancestry.com, Year: 1920; Census Place: Albertville, Marshall, Alabama; Roll: T625_28; Page: 26B; Enumeration District: 122; Image:. Birth date: about 1867 Birth place: Alabama Residence date: 1920 Residence place: Albertville, Marshall, Alabama.

444		Ancestry.com, 1930 United States Federal Census (Online publication - Provo, UT, USA: Ancestry.com Operations Inc, 2002. Original data - United States of America, Bureau of the Census. Fifteenth Census of the United States, 1930. Washington, D.C.: National Archives and Records Administration, 1930. T626,), Ancestry.com, http://www.Ancestry.com, Year: 1930; Census Place: Albertville, Marshall, Alabama; Roll: 39; Page: 1A; Enumeration District: 7; Image: 725.0. Birth date: about 1867 Birth place: Alabama Residence date: 1930 Residence place: Albertville, Marshall, Alabama.

445		Ancestry.com, 1900 United States Federal Census (Online publication - Provo, UT, USA: Ancestry.com Operations Inc, 2004. Original data - United States of America, Bureau of the Census. Twelfth Census of the United States, 1900. Washington, D.C.: National Archives and Records Administration, 1900. T623, 18), Ancestry.com, http://www.Ancestry.com, Year: 1900; Census Place: Rock Spring, Marshall, Alabama; Roll: T623_30; Page: 5A; Enumeration District: 90. Birth date: Jun 1868 Birth place: Alabama Marriage date: 1892 Marriage place: Residence date: 1900 Residence place: Rock Spring, Marshall, Alabama.

446		Ancestry.com and The Church of Jesus Christ of Latter-day Saints, 1880 United States Federal Census (Online publication - Provo, UT, USA: Ancestry.com Operations Inc, 2010. 1880 U.S. Census Index provided by The Church of Jesus Christ of Latter-day Saints © Copyright 1999 Intellectual Reserve, Inc. All rights reserved. All use is subject to the limited), Ancestry.com, http://www.Ancestry.com, Year: 1880; Census Place: June Bug, Calhoun, Alabama; Roll: 4; Family History Film: 1254004; Page: 534D; Enumeration District: 6; Image: 0629. Birth date: about 1868 Birth place: Alabama Residence date: 1880 Residence place: June Bug, Calhoun, Alabama, United States.

447		Ancestry.com, 1920 United States Federal Census (Online publication - Provo, UT, USA: Ancestry.com Operations Inc, 2010. Images reproduced by FamilySearch. Original data - Fourteenth Census of the United States, 1920. (NARA microfilm publication T625, 2076 rolls). Records of the Bureau of the Census, Record), Ancestry.com, http://www.Ancestry.com, Year: 1920; Census Place: Weavers, Calhoun, Alabama; Roll: T625_5; Page: 5B; Enumeration District: 4; Image:. Birth date: about 1868 Birth place: Alabama Residence date: 1920 Residence place: Weavers, Calhoun, Alabama.

448		Ancestry.com, 1910 United States Federal Census (Online publication - Provo, UT, USA: Ancestry.com Operations Inc, 2006. Original data - Thirteenth Census of the United States, 1910 (NARA microfilm publication T624, 1,178 rolls). Records of the Bureau of the Census, Record Group 29. National Archives, Washington), Ancestry.com, http://www.Ancestry.com, Year: 1910; Census Place: Weaver, Calhoun, Alabama; Roll: ; Page: ; Enumeration District: ; Image:. Birth date: about 1868 Birth place: Alabama Residence date: 1910 Residence place: Weaver, Calhoun, Alabama.

449		Ancestry.com, Alabama Deaths, 1908-59 (Online publication - Provo, UT, USA: Ancestry.com Operations Inc, 2000. Original data - State of Alabama. Index of Vital Records for Alabama: Deaths, 1908-1959. Montgomery, AL, USA: State of Alabama Center for Health Statistics, Record Services Division. Original), Ancestry.com, http://www.Ancestry.com, Death date: 08 Apr 1949 Death place: Calhoun.

450		Ancestry.com, Alabama Deaths, 1908-59 (Online publication - Provo, UT, USA: Ancestry.com Operations Inc, 2000. Original data - State of Alabama. Index of Vital Records for Alabama: Deaths, 1908-1959. Montgomery, AL, USA: State of Alabama Center for Health Statistics, Record Services Division. Original), Ancestry.com, http://www.Ancestry.com, Death date: 27 Jul 1956 Death place: Calhoun.

451		Ancestry.com and The Church of Jesus Christ of Latter-day Saints, 1880 United States Federal Census (Online publication - Provo, UT, USA: Ancestry.com Operations Inc, 2010. 1880 U.S. Census Index provided by The Church of Jesus Christ of Latter-day Saints © Copyright 1999 Intellectual Reserve, Inc. All rights reserved. All use is subject to the limited), Ancestry.com, http://www.Ancestry.com, Year: 1880; Census Place: June Bug, Calhoun, Alabama; Roll: 4;

Family History Film: 1254004; Page: 534D; Enumeration District: 6; Image: 0629. Birth date: about 1873 Birth place: Alabama Residence date: 1880 Residence place: June Bug, Calhoun, Alabama, United States.

452   Ancestry.com, 1900 United States Federal Census (Online publication - Provo, UT, USA: Ancestry.com Operations Inc, 2004. Original data - United States of America, Bureau of the Census. Twelfth Census of the United States, 1900. Washington, D.C.: National Archives and Records Administration, 1900. T623, 18), Ancestry.com, http://www.Ancestry.com, Year: 1900; Census Place: Friendship, Marshall, Alabama; Roll: T623_30; Page: 5A; Enumeration District: 92. Birth date: Aug 1871 Birth place: Alabama Marriage date: 1889 Marriage place: Residence date: 1900 Residence place: Friendship, Marshall, Alabama.

453   Ancestry.com, 1900 United States Federal Census (Online publication - Provo, UT, USA: Ancestry.com Operations Inc, 2004. Original data - United States of America, Bureau of the Census. Twelfth Census of the United States, 1900. Washington, D.C.: National Archives and Records Administration, 1900. T623, 18), Ancestry.com, http://www.Ancestry.com, Year: 1900; Census Place: Friendship, Marshall, Alabama; Roll: T623_30; Page: 5A; Enumeration District: 92. Birth date: Dec 1847 Birth place: Tennessee Marriage date: 1889 Marriage place: Residence date: 1900 Residence place: Friendship, Marshall, Alabama.

454   Ancestry.com, 1900 United States Federal Census (Online publication - Provo, UT, USA: Ancestry.com Operations Inc, 2004. Original data - United States of America, Bureau of the Census. Twelfth Census of the United States, 1900. Washington, D.C.: National Archives and Records Administration, 1900. T623, 18), Ancestry.com, http://www.Ancestry.com, Year: 1900; Census Place: Reed Brake, Marshall, Alabama; Roll: T623_30; Page: 8A; Enumeration District: 97. Birth date: Mar 1876 Birth place: Alabama Residence date: 1900 Residence place: Reed Brake, Marshall, Alabama.

455   Ancestry.com, 1910 United States Federal Census (Online publication - Provo, UT, USA: Ancestry.com Operations Inc, 2006. Original data - Thirteenth Census of the United States, 1910 (NARA microfilm publication T624, 1,178 rolls). Records of the Bureau of the Census, Record Group 29. National Archives, Washington), Ancestry.com, http://www.Ancestry.com, Year: 1910; Census Place: Alabama Ward 2, Etowah, Alabama; Roll: ; Page: ; Enumeration District: ; Image:. Birth date: about 1875 Birth place: Alabama Residence date: 1910 Residence place: Alabama Ward 2, Etowah, Alabama.

456   Ancestry.com and The Church of Jesus Christ of Latter-day Saints, 1880 United States Federal Census (Online publication - Provo, UT, USA: Ancestry.com Operations Inc, 2010. 1880 U.S. Census Index provided by The Church of Jesus Christ of Latter-day Saints © Copyright 1999 Intellectual Reserve, Inc. All rights reserved. All use is subject to the limited), Ancestry.com, http://www.Ancestry.com, Year: 1880; Census Place: June Bug, Calhoun, Alabama; Roll: 4; Family History Film: 1254004; Page: 534D; Enumeration District: 6; Image: 0629. Birth date: about 1874 Birth place: Alabama Residence date: 1880 Residence place: June Bug, Calhoun, Alabama, United States.

457   Ancestry.com, 1920 United States Federal Census (Online publication - Provo, UT, USA: Ancestry.com Operations Inc, 2010. Images reproduced by FamilySearch. Original data - Fourteenth Census of the United States, 1920. (NARA microfilm publication T625, 2076 rolls). Records of the Bureau of the Census, Record), Ancestry.com, http://www.Ancestry.com, Year: 1920; Census Place: Albertville, Marshall, Alabama; Roll: T625_28; Page: 9A; Enumeration District: 122; Image:. Birth date: about 1876 Birth place: Alabama Residence date: 1920 Residence place: Albertville, Marshall, Alabama.

458   Ancestry.com, 1910 United States Federal Census (Online publication - Provo, UT, USA: Ancestry.com Operations Inc, 2006. Original data - Thirteenth Census of the United States, 1910 (NARA microfilm publication T624, 1,178 rolls). Records of the Bureau of the Census, Record Group 29. National Archives, Washington), Ancestry.com, http://www.Ancestry.com, Year: 1910; Census Place: Weaver, Calhoun, Alabama; Roll: ; Page: ; Enumeration District: ; Image:. Birth date: about 1876 Birth place: Alabama Residence date: 1910 Residence place: Weaver, Calhoun, Alabama.

459   Ancestry.com and The Church of Jesus Christ of Latter-day Saints, 1880 United States Federal Census (Online publication - Provo, UT, USA: Ancestry.com Operations Inc, 2010. 1880 U.S. Census Index provided by The Church of Jesus Christ of Latter-day Saints © Copyright 1999 Intellectual Reserve, Inc. All rights reserved. All use is subject to the limited), Ancestry.com, http://www.Ancestry.com, Year: 1880; Census Place: June Bug, Calhoun, Alabama; Roll: 4; Family History Film: 1254004; Page: 534D; Enumeration District: 6; Image: 0629. Birth date: about 1876 Birth place: Alabama Residence date: 1880 Residence place: June Bug, Calhoun, Alabama, United States.

460   Ancestry.com, 1920 United States Federal Census (Online publication - Provo, UT, USA: Ancestry.com Operations Inc, 2010. Images reproduced by FamilySearch. Original data - Fourteenth Census of the United States, 1920. (NARA microfilm publication T625, 2076 rolls). Records of the Bureau of the Census, Record), Ancestry.com, http://www.Ancestry.com, Year: 1920; Census Place: Weavers, Calhoun, Alabama; Roll: T625_5; Page: 8B; Enumeration District: 4; Image:. Birth date: about 1876 Birth place: Alabama Residence date: 1920 Residence place: Weavers, Calhoun, Alabama.

461   Ancestry.com, 1900 United States Federal Census (Online publication - Provo, UT, USA: Ancestry.com Operations Inc, 2004. Original data - United States of America, Bureau of the Census. Twelfth Census of the United States, 1900. Washington, D.C.: National Archives and Records Administration, 1900. T623, 18), Ancestry.com, http://www.Ancestry.com, Year: 1900; Census Place: Weavers, Calhoun, Alabama; Roll: T623_5; Page: 3A; Enumeration District: 27. Birth date: Mar 1879 Birth place: Alabama Marriage date: 1891 Marriage place: Residence date: 1900 Residence place: Weavers, Calhoun, Alabama.

462   Ancestry.com, Alabama Deaths, 1908-59 (Online publication - Provo, UT, USA: Ancestry.com Operations Inc, 2000. Original data - State of Alabama. Index of Vital Records for Alabama: Deaths, 1908-1959. Montgomery, AL, USA:

State of Alabama Center for Health Statistics, Record Services Division. Original), Ancestry.com, http://www.Ancestry.com, Death date: 24 Mar 1947 Death place: Calhoun.

463   Ancestry.com, 1900 United States Federal Census (Online publication - Provo, UT, USA: Ancestry.com Operations Inc, 2004. Original data - United States of America, Bureau of the Census. Twelfth Census of the United States, 1900. Washington, D.C.: National Archives and Records Administration, 1900. T623, 18), Ancestry.com, http://www.Ancestry.com, Year: 1900; Census Place: Weavers, Calhoun, Alabama; Roll: T623_5; Page: 3A; Enumeration District: 27. Birth date: May 1870 Birth place: Alabama Marriage date: 1891 Marriage place: Residence date: 1900 Residence place: Weavers, Calhoun, Alabama.

464   Ancestry.com and The Church of Jesus Christ of Latter-day Saints, 1880 United States Federal Census (Online publication - Provo, UT, USA: Ancestry.com Operations Inc, 2010. 1880 U.S. Census Index provided by The Church of Jesus Christ of Latter-day Saints © Copyright 1999 Intellectual Reserve, Inc. All rights reserved. All use is subject to the limited), Ancestry.com, http://www.Ancestry.com, Year: 1880; Census Place: June Bug, Calhoun, Alabama; Roll: 4; Family History Film: 1254004; Page: 534D; Enumeration District: 6; Image: 0629. Birth date: about 1880 Birth place: Alabama Residence date: 1880 Residence place: June Bug, Calhoun, Alabama, United States.

465   Ancestry.com, 1930 United States Federal Census (Online publication - Provo, UT, USA: Ancestry.com Operations Inc, 2002. Original data - United States of America, Bureau of the Census. Fifteenth Census of the United States, 1930. Washington, D.C.: National Archives and Records Administration, 1930. T626,), Ancestry.com, http://www.Ancestry.com, Year: 1930; Census Place: Jay Bird, Marshall, Alabama; Roll: 39; Page: 5A; Enumeration District: 8; Image: 757.0. Birth date: about 1885 Birth place: Alabama Residence date: 1930 Residence place: Jay Bird, Marshall, Alabama.

466   Ancestry.com, 1900 United States Federal Census (Online publication - Provo, UT, USA: Ancestry.com Operations Inc, 2004. Original data - United States of America, Bureau of the Census. Twelfth Census of the United States, 1900. Washington, D.C.: National Archives and Records Administration, 1900. T623, 18), Ancestry.com, http://www.Ancestry.com, Year: 1900; Census Place: Reed Brake, Marshall, Alabama; Roll: T623_30; Page: 8A; Enumeration District: 97. Birth date: Mar 1886 Birth place: Alabama Residence date: 1900 Residence place: Reed Brake, Marshall, Alabama.

467   Ancestry.com, World War I Draft Registration Cards, 1917-1918 (Online publication - Provo, UT, USA: Ancestry.com Operations Inc, 2005. Original data - United States, Selective Service System. World War I Selective Service System Draft Registration Cards, 1917-1918. Washington, D.C.: National Archives and Records Administration), Ancestry.com, http://www.Ancestry.com, Registration Location: Calhoun County, Alabama; Roll: 1509363; Draft Board: 0. Birth date: 29 Mar 1885 Birth place: Residence date: Residence place: Calhoun, Alabama.

468   Ancestry.com, 1920 United States Federal Census (Online publication - Provo, UT, USA: Ancestry.com Operations Inc, 2010. Images reproduced by FamilySearch. Original data - Fourteenth Census of the United States, 1920. (NARA microfilm publication T625, 2076 rolls). Records of the Bureau of the Census, Record), Ancestry.com, http://www.Ancestry.com, Year: 1920; Census Place: Lincoln, Talladega, Alabama; Roll: T625_41; Page: 1A; Enumeration District: 129; Image:. Birth date: about 1887 Birth place: Alabama Residence date: 1920 Residence place: Lincoln, Talladega, Alabama.

469   Ancestry.com, 1910 United States Federal Census (Online publication - Provo, UT, USA: Ancestry.com Operations Inc, 2006. Original data - Thirteenth Census of the United States, 1910 (NARA microfilm publication T624, 1,178 rolls). Records of the Bureau of the Census, Record Group 29. National Archives, Washington), Ancestry.com, http://www.Ancestry.com, Year: 1910; Census Place: Precinct 1, Talladega, Alabama; Roll: ; Page: ; Enumeration District: ; Image:. Birth date: about 1886 Birth place: Alabama Residence date: 1910 Residence place: Precinct 1, Talladega, Alabama.

470   Ancestry.com, Alabama Deaths, 1908-59 (Online publication - Provo, UT, USA: Ancestry.com Operations Inc, 2000. Original data - State of Alabama. Index of Vital Records for Alabama: Deaths, 1908-1959. Montgomery, AL, USA: State of Alabama Center for Health Statistics, Record Services Division. Original), Ancestry.com, http://www.Ancestry.com, Death date: 08 Feb 1955 Death place: Etowah.

471   Ancestry.com and The Church of Jesus Christ of Latter-day Saints, 1880 United States Federal Census (Online publication - Provo, UT, USA: Ancestry.com Operations Inc, 2010. 1880 U.S. Census Index provided by The Church of Jesus Christ of Latter-day Saints © Copyright 1999 Intellectual Reserve, Inc. All rights reserved. All use is subject to the limited), Ancestry.com, http://www.Ancestry.com, Year: 1880; Census Place: 6th Ward, Lincoln, Louisiana; Roll: 456; Family History Film: 1254456; Page: 28C; Enumeration District: 38; Image: 0058. Birth date: about 1837 Birth place: Georgia Residence date: 1880 Residence place: 6th Ward, Lincoln, Louisiana, United States.

472   Ancestry.com, 1860 United States Federal Census (Online publication - Provo, UT, USA: Ancestry.com Operations, Inc., 2009. Images reproduced by FamilySearch. Original data - 1860 U.S. census, population schedule. NARA microfilm publication M653, 1,438 rolls. Washington, D.C.: National Archives and Records), Ancestry.com, http://www.Ancestry.com, Year: 1860; Census Place: Moss, Columbia, Arkansas; Roll: ; Page: 309; Image: 311. Birth date: about 1836 Birth place: Georgia Residence date: 1860 Residence place: Moss, Columbia, Arkansas, United States.

473   Ancestry.com, 1900 United States Federal Census (Online publication - Provo, UT, USA: Ancestry.com Operations Inc, 2004. Original data - United States of America, Bureau of the Census. Twelfth Census of the United States, 1900. Washington, D.C.: National Archives and Records Administration, 1900. T623, 18), Ancestry.com, http://www.Ancestry.com, Year: 1900; Census Place: Police Jury Ward 8, Claiborne, Louisiana; Roll: T623_562; Page:

11A; Enumeration District: 27. Birth date: Aug 1836 Birth place: Georgia Marriage date: 1854 Marriage place: Residence date: 1900 Residence place: Ward 8 (South Half), Claiborne, Louisiana.

474   Ancestry.com, 1910 United States Federal Census (Online publication - Provo, UT, USA: Ancestry.com Operations Inc, 2006. Original data - Thirteenth Census of the United States, 1910 (NARA microfilm publication T624, 1,178 rolls). Records of the Bureau of the Census, Record Group 29. National Archives, Washington), Ancestry.com, http://www.Ancestry.com, Year: 1910; Census Place: Police Jury Ward 4, Union, Louisiana; Roll: ; Page: ; Enumeration District: ; Image:. Birth date: 1836 Birth place: Louisiana Residence date: 1910 Residence place: Police Jury Ward 4, Union, Louisiana.

475   Ancestry.com and The Church of Jesus Christ of Latter-day Saints, 1880 United States Federal Census (Online publication - Provo, UT, USA: Ancestry.com Operations Inc, 2010. 1880 U.S. Census Index provided by The Church of Jesus Christ of Latter-day Saints © Copyright 1999 Intellectual Reserve, Inc. All rights reserved. All use is subject to the limited), Ancestry.com, http://www.Ancestry.com, Year: 1880; Census Place: 6th Ward, Lincoln, Louisiana; Roll: 456; Family History Film: 1254456; Page: 28C; Enumeration District: 38; Image: 0058. Birth date: about 1856 Birth place: Georgia Residence date: 1880 Residence place: 6th Ward, Lincoln, Louisiana, United States.

476   Ancestry.com and The Church of Jesus Christ of Latter-day Saints, 1880 United States Federal Census (Online publication - Provo, UT, USA: Ancestry.com Operations Inc, 2010. 1880 U.S. Census Index provided by The Church of Jesus Christ of Latter-day Saints © Copyright 1999 Intellectual Reserve, Inc. All rights reserved. All use is subject to the limited), Ancestry.com, http://www.Ancestry.com, Year: 1880; Census Place: 6th Ward, Lincoln, Louisiana; Roll: 456; Family History Film: 1254456; Page: 28C; Enumeration District: 38; Image: 0058. Birth date: about 1858 Birth place: Georgia Residence date: 1880 Residence place: 6th Ward, Lincoln, Louisiana, United States.

477   Ancestry.com and The Church of Jesus Christ of Latter-day Saints, 1880 United States Federal Census (Online publication - Provo, UT, USA: Ancestry.com Operations Inc, 2010. 1880 U.S. Census Index provided by The Church of Jesus Christ of Latter-day Saints © Copyright 1999 Intellectual Reserve, Inc. All rights reserved. All use is subject to the limited), Ancestry.com, http://www.Ancestry.com, Year: 1880; Census Place: 6th Ward, Lincoln, Louisiana; Roll: 456; Family History Film: 1254456; Page: 28C; Enumeration District: 38; Image: 0058. Birth date: about 1863 Birth place: Arkansas Residence date: 1880 Residence place: 6th Ward, Lincoln, Louisiana, United States.

478   Ancestry.com and The Church of Jesus Christ of Latter-day Saints, 1880 United States Federal Census (Online publication - Provo, UT, USA: Ancestry.com Operations Inc, 2010. 1880 U.S. Census Index provided by The Church of Jesus Christ of Latter-day Saints © Copyright 1999 Intellectual Reserve, Inc. All rights reserved. All use is subject to the limited), Ancestry.com, http://www.Ancestry.com, Year: 1880; Census Place: 6th Ward, Lincoln, Louisiana; Roll: 456; Family History Film: 1254456; Page: 28C; Enumeration District: 38; Image: 0058. Birth date: about 1866 Birth place: Louisiana Residence date: 1880 Residence place: 6th Ward, Lincoln, Louisiana, United States.

479   Ancestry.com and The Church of Jesus Christ of Latter-day Saints, 1880 United States Federal Census (Online publication - Provo, UT, USA: Ancestry.com Operations Inc, 2010. 1880 U.S. Census Index provided by The Church of Jesus Christ of Latter-day Saints © Copyright 1999 Intellectual Reserve, Inc. All rights reserved. All use is subject to the limited), Ancestry.com, http://www.Ancestry.com, Year: 1880; Census Place: 6th Ward, Lincoln, Louisiana; Roll: 456; Family History Film: 1254456; Page: 28C; Enumeration District: 38; Image: 0058. Birth date: about 1868 Birth place: Louisiana Residence date: 1880 Residence place: 6th Ward, Lincoln, Louisiana, United States.

480   Ancestry.com and The Church of Jesus Christ of Latter-day Saints, 1880 United States Federal Census (Online publication - Provo, UT, USA: Ancestry.com Operations Inc, 2010. 1880 U.S. Census Index provided by The Church of Jesus Christ of Latter-day Saints © Copyright 1999 Intellectual Reserve, Inc. All rights reserved. All use is subject to the limited), Ancestry.com, http://www.Ancestry.com, Year: 1880; Census Place: 6th Ward, Lincoln, Louisiana; Roll: 456; Family History Film: 1254456; Page: 28C; Enumeration District: 38; Image: 0058. Birth date: about 1870 Birth place: Louisiana Residence date: 1880 Residence place: 6th Ward, Lincoln, Louisiana, United States.

481   Ancestry.com and The Church of Jesus Christ of Latter-day Saints, 1880 United States Federal Census (Online publication - Provo, UT, USA: Ancestry.com Operations Inc, 2010. 1880 U.S. Census Index provided by The Church of Jesus Christ of Latter-day Saints © Copyright 1999 Intellectual Reserve, Inc. All rights reserved. All use is subject to the limited), Ancestry.com, http://www.Ancestry.com, Year: 1880; Census Place: 6th Ward, Lincoln, Louisiana; Roll: 456; Family History Film: 1254456; Page: 28C; Enumeration District: 38; Image: 0058. Birth date: about 1872 Birth place: Louisiana Residence date: 1880 Residence place: 6th Ward, Lincoln, Louisiana, United States.

482   Ancestry.com, 1900 United States Federal Census (Online publication - Provo, UT, USA: Ancestry.com Operations Inc, 2004. Original data - United States of America, Bureau of the Census. Twelfth Census of the United States, 1900. Washington, D.C.: National Archives and Records Administration, 1900. T623, 18), Ancestry.com, http://www.Ancestry.com, Year: 1900; Census Place: Police Jury Ward 8, Claiborne, Louisiana; Roll: T623_562; Page: 11A; Enumeration District: 27. Birth date: Jan 1873 Birth place: Louisiana Residence date: 1900 Residence place: Ward 8 (South Half), Claiborne, Louisiana.

483   Ancestry.com and The Church of Jesus Christ of Latter-day Saints, 1880 United States Federal Census (Online publication - Provo, UT, USA: Ancestry.com Operations Inc, 2010. 1880 U.S. Census Index provided by The Church of Jesus Christ of Latter-day Saints © Copyright 1999 Intellectual Reserve, Inc. All rights reserved. All use is subject to the limited), Ancestry.com, http://www.Ancestry.com, Year: 1880; Census Place: 6th Ward, Lincoln, Louisiana; Roll: 456; Family History Film: 1254456; Page: 28C; Enumeration District: 38; Image: 0058. Birth date: about 1874 Birth place: Louisiana Residence date: 1880 Residence place: 6th Ward, Lincoln, Louisiana, United States.

484   Ancestry.com and The Church of Jesus Christ of Latter-day Saints, 1880 United States Federal Census (Online publication - Provo, UT, USA: Ancestry.com Operations Inc, 2010. 1880 U.S. Census Index provided by The Church of Jesus Christ of Latter-day Saints © Copyright 1999 Intellectual Reserve, Inc. All rights reserved. All use is subject to the limited), Ancestry.com, http://www.Ancestry.com, Year: 1880; Census Place: 6th Ward, Lincoln, Louisiana; Roll: 456; Family History Film: 1254456; Page: 28C; Enumeration District: 38; Image: 0058. Birth date: about 1879 Birth place: Louisiana Residence date: 1880 Residence place: 6th Ward, Lincoln, Louisiana, United States.

485   Ancestry.com, 1850 United States Federal Census (Online publication - Provo, UT, USA: Ancestry.com Operations, Inc., 2009. Images reproduced by FamilySearch. Original data - Seventh Census of the United States, 1850; (National Archives Microfilm Publication M432, 1009 rolls); Records of the Bureau of the), Ancestry.com, http://www.Ancestry.com, Year: 1850; Census Place: Division 59, Meriwether, Georgia; Roll: M432_77; Page: 335B; Image:. Birth date: about 1828 Birth place: Georgia Residence date: 1850 Residence place: Division 59, Meriwether, Georgia.

486   Ancestry.com, 1850 United States Federal Census (Online publication - Provo, UT, USA: Ancestry.com Operations, Inc., 2009. Images reproduced by FamilySearch. Original data - Seventh Census of the United States, 1850; (National Archives Microfilm Publication M432, 1009 rolls); Records of the Bureau of the), Ancestry.com, http://www.Ancestry.com, Year: 1850; Census Place: Division 59, Meriwether, Georgia; Roll: M432_77; Page: 335B; Image:. Birth date: about 1846 Birth place: Georgia Residence date: 1850 Residence place: Division 59, Meriwether, Georgia.

487   Ancestry.com and The Church of Jesus Christ of Latter-day Saints, 1880 United States Federal Census (Online publication - Provo, UT, USA: Ancestry.com Operations Inc, 2010. 1880 U.S. Census Index provided by The Church of Jesus Christ of Latter-day Saints © Copyright 1999 Intellectual Reserve, Inc. All rights reserved. All use is subject to the limited), Ancestry.com, http://www.Ancestry.com, Year: 1880; Census Place: 4th Ward, Union, Louisiana; Roll: 473; Family History Film: 1254473; Page: 480A; Enumeration District: 88; Image: 0242. Birth date: about 1846 Birth place: Georgia Residence date: 1880 Residence place: 4th Ward, Union, Louisiana, United States.

488   Ancestry.com, 1900 United States Federal Census (Online publication - Provo, UT, USA: Ancestry.com Operations Inc, 2004. Original data - United States of America, Bureau of the Census. Twelfth Census of the United States, 1900. Washington, D.C.: National Archives and Records Administration, 1900. T623, 18), Ancestry.com, http://www.Ancestry.com, Year: 1900; Census Place: Police Jury Ward 4, Union, Louisiana; Roll: T623_585; Page: 15B; Enumeration District: 122. Birth date: Oct 1845 Birth place: Georgia Marriage date: 1870 Marriage place: Residence date: 1900 Residence place: Bernice Town, Union, Louisiana.

489   Ancestry.com, 1910 United States Federal Census (Online publication - Provo, UT, USA: Ancestry.com Operations Inc, 2006. Original data - Thirteenth Census of the United States, 1910 (NARA microfilm publication T624, 1,178 rolls). Records of the Bureau of the Census, Record Group 29. National Archives, Washington), Ancestry.com, http://www.Ancestry.com, Year: 1910; Census Place: Police Jury Ward 4, Union, Louisiana; Roll: ; Page: ; Enumeration District: ; Image:. Birth date: about 1846 Birth place: Georgia Residence date: 1910 Residence place: Police Jury Ward 4, Union, Louisiana.

490   Ancestry.com, 1860 United States Federal Census (Online publication - Provo, UT, USA: Ancestry.com Operations, Inc., 2009. Images reproduced by FamilySearch. Original data - 1860 U.S. census, population schedule. NARA microfilm publication M653, 1,438 rolls. Washington, D.C.: National Archives and Records), Ancestry.com, http://www.Ancestry.com, Year: 1860; Census Place: Moss, Columbia, Arkansas; Roll: ; Page: 309; Image: 311. Birth date: about 1845 Birth place: Georgia Residence date: 1860 Residence place: Moss, Columbia, Arkansas, United States.

491   Ancestry.com, 1850 United States Federal Census (Online publication - Provo, UT, USA: Ancestry.com Operations, Inc., 2009. Images reproduced by FamilySearch. Original data - Seventh Census of the United States, 1850; (National Archives Microfilm Publication M432, 1009 rolls); Records of the Bureau of the), Ancestry.com, http://www.Ancestry.com, Year: 1850; Census Place: Division 59, Meriwether, Georgia; Roll: M432_77; Page: 335B; Image:. Birth date: about 1847 Birth place: Georgia Residence date: 1850 Residence place: Division 59, Meriwether, Georgia.

492   Ancestry.com, 1860 United States Federal Census (Online publication - Provo, UT, USA: Ancestry.com Operations, Inc., 2009. Images reproduced by FamilySearch. Original data - 1860 U.S. census, population schedule. NARA microfilm publication M653, 1,438 rolls. Washington, D.C.: National Archives and Records), Ancestry.com, http://www.Ancestry.com, Year: 1860; Census Place: Moss, Columbia, Arkansas; Roll: ; Page: 309; Image: 311. Birth date: about 1847 Birth place: Georgia Residence date: 1860 Residence place: Moss, Columbia, Arkansas, United States.

493   Ancestry.com, 1850 United States Federal Census (Online publication - Provo, UT, USA: Ancestry.com Operations, Inc., 2009. Images reproduced by FamilySearch. Original data - Seventh Census of the United States, 1850; (National Archives Microfilm Publication M432, 1009 rolls); Records of the Bureau of the), Ancestry.com, http://www.Ancestry.com, Year: 1850; Census Place: Division 59, Meriwether, Georgia; Roll: M432_77; Page: 335B; Image:. Birth date: about 1848 Birth place: Georgia Residence date: 1850 Residence place: Division 59, Meriwether, Georgia.

494   Ancestry.com, 1860 United States Federal Census (Online publication - Provo, UT, USA: Ancestry.com Operations, Inc., 2009. Images reproduced by FamilySearch. Original data - 1860 U.S. census, population schedule. NARA microfilm publication M653, 1,438 rolls. Washington, D.C.: National Archives and Records), Ancestry.com, http://www.Ancestry.com, Year: 1860; Census Place: Moss, Columbia, Arkansas; Roll: ; Page: 309; Image: 311. Birth date: about 1848 Birth place: Georgia Residence date: 1860 Residence place: Moss, Columbia, Arkansas, United States.

495   Dodd, Jordan, Liahona Research, comp, Louisiana Marriage Records, 1851-1900 (Online publication - Provo, UT, USA: Ancestry.com Operations Inc, 2000. Original data - See Extended Description for original data sources listed by county. Original data: See Extended Description for original data sources listed by county.), Ancestry.com, http://www.Ancestry.com, Marriage date: 23/11/1873 Marriage place: Lincoln, LA.

496   Ancestry.com, 1860 United States Federal Census (Online publication - Provo, UT, USA: Ancestry.com Operations, Inc., 2009. Images reproduced by FamilySearch. Original data - 1860 U.S. census, population schedule. NARA microfilm publication M653, 1,438 rolls. Washington, D.C.: National Archives and Records), Ancestry.com, http://www.Ancestry.com, Year: 1860; Census Place: Moss, Columbia, Arkansas; Roll: ; Page: 309; Image: 311. Name: Henry Moncrief Birth: about 1849 in Georgia Death:.

497   Ancestry.com, 1870 United States Federal Census (Online publication - Provo, UT, USA: Ancestry.com Operations, Inc., 2009. Images reproduced by FamilySearch. Original data - 1870 U.S. census, population schedules. NARA microfilm publication M593, 1,761 rolls. Washington, D.C.: National Archives and Record), Ancestry.com, http://www.Ancestry.com, Year: 1870; Census Place: Ward 4, Union, Louisiana; Roll: M593_; Page: ; Image:. Birth date: about 1849 Birth place: Georgia Residence date: 1870 Residence place: Ward 4, Union, Louisiana, United States.

498   Ancestry.com, 1900 United States Federal Census (Online publication - Provo, UT, USA: Ancestry.com Operations Inc, 2004. Original data - United States of America, Bureau of the Census. Twelfth Census of the United States, 1900. Washington, D.C.: National Archives and Records Administration, 1900. T623, 18), Ancestry.com, http://www.Ancestry.com, Year: 1900; Census Place: Police Jury Ward 8, Claiborne, Louisiana; Roll: T623_562; Page: 11A; Enumeration District: 27. Birth date: Jun 1849 Birth place: Georgia Marriage date: 1869 Marriage place: Residence date: 1900 Residence place: Ward 8 (South Half), Claiborne, Louisiana.

499   Ancestry.com, Louisiana Statewide Death Index, 1900-1949 (Online publication - Provo, UT, USA: Ancestry.com Operations Inc, 2002. Original data - State of Louisiana, Secretary of State, Division of Archives, Records Management, and History. Vital Records Indices. Baton Rouge, LA, USA. Original data: State of Louisiana), Ancestry.com, http://www.Ancestry.com, Birth date: 1849 Birth place: Death date: 11 Mar 1921 Death place: Louisiana.

500   Ancestry.com, 1850 United States Federal Census (Online publication - Provo, UT, USA: Ancestry.com Operations, Inc., 2009. Images reproduced by FamilySearch. Original data - Seventh Census of the United States, 1850; (National Archives Microfilm Publication M432, 1009 rolls); Records of the Bureau of the), Ancestry.com, http://www.Ancestry.com, Year: 1850; Census Place: Division 59, Meriwether, Georgia; Roll: M432_77; Page: 335B; Image:. Birth date: about 1849 Birth place: Georgia Residence date: 1850 Residence place: Division 59, Meriwether, Georgia.

501   Ancestry.com and The Church of Jesus Christ of Latter-day Saints, 1880 United States Federal Census (Online publication - Provo, UT, USA: Ancestry.com Operations Inc, 2010. 1880 U.S. Census Index provided by The Church of Jesus Christ of Latter-day Saints © Copyright 1999 Intellectual Reserve, Inc. All rights reserved. All use is subject to the limited), Ancestry.com, http://www.Ancestry.com, Year: 1880; Census Place: 8th Ward, Claiborne, Louisiana; Roll: 451; Family History Film: 1254451; Page: 403A; Enumeration District: 16; Image: 0600. Birth date: about 1850 Birth place: Georgia Residence date: 1880 Residence place: 8th Ward, Claiborne, Louisiana, United States.

502   Ancestry.com, 1910 United States Federal Census (Online publication - Provo, UT, USA: Ancestry.com Operations Inc, 2006. Original data - Thirteenth Census of the United States, 1910 (NARA microfilm publication T624, 1,178 rolls). Records of the Bureau of the Census, Record Group 29. National Archives, Washington), Ancestry.com, http://www.Ancestry.com, Year: 1910; Census Place: Police Jury Ward 8, Claiborne, Louisiana; Roll: ; Page: ; Enumeration District: ; Image:. Birth date: 1848 Birth place: Georgia Residence date: 1910 Residence place: Police Jury Ward 8, Claiborne, Louisiana.

503   Ancestry.com, 1920 United States Federal Census (Online publication - Provo, UT, USA: Ancestry.com Operations Inc, 2010. Images reproduced by FamilySearch. Original data - Fourteenth Census of the United States, 1920. (NARA microfilm publication T625, 2076 rolls). Records of the Bureau of the Census, Record), Ancestry.com, http://www.Ancestry.com, Year: 1920; Census Place: Police Jury Ward 8, Claiborne, Louisiana; Roll: T625_609; Page: 11B; Enumeration District: 98; Image:. Birth date: about 1850 Birth place: Georgia Residence date: 1920 Residence place: Police Jury Ward 8, Claiborne, Louisiana.

504   Ancestry.com and The Church of Jesus Christ of Latter-day Saints, 1880 United States Federal Census (Online publication - Provo, UT, USA: Ancestry.com Operations Inc, 2010. 1880 U.S. Census Index provided by The Church of Jesus Christ of Latter-day Saints © Copyright 1999 Intellectual Reserve, Inc. All rights reserved. All use is subject to the limited), Ancestry.com, http://www.Ancestry.com, Year: 1880; Census Place: Clanton, Chilton, Alabama; Roll: 6; Family History Film: 1254006; Page: 74A; Enumeration District: 29; Image: 0595. Birth date: about 1825 Birth place: Indiana Residence date: 1880 Residence place: Clanton, Chilton, Alabama, United States.

505   Ancestry.com, 1860 United States Federal Census (Online publication - Provo, UT, USA: Ancestry.com Operations, Inc., 2009. Images reproduced by FamilySearch. Original data - 1860 U.S. census, population schedule. NARA microfilm publication M653, 1,438 rolls. Washington, D.C.: National Archives and Records), Ancestry.com, http://www.Ancestry.com, Year: 1860; Census Place: Division 1, Montgomery, Alabama; Roll: ; Page: 217; Image: 217. Birth date: about 1828 Birth place: Indiana Residence date: 1860 Residence place: Division 1, Montgomery, Alabama, United States.

506   Ancestry.com and The Church of Jesus Christ of Latter-day Saints, 1880 United States Federal Census (Online publication - Provo, UT, USA: Ancestry.com Operations Inc, 2010. 1880 U.S. Census Index provided by The Church of Jesus Christ of Latter-day Saints © Copyright 1999 Intellectual Reserve, Inc. All rights reserved. All use is subject to the

limited), Ancestry.com, http://www.Ancestry.com, Year: 1880; Census Place: Clanton, Chilton, Alabama; Roll: 6; Family History Film: 1254006; Page: 74A; Enumeration District: 29; Image: 0595. Birth date: about 1856 Birth place: Alabama Residence date: 1880 Residence place: Clanton, Chilton, Alabama, United States.

507   Ancestry.com, 1900 United States Federal Census (Online publication - Provo, UT, USA: Ancestry.com Operations Inc, 2004. Original data - United States of America, Bureau of the Census. Twelfth Census of the United States, 1900. Washington, D.C.: National Archives and Records Administration, 1900. T623, 18), Ancestry.com, http://www.Ancestry.com, Year: 1900; Census Place: Clanton, Chilton, Alabama; Roll: T623_7; Page: 20A; Enumeration District: 27. Birth date: Aug 1855 Birth place: Alabama Residence date: 1900 Residence place: Clanton Town, Chilton, Alabama.

508   Ancestry.com, 1860 United States Federal Census (Online publication - Provo, UT, USA: Ancestry.com Operations, Inc., 2009. Images reproduced by FamilySearch. Original data - 1860 U.S. census, population schedule. NARA microfilm publication M653, 1,438 rolls. Washington, D.C.: National Archives and Records), Ancestry.com, http://www.Ancestry.com, Year: 1860; Census Place: Division 1, Montgomery, Alabama; Roll: ; Page: 217; Image: 217. Birth date: about 1856 Birth place: Alabama Residence date: 1860 Residence place: Division 1, Montgomery, Alabama, United States.

509   Ancestry.com, 1860 United States Federal Census (Online publication - Provo, UT, USA: Ancestry.com Operations, Inc., 2009. Images reproduced by FamilySearch. Original data - 1860 U.S. census, population schedule. NARA microfilm publication M653, 1,438 rolls. Washington, D.C.: National Archives and Records), Ancestry.com, http://www.Ancestry.com, Year: 1860; Census Place: Division 1, Montgomery, Alabama; Roll: ; Page: 217; Image: 217. Birth date: about 1858 Birth place: Alabama Residence date: 1860 Residence place: Division 1, Montgomery, Alabama, United States.

510   Ancestry.com, 1910 United States Federal Census (Online publication - Provo, UT, USA: Ancestry.com Operations Inc, 2006. Original data - Thirteenth Census of the United States, 1910 (NARA microfilm publication T624, 1,178 rolls). Records of the Bureau of the Census, Record Group 29. National Archives, Washington), Ancestry.com, http://www.Ancestry.com, Year: 1910; Census Place: Precinct 4, Chilton, Alabama; Roll: ; Page: ; Enumeration District: ; Image:. Birth date: about 1862 Birth place: Alabama Residence date: 1910 Residence place: Precinct 4, Chilton, Alabama.

511   Ancestry.com, 1870 United States Federal Census (Online publication - Provo, UT, USA: Ancestry.com Operations, Inc., 2009. Images reproduced by FamilySearch. Original data - 1870 U.S. census, population schedules. NARA microfilm publication M593, 1,761 rolls. Washington, D.C.: National Archives and Record), Ancestry.com, http://www.Ancestry.com, Year: 1870; Census Place: Montgomery Ward 5, Montgomery, Alabama; Roll: M593_; Page: ; Image:. Birth date: about 1858 Birth place: Alabama Residence date: 1870 Residence place: Montgomery Ward 5, Montgomery, Alabama, United States.

512   Ancestry.com and The Church of Jesus Christ of Latter-day Saints, 1880 United States Federal Census (Online publication - Provo, UT, USA: Ancestry.com Operations Inc, 2010. 1880 U.S. Census Index provided by The Church of Jesus Christ of Latter-day Saints © Copyright 1999 Intellectual Reserve, Inc. All rights reserved. All use is subject to the limited), Ancestry.com, http://www.Ancestry.com, Year: 1880; Census Place: Clanton, Chilton, Alabama; Roll: 6; Family History Film: 1254006; Page: 74A; Enumeration District: 29; Image: 0595. Birth date: about 1861 Birth place: Alabama Residence date: 1880 Residence place: Clanton, Chilton, Alabama, United States.

513   Ancestry.com, 1900 United States Federal Census (Online publication - Provo, UT, USA: Ancestry.com Operations Inc, 2004. Original data - United States of America, Bureau of the Census. Twelfth Census of the United States, 1900. Washington, D.C.: National Archives and Records Administration, 1900. T623, 18), Ancestry.com, http://www.Ancestry.com, Year: 1900; Census Place: Clanton, Chilton, Alabama; Roll: T623_7; Page: 20A; Enumeration District: 27. Birth date: Dec 1871 Birth place: Alabama Residence date: 1900 Residence place: Clanton Town, Chilton, Alabama.

514   Ancestry.com and The Church of Jesus Christ of Latter-day Saints, 1880 United States Federal Census (Online publication - Provo, UT, USA: Ancestry.com Operations Inc, 2010. 1880 U.S. Census Index provided by The Church of Jesus Christ of Latter-day Saints © Copyright 1999 Intellectual Reserve, Inc. All rights reserved. All use is subject to the limited), Ancestry.com, http://www.Ancestry.com, Year: 1880; Census Place: Clanton, Chilton, Alabama; Roll: 6; Family History Film: 1254006; Page: 74A; Enumeration District: 29; Image: 0595. Birth date: about 1870 Birth place: Alabama Residence date: 1880 Residence place: Clanton, Chilton, Alabama, United States.

515   Ancestry.com, 1900 United States Federal Census (Online publication - Provo, UT, USA: Ancestry.com Operations Inc, 2004. Original data - United States of America, Bureau of the Census. Twelfth Census of the United States, 1900. Washington, D.C.: National Archives and Records Administration, 1900. T623, 18), Ancestry.com, http://www.Ancestry.com, Year: 1900; Census Place: Orizaba, Tippah, Mississippi; Roll: T623_829; Page: 5B; Enumeration District: 108. Birth date: Sep 1867 Birth place: Mississippi Marriage date: 1889 Marriage place: Residence date: 1900 Residence place: Orizaba, Tippah, Mississippi.

516   Ancestry.com, 1910 United States Federal Census (Online publication - Provo, UT, USA: Ancestry.com Operations Inc, 2006. Original data - Thirteenth Census of the United States, 1910 (NARA microfilm publication T624, 1,178 rolls). Records of the Bureau of the Census, Record Group 29. National Archives, Washington), Ancestry.com, http://www.Ancestry.com, Year: 1910; Census Place: Beat 3, Tippah, Mississippi; Roll: ; Page: ; Enumeration District: ; Image:. Birth date: about 1869 Birth place: Mississippi Residence date: 1910 Residence place: Beat 3, Tippah, Mississippi.

517   Ancestry.com, 1920 United States Federal Census (Online publication - Provo, UT, USA: Ancestry.com Operations Inc, 2010. Images reproduced by FamilySearch. Original data - Fourteenth Census of the United States, 1920. (NARA microfilm publication T625, 2076 rolls). Records of the Bureau of the Census, Record), Ancestry.com, http://www.Ancestry.com, Year: 1920; Census Place: Halls, Lauderdale, Tennessee; Roll: T625_1751; Page: 14B; Enumeration District: 105; Image:. Birth date: about 1866 Birth place: Mississippi Residence date: 1920 Residence place: Halls, Lauderdale, Tennessee.

518   Ancestry.com, Social Security Death Index (Online publication - Provo, UT, USA: Ancestry.com Operations Inc, 2010. Original data - Social Security Administration. Social Security Death Index, Master File. Social Security Administration. Original data: Social Security Administration. Social Security D), Ancestry.com, http://www.Ancestry.com, Number: 412-03-8351; Issue State: Tennessee; Issue Date: Before 1951. Birth date: 3 Sep 1874 Birth place: Death date: Nov 1973 Death place: Memphis, Shelby, Tennessee, United States of America.

519   Ancestry.com, 1900 United States Federal Census (Online publication - Provo, UT, USA: Ancestry.com Operations Inc, 2004. Original data - United States of America, Bureau of the Census. Twelfth Census of the United States, 1900. Washington, D.C.: National Archives and Records Administration, 1900. T623, 18), Ancestry.com, http://www.Ancestry.com, Year: 1900; Census Place: Quitman, Clarke, Mississippi; Roll: T623_804; Page: 5B; Enumeration District: 1. Birth date: Jan 1880 Birth place: Mississippi Marriage date: 1899 Marriage place: Residence date: 1900 Residence place: Quitman, Clarke, Mississippi.

520   Ancestry.com, Social Security Death Index (Online publication - Provo, UT, USA: Ancestry.com Operations Inc, 2010. Original data - Social Security Administration. Social Security Death Index, Master File. Social Security Administration. Original data: Social Security Administration. Social Security D), Ancestry.com, http://www.Ancestry.com, Number: 414-10-6356; Issue State: Tennessee; Issue Date: Before 1951. Birth date: 18 Oct 1880 Birth place: Death date: Apr 1983 Death place: Germantown, Shelby, Tennessee, United States of America.

521   Ancestry.com, 1900 United States Federal Census (Online publication - Provo, UT, USA: Ancestry.com Operations Inc, 2004. Original data - United States of America, Bureau of the Census. Twelfth Census of the United States, 1900. Washington, D.C.: National Archives and Records Administration, 1900. T623, 18), Ancestry.com, http://www.Ancestry.com, Year: 1900; Census Place: Quitman, Clarke, Mississippi; Roll: T623_804; Page: 5B; Enumeration District: 1. Birth date: Nov 1872 Birth place: Alabama Marriage date: 1899 Marriage place: Residence date: 1900 Residence place: Quitman, Clarke, Mississippi.

522   Ancestry.com and The Church of Jesus Christ of Latter-day Saints, 1880 United States Federal Census (Online publication - Provo, UT, USA: Ancestry.com Operations Inc, 2010. 1880 U.S. Census Index provided by The Church of Jesus Christ of Latter-day Saints © Copyright 1999 Intellectual Reserve, Inc. All rights reserved. All use is subject to the limited), Ancestry.com, http://www.Ancestry.com, Year: 1880; Census Place: Albany, Union, Mississippi; Roll: 666; Family History Film: 1254666; Page: 260A; Enumeration District: 202; Image: 0660. Birth date: about 1831 Birth place: South Carolina Residence date: 1880 Residence place: Albany, Union, Mississippi, United States.

523   Ancestry.com, 1860 United States Federal Census (Online publication - Provo, UT, USA: Ancestry.com Operations, Inc., 2009. Images reproduced by FamilySearch. Original data - 1860 U.S. census, population schedule. NARA microfilm publication M653, 1,438 rolls. Washington, D.C.: National Archives and Records), Ancestry.com, http://www.Ancestry.com, Year: 1860; Census Place: , Pontotoc, Mississippi; Roll: ; Page: 715; Image: 235. Birth date: about 1831 Birth place: South Carolina Residence date: 1860 Residence place: Pontotoc, Mississippi, United States.

524   Ancestry.com and The Church of Jesus Christ of Latter-day Saints, 1880 United States Federal Census (Online publication - Provo, UT, USA: Ancestry.com Operations Inc, 2010. 1880 U.S. Census Index provided by The Church of Jesus Christ of Latter-day Saints © Copyright 1999 Intellectual Reserve, Inc. All rights reserved. All use is subject to the limited), Ancestry.com, http://www.Ancestry.com, Year: 1880; Census Place: Albany, Union, Mississippi; Roll: 666; Family History Film: 1254666; Page: 260A; Enumeration District: 202; Image: 0660. Birth date: about 1855 Birth place: Mississippi Residence date: 1880 Residence place: Albany, Union, Mississippi, United States.

525   Ancestry.com, 1860 United States Federal Census (Online publication - Provo, UT, USA: Ancestry.com Operations, Inc., 2009. Images reproduced by FamilySearch. Original data - 1860 U.S. census, population schedule. NARA microfilm publication M653, 1,438 rolls. Washington, D.C.: National Archives and Records), Ancestry.com, http://www.Ancestry.com, Year: 1860; Census Place: , Pontotoc, Mississippi; Roll: ; Page: 847; Image: 369. Birth date: about 1853 Birth place: Mississippi Residence date: 1860 Residence place: Pontotoc, Mississippi, United States.

526   Ancestry.com, 1920 United States Federal Census (Online publication - Provo, UT, USA: Ancestry.com Operations Inc, 2010. Images reproduced by FamilySearch. Original data - Fourteenth Census of the United States, 1920. (NARA microfilm publication T625, 2076 rolls). Records of the Bureau of the Census, Record), Ancestry.com, http://www.Ancestry.com, Year: 1920; Census Place: New Albany, Union, Mississippi; Roll: T625_897; Page: 22B; Enumeration District: 118; Image:. Birth date: about 1854 Birth place: Mississippi Residence date: 1920 Residence place: New Albany, Union, Mississippi.

527   Ancestry.com, 1860 United States Federal Census (Online publication - Provo, UT, USA: Ancestry.com Operations, Inc., 2009. Images reproduced by FamilySearch. Original data - 1860 U.S. census, population schedule. NARA microfilm publication M653, 1,438 rolls. Washington, D.C.: National Archives and Records), Ancestry.com, http://www.Ancestry.com, Year: 1860; Census Place: Northern Division, Tippah, Mississippi; Roll: ; Page: 511; Image: 71. Birth date: about 1855 Birth place: Mississippi Residence date: 1860 Residence place: Northern Division, Tippah, Mississippi, United States.

528   Ancestry.com and The Church of Jesus Christ of Latter-day Saints, 1880 United States Federal Census (Online publication - Provo, UT, USA: Ancestry.com Operations Inc, 2010. 1880 U.S. Census Index provided by The Church of Jesus Christ of Latter-day Saints © Copyright 1999 Intellectual Reserve, Inc. All rights reserved. All use is subject to the limited), Ancestry.com, http://www.Ancestry.com, Year: 1880; Census Place: Albany, Union, Mississippi; Roll: 666; Family History Film: 1254666; Page: 260A; Enumeration District: 202; Image: 0660. Birth date: about 1858 Birth place: Mississippi Residence date: 1880 Residence place: Albany, Union, Mississippi, United States.

529   Ancestry.com and The Church of Jesus Christ of Latter-day Saints, 1880 United States Federal Census (Online publication - Provo, UT, USA: Ancestry.com Operations Inc, 2010. 1880 U.S. Census Index provided by The Church of Jesus Christ of Latter-day Saints © Copyright 1999 Intellectual Reserve, Inc. All rights reserved. All use is subject to the limited), Ancestry.com, http://www.Ancestry.com, Year: 1880; Census Place: Albany, Union, Mississippi; Roll: 666; Family History Film: 1254666; Page: 260A; Enumeration District: 202; Image: 0660. Birth date: about 1862 Birth place: Mississippi Residence date: 1880 Residence place: Albany, Union, Mississippi, United States.

530   Ancestry.com and The Church of Jesus Christ of Latter-day Saints, 1880 United States Federal Census (Online publication - Provo, UT, USA: Ancestry.com Operations Inc, 2010. 1880 U.S. Census Index provided by The Church of Jesus Christ of Latter-day Saints © Copyright 1999 Intellectual Reserve, Inc. All rights reserved. All use is subject to the limited), Ancestry.com, http://www.Ancestry.com, Year: 1880; Census Place: Albany, Union, Mississippi; Roll: 666; Family History Film: 1254666; Page: 260A; Enumeration District: 202; Image: 0660. Birth date: about 1864 Birth place: Mississippi Residence date: 1880 Residence place: Albany, Union, Mississippi, United States.

531   Ancestry.com and The Church of Jesus Christ of Latter-day Saints, 1880 United States Federal Census (Online publication - Provo, UT, USA: Ancestry.com Operations Inc, 2010. 1880 U.S. Census Index provided by The Church of Jesus Christ of Latter-day Saints © Copyright 1999 Intellectual Reserve, Inc. All rights reserved. All use is subject to the limited), Ancestry.com, http://www.Ancestry.com, Year: 1880; Census Place: Albany, Union, Mississippi; Roll: 666; Family History Film: 1254666; Page: 260A; Enumeration District: 202; Image: 0660. Birth date: about 1868 Birth place: Mississippi Residence date: 1880 Residence place: Albany, Union, Mississippi, United States.

532   Ancestry.com and The Church of Jesus Christ of Latter-day Saints, 1880 United States Federal Census (Online publication - Provo, UT, USA: Ancestry.com Operations Inc, 2010. 1880 U.S. Census Index provided by The Church of Jesus Christ of Latter-day Saints © Copyright 1999 Intellectual Reserve, Inc. All rights reserved. All use is subject to the limited), Ancestry.com, http://www.Ancestry.com, Year: 1880; Census Place: Albany, Union, Mississippi; Roll: 666; Family History Film: 1254666; Page: 260A; Enumeration District: 202; Image: 0660. Birth date: about 1869 Birth place: Mississippi Residence date: 1880 Residence place: Albany, Union, Mississippi, United States.

533   Ancestry.com, 1870 United States Federal Census (Online publication - Provo, UT, USA: Ancestry.com Operations, Inc., 2009. Images reproduced by FamilySearch. Original data - 1870 U.S. census, population schedules. NARA microfilm publication M593, 1,761 rolls. Washington, D.C.: National Archives and Record), Ancestry.com, http://www.Ancestry.com, Year: 1870; Census Place: , Red River, Texas; Roll: M593_; Page: ; Image:. Birth date: about 1843 Birth place: Alabama Residence date: 1870 Residence place: Red River, Texas, United States.

534   Hunting For Bears, comp., Mississippi Marriages, 1776-1935 (Online publication - Provo, UT, USA: Ancestry.com Operations Inc, 2004. Original data - Mississippi marriage information taken from county courthouse records. Many of these records were extracted from copies of the original records in microfilm, microfiche,), Ancestry.com, http://www.Ancestry.com, Marriage date: 11 Oct 1859 Marriage place: Pontotoc, Mississippi.

535   Ancestry.com, 1900 United States Federal Census (Online publication - Provo, UT, USA: Ancestry.com Operations Inc, 2004. Original data - United States of America, Bureau of the Census. Twelfth Census of the United States, 1900. Washington, D.C.: National Archives and Records Administration, 1900. T623, 18), Ancestry.com, http://www.Ancestry.com, Year: 1900; Census Place: Justice Precinct 6, Hopkins, Texas; Roll: T623_1646; Page: 3A; Enumeration District: 57.

536   Ancestry.com, 1900 United States Federal Census (Online publication - Provo, UT, USA: Ancestry.com Operations Inc, 2004. Original data - United States of America, Bureau of the Census. Twelfth Census of the United States, 1900. Washington, D.C.: National Archives and Records Administration, 1900. T623, 18), Ancestry.com, http://www.Ancestry.com, Year: 1900; Census Place: Clay, Dunklin, Missouri; Roll: T623_853; Page: B; Enumeration District: 40. Birth date: Dec 1853 Birth place: Mississippi Marriage date: 1876 Marriage place: Residence date: 1900 Residence place: Clay, Dunklin, Missouri.

537   Ancestry.com, 1860 United States Federal Census (Online publication - Provo, UT, USA: Ancestry.com Operations, Inc., 2009. Images reproduced by FamilySearch. Original data - 1860 U.S. census, population schedule. NARA microfilm publication M653, 1,438 rolls. Washington, D.C.: National Archives and Records), Ancestry.com, http://www.Ancestry.com, Year: 1860; Census Place: , Pontotoc, Mississippi; Roll: ; Page: 601; Image: 121. Birth date: about 1853 Birth place: Mississippi Residence date: 1860 Residence place: Pontotoc, Mississippi, United States.

538   Ancestry.com and The Church of Jesus Christ of Latter-day Saints, 1880 United States Federal Census (Online publication - Provo, UT, USA: Ancestry.com Operations Inc, 2010. 1880 U.S. Census Index provided by The Church of Jesus Christ of Latter-day Saints © Copyright 1999 Intellectual Reserve, Inc. All rights reserved. All use is subject to the limited), Ancestry.com, http://www.Ancestry.com, Year: 1880; Census Place: Precinct 6, Hopkins, Texas; Roll: 1311; Family History Film: 1255311; Page: 212B; Enumeration District: 61; Image:. Birth date: about 1863 Birth place: Mississippi Residence date: 1880 Residence place: Precinct 6, Hopkins, Texas, United States.

539   Ancestry.com, 1900 United States Federal Census (Online publication - Provo, UT, USA: Ancestry.com Operations Inc, 2004. Original data - United States of America, Bureau of the Census. Twelfth Census of the United

States, 1900. Washington, D.C.: National Archives and Records Administration, 1900. T623, 18), Ancestry.com, http://www.Ancestry.com, Year: 1900; Census Place: Justice Precinct 6, Hopkins, Texas; Roll: T623_1646; Page: 3A; Enumeration District: 57. Birth date: Oct 1862 Birth place: Mississippi Marriage date: 1879 Marriage place: Residence date: 1900 Residence place: Justice Precinct 6, Hopkins, Texas.

540   Ancestry.com, 1930 United States Federal Census (Online publication - Provo, UT, USA: Ancestry.com Operations Inc, 2002. Original data - United States of America, Bureau of the Census. Fifteenth Census of the United States, 1930. Washington, D.C.: National Archives and Records Administration, 1930. T626,), Ancestry.com, http://www.Ancestry.com, Year: 1930; Census Place: Precinct 6, Hopkins, Texas; Roll: 2358; Page: 11A; Enumeration District: 23; Image: 506.0. Birth date: about 1862 Birth place: Residence date: 1930 Residence place: Precinct 6, Hopkins, Texas.

541   Ancestry.com, 1920 United States Federal Census (Online publication - Provo, UT, USA: Ancestry.com Operations Inc, 2010. Images reproduced by FamilySearch. Original data - Fourteenth Census of the United States, 1920. (NARA microfilm publication T625, 2076 rolls). Records of the Bureau of the Census, Record), Ancestry.com, http://www.Ancestry.com, Year: 1920; Census Place: Justice Precinct 6, Hopkins, Texas; Roll: T625_1817; Page: 3A; Enumeration District: 79; Image:. Birth date: about 1862 Birth place: Mississippi Residence date: 1920 Residence place: Justice Precinct 6, Hopkins, Texas.

542   Ancestry.com, 1900 United States Federal Census (Online publication - Provo, UT, USA: Ancestry.com Operations Inc, 2004. Original data - United States of America, Bureau of the Census. Twelfth Census of the United States, 1900. Washington, D.C.: National Archives and Records Administration, 1900. T623, 18), Ancestry.com, http://www.Ancestry.com, Year: 1900; Census Place: Justice Precinct 6, Hopkins, Texas; Roll: T623_1646; Page: 3A; Enumeration District: 57. Birth date: Jun 1858 Birth place: Texas Marriage date: 1879 Marriage place: Residence date: 1900 Residence place: Justice Precinct 6, Hopkins, Texas.

543   Ancestry.com and The Church of Jesus Christ of Latter-day Saints, 1880 United States Federal Census (Online publication - Provo, UT, USA: Ancestry.com Operations Inc, 2010. 1880 U.S. Census Index provided by The Church of Jesus Christ of Latter-day Saints © Copyright 1999 Intellectual Reserve, Inc. All rights reserved. All use is subject to the limited), Ancestry.com, http://www.Ancestry.com, Year: 1880; Census Place: District 2, Dyer, Tennessee; Roll: 1253; Family History Film: 1255253; Page: 17A; Enumeration District: 5; Image:. Birth date: about 1842 Birth place: Mississippi Residence date: 1880 Residence place: District 2, Dyer, Tennessee, United States.

544   Ancestry.com and The Church of Jesus Christ of Latter-day Saints, 1880 United States Federal Census (Online publication - Provo, UT, USA: Ancestry.com Operations Inc, 2010. 1880 U.S. Census Index provided by The Church of Jesus Christ of Latter-day Saints © Copyright 1999 Intellectual Reserve, Inc. All rights reserved. All use is subject to the limited), Ancestry.com, http://www.Ancestry.com, Year: 1880; Census Place: District 2, Dyer, Tennessee; Roll: 1253; Family History Film: 1255253; Page: 17A; Enumeration District: 5; Image:. Birth date: about 1866 Birth place: Tennessee Residence date: 1880 Residence place: District 2, Dyer, Tennessee, United States.

545   Ancestry.com and The Church of Jesus Christ of Latter-day Saints, 1880 United States Federal Census (Online publication - Provo, UT, USA: Ancestry.com Operations Inc, 2010. 1880 U.S. Census Index provided by The Church of Jesus Christ of Latter-day Saints © Copyright 1999 Intellectual Reserve, Inc. All rights reserved. All use is subject to the limited), Ancestry.com, http://www.Ancestry.com, Year: 1880; Census Place: District 2, Dyer, Tennessee; Roll: 1253; Family History Film: 1255253; Page: 17A; Enumeration District: 5; Image:. Birth date: about 1872 Birth place: Tennessee Residence date: 1880 Residence place: District 2, Dyer, Tennessee, United States.

546   Ancestry.com and The Church of Jesus Christ of Latter-day Saints, 1880 United States Federal Census (Online publication - Provo, UT, USA: Ancestry.com Operations Inc, 2010. 1880 U.S. Census Index provided by The Church of Jesus Christ of Latter-day Saints © Copyright 1999 Intellectual Reserve, Inc. All rights reserved. All use is subject to the limited), Ancestry.com, http://www.Ancestry.com, Year: 1880; Census Place: District 2, Dyer, Tennessee; Roll: 1253; Family History Film: 1255253; Page: 17A; Enumeration District: 5; Image:. Birth date: about 1874 Birth place: Tennessee Residence date: 1880 Residence place: District 2, Dyer, Tennessee, United States.

547   Ancestry.com and The Church of Jesus Christ of Latter-day Saints, 1880 United States Federal Census (Online publication - Provo, UT, USA: Ancestry.com Operations Inc, 2010. 1880 U.S. Census Index provided by The Church of Jesus Christ of Latter-day Saints © Copyright 1999 Intellectual Reserve, Inc. All rights reserved. All use is subject to the limited), Ancestry.com, http://www.Ancestry.com, Year: 1880; Census Place: Ball Play, Etowah, Alabama; Roll: 13; Family History Film: 1254013; Page: 319A; Enumeration District: 66; Image:. Birth date: about 1843 Birth place: Tennessee Residence date: 1880 Residence place: Ball Play, Etowah, Alabama, United States.

548   Ancestry.com and The Church of Jesus Christ of Latter-day Saints, 1880 United States Federal Census (Online publication - Provo, UT, USA: Ancestry.com Operations Inc, 2010. 1880 U.S. Census Index provided by The Church of Jesus Christ of Latter-day Saints © Copyright 1999 Intellectual Reserve, Inc. All rights reserved. All use is subject to the limited), Ancestry.com, http://www.Ancestry.com, Year: 1880; Census Place: Ball Play, Etowah, Alabama; Roll: 13; Family History Film: 1254013; Page: 319A; Enumeration District: 66; Image:. Birth date: about 1866 Birth place: Alabama Residence date: 1880 Residence place: Ball Play, Etowah, Alabama, United States.

549   Ancestry.com and The Church of Jesus Christ of Latter-day Saints, 1880 United States Federal Census (Online publication - Provo, UT, USA: Ancestry.com Operations Inc, 2010. 1880 U.S. Census Index provided by The Church of Jesus Christ of Latter-day Saints © Copyright 1999 Intellectual Reserve, Inc. All rights reserved. All use is subject to the limited), Ancestry.com, http://www.Ancestry.com, Year: 1880; Census Place: Ball Play, Etowah, Alabama; Roll: 13; Family

History Film: 1254013; Page: 319A; Enumeration District: 66; Image:. Birth date: about 1865 Birth place: Alabama Residence date: 1880 Residence place: Ball Play, Etowah, Alabama, United States.

550   Ancestry.com and The Church of Jesus Christ of Latter-day Saints, 1880 United States Federal Census (Online publication - Provo, UT, USA: Ancestry.com Operations Inc, 2010. 1880 U.S. Census Index provided by The Church of Jesus Christ of Latter-day Saints © Copyright 1999 Intellectual Reserve, Inc. All rights reserved. All use is subject to the limited), Ancestry.com, http://www.Ancestry.com, Year: 1880; Census Place: Ball Play, Etowah, Alabama; Roll: 13; Family History Film: 1254013; Page: 319A; Enumeration District: 66; Image:. Birth date: about 1867 Birth place: Alabama Residence date: 1880 Residence place: Ball Play, Etowah, Alabama, United States.

551   Ancestry.com and The Church of Jesus Christ of Latter-day Saints, 1880 United States Federal Census (Online publication - Provo, UT, USA: Ancestry.com Operations Inc, 2010. 1880 U.S. Census Index provided by The Church of Jesus Christ of Latter-day Saints © Copyright 1999 Intellectual Reserve, Inc. All rights reserved. All use is subject to the limited), Ancestry.com, http://www.Ancestry.com, Year: 1880; Census Place: Ball Play, Etowah, Alabama; Roll: 13; Family History Film: 1254013; Page: 319A; Enumeration District: 66; Image:. Birth date: about 1869 Birth place: Alabama Residence date: 1880 Residence place: Ball Play, Etowah, Alabama, United States.

552   Ancestry.com, 1900 United States Federal Census (Online publication - Provo, UT, USA: Ancestry.com Operations Inc, 2004. Original data - United States of America, Bureau of the Census. Twelfth Census of the United States, 1900. Washington, D.C.: National Archives and Records Administration, 1900. T623, 18), Ancestry.com, http://www.Ancestry.com, Year: 1900; Census Place: Hokes Bluff, Etowah, Alabama; Roll: T623_15; Page: 14B; Enumeration District: 151. Birth date: Apr 1869 Birth place: Alabama Residence date: 1900 Residence place: Precinct 4 Hokes Bluff, Etowah, Alabama.

553   Ancestry.com and The Church of Jesus Christ of Latter-day Saints, 1880 United States Federal Census (Online publication - Provo, UT, USA: Ancestry.com Operations Inc, 2010. 1880 U.S. Census Index provided by The Church of Jesus Christ of Latter-day Saints © Copyright 1999 Intellectual Reserve, Inc. All rights reserved. All use is subject to the limited), Ancestry.com, http://www.Ancestry.com, Year: 1880; Census Place: Ball Play, Etowah, Alabama; Roll: 13; Family History Film: 1254013; Page: 319A; Enumeration District: 66; Image:. Birth date: about 1874 Birth place: Alabama Residence date: 1880 Residence place: Ball Play, Etowah, Alabama, United States.

554   Ancestry.com, 1900 United States Federal Census (Online publication - Provo, UT, USA: Ancestry.com Operations Inc, 2004. Original data - United States of America, Bureau of the Census. Twelfth Census of the United States, 1900. Washington, D.C.: National Archives and Records Administration, 1900. T623, 18), Ancestry.com, http://www.Ancestry.com, Year: 1900; Census Place: Hokes Bluff, Etowah, Alabama; Roll: T623_15; Page: 14B; Enumeration District: 151. Birth date: Oct 1874 Birth place: Alabama Residence date: 1900 Residence place: Precinct 4 Hokes Bluff, Etowah, Alabama.

555   Ancestry.com, 1910 United States Federal Census (Online publication - Provo, UT, USA: Ancestry.com Operations Inc, 2006. Original data - Thirteenth Census of the United States, 1910 (NARA microfilm publication T624, 1,178 rolls). Records of the Bureau of the Census, Record Group 29. National Archives, Washington), Ancestry.com, http://www.Ancestry.com, Year: 1910; Census Place: Cox, Etowah, Alabama; Roll: ; Page: ; Enumeration District: ; Image:. Birth date: about 1875 Birth place: Alabama Residence date: 1910 Residence place: Cox, Etowah, Alabama.

556   Ancestry.com, 1930 United States Federal Census (Online publication - Provo, UT, USA: Ancestry.com Operations Inc, 2002. Original data - United States of America, Bureau of the Census. Fifteenth Census of the United States, 1930. Washington, D.C.: National Archives and Records Administration, 1930. T626,), Ancestry.com, http://www.Ancestry.com, Year: 1930; Census Place: Cox, Etowah, Alabama; Roll: 16; Page: 2B; Enumeration District: 23; Image: 724.0. Birth date: about 1873 Birth place: Alabama Residence date: 1930 Residence place: Cox, Etowah, Alabama.

557   Ancestry.com and The Church of Jesus Christ of Latter-day Saints, 1880 United States Federal Census (Online publication - Provo, UT, USA: Ancestry.com Operations Inc, 2010. 1880 U.S. Census Index provided by The Church of Jesus Christ of Latter-day Saints © Copyright 1999 Intellectual Reserve, Inc. All rights reserved. All use is subject to the limited), Ancestry.com, http://www.Ancestry.com, Year: 1880; Census Place: Ball Play, Etowah, Alabama; Roll: 13; Family History Film: 1254013; Page: 319A; Enumeration District: 66; Image:. Birth date: about 1876 Birth place: Alabama Residence date: 1880 Residence place: Ball Play, Etowah, Alabama, United States.

558   Ancestry.com and The Church of Jesus Christ of Latter-day Saints, 1880 United States Federal Census (Online publication - Provo, UT, USA: Ancestry.com Operations Inc, 2010. 1880 U.S. Census Index provided by The Church of Jesus Christ of Latter-day Saints © Copyright 1999 Intellectual Reserve, Inc. All rights reserved. All use is subject to the limited), Ancestry.com, http://www.Ancestry.com, Year: 1880; Census Place: Ball Play, Etowah, Alabama; Roll: 13; Family History Film: 1254013; Page: 319A; Enumeration District: 66; Image:. Birth date: about 1877 Birth place: Alabama Residence date: 1880 Residence place: Ball Play, Etowah, Alabama, United States.

559   Ancestry.com, 1900 United States Federal Census (Online publication - Provo, UT, USA: Ancestry.com Operations Inc, 2004. Original data - United States of America, Bureau of the Census. Twelfth Census of the United States, 1900. Washington, D.C.: National Archives and Records Administration, 1900. T623, 18), Ancestry.com, http://www.Ancestry.com, Year: 1900; Census Place: Hokes Bluff, Etowah, Alabama; Roll: T623_15; Page: 14B; Enumeration District: 151. Birth date: Dec 1876 Birth place: Alabama Residence date: 1900 Residence place: Precinct 4 Hokes Bluff, Etowah, Alabama.

560   Ancestry.com, 1900 United States Federal Census (Online publication - Provo, UT, USA: Ancestry.com Operations Inc, 2004. Original data - United States of America, Bureau of the Census. Twelfth Census of the United

States, 1900. Washington, D.C.: National Archives and Records Administration, 1900. T623, 18), Ancestry.com, http://www.Ancestry.com, Year: 1900; Census Place: Hokes Bluff, Etowah, Alabama; Roll: T623_15; Page: 14B; Enumeration District: 151. Birth date: Oct 1883 Birth place: Alabama Residence date: 1900 Residence place: Precinct 4 Hokes Bluff, Etowah, Alabama.

561   Ancestry.com, 1920 United States Federal Census (Online publication - Provo, UT, USA: Ancestry.com Operations Inc, 2010. Images reproduced by FamilySearch. Original data - Fourteenth Census of the United States, 1920. (NARA microfilm publication T625, 2076 rolls). Records of the Bureau of the Census, Record), Ancestry.com, http://www.Ancestry.com, Year: 1920; Census Place: Louisville, Barbour, Alabama; Roll: T625_3; Page: 12A; Enumeration District: 17; Image:. Birth date: about 1865 Birth place: Alabama Residence date: 1920 Residence place: Louisville, Barbour, Alabama.

562   Ancestry.com, 1920 United States Federal Census (Online publication - Provo, UT, USA: Ancestry.com Operations Inc, 2010. Images reproduced by FamilySearch. Original data - Fourteenth Census of the United States, 1920. (NARA microfilm publication T625, 2076 rolls). Records of the Bureau of the Census, Record), Ancestry.com, http://www.Ancestry.com, Year: 1920; Census Place: Louisville, Barbour, Alabama; Roll: T625_3; Page: 12A; Enumeration District: 17; Image:. Birth date: about 1904 Birth place: Alabama Residence date: 1920 Residence place: Louisville, Barbour, Alabama.

563   Ancestry.com, 1900 United States Federal Census (Online publication - Provo, UT, USA: Ancestry.com Operations Inc, 2004. Original data - United States of America, Bureau of the Census. Twelfth Census of the United States, 1900. Washington, D.C.: National Archives and Records Administration, 1900. T623, 18), Ancestry.com, http://www.Ancestry.com, Year: 1900; Census Place: Justice Precinct 1, Camp, Texas; Roll: T623_1618; Page: 19A; Enumeration District: 13. Birth date: Mar 1880 Birth place: Alabama Residence date: 1900 Residence place: Justice Precinct 1 (Excl. Pittsburg Town), Camp, Texas.

564   Ancestry.com, 1900 United States Federal Census (Online publication - Provo, UT, USA: Ancestry.com Operations Inc, 2004. Original data - United States of America, Bureau of the Census. Twelfth Census of the United States, 1900. Washington, D.C.: National Archives and Records Administration, 1900. T623, 18), Ancestry.com, http://www.Ancestry.com, Year: 1900; Census Place: Justice Precinct 1, Camp, Texas; Roll: T623_1618; Page: 19A; Enumeration District: 13. Birth date: Oct 1881 Birth place: Alabama Residence date: 1900 Residence place: Justice Precinct 1 (Excl. Pittsburg Town), Camp, Texas.

565   Ancestry.com, 1900 United States Federal Census (Online publication - Provo, UT, USA: Ancestry.com Operations Inc, 2004. Original data - United States of America, Bureau of the Census. Twelfth Census of the United States, 1900. Washington, D.C.: National Archives and Records Administration, 1900. T623, 18), Ancestry.com, http://www.Ancestry.com, Year: 1900; Census Place: Justice Precinct 1, Camp, Texas; Roll: T623_1618; Page: 19A; Enumeration District: 13. Birth date: Sep 1883 Birth place: Alabama Residence date: 1900 Residence place: Justice Precinct 1 (Excl. Pittsburg Town), Camp, Texas.

566   Ancestry.com, 1900 United States Federal Census (Online publication - Provo, UT, USA: Ancestry.com Operations Inc, 2004. Original data - United States of America, Bureau of the Census. Twelfth Census of the United States, 1900. Washington, D.C.: National Archives and Records Administration, 1900. T623, 18), Ancestry.com, http://www.Ancestry.com, Year: 1900; Census Place: Justice Precinct 1, Camp, Texas; Roll: T623_1618; Page: 19A; Enumeration District: 13. Birth date: Feb 1887 Birth place: Alabama Residence date: 1900 Residence place: Justice Precinct 1 (Excl. Pittsburg Town), Camp, Texas.

567   Ancestry.com, 1900 United States Federal Census (Online publication - Provo, UT, USA: Ancestry.com Operations Inc, 2004. Original data - United States of America, Bureau of the Census. Twelfth Census of the United States, 1900. Washington, D.C.: National Archives and Records Administration, 1900. T623, 18), Ancestry.com, http://www.Ancestry.com, Year: 1900; Census Place: Justice Precinct 1, Camp, Texas; Roll: T623_1618; Page: 19A; Enumeration District: 13. Birth date: Dec 1888 Birth place: Alabama Residence date: 1900 Residence place: Justice Precinct 1 (Excl. Pittsburg Town), Camp, Texas.

568   Ancestry.com, 1900 United States Federal Census (Online publication - Provo, UT, USA: Ancestry.com Operations Inc, 2004. Original data - United States of America, Bureau of the Census. Twelfth Census of the United States, 1900. Washington, D.C.: National Archives and Records Administration, 1900. T623, 18), Ancestry.com, http://www.Ancestry.com, Year: 1900; Census Place: Justice Precinct 1, Camp, Texas; Roll: T623_1618; Page: 19A; Enumeration District: 13. Birth date: Aug 1891 Birth place: Alabama Residence date: 1900 Residence place: Justice Precinct 1 (Excl. Pittsburg Town), Camp, Texas.

569   Ancestry.com, 1900 United States Federal Census (Online publication - Provo, UT, USA: Ancestry.com Operations Inc, 2004. Original data - United States of America, Bureau of the Census. Twelfth Census of the United States, 1900. Washington, D.C.: National Archives and Records Administration, 1900. T623, 18), Ancestry.com, http://www.Ancestry.com, Year: 1900; Census Place: Justice Precinct 1, Camp, Texas; Roll: T623_1618; Page: 19A; Enumeration District: 13. Birth date: Dec 1893 Birth place: Alabama Residence date: 1900 Residence place: Justice Precinct 1 (Excl. Pittsburg Town), Camp, Texas.

570   Ancestry.com, 1900 United States Federal Census (Online publication - Provo, UT, USA: Ancestry.com Operations Inc, 2004. Original data - United States of America, Bureau of the Census. Twelfth Census of the United States, 1900. Washington, D.C.: National Archives and Records Administration, 1900. T623, 18), Ancestry.com, http://www.Ancestry.com, Year: 1900; Census Place: Justice Precinct 1, Camp, Texas; Roll: T623_1618; Page: 19A;

Enumeration District: 13. Birth date: Oct 1896 Birth place: Alabama Residence date: 1900 Residence place: Justice Precinct 1 (Excl. Pittsburg Town), Camp, Texas.

571   Ancestry.com and The Church of Jesus Christ of Latter-day Saints, 1880 United States Federal Census (Online publication - Provo, UT, USA: Ancestry.com Operations Inc, 2010. 1880 U.S. Census Index provided by The Church of Jesus Christ of Latter-day Saints © Copyright 1999 Intellectual Reserve, Inc. All rights reserved. All use is subject to the limited), Ancestry.com, http://www.Ancestry.com, Year: 1880; Census Place: Gadsden and Turkey Town, Etowah, Alabama; Roll: 13; Family History Film: 1254013; Page: 327B; Enumeration District: 66; Image:. Birth date: about 1855 Birth place: Alabama Residence date: 1880 Residence place: Gadsden and Turkey Town, Etowah, Alabama, United States.

572   Ancestry.com and The Church of Jesus Christ of Latter-day Saints, 1880 United States Federal Census (Online publication - Provo, UT, USA: Ancestry.com Operations Inc, 2010. 1880 U.S. Census Index provided by The Church of Jesus Christ of Latter-day Saints © Copyright 1999 Intellectual Reserve, Inc. All rights reserved. All use is subject to the limited), Ancestry.com, http://www.Ancestry.com, Year: 1880; Census Place: Gadsden and Turkey Town, Etowah, Alabama; Roll: 13; Family History Film: 1254013; Page: 327B; Enumeration District: 66; Image:. Birth date: about 1876 Birth place: Alabama Residence date: 1880 Residence place: Gadsden and Turkey Town, Etowah, Alabama, United States.

573   Ancestry.com, 1900 United States Federal Census (Online publication - Provo, UT, USA: Ancestry.com Operations Inc, 2004. Original data - United States of America, Bureau of the Census. Twelfth Census of the United States, 1900. Washington, D.C.: National Archives and Records Administration, 1900. T623, 18), Ancestry.com, http://www.Ancestry.com, Year: 1900; Census Place: Justice Precinct 1, Camp, Texas; Roll: T623_1618; Page: 19A; Enumeration District: 13. Birth date: Jan 1877 Birth place: Alabama Residence date: 1900 Residence place: Justice Precinct 1 (Excl. Pittsburg Town), Camp, Texas.

574   Ancestry.com and The Church of Jesus Christ of Latter-day Saints, 1880 United States Federal Census (Online publication - Provo, UT, USA: Ancestry.com Operations Inc, 2010. 1880 U.S. Census Index provided by The Church of Jesus Christ of Latter-day Saints © Copyright 1999 Intellectual Reserve, Inc. All rights reserved. All use is subject to the limited), Ancestry.com, http://www.Ancestry.com, Year: 1880; Census Place: Gadsden and Turkey Town, Etowah, Alabama; Roll: 13; Family History Film: 1254013; Page: 327B; Enumeration District: 66; Image:. Birth date: about 1878 Birth place: Alabama Residence date: 1880 Residence place: Gadsden and Turkey Town, Etowah, Alabama, United States.

575   Ancestry.com and The Church of Jesus Christ of Latter-day Saints, 1880 United States Federal Census (Online publication - Provo, UT, USA: Ancestry.com Operations Inc, 2010. 1880 U.S. Census Index provided by The Church of Jesus Christ of Latter-day Saints © Copyright 1999 Intellectual Reserve, Inc. All rights reserved. All use is subject to the limited), Ancestry.com, http://www.Ancestry.com, Year: 1880; Census Place: Gadsden and Turkey Town, Etowah, Alabama; Roll: 13; Family History Film: 1254013; Page: 327B; Enumeration District: 66; Image:. Birth date: about 1880 Birth place: Alabama Residence date: 1880 Residence place: Gadsden and Turkey Town, Etowah, Alabama, United States.

576   Ancestry.com, 1920 United States Federal Census (Online publication - Provo, UT, USA: Ancestry.com Operations Inc, 2010. Images reproduced by FamilySearch. Original data - Fourteenth Census of the United States, 1920. (NARA microfilm publication T625, 2076 rolls). Records of the Bureau of the Census, Record), Ancestry.com, http://www.Ancestry.com, Year: 1920; Census Place: Hokes Bluff, Etowah, Alabama; Roll: T625_15; Page: 9A; Enumeration District: 99; Image:. Birth date: about 1872 Birth place: Alabama Residence date: 1920 Residence place: Hokes Bluff, Etowah, Alabama.

577   Ancestry.com and The Church of Jesus Christ of Latter-day Saints, 1880 United States Federal Census (Online publication - Provo, UT, USA: Ancestry.com Operations Inc, 2010. 1880 U.S. Census Index provided by The Church of Jesus Christ of Latter-day Saints © Copyright 1999 Intellectual Reserve, Inc. All rights reserved. All use is subject to the limited), Ancestry.com, http://www.Ancestry.com, Year: 1880; Census Place: , Cherokee, Alabama; Roll: 6; Family History Film: 1254006; Page: 441D; Enumeration District: 30; Image:. Birth date: about 1848 Birth place: Alabama Residence date: 1880 Residence place: Cherokee, Alabama, United States.

578   Ancestry.com, 1920 United States Federal Census (Online publication - Provo, UT, USA: Ancestry.com Operations Inc, 2010. Images reproduced by FamilySearch. Original data - Fourteenth Census of the United States, 1920. (NARA microfilm publication T625, 2076 rolls). Records of the Bureau of the Census, Record), Ancestry.com, http://www.Ancestry.com, Year: 1920; Census Place: Hokes Bluff, Etowah, Alabama; Roll: T625_15; Page: 9A; Enumeration District: 99; Image:. Birth date: about 1866 Birth place: Alabama Residence date: 1920 Residence place: Hokes Bluff, Etowah, Alabama.

579   Ancestry.com and The Church of Jesus Christ of Latter-day Saints, 1880 United States Federal Census (Online publication - Provo, UT, USA: Ancestry.com Operations Inc, 2010. 1880 U.S. Census Index provided by The Church of Jesus Christ of Latter-day Saints © Copyright 1999 Intellectual Reserve, Inc. All rights reserved. All use is subject to the limited), Ancestry.com, http://www.Ancestry.com, Year: 1880; Census Place: , Cherokee, Alabama; Roll: 6; Family History Film: 1254006; Page: 441D; Enumeration District: 30; Image:. Birth date: about 1866 Birth place: Alabama Residence date: 1880 Residence place: Cherokee, Alabama, United States.

580   Ancestry.com, 1900 United States Federal Census (Online publication - Provo, UT, USA: Ancestry.com Operations Inc, 2004. Original data - United States of America, Bureau of the Census. Twelfth Census of the United States, 1900. Washington, D.C.: National Archives and Records Administration, 1900. T623, 18), Ancestry.com,

http://www.Ancestry.com, Year: 1900; Census Place: Hokes Bluff, Etowah, Alabama; Roll: T623_15; Page: 9B; Enumeration District: 151. Birth date: Apr 1865 Birth place: Alabama Marriage date: 1897 Marriage place: Residence date: 1900 Residence place: Precinct 4 Hokes Bluff, Etowah, Alabama.

581   Ancestry.com, 1930 United States Federal Census (Online publication - Provo, UT, USA: Ancestry.com Operations Inc, 2002. Original data - United States of America, Bureau of the Census. Fifteenth Census of the United States, 1930. Washington, D.C.: National Archives and Records Administration, 1930. T626,), Ancestry.com, http://www.Ancestry.com, Year: 1930; Census Place: Hokes Bluff, Etowah, Alabama; Roll: 16; Page: 8B; Enumeration District: 16; Image: 608.0. Birth date: about 1866 Birth place: Alabama Residence date: 1930 Residence place: Hokes Bluff, Etowah, Alabama.

582   Ancestry.com and The Church of Jesus Christ of Latter-day Saints, 1880 United States Federal Census (Online publication - Provo, UT, USA: Ancestry.com Operations Inc, 2010. 1880 U.S. Census Index provided by The Church of Jesus Christ of Latter-day Saints © Copyright 1999 Intellectual Reserve, Inc. All rights reserved. All use is subject to the limited), Ancestry.com, http://www.Ancestry.com, Year: 1880; Census Place: , Cherokee, Alabama; Roll: 6; Family History Film: 1254006; Page: 441D; Enumeration District: 30; Image:. Birth date: about 1869 Birth place: Alabama Residence date: 1880 Residence place: Cherokee, Alabama, United States.

583   Ancestry.com and The Church of Jesus Christ of Latter-day Saints, 1880 United States Federal Census (Online publication - Provo, UT, USA: Ancestry.com Operations Inc, 2010. 1880 U.S. Census Index provided by The Church of Jesus Christ of Latter-day Saints © Copyright 1999 Intellectual Reserve, Inc. All rights reserved. All use is subject to the limited), Ancestry.com, http://www.Ancestry.com, Year: 1880; Census Place: , Cherokee, Alabama; Roll: 6; Family History Film: 1254006; Page: 441D; Enumeration District: 30; Image:. Birth date: about 1872 Birth place: Alabama Residence date: 1880 Residence place: Cherokee, Alabama, United States.

584   Ancestry.com and The Church of Jesus Christ of Latter-day Saints, 1880 United States Federal Census (Online publication - Provo, UT, USA: Ancestry.com Operations Inc, 2010. 1880 U.S. Census Index provided by The Church of Jesus Christ of Latter-day Saints © Copyright 1999 Intellectual Reserve, Inc. All rights reserved. All use is subject to the limited), Ancestry.com, http://www.Ancestry.com, Year: 1880; Census Place: , Cherokee, Alabama; Roll: 6; Family History Film: 1254006; Page: 441D; Enumeration District: 30; Image:. Birth date: about 1876 Birth place: Alabama Residence date: 1880 Residence place: Cherokee, Alabama, United States.

585   Ancestry.com, 1920 United States Federal Census (Online publication - Provo, UT, USA: Ancestry.com Operations Inc, 2010. Images reproduced by FamilySearch. Original data - Fourteenth Census of the United States, 1920. (NARA microfilm publication T625, 2076 rolls). Records of the Bureau of the Census, Record), Ancestry.com, http://www.Ancestry.com, Year: 1920; Census Place: Greens Schoolhouse, Calhoun, Alabama; Roll: T625_5; Page: 1A; Enumeration District: 10; Image:. Birth date: about 1883 Birth place: Alabama Residence date: 1920 Residence place: Greens Schoolhouse, Calhoun, Alabama.

586   Ancestry.com, 1910 United States Federal Census (Online publication - Provo, UT, USA: Ancestry.com Operations Inc, 2006. Original data - Thirteenth Census of the United States, 1910 (NARA microfilm publication T624, 1,178 rolls). Records of the Bureau of the Census, Record Group 29. National Archives, Washington), Ancestry.com, http://www.Ancestry.com, Year: 1910; Census Place: Greens Schoolhouse, Calhoun, Alabama; Roll: ; Page: ; Enumeration District: ; Image:. Birth date: about 1882 Birth place: Alabama Residence date: 1910 Residence place: Greens Schoolhouse, Calhoun, Alabama.

587   Ancestry.com, Alabama Deaths, 1908-59 (Online publication - Provo, UT, USA: Ancestry.com Operations Inc, 2000. Original data - State of Alabama. Index of Vital Records for Alabama: Deaths, 1908-1959. Montgomery, AL, USA: State of Alabama Center for Health Statistics, Record Services Division. Original), Ancestry.com, http://www.Ancestry.com, Death date: 25 Apr 1957 Death place: Etowah.

588   Ancestry.com, 1870 United States Federal Census (Online publication - Provo, UT, USA: Ancestry.com Operations, Inc., 2009. Images reproduced by FamilySearch. Original data - 1870 U.S. census, population schedules. NARA microfilm publication M593, 1,761 rolls. Washington, D.C.: National Archives and Record), Ancestry.com, http://www.Ancestry.com, Year: 1870; Census Place: Township 12 Range 7, Etowah, Alabama; Roll: M593_; Page: ; Image:. Birth date: about 1835 Birth place: Georgia Residence date: 1870 Residence place: Township 12 Range 7, Etowah, Alabama, United States.

589   Ancestry.com, 1860 United States Federal Census (Online publication - Provo, UT, USA: Ancestry.com Operations, Inc., 2009. Images reproduced by FamilySearch. Original data - 1860 U.S. census, population schedule. NARA microfilm publication M653, 1,438 rolls. Washington, D.C.: National Archives and Records), Ancestry.com, http://www.Ancestry.com, Year: 1860; Census Place: Ranges 8 and 9, Calhoun, Alabama; Roll: ; Page: 417; Image: 137. Birth date: about 1833 Birth place: Georgia Residence date: 1860 Residence place: Ranges 8 and 9, Calhoun, Alabama, United States.

590   Ancestry.com, 1850 United States Federal Census (Online publication - Provo, UT, USA: Ancestry.com Operations, Inc., 2009. Images reproduced by FamilySearch. Original data - Seventh Census of the United States, 1850; (National Archives Microfilm Publication M432, 1009 rolls); Records of the Bureau of the), Ancestry.com, http://www.Ancestry.com, Year: 1850; Census Place: District 27, Cherokee, Alabama; Roll: M432_3; Page: 84B; Image:. Birth date: about 1829 Birth place: Georgia Residence date: 1850 Residence place: District 27, Cherokee, Alabama.

591   Ancestry.com, 1900 United States Federal Census (Online publication - Provo, UT, USA: Ancestry.com Operations Inc, 2004. Original data - United States of America, Bureau of the Census. Twelfth Census of the United States, 1900. Washington, D.C.: National Archives and Records Administration, 1900. T623, 18), Ancestry.com,

http://www.Ancestry.com, Year: 1900; Census Place: Hokes Bluff, Etowah, Alabama; Roll: T623_15; Page: 9A; Enumeration District: 151. Birth date: Aug 1830 Birth place: Alabama Residence date: 1900 Residence place: Hokes Bluff, Etowah, Alabama.

592   Ancestry.com, 1910 United States Federal Census (Online publication - Provo, UT, USA: Ancestry.com Operations Inc, 2006. Original data - Thirteenth Census of the United States, 1910 (NARA microfilm publication T624, 1,178 rolls). Records of the Bureau of the Census, Record Group 29. National Archives, Washington), Ancestry.com, http://www.Ancestry.com, Year: 1910; Census Place: Corinth, DeKalb, Alabama; Roll: ; Page: ; Enumeration District: ; Image:. Birth date: about 1855 Birth place: Alabama Residence date: 1910 Residence place: Corinth, DeKalb, Alabama.

593   Ancestry.com, 1870 United States Federal Census (Online publication - Provo, UT, USA: Ancestry.com Operations, Inc., 2009. Images reproduced by FamilySearch. Original data - 1870 U.S. census, population schedules. NARA microfilm publication M593, 1,761 rolls. Washington, D.C.: National Archives and Record), Ancestry.com, http://www.Ancestry.com, Year: 1870; Census Place: Township 12 Range 7, Etowah, Alabama; Roll: M593_; Page: ; Image:. Birth date: about 1853 Birth place: Alabama Residence date: 1870 Residence place: Township 12 Range 7, Etowah, Alabama, United States.

594   Ancestry.com, 1860 United States Federal Census (Online publication - Provo, UT, USA: Ancestry.com Operations, Inc., 2009. Images reproduced by FamilySearch. Original data - 1860 U.S. census, population schedule. NARA microfilm publication M653, 1,438 rolls. Washington, D.C.: National Archives and Records), Ancestry.com, http://www.Ancestry.com, Year: 1860; Census Place: Ranges 8 and 9, Calhoun, Alabama; Roll: ; Page: 417; Image: 137. Birth date: about 1851 Birth place: Alabama Residence date: 1860 Residence place: Ranges 8 and 9, Calhoun, Alabama, United States.

595   Ancestry.com, 1920 United States Federal Census (Online publication - Provo, UT, USA: Ancestry.com Operations Inc, 2010. Images reproduced by FamilySearch. Original data - Fourteenth Census of the United States, 1920. (NARA microfilm publication T625, 2076 rolls). Records of the Bureau of the Census, Record), Ancestry.com, http://www.Ancestry.com, Year: 1920; Census Place: Corinth, DeKalb, Alabama; Roll: T625_12; Page: 18A; Enumeration District: 86; Image:. Birth date: about 1857 Birth place: Alabama Residence date: 1920 Residence place: Corinth, DeKalb, Alabama.

596   Ancestry.com, Alabama Marriage Collection, 1800-1969 (Online publication - Provo, UT, USA: Ancestry.com Operations Inc, 2006. Original data - Alabama Center for Health Statistics. Alabama Marriage Index, 1936-1969. Alabama Center for Health Statistics, Montgomery, Alabama. Dodd, Jordan R., et. al. Early America), Ancestry.com, http://www.Ancestry.com, Marriage date: 29 Nov 1889 Marriage place: Dekalb, Alabama.

597   Dodd, Jordan R., comp., Alabama Marriages, 1809-1920 (Selected Counties) (Online publication - Provo, UT, USA: The Generations Network, Inc., 1999. Original data - Early American Marriages: Alabama, 1800 to 1920. Original data: Early American Marriages: Alabama, 1800 to 1920), Ancestry.com, http://www.Ancestry.com, Marriage date: 29 Nov 1889 Marriage place: Dekalb.

598   Ancestry.com, 1850 United States Federal Census (Online publication - Provo, UT, USA: Ancestry.com Operations, Inc., 2009. Images reproduced by FamilySearch. Original data - Seventh Census of the United States, 1850; (National Archives Microfilm Publication M432, 1009 rolls); Records of the Bureau of the), Ancestry.com, http://www.Ancestry.com, Year: 1850; Census Place: District 27, Cherokee, Alabama; Roll: M432_3; Page: 84B; Image:. Birth date: about 1847 Birth place: Alabama Residence date: 1850 Residence place: District 27, Cherokee, Alabama.

599   Ancestry.com, 1860 United States Federal Census (Online publication - Provo, UT, USA: Ancestry.com Operations, Inc., 2009. Images reproduced by FamilySearch. Original data - 1860 U.S. census, population schedule. NARA microfilm publication M653, 1,438 rolls. Washington, D.C.: National Archives and Records), Ancestry.com, http://www.Ancestry.com, Year: 1860; Census Place: Ranges 8 and 9, Calhoun, Alabama; Roll: ; Page: 417; Image: 137. Birth date: about 1847 Birth place: Alabama Residence date: 1860 Residence place: Ranges 8 and 9, Calhoun, Alabama, United States.

600   Ancestry.com, 1870 United States Federal Census (Online publication - Provo, UT, USA: Ancestry.com Operations, Inc., 2009. Images reproduced by FamilySearch. Original data - 1870 U.S. census, population schedules. NARA microfilm publication M593, 1,761 rolls. Washington, D.C.: National Archives and Record), Ancestry.com, http://www.Ancestry.com, Year: 1870; Census Place: Township 15, Calhoun, Alabama; Roll: M593_; Page: ; Image:. Birth date: about 1848 Birth place: Alabama Residence date: 1870 Residence place: Township 15, Calhoun, Alabama, United States.

601   Ancestry.com and The Church of Jesus Christ of Latter-day Saints, 1880 United States Federal Census (Online publication - Provo, UT, USA: Ancestry.com Operations Inc, 2010. 1880 U.S. Census Index provided by The Church of Jesus Christ of Latter-day Saints © Copyright 1999 Intellectual Reserve, Inc. All rights reserved. All use is subject to the limited), Ancestry.com, http://www.Ancestry.com, Year: 1880; Census Place: Beat 2, Warren, Mississippi; Roll: 667; Family History Film: 1254667; Page: 472B; Enumeration District: 74; Image: 0297. Birth date: about 1848 Birth place: Alabama Residence date: 1880 Residence place: Beat 2, Warren, Mississippi, United States.

602   Ancestry.com, 1900 United States Federal Census (Online publication - Provo, UT, USA: Ancestry.com Operations Inc, 2004. Original data - United States of America, Bureau of the Census. Twelfth Census of the United States, 1900. Washington, D.C.: National Archives and Records Administration, 1900. T623, 18), Ancestry.com, http://www.Ancestry.com, Year: 1900; Census Place: Beat 2, Warren, Mississippi; Roll: T623_831; Page: 10B; Enumeration District: 126. Birth date: Oct 1848 Birth place: Alabama Marriage date: 1865 Marriage place: Residence date: 1900 Residence place: Beat 2, Warren, Mississippi.

603   Ancestry.com, Louisiana Statewide Death Index, 1900-1949 (Online publication - Provo, UT, USA: Ancestry.com Operations Inc, 2002. Original data - State of Louisiana, Secretary of State, Division of Archives, Records Management, and History. Vital Records Indices. Baton Rouge, LA, USA. Original data: State of Louisiana), Ancestry.com, http://www.Ancestry.com, Birth date: 1849 Birth place: Death date: 25 Feb 1926 Death place: Louisiana.

604   Ancestry.com, 1910 United States Federal Census (Online publication - Provo, UT, USA: Ancestry.com Operations Inc, 2006. Original data - Thirteenth Census of the United States, 1910 (NARA microfilm publication T624, 1,178 rolls). Records of the Bureau of the Census, Record Group 29. National Archives, Washington), Ancestry.com, http://www.Ancestry.com, Year: 1910; Census Place: Police Jury Ward 5, Ouachita, Louisiana; Roll: ; Page: ; Enumeration District: ; Image:. Birth date: about 1849 Birth place: Alabama Residence date: 1910 Residence place: Police Jury Ward 5, Ouachita, Louisiana.

605   Ancestry.com, Alabama Marriage Collection, 1800-1969 (Online publication - Provo, UT, USA: Ancestry.com Operations Inc, 2006. Original data - Alabama Center for Health Statistics. Alabama Marriage Index, 1936-1969. Alabama Center for Health Statistics, Montgomery, Alabama. Dodd, Jordan R., et. al. Early America), Ancestry.com, http://www.Ancestry.com, Marriage date: 17 Jan 1865 Marriage place: Calhoun, Alabama.

606   Ancestry.com and The Church of Jesus Christ of Latter-day Saints, 1880 United States Federal Census (Online publication - Provo, UT, USA: Ancestry.com Operations Inc, 2010. 1880 U.S. Census Index provided by The Church of Jesus Christ of Latter-day Saints © Copyright 1999 Intellectual Reserve, Inc. All rights reserved. All use is subject to the limited), Ancestry.com, http://www.Ancestry.com, Year: 1880; Census Place: Greenwood, Etowah, Alabama; Roll: 13; Family History Film: 1254013; Page: 405A; Enumeration District: 72; Image: 0317. Birth date: about 1851 Birth place: Alabama Residence date: 1880 Residence place: Greenwood, Etowah, Alabama, United States.

607   Ancestry.com, 1850 United States Federal Census (Online publication - Provo, UT, USA: Ancestry.com Operations, Inc., 2009. Images reproduced by FamilySearch. Original data - Seventh Census of the United States, 1850; (National Archives Microfilm Publication M432, 1009 rolls); Records of the Bureau of the), Ancestry.com, http://www.Ancestry.com, Year: 1850; Census Place: District 27, Cherokee, Alabama; Roll: M432_3; Page: 84B; Image:. Birth date: about 1850 Birth place: Alabama Residence date: 1850 Residence place: District 27, Cherokee, Alabama.

608   Ancestry.com, 1860 United States Federal Census (Online publication - Provo, UT, USA: Ancestry.com Operations, Inc., 2009. Images reproduced by FamilySearch. Original data - 1860 U.S. census, population schedule. NARA microfilm publication M653, 1,438 rolls. Washington, D.C.: National Archives and Records), Ancestry.com, http://www.Ancestry.com, Year: 1860; Census Place: Ranges 8 and 9, Calhoun, Alabama; Roll: ; Page: 417; Image: 137. Birth date: about 1849 Birth place: Alabama Residence date: 1860 Residence place: Ranges 8 and 9, Calhoun, Alabama, United States.

609   Ancestry.com, 1870 United States Federal Census (Online publication - Provo, UT, USA: Ancestry.com Operations, Inc., 2009. Images reproduced by FamilySearch. Original data - 1870 U.S. census, population schedules. NARA microfilm publication M593, 1,761 rolls. Washington, D.C.: National Archives and Record), Ancestry.com, http://www.Ancestry.com, Year: 1870; Census Place: Township 12 Range 7, Etowah, Alabama; Roll: M593_; Page: ; Image:. Birth date: about 1850 Birth place: Alabama Residence date: 1870 Residence place: Township 12 Range 7, Etowah, Alabama, United States.

610   Ancestry.com, U.S. General Land Office Records, 1796-1907 (Online publication - Provo, UT, USA: Ancestry.com Operations Inc, 2008. Original data - United States. Bureau of Land Management, General Land Office Records. Automated Records Project; Federal Land Patents, State Volumes. Springfield, Virginia: Bureau of L), Ancestry.com, http://www.Ancestry.com, Residence date: Residence place: United States.

611   Ancestry.com and The Church of Jesus Christ of Latter-day Saints, 1880 United States Federal Census (Online publication - Provo, UT, USA: Ancestry.com Operations Inc, 2010. 1880 U.S. Census Index provided by The Church of Jesus Christ of Latter-day Saints © Copyright 1999 Intellectual Reserve, Inc. All rights reserved. All use is subject to the limited), Ancestry.com, http://www.Ancestry.com, Year: 1880; Census Place: Hokes Bluff and Turkey Town, Etowah, Alabama; Roll: 13; Family History Film: 1254013; Page: 323B; Enumeration District: 66; Image: 0154. Birth date: about 1853 Birth place: Alabama Residence date: 1880 Residence place: Hokes Bluff and Turkey Town, Etowah, Alabama, United States.

612   Ancestry.com, 1900 United States Federal Census (Online publication - Provo, UT, USA: Ancestry.com Operations Inc, 2004. Original data - United States of America, Bureau of the Census. Twelfth Census of the United States, 1900. Washington, D.C.: National Archives and Records Administration, 1900. T623, 18), Ancestry.com, http://www.Ancestry.com, Year: 1900; Census Place: Hokes Bluff, Etowah, Alabama; Roll: T623_15; Page: 9B; Enumeration District: 151. Birth date: Feb 1852 Birth place: Alabama Residence date: 1900 Residence place: Hokes Bluff, Etowah, Alabama.

613   Ancestry.com, Alabama Marriage Collection, 1800-1969 (Online publication - Provo, UT, USA: Ancestry.com Operations Inc, 2006. Original data - Alabama Center for Health Statistics. Alabama Marriage Index, 1936-1969. Alabama Center for Health Statistics, Montgomery, Alabama. Dodd, Jordan R., et. al. Early America), Ancestry.com, http://www.Ancestry.com, Marriage date: 21 Nov 1875 Marriage place: Etowah, Alabama.

614   Ancestry.com, 1860 United States Federal Census (Online publication - Provo, UT, USA: Ancestry.com Operations, Inc., 2009. Images reproduced by FamilySearch. Original data - 1860 U.S. census, population schedule. NARA microfilm publication M653, 1,438 rolls. Washington, D.C.: National Archives and Records), Ancestry.com, http://www.Ancestry.com, Year: 1860; Census Place: Ranges 8 and 9, Calhoun, Alabama; Roll: ; Page: 417; Image: 137.

Birth date: about 1854 Birth place: Alabama Residence date: 1860 Residence place: Ranges 8 and 9, Calhoun, Alabama, United States.

615   Ancestry.com, 1870 United States Federal Census (Online publication - Provo, UT, USA: Ancestry.com Operations, Inc., 2009. Images reproduced by FamilySearch. Original data - 1870 U.S. census, population schedules. NARA microfilm publication M593, 1,761 rolls. Washington, D.C.: National Archives and Record), Ancestry.com, http://www.Ancestry.com, Year: 1870; Census Place: Township 12 Range 7, Etowah, Alabama; Roll: M593_; Page: ; Image:. Birth date: about 1858 Birth place: Alabama Residence date: 1870 Residence place: Township 12 Range 7, Etowah, Alabama, United States.

616   Ancestry.com, Alabama Marriage Collection, 1800-1969 (Online publication - Provo, UT, USA: Ancestry.com Operations Inc, 2006. Original data - Alabama Center for Health Statistics. Alabama Marriage Index, 1936-1969. Alabama Center for Health Statistics, Montgomery, Alabama. Dodd, Jordan R., et. al. Early America), Ancestry.com, http://www.Ancestry.com, Marriage date: 21 Nov 1875 Marriage place: Etowah, Alabama.

617   Ancestry.com, Alabama Marriage Collection, 1800-1969 (Online publication - Provo, UT, USA: Ancestry.com Operations Inc, 2006. Original data - Alabama Center for Health Statistics. Alabama Marriage Index, 1936-1969. Alabama Center for Health Statistics, Montgomery, Alabama. Dodd, Jordan R., et. al. Early America), Ancestry.com, http://www.Ancestry.com, Marriage date: 10 Apr 1879 Marriage place: Etowah, Alabama.

618   Ancestry.com, Alabama Marriage Collection, 1800-1969 (Online publication - Provo, UT, USA: Ancestry.com Operations Inc, 2006. Original data - Alabama Center for Health Statistics. Alabama Marriage Index, 1936-1969. Alabama Center for Health Statistics, Montgomery, Alabama. Dodd, Jordan R., et. al. Early America), Ancestry.com, http://www.Ancestry.com, Marriage date: 10 Apr 1879 Marriage place: Etowah, Alabama.

619   Ancestry.com, 1860 United States Federal Census (Online publication - Provo, UT, USA: Ancestry.com Operations, Inc., 2009. Images reproduced by FamilySearch. Original data - 1860 U.S. census, population schedule. NARA microfilm publication M653, 1,438 rolls. Washington, D.C.: National Archives and Records), Ancestry.com, http://www.Ancestry.com, Year: 1860; Census Place: Ranges 8 and 9, Calhoun, Alabama; Roll: ; Page: 417; Image: 137. Birth date: about 1857 Birth place: Alabama Residence date: 1860 Residence place: Ranges 8 and 9, Calhoun, Alabama, United States.

620   Ancestry.com, 1900 United States Federal Census (Online publication - Provo, UT, USA: Ancestry.com Operations Inc, 2004. Original data - United States of America, Bureau of the Census. Twelfth Census of the United States, 1900. Washington, D.C.: National Archives and Records Administration, 1900. T623, 18), Ancestry.com, http://www.Ancestry.com, Year: 1900; Census Place: Turkeytown, Etowah, Alabama; Roll: T623_16; Page: 4A; Enumeration District: 154. Birth date: Apr 1857 Birth place: Alabama Marriage date: 1879 Marriage place: Residence date: 1900 Residence place: Turkeytown, Etowah, Alabama.

621   Ancestry.com, Alabama Deaths, 1908-59 (Online publication - Provo, UT, USA: Ancestry.com Operations Inc, 2000. Original data - State of Alabama. Index of Vital Records for Alabama: Deaths, 1908-1959. Montgomery, AL, USA: State of Alabama Center for Health Statistics, Record Services Division. Original), Ancestry.com, http://www.Ancestry.com.

622   Ancestry.com, U.S. General Land Office Records, 1796-1907 (Online publication - Provo, UT, USA: Ancestry.com Operations Inc, 2008. Original data - United States. Bureau of Land Management, General Land Office Records. Automated Records Project; Federal Land Patents, State Volumes. Springfield, Virginia: Bureau of L), Ancestry.com, http://www.Ancestry.com, Residence date: Residence place: United States.

623   United States, Bureau of Land Management, Alabama Land Records (Online publication - Provo, UT, USA: Ancestry.com Operations Inc, 1997. Original data - United States. Bureau of Land Management. Alabama Pre-1908 Homestead and Cash Entry Patent and Cadastral Survey Plat Index. General Land Office Automated Records Project), Ancestry.com, http://www.Ancestry.com.

624   Dodd, Jordan R., comp., Alabama Marriages, 1809-1920 (Selected Counties) (Online publication - Provo, UT, USA: The Generations Network, Inc., 1999. Original data - Early American Marriages: Alabama, 1800 to 1920. Original data: Early American Marriages: Alabama, 1800 to 1920), Ancestry.com, http://www.Ancestry.com, Marriage date: 10 Apr 1879 Marriage place: Etowah.

625   Ancestry.com, Alabama Marriage Collection, 1800-1969 (Online publication - Provo, UT, USA: Ancestry.com Operations Inc, 2006. Original data - Alabama Center for Health Statistics. Alabama Marriage Index, 1936-1969. Alabama Center for Health Statistics, Montgomery, Alabama. Dodd, Jordan R., et. al. Early America), Ancestry.com, http://www.Ancestry.com, Date.

626   Ancestry.com, Alabama Deaths, 1908-59 (Online publication - Provo, UT, USA: Ancestry.com Operations Inc, 2000. Original data - State of Alabama. Index of Vital Records for Alabama: Deaths, 1908-1959. Montgomery, AL, USA: State of Alabama Center for Health Statistics, Record Services Division. Original), Ancestry.com, http://www.Ancestry.com, Death date: Jan 1926 Death place: Calhoun.

627   Ancestry.com, Alabama Marriage Collection, 1800-1969 (Online publication - Provo, UT, USA: Ancestry.com Operations Inc, 2006. Original data - Alabama Center for Health Statistics. Alabama Marriage Index, 1936-1969. Alabama Center for Health Statistics, Montgomery, Alabama. Dodd, Jordan R., et. al. Early America), Ancestry.com, http://www.Ancestry.com, Marriage date: 29 Dec 1881 Marriage place: Etowah, Alabama.

628   Ancestry.com, 1870 United States Federal Census (Online publication - Provo, UT, USA: Ancestry.com Operations, Inc., 2009. Images reproduced by FamilySearch. Original data - 1870 U.S. census, population schedules. NARA microfilm publication M593, 1,761 rolls. Washington, D.C.: National Archives and Record), Ancestry.com, http://www.Ancestry.com, Year: 1870; Census Place: Township 12 Range 7, Etowah, Alabama; Roll: M593_; Page: ; Image:. Birth date: about 1863 Birth place: Alabama Residence date: 1870 Residence place: Township 12 Range 7, Etowah, Alabama, United States.

629   Ancestry.com, 1910 United States Federal Census (Online publication - Provo, UT, USA: Ancestry.com Operations Inc, 2006. Original data - Thirteenth Census of the United States, 1910 (NARA microfilm publication T624, 1,178 rolls). Records of the Bureau of the Census, Record Group 29. National Archives, Washington), Ancestry.com, http://www.Ancestry.com, Year: 1910; Census Place: Piedmont, Calhoun, Alabama; Roll: ; Page: ; Enumeration District: ; Image:. Birth date: 1859 Birth place: Georgia Residence date: 1910 Residence place: Piedmont, Calhoun, Alabama.

630   Ancestry.com, 1870 United States Federal Census (Online publication - Provo, UT, USA: Ancestry.com Operations, Inc., 2009. Images reproduced by FamilySearch. Original data - 1870 U.S. census, population schedules. NARA microfilm publication M593, 1,761 rolls. Washington, D.C.: National Archives and Record), Ancestry.com, http://www.Ancestry.com, Year: 1870; Census Place: Subdivision 71, Jackson, Georgia; Roll: M593_; Page: ; Image:. Birth date: about 1861 Birth place: Georgia Residence date: 1870 Residence place: Subdivision 71, Jackson, Georgia, United States.

631   Ancestry.com, 1920 United States Federal Census (Online publication - Provo, UT, USA: Ancestry.com Operations Inc, 2010. Images reproduced by FamilySearch. Original data - Fourteenth Census of the United States, 1920. (NARA microfilm publication T625, 2076 rolls). Records of the Bureau of the Census, Record), Ancestry.com, http://www.Ancestry.com, Year: 1920; Census Place: Jacksonville, Calhoun, Alabama; Roll: T625_5; Page: 22A; Enumeration District: 2; Image:. Birth date: about 1860 Birth place: Georgia Residence date: 1920 Residence place: Jacksonville, Calhoun, Alabama.

632   Ancestry.com, 1930 United States Federal Census (Online publication - Provo, UT, USA: Ancestry.com Operations Inc, 2002. Original data - United States of America, Bureau of the Census. Fifteenth Census of the United States, 1930. Washington, D.C.: National Archives and Records Administration, 1930. T626,), Ancestry.com, http://www.Ancestry.com, Year: 1930; Census Place: Greens Schoolhouse, Calhoun, Alabama; Roll: 5; Page: 8B; Enumeration District: 11; Image: 257.0. Birth date: about 1862 Birth place: Residence date: 1930 Residence place: Greens Schoolhouse, Calhoun, Alabama.

633   Ancestry.com, Alabama Deaths, 1908-59 (Online publication - Provo, UT, USA: Ancestry.com Operations Inc, 2000. Original data - State of Alabama. Index of Vital Records for Alabama: Deaths, 1908-1959. Montgomery, AL, USA: State of Alabama Center for Health Statistics, Record Services Division. Original), Ancestry.com, http://www.Ancestry.com, Death date: Jan 1939 Death place: Cherokee.

634   Ancestry.com, 1900 United States Federal Census (Online publication - Provo, UT, USA: Ancestry.com Operations Inc, 2004. Original data - United States of America, Bureau of the Census. Twelfth Census of the United States, 1900. Washington, D.C.: National Archives and Records Administration, 1900. T623, 18), Ancestry.com, http://www.Ancestry.com, Year: 1900; Census Place: Coloma, Cherokee, Alabama; Roll: T623_6; Page: 1A; Enumeration District: 122. Birth date: Mar 1885 Birth place: Alabama Residence date: 1900 Residence place: Precinct 7 Coloma, Cherokee, Alabama.

635   Ancestry.com, 1930 United States Federal Census (Online publication - Provo, UT, USA: Ancestry.com Operations Inc, 2002. Original data - United States of America, Bureau of the Census. Fifteenth Census of the United States, 1930. Washington, D.C.: National Archives and Records Administration, 1930. T626,), Ancestry.com, http://www.Ancestry.com, Year: 1930; Census Place: Greens Schoolhouse, Calhoun, Alabama; Roll: 5; Page: 8A; Enumeration District: 11; Image: 256.0. Birth date: about 1885 Birth place: Alabama Residence date: 1930 Residence place: Greens Schoolhouse, Calhoun, Alabama.

636   Ancestry.com, 1920 United States Federal Census (Online publication - Provo, UT, USA: Ancestry.com Operations Inc, 2010. Images reproduced by FamilySearch. Original data - Fourteenth Census of the United States, 1920. (NARA microfilm publication T625, 2076 rolls). Records of the Bureau of the Census, Record), Ancestry.com, http://www.Ancestry.com, Year: 1920; Census Place: Greens Schoolhouse, Calhoun, Alabama; Roll: T625_5; Page: 3B; Enumeration District: 10; Image:. Birth date: about 1886 Birth place: Alabama Residence date: 1920 Residence place: Greens Schoolhouse, Calhoun, Alabama.

637   Ancestry.com, 1910 United States Federal Census (Online publication - Provo, UT, USA: Ancestry.com Operations Inc, 2006. Original data - Thirteenth Census of the United States, 1910 (NARA microfilm publication T624, 1,178 rolls). Records of the Bureau of the Census, Record Group 29. National Archives, Washington), Ancestry.com, http://www.Ancestry.com, Year: 1910; Census Place: Piedmont, Calhoun, Alabama; Roll: ; Page: ; Enumeration District: ; Image:. Birth date: 1887 Birth place: Alabama Residence date: 1910 Residence place: Piedmont, Calhoun, Alabama.

638   Ancestry.com, 1900 United States Federal Census (Online publication - Provo, UT, USA: Ancestry.com Operations Inc, 2004. Original data - United States of America, Bureau of the Census. Twelfth Census of the United States, 1900. Washington, D.C.: National Archives and Records Administration, 1900. T623, 18), Ancestry.com, http://www.Ancestry.com, Year: 1900; Census Place: Coloma, Cherokee, Alabama; Roll: T623_6; Page: 1A; Enumeration District: 122. Birth date: Dec 1886 Birth place: Alabama Residence date: 1900 Residence place: Precinct 7 Coloma, Cherokee, Alabama.

639   Ancestry.com, World War I Draft Registration Cards, 1917-1918 (Online publication - Provo, UT, USA: Ancestry.com Operations Inc, 2005. Original data - United States, Selective Service System. World War I Selective Service System Draft Registration Cards, 1917-1918. Washington, D.C.: National Archives and Records Administration), Ancestry.com, http://www.Ancestry.com, Registration Location: Calhoun County, Alabama; Roll: 1509362; Draft Board: 0. Birth date: 12 Nov 1886 Birth place: Alabama; United States of America Residence date: Residence place: Calhoun, Alabama.

640   Ancestry.com, 1920 United States Federal Census (Online publication - Provo, UT, USA: Ancestry.com Operations Inc, 2010. Images reproduced by FamilySearch. Original data - Fourteenth Census of the United States, 1920. (NARA microfilm publication T625, 2076 rolls). Records of the Bureau of the Census, Record), Ancestry.com, http://www.Ancestry.com, Year: 1920; Census Place: Piedmont, Calhoun, Alabama; Roll: T625_5; Page: 11A; Enumeration District: 12; Image:. Birth date: about 1887 Birth place: Alabama Residence date: 1920 Residence place: Piedmont, Calhoun, Alabama.

641   Ancestry.com, 1930 United States Federal Census (Online publication - Provo, UT, USA: Ancestry.com Operations Inc, 2002. Original data - United States of America, Bureau of the Census. Fifteenth Census of the United States, 1930. Washington, D.C.: National Archives and Records Administration, 1930. T626,), Ancestry.com, http://www.Ancestry.com, Year: 1930; Census Place: Snows, Calhoun, Alabama; Roll: 5; Page: 4A; Enumeration District: 43; Image: 534.0. Birth date: about 1885 Birth place: Alabama Residence date: 1930 Residence place: Snows, Calhoun, Alabama.

642   Ancestry.com, Alabama Deaths, 1908-59 (Online publication - Provo, UT, USA: Ancestry.com Operations Inc, 2000. Original data - State of Alabama. Index of Vital Records for Alabama: Deaths, 1908-1959. Montgomery, AL, USA: State of Alabama Center for Health Statistics, Record Services Division. Original), Ancestry.com, http://www.Ancestry.com, Death date: Feb 1935 Death place: Calhoun.

643   Ancestry.com, 1900 United States Federal Census (Online publication - Provo, UT, USA: Ancestry.com Operations Inc, 2004. Original data - United States of America, Bureau of the Census. Twelfth Census of the United States, 1900. Washington, D.C.: National Archives and Records Administration, 1900. T623, 18), Ancestry.com, http://www.Ancestry.com, Year: 1900; Census Place: Coloma, Cherokee, Alabama; Roll: T623_6; Page: 1A; Enumeration District: 122. Birth date: Feb 1889 Birth place: Alabama Residence date: 1900 Residence place: Precinct 7 Coloma, Cherokee, Alabama.

644   Ancestry.com, 1910 United States Federal Census (Online publication - Provo, UT, USA: Ancestry.com Operations Inc, 2006. Original data - Thirteenth Census of the United States, 1910 (NARA microfilm publication T624, 1,178 rolls). Records of the Bureau of the Census, Record Group 29. National Archives, Washington), Ancestry.com, http://www.Ancestry.com, Year: 1910; Census Place: Piedmont, Calhoun, Alabama; Roll: ; Page: ; Enumeration District: ; Image:. Birth date: 1889 Birth place: Alabama Residence date: 1910 Residence place: Piedmont, Calhoun, Alabama.

645   Ancestry.com, 1900 United States Federal Census (Online publication - Provo, UT, USA: Ancestry.com Operations Inc, 2004. Original data - United States of America, Bureau of the Census. Twelfth Census of the United States, 1900. Washington, D.C.: National Archives and Records Administration, 1900. T623, 18), Ancestry.com, http://www.Ancestry.com, Year: 1900; Census Place: Coloma, Cherokee, Alabama; Roll: T623_6; Page: 1A; Enumeration District: 122. Birth date: Nov 1891 Birth place: Alabama Residence date: 1900 Residence place: Precinct 7 Coloma, Cherokee, Alabama.

646   Ancestry.com, 1900 United States Federal Census (Online publication - Provo, UT, USA: Ancestry.com Operations Inc, 2004. Original data - United States of America, Bureau of the Census. Twelfth Census of the United States, 1900. Washington, D.C.: National Archives and Records Administration, 1900. T623, 18), Ancestry.com, http://www.Ancestry.com, Year: 1900; Census Place: Coloma, Cherokee, Alabama; Roll: T623_6; Page: 1A; Enumeration District: 122. Birth date: Jan 1893 Birth place: Alabama Residence date: 1900 Residence place: Precinct 7 Coloma, Cherokee, Alabama.

647   Ancestry.com, 1900 United States Federal Census (Online publication - Provo, UT, USA: Ancestry.com Operations Inc, 2004. Original data - United States of America, Bureau of the Census. Twelfth Census of the United States, 1900. Washington, D.C.: National Archives and Records Administration, 1900. T623, 18), Ancestry.com, http://www.Ancestry.com, Year: 1900; Census Place: Coloma, Cherokee, Alabama; Roll: T623_6; Page: 1A; Enumeration District: 122. Birth date: Mar 1896 Birth place: Alabama Residence date: 1900 Residence place: Precinct 7 Coloma, Cherokee, Alabama.

648   Ancestry.com, 1920 United States Federal Census (Online publication - Provo, UT, USA: Ancestry.com Operations Inc, 2010. Images reproduced by FamilySearch. Original data - Fourteenth Census of the United States, 1920. (NARA microfilm publication T625, 2076 rolls). Records of the Bureau of the Census, Record), Ancestry.com, http://www.Ancestry.com, Year: 1920; Census Place: Jacksonville, Calhoun, Alabama; Roll: T625_5; Page: 22A; Enumeration District: 2; Image:. Birth date: about 1896 Birth place: Alabama Residence date: 1920 Residence place: Jacksonville, Calhoun, Alabama.

649   Ancestry.com, 1910 United States Federal Census (Online publication - Provo, UT, USA: Ancestry.com Operations Inc, 2006. Original data - Thirteenth Census of the United States, 1910 (NARA microfilm publication T624, 1,178 rolls). Records of the Bureau of the Census, Record Group 29. National Archives, Washington), Ancestry.com, http://www.Ancestry.com, Year: 1910; Census Place: Piedmont, Calhoun, Alabama; Roll: ; Page: ; Enumeration District: ; Image:. Birth date: 1896 Birth place: Alabama Residence date: 1910 Residence place: Piedmont, Calhoun, Alabama.

650	Ancestry.com, Social Security Death Index (Online publication - Provo, UT, USA: Ancestry.com Operations Inc, 2010. Original data - Social Security Administration. Social Security Death Index, Master File. Social Security Administration. Original data: Social Security Administration. Social Security D), Ancestry.com, http://www.Ancestry.com, Number: 253-09-8400; Issue State: Georgia; Issue Date: Before 1951. Birth date: 22 Mar 1896 Birth place: Death date: Mar 1978 Death place: Anniston, Calhoun, Alabama, United States of America.

651	Ancestry.com, 1930 United States Federal Census (Online publication - Provo, UT, USA: Ancestry.com Operations Inc, 2002. Original data - United States of America, Bureau of the Census. Fifteenth Census of the United States, 1930. Washington, D.C.: National Archives and Records Administration, 1930. T626,), Ancestry.com, http://www.Ancestry.com, Year: 1930; Census Place: Chattanooga, Hamilton, Tennessee; Roll: 2252; Page: 24A; Enumeration District: 47; Image: 163.0. Birth date: about 1895 Birth place: Alabama Residence date: 1930 Residence place: Chattanooga, Hamilton, Tennessee.

652	Ancestry.com, 1900 United States Federal Census (Online publication - Provo, UT, USA: Ancestry.com Operations Inc, 2004. Original data - United States of America, Bureau of the Census. Twelfth Census of the United States, 1900. Washington, D.C.: National Archives and Records Administration, 1900. T623, 18), Ancestry.com, http://www.Ancestry.com, Year: 1900; Census Place: Coloma, Cherokee, Alabama; Roll: T623_6; Page: 1A; Enumeration District: 122. Birth date: Apr 1899 Birth place: Alabama Residence date: 1900 Residence place: Precinct 7 Coloma, Cherokee, Alabama.

653	Ancestry.com, 1920 United States Federal Census (Online publication - Provo, UT, USA: Ancestry.com Operations Inc, 2010. Images reproduced by FamilySearch. Original data - Fourteenth Census of the United States, 1920. (NARA microfilm publication T625, 2076 rolls). Records of the Bureau of the Census, Record), Ancestry.com, http://www.Ancestry.com, Year: 1920; Census Place: Gadsden Ward 4, Etowah, Alabama; Roll: T625_15; Page: 11B; Enumeration District: 94; Image:. Birth date: about 1871 Birth place: Georgia Residence date: 1920 Residence place: Gadsden Ward 4, Etowah, Alabama.

654	Ancestry.com, 1930 United States Federal Census (Online publication - Provo, UT, USA: Ancestry.com Operations Inc, 2002. Original data - United States of America, Bureau of the Census. Fifteenth Census of the United States, 1930. Washington, D.C.: National Archives and Records Administration, 1930. T626,), Ancestry.com, http://www.Ancestry.com, Year: 1930; Census Place: Gadsden, Etowah, Alabama; Roll: 16; Page: 21B; Enumeration District: 9; Image: 420.0.	Birth date: about 1871 Birth place: Residence date: 1930 Residence place: Gadsden, Etowah, Alabama.

655	Ancestry.com, 1920 United States Federal Census (Online publication - Provo, UT, USA: Ancestry.com Operations Inc, 2010. Images reproduced by FamilySearch. Original data - Fourteenth Census of the United States, 1920. (NARA microfilm publication T625, 2076 rolls). Records of the Bureau of the Census, Record), Ancestry.com, http://www.Ancestry.com, Year: 1920; Census Place: Gadsden Ward 4, Etowah, Alabama; Roll: T625_15; Page: 11B; Enumeration District: 94; Image:. Birth date: about 1899 Birth place: Alabama Residence date: 1920 Residence place: Gadsden Ward 4, Etowah, Alabama.

656	Ancestry.com, 1920 United States Federal Census (Online publication - Provo, UT, USA: Ancestry.com Operations Inc, 2010. Images reproduced by FamilySearch. Original data - Fourteenth Census of the United States, 1920. (NARA microfilm publication T625, 2076 rolls). Records of the Bureau of the Census, Record), Ancestry.com, http://www.Ancestry.com, Year: 1920; Census Place: Gadsden Ward 4, Etowah, Alabama; Roll: T625_15; Page: 11B; Enumeration District: 94; Image:. Birth date: about 1907 Birth place: Alabama Residence date: 1920 Residence place: Gadsden Ward 4, Etowah, Alabama.

657	Ancestry.com, 1930 United States Federal Census (Online publication - Provo, UT, USA: Ancestry.com Operations Inc, 2002. Original data - United States of America, Bureau of the Census. Fifteenth Census of the United States, 1930. Washington, D.C.: National Archives and Records Administration, 1930. T626,), Ancestry.com, http://www.Ancestry.com, Year: 1930; Census Place: Gadsden, Etowah, Alabama; Roll: 16; Page: 21B; Enumeration District: 9; Image: 420.0. Birth date: about 1907 Birth place: Residence date: 1930 Residence place: Gadsden, Etowah, Alabama.

658	Ancestry.com, 1910 United States Federal Census (Online publication - Provo, UT, USA: Ancestry.com Operations Inc, 2006. Original data - Thirteenth Census of the United States, 1910 (NARA microfilm publication T624, 1,178 rolls). Records of the Bureau of the Census, Record Group 29. National Archives, Washington), Ancestry.com, http://www.Ancestry.com, Year: 1910; Census Place: Coalgate Ward 2, Coal, Oklahoma; Roll: ; Page: ; Enumeration District: ; Image:. Birth date: 1868 Birth place: Alabama Residence date: 1910 Residence place: Coalgate Ward 2, Coal, Oklahoma.

659	Ancestry.com, 1920 United States Federal Census (Online publication - Provo, UT, USA: Ancestry.com Operations Inc, 2010. Images reproduced by FamilySearch. Original data - Fourteenth Census of the United States, 1920. (NARA microfilm publication T625, 2076 rolls). Records of the Bureau of the Census, Record), Ancestry.com, http://www.Ancestry.com, Year: 1920; Census Place: Henry, Okmulgee, Oklahoma; Roll: T625_1476; Page: 10B; Enumeration District: 113; Image:. Birth date: about 1868 Birth place: Alabama Residence date: 1920 Residence place: Henry, Okmulgee, Oklahoma.

660	Ancestry.com, 1930 United States Federal Census (Online publication - Provo, UT, USA: Ancestry.com Operations Inc, 2002. Original data - United States of America, Bureau of the Census. Fifteenth Census of the United States, 1930. Washington, D.C.: National Archives and Records Administration, 1930. T626,), Ancestry.com, http://www.Ancestry.com, Year: 1930; Census Place: Borger, Hutchinson, Texas; Roll: 2360; Page: 13B; Enumeration

District: 2; Image: 551.0. Birth date: about 1868 Birth place: Alabama Residence date: 1930 Residence place: Borger, Hutchinson, Texas.

661   Ancestry.com, 1870 United States Federal Census (Online publication - Provo, UT, USA: Ancestry.com Operations, Inc., 2009. Images reproduced by FamilySearch. Original data - 1870 U.S. census, population schedules. NARA microfilm publication M593, 1,761 rolls. Washington, D.C.: National Archives and Record), Ancestry.com, http://www.Ancestry.com, Year: 1870; Census Place: Township 12 Range 9, Cherokee, Alabama; Roll: M593_; Page: ; Image:. Birth date: about 1869 Birth place: Alabama Residence date: 1870 Residence place: Township 12 Range 9, Cherokee, Alabama, United States.

662   Ancestry.com and The Church of Jesus Christ of Latter-day Saints, 1880 United States Federal Census (Online publication - Provo, UT, USA: Ancestry.com Operations Inc, 2010. 1880 U.S. Census Index provided by The Church of Jesus Christ of Latter-day Saints © Copyright 1999 Intellectual Reserve, Inc. All rights reserved. All use is subject to the limited), Ancestry.com, http://www.Ancestry.com, Year: 1880; Census Place: , Cherokee, Alabama; Roll: 6; Family History Film: 1254006; Page: 441C; Enumeration District: 30; Image:. Birth date: about 1868 Birth place: Alabama Residence date: 1880 Residence place: Cherokee, Alabama, United States.

663   Ancestry.com, Social Security Death Index (Online publication - Provo, UT, USA: Ancestry.com Operations Inc, 2010. Original data - Social Security Administration. Social Security Death Index, Master File. Social Security Administration. Original data: Social Security Administration. Social Security D), Ancestry.com, http://www.Ancestry.com, Number: 441-01-1843; Issue State: Oklahoma; Issue Date: Before 1951. Birth date: 31 May 1893 Birth place: Death date: Nov 1979 Death place: Henryetta, Okmulgee, Oklahoma, United States of America.

664   Ancestry.com, World War I Draft Registration Cards, 1917-1918 (Online publication - Provo, UT, USA: Ancestry.com Operations Inc, 2005. Original data - United States, Selective Service System. World War I Selective Service System Draft Registration Cards, 1917-1918. Washington, D.C.: National Archives and Records Administration), Ancestry.com, http://www.Ancestry.com, Registration Location: Atoka County, Oklahoma; Roll: 1851605; Draft Board: 0. Birth date: 31 May 1893 Birth place: Texas; United States of America Residence date: Residence place: Atoka, Oklahoma.

665   Ancestry.com, 1910 United States Federal Census (Online publication - Provo, UT, USA: Ancestry.com Operations Inc, 2006. Original data - Thirteenth Census of the United States, 1910 (NARA microfilm publication T624, 1,178 rolls). Records of the Bureau of the Census, Record Group 29. National Archives, Washington), Ancestry.com, http://www.Ancestry.com, Year: 1910; Census Place: Coalgate Ward 2, Coal, Oklahoma; Roll: ; Page: ; Enumeration District: ; Image:. Birth date: 1894 Birth place: Texas Residence date: 1910 Residence place: Coalgate Ward 2, Coal, Oklahoma.

666   Ancestry.com, 1920 United States Federal Census (Online publication - Provo, UT, USA: Ancestry.com Operations Inc, 2010. Images reproduced by FamilySearch. Original data - Fourteenth Census of the United States, 1920. (NARA microfilm publication T625, 2076 rolls). Records of the Bureau of the Census, Record), Ancestry.com, http://www.Ancestry.com, Year: 1920; Census Place: Henryetta Ward 1, Okmulgee, Oklahoma; Roll: T625_1476; Page: 5B; Enumeration District: 115; Image:. Birth date: about 1894 Birth place: Texas Residence date: 1920 Residence place: Henryetta Ward 1, Okmulgee, Oklahoma.

667   Ancestry.com, 1930 United States Federal Census (Online publication - Provo, UT, USA: Ancestry.com Operations Inc, 2002. Original data - United States of America, Bureau of the Census. Fifteenth Census of the United States, 1930. Washington, D.C.: National Archives and Records Administration, 1930. T626,), Ancestry.com, http://www.Ancestry.com, Year: 1930; Census Place: Henryetta, Okmulgee, Oklahoma; Roll: 1921; Page: 18A; Enumeration District: 17; Image: 1054.0. Birth date: about 1894 Birth place: Texas Residence date: 1930 Residence place: Henryetta, Okmulgee, Oklahoma.

668   Ancestry.com, 1910 United States Federal Census (Online publication - Provo, UT, USA: Ancestry.com Operations Inc, 2006. Original data - Thirteenth Census of the United States, 1910 (NARA microfilm publication T624, 1,178 rolls). Records of the Bureau of the Census, Record Group 29. National Archives, Washington), Ancestry.com, http://www.Ancestry.com, Year: 1910; Census Place: Coalgate Ward 2, Coal, Oklahoma; Roll: ; Page: ; Enumeration District: ; Image:. Birth date: 1895 Birth place: Texas Residence date: 1910 Residence place: Coalgate Ward 2, Coal, Oklahoma.

669   Ancestry.com, 1910 United States Federal Census (Online publication - Provo, UT, USA: Ancestry.com Operations Inc, 2006. Original data - Thirteenth Census of the United States, 1910 (NARA microfilm publication T624, 1,178 rolls). Records of the Bureau of the Census, Record Group 29. National Archives, Washington), Ancestry.com, http://www.Ancestry.com, Year: 1910; Census Place: Coalgate Ward 2, Coal, Oklahoma; Roll: ; Page: ; Enumeration District: ; Image:. Birth date: 1897 Birth place: Texas Residence date: 1910 Residence place: Coalgate Ward 2, Coal, Oklahoma.

670   Ancestry.com, 1920 United States Federal Census (Online publication - Provo, UT, USA: Ancestry.com Operations Inc, 2010. Images reproduced by FamilySearch. Original data - Fourteenth Census of the United States, 1920. (NARA microfilm publication T625, 2076 rolls). Records of the Bureau of the Census, Record), Ancestry.com, http://www.Ancestry.com, Year: 1920; Census Place: Henryetta Ward 1, Okmulgee, Oklahoma; Roll: T625_1476; Page: 5A; Enumeration District: 115; Image:. Birth date: about 1897 Birth place: Texas Residence date: 1920 Residence place: Henryetta Ward 1, Okmulgee, Oklahoma.

671   Ancestry.com, Social Security Death Index (Online publication - Provo, UT, USA: Ancestry.com Operations Inc, 2010. Original data - Social Security Administration. Social Security Death Index, Master File. Social Security

Administration. Original data: Social Security Administration. Social Security D), Ancestry.com, http://www.Ancestry.com, Number: 525-38-4279; Issue State: New Mexico; Issue Date: Before 1951. Birth date: 19 May 1896 Birth place: Death date: 22 Aug 1990 Death place: Tempe, Maricopa, Arizona, United States of America.

672   Ancestry.com, 1930 United States Federal Census (Online publication - Provo, UT, USA: Ancestry.com Operations Inc, 2002. Original data - United States of America, Bureau of the Census. Fifteenth Census of the United States, 1930. Washington, D.C.: National Archives and Records Administration, 1930. T626,), Ancestry.com, http://www.Ancestry.com, Year: 1930; Census Place: Hobbs, Lea, New Mexico; Roll: 1395; Page: 2B; Enumeration District: 18; Image: 1029.0. Birth date: about 1898 Birth place: Residence date: 1930 Residence place: Hobbs, Lea, New Mexico.

673   Ancestry.com, 1910 United States Federal Census (Online publication - Provo, UT, USA: Ancestry.com Operations Inc, 2006. Original data - Thirteenth Census of the United States, 1910 (NARA microfilm publication T624, 1,178 rolls). Records of the Bureau of the Census, Record Group 29. National Archives, Washington), Ancestry.com, http://www.Ancestry.com, Year: 1910; Census Place: Coalgate Ward 2, Coal, Oklahoma; Roll: ; Page: ; Enumeration District: ; Image:. Birth date: 1900 Birth place: Texas Residence date: 1910 Residence place: Coalgate Ward 2, Coal, Oklahoma.

674   Ancestry.com, World War I Draft Registration Cards, 1917-1918 (Online publication - Provo, UT, USA: Ancestry.com Operations Inc, 2005. Original data - United States, Selective Service System. World War I Selective Service System Draft Registration Cards, 1917-1918. Washington, D.C.: National Archives and Records Administration), Ancestry.com, http://www.Ancestry.com, Registration Location: Okmulgee County, Oklahoma; Roll: 1852064; Draft Board: 0. Birth date: 09 Nov 1899 Birth place: Residence date: Residence place: Okmulgee, Oklahoma.

675   Ancestry.com, Social Security Death Index (Online publication - Provo, UT, USA: Ancestry.com Operations Inc, 2010. Original data - Social Security Administration. Social Security Death Index, Master File. Social Security Administration. Original data: Social Security Administration. Social Security D), Ancestry.com, http://www.Ancestry.com, Number: 457-01-9707; Issue State: Texas; Issue Date: Before 1951. Birth date: 9 Nov 1899 Birth place: Death date: Jun 1974 Death place: Raton, Colfax, New Mexico, United States of America.

676   Ancestry.com, 1930 United States Federal Census (Online publication - Provo, UT, USA: Ancestry.com Operations Inc, 2002. Original data - United States of America, Bureau of the Census. Fifteenth Census of the United States, 1930. Washington, D.C.: National Archives and Records Administration, 1930. T626,), Ancestry.com, http://www.Ancestry.com, Year: 1930; Census Place: Borger, Hutchinson, Texas; Roll: 2360; Page: 1B; Enumeration District: 3; Image: 576.0. Birth date: about 1900 Birth place: Texas Residence date: 1930 Residence place: Borger, Hutchinson, Texas.

677   Ancestry.com, 1920 United States Federal Census (Online publication - Provo, UT, USA: Ancestry.com Operations Inc, 2010. Images reproduced by FamilySearch. Original data - Fourteenth Census of the United States, 1920. (NARA microfilm publication T625, 2076 rolls). Records of the Bureau of the Census, Record), Ancestry.com, http://www.Ancestry.com, Year: 1920; Census Place: Henryetta Ward 1, Okmulgee, Oklahoma; Roll: T625_1476; Page: 4B; Enumeration District: 115; Image:. Birth date: about 1899 Birth place: Texas Residence date: 1920 Residence place: Henryetta Ward 1, Okmulgee, Oklahoma.

678   Ancestry.com, 1910 United States Federal Census (Online publication - Provo, UT, USA: Ancestry.com Operations Inc, 2006. Original data - Thirteenth Census of the United States, 1910 (NARA microfilm publication T624, 1,178 rolls). Records of the Bureau of the Census, Record Group 29. National Archives, Washington), Ancestry.com, http://www.Ancestry.com, Year: 1910; Census Place: Coalgate Ward 2, Coal, Oklahoma; Roll: ; Page: ; Enumeration District: ; Image:. Birth date: 1903 Birth place: Oklahoma Residence date: 1910 Residence place: Coalgate Ward 2, Coal, Oklahoma.

679   Ancestry.com, 1920 United States Federal Census (Online publication - Provo, UT, USA: Ancestry.com Operations Inc, 2010. Images reproduced by FamilySearch. Original data - Fourteenth Census of the United States, 1920. (NARA microfilm publication T625, 2076 rolls). Records of the Bureau of the Census, Record), Ancestry.com, http://www.Ancestry.com, Year: 1920; Census Place: Henry, Okmulgee, Oklahoma; Roll: T625_1476; Page: 10B; Enumeration District: 113; Image:. Birth date: about 1904 Birth place: Oklahoma Residence date: 1920 Residence place: Henry, Okmulgee, Oklahoma.

680   Ancestry.com, 1910 United States Federal Census (Online publication - Provo, UT, USA: Ancestry.com Operations Inc, 2006. Original data - Thirteenth Census of the United States, 1910 (NARA microfilm publication T624, 1,178 rolls). Records of the Bureau of the Census, Record Group 29. National Archives, Washington), Ancestry.com, http://www.Ancestry.com, Year: 1910; Census Place: Coalgate Ward 2, Coal, Oklahoma; Roll: ; Page: ; Enumeration District: ; Image:. Birth date: 1907 Birth place: Oklahoma Residence date: 1910 Residence place: Coalgate Ward 2, Coal, Oklahoma.

681   Ancestry.com, Social Security Death Index (Online publication - Provo, UT, USA: Ancestry.com Operations Inc, 2010. Original data - Social Security Administration. Social Security Death Index, Master File. Social Security Administration. Original data: Social Security Administration. Social Security D), Ancestry.com, http://www.Ancestry.com, Number: 457-01-9725; Issue State: Texas; Issue Date: Before 1951. Birth date: 29 May 1906 Birth place: Death date: Feb 1984 Death place: Fort Myers, Lee, Florida, United States of America.

682   Ancestry.com, Florida Death Index, 1877-1998 (Online publication - Provo, UT, USA: Ancestry.com Operations Inc, 2004. Original data - State of Florida. Florida Death Index, 1877-1998. Florida: Florida Department of Health, Office of

Vital Records, 1998. Original data: State of Florida. Florida Death Ind), Ancestry.com, http://www.Ancestry.com, Birth date: 29 May 1906 Birth place: Death date: 3 Feb 1984 Death place: Lee, Florida, United States.

683 Ancestry.com, 1920 United States Federal Census (Online publication - Provo, UT, USA: Ancestry.com Operations Inc, 2010. Images reproduced by FamilySearch. Original data - Fourteenth Census of the United States, 1920. (NARA microfilm publication T625, 2076 rolls). Records of the Bureau of the Census, Record), Ancestry.com, http://www.Ancestry.com, Year: 1920; Census Place: Henry, Okmulgee, Oklahoma; Roll: T625_1476; Page: 10B; Enumeration District: 113; Image:. Birth date: about 1907 Birth place: Oklahoma Residence date: 1920 Residence place: Henry, Okmulgee, Oklahoma.

684 Ancestry.com, 1910 United States Federal Census (Online publication - Provo, UT, USA: Ancestry.com Operations Inc, 2006. Original data - Thirteenth Census of the United States, 1910 (NARA microfilm publication T624, 1,178 rolls). Records of the Bureau of the Census, Record Group 29. National Archives, Washington), Ancestry.com, http://www.Ancestry.com, Year: 1910; Census Place: Coalgate Ward 2, Coal, Oklahoma; Roll: ; Page: ; Enumeration District: ; Image:. Birth date: 1909 Birth place: Oklahoma Residence date: 1910 Residence place: Coalgate Ward 2, Coal, Oklahoma.

685 Ancestry.com, 1920 United States Federal Census (Online publication - Provo, UT, USA: Ancestry.com Operations Inc, 2010. Images reproduced by FamilySearch. Original data - Fourteenth Census of the United States, 1920. (NARA microfilm publication T625, 2076 rolls). Records of the Bureau of the Census, Record), Ancestry.com, http://www.Ancestry.com, Year: 1920; Census Place: Henry, Okmulgee, Oklahoma; Roll: T625_1476; Page: 10B; Enumeration District: 113; Image:. Birth date: about 1910 Birth place: Oklahoma Residence date: 1920 Residence place: Henry, Okmulgee, Oklahoma.

686 Ancestry.com, 1930 United States Federal Census (Online publication - Provo, UT, USA: Ancestry.com Operations Inc, 2002. Original data - United States of America, Bureau of the Census. Fifteenth Census of the United States, 1930. Washington, D.C.: National Archives and Records Administration, 1930. T626,), Ancestry.com, http://www.Ancestry.com, Year: 1930; Census Place: Borger, Hutchinson, Texas; Roll: 2360; Page: 13B; Enumeration District: 2; Image: 551.0. Birth date: about 1909 Birth place: Residence date: 1930 Residence place: Borger, Hutchinson, Texas.

687 Ancestry.com, 1920 United States Federal Census (Online publication - Provo, UT, USA: Ancestry.com Operations Inc, 2010. Images reproduced by FamilySearch. Original data - Fourteenth Census of the United States, 1920. (NARA microfilm publication T625, 2076 rolls). Records of the Bureau of the Census, Record), Ancestry.com, http://www.Ancestry.com, Year: 1920; Census Place: Henry, Okmulgee, Oklahoma; Roll: T625_1476; Page: 10B; Enumeration District: 113; Image:. Birth date: about 1914 Birth place: Oklahoma Residence date: 1920 Residence place: Henry, Okmulgee, Oklahoma.

688 Ancestry.com, 1920 United States Federal Census (Online publication - Provo, UT, USA: Ancestry.com Operations Inc, 2010. Images reproduced by FamilySearch. Original data - Fourteenth Census of the United States, 1920. (NARA microfilm publication T625, 2076 rolls). Records of the Bureau of the Census, Record), Ancestry.com, http://www.Ancestry.com, Year: 1920; Census Place: Henry, Okmulgee, Oklahoma; Roll: T625_1476; Page: 10B; Enumeration District: 113; Image:. Birth date: about 1916 Birth place: Oklahoma Residence date: 1920 Residence place: Henry, Okmulgee, Oklahoma.

689 Ancestry.com, 1910 United States Federal Census (Online publication - Provo, UT, USA: Ancestry.com Operations Inc, 2006. Original data - Thirteenth Census of the United States, 1910 (NARA microfilm publication T624, 1,178 rolls). Records of the Bureau of the Census, Record Group 29. National Archives, Washington), Ancestry.com, http://www.Ancestry.com, Year: 1910; Census Place: Coloma, Cherokee, Alabama; Roll: ; Page: ; Enumeration District: ; Image:. Birth date: 1879 Birth place: Alabama Residence date: 1910 Residence place: Coloma, Cherokee, Alabama.

690 Ancestry.com, 1910 United States Federal Census (Online publication - Provo, UT, USA: Ancestry.com Operations Inc, 2006. Original data - Thirteenth Census of the United States, 1910 (NARA microfilm publication T624, 1,178 rolls). Records of the Bureau of the Census, Record Group 29. National Archives, Washington), Ancestry.com, http://www.Ancestry.com, Year: 1910; Census Place: Coloma, Cherokee, Alabama; Roll: ; Page: ; Enumeration District: ; Image:. Birth date: 1902 Birth place: Alabama Residence date: 1910 Residence place: Coloma, Cherokee, Alabama.

691 Ancestry.com, 1910 United States Federal Census (Online publication - Provo, UT, USA: Ancestry.com Operations Inc, 2006. Original data - Thirteenth Census of the United States, 1910 (NARA microfilm publication T624, 1,178 rolls). Records of the Bureau of the Census, Record Group 29. National Archives, Washington), Ancestry.com, http://www.Ancestry.com, Year: 1910; Census Place: Coloma, Cherokee, Alabama; Roll: ; Page: ; Enumeration District: ; Image:. Birth date: 1904 Birth place: Alabama Residence date: 1910 Residence place: Coloma, Cherokee, Alabama.

692 Ancestry.com, 1910 United States Federal Census (Online publication - Provo, UT, USA: Ancestry.com Operations Inc, 2006. Original data - Thirteenth Census of the United States, 1910 (NARA microfilm publication T624, 1,178 rolls). Records of the Bureau of the Census, Record Group 29. National Archives, Washington), Ancestry.com, http://www.Ancestry.com, Year: 1910; Census Place: Coloma, Cherokee, Alabama; Roll: ; Page: ; Enumeration District: ; Image:. Birth date: 1906 Birth place: Alabama Residence date: 1910 Residence place: Coloma, Cherokee, Alabama.

693 Ancestry.com, 1910 United States Federal Census (Online publication - Provo, UT, USA: Ancestry.com Operations Inc, 2006. Original data - Thirteenth Census of the United States, 1910 (NARA microfilm publication T624, 1,178 rolls). Records of the Bureau of the Census, Record Group 29. National Archives, Washington), Ancestry.com, http://www.Ancestry.com, Year: 1910; Census Place: Coloma, Cherokee, Alabama; Roll: ; Page: ; Enumeration District: ;

Image:. Birth date: about 1910 Birth place: Alabama Residence date: 1910 Residence place: Coloma, Cherokee, Alabama.

694   Ancestry.com and The Church of Jesus Christ of Latter-day Saints, 1880 United States Federal Census (Online publication - Provo, UT, USA: Ancestry.com Operations Inc, 2010. 1880 U.S. Census Index provided by The Church of Jesus Christ of Latter-day Saints © Copyright 1999 Intellectual Reserve, Inc. All rights reserved. All use is subject to the limited), Ancestry.com, http://www.Ancestry.com, Year: 1880; Census Place: June Bug, Calhoun, Alabama; Roll: 4; Family History Film: 1254004; Page: 535A; Enumeration District: 6; Image: 0630. Birth date: about 1840 Birth place: North Carolina Residence date: 1880 Residence place: June Bug, Calhoun, Alabama, United States.

695   Ancestry.com and The Church of Jesus Christ of Latter-day Saints, 1880 United States Federal Census (Online publication - Provo, UT, USA: Ancestry.com Operations Inc, 2010. 1880 U.S. Census Index provided by The Church of Jesus Christ of Latter-day Saints © Copyright 1999 Intellectual Reserve, Inc. All rights reserved. All use is subject to the limited), Ancestry.com, http://www.Ancestry.com, Year: 1880; Census Place: June Bug, Calhoun, Alabama; Roll: 4; Family History Film: 1254004; Page: 535A; Enumeration District: 6; Image: 0630. Birth date: about 1872 Birth place: Alabama Residence date: 1880 Residence place: June Bug, Calhoun, Alabama, United States.

696   Ancestry.com and The Church of Jesus Christ of Latter-day Saints, 1880 United States Federal Census (Online publication - Provo, UT, USA: Ancestry.com Operations Inc, 2010. 1880 U.S. Census Index provided by The Church of Jesus Christ of Latter-day Saints © Copyright 1999 Intellectual Reserve, Inc. All rights reserved. All use is subject to the limited), Ancestry.com, http://www.Ancestry.com, Year: 1880; Census Place: June Bug, Calhoun, Alabama; Roll: 4; Family History Film: 1254004; Page: 535A; Enumeration District: 6; Image: 0630. Birth date: about 1874 Birth place: Alabama Residence date: 1880 Residence place: June Bug, Calhoun, Alabama, United States.

697   Ancestry.com and The Church of Jesus Christ of Latter-day Saints, 1880 United States Federal Census (Online publication - Provo, UT, USA: Ancestry.com Operations Inc, 2010. 1880 U.S. Census Index provided by The Church of Jesus Christ of Latter-day Saints © Copyright 1999 Intellectual Reserve, Inc. All rights reserved. All use is subject to the limited), Ancestry.com, http://www.Ancestry.com, Year: 1880; Census Place: June Bug, Calhoun, Alabama; Roll: 4; Family History Film: 1254004; Page: 535A; Enumeration District: 6; Image: 0630. Birth date: about 1876 Birth place: Alabama Residence date: 1880 Residence place: June Bug, Calhoun, Alabama, United States.

698   Ancestry.com and The Church of Jesus Christ of Latter-day Saints, 1880 United States Federal Census (Online publication - Provo, UT, USA: Ancestry.com Operations Inc, 2010. 1880 U.S. Census Index provided by The Church of Jesus Christ of Latter-day Saints © Copyright 1999 Intellectual Reserve, Inc. All rights reserved. All use is subject to the limited), Ancestry.com, http://www.Ancestry.com, Year: 1880; Census Place: June Bug, Calhoun, Alabama; Roll: 4; Family History Film: 1254004; Page: 535A; Enumeration District: 6; Image: 0630. Birth date: about 1878 Birth place: Alabama Residence date: 1880 Residence place: June Bug, Calhoun, Alabama, United States.

699   Ancestry.com, 1920 United States Federal Census (Online publication - Provo, UT, USA: Ancestry.com Operations Inc, 2010. Images reproduced by FamilySearch. Original data - Fourteenth Census of the United States, 1920. (NARA microfilm publication T625, 2076 rolls). Records of the Bureau of the Census, Record), Ancestry.com, http://www.Ancestry.com, Year: 1920; Census Place: Renfroe, Talladega, Alabama; Roll: T625_41; Page: 7A; Enumeration District: 141; Image:. Birth date: about 1851 Birth place: Alabama Residence date: 1920 Residence place: Renfroe, Talladega, Alabama.

700   Ancestry.com, 1870 United States Federal Census (Online publication - Provo, UT, USA: Ancestry.com Operations, Inc., 2009. Images reproduced by FamilySearch. Original data - 1870 U.S. census, population schedules. NARA microfilm publication M593, 1,761 rolls. Washington, D.C.: National Archives and Record), Ancestry.com, http://www.Ancestry.com, Year: 1870; Census Place: Township 19 Range 4, Talladega, Alabama; Roll: M593_; Page: ; Image:. Birth date: about 1851 Birth place: Alabama Residence date: 1870 Residence place: Township 19 Range 4, Talladega, Alabama, United States.

701   Ancestry.com, 1930 United States Federal Census (Online publication - Provo, UT, USA: Ancestry.com Operations Inc, 2002. Original data - United States of America, Bureau of the Census. Fifteenth Census of the United States, 1930. Washington, D.C.: National Archives and Records Administration, 1930. T626,), Ancestry.com, http://www.Ancestry.com, Year: 1930; Census Place: Renfroe, Talladega, Alabama; Roll: 49; Page: 6A; Enumeration District: 18; Image: 993.0. Birth date: about 1872 Birth place: Alabama Residence date: 1930 Residence place: Renfroe, Talladega, Alabama.

702   Ancestry.com, 1920 United States Federal Census (Online publication - Provo, UT, USA: Ancestry.com Operations Inc, 2010. Images reproduced by FamilySearch. Original data - Fourteenth Census of the United States, 1920. (NARA microfilm publication T625, 2076 rolls). Records of the Bureau of the Census, Record), Ancestry.com, http://www.Ancestry.com, Year: 1920; Census Place: Renfroe, Talladega, Alabama; Roll: T625_41; Page: 9A; Enumeration District: 141; Image:. Birth date: about 1873 Birth place: Alabama Residence date: 1920 Residence place: Renfroe, Talladega, Alabama.

703   Ancestry.com, 1900 United States Federal Census (Online publication - Provo, UT, USA: Ancestry.com Operations Inc, 2004. Original data - United States of America, Bureau of the Census. Twelfth Census of the United States, 1900. Washington, D.C.: National Archives and Records Administration, 1900. T623, 18), Ancestry.com, http://www.Ancestry.com, Year: 1900; Census Place: Cast, Talladega, Alabama; Roll: T623_40; Page: 10B; Enumeration District: 92. Birth date: Mar 1872 Birth place: Alabama Marriage date: 1895 Marriage place: Residence date: 1900 Residence place: Cast, Talladega, Alabama.

704   Ancestry.com, Alabama Deaths, 1908-59 (Online publication - Provo, UT, USA: Ancestry.com Operations Inc, 2000. Original data - State of Alabama. Index of Vital Records for Alabama: Deaths, 1908-1959. Montgomery, AL, USA: State of Alabama Center for Health Statistics, Record Services Division. Original), Ancestry.com, http://www.Ancestry.com, Death date: Dec 1933 Death place: Talladega.

705   Ancestry.com, 1930 United States Federal Census (Online publication - Provo, UT, USA: Ancestry.com Operations Inc, 2002. Original data - United States of America, Bureau of the Census. Fifteenth Census of the United States, 1930. Washington, D.C.: National Archives and Records Administration, 1930. T626,), Ancestry.com, http://www.Ancestry.com, Year: 1930; Census Place: Talladega, Talladega, Alabama; Roll: 49; Page: 1B; Enumeration District: 13; Image: 803.0. Birth date: about 1879 Birth place: Alabama Residence date: 1930 Residence place: Talladega, Talladega, Alabama.

706   Ancestry.com, World War I Draft Registration Cards, 1917-1918 (Online publication - Provo, UT, USA: Ancestry.com Operations Inc, 2005. Original data - United States, Selective Service System. World War I Selective Service System Draft Registration Cards, 1917-1918. Washington, D.C.: National Archives and Records Administration), Ancestry.com, http://www.Ancestry.com, Registration Location: Talladega County, Alabama; Roll: 1509440; Draft Board: 0. Birth date: 22 Apr 1878 Birth place: Residence date: Residence place: Talladega, Alabama.

707   Ancestry.com, Alabama Deaths, 1908-59 (Online publication - Provo, UT, USA: Ancestry.com Operations Inc, 2000. Original data - State of Alabama. Index of Vital Records for Alabama: Deaths, 1908-1959. Montgomery, AL, USA: State of Alabama Center for Health Statistics, Record Services Division. Original), Ancestry.com, http://www.Ancestry.com, Death date: 11 Mar 1945 Death place: Talladega.

708   Ancestry.com, 1910 United States Federal Census (Online publication - Provo, UT, USA: Ancestry.com Operations Inc, 2006. Original data - Thirteenth Census of the United States, 1910 (NARA microfilm publication T624, 1,178 rolls). Records of the Bureau of the Census, Record Group 29. National Archives, Washington), Ancestry.com, http://www.Ancestry.com, Year: 1910; Census Place: Anniston Ward 1, Calhoun, Alabama; Roll: ; Page: ; Enumeration District: ; Image:. Birth date: about 1876 Birth place: Alabama Residence date: 1910 Residence place: Anniston Ward 1, Calhoun, Alabama.

709   Ancestry.com, 1900 United States Federal Census (Online publication - Provo, UT, USA: Ancestry.com Operations Inc, 2004. Original data - United States of America, Bureau of the Census. Twelfth Census of the United States, 1900. Washington, D.C.: National Archives and Records Administration, 1900. T623, 18), Ancestry.com, http://www.Ancestry.com, Year: 1900; Census Place: Cold Water, Calhoun, Alabama; Roll: T623_5; Page: 2A; Enumeration District: 28. Birth date: Feb 1876 Birth place: Georgia Marriage date: 1891 Marriage place: Residence date: 1900 Residence place: Cold Water, Calhoun, Alabama.

710   Ancestry.com, 1900 United States Federal Census (Online publication - Provo, UT, USA: Ancestry.com Operations Inc, 2004. Original data - United States of America, Bureau of the Census. Twelfth Census of the United States, 1900. Washington, D.C.: National Archives and Records Administration, 1900. T623, 18), Ancestry.com, http://www.Ancestry.com, Year: 1900; Census Place: Cold Water, Calhoun, Alabama; Roll: T623_5; Page: 2A; Enumeration District: 28. Birth date: Feb 1893 Birth place: Alabama Residence date: 1900 Residence place: Cold Water, Calhoun, Alabama.

711   Ancestry.com, 1900 United States Federal Census (Online publication - Provo, UT, USA: Ancestry.com Operations Inc, 2004. Original data - United States of America, Bureau of the Census. Twelfth Census of the United States, 1900. Washington, D.C.: National Archives and Records Administration, 1900. T623, 18), Ancestry.com, http://www.Ancestry.com, Year: 1900; Census Place: Cold Water, Calhoun, Alabama; Roll: T623_5; Page: 2A; Enumeration District: 28. Birth date: Dec 1894 Birth place: Alabama Residence date: 1900 Residence place: Cold Water, Calhoun, Alabama.

712   Ancestry.com, 1910 United States Federal Census (Online publication - Provo, UT, USA: Ancestry.com Operations Inc, 2006. Original data - Thirteenth Census of the United States, 1910 (NARA microfilm publication T624, 1,178 rolls). Records of the Bureau of the Census, Record Group 29. National Archives, Washington), Ancestry.com, http://www.Ancestry.com, Year: 1910; Census Place: Anniston Ward 1, Calhoun, Alabama; Roll: ; Page: ; Enumeration District: ; Image:. Birth date: about 1893 Birth place: Alabama Residence date: 1910 Residence place: Anniston Ward 1, Calhoun, Alabama.

713   Ancestry.com, 1910 United States Federal Census (Online publication - Provo, UT, USA: Ancestry.com Operations Inc, 2006. Original data - Thirteenth Census of the United States, 1910 (NARA microfilm publication T624, 1,178 rolls). Records of the Bureau of the Census, Record Group 29. National Archives, Washington), Ancestry.com, http://www.Ancestry.com, Year: 1910; Census Place: Anniston Ward 1, Calhoun, Alabama; Roll: ; Page: ; Enumeration District: ; Image:. Birth date: about 1895 Birth place: Alabama Residence date: 1910 Residence place: Anniston Ward 1, Calhoun, Alabama.

714   Ancestry.com, 1900 United States Federal Census (Online publication - Provo, UT, USA: Ancestry.com Operations Inc, 2004. Original data - United States of America, Bureau of the Census. Twelfth Census of the United States, 1900. Washington, D.C.: National Archives and Records Administration, 1900. T623, 18), Ancestry.com, http://www.Ancestry.com, Year: 1900; Census Place: Cold Water, Calhoun, Alabama; Roll: T623_5; Page: 2A; Enumeration District: 28. Birth date: Dec 1896 Birth place: Alabama Residence date: 1900 Residence place: Cold Water, Calhoun, Alabama.

715   Ancestry.com, 1910 United States Federal Census (Online publication - Provo, UT, USA: Ancestry.com Operations Inc, 2006. Original data - Thirteenth Census of the United States, 1910 (NARA microfilm publication T624,

1,178 rolls). Records of the Bureau of the Census, Record Group 29. National Archives, Washington), Ancestry.com, http://www.Ancestry.com, Year: 1910; Census Place: Anniston Ward 1, Calhoun, Alabama; Roll: ; Page: ; Enumeration District: ; Image:. Birth date: about 1897 Birth place: Alabama Residence date: 1910 Residence place: Anniston Ward 1, Calhoun, Alabama.

716   Ancestry.com, Social Security Death Index (Online publication - Provo, UT, USA: Ancestry.com Operations Inc, 2010. Original data - Social Security Administration. Social Security Death Index, Master File. Social Security Administration. Original data: Social Security Administration. Social Security D), Ancestry.com, http://www.Ancestry.com, Number: 298-26-9930; Issue State: Ohio; Issue Date: Before 1951. Birth date: 7 Dec 1896 Birth place: Death date: Mar 1983 Death place: Plant City, Hillsborough, Florida, United States of America.

717   Ancestry.com, Florida Death Index, 1877-1998 (Online publication - Provo, UT, USA: Ancestry.com Operations Inc, 2004. Original data - State of Florida. Florida Death Index, 1877-1998. Florida: Florida Department of Health, Office of Vital Records, 1998. Original data: State of Florida. Florida Death Ind), Ancestry.com, http://www.Ancestry.com, Birth date: 7 Dec 1896 Birth place: Death date: 16 Mar 1983 Death place: Pinellas, Florida, United States.

718   Ancestry.com, 1920 United States Federal Census (Online publication - Provo, UT, USA: Ancestry.com Operations Inc, 2010. Images reproduced by FamilySearch. Original data - Fourteenth Census of the United States, 1920. (NARA microfilm publication T625, 2076 rolls). Records of the Bureau of the Census, Record), Ancestry.com, http://www.Ancestry.com, Year: 1920; Census Place: Radford, Radford (Independent City), Virginia; Roll: T625_1908; Page: 18A; Enumeration District: 18; Image:. Birth date: about 1897 Birth place: Alabama Residence date: 1920 Residence place: Radford, Radford (Independent City), Virginia.

719   Ancestry.com, 1900 United States Federal Census (Online publication - Provo, UT, USA: Ancestry.com Operations Inc, 2004. Original data - United States of America, Bureau of the Census. Twelfth Census of the United States, 1900. Washington, D.C.: National Archives and Records Administration, 1900. T623, 18), Ancestry.com, http://www.Ancestry.com, Year: 1900; Census Place: Cold Water, Calhoun, Alabama; Roll: T623_5; Page: 2A; Enumeration District: 28. Birth date: Jun 1899 Birth place: Alabama Residence date: 1900 Residence place: Cold Water, Calhoun, Alabama.

720   Ancestry.com, 1910 United States Federal Census (Online publication - Provo, UT, USA: Ancestry.com Operations Inc, 2006. Original data - Thirteenth Census of the United States, 1910 (NARA microfilm publication T624, 1,178 rolls). Records of the Bureau of the Census, Record Group 29. National Archives, Washington), Ancestry.com, http://www.Ancestry.com, Year: 1910; Census Place: Anniston Ward 1, Calhoun, Alabama; Roll: ; Page: ; Enumeration District: ; Image:. Birth date: about 1900 Birth place: Alabama Residence date: 1910 Residence place: Anniston Ward 1, Calhoun, Alabama.

721   Ancestry.com, World War I Draft Registration Cards, 1917-1918 (Online publication - Provo, UT, USA: Ancestry.com Operations Inc, 2005. Original data - United States, Selective Service System. World War I Selective Service System Draft Registration Cards, 1917-1918. Washington, D.C.: National Archives and Records Administration), Ancestry.com, http://www.Ancestry.com, Registration Location: Calhoun County, Alabama; Roll: 1509363; Draft Board: 0. Birth date: 23 Jun 1899 Birth place: Residence date: Residence place: Calhoun, Alabama.

722   Ancestry.com, 1910 United States Federal Census (Online publication - Provo, UT, USA: Ancestry.com Operations Inc, 2006. Original data - Thirteenth Census of the United States, 1910 (NARA microfilm publication T624, 1,178 rolls). Records of the Bureau of the Census, Record Group 29. National Archives, Washington), Ancestry.com, http://www.Ancestry.com, Year: 1910; Census Place: Anniston Ward 1, Calhoun, Alabama; Roll: ; Page: ; Enumeration District: ; Image:. Birth date: about 1902 Birth place: Alabama Residence date: 1910 Residence place: Anniston Ward 1, Calhoun, Alabama.

723   Ancestry.com, 1910 United States Federal Census (Online publication - Provo, UT, USA: Ancestry.com Operations Inc, 2006. Original data - Thirteenth Census of the United States, 1910 (NARA microfilm publication T624, 1,178 rolls). Records of the Bureau of the Census, Record Group 29. National Archives, Washington), Ancestry.com, http://www.Ancestry.com, Year: 1910; Census Place: Anniston Ward 1, Calhoun, Alabama; Roll: ; Page: ; Enumeration District: ; Image:. Birth date: about 1904 Birth place: Alabama Residence date: 1910 Residence place: Anniston Ward 1, Calhoun, Alabama.

724   Ancestry.com, California Death Index, 1940-1997 (Online publication - Provo, UT, USA: Ancestry.com Operations Inc, 2000. Original data - State of California. California Death Index, 1940-1997. Sacramento, CA, USA: State of California Department of Health Services, Center for Health Statistics. Original data), Ancestry.com, http://www.Ancestry.com, Birth date: 31 Aug 1903 Birth place: Alabama Death date: 22 Dec 1987 Death place: San Joaquin, California.

725   Ancestry.com, 1930 United States Federal Census (Online publication - Provo, UT, USA: Ancestry.com Operations Inc, 2002. Original data - United States of America, Bureau of the Census. Fifteenth Census of the United States, 1930. Washington, D.C.: National Archives and Records Administration, 1930. T626,), Ancestry.com, http://www.Ancestry.com, Year: 1930; Census Place: Militia District 1104, Chattahoochee, Georgia; Roll: 345; Page: 30A; Enumeration District: 5; Image: 663.0. Birth date: about 1906 Birth place: Alabama Residence date: 1930 Residence place: Militia District 1104, Chattahoochee, Georgia.

726   Ancestry.com, 1910 United States Federal Census (Online publication - Provo, UT, USA: Ancestry.com Operations Inc, 2006. Original data - Thirteenth Census of the United States, 1910 (NARA microfilm publication T624, 1,178 rolls). Records of the Bureau of the Census, Record Group 29. National Archives, Washington), Ancestry.com, http://www.Ancestry.com, Year: 1910; Census Place: Anniston Ward 1, Calhoun, Alabama; Roll: ; Page: ; Enumeration

District: ; Image:. Birth date: about 1906 Birth place: Alabama Residence date: 1910 Residence place: Anniston Ward 1, Calhoun, Alabama.

727	Ancestry.com, 1920 United States Federal Census (Online publication - Provo, UT, USA: Ancestry.com Operations Inc, 2010. Images reproduced by FamilySearch. Original data - Fourteenth Census of the United States, 1920. (NARA microfilm publication T625, 2076 rolls). Records of the Bureau of the Census, Record), Ancestry.com, http://www.Ancestry.com, Year: 1920; Census Place: Munford, Talladega, Alabama; Roll: T625_41; Page: 19A; Enumeration District: 155; Image:. Birth date: about 1907 Birth place: Alabama Residence date: 1920 Residence place: Munford, Talladega, Alabama.

728	Ancestry.com, 1910 United States Federal Census (Online publication - Provo, UT, USA: Ancestry.com Operations Inc, 2006. Original data - Thirteenth Census of the United States, 1910 (NARA microfilm publication T624, 1,178 rolls). Records of the Bureau of the Census, Record Group 29. National Archives, Washington), Ancestry.com, http://www.Ancestry.com, Year: 1910; Census Place: Anniston Ward 1, Calhoun, Alabama; Roll: ; Page: ; Enumeration District: ; Image:. Birth date: about 1909 Birth place: Alabama Residence date: 1910 Residence place: Anniston Ward 1, Calhoun, Alabama.

729	Ancestry.com and The Church of Jesus Christ of Latter-day Saints, 1880 United States Federal Census (Online publication - Provo, UT, USA: Ancestry.com Operations Inc, 2010. 1880 U.S. Census Index provided by The Church of Jesus Christ of Latter-day Saints © Copyright 1999 Intellectual Reserve, Inc. All rights reserved. All use is subject to the limited), Ancestry.com, http://www.Ancestry.com, Year: 1880; Census Place: June Bug, Calhoun, Alabama; Roll: 4; Family History Film: 1254004; Page: 535A; Enumeration District: 6; Image: 0630. Birth date: about 1878 Birth place: Alabama Residence date: 1880 Residence place: June Bug, Calhoun, Alabama, United States.

730	Ancestry.com, World War I Draft Registration Cards, 1917-1918 (Online publication - Provo, UT, USA: Ancestry.com Operations Inc, 2005. Original data - United States, Selective Service System. World War I Selective Service System Draft Registration Cards, 1917-1918. Washington, D.C.: National Archives and Records Administration), Ancestry.com, http://www.Ancestry.com, Registration Location: Calhoun County, Alabama; Roll: 1509363; Draft Board: 0. Birth date: 25 Aug 1878 Birth place: Residence date: Residence place: Calhoun, Alabama.

731	Ancestry.com, 1920 United States Federal Census (Online publication - Provo, UT, USA: Ancestry.com Operations Inc, 2010. Images reproduced by FamilySearch. Original data - Fourteenth Census of the United States, 1920. (NARA microfilm publication T625, 2076 rolls). Records of the Bureau of the Census, Record), Ancestry.com, http://www.Ancestry.com, Year: 1920; Census Place: Anniston Ward 2, Calhoun, Alabama; Roll: T625_5; Page: 18A; Enumeration District: 23; Image:. Birth date: about 1879 Birth place: Alabama Residence date: 1920 Residence place: Anniston Ward 2, Calhoun, Alabama.

732	Ancestry.com, 1910 United States Federal Census (Online publication - Provo, UT, USA: Ancestry.com Operations Inc, 2006. Original data - Thirteenth Census of the United States, 1910 (NARA microfilm publication T624, 1,178 rolls). Records of the Bureau of the Census, Record Group 29. National Archives, Washington), Ancestry.com, http://www.Ancestry.com, Year: 1910; Census Place: Anniston Ward 1, Calhoun, Alabama; Roll: ; Page: ; Enumeration District: ; Image:. Birth date: about 1878 Birth place: Alabama Residence date: 1910 Residence place: Anniston Ward 1, Calhoun, Alabama.

733	Ancestry.com, 1930 United States Federal Census (Online publication - Provo, UT, USA: Ancestry.com Operations Inc, 2002. Original data - United States of America, Bureau of the Census. Fifteenth Census of the United States, 1930. Washington, D.C.: National Archives and Records Administration, 1930. T626,), Ancestry.com, http://www.Ancestry.com, Year: 1930; Census Place: Anniston, Calhoun, Alabama; Roll: 5; Page: 10B; Enumeration District: 24; Image: 654.0. Birth date: about 1879 Birth place: Alabama Residence date: 1930 Residence place: Anniston, Calhoun, Alabama.

734	Ancestry.com, Alabama Deaths, 1908-59 (Online publication - Provo, UT, USA: Ancestry.com Operations Inc, 2000. Original data - State of Alabama. Index of Vital Records for Alabama: Deaths, 1908-1959. Montgomery, AL, USA: State of Alabama Center for Health Statistics, Record Services Division. Original), Ancestry.com, http://www.Ancestry.com, Death date: Jun 1932 Death place: Calhoun.

735	Ancestry.com, 1900 United States Federal Census (Online publication - Provo, UT, USA: Ancestry.com Operations Inc, 2004. Original data - United States of America, Bureau of the Census. Twelfth Census of the United States, 1900. Washington, D.C.: National Archives and Records Administration, 1900. T623, 18), Ancestry.com, http://www.Ancestry.com, Year: 1900; Census Place: Cold Water, Calhoun, Alabama; Roll: T623_5; Page: 2A; Enumeration District: 28. Birth date: Jun 1882 Birth place: Alabama Residence date: 1900 Residence place: Cold Water, Calhoun, Alabama.

736	Ancestry.com, 1910 United States Federal Census (Online publication - Provo, UT, USA: Ancestry.com Operations Inc, 2006. Original data - Thirteenth Census of the United States, 1910 (NARA microfilm publication T624, 1,178 rolls). Records of the Bureau of the Census, Record Group 29. National Archives, Washington), Ancestry.com, http://www.Ancestry.com, Year: 1910; Census Place: Precinct 9, Mobile, Alabama; Roll: ; Page: ; Enumeration District: ; Image:. Birth date: about 1883 Birth place: Alabama Residence date: 1910 Residence place: Precinct 9, Mobile, Alabama.

737	Ancestry.com, 1900 United States Federal Census (Online publication - Provo, UT, USA: Ancestry.com Operations Inc, 2004. Original data - United States of America, Bureau of the Census. Twelfth Census of the United States, 1900. Washington, D.C.: National Archives and Records Administration, 1900. T623, 18), Ancestry.com, http://www.Ancestry.com, Year: 1900; Census Place: Cold Water, Calhoun, Alabama; Roll: T623_5; Page: 2A;

Enumeration District: 28. Birth date: Jan 1884 Birth place: Alabama Residence date: 1900 Residence place: Cold Water, Calhoun, Alabama.

738   Ancestry.com, 1900 United States Federal Census (Online publication - Provo, UT, USA: Ancestry.com Operations Inc, 2004. Original data - United States of America, Bureau of the Census. Twelfth Census of the United States, 1900. Washington, D.C.: National Archives and Records Administration, 1900. T623, 18), Ancestry.com, http://www.Ancestry.com, Year: 1900; Census Place: Cold Water, Calhoun, Alabama; Roll: T623_5; Page: 2A; Enumeration District: 28. Birth date: Nov 1887 Birth place: Alabama Residence date: 1900 Residence place: Cold Water, Calhoun, Alabama.

739   Ancestry.com, 1900 United States Federal Census (Online publication - Provo, UT, USA: Ancestry.com Operations Inc, 2004. Original data - United States of America, Bureau of the Census. Twelfth Census of the United States, 1900. Washington, D.C.: National Archives and Records Administration, 1900. T623, 18), Ancestry.com, http://www.Ancestry.com, Year: 1900; Census Place: Cold Water, Calhoun, Alabama; Roll: T623_5; Page: 2A; Enumeration District: 28. Birth date: Jan 1890 Birth place: Alabama Residence date: 1900 Residence place: Cold Water, Calhoun, Alabama.

740   Ancestry.com, 1920 United States Federal Census (Online publication - Provo, UT, USA: Ancestry.com Operations Inc, 2010. Images reproduced by FamilySearch. Original data - Fourteenth Census of the United States, 1920. (NARA microfilm publication T625, 2076 rolls). Records of the Bureau of the Census, Record), Ancestry.com, http://www.Ancestry.com, Year: 1920; Census Place: Anniston Ward 2, Calhoun, Alabama; Roll: T625_5; Page: 8A; Enumeration District: 23; Image:. Birth date: about 1876 Birth place: Alabama Residence date: 1920 Residence place: Anniston Ward 2, Calhoun, Alabama.

741   Ancestry.com, 1920 United States Federal Census (Online publication - Provo, UT, USA: Ancestry.com Operations Inc, 2010. Images reproduced by FamilySearch. Original data - Fourteenth Census of the United States, 1920. (NARA microfilm publication T625, 2076 rolls). Records of the Bureau of the Census, Record), Ancestry.com, http://www.Ancestry.com, Year: 1920; Census Place: Anniston Ward 2, Calhoun, Alabama; Roll: T625_5; Page: 8A; Enumeration District: 23; Image:. Birth date: about 1899 Birth place: Alabama Residence date: 1920 Residence place: Anniston Ward 2, Calhoun, Alabama.

742   Ancestry.com, 1920 United States Federal Census (Online publication - Provo, UT, USA: Ancestry.com Operations Inc, 2010. Images reproduced by FamilySearch. Original data - Fourteenth Census of the United States, 1920. (NARA microfilm publication T625, 2076 rolls). Records of the Bureau of the Census, Record), Ancestry.com, http://www.Ancestry.com, Year: 1920; Census Place: Anniston Ward 2, Calhoun, Alabama; Roll: T625_5; Page: 8A; Enumeration District: 23; Image:. Birth date: about 1899 Birth place: Alabama Residence date: 1920 Residence place: Anniston Ward 2, Calhoun, Alabama.

743   Ancestry.com, 1920 United States Federal Census (Online publication - Provo, UT, USA: Ancestry.com Operations Inc, 2010. Images reproduced by FamilySearch. Original data - Fourteenth Census of the United States, 1920. (NARA microfilm publication T625, 2076 rolls). Records of the Bureau of the Census, Record), Ancestry.com, http://www.Ancestry.com, Year: 1920; Census Place: Anniston Ward 2, Calhoun, Alabama; Roll: T625_5; Page: 8A; Enumeration District: 23; Image:. Birth date: about 1910 Birth place: Alabama Residence date: 1920 Residence place: Anniston Ward 2, Calhoun, Alabama.

744   Ancestry.com, 1900 United States Federal Census (Online publication - Provo, UT, USA: Ancestry.com Operations Inc, 2004. Original data - United States of America, Bureau of the Census. Twelfth Census of the United States, 1900. Washington, D.C.: National Archives and Records Administration, 1900. T623, 18), Ancestry.com, http://www.Ancestry.com, Year: 1900; Census Place: Mine Creek, Hempstead, Arkansas; Roll: T623_60; Page: 7A; Enumeration District: 46. Birth date: Mar 1884 Birth place: Alabama Residence date: 1900 Residence place: Mine Creek, Hempstead, Arkansas.

745   Ancestry.com, 1920 United States Federal Census (Online publication - Provo, UT, USA: Ancestry.com Operations Inc, 2010. Images reproduced by FamilySearch. Original data - Fourteenth Census of the United States, 1920. (NARA microfilm publication T625, 2076 rolls). Records of the Bureau of the Census, Record), Ancestry.com, http://www.Ancestry.com, Year: 1920; Census Place: Redland, Hempstead, Arkansas; Roll: T625_64; Page: 6A; Enumeration District: 105; Image:. Birth date: about 1885 Birth place: Alabama Residence date: 1920 Residence place: Redland, Hempstead, Arkansas.

746   Ancestry.com, 1920 United States Federal Census (Online publication - Provo, UT, USA: Ancestry.com Operations Inc, 2010. Images reproduced by FamilySearch. Original data - Fourteenth Census of the United States, 1920. (NARA microfilm publication T625, 2076 rolls). Records of the Bureau of the Census, Record), Ancestry.com, http://www.Ancestry.com, Year: 1920; Census Place: Justice Precinct 1, Tarrant, Texas; Roll: T625_1848; Page: 41A; Enumeration District: 87; Image:. Birth date: about 1888 Birth place: Alabama Residence date: 1920 Residence place: Justice Precinct 1, Tarrant, Texas.

747   Ancestry.com, 1900 United States Federal Census (Online publication - Provo, UT, USA: Ancestry.com Operations Inc, 2004. Original data - United States of America, Bureau of the Census. Twelfth Census of the United States, 1900. Washington, D.C.: National Archives and Records Administration, 1900. T623, 18), Ancestry.com, http://www.Ancestry.com, Year: 1900; Census Place: Mine Creek, Hempstead, Arkansas; Roll: T623_60; Page: 7A; Enumeration District: 46. Birth date: Aug 1887 Birth place: Alabama Residence date: 1900 Residence place: Mine Creek, Hempstead, Arkansas.

748   Ancestry.com, World War I Draft Registration Cards, 1917-1918 (Online publication - Provo, UT, USA: Ancestry.com Operations Inc, 2005. Original data - United States, Selective Service System. World War I Selective Service System Draft Registration Cards, 1917-1918. Washington, D.C.: National Archives and Records Administration), Ancestry.com, http://www.Ancestry.com, Registration Location: Calhoun County, Alabama; Roll: 1509363; Draft Board: 0. Birth date: 17 Aug 1887 Birth place: Residence date: Residence place: Calhoun, Alabama.

749   Ancestry.com, 1930 United States Federal Census (Online publication - Provo, UT, USA: Ancestry.com Operations Inc, 2002. Original data - United States of America, Bureau of the Census. Fifteenth Census of the United States, 1930. Washington, D.C.: National Archives and Records Administration, 1930. T626,), Ancestry.com, http://www.Ancestry.com, Year: 1930; Census Place: Jonesboro, Craighead, Arkansas; Roll: 70; Page: 11A; Enumeration District: 16; Image: 619.0. Birth date: about 1888 Birth place: Alabama Residence date: 1930 Residence place: Jonesboro, Craighead, Arkansas.

750   Ancestry.com, 1900 United States Federal Census (Online publication - Provo, UT, USA: Ancestry.com Operations Inc, 2004. Original data - United States of America, Bureau of the Census. Twelfth Census of the United States, 1900. Washington, D.C.: National Archives and Records Administration, 1900. T623, 18), Ancestry.com, http://www.Ancestry.com, Year: 1900; Census Place: Mine Creek, Hempstead, Arkansas; Roll: T623_60; Page: 7A; Enumeration District: 46. Birth date: Jul 1892 Birth place: Alabama Residence date: 1900 Residence place: Mine Creek, Hempstead, Arkansas.

751   Ancestry.com, Social Security Death Index (Online publication - Provo, UT, USA: Ancestry.com Operations Inc, 2010. Original data - Social Security Administration. Social Security Death Index, Master File. Social Security Administration. Original data: Social Security Administration. Social Security D), Ancestry.com, http://www.Ancestry.com, Number: 416-07-4511; Issue State: Alabama; Issue Date: Before 1951. Birth date: 8 Jul 1890 Birth place: Death date: Mar 1965 Death place:.

752   Ancestry.com, World War I Draft Registration Cards, 1917-1918 (Online publication - Provo, UT, USA: Ancestry.com Operations Inc, 2005. Original data - United States, Selective Service System. World War I Selective Service System Draft Registration Cards, 1917-1918. Washington, D.C.: National Archives and Records Administration), Ancestry.com, http://www.Ancestry.com, Registration Location: Troup County, Georgia; Roll: 1558648; Draft Board: 0. Birth date: 8 Jul 1890 Birth place: Residence date: Residence place: Troup, Georgia.

753   Ancestry.com, 1930 United States Federal Census (Online publication - Provo, UT, USA: Ancestry.com Operations Inc, 2002. Original data - United States of America, Bureau of the Census. Fifteenth Census of the United States, 1930. Washington, D.C.: National Archives and Records Administration, 1930. T626,), Ancestry.com, http://www.Ancestry.com, Year: 1930; Census Place: Anniston, Calhoun, Alabama; Roll: 5; Page: 2B; Enumeration District: 23; Image: 612.0. Birth date: about 1891 Birth place: Alabama Residence date: 1930 Residence place: Anniston, Calhoun, Alabama.

754   Ancestry.com, 1920 United States Federal Census (Online publication - Provo, UT, USA: Ancestry.com Operations Inc, 2010. Images reproduced by FamilySearch. Original data - Fourteenth Census of the United States, 1920. (NARA microfilm publication T625, 2076 rolls). Records of the Bureau of the Census, Record), Ancestry.com, http://www.Ancestry.com, Year: 1920; Census Place: La Grange, Troup, Georgia; Roll: T625_281; Page: 2A; Enumeration District: 137; Image:. Birth date: about 1891 Birth place: Alabama Residence date: 1920 Residence place: La Grange, Troup, Georgia.

755   Ancestry.com, Florida Death Index, 1877-1998 (Online publication - Provo, UT, USA: Ancestry.com Operations Inc, 2004. Original data - State of Florida. Florida Death Index, 1877-1998. Florida: Florida Department of Health, Office of Vital Records, 1998. Original data: State of Florida. Florida Death Ind), Ancestry.com, http://www.Ancestry.com, Death date: Mar 1965 Death place: Gadsden, Florida, United States.

756   Ancestry.com, 1910 United States Federal Census (Online publication - Provo, UT, USA: Ancestry.com Operations Inc, 2006. Original data - Thirteenth Census of the United States, 1910 (NARA microfilm publication T624, 1,178 rolls). Records of the Bureau of the Census, Record Group 29. National Archives, Washington), Ancestry.com, http://www.Ancestry.com, Year: 1910; Census Place: Redland, Hempstead, Arkansas; Roll: ; Page: ; Enumeration District: ; Image:. Birth date: 1881 Birth place: Indiana Residence date: 1910 Residence place: Redland, Hempstead, Arkansas.

757   Ancestry.com, 1900 United States Federal Census (Online publication - Provo, UT, USA: Ancestry.com Operations Inc, 2004. Original data - United States of America, Bureau of the Census. Twelfth Census of the United States, 1900. Washington, D.C.: National Archives and Records Administration, 1900. T623, 18), Ancestry.com, http://www.Ancestry.com, Year: 1900; Census Place: Mine Creek, Hempstead, Arkansas; Roll: T623_60; Page: 7A; Enumeration District: 46. Birth date: Oct 1879 Birth place: Indiana Residence date: 1900 Residence place: Mine Creek, Hempstead, Arkansas.

758   Ancestry.com, Social Security Death Index (Online publication - Provo, UT, USA: Ancestry.com Operations Inc, 2010. Original data - Social Security Administration. Social Security Death Index, Master File. Social Security Administration. Original data: Social Security Administration. Social Security D), Ancestry.com, http://www.Ancestry.com, Number: 430-94-2880; Issue State: Arkansas; Issue Date: 1965. Birth date: 11 Oct 1879 Birth place: Death date: 15 Mar 1970 Death place: McCaskill, Hempstead, Arkansas, United States of America.

759   Dodd, Jordan, Liahona Research, comp., Arkansas Marriages, 1851-1900 (Online publication - Provo, UT, USA: The Generations Network, Inc., 2001. Original data - See the extended description for original data sources listed by county. Original data: See the extended description for original data sources listed by county.), Ancestry.com, http://www.Ancestry.com, Marriage date: 12 Jul 1899 Marriage place: Hempstead, AR.

760	Ancestry.com, 1910 United States Federal Census (Online publication - Provo, UT, USA: Ancestry.com Operations Inc, 2006. Original data - Thirteenth Census of the United States, 1910 (NARA microfilm publication T624, 1,178 rolls). Records of the Bureau of the Census, Record Group 29. National Archives, Washington), Ancestry.com, http://www.Ancestry.com, Year: 1910; Census Place: Redland, Hempstead, Arkansas; Roll: ; Page: ; Enumeration District: ; Image:. Birth date: 1900 Birth place: Arkansas Residence date: 1910 Residence place: Redland, Hempstead, Arkansas.

761	Ancestry.com, 1930 United States Federal Census (Online publication - Provo, UT, USA: Ancestry.com Operations Inc, 2002. Original data - United States of America, Bureau of the Census. Fifteenth Census of the United States, 1930. Washington, D.C.: National Archives and Records Administration, 1930. T626,), Ancestry.com, http://www.Ancestry.com, Year: 1930; Census Place: Hope, Hempstead, Arkansas; Roll: 76; Page: 12A; Enumeration District: 6; Image: 722.0. Birth date: about 1905 Birth place: Arkansas Residence date: 1930 Residence place: Hope, Hempstead, Arkansas.

762	Ancestry.com, 1910 United States Federal Census (Online publication - Provo, UT, USA: Ancestry.com Operations Inc, 2006. Original data - Thirteenth Census of the United States, 1910 (NARA microfilm publication T624, 1,178 rolls). Records of the Bureau of the Census, Record Group 29. National Archives, Washington), Ancestry.com, http://www.Ancestry.com, Year: 1910; Census Place: Redland, Hempstead, Arkansas; Roll: ; Page: ; Enumeration District: ; Image:. Birth date: 1904 Birth place: Arkansas Residence date: 1910 Residence place: Redland, Hempstead, Arkansas.

763	Ancestry.com, Social Security Death Index (Online publication - Provo, UT, USA: Ancestry.com Operations Inc, 2010. Original data - Social Security Administration. Social Security Death Index, Master File. Social Security Administration. Original data: Social Security Administration. Social Security D), Ancestry.com, http://www.Ancestry.com, Number: 429-14-5762; Issue State: Arkansas; Issue Date: Before 1951. Birth date: 5 Feb 1906 Birth place: Death date: Jul 1981 Death place: McCaskill, Hempstead, Arkansas, United States of America.

764	Ancestry.com, 1920 United States Federal Census (Online publication - Provo, UT, USA: Ancestry.com Operations Inc, 2010. Images reproduced by FamilySearch. Original data - Fourteenth Census of the United States, 1920. (NARA microfilm publication T625, 2076 rolls). Records of the Bureau of the Census, Record), Ancestry.com, http://www.Ancestry.com, Year: 1920; Census Place: Redland, Hempstead, Arkansas; Roll: T625_64; Page: 13B; Enumeration District: 105; Image:. Birth date: about 1906 Birth place: Arkansas Residence date: 1920 Residence place: Redland, Hempstead, Arkansas.

765	Ancestry.com, Texas Land Title Abstracts (Online publication - Provo, UT, USA: Ancestry.com Operations Inc, 2000. Original data - Texas General Land Office. Abstracts of all original Texas Land Titles comprising Grants and Locations. Austin, TX, USA. Original data: Texas General Land Office. Abstract), Ancestry.com, http://www.Ancestry.com.

766	Ancestry.com, 1910 United States Federal Census (Online publication - Provo, UT, USA: Ancestry.com Operations Inc, 2006. Original data - Thirteenth Census of the United States, 1910 (NARA microfilm publication T624, 1,178 rolls). Records of the Bureau of the Census, Record Group 29. National Archives, Washington), Ancestry.com, http://www.Ancestry.com, Year: 1910; Census Place: Redland, Hempstead, Arkansas; Roll: ; Page: ; Enumeration District: ; Image:. Birth date: 1906 Birth place: Arkansas Residence date: 1910 Residence place: Redland, Hempstead, Arkansas.

767	Ancestry.com, 1930 United States Federal Census (Online publication - Provo, UT, USA: Ancestry.com Operations Inc, 2002. Original data - United States of America, Bureau of the Census. Fifteenth Census of the United States, 1930. Washington, D.C.: National Archives and Records Administration, 1930. T626,), Ancestry.com, http://www.Ancestry.com, Year: 1930; Census Place: Saline, Pike, Arkansas; Roll: 88; Page: 7A; Enumeration District: 14; Image: 475.0. Birth date: about 1906 Birth place: Arkansas Residence date: 1930 Residence place: Saline, Pike, Arkansas.

768	Ancestry.com, 1910 United States Federal Census (Online publication - Provo, UT, USA: Ancestry.com Operations Inc, 2006. Original data - Thirteenth Census of the United States, 1910 (NARA microfilm publication T624, 1,178 rolls). Records of the Bureau of the Census, Record Group 29. National Archives, Washington), Ancestry.com, http://www.Ancestry.com, Year: 1910; Census Place: Redland, Hempstead, Arkansas; Roll: ; Page: ; Enumeration District: ; Image:. Birth date: 1909 Birth place: Arkansas Residence date: 1910 Residence place: Redland, Hempstead, Arkansas.

769	Ancestry.com, 1910 United States Federal Census (Online publication - Provo, UT, USA: Ancestry.com Operations Inc, 2006. Original data - Thirteenth Census of the United States, 1910 (NARA microfilm publication T624, 1,178 rolls). Records of the Bureau of the Census, Record Group 29. National Archives, Washington), Ancestry.com, http://www.Ancestry.com, Year: 1910; Census Place: Anniston Ward 1, Calhoun, Alabama; Roll: ; Page: ; Enumeration District: ; Image:. Birth date: about 1870 Birth place: Alabama Residence date: 1910 Residence place: Anniston Ward 1, Calhoun, Alabama.

770	Ancestry.com, 1900 United States Federal Census (Online publication - Provo, UT, USA: Ancestry.com Operations Inc, 2004. Original data - United States of America, Bureau of the Census. Twelfth Census of the United States, 1900. Washington, D.C.: National Archives and Records Administration, 1900. T623, 18), Ancestry.com, http://www.Ancestry.com, Year: 1900; Census Place: Anniston Ward 1, Calhoun, Alabama; Roll: T623_5; Page: 10B; Enumeration District: 42. Birth date: Feb 1870 Birth place: Alabama Marriage date: 1888 Marriage place: Residence date: 1900 Residence place: Anniston Ward 1, Calhoun, Alabama.

771	Ancestry.com, 1900 United States Federal Census (Online publication - Provo, UT, USA: Ancestry.com Operations Inc, 2004. Original data - United States of America, Bureau of the Census. Twelfth Census of the United States, 1900. Washington, D.C.: National Archives and Records Administration, 1900. T623, 18), Ancestry.com, http://www.Ancestry.com, Year: 1900; Census Place: Anniston Ward 1, Calhoun, Alabama; Roll: T623_5; Page: 10B;

Enumeration District: 42. Birth date: Sep 1893 Birth place: Alabama Residence date: 1900 Residence place: Anniston Ward 1, Calhoun, Alabama.

772   Ancestry.com, 1910 United States Federal Census (Online publication - Provo, UT, USA: Ancestry.com Operations Inc, 2006. Original data - Thirteenth Census of the United States, 1910 (NARA microfilm publication T624, 1,178 rolls). Records of the Bureau of the Census, Record Group 29. National Archives, Washington), Ancestry.com, http://www.Ancestry.com, Year: 1910; Census Place: Anniston Ward 1, Calhoun, Alabama; Roll: ; Page: ; Enumeration District: ; Image:. Birth date: about 1894 Birth place: Alabama Residence date: 1910 Residence place: Anniston Ward 1, Calhoun, Alabama.

773   Ancestry.com, 1920 United States Federal Census (Online publication - Provo, UT, USA: Ancestry.com Operations Inc, 2010. Images reproduced by FamilySearch. Original data - Fourteenth Census of the United States, 1920. (NARA microfilm publication T625, 2076 rolls). Records of the Bureau of the Census, Record), Ancestry.com, http://www.Ancestry.com, Year: 1920; Census Place: Greens Schoolhouse, Calhoun, Alabama; Roll: T625_5; Page: 7B; Enumeration District: 10; Image:. Birth date: about 1884 Birth place: Mississippi Residence date: 1920 Residence place: Greens Schoolhouse, Calhoun, Alabama.

774   Ancestry.com, 1930 United States Federal Census (Online publication - Provo, UT, USA: Ancestry.com Operations Inc, 2002. Original data - United States of America, Bureau of the Census. Fifteenth Census of the United States, 1930. Washington, D.C.: National Archives and Records Administration, 1930. T626,), Ancestry.com, http://www.Ancestry.com, Year: 1930; Census Place: Anniston, Calhoun, Alabama; Roll: 5; Page: 8B; Enumeration District: 37; Image: 1096.0. Birth date: about 1884 Birth place: Alabama Residence date: 1930 Residence place: Anniston, Calhoun, Alabama.

775   Ancestry.com, 1920 United States Federal Census (Online publication - Provo, UT, USA: Ancestry.com Operations Inc, 2010. Images reproduced by FamilySearch. Original data - Fourteenth Census of the United States, 1920. (NARA microfilm publication T625, 2076 rolls). Records of the Bureau of the Census, Record), Ancestry.com, http://www.Ancestry.com, Year: 1920; Census Place: Greens Schoolhouse, Calhoun, Alabama; Roll: T625_5; Page: 6B; Enumeration District: 10; Image:. Birth date: about 1886 Birth place: Alabama Residence date: 1920 Residence place: Greens Schoolhouse, Calhoun, Alabama.

776   Ancestry.com, 1910 United States Federal Census (Online publication - Provo, UT, USA: Ancestry.com Operations Inc, 2006. Original data - Thirteenth Census of the United States, 1910 (NARA microfilm publication T624, 1,178 rolls). Records of the Bureau of the Census, Record Group 29. National Archives, Washington), Ancestry.com, http://www.Ancestry.com, Year: 1910; Census Place: Ballplay, Etowah, Alabama; Roll: ; Page: ; Enumeration District: ; Image:. Birth date: 1885 Birth place: Alabama Residence date: 1910 Residence place: Ballplay, Etowah, Alabama.

777   Ancestry.com, 1930 United States Federal Census (Online publication - Provo, UT, USA: Ancestry.com Operations Inc, 2002. Original data - United States of America, Bureau of the Census. Fifteenth Census of the United States, 1930. Washington, D.C.: National Archives and Records Administration, 1930. T626,), Ancestry.com, http://www.Ancestry.com, Year: 1930; Census Place: Greens Schoolhouse, Calhoun, Alabama; Roll: 5; Page: 5B; Enumeration District: 11; Image: 251.0. Birth date: about 1885 Birth place: Alabama Residence date: 1930 Residence place: Greens Schoolhouse, Calhoun, Alabama.

778   Ancestry.com, 1910 United States Federal Census (Online publication - Provo, UT, USA: Ancestry.com Operations Inc, 2006. Original data - Thirteenth Census of the United States, 1910 (NARA microfilm publication T624, 1,178 rolls). Records of the Bureau of the Census, Record Group 29. National Archives, Washington), Ancestry.com, http://www.Ancestry.com, Year: 1910; Census Place: Greens Schoolhouse, Calhoun, Alabama; Roll: ; Page: ; Enumeration District: ; Image:. Birth date: about 1892 Birth place: Alabama Residence date: 1910 Residence place: Greens Schoolhouse, Calhoun, Alabama.

779   Ancestry.com, 1920 United States Federal Census (Online publication - Provo, UT, USA: Ancestry.com Operations Inc, 2010. Images reproduced by FamilySearch. Original data - Fourteenth Census of the United States, 1920. (NARA microfilm publication T625, 2076 rolls). Records of the Bureau of the Census, Record), Ancestry.com, http://www.Ancestry.com, Year: 1920; Census Place: Greens Schoolhouse, Calhoun, Alabama; Roll: T625_5; Page: 3B; Enumeration District: 10; Image:. Birth date: about 1890 Birth place: Alabama Residence date: 1920 Residence place: Greens Schoolhouse, Calhoun, Alabama.

780   Ancestry.com, Alabama Deaths, 1908-59 (Online publication - Provo, UT, USA: Ancestry.com Operations Inc, 2000. Original data - State of Alabama. Index of Vital Records for Alabama: Deaths, 1908-1959. Montgomery, AL, USA: State of Alabama Center for Health Statistics, Record Services Division. Original), Ancestry.com, http://www.Ancestry.com, Death date: 23 Mar 1916 Death place: Calhoun.

781   Ancestry.com, 1900 United States Federal Census (Online publication - Provo, UT, USA: Ancestry.com Operations Inc, 2004. Original data - United States of America, Bureau of the Census. Twelfth Census of the United States, 1900. Washington, D.C.: National Archives and Records Administration, 1900. T623, 18), Ancestry.com, http://www.Ancestry.com, Year: 1900; Census Place: Allen, Calhoun, Alabama; Roll: T623_5; Page: 1B; Enumeration District: 32. Birth date: Mar 1852 Birth place: Georgia Marriage date: 1875 Marriage place: Residence date: 1900 Residence place: Precinct 8 Green's Schoolhouse, Calhoun, Alabama.

782   Ancestry.com, 1860 United States Federal Census (Online publication - Provo, UT, USA: Ancestry.com Operations, Inc., 2009. Images reproduced by FamilySearch. Original data - 1860 U.S. census, population schedule. NARA microfilm publication M653, 1,438 rolls. Washington, D.C.: National Archives and Records), Ancestry.com, http://www.Ancestry.com, Year: 1860; Census Place: Township 14 Range 12, Calhoun, Alabama; Roll: ; Page: 473;

Image: 193. Birth date: about 1852 Birth place: Georgia Residence date: 1860 Residence place: Township 14 Range 12, Calhoun, Alabama, United States.

783   Ancestry.com, 1870 United States Federal Census (Online publication - Provo, UT, USA: Ancestry.com Operations, Inc., 2009. Images reproduced by FamilySearch. Original data - 1870 U.S. census, population schedules. NARA microfilm publication M593, 1,761 rolls. Washington, D.C.: National Archives and Record), Ancestry.com, http://www.Ancestry.com, Year: 1870; Census Place: Township 14 Range 12, Cleburne, Alabama; Roll: M593_; Page: ; Image:. Birth date: about 1855 Birth place: Georgia Residence date: 1870 Residence place: Township 14 Range 12, Cleburne, Alabama, United States.

784   Ancestry.com and The Church of Jesus Christ of Latter-day Saints, 1880 United States Federal Census (Online publication - Provo, UT, USA: Ancestry.com Operations Inc, 2010. 1880 U.S. Census Index provided by The Church of Jesus Christ of Latter-day Saints © Copyright 1999 Intellectual Reserve, Inc. All rights reserved. All use is subject to the limited), Ancestry.com, http://www.Ancestry.com, Year: 1880; Census Place: District 1105, Webster, Georgia; Roll: 171; Family History Film: 1254171; Page: 456B; Enumeration District: 86; Image: 0296. Birth date: about 1852 Birth place: Georgia Residence date: 1880 Residence place: District 1105, Webster, Georgia, United States.

785   Ancestry.com and The Church of Jesus Christ of Latter-day Saints, 1880 United States Federal Census (Online publication - Provo, UT, USA: Ancestry.com Operations Inc, 2010. 1880 U.S. Census Index provided by The Church of Jesus Christ of Latter-day Saints © Copyright 1999 Intellectual Reserve, Inc. All rights reserved. All use is subject to the limited), Ancestry.com, http://www.Ancestry.com, Year: 1880; Census Place: District 1105, Webster, Georgia; Roll: 171; Family History Film: 1254171; Page: 456B; Enumeration District: 86; Image: 0296. Birth date: about 1873 Birth place: Georgia Residence date: 1880 Residence place: District 1105, Webster, Georgia, United States.

786   Ancestry.com, 1910 United States Federal Census (Online publication - Provo, UT, USA: Ancestry.com Operations Inc, 2006. Original data - Thirteenth Census of the United States, 1910 (NARA microfilm publication T624, 1,178 rolls). Records of the Bureau of the Census, Record Group 29. National Archives, Washington), Ancestry.com, http://www.Ancestry.com, Year: 1910; Census Place: Greens Schoolhouse, Calhoun, Alabama; Roll: ; Page: ; Enumeration District: ; Image:. Birth date: about 1875 Birth place: Alabama Residence date: 1910 Residence place: Greens Schoolhouse, Calhoun, Alabama.

787   Ancestry.com and The Church of Jesus Christ of Latter-day Saints, 1880 United States Federal Census (Online publication - Provo, UT, USA: Ancestry.com Operations Inc, 2010. 1880 U.S. Census Index provided by The Church of Jesus Christ of Latter-day Saints © Copyright 1999 Intellectual Reserve, Inc. All rights reserved. All use is subject to the limited), Ancestry.com, http://www.Ancestry.com, Year: 1880; Census Place: District 1105, Webster, Georgia; Roll: 171; Family History Film: 1254171; Page: 456B; Enumeration District: 86; Image: 0296. Birth date: about 1875 Birth place: Georgia Residence date: 1880 Residence place: District 1105, Webster, Georgia, United States.

788   Ancestry.com, 1920 United States Federal Census (Online publication - Provo, UT, USA: Ancestry.com Operations Inc, 2010. Images reproduced by FamilySearch. Original data - Fourteenth Census of the United States, 1920. (NARA microfilm publication T625, 2076 rolls). Records of the Bureau of the Census, Record), Ancestry.com, http://www.Ancestry.com, Year: 1920; Census Place: Gum Spring, Etowah, Alabama; Roll: T625_15; Page: 4B; Enumeration District: 110; Image:. Birth date: about 1878 Birth place: Alabama Residence date: 1920 Residence place: Gum Spring, Etowah, Alabama.

789   Ancestry.com, 1900 United States Federal Census (Online publication - Provo, UT, USA: Ancestry.com Operations Inc, 2004. Original data - United States of America, Bureau of the Census. Twelfth Census of the United States, 1900. Washington, D.C.: National Archives and Records Administration, 1900. T623, 18), Ancestry.com, http://www.Ancestry.com, Year: 1900; Census Place: Allen, Calhoun, Alabama; Roll: T623_5; Page: 3B; Enumeration District: 32. Birth date: May 1867 Birth place: Alabama Marriage date: 1891 Marriage place: Residence date: 1900 Residence place: Allen, Calhoun, Alabama.

790   Ancestry.com, 1910 United States Federal Census (Online publication - Provo, UT, USA: Ancestry.com Operations Inc, 2006. Original data - Thirteenth Census of the United States, 1910 (NARA microfilm publication T624, 1,178 rolls). Records of the Bureau of the Census, Record Group 29. National Archives, Washington), Ancestry.com, http://www.Ancestry.com, Year: 1910; Census Place: De Armanville, Calhoun, Alabama; Roll: ; Page: ; Enumeration District: ; Image:. Birth date: about 1877 Birth place: Alabama Residence date: 1910 Residence place: De Armanville, Calhoun, Alabama.

791   Ancestry.com, 1900 United States Federal Census (Online publication - Provo, UT, USA: Ancestry.com Operations Inc, 2004. Original data - United States of America, Bureau of the Census. Twelfth Census of the United States, 1900. Washington, D.C.: National Archives and Records Administration, 1900. T623, 18), Ancestry.com, http://www.Ancestry.com, Year: 1900; Census Place: Allen, Calhoun, Alabama; Roll: T623_5; Page: 3B; Enumeration District: 32. Birth date: Sep 1871 Birth place: Alabama Marriage date: 1891 Marriage place: Residence date: 1900 Residence place: Allen, Calhoun, Alabama.

792   Ancestry.com, 1900 United States Federal Census (Online publication - Provo, UT, USA: Ancestry.com Operations Inc, 2004. Original data - United States of America, Bureau of the Census. Twelfth Census of the United States, 1900. Washington, D.C.: National Archives and Records Administration, 1900. T623, 18), Ancestry.com, http://www.Ancestry.com, Year: 1900; Census Place: Allen, Calhoun, Alabama; Roll: T623_5; Page: 1A; Enumeration District: 32. Birth date: Mar 1879 Birth place: Alabama Residence date: 1900 Residence place: Precinct 8 Green's Schoolhouse, Calhoun, Alabama.

793   Ancestry.com, 1910 United States Federal Census (Online publication - Provo, UT, USA: Ancestry.com Operations Inc, 2006. Original data - Thirteenth Census of the United States, 1910 (NARA microfilm publication T624, 1,178 rolls). Records of the Bureau of the Census, Record Group 29. National Archives, Washington), Ancestry.com, http://www.Ancestry.com, Year: 1910; Census Place: Greens Schoolhouse, Calhoun, Alabama; Roll: ; Page: ; Enumeration District: ; Image:. Birth date: about 1879 Birth place: Alabama Residence date: 1910 Residence place: Greens Schoolhouse, Calhoun, Alabama.

794   Ancestry.com, 1920 United States Federal Census (Online publication - Provo, UT, USA: Ancestry.com Operations Inc, 2010. Images reproduced by FamilySearch. Original data - Fourteenth Census of the United States, 1920. (NARA microfilm publication T625, 2076 rolls). Records of the Bureau of the Census, Record), Ancestry.com, http://www.Ancestry.com, Year: 1920; Census Place: Oxford, Calhoun, Alabama; Roll: T625_5; Page: 10A; Enumeration District: 16; Image:. Birth date: about 1880 Birth place: Alabama Residence date: 1920 Residence place: Oxford, Calhoun, Alabama.

795   Ancestry.com, 1900 United States Federal Census (Online publication - Provo, UT, USA: Ancestry.com Operations Inc, 2004. Original data - United States of America, Bureau of the Census. Twelfth Census of the United States, 1900. Washington, D.C.: National Archives and Records Administration, 1900. T623, 18), Ancestry.com, http://www.Ancestry.com, Year: 1900; Census Place: Allen, Calhoun, Alabama; Roll: T623_5; Page: 3B; Enumeration District: 32. Birth date: Mar 1881 Birth place: Alabama Marriage date: 1897 Marriage place: Residence date: 1900 Residence place: Precinct 8 Green's Schoolhouse, Calhoun, Alabama.

796   Ancestry.com, 1910 United States Federal Census (Online publication - Provo, UT, USA: Ancestry.com Operations Inc, 2006. Original data - Thirteenth Census of the United States, 1910 (NARA microfilm publication T624, 1,178 rolls). Records of the Bureau of the Census, Record Group 29. National Archives, Washington), Ancestry.com, http://www.Ancestry.com, Year: 1910; Census Place: Greens Schoolhouse, Calhoun, Alabama; Roll: ; Page: ; Enumeration District: ; Image:. Birth date: about 1886 Birth place: Alabama Residence date: 1910 Residence place: Greens Schoolhouse, Calhoun, Alabama.

797   Ancestry.com, 1900 United States Federal Census (Online publication - Provo, UT, USA: Ancestry.com Operations Inc, 2004. Original data - United States of America, Bureau of the Census. Twelfth Census of the United States, 1900. Washington, D.C.: National Archives and Records Administration, 1900. T623, 18), Ancestry.com, http://www.Ancestry.com, Year: 1900; Census Place: Allen, Calhoun, Alabama; Roll: T623_5; Page: 3B; Enumeration District: 32. Birth date: Jul 1873 Birth place: Alabama Marriage date: 1897 Marriage place: Residence date: 1900 Residence place: Precinct 8 Green's Schoolhouse, Calhoun, Alabama.

798   Ancestry.com, 1900 United States Federal Census (Online publication - Provo, UT, USA: Ancestry.com Operations Inc, 2004. Original data - United States of America, Bureau of the Census. Twelfth Census of the United States, 1900. Washington, D.C.: National Archives and Records Administration, 1900. T623, 18), Ancestry.com, http://www.Ancestry.com, Year: 1900; Census Place: Allen, Calhoun, Alabama; Roll: T623_5; Page: 1B; Enumeration District: 32. Birth date: Mar 1887 Birth place: Alabama Residence date: 1900 Residence place: Precinct 8 Green's Schoolhouse, Calhoun, Alabama.

799   Ancestry.com, Alabama Deaths, 1908-59 (Online publication - Provo, UT, USA: Ancestry.com Operations Inc, 2000. Original data - State of Alabama. Index of Vital Records for Alabama: Deaths, 1908-1959. Montgomery, AL, USA: State of Alabama Center for Health Statistics, Record Services Division. Original), Ancestry.com, http://www.Ancestry.com, Death date: Mar 1934 Death place: Calhoun.

800   Ancestry.com, 1900 United States Federal Census (Online publication - Provo, UT, USA: Ancestry.com Operations Inc, 2004. Original data - United States of America, Bureau of the Census. Twelfth Census of the United States, 1900. Washington, D.C.: National Archives and Records Administration, 1900. T623, 18), Ancestry.com, http://www.Ancestry.com, Year: 1900; Census Place: Allen, Calhoun, Alabama; Roll: T623_5; Page: 1B; Enumeration District: 32. Birth date: Feb 1883 Birth place: Alabama Residence date: 1900 Residence place: Precinct 8 Green's Schoolhouse, Calhoun, Alabama.

801   Ancestry.com, World War I Draft Registration Cards, 1917-1918 (Online publication - Provo, UT, USA: Ancestry.com Operations Inc, 2005. Original data - United States, Selective Service System. World War I Selective Service System Draft Registration Cards, 1917-1918. Washington, D.C.: National Archives and Records Administration), Ancestry.com, http://www.Ancestry.com, Registration Location: Etowah County, Alabama; Roll: 1509384; Draft Board: 0. Birth date: 4 Nov 1890 Birth place: Alabama Residence date: Residence place: Etowah, Alabama.

802   Ancestry.com, 1910 United States Federal Census (Online publication - Provo, UT, USA: Ancestry.com Operations Inc, 2006. Original data - Thirteenth Census of the United States, 1910 (NARA microfilm publication T624, 1,178 rolls). Records of the Bureau of the Census, Record Group 29. National Archives, Washington), Ancestry.com, http://www.Ancestry.com, Year: 1910; Census Place: Greens Schoolhouse, Calhoun, Alabama; Roll: ; Page: ; Enumeration District: ; Image:. Birth date: about 1890 Birth place: Alabama Residence date: 1910 Residence place: Greens Schoolhouse, Calhoun, Alabama.

803   Ancestry.com, 1920 United States Federal Census (Online publication - Provo, UT, USA: Ancestry.com Operations Inc, 2010. Images reproduced by FamilySearch. Original data - Fourteenth Census of the United States, 1920. (NARA microfilm publication T625, 2076 rolls). Records of the Bureau of the Census, Record), Ancestry.com, http://www.Ancestry.com, Year: 1920; Census Place: Ball Play, Etowah, Alabama; Roll: T625_15; Page: 3B; Enumeration District: 100; Image:. Birth date: about 1890 Birth place: Alabama Residence date: 1920 Residence place: Ball Play, Etowah, Alabama.

804   Ancestry.com, 1900 United States Federal Census (Online publication - Provo, UT, USA: Ancestry.com Operations Inc, 2004. Original data - United States of America, Bureau of the Census. Twelfth Census of the United States, 1900. Washington, D.C.: National Archives and Records Administration, 1900. T623, 18), Ancestry.com, http://www.Ancestry.com, Year: 1900; Census Place: Allen, Calhoun, Alabama; Roll: T623_5; Page: 1B; Enumeration District: 32. Birth date: Sep 1890 Birth place: Alabama Residence date: 1900 Residence place: Precinct 8 Green's Schoolhouse, Calhoun, Alabama.

805   Ancestry.com, 1900 United States Federal Census (Online publication - Provo, UT, USA: Ancestry.com Operations Inc, 2004. Original data - United States of America, Bureau of the Census. Twelfth Census of the United States, 1900. Washington, D.C.: National Archives and Records Administration, 1900. T623, 18), Ancestry.com, http://www.Ancestry.com, Year: 1900; Census Place: Allen, Calhoun, Alabama; Roll: T623_5; Page: 1B; Enumeration District: 32. Birth date: Jan 1892 Birth place: Alabama Residence date: 1900 Residence place: Precinct 8 Green's Schoolhouse, Calhoun, Alabama.

806   Ancestry.com, 1910 United States Federal Census (Online publication - Provo, UT, USA: Ancestry.com Operations Inc, 2006. Original data - Thirteenth Census of the United States, 1910 (NARA microfilm publication T624, 1,178 rolls). Records of the Bureau of the Census, Record Group 29. National Archives, Washington), Ancestry.com, http://www.Ancestry.com, Year: 1910; Census Place: Greens Schoolhouse, Calhoun, Alabama; Roll: ; Page: ; Enumeration District: ; Image:. Birth date: about 1892 Birth place: Alabama Residence date: 1910 Residence place: Greens Schoolhouse, Calhoun, Alabama.

807   Ancestry.com, World War I Draft Registration Cards, 1917-1918 (Online publication - Provo, UT, USA: Ancestry.com Operations Inc, 2005. Original data - United States, Selective Service System. World War I Selective Service System Draft Registration Cards, 1917-1918. Washington, D.C.: National Archives and Records Administration), Ancestry.com, http://www.Ancestry.com, Registration Location: Etowah County, Alabama; Roll: 1509384; Draft Board: 0. Birth date: 7 Jan 1892 Birth place: Alabama Residence date: Residence place: Etowah, Alabama.

808   Ancestry.com, 1900 United States Federal Census (Online publication - Provo, UT, USA: Ancestry.com Operations Inc, 2004. Original data - United States of America, Bureau of the Census. Twelfth Census of the United States, 1900. Washington, D.C.: National Archives and Records Administration, 1900. T623, 18), Ancestry.com, http://www.Ancestry.com, Year: 1900; Census Place: Allen, Calhoun, Alabama; Roll: T623_5; Page: 1B; Enumeration District: 32. Birth date: Jan 1892 Birth place: Alabama Residence date: 1900 Residence place: Precinct 8 Green's Schoolhouse, Calhoun, Alabama.

809   Ancestry.com, 1910 United States Federal Census (Online publication - Provo, UT, USA: Ancestry.com Operations Inc, 2006. Original data - Thirteenth Census of the United States, 1910 (NARA microfilm publication T624, 1,178 rolls). Records of the Bureau of the Census, Record Group 29. National Archives, Washington), Ancestry.com, http://www.Ancestry.com, Year: 1910; Census Place: Greens Schoolhouse, Calhoun, Alabama; Roll: ; Page: ; Enumeration District: ; Image:. Birth date: about 1894 Birth place: Alabama Residence date: 1910 Residence place: Greens Schoolhouse, Calhoun, Alabama.

810   Ancestry.com, World War I Draft Registration Cards, 1917-1918 (Online publication - Provo, UT, USA: Ancestry.com Operations Inc, 2005. Original data - United States, Selective Service System. World War I Selective Service System Draft Registration Cards, 1917-1918. Washington, D.C.: National Archives and Records Administration), Ancestry.com, http://www.Ancestry.com, Registration Location: Calhoun County, Alabama; Roll: 1509363; Draft Board: 0. Birth date: 4 Mar 1894 Birth place: Alabama Residence date: Residence place: Calhoun, Alabama.

811   Ancestry.com, 1920 United States Federal Census (Online publication - Provo, UT, USA: Ancestry.com Operations Inc, 2010. Images reproduced by FamilySearch. Original data - Fourteenth Census of the United States, 1920. (NARA microfilm publication T625, 2076 rolls). Records of the Bureau of the Census, Record), Ancestry.com, http://www.Ancestry.com, Year: 1920; Census Place: Greens Schoolhouse, Calhoun, Alabama; Roll: T625_5; Page: 4B; Enumeration District: 10; Image:. Birth date: about 1895 Birth place: Alabama Residence date: 1920 Residence place: Greens Schoolhouse, Calhoun, Alabama.

812   Ancestry.com, 1930 United States Federal Census (Online publication - Provo, UT, USA: Ancestry.com Operations Inc, 2002. Original data - United States of America, Bureau of the Census. Fifteenth Census of the United States, 1930. Washington, D.C.: National Archives and Records Administration, 1930. T626,), Ancestry.com, http://www.Ancestry.com, Year: 1930; Census Place: Greens Schoolhouse, Calhoun, Alabama; Roll: 5; Page: 4B; Enumeration District: 11; Image: 249.0. Birth date: about 1894 Birth place: Alabama Residence date: 1930 Residence place: Greens Schoolhouse, Calhoun, Alabama.

813   Ancestry.com, 1910 United States Federal Census (Online publication - Provo, UT, USA: Ancestry.com Operations Inc, 2006. Original data - Thirteenth Census of the United States, 1910 (NARA microfilm publication T624, 1,178 rolls). Records of the Bureau of the Census, Record Group 29. National Archives, Washington), Ancestry.com, http://www.Ancestry.com, Year: 1910; Census Place: Greens Schoolhouse, Calhoun, Alabama; Roll: ; Page: ; Enumeration District: ; Image:. Birth date: about 1886 Birth place: Alabama Residence date: 1910 Residence place: Greens Schoolhouse, Calhoun, Alabama.

814   Ancestry.com, 1920 United States Federal Census (Online publication - Provo, UT, USA: Ancestry.com Operations Inc, 2010. Images reproduced by FamilySearch. Original data - Fourteenth Census of the United States, 1920. (NARA microfilm publication T625, 2076 rolls). Records of the Bureau of the Census, Record), Ancestry.com, http://www.Ancestry.com, Year: 1920; Census Place: Oxford, Calhoun, Alabama; Roll: T625_5; Page: 10A; Enumeration

District: 16; Image:. Birth date: about 1885 Birth place: Alabama Residence date: 1920 Residence place: Oxford, Calhoun, Alabama.

815   Ancestry.com, Social Security Death Index (Online publication - Provo, UT, USA: Ancestry.com Operations Inc, 2010. Original data - Social Security Administration. Social Security Death Index, Master File. Social Security Administration. Original data: Social Security Administration. Social Security D), Ancestry.com, http://www.Ancestry.com, Number: 416-86-7690; Issue State: Alabama; Issue Date: 1973. Birth date: 22 May 1885 Birth place: Death date: Feb 1978 Death place: Weaver, Calhoun, Alabama, United States of America.

816   Ancestry.com, 1900 United States Federal Census (Online publication - Provo, UT, USA: Ancestry.com Operations Inc, 2004. Original data - United States of America, Bureau of the Census. Twelfth Census of the United States, 1900. Washington, D.C.: National Archives and Records Administration, 1900. T623, 18), Ancestry.com, http://www.Ancestry.com, Year: 1900; Census Place: Anniston Ward 2, Calhoun, Alabama; Roll: _; Page: 1A; Enumeration District: 43. Birth date: May 1885 Birth place: Alabama Residence date: 1900 Residence place: Anniston City, Calhoun, Alabama.

817   Ancestry.com, 1910 United States Federal Census (Online publication - Provo, UT, USA: Ancestry.com Operations Inc, 2006. Original data - Thirteenth Census of the United States, 1910 (NARA microfilm publication T624, 1,178 rolls). Records of the Bureau of the Census, Record Group 29. National Archives, Washington), Ancestry.com, http://www.Ancestry.com, Year: 1910; Census Place: Ballplay, Etowah, Alabama; Roll: ; Page: ; Enumeration District: ; Image:. Birth date: about 1862 Birth place: Alabama Residence date: 1910 Residence place: Ballplay, Etowah, Alabama.

818   Ancestry.com, 1870 United States Federal Census (Online publication - Provo, UT, USA: Ancestry.com Operations, Inc., 2009. Images reproduced by FamilySearch. Original data - 1870 U.S. census, population schedules. NARA microfilm publication M593, 1,761 rolls. Washington, D.C.: National Archives and Record), Ancestry.com, http://www.Ancestry.com, Year: 1870; Census Place: Precinct 8, Calhoun, Alabama; Roll: M593_; Page: ; Image:. Birth date: about 1864 Birth place: Alabama Residence date: 1870 Residence place: Precinct 8, Calhoun, Alabama, United States.

819   Ancestry.com, 1920 United States Federal Census (Online publication - Provo, UT, USA: Ancestry.com Operations Inc, 2010. Images reproduced by FamilySearch. Original data - Fourteenth Census of the United States, 1920. (NARA microfilm publication T625, 2076 rolls). Records of the Bureau of the Census, Record), Ancestry.com, http://www.Ancestry.com, Year: 1920; Census Place: Greens Schoolhouse, Calhoun, Alabama; Roll: T625_5; Page: 7B; Enumeration District: 10; Image:. Birth date: about 1863 Birth place: Alabama Residence date: 1920 Residence place: Greens Schoolhouse, Calhoun, Alabama.

820   Ancestry.com, 1930 United States Federal Census (Online publication - Provo, UT, USA: Ancestry.com Operations Inc, 2002. Original data - United States of America, Bureau of the Census. Fifteenth Census of the United States, 1930. Washington, D.C.: National Archives and Records Administration, 1930. T626,), Ancestry.com, http://www.Ancestry.com, Year: 1930; Census Place: Hollingsworth, Calhoun, Alabama; Roll: 5; Page: 1B; Enumeration District: 10; Image: 225.0. Birth date: about 1863 Birth place: Alabama Residence date: 1930 Residence place: Hollingsworth, Calhoun, Alabama.

821   Ancestry.com, Alabama Deaths, 1908-59 (Online publication - Provo, UT, USA: Ancestry.com Operations Inc, 2000. Original data - State of Alabama. Index of Vital Records for Alabama: Deaths, 1908-1959. Montgomery, AL, USA: State of Alabama Center for Health Statistics, Record Services Division. Original), Ancestry.com, http://www.Ancestry.com, Death date: 24 Aug 1944 Death place: Calhoun.

822   Ancestry.com, 1900 United States Federal Census (Online publication - Provo, UT, USA: Ancestry.com Operations Inc, 2004. Original data - United States of America, Bureau of the Census. Twelfth Census of the United States, 1900. Washington, D.C.: National Archives and Records Administration, 1900. T623, 18), Ancestry.com, http://www.Ancestry.com, Year: 1900; Census Place: Anniston Ward 2, Calhoun, Alabama; Roll: T623_5; Page: 1B; Enumeration District: 43. Birth date: Apr 1887 Birth place: Alabama Residence date: 1900 Residence place: Anniston City, Calhoun, Alabama.

823   Ancestry.com, 1900 United States Federal Census (Online publication - Provo, UT, USA: Ancestry.com Operations Inc, 2004. Original data - United States of America, Bureau of the Census. Twelfth Census of the United States, 1900. Washington, D.C.: National Archives and Records Administration, 1900. T623, 18), Ancestry.com, http://www.Ancestry.com, Year: 1900; Census Place: Anniston Ward 2, Calhoun, Alabama; Roll: T623_5; Page: 1B; Enumeration District: 43. Birth date: Apr 1888 Birth place: Alabama Residence date: 1900 Residence place: Anniston City, Calhoun, Alabama.

824   Ancestry.com, 1910 United States Federal Census (Online publication - Provo, UT, USA: Ancestry.com Operations Inc, 2006. Original data - Thirteenth Census of the United States, 1910 (NARA microfilm publication T624, 1,178 rolls). Records of the Bureau of the Census, Record Group 29. National Archives, Washington), Ancestry.com, http://www.Ancestry.com, Year: 1910; Census Place: Ballplay, Etowah, Alabama; Roll: ; Page: ; Enumeration District: ; Image:. Birth date: about 1888 Birth place: Alabama Residence date: 1910 Residence place: Ballplay, Etowah, Alabama.

825   Ancestry.com, 1900 United States Federal Census (Online publication - Provo, UT, USA: Ancestry.com Operations Inc, 2004. Original data - United States of America, Bureau of the Census. Twelfth Census of the United States, 1900. Washington, D.C.: National Archives and Records Administration, 1900. T623, 18), Ancestry.com, http://www.Ancestry.com, Year: 1900; Census Place: Anniston Ward 2, Calhoun, Alabama; Roll: T623_5; Page: 1B; Enumeration District: 43. Birth date: Jul 1889 Birth place: Alabama Residence date: 1900 Residence place: Anniston City, Calhoun, Alabama.

826   Ancestry.com, 1920 United States Federal Census (Online publication - Provo, UT, USA: Ancestry.com Operations Inc, 2010. Images reproduced by FamilySearch. Original data - Fourteenth Census of the United States, 1920. (NARA microfilm publication T625, 2076 rolls). Records of the Bureau of the Census, Record), Ancestry.com, http://www.Ancestry.com, Year: 1920; Census Place: Greens Schoolhouse, Calhoun, Alabama; Roll: T625_5; Page: 6B; Enumeration District: 10; Image:. Birth date: about 1890 Birth place: Alabama Residence date: 1920 Residence place: Greens Schoolhouse, Calhoun, Alabama.

827   Ancestry.com, 1910 United States Federal Census (Online publication - Provo, UT, USA: Ancestry.com Operations Inc, 2006. Original data - Thirteenth Census of the United States, 1910 (NARA microfilm publication T624, 1,178 rolls). Records of the Bureau of the Census, Record Group 29. National Archives, Washington), Ancestry.com, http://www.Ancestry.com, Year: 1910; Census Place: Ballplay, Etowah, Alabama; Roll: ; Page: ; Enumeration District: ; Image:. Birth date: 1889 Birth place: Alabama Residence date: 1910 Residence place: Ballplay, Etowah, Alabama.

828   Ancestry.com, 1930 United States Federal Census (Online publication - Provo, UT, USA: Ancestry.com Operations Inc, 2002. Original data - United States of America, Bureau of the Census. Fifteenth Census of the United States, 1930. Washington, D.C.: National Archives and Records Administration, 1930. T626,), Ancestry.com, http://www.Ancestry.com, Year: 1930; Census Place: Greens Schoolhouse, Calhoun, Alabama; Roll: 5; Page: 5B; Enumeration District: 11; Image: 251.0. Birth date: about 1890 Birth place: Residence date: 1930 Residence place: Greens Schoolhouse, Calhoun, Alabama.

829   Ancestry.com, Alabama Deaths, 1908-59 (Online publication - Provo, UT, USA: Ancestry.com Operations Inc, 2000. Original data - State of Alabama. Index of Vital Records for Alabama: Deaths, 1908-1959. Montgomery, AL, USA: State of Alabama Center for Health Statistics, Record Services Division. Original), Ancestry.com, http://www.Ancestry.com, Death date: 15 Sep 1948 Death place: Calhoun.

830   Ancestry.com, 1900 United States Federal Census (Online publication - Provo, UT, USA: Ancestry.com Operations Inc, 2004. Original data - United States of America, Bureau of the Census. Twelfth Census of the United States, 1900. Washington, D.C.: National Archives and Records Administration, 1900. T623, 18), Ancestry.com, http://www.Ancestry.com, Year: 1900; Census Place: Anniston Ward 2, Calhoun, Alabama; Roll: T623_5; Page: 1B; Enumeration District: 43. Birth date: Jan 1892 Birth place: Alabama Residence date: 1900 Residence place: Anniston City, Calhoun, Alabama.

831   Ancestry.com, 1900 United States Federal Census (Online publication - Provo, UT, USA: Ancestry.com Operations Inc, 2004. Original data - United States of America, Bureau of the Census. Twelfth Census of the United States, 1900. Washington, D.C.: National Archives and Records Administration, 1900. T623, 18), Ancestry.com, http://www.Ancestry.com, Year: 1900; Census Place: Anniston Ward 2, Calhoun, Alabama; Roll: T623_5; Page: 1B; Enumeration District: 43. Birth date: May 1893 Birth place: Alabama Residence date: 1900 Residence place: Anniston City, Calhoun, Alabama.

832   Ancestry.com, 1910 United States Federal Census (Online publication - Provo, UT, USA: Ancestry.com Operations Inc, 2006. Original data - Thirteenth Census of the United States, 1910 (NARA microfilm publication T624, 1,178 rolls). Records of the Bureau of the Census, Record Group 29. National Archives, Washington), Ancestry.com, http://www.Ancestry.com, Year: 1910; Census Place: Ballplay, Etowah, Alabama; Roll: ; Page: ; Enumeration District: ; Image:. Birth date: about 1893 Birth place: Alabama Residence date: 1910 Residence place: Ballplay, Etowah, Alabama.

833   Ancestry.com, 1900 United States Federal Census (Online publication - Provo, UT, USA: Ancestry.com Operations Inc, 2004. Original data - United States of America, Bureau of the Census. Twelfth Census of the United States, 1900. Washington, D.C.: National Archives and Records Administration, 1900. T623, 18), Ancestry.com, http://www.Ancestry.com, Year: 1900; Census Place: Anniston Ward 2, Calhoun, Alabama; Roll: T623_5; Page: 1B; Enumeration District: 43. Birth date: Aug 1893 Birth place: Alabama Residence date: 1900 Residence place: Anniston City, Calhoun, Alabama.

834   Ancestry.com, 1910 United States Federal Census (Online publication - Provo, UT, USA: Ancestry.com Operations Inc, 2006. Original data - Thirteenth Census of the United States, 1910 (NARA microfilm publication T624, 1,178 rolls). Records of the Bureau of the Census, Record Group 29. National Archives, Washington), Ancestry.com, http://www.Ancestry.com, Year: 1910; Census Place: Ballplay, Etowah, Alabama; Roll: ; Page: ; Enumeration District: ; Image:. Birth date: about 1894 Birth place: Alabama Residence date: 1910 Residence place: Ballplay, Etowah, Alabama.

835   Ancestry.com, 1910 United States Federal Census (Online publication - Provo, UT, USA: Ancestry.com Operations Inc, 2006. Original data - Thirteenth Census of the United States, 1910 (NARA microfilm publication T624, 1,178 rolls). Records of the Bureau of the Census, Record Group 29. National Archives, Washington), Ancestry.com, http://www.Ancestry.com, Year: 1910; Census Place: Ballplay, Etowah, Alabama; Roll: ; Page: ; Enumeration District: ; Image:. Birth date: about 1896 Birth place: Alabama Residence date: 1910 Residence place: Ballplay, Etowah, Alabama.

836   Ancestry.com, 1900 United States Federal Census (Online publication - Provo, UT, USA: Ancestry.com Operations Inc, 2004. Original data - United States of America, Bureau of the Census. Twelfth Census of the United States, 1900. Washington, D.C.: National Archives and Records Administration, 1900. T623, 18), Ancestry.com, http://www.Ancestry.com, Year: 1900; Census Place: Anniston Ward 2, Calhoun, Alabama; Roll: T623_5; Page: 1B; Enumeration District: 43. Birth date: Feb 1896 Birth place: Alabama Residence date: 1900 Residence place: Anniston City, Calhoun, Alabama.

837   Ancestry.com, 1910 United States Federal Census (Online publication - Provo, UT, USA: Ancestry.com Operations Inc, 2006. Original data - Thirteenth Census of the United States, 1910 (NARA microfilm publication T624, 1,178 rolls). Records of the Bureau of the Census, Record Group 29. National Archives, Washington), Ancestry.com,

http://www.Ancestry.com, Year: 1910; Census Place: Ballplay, Etowah, Alabama; Roll: ; Page: ; Enumeration District: ; Image:. Birth date: about 1898 Birth place: Alabama Residence date: 1910 Residence place: Ballplay, Etowah, Alabama.

838   Ancestry.com, 1900 United States Federal Census (Online publication - Provo, UT, USA: Ancestry.com Operations Inc, 2004. Original data - United States of America, Bureau of the Census. Twelfth Census of the United States, 1900. Washington, D.C.: National Archives and Records Administration, 1900. T623, 18), Ancestry.com, http://www.Ancestry.com, Year: 1900; Census Place: Anniston Ward 2, Calhoun, Alabama; Roll: T623_5; Page: 1B; Enumeration District: 43. Birth date: Aug 1897 Birth place: Alabama Residence date: 1900 Residence place: Anniston City, Calhoun, Alabama.

839   Ancestry.com, 1910 United States Federal Census (Online publication - Provo, UT, USA: Ancestry.com Operations Inc, 2006. Original data - Thirteenth Census of the United States, 1910 (NARA microfilm publication T624, 1,178 rolls). Records of the Bureau of the Census, Record Group 29. National Archives, Washington), Ancestry.com, http://www.Ancestry.com, Year: 1910; Census Place: Ballplay, Etowah, Alabama; Roll: ; Page: ; Enumeration District: ; Image:. Birth date: about 1900 Birth place: Alabama Residence date: 1910 Residence place: Ballplay, Etowah, Alabama.

840   Ancestry.com, 1930 United States Federal Census (Online publication - Provo, UT, USA: Ancestry.com Operations Inc, 2002. Original data - United States of America, Bureau of the Census. Fifteenth Census of the United States, 1930. Washington, D.C.: National Archives and Records Administration, 1930. T626,), Ancestry.com, http://www.Ancestry.com, Year: 1930; Census Place: Hollingsworth, Calhoun, Alabama; Roll: 5; Page: 1B; Enumeration District: 10; Image: 225.0. Birth date: about 1901 Birth place: Residence date: 1930 Residence place: Hollingsworth, Calhoun, Alabama.

841   Ancestry.com, 1920 United States Federal Census (Online publication - Provo, UT, USA: Ancestry.com Operations Inc, 2010. Images reproduced by FamilySearch. Original data - Fourteenth Census of the United States, 1920. (NARA microfilm publication T625, 2076 rolls). Records of the Bureau of the Census, Record), Ancestry.com, http://www.Ancestry.com, Year: 1920; Census Place: Greens Schoolhouse, Calhoun, Alabama; Roll: T625_5; Page: 7B; Enumeration District: 10; Image:. Birth date: about 1904 Birth place: Alabama Residence date: 1920 Residence place: Greens Schoolhouse, Calhoun, Alabama.

842   Ancestry.com, 1910 United States Federal Census (Online publication - Provo, UT, USA: Ancestry.com Operations Inc, 2006. Original data - Thirteenth Census of the United States, 1910 (NARA microfilm publication T624, 1,178 rolls). Records of the Bureau of the Census, Record Group 29. National Archives, Washington), Ancestry.com, http://www.Ancestry.com, Year: 1910; Census Place: Ballplay, Etowah, Alabama; Roll: ; Page: ; Enumeration District: ; Image:. Birth date: 1903 Birth place: Alabama Residence date: 1910 Residence place: Ballplay, Etowah, Alabama.

843   Ancestry.com, 1900 United States Federal Census (Online publication - Provo, UT, USA: Ancestry.com Operations Inc, 2004. Original data - United States of America, Bureau of the Census. Twelfth Census of the United States, 1900. Washington, D.C.: National Archives and Records Administration, 1900. T623, 18), Ancestry.com, http://www.Ancestry.com, Year: 1900; Census Place: Oxford, Calhoun, Alabama; Roll: T623_5; Page: 8B; Enumeration District: 37. Birth date: Jan 1850 Birth place: Alabama Marriage date: 1869 Marriage place: Residence date: 1900 Residence place: Precinct 13 (Excl. Hobson & Oxford Towns), Calhoun, Alabama.

844   Ancestry.com, 1910 United States Federal Census (Online publication - Provo, UT, USA: Ancestry.com Operations Inc, 2006. Original data - Thirteenth Census of the United States, 1910 (NARA microfilm publication T624, 1,178 rolls). Records of the Bureau of the Census, Record Group 29. National Archives, Washington), Ancestry.com, http://www.Ancestry.com, Year: 1910; Census Place: Oxford, Calhoun, Alabama; Roll: ; Page: ; Enumeration District: ; Image:. Birth date: about 1850 Birth place: Mississippi Residence date: 1910 Residence place: Oxford, Calhoun, Alabama.

845   Ancestry.com, 1920 United States Federal Census (Online publication - Provo, UT, USA: Ancestry.com Operations Inc, 2010. Images reproduced by FamilySearch. Original data - Fourteenth Census of the United States, 1920. (NARA microfilm publication T625, 2076 rolls). Records of the Bureau of the Census, Record), Ancestry.com, http://www.Ancestry.com, Year: 1920; Census Place: Silver Run, Talladega, Alabama; Roll: T625_41; Page: 3B; Enumeration District: 131; Image:. Birth date: about 1850 Birth place: Alabama Residence date: 1920 Residence place: Silver Run, Talladega, Alabama.

846   Ancestry.com, 1900 United States Federal Census (Online publication - Provo, UT, USA: Ancestry.com Operations Inc, 2004. Original data - United States of America, Bureau of the Census. Twelfth Census of the United States, 1900. Washington, D.C.: National Archives and Records Administration, 1900. T623, 18), Ancestry.com, http://www.Ancestry.com, Year: 1900; Census Place: Oxford, Calhoun, Alabama; Roll: T623_5; Page: 8B; Enumeration District: 37. Birth date: Dec 1879 Birth place: Alabama Residence date: 1900 Residence place: Precinct 13 (Excl. Hobson & Oxford Towns), Calhoun, Alabama.

847   Ancestry.com, 1900 United States Federal Census (Online publication - Provo, UT, USA: Ancestry.com Operations Inc, 2004. Original data - United States of America, Bureau of the Census. Twelfth Census of the United States, 1900. Washington, D.C.: National Archives and Records Administration, 1900. T623, 18), Ancestry.com, http://www.Ancestry.com, Year: 1900; Census Place: Oxford, Calhoun, Alabama; Roll: T623_5; Page: 8B; Enumeration District: 37. Birth date: Aug 1886 Birth place: Alabama Residence date: 1900 Residence place: Precinct 13 (Excl. Hobson & Oxford Towns), Calhoun, Alabama.

848   Ancestry.com, 1910 United States Federal Census (Online publication - Provo, UT, USA: Ancestry.com Operations Inc, 2006. Original data - Thirteenth Census of the United States, 1910 (NARA microfilm publication T624, 1,178 rolls). Records of the Bureau of the Census, Record Group 29. National Archives, Washington), Ancestry.com,

http://www.Ancestry.com, Year: 1910; Census Place: Oxford, Calhoun, Alabama; Roll: ; Page: ; Enumeration District: ; Image:. Birth date: about 1887 Birth place: Alabama Residence date: 1910 Residence place: Oxford, Calhoun, Alabama.

849   Ancestry.com, 1900 United States Federal Census (Online publication - Provo, UT, USA: Ancestry.com Operations Inc, 2004. Original data - United States of America, Bureau of the Census. Twelfth Census of the United States, 1900. Washington, D.C.: National Archives and Records Administration, 1900. T623, 18), Ancestry.com, http://www.Ancestry.com, Year: 1900; Census Place: Oxford, Calhoun, Alabama; Roll: T623_5; Page: 8B; Enumeration District: 37. Birth date: Dec 1888 Birth place: Alabama Residence date: 1900 Residence place: Precinct 13 (Excl. Hobson & Oxford Towns), Calhoun, Alabama.

850   Ancestry.com, 1900 United States Federal Census (Online publication - Provo, UT, USA: Ancestry.com Operations Inc, 2004. Original data - United States of America, Bureau of the Census. Twelfth Census of the United States, 1900. Washington, D.C.: National Archives and Records Administration, 1900. T623, 18), Ancestry.com, http://www.Ancestry.com, Year: 1900; Census Place: Oxford, Calhoun, Alabama; Roll: T623_5; Page: 8B; Enumeration District: 37. Birth date: Aug 1890 Birth place: Alabama Residence date: 1900 Residence place: Precinct 13 (Excl. Hobson & Oxford Towns), Calhoun, Alabama.

851   Ancestry.com, 1910 United States Federal Census (Online publication - Provo, UT, USA: Ancestry.com Operations Inc, 2006. Original data - Thirteenth Census of the United States, 1910 (NARA microfilm publication T624, 1,178 rolls). Records of the Bureau of the Census, Record Group 29. National Archives, Washington), Ancestry.com, http://www.Ancestry.com, Year: 1910; Census Place: Oxford, Calhoun, Alabama; Roll: ; Page: ; Enumeration District: ; Image:. Birth date: about 1890 Birth place: Alabama Residence date: 1910 Residence place: Oxford, Calhoun, Alabama.

852   Ancestry.com, 1920 United States Federal Census (Online publication - Provo, UT, USA: Ancestry.com Operations Inc, 2010. Images reproduced by FamilySearch. Original data - Fourteenth Census of the United States, 1920. (NARA microfilm publication T625, 2076 rolls). Records of the Bureau of the Census, Record), Ancestry.com, http://www.Ancestry.com, Year: 1920; Census Place: Silver Run, Talladega, Alabama; Roll: T625_41; Page: 3B; Enumeration District: 131; Image:. Birth date: about 1892 Birth place: Alabama Residence date: 1920 Residence place: Silver Run, Talladega, Alabama.

853   Ancestry.com, 1900 United States Federal Census (Online publication - Provo, UT, USA: Ancestry.com Operations Inc, 2004. Original data - United States of America, Bureau of the Census. Twelfth Census of the United States, 1900. Washington, D.C.: National Archives and Records Administration, 1900. T623, 18), Ancestry.com, http://www.Ancestry.com, Year: 1900; Census Place: Oxford, Calhoun, Alabama; Roll: T623_5; Page: 10B; Enumeration District: 37. Birth date: Jul 1887 Birth place: Alabama Residence date: 1900 Residence place: Precinct 13 (Excl. Hobson & Oxford Towns), Calhoun, Alabama.

854   Ancestry.com, 1900 United States Federal Census (Online publication - Provo, UT, USA: Ancestry.com Operations Inc, 2004. Original data - United States of America, Bureau of the Census. Twelfth Census of the United States, 1900. Washington, D.C.: National Archives and Records Administration, 1900. T623, 18), Ancestry.com, http://www.Ancestry.com, Year: 1900; Census Place: Oxford, Calhoun, Alabama; Roll: T623_5; Page: 10B; Enumeration District: 37. Birth date: Jun 1877 Birth place: Alabama Marriage date: 1899 Marriage place: Residence date: 1900 Residence place: Precinct 13 (Excl. Hobson & Oxford Towns), Calhoun, Alabama.

855   Ancestry.com and The Church of Jesus Christ of Latter-day Saints, 1880 United States Federal Census (Online publication - Provo, UT, USA: Ancestry.com Operations Inc, 2010. 1880 U.S. Census Index provided by The Church of Jesus Christ of Latter-day Saints © Copyright 1999 Intellectual Reserve, Inc. All rights reserved. All use is subject to the limited), Ancestry.com, http://www.Ancestry.com, Year: 1880; Census Place: Allens, Calhoun, Alabama; Roll: 5; Family History Film: 1254005; Page: 645A; Enumeration District: 10; Image: 0031. Birth date: about 1878 Birth place: Alabama Residence date: 1880 Residence place: Allens, Calhoun, Alabama, United States.

856   Ancestry.com and The Church of Jesus Christ of Latter-day Saints, 1880 United States Federal Census (Online publication - Provo, UT, USA: Ancestry.com Operations Inc, 2010. 1880 U.S. Census Index provided by The Church of Jesus Christ of Latter-day Saints © Copyright 1999 Intellectual Reserve, Inc. All rights reserved. All use is subject to the limited), Ancestry.com, http://www.Ancestry.com, Year: 1880; Census Place: Allens, Calhoun, Alabama; Roll: 5; Family History Film: 1254005; Page: 645B; Enumeration District: 10; Image: 0032. Birth date: about 1880 Birth place: Alabama Residence date: 1880 Residence place: Allens, Calhoun, Alabama, United States.

857   Ancestry.com, 1900 United States Federal Census (Online publication - Provo, UT, USA: Ancestry.com Operations Inc, 2004. Original data - United States of America, Bureau of the Census. Twelfth Census of the United States, 1900. Washington, D.C.: National Archives and Records Administration, 1900. T623, 18), Ancestry.com, http://www.Ancestry.com, Year: 1900; Census Place: Oxford, Calhoun, Alabama; Roll: T623_5; Page: 10B; Enumeration District: 37. Birth date: Nov 1879 Birth place: Alabama Residence date: 1900 Residence place: Precinct 13 (Excl. Hobson & Oxford Towns), Calhoun, Alabama.

858   Ancestry.com, 1910 United States Federal Census (Online publication - Provo, UT, USA: Ancestry.com Operations Inc, 2006. Original data - Thirteenth Census of the United States, 1910 (NARA microfilm publication T624, 1,178 rolls). Records of the Bureau of the Census, Record Group 29. National Archives, Washington), Ancestry.com, http://www.Ancestry.com, Year: 1910; Census Place: Oxford, Calhoun, Alabama; Roll: ; Page: ; Enumeration District: ; Image:. Birth date: about 1880 Birth place: Alabama Residence date: 1910 Residence place: Oxford, Calhoun, Alabama.

859   Ancestry.com, 1920 United States Federal Census (Online publication - Provo, UT, USA: Ancestry.com Operations Inc, 2010. Images reproduced by FamilySearch. Original data - Fourteenth Census of the United States, 1920. (NARA microfilm publication T625, 2076 rolls). Records of the Bureau of the Census, Record), Ancestry.com,

http://www.Ancestry.com, Year: 1920; Census Place: Oxford, Calhoun, Alabama; Roll: T625_5; Page: 10B; Enumeration District: 16; Image:. Birth date: about 1879 Birth place: Alabama Residence date: 1920 Residence place: Oxford, Calhoun, Alabama.

860   Ancestry.com, 1930 United States Federal Census (Online publication - Provo, UT, USA: Ancestry.com Operations Inc, 2002. Original data - United States of America, Bureau of the Census. Fifteenth Census of the United States, 1930. Washington, D.C.: National Archives and Records Administration, 1930. T626,), Ancestry.com, http://www.Ancestry.com, Year: 1930; Census Place: Oxford, Calhoun, Alabama; Roll: 5; Page: 1A; Enumeration District: 20; Image: 476.0. Birth date: about 1880 Birth place: Alabama Residence date: 1930 Residence place: Oxford, Calhoun, Alabama.

861   Ancestry.com, 1900 United States Federal Census (Online publication - Provo, UT, USA: Ancestry.com Operations Inc, 2004. Original data - United States of America, Bureau of the Census. Twelfth Census of the United States, 1900. Washington, D.C.: National Archives and Records Administration, 1900. T623, 18), Ancestry.com, http://www.Ancestry.com, Year: 1900; Census Place: Oxford, Calhoun, Alabama; Roll: T623_5; Page: 10B; Enumeration District: 37. Birth date: Nov 1884 Birth place: Alabama Residence date: 1900 Residence place: Precinct 13 (Excl. Hobson & Oxford Towns), Calhoun, Alabama.

862   Ancestry.com, 1900 United States Federal Census (Online publication - Provo, UT, USA: Ancestry.com Operations Inc, 2004. Original data - United States of America, Bureau of the Census. Twelfth Census of the United States, 1900. Washington, D.C.: National Archives and Records Administration, 1900. T623, 18), Ancestry.com, http://www.Ancestry.com, Year: 1900; Census Place: Oxford, Calhoun, Alabama; Roll: T623_5; Page: 10B; Enumeration District: 37. Birth date: Oct 1891 Birth place: Alabama Residence date: 1900 Residence place: Precinct 13 (Excl. Hobson & Oxford Towns), Calhoun, Alabama.

863   Ancestry.com, World War I Draft Registration Cards, 1917-1918 (Online publication - Provo, UT, USA: Ancestry.com Operations Inc, 2005. Original data - United States, Selective Service System. World War I Selective Service System Draft Registration Cards, 1917-1918. Washington, D.C.: National Archives and Records Administration), Ancestry.com, http://www.Ancestry.com, Registration Location: Calhoun County, Alabama; Roll: 1509363; Draft Board: 0. Birth date: 15 Oct 1892 Birth place: Alabama; United States of America Residence date: Residence place: Calhoun, Alabama.

864   Ancestry.com, 1900 United States Federal Census (Online publication - Provo, UT, USA: Ancestry.com Operations Inc, 2004. Original data - United States of America, Bureau of the Census. Twelfth Census of the United States, 1900. Washington, D.C.: National Archives and Records Administration, 1900. T623, 18), Ancestry.com, http://www.Ancestry.com, Year: 1900; Census Place: Oxford, Calhoun, Alabama; Roll: T623_5; Page: 10B; Enumeration District: 37. Birth date: Apr 1895 Birth place: Alabama Residence date: 1900 Residence place: Precinct 13 (Excl. Hobson & Oxford Towns), Calhoun, Alabama.

865   Ancestry.com, 1900 United States Federal Census (Online publication - Provo, UT, USA: Ancestry.com Operations Inc, 2004. Original data - United States of America, Bureau of the Census. Twelfth Census of the United States, 1900. Washington, D.C.: National Archives and Records Administration, 1900. T623, 18), Ancestry.com, http://www.Ancestry.com, Year: 1900; Census Place: Oxford, Calhoun, Alabama; Roll: T623_5; Page: 10B; Enumeration District: 37. Birth date: Jun 1898 Birth place: Alabama Residence date: 1900 Residence place: Precinct 13 (Excl. Hobson & Oxford Towns), Calhoun, Alabama.

866   Ancestry.com, 1920 United States Federal Census (Online publication - Provo, UT, USA: Ancestry.com Operations Inc, 2010. Images reproduced by FamilySearch. Original data - Fourteenth Census of the United States, 1920. (NARA microfilm publication T625, 2076 rolls). Records of the Bureau of the Census, Record), Ancestry.com, http://www.Ancestry.com, Year: 1920; Census Place: Oxford, Calhoun, Alabama; Roll: T625_5; Page: 11A; Enumeration District: 16; Image:. Birth date: about 1899 Birth place: Alabama Residence date: 1920 Residence place: Oxford, Calhoun, Alabama.

867   Ancestry.com, Social Security Death Index (Online publication - Provo, UT, USA: Ancestry.com Operations Inc, 2010. Original data - Social Security Administration. Social Security Death Index, Master File. Social Security Administration. Original data: Social Security Administration. Social Security D), Ancestry.com, http://www.Ancestry.com, Number: 422-18-3129; Issue State: Alabama; Issue Date: Before 1951. Birth date: 10 Jun 1898 Birth place: Death date: 1 Jun 1964 Death place: Alabama, United States of America.

868   Ancestry.com, 1910 United States Federal Census (Online publication - Provo, UT, USA: Ancestry.com Operations Inc, 2006. Original data - Thirteenth Census of the United States, 1910 (NARA microfilm publication T624, 1,178 rolls). Records of the Bureau of the Census, Record Group 29. National Archives, Washington), Ancestry.com, http://www.Ancestry.com, Year: 1910; Census Place: Oxford, Calhoun, Alabama; Roll: ; Page: ; Enumeration District: ; Image:. Birth date: about 1899 Birth place: Alabama Residence date: 1910 Residence place: Oxford, Calhoun, Alabama.

869   Ancestry.com, 1920 United States Federal Census (Online publication - Provo, UT, USA: Ancestry.com Operations Inc, 2010. Images reproduced by FamilySearch. Original data - Fourteenth Census of the United States, 1920. (NARA microfilm publication T625, 2076 rolls). Records of the Bureau of the Census, Record), Ancestry.com, http://www.Ancestry.com, Year: 1920; Census Place: Oxford, Calhoun, Alabama; Roll: T625_5; Page: 11A; Enumeration District: 16; Image:. Birth date: about 1901 Birth place: Alabama Residence date: 1920 Residence place: Oxford, Calhoun, Alabama.

870   Ancestry.com, 1930 United States Federal Census (Online publication - Provo, UT, USA: Ancestry.com Operations Inc, 2002. Original data - United States of America, Bureau of the Census. Fifteenth Census of the United

States, 1930. Washington, D.C.: National Archives and Records Administration, 1930. T626,), Ancestry.com, http://www.Ancestry.com, Year: 1930; Census Place: Oxford, Calhoun, Alabama; Roll: 5; Page: 3A; Enumeration District: 20; Image: 480.0. Birth date: about 1901 Birth place: Residence date: 1930 Residence place: Oxford, Calhoun, Alabama.

871   Ancestry.com, 1910 United States Federal Census (Online publication - Provo, UT, USA: Ancestry.com Operations Inc, 2006. Original data - Thirteenth Census of the United States, 1910 (NARA microfilm publication T624, 1,178 rolls). Records of the Bureau of the Census, Record Group 29. National Archives, Washington), Ancestry.com, http://www.Ancestry.com, Year: 1910; Census Place: Oxford, Calhoun, Alabama; Roll: ; Page: ; Enumeration District: ; Image:. Birth date: about 1901 Birth place: Alabama Residence date: 1910 Residence place: Oxford, Calhoun, Alabama.

872   Ancestry.com, 1920 United States Federal Census (Online publication - Provo, UT, USA: Ancestry.com Operations Inc, 2010. Images reproduced by FamilySearch. Original data - Fourteenth Census of the United States, 1920. (NARA microfilm publication T625, 2076 rolls). Records of the Bureau of the Census, Record), Ancestry.com, http://www.Ancestry.com, Year: 1920; Census Place: Oxford, Calhoun, Alabama; Roll: T625_5; Page: 11A; Enumeration District: 16; Image:. Birth date: about 1904 Birth place: Alabama Residence date: 1920 Residence place: Oxford, Calhoun, Alabama.

873   Ancestry.com, 1900 United States Federal Census (Online publication - Provo, UT, USA: Ancestry.com Operations Inc, 2004. Original data - United States of America, Bureau of the Census. Twelfth Census of the United States, 1900. Washington, D.C.: National Archives and Records Administration, 1900. T623, 18), Ancestry.com, http://www.Ancestry.com, Year: 1900; Census Place: Bluff Eye, Talladega, Alabama; Roll: T623_40; Page: 10A; Enumeration District: 84. Birth date: Nov 1866 Birth place: Alabama Marriage date: 1885 Marriage place: Residence date: 1900 Residence place: Bluff Eye, Talladega, Alabama.

874   Ancestry.com, 1900 United States Federal Census (Online publication - Provo, UT, USA: Ancestry.com Operations Inc, 2004. Original data - United States of America, Bureau of the Census. Twelfth Census of the United States, 1900. Washington, D.C.: National Archives and Records Administration, 1900. T623, 18), Ancestry.com, http://www.Ancestry.com, Year: 1900; Census Place: Bluff Eye, Talladega, Alabama; Roll: T623_40; Page: 10A; Enumeration District: 84. Birth date: Mar 1886 Birth place: Alabama Residence date: 1900 Residence place: Bluff Eye, Talladega, Alabama.

875   Ancestry.com, 1900 United States Federal Census (Online publication - Provo, UT, USA: Ancestry.com Operations Inc, 2004. Original data - United States of America, Bureau of the Census. Twelfth Census of the United States, 1900. Washington, D.C.: National Archives and Records Administration, 1900. T623, 18), Ancestry.com, http://www.Ancestry.com, Year: 1900; Census Place: Bluff Eye, Talladega, Alabama; Roll: T623_40; Page: 10A; Enumeration District: 84. Birth date: Jan 1888 Birth place: Alabama Residence date: 1900 Residence place: Bluff Eye, Talladega, Alabama.

876   Ancestry.com, 1900 United States Federal Census (Online publication - Provo, UT, USA: Ancestry.com Operations Inc, 2004. Original data - United States of America, Bureau of the Census. Twelfth Census of the United States, 1900. Washington, D.C.: National Archives and Records Administration, 1900. T623, 18), Ancestry.com, http://www.Ancestry.com, Year: 1900; Census Place: Bluff Eye, Talladega, Alabama; Roll: T623_40; Page: 10A; Enumeration District: 84. Birth date: Apr 1890 Birth place: Alabama Residence date: 1900 Residence place: Bluff Eye, Talladega, Alabama.

877   Ancestry.com, 1900 United States Federal Census (Online publication - Provo, UT, USA: Ancestry.com Operations Inc, 2004. Original data - United States of America, Bureau of the Census. Twelfth Census of the United States, 1900. Washington, D.C.: National Archives and Records Administration, 1900. T623, 18), Ancestry.com, http://www.Ancestry.com, Year: 1900; Census Place: Bluff Eye, Talladega, Alabama; Roll: T623_40; Page: 10A; Enumeration District: 84. Birth date: May 1892 Birth place: Alabama Residence date: 1900 Residence place: Bluff Eye, Talladega, Alabama.

878   Ancestry.com, 1900 United States Federal Census (Online publication - Provo, UT, USA: Ancestry.com Operations Inc, 2004. Original data - United States of America, Bureau of the Census. Twelfth Census of the United States, 1900. Washington, D.C.: National Archives and Records Administration, 1900. T623, 18), Ancestry.com, http://www.Ancestry.com, Year: 1900; Census Place: Bluff Eye, Talladega, Alabama; Roll: T623_40; Page: 10A; Enumeration District: 84. Birth date: Jun 1893 Birth place: Alabama Residence date: 1900 Residence place: Bluff Eye, Talladega, Alabama.

879   Ancestry.com, 1900 United States Federal Census (Online publication - Provo, UT, USA: Ancestry.com Operations Inc, 2004. Original data - United States of America, Bureau of the Census. Twelfth Census of the United States, 1900. Washington, D.C.: National Archives and Records Administration, 1900. T623, 18), Ancestry.com, http://www.Ancestry.com, Year: 1900; Census Place: Bluff Eye, Talladega, Alabama; Roll: T623_40; Page: 10A; Enumeration District: 84. Birth date: Nov 1897 Birth place: Alabama Residence date: 1900 Residence place: Bluff Eye, Talladega, Alabama.

880   Ancestry.com, World War I Draft Registration Cards, 1917-1918 (Online publication - Provo, UT, USA: Ancestry.com Operations Inc, 2005. Original data - United States, Selective Service System. World War I Selective Service System Draft Registration Cards, 1917-1918. Washington, D.C.: National Archives and Records Administration), Ancestry.com, http://www.Ancestry.com, Registration Location: Lincoln County, Louisiana; Roll: 1684810; Draft Board: 0. Birth date: 6 Sep 1880 Birth place: Residence date: Residence place: Lincoln, Louisiana.

881   Ancestry.com, Louisiana Statewide Death Index, 1900-1949 (Online publication - Provo, UT, USA: Ancestry.com Operations Inc, 2002. Original data - State of Louisiana, Secretary of State, Division of Archives, Records

189

Management, and History. Vital Records Indices. Baton Rouge, LA, USA. Original data: State of Louisiana), Ancestry.com, http://www.Ancestry.com, Birth date: 1883 Birth place: Death date: 14 Aug 1918 Death place: Louisiana.

882   Ancestry.com, Social Security Death Index (Online publication - Provo, UT, USA: Ancestry.com Operations Inc, 2010. Original data - Social Security Administration. Social Security Death Index, Master File. Social Security Administration. Original data: Social Security Administration. Social Security D), Ancestry.com, http://www.Ancestry.com, Number: 465-10-8935; Issue State: Texas; Issue Date: Before 1951. Birth date: 15 Mar 1885 Birth place: Death date: Oct 1967 Death place: Shreveport, Caddo, Louisiana, United States of America.

883   Ancestry.com, 1900 United States Federal Census (Online publication - Provo, UT, USA: Ancestry.com Operations Inc, 2004. Original data - United States of America, Bureau of the Census. Twelfth Census of the United States, 1900. Washington, D.C.: National Archives and Records Administration, 1900. T623, 18), Ancestry.com, http://www.Ancestry.com, Year: 1900; Census Place: Talladega, Talladega, Alabama; Roll: T623_40; Page: 22A; Enumeration District: 90. Birth date: May 1860 Birth place: Alabama Marriage date: 1877 Marriage place: Residence date: 1900 Residence place: Talladega, Talladega, Alabama.

884   Ancestry.com, 1900 United States Federal Census (Online publication - Provo, UT, USA: Ancestry.com Operations Inc, 2004. Original data - United States of America, Bureau of the Census. Twelfth Census of the United States, 1900. Washington, D.C.: National Archives and Records Administration, 1900. T623, 18), Ancestry.com, http://www.Ancestry.com, Year: 1900; Census Place: Talladega, Talladega, Alabama; Roll: T623_40; Page: 22A; Enumeration District: 90. Birth date: Jun 1881 Birth place: Alabama Residence date: 1900 Residence place: Talladega, Talladega, Alabama.

885   Ancestry.com, 1900 United States Federal Census (Online publication - Provo, UT, USA: Ancestry.com Operations Inc, 2004. Original data - United States of America, Bureau of the Census. Twelfth Census of the United States, 1900. Washington, D.C.: National Archives and Records Administration, 1900. T623, 18), Ancestry.com, http://www.Ancestry.com, Year: 1900; Census Place: Talladega, Talladega, Alabama; Roll: T623_40; Page: 22A; Enumeration District: 90. Birth date: Jun 1883 Birth place: Alabama Marriage date: 1898 Marriage place: Residence date: 1900 Residence place: Talladega, Talladega, Alabama.

886   Ancestry.com, 1900 United States Federal Census (Online publication - Provo, UT, USA: Ancestry.com Operations Inc, 2004. Original data - United States of America, Bureau of the Census. Twelfth Census of the United States, 1900. Washington, D.C.: National Archives and Records Administration, 1900. T623, 18), Ancestry.com, http://www.Ancestry.com, Year: 1900; Census Place: Talladega, Talladega, Alabama; Roll: T623_40; Page: 22A; Enumeration District: 90. Birth date: May 1886 Birth place: Alabama Residence date: 1900 Residence place: Talladega, Talladega, Alabama.

887   Ancestry.com, 1900 United States Federal Census (Online publication - Provo, UT, USA: Ancestry.com Operations Inc, 2004. Original data - United States of America, Bureau of the Census. Twelfth Census of the United States, 1900. Washington, D.C.: National Archives and Records Administration, 1900. T623, 18), Ancestry.com, http://www.Ancestry.com, Year: 1900; Census Place: Talladega, Talladega, Alabama; Roll: T623_40; Page: 22A; Enumeration District: 90. Birth date: Apr 1888 Birth place: Alabama Residence date: 1900 Residence place: Talladega, Talladega, Alabama.

888   Ancestry.com, 1900 United States Federal Census (Online publication - Provo, UT, USA: Ancestry.com Operations Inc, 2004. Original data - United States of America, Bureau of the Census. Twelfth Census of the United States, 1900. Washington, D.C.: National Archives and Records Administration, 1900. T623, 18), Ancestry.com, http://www.Ancestry.com, Year: 1900; Census Place: Talladega, Talladega, Alabama; Roll: T623_40; Page: 22A; Enumeration District: 90. Birth date: Dec 1891 Birth place: Alabama Residence date: 1900 Residence place: Talladega, Talladega, Alabama.

889   Ancestry.com, 1900 United States Federal Census (Online publication - Provo, UT, USA: Ancestry.com Operations Inc, 2004. Original data - United States of America, Bureau of the Census. Twelfth Census of the United States, 1900. Washington, D.C.: National Archives and Records Administration, 1900. T623, 18), Ancestry.com, http://www.Ancestry.com, Year: 1900; Census Place: Talladega, Talladega, Alabama; Roll: T623_40; Page: 22A; Enumeration District: 90. Birth date: Jun 1897 Birth place: Alabama Residence date: 1900 Residence place: Talladega, Talladega, Alabama.

890   Ancestry.com, 1900 United States Federal Census (Online publication - Provo, UT, USA: Ancestry.com Operations Inc, 2004. Original data - United States of America, Bureau of the Census. Twelfth Census of the United States, 1900. Washington, D.C.: National Archives and Records Administration, 1900. T623, 18), Ancestry.com, http://www.Ancestry.com, Year: 1900; Census Place: Munford, Talladega, Alabama; Roll: T623_41; Page: 14A; Enumeration District: 100. Birth date: Sep 1879 Birth place: Alabama Marriage date: 1899 Marriage place: Residence date: 1900 Residence place: Munford, Talladega, Alabama.

891   Ancestry.com, 1920 United States Federal Census (Online publication - Provo, UT, USA: Ancestry.com Operations Inc, 2010. Images reproduced by FamilySearch. Original data - Fourteenth Census of the United States, 1920. (NARA microfilm publication T625, 2076 rolls). Records of the Bureau of the Census, Record), Ancestry.com, http://www.Ancestry.com, Year: 1920; Census Place: Oxford, Calhoun, Alabama; Roll: T625_5; Page: 10B; Enumeration District: 16; Image:. Birth date: about 1879 Birth place: Alabama Residence date: 1920 Residence place: Oxford, Calhoun, Alabama.

892   Ancestry.com, 1930 United States Federal Census (Online publication - Provo, UT, USA: Ancestry.com Operations Inc, 2002. Original data - United States of America, Bureau of the Census. Fifteenth Census of the United

States, 1930. Washington, D.C.: National Archives and Records Administration, 1930. T626,), Ancestry.com, http://www.Ancestry.com, Year: 1930; Census Place: Alexandria, Calhoun, Alabama; Roll: 5; Page: 5A; Enumeration District: 4; Image: 100.0. Birth date: about 1879 Birth place: Residence date: 1930 Residence place: Alexandria, Calhoun, Alabama.

893   Ancestry.com, 1920 United States Federal Census (Online publication - Provo, UT, USA: Ancestry.com Operations Inc, 2010. Images reproduced by FamilySearch. Original data - Fourteenth Census of the United States, 1920. (NARA microfilm publication T625, 2076 rolls). Records of the Bureau of the Census, Record), Ancestry.com, http://www.Ancestry.com, Year: 1920; Census Place: Oxford, Calhoun, Alabama; Roll: T625_5; Page: 10B; Enumeration District: 16; Image:. Birth date: about 1902 Birth place: Alabama Residence date: 1920 Residence place: Oxford, Calhoun, Alabama.

894   Ancestry.com, 1920 United States Federal Census (Online publication - Provo, UT, USA: Ancestry.com Operations Inc, 2010. Images reproduced by FamilySearch. Original data - Fourteenth Census of the United States, 1920. (NARA microfilm publication T625, 2076 rolls). Records of the Bureau of the Census, Record), Ancestry.com, http://www.Ancestry.com, Year: 1920; Census Place: Oxford, Calhoun, Alabama; Roll: T625_5; Page: 10B; Enumeration District: 16; Image:. Birth date: about 1902 Birth place: Arkansas Residence date: 1920 Residence place: Oxford, Calhoun, Alabama.

895   Ancestry.com, 1920 United States Federal Census (Online publication - Provo, UT, USA: Ancestry.com Operations Inc, 2010. Images reproduced by FamilySearch. Original data - Fourteenth Census of the United States, 1920. (NARA microfilm publication T625, 2076 rolls). Records of the Bureau of the Census, Record), Ancestry.com, http://www.Ancestry.com, Year: 1920; Census Place: Oxford, Calhoun, Alabama; Roll: T625_5; Page: 10B; Enumeration District: 16; Image:. Birth date: about 1906 Birth place: Arkansas Residence date: 1920 Residence place: Oxford, Calhoun, Alabama.

896   Ancestry.com, 1920 United States Federal Census (Online publication - Provo, UT, USA: Ancestry.com Operations Inc, 2010. Images reproduced by FamilySearch. Original data - Fourteenth Census of the United States, 1920. (NARA microfilm publication T625, 2076 rolls). Records of the Bureau of the Census, Record), Ancestry.com, http://www.Ancestry.com, Year: 1920; Census Place: Oxford, Calhoun, Alabama; Roll: T625_5; Page: 10B; Enumeration District: 16; Image:. Birth date: about 1908 Birth place: Arkansas Residence date: 1920 Residence place: Oxford, Calhoun, Alabama.

897   Ancestry.com, 1920 United States Federal Census (Online publication - Provo, UT, USA: Ancestry.com Operations Inc, 2010. Images reproduced by FamilySearch. Original data - Fourteenth Census of the United States, 1920. (NARA microfilm publication T625, 2076 rolls). Records of the Bureau of the Census, Record), Ancestry.com, http://www.Ancestry.com, Year: 1920; Census Place: Oxford, Calhoun, Alabama; Roll: T625_5; Page: 10B; Enumeration District: 16; Image:. Birth date: about 1910 Birth place: Arkansas Residence date: 1920 Residence place: Oxford, Calhoun, Alabama.

898   Ancestry.com, 1930 United States Federal Census (Online publication - Provo, UT, USA: Ancestry.com Operations Inc, 2002. Original data - United States of America, Bureau of the Census. Fifteenth Census of the United States, 1930. Washington, D.C.: National Archives and Records Administration, 1930. T626,), Ancestry.com, http://www.Ancestry.com, Year: 1930; Census Place: Alexandria, Calhoun, Alabama; Roll: 5; Page: 5A; Enumeration District: 4; Image: 100.0. Birth date: about 1910 Birth place: Residence date: 1930 Residence place: Alexandria, Calhoun, Alabama.

899   Ancestry.com, 1920 United States Federal Census (Online publication - Provo, UT, USA: Ancestry.com Operations Inc, 2010. Images reproduced by FamilySearch. Original data - Fourteenth Census of the United States, 1920. (NARA microfilm publication T625, 2076 rolls). Records of the Bureau of the Census, Record), Ancestry.com, http://www.Ancestry.com, Year: 1920; Census Place: Oxford, Calhoun, Alabama; Roll: T625_5; Page: 10B; Enumeration District: 16; Image:. Birth date: about 1911 Birth place: Arkansas Residence date: 1920 Residence place: Oxford, Calhoun, Alabama.

900   Ancestry.com, 1920 United States Federal Census (Online publication - Provo, UT, USA: Ancestry.com Operations Inc, 2010. Images reproduced by FamilySearch. Original data - Fourteenth Census of the United States, 1920. (NARA microfilm publication T625, 2076 rolls). Records of the Bureau of the Census, Record), Ancestry.com, http://www.Ancestry.com, Year: 1920; Census Place: Oxford, Calhoun, Alabama; Roll: T625_5; Page: 10B; Enumeration District: 16; Image:. Birth date: about 1914 Birth place: Arkansas Residence date: 1920 Residence place: Oxford, Calhoun, Alabama.

901   Ancestry.com, 1930 United States Federal Census (Online publication - Provo, UT, USA: Ancestry.com Operations Inc, 2002. Original data - United States of America, Bureau of the Census. Fifteenth Census of the United States, 1930. Washington, D.C.: National Archives and Records Administration, 1930. T626,), Ancestry.com, http://www.Ancestry.com, Year: 1930; Census Place: Alexandria, Calhoun, Alabama; Roll: 5; Page: 5A; Enumeration District: 4; Image: 100.0. Birth date: about 1914 Birth place: Residence date: 1930 Residence place: Alexandria, Calhoun, Alabama.

902   Ancestry.com, 1930 United States Federal Census (Online publication - Provo, UT, USA: Ancestry.com Operations Inc, 2002. Original data - United States of America, Bureau of the Census. Fifteenth Census of the United States, 1930. Washington, D.C.: National Archives and Records Administration, 1930. T626,), Ancestry.com, http://www.Ancestry.com, Year: 1930; Census Place: Alexandria, Calhoun, Alabama; Roll: 5; Page: 5A; Enumeration

District: 4; Image: 100.0. Birth date: about 1916 Birth place: Residence date: 1930 Residence place: Alexandria, Calhoun, Alabama.

903   Ancestry.com, 1920 United States Federal Census (Online publication - Provo, UT, USA: Ancestry.com Operations Inc, 2010. Images reproduced by FamilySearch. Original data - Fourteenth Census of the United States, 1920. (NARA microfilm publication T625, 2076 rolls). Records of the Bureau of the Census, Record), Ancestry.com, http://www.Ancestry.com, Year: 1920; Census Place: Oxford, Calhoun, Alabama; Roll: T625_5; Page: 10B; Enumeration District: 16; Image:. Birth date: about 1920 Birth place: Alabama Residence date: 1920 Residence place: Oxford, Calhoun, Alabama.

904   Ancestry.com, 1930 United States Federal Census (Online publication - Provo, UT, USA: Ancestry.com Operations Inc, 2002. Original data - United States of America, Bureau of the Census. Fifteenth Census of the United States, 1930. Washington, D.C.: National Archives and Records Administration, 1930. T626,), Ancestry.com, http://www.Ancestry.com, Year: 1930; Census Place: Alexandria, Calhoun, Alabama; Roll: 5; Page: 5A; Enumeration District: 4; Image: 100.0. Birth date: about 1920 Birth place: Residence date: 1930 Residence place: Alexandria, Calhoun, Alabama.

905   Ancestry.com, 1900 United States Federal Census (Online publication - Provo, UT, USA: Ancestry.com Operations Inc, 2004. Original data - United States of America, Bureau of the Census. Twelfth Census of the United States, 1900. Washington, D.C.: National Archives and Records Administration, 1900. T623, 18), Ancestry.com, http://www.Ancestry.com, Year: 1900; Census Place: Weavers, Calhoun, Alabama; Roll: T623_5; Page: 5A; Enumeration District: 27. Birth date: Jun 1861 Birth place: Alabama Marriage date: 1879 Marriage place: Residence date: 1900 Residence place: Weavers, Calhoun, Alabama.

906   Ancestry.com, 1920 United States Federal Census (Online publication - Provo, UT, USA: Ancestry.com Operations Inc, 2010. Images reproduced by FamilySearch. Original data - Fourteenth Census of the United States, 1920. (NARA microfilm publication T625, 2076 rolls). Records of the Bureau of the Census, Record), Ancestry.com, http://www.Ancestry.com, Year: 1920; Census Place: Anniston Ward 5, Calhoun, Alabama; Roll: T625_5; Page: 5A; Enumeration District: 156; Image:. Birth date: about 1862 Birth place: Alabama Residence date: 1920 Residence place: Anniston Ward 5, Calhoun, Alabama.

907   Ancestry.com and The Church of Jesus Christ of Latter-day Saints, 1880 United States Federal Census (Online publication - Provo, UT, USA: Ancestry.com Operations Inc, 2010. 1880 U.S. Census Index provided by The Church of Jesus Christ of Latter-day Saints © Copyright 1999 Intellectual Reserve, Inc. All rights reserved. All use is subject to the limited), Ancestry.com, http://www.Ancestry.com, Year: 1880; Census Place: June Bug, Calhoun, Alabama; Roll: 4; Family History Film: 1254004; Page: 533B; Enumeration District: 6; Image: 0627. Birth date: about 1859 Birth place: Alabama Residence date: 1880 Residence place: June Bug, Calhoun, Alabama, United States.

908   Ancestry.com, 1930 United States Federal Census (Online publication - Provo, UT, USA: Ancestry.com Operations Inc, 2002. Original data - United States of America, Bureau of the Census. Fifteenth Census of the United States, 1930. Washington, D.C.: National Archives and Records Administration, 1930. T626,), Ancestry.com, http://www.Ancestry.com, Year: 1930; Census Place: Oxford, Calhoun, Alabama; Roll: 5; Page: 7A; Enumeration District: 19; Image: 462.0. Birth date: about 1862 Birth place: Residence date: 1930 Residence place: Oxford, Calhoun, Alabama.

909   Ancestry.com, 1870 United States Federal Census (Online publication - Provo, UT, USA: Ancestry.com Operations, Inc., 2009. Images reproduced by FamilySearch. Original data - 1870 U.S. census, population schedules. NARA microfilm publication M593, 1,761 rolls. Washington, D.C.: National Archives and Record), Ancestry.com, http://www.Ancestry.com, Year: 1870; Census Place: Township 15, Calhoun, Alabama; Roll: M593_; Page: ; Image:. Birth date: about 1861 Birth place: Alabama Residence date: 1870 Residence place: Township 15, Calhoun, Alabama, United States.

910   Ancestry.com, 1910 United States Federal Census (Online publication - Provo, UT, USA: Ancestry.com Operations Inc, 2006. Original data - Thirteenth Census of the United States, 1910 (NARA microfilm publication T624, 1,178 rolls). Records of the Bureau of the Census, Record Group 29. National Archives, Washington), Ancestry.com, http://www.Ancestry.com, Year: 1910; Census Place: Weaver, Calhoun, Alabama; Roll: ; Page: ; Enumeration District: ; Image:. Birth date: about 1862 Birth place: Alabama Residence date: 1910 Residence place: Weaver, Calhoun, Alabama.

911   Ancestry.com, Alabama Deaths, 1908-59 (Online publication - Provo, UT, USA: Ancestry.com Operations Inc, 2000. Original data - State of Alabama. Index of Vital Records for Alabama: Deaths, 1908-1959. Montgomery, AL, USA: State of Alabama Center for Health Statistics, Record Services Division. Original), Ancestry.com, http://www.Ancestry.com, Death date: Nov 1933 Death place: Calhoun.

912   Ancestry.com, 1930 United States Federal Census (Online publication - Provo, UT, USA: Ancestry.com Operations Inc, 2002. Original data - United States of America, Bureau of the Census. Fifteenth Census of the United States, 1930. Washington, D.C.: National Archives and Records Administration, 1930. T626,), Ancestry.com, http://www.Ancestry.com, Year: 1930; Census Place: Weavers, Calhoun, Alabama; Roll: 5; Page: 4A; Enumeration District: 5; Image: 128.0. Birth date: about 1880 Birth place: Residence date: 1930 Residence place: Weavers, Calhoun, Alabama.

913   Ancestry.com, Social Security Death Index (Online publication - Provo, UT, USA: Ancestry.com Operations Inc, 2010. Original data - Social Security Administration. Social Security Death Index, Master File. Social Security Administration. Original data: Social Security Administration. Social Security D), Ancestry.com, http://www.Ancestry.com, Number: 261-60-6484; Issue State: Florida; Issue Date: 1956. Birth date: 24 Nov 1879 Birth place: Death date: Jan 1975 Death place: Homestead, Miami-Dade, Florida, United States of America.

914	Ancestry.com, 1920 United States Federal Census (Online publication - Provo, UT, USA: Ancestry.com Operations Inc, 2010. Images reproduced by FamilySearch. Original data - Fourteenth Census of the United States, 1920. (NARA microfilm publication T625, 2076 rolls). Records of the Bureau of the Census, Record), Ancestry.com, http://www.Ancestry.com, Year: 1920; Census Place: Weavers, Calhoun, Alabama; Roll: T625_5; Page: 10B; Enumeration District: 4; Image:. Birth date: about 1880 Birth place: Alabama Residence date: 1920 Residence place: Weavers, Calhoun, Alabama.

915	Ancestry.com and The Church of Jesus Christ of Latter-day Saints, 1880 United States Federal Census (Online publication - Provo, UT, USA: Ancestry.com Operations Inc, 2010. 1880 U.S. Census Index provided by The Church of Jesus Christ of Latter-day Saints © Copyright 1999 Intellectual Reserve, Inc. All rights reserved. All use is subject to the limited), Ancestry.com, http://www.Ancestry.com, Year: 1880; Census Place: June Bug, Calhoun, Alabama; Roll: 4; Family History Film: 1254004; Page: 533B; Enumeration District: 6; Image: 0627. Birth date: about 1879 Birth place: Alabama Residence date: 1880 Residence place: June Bug, Calhoun, Alabama, United States.

916	Ancestry.com, Florida Death Index, 1877-1998 (Online publication - Provo, UT, USA: Ancestry.com Operations Inc, 2004. Original data - State of Florida. Florida Death Index, 1877-1998. Florida: Florida Department of Health, Office of Vital Records, 1998. Original data: State of Florida. Florida Death Ind), Ancestry.com, http://www.Ancestry.com, Birth date: 24 Nov 1879 Birth place: Death date: 7 Jan 1975 Death place: Dade, Florida, United States.

917	Ancestry.com, 1900 United States Federal Census (Online publication - Provo, UT, USA: Ancestry.com Operations Inc, 2004. Original data - United States of America, Bureau of the Census. Twelfth Census of the United States, 1900. Washington, D.C.: National Archives and Records Administration, 1900. T623, 18), Ancestry.com, http://www.Ancestry.com, Year: 1900; Census Place: Weavers, Calhoun, Alabama; Roll: T623_5; Page: 4B; Enumeration District: 27. Birth date: Nov 1879 Birth place: Alabama Marriage date: 1899 Marriage place: Residence date: 1900 Residence place: Weavers, Calhoun, Alabama.

918	Ancestry.com, 1910 United States Federal Census (Online publication - Provo, UT, USA: Ancestry.com Operations Inc, 2006. Original data - Thirteenth Census of the United States, 1910 (NARA microfilm publication T624, 1,178 rolls). Records of the Bureau of the Census, Record Group 29. National Archives, Washington), Ancestry.com, http://www.Ancestry.com, Year: 1910; Census Place: Weaver, Calhoun, Alabama; Roll: ; Page: ; Enumeration District: ; Image:. Birth date: about 1879 Birth place: Alabama Residence date: 1910 Residence place: Weaver, Calhoun, Alabama.

919	Ancestry.com, 1900 United States Federal Census (Online publication - Provo, UT, USA: Ancestry.com Operations Inc, 2004. Original data - United States of America, Bureau of the Census. Twelfth Census of the United States, 1900. Washington, D.C.: National Archives and Records Administration, 1900. T623, 18), Ancestry.com, http://www.Ancestry.com, Year: 1900; Census Place: Weavers, Calhoun, Alabama; Roll: T623_5; Page: 4B; Enumeration District: 27. Birth date: Nov 1875 Birth place: Alabama Marriage date: 1899 Marriage place: Residence date: 1900 Residence place: Weavers, Calhoun, Alabama.

920	Ancestry.com, 1900 United States Federal Census (Online publication - Provo, UT, USA: Ancestry.com Operations Inc, 2004. Original data - United States of America, Bureau of the Census. Twelfth Census of the United States, 1900. Washington, D.C.: National Archives and Records Administration, 1900. T623, 18), Ancestry.com, http://www.Ancestry.com, Year: 1900; Census Place: Weavers, Calhoun, Alabama; Roll: T623_5; Page: 5A; Enumeration District: 27. Birth date: Sep 1882 Birth place: Alabama Residence date: 1900 Residence place: Weavers, Calhoun, Alabama.

921	Ancestry.com, 1910 United States Federal Census (Online publication - Provo, UT, USA: Ancestry.com Operations Inc, 2006. Original data - Thirteenth Census of the United States, 1910 (NARA microfilm publication T624, 1,178 rolls). Records of the Bureau of the Census, Record Group 29. National Archives, Washington), Ancestry.com, http://www.Ancestry.com, Year: 1910; Census Place: Weaver, Calhoun, Alabama; Roll: ; Page: ; Enumeration District: ; Image:. Birth date: about 1883 Birth place: Alabama Residence date: 1910 Residence place: Weaver, Calhoun, Alabama.

922	Ancestry.com, 1900 United States Federal Census (Online publication - Provo, UT, USA: Ancestry.com Operations Inc, 2004. Original data - United States of America, Bureau of the Census. Twelfth Census of the United States, 1900. Washington, D.C.: National Archives and Records Administration, 1900. T623, 18), Ancestry.com, http://www.Ancestry.com, Year: 1900; Census Place: Weavers, Calhoun, Alabama; Roll: T623_5; Page: 5A; Enumeration District: 27. Birth date: Oct 1885 Birth place: Alabama Residence date: 1900 Residence place: Weavers, Calhoun, Alabama.

923	Ancestry.com, 1920 United States Federal Census (Online publication - Provo, UT, USA: Ancestry.com Operations Inc, 2010. Images reproduced by FamilySearch. Original data - Fourteenth Census of the United States, 1920. (NARA microfilm publication T625, 2076 rolls). Records of the Bureau of the Census, Record), Ancestry.com, http://www.Ancestry.com, Year: 1920; Census Place: Menlo, Chattooga, Georgia; Roll: T625_242; Page: 3B; Enumeration District: 34; Image:. Birth date: about 1887 Birth place: Alabama Residence date: 1920 Residence place: Menlo, Chattooga, Georgia.

924	Ancestry.com, 1910 United States Federal Census (Online publication - Provo, UT, USA: Ancestry.com Operations Inc, 2006. Original data - Thirteenth Census of the United States, 1910 (NARA microfilm publication T624, 1,178 rolls). Records of the Bureau of the Census, Record Group 29. National Archives, Washington), Ancestry.com, http://www.Ancestry.com, Year: 1910; Census Place: Jacksonville, Calhoun, Alabama; Roll: ; Page: ; Enumeration District: ; Image:. Birth date: about 1886 Birth place: Alabama Residence date: 1910 Residence place: Jacksonville, Calhoun, Alabama.

925   Ancestry.com, Georgia Deaths, 1919-98 (Online publication - Provo, UT, USA: Ancestry.com Operations Inc, 2001. Original data - State of Georgia. Indexes of Vital Records for Georgia: Deaths, 1919-1998. Georgia, USA: Georgia Health Department, Office of Vital Records, 1998. Original data: State of), Ancestry.com, http://www.Ancestry.com, Certificate number: 02314. Birth date: about 1885 Birth place: Death date: 02 Jan 1960 Death place: Troup, Georgia Residence date: Residence place: Troup.

926   Ancestry.com, 1930 United States Federal Census (Online publication - Provo, UT, USA: Ancestry.com Operations Inc, 2002. Original data - United States of America, Bureau of the Census. Fifteenth Census of the United States, 1930. Washington, D.C.: National Archives and Records Administration, 1930. T626,), Ancestry.com, http://www.Ancestry.com, Year: 1930; Census Place: Rome, Floyd, Georgia; Roll: 356; Page: 2A; Enumeration District: 21; Image: 594.0. Birth date: about 1887 Birth place: Alabama Residence date: 1930 Residence place: Rome, Floyd, Georgia.

927   Ancestry.com, 1900 United States Federal Census (Online publication - Provo, UT, USA: Ancestry.com Operations Inc, 2004. Original data - United States of America, Bureau of the Census. Twelfth Census of the United States, 1900. Washington, D.C.: National Archives and Records Administration, 1900. T623, 18), Ancestry.com, http://www.Ancestry.com, Year: 1900; Census Place: Weavers, Calhoun, Alabama; Roll: T623_5; Page: 5A; Enumeration District: 27. Birth date: Mar 1889 Birth place: Alabama Residence date: 1900 Residence place: Weavers, Calhoun, Alabama.

928   Ancestry.com, Social Security Death Index (Online publication - Provo, UT, USA: Ancestry.com Operations Inc, 2010. Original data - Social Security Administration. Social Security Death Index, Master File. Social Security Administration. Original data: Social Security Administration. Social Security D), Ancestry.com, http://www.Ancestry.com, Number: 421-07-5407; Issue State: Alabama; Issue Date: Before 1951. Birth date: 23 Dec 1890 Birth place: Death date: Dec 1963 Death place: Alabama, United States of America.

929   Ancestry.com, 1910 United States Federal Census (Online publication - Provo, UT, USA: Ancestry.com Operations Inc, 2006. Original data - Thirteenth Census of the United States, 1910 (NARA microfilm publication T624, 1,178 rolls). Records of the Bureau of the Census, Record Group 29. National Archives, Washington), Ancestry.com, http://www.Ancestry.com, Year: 1910; Census Place: Weaver, Calhoun, Alabama; Roll: ; Page: ; Enumeration District: ; Image:. Birth date: about 1893 Birth place: Alabama Residence date: 1910 Residence place: Weaver, Calhoun, Alabama.

930   Ancestry.com, 1900 United States Federal Census (Online publication - Provo, UT, USA: Ancestry.com Operations Inc, 2004. Original data - United States of America, Bureau of the Census. Twelfth Census of the United States, 1900. Washington, D.C.: National Archives and Records Administration, 1900. T623, 18), Ancestry.com, http://www.Ancestry.com, Year: 1900; Census Place: Weavers, Calhoun, Alabama; Roll: T623_5; Page: 5A; Enumeration District: 27. Birth date: Dec 1890 Birth place: Alabama Residence date: 1900 Residence place: Weavers, Calhoun, Alabama.

931   Ancestry.com, 1910 United States Federal Census (Online publication - Provo, UT, USA: Ancestry.com Operations Inc, 2006. Original data - Thirteenth Census of the United States, 1910 (NARA microfilm publication T624, 1,178 rolls). Records of the Bureau of the Census, Record Group 29. National Archives, Washington), Ancestry.com, http://www.Ancestry.com, Year: 1910; Census Place: Weaver, Calhoun, Alabama; Roll: ; Page: ; Enumeration District: ; Image:. Birth date: about 1891 Birth place: Alabama Residence date: 1910 Residence place: Weaver, Calhoun, Alabama.

932   Ancestry.com, 1910 United States Federal Census (Online publication - Provo, UT, USA: Ancestry.com Operations Inc, 2006. Original data - Thirteenth Census of the United States, 1910 (NARA microfilm publication T624, 1,178 rolls). Records of the Bureau of the Census, Record Group 29. National Archives, Washington), Ancestry.com, http://www.Ancestry.com, Year: 1910; Census Place: Weaver, Calhoun, Alabama; Roll: ; Page: ; Enumeration District: ; Image:. Birth date: about 1898 Birth place: Alabama Residence date: 1910 Residence place: Weaver, Calhoun, Alabama.

933   Ancestry.com, 1900 United States Federal Census (Online publication - Provo, UT, USA: Ancestry.com Operations Inc, 2004. Original data - United States of America, Bureau of the Census. Twelfth Census of the United States, 1900. Washington, D.C.: National Archives and Records Administration, 1900. T623, 18), Ancestry.com, http://www.Ancestry.com, Year: 1900; Census Place: Weavers, Calhoun, Alabama; Roll: T623_5; Page: 5A; Enumeration District: 27. Birth date: May 1896 Birth place: Alabama Residence date: 1900 Residence place: Weavers, Calhoun, Alabama.

934   Ancestry.com, 1910 United States Federal Census (Online publication - Provo, UT, USA: Ancestry.com Operations Inc, 2006. Original data - Thirteenth Census of the United States, 1910 (NARA microfilm publication T624, 1,178 rolls). Records of the Bureau of the Census, Record Group 29. National Archives, Washington), Ancestry.com, http://www.Ancestry.com, Year: 1910; Census Place: Weaver, Calhoun, Alabama; Roll: ; Page: ; Enumeration District: ; Image:. Birth date: about 1895 Birth place: Alabama Residence date: 1910 Residence place: Weaver, Calhoun, Alabama.

935   Ancestry.com, 1900 United States Federal Census (Online publication - Provo, UT, USA: Ancestry.com Operations Inc, 2004. Original data - United States of America, Bureau of the Census. Twelfth Census of the United States, 1900. Washington, D.C.: National Archives and Records Administration, 1900. T623, 18), Ancestry.com, http://www.Ancestry.com, Year: 1900; Census Place: Polkville, Calhoun, Alabama; Roll: T623_5; Page: 3A; Enumeration District: 29. Birth date: Mar 1854 Birth place: Alabama Marriage date: 1870 Marriage place: Residence date: 1900 Residence place: Polkville, Calhoun, Alabama.

936   Ancestry.com, 1910 United States Federal Census (Online publication - Provo, UT, USA: Ancestry.com Operations Inc, 2006. Original data - Thirteenth Census of the United States, 1910 (NARA microfilm publication T624, 1,178 rolls). Records of the Bureau of the Census, Record Group 29. National Archives, Washington), Ancestry.com,

http://www.Ancestry.com, Year: 1910; Census Place: Polkville, Calhoun, Alabama; Roll: ; Page: ; Enumeration District: ; Image:. Birth date: about 1854 Birth place: Alabama Residence date: 1910 Residence place: Polkville, Calhoun, Alabama.

937   Ancestry.com, Alabama Deaths, 1908-59 (Online publication - Provo, UT, USA: Ancestry.com Operations Inc, 2000. Original data - State of Alabama. Index of Vital Records for Alabama: Deaths, 1908-1959. Montgomery, AL, USA: State of Alabama Center for Health Statistics, Record Services Division. Original), Ancestry.com, http://www.Ancestry.com, Death date: Feb 1926 Death place: Calhoun.

938   Ancestry.com, 1860 United States Federal Census (Online publication - Provo, UT, USA: Ancestry.com Operations, Inc., 2009. Images reproduced by FamilySearch. Original data - 1860 U.S. census, population schedule. NARA microfilm publication M653, 1,438 rolls. Washington, D.C.: National Archives and Records), Ancestry.com, http://www.Ancestry.com, Year: 1860; Census Place: Ranges 8 and 9, Calhoun, Alabama; Roll: ; Page: 406; Image: 126. Birth date: about 1853 Birth place: Alabama Residence date: 1860 Residence place: Ranges 8 and 9, Calhoun, Alabama, United States.

939   Ancestry.com, 1920 United States Federal Census (Online publication - Provo, UT, USA: Ancestry.com Operations Inc, 2010. Images reproduced by FamilySearch. Original data - Fourteenth Census of the United States, 1920. (NARA microfilm publication T625, 2076 rolls). Records of the Bureau of the Census, Record), Ancestry.com, http://www.Ancestry.com, Year: 1920; Census Place: Polkville, Calhoun, Alabama; Roll: T625_5; Page: 1B; Enumeration District: 7; Image:. Birth date: about 1854 Birth place: Alabama Residence date: 1920 Residence place: Polkville, Calhoun, Alabama.

940   Ancestry.com, 1920 United States Federal Census (Online publication - Provo, UT, USA: Ancestry.com Operations Inc, 2010. Images reproduced by FamilySearch. Original data - Fourteenth Census of the United States, 1920. (NARA microfilm publication T625, 2076 rolls). Records of the Bureau of the Census, Record), Ancestry.com, http://www.Ancestry.com, Year: 1920; Census Place: Polkville, Calhoun, Alabama; Roll: T625_5; Page: 2A; Enumeration District: 7; Image:. Birth date: about 1874 Birth place: Alabama Residence date: 1920 Residence place: Polkville, Calhoun, Alabama.

941   Ancestry.com, 1900 United States Federal Census (Online publication - Provo, UT, USA: Ancestry.com Operations Inc, 2004. Original data - United States of America, Bureau of the Census. Twelfth Census of the United States, 1900. Washington, D.C.: National Archives and Records Administration, 1900. T623, 18), Ancestry.com, http://www.Ancestry.com, Year: 1900; Census Place: Polkville, Calhoun, Alabama; Roll: T623_5; Page: 5A; Enumeration District: 29. Birth date: Aug 1873 Birth place: Alabama Marriage date: 1896 Marriage place: Residence date: 1900 Residence place: Polkville, Calhoun, Alabama.

942   Ancestry.com, 1910 United States Federal Census (Online publication - Provo, UT, USA: Ancestry.com Operations Inc, 2006. Original data - Thirteenth Census of the United States, 1910 (NARA microfilm publication T624, 1,178 rolls). Records of the Bureau of the Census, Record Group 29. National Archives, Washington), Ancestry.com, http://www.Ancestry.com, Year: 1910; Census Place: Polkville, Calhoun, Alabama; Roll: ; Page: ; Enumeration District: ; Image:. Birth date: about 1874 Birth place: Alabama Residence date: 1910 Residence place: Polkville, Calhoun, Alabama.

943   Ancestry.com, Alabama Deaths, 1908-59 (Online publication - Provo, UT, USA: Ancestry.com Operations Inc, 2000. Original data - State of Alabama. Index of Vital Records for Alabama: Deaths, 1908-1959. Montgomery, AL, USA: State of Alabama Center for Health Statistics, Record Services Division. Original), Ancestry.com, http://www.Ancestry.com, Death date: Oct 1938 Death place: Calhoun.

944   Ancestry.com, 1900 United States Federal Census (Online publication - Provo, UT, USA: Ancestry.com Operations Inc, 2004. Original data - United States of America, Bureau of the Census. Twelfth Census of the United States, 1900. Washington, D.C.: National Archives and Records Administration, 1900. T623, 18), Ancestry.com, http://www.Ancestry.com, Year: 1900; Census Place: Polkville, Calhoun, Alabama; Roll: T623_5; Page: 3B; Enumeration District: 29. Birth date: Apr 1880 Birth place: Alabama Residence date: 1900 Residence place: Polkville, Calhoun, Alabama.

945   Ancestry.com, 1900 United States Federal Census (Online publication - Provo, UT, USA: Ancestry.com Operations Inc, 2004. Original data - United States of America, Bureau of the Census. Twelfth Census of the United States, 1900. Washington, D.C.: National Archives and Records Administration, 1900. T623, 18), Ancestry.com, http://www.Ancestry.com, Year: 1900; Census Place: Polkville, Calhoun, Alabama; Roll: T623_5; Page: 3B; Enumeration District: 29. Birth date: Jun 1882 Birth place: Alabama Residence date: 1900 Residence place: Polkville, Calhoun, Alabama.

946   Ancestry.com, Social Security Death Index (Online publication - Provo, UT, USA: Ancestry.com Operations Inc, 2010. Original data - Social Security Administration. Social Security Death Index, Master File. Social Security Administration. Original data: Social Security Administration. Social Security D), Ancestry.com, http://www.Ancestry.com, Number: 419-05-3922; Issue State: Alabama; Issue Date: Before 1951. Birth date: 6 Feb 1884 Birth place: Death date: Mar 1964 Death place: Alabama, United States of America.

947   Ancestry.com, 1900 United States Federal Census (Online publication - Provo, UT, USA: Ancestry.com Operations Inc, 2004. Original data - United States of America, Bureau of the Census. Twelfth Census of the United States, 1900. Washington, D.C.: National Archives and Records Administration, 1900. T623, 18), Ancestry.com, http://www.Ancestry.com, Year: 1900; Census Place: Polkville, Calhoun, Alabama; Roll: T623_5; Page: 3B; Enumeration District: 29. Birth date: Feb 1884 Birth place: Alabama Residence date: 1900 Residence place: Polkville, Calhoun, Alabama.

948	Ancestry.com, 1900 United States Federal Census (Online publication - Provo, UT, USA: Ancestry.com Operations Inc, 2004. Original data - United States of America, Bureau of the Census. Twelfth Census of the United States, 1900. Washington, D.C.: National Archives and Records Administration, 1900. T623, 18), Ancestry.com, http://www.Ancestry.com, Year: 1900; Census Place: Polkville, Calhoun, Alabama; Roll: T623_5; Page: 3B; Enumeration District: 29. Birth date: Oct 1886 Birth place: Alabama Residence date: 1900 Residence place: Polkville, Calhoun, Alabama.

949	Ancestry.com, 1920 United States Federal Census (Online publication - Provo, UT, USA: Ancestry.com Operations Inc, 2010. Images reproduced by FamilySearch. Original data - Fourteenth Census of the United States, 1920. (NARA microfilm publication T625, 2076 rolls). Records of the Bureau of the Census, Record), Ancestry.com, http://www.Ancestry.com, Year: 1920; Census Place: Polkville, Calhoun, Alabama; Roll: T625_5; Page: 1B; Enumeration District: 7; Image:. Birth date: about 1889 Birth place: Alabama Residence date: 1920 Residence place: Polkville, Calhoun, Alabama.

950	Ancestry.com, 1900 United States Federal Census (Online publication - Provo, UT, USA: Ancestry.com Operations Inc, 2004. Original data - United States of America, Bureau of the Census. Twelfth Census of the United States, 1900. Washington, D.C.: National Archives and Records Administration, 1900. T623, 18), Ancestry.com, http://www.Ancestry.com, Year: 1900; Census Place: Polkville, Calhoun, Alabama; Roll: T623_5; Page: 3B; Enumeration District: 29. Birth date: Aug 1888 Birth place: Alabama Residence date: 1900 Residence place: Polkville, Calhoun, Alabama.

951	Ancestry.com, World War I Draft Registration Cards, 1917-1918 (Online publication - Provo, UT, USA: Ancestry.com Operations Inc, 2005. Original data - United States, Selective Service System. World War I Selective Service System Draft Registration Cards, 1917-1918. Washington, D.C.: National Archives and Records Administration), Ancestry.com, http://www.Ancestry.com, Registration Location: Calhoun County, Alabama; Roll: 1509362; Draft Board: 0. Birth date: 22 Aug 1888 Birth place: Residence date: Residence place: Calhoun, Alabama.

952	Ancestry.com, 1910 United States Federal Census (Online publication - Provo, UT, USA: Ancestry.com Operations Inc, 2006. Original data - Thirteenth Census of the United States, 1910 (NARA microfilm publication T624, 1,178 rolls). Records of the Bureau of the Census, Record Group 29. National Archives, Washington), Ancestry.com, http://www.Ancestry.com, Year: 1910; Census Place: Anniston Ward 2, Calhoun, Alabama; Roll: ; Page: ; Enumeration District: ; Image:. Birth date: about 1888 Birth place: Alabama Residence date: 1910 Residence place: Anniston Ward 2, Calhoun, Alabama.

953	Ancestry.com, Alabama Deaths, 1908-59 (Online publication - Provo, UT, USA: Ancestry.com Operations Inc, 2000. Original data - State of Alabama. Index of Vital Records for Alabama: Deaths, 1908-1959. Montgomery, AL, USA: State of Alabama Center for Health Statistics, Record Services Division. Original), Ancestry.com, http://www.Ancestry.com, Death date: Nov 1925 Death place: Calhoun.

954	Ancestry.com, 1910 United States Federal Census (Online publication - Provo, UT, USA: Ancestry.com Operations Inc, 2006. Original data - Thirteenth Census of the United States, 1910 (NARA microfilm publication T624, 1,178 rolls). Records of the Bureau of the Census, Record Group 29. National Archives, Washington), Ancestry.com, http://www.Ancestry.com, Year: 1910; Census Place: Albertville, Marshall, Alabama; Roll: ; Page: ; Enumeration District: ; Image:. Birth date: about 1876 Birth place: Alabama Residence date: 1910 Residence place: Albertville, Marshall, Alabama.

955	Ancestry.com, 1900 United States Federal Census (Online publication - Provo, UT, USA: Ancestry.com Operations Inc, 2004. Original data - United States of America, Bureau of the Census. Twelfth Census of the United States, 1900. Washington, D.C.: National Archives and Records Administration, 1900. T623, 18), Ancestry.com, http://www.Ancestry.com, Year: 1900; Census Place: Rock Spring, Marshall, Alabama; Roll: T623_30; Page: 5A; Enumeration District: 90. Birth date: Mar 1875 Birth place: Alabama Marriage date: 1891 Marriage place: Residence date: 1900 Residence place: Rock Spring, Marshall, Alabama.

956	Ancestry.com, 1920 United States Federal Census (Online publication - Provo, UT, USA: Ancestry.com Operations Inc, 2010. Images reproduced by FamilySearch. Original data - Fourteenth Census of the United States, 1920. (NARA microfilm publication T625, 2076 rolls). Records of the Bureau of the Census, Record), Ancestry.com, http://www.Ancestry.com, Year: 1920; Census Place: Albertville, Marshall, Alabama; Roll: T625_28; Page: 26B; Enumeration District: 122; Image:. Birth date: about 1874 Birth place: Arkansas Residence date: 1920 Residence place: Albertville, Marshall, Alabama.

957	Ancestry.com, 1930 United States Federal Census (Online publication - Provo, UT, USA: Ancestry.com Operations Inc, 2002. Original data - United States of America, Bureau of the Census. Fifteenth Census of the United States, 1930. Washington, D.C.: National Archives and Records Administration, 1930. T626,), Ancestry.com, http://www.Ancestry.com, Year: 1930; Census Place: Albertville, Marshall, Alabama; Roll: 39; Page: 1A; Enumeration District: 7; Image: 725.0. Birth date: about 1874 Birth place: Residence date: 1930 Residence place: Albertville, Marshall, Alabama.

958	Ancestry.com, Alabama Deaths, 1908-59 (Online publication - Provo, UT, USA: Ancestry.com Operations Inc, 2000. Original data - State of Alabama. Index of Vital Records for Alabama: Deaths, 1908-1959. Montgomery, AL, USA: State of Alabama Center for Health Statistics, Record Services Division. Original), Ancestry.com, http://www.Ancestry.com, Death date: 24 Oct 1958 Death place: Marshall.

959	Ancestry.com, 1900 United States Federal Census (Online publication - Provo, UT, USA: Ancestry.com Operations Inc, 2004. Original data - United States of America, Bureau of the Census. Twelfth Census of the United

States, 1900. Washington, D.C.: National Archives and Records Administration, 1900. T623, 18), Ancestry.com, http://www.Ancestry.com, Year: 1900; Census Place: Rock Spring, Marshall, Alabama; Roll: T623_30; Page: 5A; Enumeration District: 90. Birth date: Jul 1892 Birth place: Alabama Residence date: 1900 Residence place: Rock Spring, Marshall, Alabama.

960   Ancestry.com, 1910 United States Federal Census (Online publication - Provo, UT, USA: Ancestry.com Operations Inc, 2006. Original data - Thirteenth Census of the United States, 1910 (NARA microfilm publication T624, 1,178 rolls). Records of the Bureau of the Census, Record Group 29. National Archives, Washington), Ancestry.com, http://www.Ancestry.com, Year: 1910; Census Place: Albertville, Marshall, Alabama; Roll: ; Page: ; Enumeration District: ; Image:. Birth date: about 1892 Birth place: Alabama Residence date: 1910 Residence place: Albertville, Marshall, Alabama.

961   Ancestry.com, 1920 United States Federal Census (Online publication - Provo, UT, USA: Ancestry.com Operations Inc, 2010. Images reproduced by FamilySearch. Original data - Fourteenth Census of the United States, 1920. (NARA microfilm publication T625, 2076 rolls). Records of the Bureau of the Census, Record), Ancestry.com, http://www.Ancestry.com, Year: 1920; Census Place: Albertville, Marshall, Alabama; Roll: T625_28; Page: 9A; Enumeration District: 122; Image:. Birth date: about 1893 Birth place: Alabama Residence date: 1920 Residence place: Albertville, Marshall, Alabama.

962   Ancestry.com, 1900 United States Federal Census (Online publication - Provo, UT, USA: Ancestry.com Operations Inc, 2004. Original data - United States of America, Bureau of the Census. Twelfth Census of the United States, 1900. Washington, D.C.: National Archives and Records Administration, 1900. T623, 18), Ancestry.com, http://www.Ancestry.com, Year: 1900; Census Place: Rock Spring, Marshall, Alabama; Roll: T623_30; Page: 5A; Enumeration District: 90. Birth date: Dec 1894 Birth place: Alabama Residence date: 1900 Residence place: Rock Spring, Marshall, Alabama.

963   Ancestry.com, 1910 United States Federal Census (Online publication - Provo, UT, USA: Ancestry.com Operations Inc, 2006. Original data - Thirteenth Census of the United States, 1910 (NARA microfilm publication T624, 1,178 rolls). Records of the Bureau of the Census, Record Group 29. National Archives, Washington), Ancestry.com, http://www.Ancestry.com, Year: 1910; Census Place: Albertville, Marshall, Alabama; Roll: ; Page: ; Enumeration District: ; Image:. Birth date: about 1894 Birth place: Alabama Residence date: 1910 Residence place: Albertville, Marshall, Alabama.

964   Ancestry.com, World War I Draft Registration Cards, 1917-1918 (Online publication - Provo, UT, USA: Ancestry.com Operations Inc, 2005. Original data - United States, Selective Service System. World War I Selective Service System Draft Registration Cards, 1917-1918. Washington, D.C.: National Archives and Records Administration), Ancestry.com, http://www.Ancestry.com, Registration Location: Marshall County, Alabama; Roll: 1509407; Draft Board: 0. Birth date: 8 Dec 1893 Birth place: Residence date: Residence place: Marshall, Alabama.

965   Ancestry.com, Alabama Deaths, 1908-59 (Online publication - Provo, UT, USA: Ancestry.com Operations Inc, 2000. Original data - State of Alabama. Index of Vital Records for Alabama: Deaths, 1908-1959. Montgomery, AL, USA: State of Alabama Center for Health Statistics, Record Services Division. Original), Ancestry.com, http://www.Ancestry.com, Death date: 15 Feb 1959 Death place: Marshall.

966   Ancestry.com, 1920 United States Federal Census (Online publication - Provo, UT, USA: Ancestry.com Operations Inc, 2010. Images reproduced by FamilySearch. Original data - Fourteenth Census of the United States, 1920. (NARA microfilm publication T625, 2076 rolls). Records of the Bureau of the Census, Record), Ancestry.com, http://www.Ancestry.com, Year: 1920; Census Place: Albertville, Marshall, Alabama; Roll: T625_28; Page: 17A; Enumeration District: 122; Image:. Birth date: about 1894 Birth place: Alabama Residence date: 1920 Residence place: Albertville, Marshall, Alabama.

967   Ancestry.com, 1930 United States Federal Census (Online publication - Provo, UT, USA: Ancestry.com Operations Inc, 2002. Original data - United States of America, Bureau of the Census. Fifteenth Census of the United States, 1930. Washington, D.C.: National Archives and Records Administration, 1930. T626,), Ancestry.com, http://www.Ancestry.com, Year: 1930; Census Place: Albertville, Marshall, Alabama; Roll: 39; Page: 1A; Enumeration District: 7; Image: 725.0. Birth date: about 1894 Birth place: Alabama Residence date: 1930 Residence place: Albertville, Marshall, Alabama.

968   Ancestry.com, 1900 United States Federal Census (Online publication - Provo, UT, USA: Ancestry.com Operations Inc, 2004. Original data - United States of America, Bureau of the Census. Twelfth Census of the United States, 1900. Washington, D.C.: National Archives and Records Administration, 1900. T623, 18), Ancestry.com, http://www.Ancestry.com, Year: 1900; Census Place: Rock Spring, Marshall, Alabama; Roll: T623_30; Page: 5A; Enumeration District: 90. Birth date: Feb 1895 Birth place: Alabama Residence date: 1900 Residence place: Rock Spring, Marshall, Alabama.

969   Ancestry.com, Alabama Deaths, 1908-59 (Online publication - Provo, UT, USA: Ancestry.com Operations Inc, 2000. Original data - State of Alabama. Index of Vital Records for Alabama: Deaths, 1908-1959. Montgomery, AL, USA: State of Alabama Center for Health Statistics, Record Services Division. Original), Ancestry.com, http://www.Ancestry.com, Death date: 06 Jul 1910 Death place: Calhoun.

970   Ancestry.com, 1900 United States Federal Census (Online publication - Provo, UT, USA: Ancestry.com Operations Inc, 2004. Original data - United States of America, Bureau of the Census. Twelfth Census of the United States, 1900. Washington, D.C.: National Archives and Records Administration, 1900. T623, 18), Ancestry.com, http://www.Ancestry.com, Year: 1900; Census Place: Rock Spring, Marshall, Alabama; Roll: T623_30; Page: 5A;

Enumeration District: 90. Birth date: Oct 1899 Birth place: Alabama Residence date: 1900 Residence place: Rock Spring, Marshall, Alabama.

971   Ancestry.com, 1910 United States Federal Census (Online publication - Provo, UT, USA: Ancestry.com Operations Inc, 2006. Original data - Thirteenth Census of the United States, 1910 (NARA microfilm publication T624, 1,178 rolls). Records of the Bureau of the Census, Record Group 29. National Archives, Washington), Ancestry.com, http://www.Ancestry.com, Year: 1910; Census Place: Albertville, Marshall, Alabama; Roll: ; Page: ; Enumeration District: ; Image:. Birth date: about 1899 Birth place: Alabama Residence date: 1910 Residence place: Albertville, Marshall, Alabama.

972   Ancestry.com, 1920 United States Federal Census (Online publication - Provo, UT, USA: Ancestry.com Operations Inc, 2010. Images reproduced by FamilySearch. Original data - Fourteenth Census of the United States, 1920. (NARA microfilm publication T625, 2076 rolls). Records of the Bureau of the Census, Record), Ancestry.com, http://www.Ancestry.com, Year: 1920; Census Place: Albertville, Marshall, Alabama; Roll: T625_28; Page: 26B; Enumeration District: 122; Image:. Birth date: about 1900 Birth place: Alabama Residence date: 1920 Residence place: Albertville, Marshall, Alabama.

973   Ancestry.com, 1930 United States Federal Census (Online publication - Provo, UT, USA: Ancestry.com Operations Inc, 2002. Original data - United States of America, Bureau of the Census. Fifteenth Census of the United States, 1930. Washington, D.C.: National Archives and Records Administration, 1930. T626,), Ancestry.com, http://www.Ancestry.com, Year: 1930; Census Place: Albertville, Marshall, Alabama; Roll: 39; Page: 1A; Enumeration District: 7; Image: 725.0. Birth date: about 1900 Birth place: Residence date: 1930 Residence place: Albertville, Marshall, Alabama.

974   Ancestry.com, Alabama Deaths, 1908-59 (Online publication - Provo, UT, USA: Ancestry.com Operations Inc, 2000. Original data - State of Alabama. Index of Vital Records for Alabama: Deaths, 1908-1959. Montgomery, AL, USA: State of Alabama Center for Health Statistics, Record Services Division. Original), Ancestry.com, http://www.Ancestry.com, Death date: Jul 1927 Death place: Marshall.

975   Ancestry.com, 1910 United States Federal Census (Online publication - Provo, UT, USA: Ancestry.com Operations Inc, 2006. Original data - Thirteenth Census of the United States, 1910 (NARA microfilm publication T624, 1,178 rolls). Records of the Bureau of the Census, Record Group 29. National Archives, Washington), Ancestry.com, http://www.Ancestry.com, Year: 1910; Census Place: Albertville, Marshall, Alabama; Roll: ; Page: ; Enumeration District: ; Image:. Birth date: about 1902 Birth place: Alabama Residence date: 1910 Residence place: Albertville, Marshall, Alabama.

976   Ancestry.com, 1920 United States Federal Census (Online publication - Provo, UT, USA: Ancestry.com Operations Inc, 2010. Images reproduced by FamilySearch. Original data - Fourteenth Census of the United States, 1920. (NARA microfilm publication T625, 2076 rolls). Records of the Bureau of the Census, Record), Ancestry.com, http://www.Ancestry.com, Year: 1920; Census Place: Albertville, Marshall, Alabama; Roll: T625_28; Page: 26B; Enumeration District: 122; Image:. Birth date: about 1902 Birth place: Alabama Residence date: 1920 Residence place: Albertville, Marshall, Alabama.

977   Ancestry.com, 1910 United States Federal Census (Online publication - Provo, UT, USA: Ancestry.com Operations Inc, 2006. Original data - Thirteenth Census of the United States, 1910 (NARA microfilm publication T624, 1,178 rolls). Records of the Bureau of the Census, Record Group 29. National Archives, Washington), Ancestry.com, http://www.Ancestry.com, Year: 1910; Census Place: Albertville, Marshall, Alabama; Roll: ; Page: ; Enumeration District: ; Image:. Birth date: about 1903 Birth place: Alabama Residence date: 1910 Residence place: Albertville, Marshall, Alabama.

978   Ancestry.com, Social Security Death Index (Online publication - Provo, UT, USA: Ancestry.com Operations Inc, 2010. Original data - Social Security Administration. Social Security Death Index, Master File. Social Security Administration. Original data: Social Security Administration. Social Security D), Ancestry.com, http://www.Ancestry.com, Number: 420-86-1334; Issue State: Alabama; Issue Date: 1973. Birth date: 23 Dec 1903 Birth place: Death date: Dec 1977 Death place: Albertville, Marshall, Alabama, United States of America.

979   Ancestry.com, Social Security Death Index (Online publication - Provo, UT, USA: Ancestry.com Operations Inc, 2010. Original data - Social Security Administration. Social Security Death Index, Master File. Social Security Administration. Original data: Social Security Administration. Social Security D), Ancestry.com, http://www.Ancestry.com, Number: 418-14-1982; Issue State: Alabama; Issue Date: Before 1951. Birth date: 19 Oct 1905 Birth place: Death date: Jan 1972 Death place: Albertville, Marshall, Alabama, United States of America.

980   Ancestry.com, 1910 United States Federal Census (Online publication - Provo, UT, USA: Ancestry.com Operations Inc, 2006. Original data - Thirteenth Census of the United States, 1910 (NARA microfilm publication T624, 1,178 rolls). Records of the Bureau of the Census, Record Group 29. National Archives, Washington), Ancestry.com, http://www.Ancestry.com, Year: 1910; Census Place: Albertville, Marshall, Alabama; Roll: ; Page: ; Enumeration District: ; Image:. Birth date: about 1906 Birth place: Alabama Residence date: 1910 Residence place: Albertville, Marshall, Alabama.

981   Ancestry.com, 1920 United States Federal Census (Online publication - Provo, UT, USA: Ancestry.com Operations Inc, 2010. Images reproduced by FamilySearch. Original data - Fourteenth Census of the United States, 1920. (NARA microfilm publication T625, 2076 rolls). Records of the Bureau of the Census, Record), Ancestry.com, http://www.Ancestry.com, Year: 1920; Census Place: Albertville, Marshall, Alabama; Roll: T625_28; Page: 26B;

Enumeration District: 122; Image:. Birth date: about 1906 Birth place: Alabama Residence date: 1920 Residence place: Albertville, Marshall, Alabama.

982   Ancestry.com, 1930 United States Federal Census (Online publication - Provo, UT, USA: Ancestry.com Operations Inc, 2002. Original data - United States of America, Bureau of the Census. Fifteenth Census of the United States, 1930. Washington, D.C.: National Archives and Records Administration, 1930. T626,), Ancestry.com, http://www.Ancestry.com, Year: 1930; Census Place: Albertville, Marshall, Alabama; Roll: 39; Page: 1A; Enumeration District: 7; Image: 725.0. Birth date: about 1907 Birth place: Residence date: 1930 Residence place: Albertville, Marshall, Alabama.

983   Ancestry.com, 1910 United States Federal Census (Online publication - Provo, UT, USA: Ancestry.com Operations Inc, 2006. Original data - Thirteenth Census of the United States, 1910 (NARA microfilm publication T624, 1,178 rolls). Records of the Bureau of the Census, Record Group 29. National Archives, Washington), Ancestry.com, http://www.Ancestry.com, Year: 1910; Census Place: Albertville, Marshall, Alabama; Roll: ; Page: ; Enumeration District: ; Image:. Birth date: about 1909 Birth place: Alabama Residence date: 1910 Residence place: Albertville, Marshall, Alabama.

984   Ancestry.com, Social Security Death Index (Online publication - Provo, UT, USA: Ancestry.com Operations Inc, 2010. Original data - Social Security Administration. Social Security Death Index, Master File. Social Security Administration. Original data: Social Security Administration. Social Security D), Ancestry.com, http://www.Ancestry.com, Number: 417-20-2326; Issue State: Alabama; Issue Date: Before 1951. Birth date: 16 Jul 1909 Birth place: Death date: Oct 1985 Death place: Wedowee, Randolph, Alabama, United States of America.

985   Ancestry.com, 1930 United States Federal Census (Online publication - Provo, UT, USA: Ancestry.com Operations Inc, 2002. Original data - United States of America, Bureau of the Census. Fifteenth Census of the United States, 1930. Washington, D.C.: National Archives and Records Administration, 1930. T626,), Ancestry.com, http://www.Ancestry.com, Year: 1930; Census Place: Turkey Creek, Stone, Arkansas; Roll: 95; Page: 1A; Enumeration District: 25; Image: 1179.0. Birth date: about 1911 Birth place: Residence date: 1930 Residence place: Turkey Creek, Stone, Arkansas.

986   Ancestry.com, Social Security Death Index (Online publication - Provo, UT, USA: Ancestry.com Operations Inc, 2010. Original data - Social Security Administration. Social Security Death Index, Master File. Social Security Administration. Original data: Social Security Administration. Social Security D), Ancestry.com, http://www.Ancestry.com, Number: 423-64-4562; Issue State: Alabama; Issue Date: 1964. Birth date: 8 Dec 1911 Birth place: Death date: 15 Jun 2001 Death place: Albertville, Marshall, Alabama, United States of America.

987   Ancestry.com, 1920 United States Federal Census (Online publication - Provo, UT, USA: Ancestry.com Operations Inc, 2010. Images reproduced by FamilySearch. Original data - Fourteenth Census of the United States, 1920. (NARA microfilm publication T625, 2076 rolls). Records of the Bureau of the Census, Record), Ancestry.com, http://www.Ancestry.com, Year: 1920; Census Place: Albertville, Marshall, Alabama; Roll: T625_28; Page: 26B; Enumeration District: 122; Image:. Birth date: about 1912 Birth place: Alabama Residence date: 1920 Residence place: Albertville, Marshall, Alabama.

988   Ancestry.com, 1930 United States Federal Census (Online publication - Provo, UT, USA: Ancestry.com Operations Inc, 2002. Original data - United States of America, Bureau of the Census. Fifteenth Census of the United States, 1930. Washington, D.C.: National Archives and Records Administration, 1930. T626,), Ancestry.com, http://www.Ancestry.com, Year: 1930; Census Place: Albertville, Marshall, Alabama; Roll: 39; Page: 1A; Enumeration District: 7; Image: 725.0. Birth date: about 1912 Birth place: Residence date: 1930 Residence place: Albertville, Marshall, Alabama.

989   Ancestry.com, Alabama Deaths, 1908-59 (Online publication - Provo, UT, USA: Ancestry.com Operations Inc, 2000. Original data - State of Alabama. Index of Vital Records for Alabama: Deaths, 1908-1959. Montgomery, AL, USA: State of Alabama Center for Health Statistics, Record Services Division. Original), Ancestry.com, http://www.Ancestry.com, Death date: 14 Jan 1915 Death place: Marshall.

990   Ancestry.com, Alabama Deaths, 1908-59 (Online publication - Provo, UT, USA: Ancestry.com Operations Inc, 2000. Original data - State of Alabama. Index of Vital Records for Alabama: Deaths, 1908-1959. Montgomery, AL, USA: State of Alabama Center for Health Statistics, Record Services Division. Original), Ancestry.com, http://www.Ancestry.com, Death date: Aug 1935 Death place: Marshall.

991   Ancestry.com, 1910 United States Federal Census (Online publication - Provo, UT, USA: Ancestry.com Operations Inc, 2006. Original data - Thirteenth Census of the United States, 1910 (NARA microfilm publication T624, 1,178 rolls). Records of the Bureau of the Census, Record Group 29. National Archives, Washington), Ancestry.com, http://www.Ancestry.com, Year: 1910; Census Place: Alabama Ward 2, Etowah, Alabama; Roll: ; Page: ; Enumeration District: ; Image:. Birth date: about 1857 Birth place: Tennessee Residence date: 1910 Residence place: Alabama Ward 2, Etowah, Alabama.

992   Ancestry.com, 1920 United States Federal Census (Online publication - Provo, UT, USA: Ancestry.com Operations Inc, 2010. Images reproduced by FamilySearch. Original data - Fourteenth Census of the United States, 1920. (NARA microfilm publication T625, 2076 rolls). Records of the Bureau of the Census, Record), Ancestry.com, http://www.Ancestry.com, Year: 1920; Census Place: Albertville, Marshall, Alabama; Roll: T625_28; Page: 9A; Enumeration District: 122; Image:. Birth date: about 1850 Birth place: Tennessee Residence date: 1920 Residence place: Albertville, Marshall, Alabama.

993	Ancestry.com, 1920 United States Federal Census (Online publication - Provo, UT, USA: Ancestry.com Operations Inc, 2010. Images reproduced by FamilySearch. Original data - Fourteenth Census of the United States, 1920. (NARA microfilm publication T625, 2076 rolls). Records of the Bureau of the Census, Record), Ancestry.com, http://www.Ancestry.com, Year: 1920; Census Place: Albertville, Marshall, Alabama; Roll: T625_28; Page: 9A; Enumeration District: 122; Image:. Birth date: about 1902 Birth place: Alabama Residence date: 1920 Residence place: Albertville, Marshall, Alabama.

994	Ancestry.com, 1910 United States Federal Census (Online publication - Provo, UT, USA: Ancestry.com Operations Inc, 2006. Original data - Thirteenth Census of the United States, 1910 (NARA microfilm publication T624, 1,178 rolls). Records of the Bureau of the Census, Record Group 29. National Archives, Washington), Ancestry.com, http://www.Ancestry.com, Year: 1910; Census Place: Alabama Ward 2, Etowah, Alabama; Roll: ; Page: ; Enumeration District: ; Image:. Birth date: about 1905 Birth place: Alabama Residence date: 1910 Residence place: Alabama Ward 2, Etowah, Alabama.

995	Ancestry.com, 1920 United States Federal Census (Online publication - Provo, UT, USA: Ancestry.com Operations Inc, 2010. Images reproduced by FamilySearch. Original data - Fourteenth Census of the United States, 1920. (NARA microfilm publication T625, 2076 rolls). Records of the Bureau of the Census, Record), Ancestry.com, http://www.Ancestry.com, Year: 1920; Census Place: Albertville, Marshall, Alabama; Roll: T625_28; Page: 9A; Enumeration District: 122; Image:. Birth date: about 1905 Birth place: Alabama Residence date: 1920 Residence place: Albertville, Marshall, Alabama.

996	Ancestry.com, 1900 United States Federal Census (Online publication - Provo, UT, USA: Ancestry.com Operations Inc, 2004. Original data - United States of America, Bureau of the Census. Twelfth Census of the United States, 1900. Washington, D.C.: National Archives and Records Administration, 1900. T623, 18), Ancestry.com, http://www.Ancestry.com, Year: 1900; Census Place: Friendship, Marshall, Alabama; Roll: T623_30; Page: 5A; Enumeration District: 92. Birth date: Dec 1878 Birth place: Georgia Residence date: 1900 Residence place: Friendship, Marshall, Alabama.

997	Ancestry.com, 1900 United States Federal Census (Online publication - Provo, UT, USA: Ancestry.com Operations Inc, 2004. Original data - United States of America, Bureau of the Census. Twelfth Census of the United States, 1900. Washington, D.C.: National Archives and Records Administration, 1900. T623, 18), Ancestry.com, http://www.Ancestry.com, Year: 1900; Census Place: Friendship, Marshall, Alabama; Roll: T623_30; Page: 5A; Enumeration District: 92. Birth date: Feb 1881 Birth place: Georgia Residence date: 1900 Residence place: Friendship, Marshall, Alabama.

998	Ancestry.com, 1900 United States Federal Census (Online publication - Provo, UT, USA: Ancestry.com Operations Inc, 2004. Original data - United States of America, Bureau of the Census. Twelfth Census of the United States, 1900. Washington, D.C.: National Archives and Records Administration, 1900. T623, 18), Ancestry.com, http://www.Ancestry.com, Year: 1900; Census Place: Friendship, Marshall, Alabama; Roll: T623_30; Page: 5A; Enumeration District: 92. Birth date: Dec 1883 Birth place: Texas Residence date: 1900 Residence place: Friendship, Marshall, Alabama.

999	Ancestry.com, 1900 United States Federal Census (Online publication - Provo, UT, USA: Ancestry.com Operations Inc, 2004. Original data - United States of America, Bureau of the Census. Twelfth Census of the United States, 1900. Washington, D.C.: National Archives and Records Administration, 1900. T623, 18), Ancestry.com, http://www.Ancestry.com, Year: 1900; Census Place: Friendship, Marshall, Alabama; Roll: T623_30; Page: 5A; Enumeration District: 92. Birth date: Nov 1893 Birth place: Alabama Residence date: 1900 Residence place: Friendship, Marshall, Alabama.

1000	Ancestry.com, 1900 United States Federal Census (Online publication - Provo, UT, USA: Ancestry.com Operations Inc, 2004. Original data - United States of America, Bureau of the Census. Twelfth Census of the United States, 1900. Washington, D.C.: National Archives and Records Administration, 1900. T623, 18), Ancestry.com, http://www.Ancestry.com, Year: 1900; Census Place: Friendship, Marshall, Alabama; Roll: T623_30; Page: 5A; Enumeration District: 92. Birth date: Apr 1895 Birth place: Alabama Residence date: 1900 Residence place: Friendship, Marshall, Alabama.

1001	Ancestry.com, 1920 United States Federal Census (Online publication - Provo, UT, USA: Ancestry.com Operations Inc, 2010. Images reproduced by FamilySearch. Original data - Fourteenth Census of the United States, 1920. (NARA microfilm publication T625, 2076 rolls). Records of the Bureau of the Census, Record), Ancestry.com, http://www.Ancestry.com, Year: 1920; Census Place: Weavers, Calhoun, Alabama; Roll: T625_5; Page: 6A; Enumeration District: 4; Image:. Birth date: about 1877 Birth place: Alabama Residence date: 1920 Residence place: Weavers, Calhoun, Alabama.

1002	Ancestry.com, Anniston Star (Anniston, Alabama) (Online publication - Provo, UT, USA: Ancestry.com Operations Inc, 2007. Original data - Anniston Star. Anniston, Alabama, United States Of America. Database created from microfilm copies of the newspaper. Original data: Anniston Star. Anniston, Alabama, Unit), Ancestry.com, http://www.Ancestry.com.

1003	Ancestry.com, Alabama Deaths, 1908-59 (Online publication - Provo, UT, USA: Ancestry.com Operations Inc, 2000. Original data - State of Alabama. Index of Vital Records for Alabama: Deaths, 1908-1959. Montgomery, AL, USA: State of Alabama Center for Health Statistics, Record Services Division. Original), Ancestry.com, http://www.Ancestry.com, Death date: 18 Sep 1945 Death place: Calhoun.

1004   Ancestry.com, 1900 United States Federal Census (Online publication - Provo, UT, USA: Ancestry.com Operations Inc, 2004. Original data - United States of America, Bureau of the Census. Twelfth Census of the United States, 1900. Washington, D.C.: National Archives and Records Administration, 1900. T623, 18), Ancestry.com, http://www.Ancestry.com, Year: 1900; Census Place: Rock Spring, Marshall, Alabama; Roll: T623_30; Page: 5A; Enumeration District: 90. Birth date: Apr 1877 Birth place: Alabama Marriage date: 1892 Marriage place: Residence date: 1900 Residence place: Rock Spring, Marshall, Alabama.

1005   Ancestry.com, 1910 United States Federal Census (Online publication - Provo, UT, USA: Ancestry.com Operations Inc, 2006. Original data - Thirteenth Census of the United States, 1910 (NARA microfilm publication T624, 1,178 rolls). Records of the Bureau of the Census, Record Group 29. National Archives, Washington), Ancestry.com, http://www.Ancestry.com, Year: 1910; Census Place: Weaver, Calhoun, Alabama; Roll: ; Page: ; Enumeration District: ; Image:. Birth date: about 1874 Birth place: Alabama Residence date: 1910 Residence place: Weaver, Calhoun, Alabama.

1006   Ancestry.com, Anniston Star (Anniston, Alabama) (Online publication - Provo, UT, USA: Ancestry.com Operations Inc, 2007. Original data - Anniston Star. Anniston, Alabama, United States Of America. Database created from microfilm copies of the newspaper. Original data: Anniston Star. Anniston, Alabama, Unit), Ancestry.com, http://www.Ancestry.com, Memoriam person from children.

1007   Ancestry.com, 1900 United States Federal Census (Online publication - Provo, UT, USA: Ancestry.com Operations Inc, 2004. Original data - United States of America, Bureau of the Census. Twelfth Census of the United States, 1900. Washington, D.C.: National Archives and Records Administration, 1900. T623, 18), Ancestry.com, http://www.Ancestry.com, Year: 1900; Census Place: Rock Spring, Marshall, Alabama; Roll: T623_30; Page: 5A; Enumeration District: 90. Birth date: May 1894 Birth place: Alabama Residence date: 1900 Residence place: Rock Spring, Marshall, Alabama.

1008   Ancestry.com, Social Security Death Index (Online publication - Provo, UT, USA: Ancestry.com Operations Inc, 2010. Original data - Social Security Administration. Social Security Death Index, Master File. Social Security Administration. Original data: Social Security Administration. Social Security Death Index, Master File. Social Security D), Ancestry.com, http://www.Ancestry.com, Number: 417-30-3474; Issue State: Alabama; Issue Date: Before 1951. Birth date: 25 May 1894 Birth place: Death date: Jun 1970 Death place: Piedmont, Calhoun, Alabama, United States of America.

1009   Ancestry.com, 1910 United States Federal Census (Online publication - Provo, UT, USA: Ancestry.com Operations Inc, 2006. Original data - Thirteenth Census of the United States, 1910 (NARA microfilm publication T624, 1,178 rolls). Records of the Bureau of the Census, Record Group 29. National Archives, Washington), Ancestry.com, http://www.Ancestry.com, Year: 1910; Census Place: Weaver, Calhoun, Alabama; Roll: ; Page: ; Enumeration District: ; Image:. Birth date: about 1894 Birth place: Alabama Residence date: 1910 Residence place: Weaver, Calhoun, Alabama.

1010   Ancestry.com, 1920 United States Federal Census (Online publication - Provo, UT, USA: Ancestry.com Operations Inc, 2010. Images reproduced by FamilySearch. Original data - Fourteenth Census of the United States, 1920. (NARA microfilm publication T625, 2076 rolls). Records of the Bureau of the Census, Record), Ancestry.com, http://www.Ancestry.com, Year: 1920; Census Place: Crumley, DeKalb, Alabama; Roll: T625_12; Page: 5B; Enumeration District: 84; Image:. Birth date: about 1895 Birth place: Alabama Residence date: 1920 Residence place: Crumley, DeKalb, Alabama.

1011   Ancestry.com, 1930 United States Federal Census (Online publication - Provo, UT, USA: Ancestry.com Operations Inc, 2002. Original data - United States of America, Bureau of the Census. Fifteenth Census of the United States, 1930. Washington, D.C.: National Archives and Records Administration, 1930. T626,), Ancestry.com, http://www.Ancestry.com, Year: 1930; Census Place: Burns Cross Roads, Calhoun, Alabama; Roll: 5; Page: 18A; Enumeration District: 7; Image: 190.0. Birth date: about 1895 Birth place: Residence date: 1930 Residence place: Burns Cross Roads, Calhoun, Alabama.

1012   Ancestry.com, 1920 United States Federal Census (Online publication - Provo, UT, USA: Ancestry.com Operations Inc, 2010. Images reproduced by FamilySearch. Original data - Fourteenth Census of the United States, 1920. (NARA microfilm publication T625, 2076 rolls). Records of the Bureau of the Census, Record), Ancestry.com, http://www.Ancestry.com, Year: 1920; Census Place: Weavers, Calhoun, Alabama; Roll: T625_5; Page: 6A; Enumeration District: 4; Image:. Birth date: about 1901 Birth place: Alabama Residence date: 1920 Residence place: Weavers, Calhoun, Alabama.

1013   Ancestry.com, World War I Draft Registration Cards, 1917-1918 (Online publication - Provo, UT, USA: Ancestry.com Operations Inc, 2005. Original data - United States, Selective Service System. World War I Selective Service System Draft Registration Cards, 1917-1918. Washington, D.C.: National Archives and Records Administration), Ancestry.com, http://www.Ancestry.com, Registration Location: Calhoun County, Alabama; Roll: 1509363; Draft Board: 0. Birth date: 5 Jun 1900 Birth place: Residence date: Residence place: Calhoun, Alabama.

1014   Ancestry.com, 1910 United States Federal Census (Online publication - Provo, UT, USA: Ancestry.com Operations Inc, 2006. Original data - Thirteenth Census of the United States, 1910 (NARA microfilm publication T624, 1,178 rolls). Records of the Bureau of the Census, Record Group 29. National Archives, Washington), Ancestry.com, http://www.Ancestry.com, Year: 1910; Census Place: Weaver, Calhoun, Alabama; Roll: ; Page: ; Enumeration District: ; Image:. Birth date: about 1901 Birth place: Alabama Residence date: 1910 Residence place: Weaver, Calhoun, Alabama.

1015   Ancestry.com, 1910 United States Federal Census (Online publication - Provo, UT, USA: Ancestry.com Operations Inc, 2006. Original data - Thirteenth Census of the United States, 1910 (NARA microfilm publication T624, 1,178 rolls). Records of the Bureau of the Census, Record Group 29. National Archives, Washington), Ancestry.com,

http://www.Ancestry.com, Year: 1910; Census Place: Weaver, Calhoun, Alabama; Roll: ; Page: ; Enumeration District: ; Image:. Birth date: about 1903 Birth place: Alabama Residence date: 1910 Residence place: Weaver, Calhoun, Alabama.

1016   Ancestry.com, Social Security Death Index (Online publication - Provo, UT, USA: Ancestry.com Operations Inc, 2010. Original data - Social Security Administration. Social Security Death Index, Master File. Social Security Administration. Original data: Social Security Administration. Social Security D), Ancestry.com, http://www.Ancestry.com, Number: 422-01-3946; Issue State: Alabama; Issue Date: Before 1951. Birth date: 3 Oct 1902 Birth place: Death date: 17 Nov 1992 Death place: Ohatchee, Calhoun, Alabama, United States of America.

1017   Ancestry.com, Anniston Star (Anniston, Alabama) (Online publication - Provo, UT, USA: Ancestry.com Operations Inc, 2007. Original data - Anniston Star. Anniston, Alabama, United States Of America. Database created from microfilm copies of the newspaper. Original data: Anniston Star. Anniston, Alabama, Unit), Ancestry.com, http://www.Ancestry.com.

1018   Ancestry.com, Anniston Star (Anniston, Alabama) (Online publication - Provo, UT, USA: Ancestry.com Operations Inc, 2007. Original data - Anniston Star. Anniston, Alabama, United States Of America. Database created from microfilm copies of the newspaper. Original data: Anniston Star. Anniston, Alabama, Unit), Ancestry.com, http://www.Ancestry.com.

1019   Ancestry.com, Social Security Death Index (Online publication - Provo, UT, USA: Ancestry.com Operations Inc, 2010. Original data - Social Security Administration. Social Security Death Index, Master File. Social Security Administration. Original data: Social Security Administration. Social Security D), Ancestry.com, http://www.Ancestry.com, Number: 418-07-5722; Issue State: Alabama; Issue Date: Before 1951. Birth date: 10 May 1904 Birth place: Death date: Jul 1984 Death place: Anniston, Calhoun, Alabama, United States of America.

1020   Ancestry.com, 1910 United States Federal Census (Online publication - Provo, UT, USA: Ancestry.com Operations Inc, 2006. Original data - Thirteenth Census of the United States, 1910 (NARA microfilm publication T624, 1,178 rolls). Records of the Bureau of the Census, Record Group 29. National Archives, Washington), Ancestry.com, http://www.Ancestry.com, Year: 1910; Census Place: Weaver, Calhoun, Alabama; Roll: ; Page: ; Enumeration District: ; Image:. Birth date: about 1905 Birth place: Alabama Residence date: 1910 Residence place: Weaver, Calhoun, Alabama.

1021   Ancestry.com, 1920 United States Federal Census (Online publication - Provo, UT, USA: Ancestry.com Operations Inc, 2010. Images reproduced by FamilySearch. Original data - Fourteenth Census of the United States, 1920. (NARA microfilm publication T625, 2076 rolls). Records of the Bureau of the Census, Record), Ancestry.com, http://www.Ancestry.com, Year: 1920; Census Place: Weavers, Calhoun, Alabama; Roll: T625_5; Page: 6A; Enumeration District: 4; Image:. Birth date: about 1905 Birth place: Alabama Residence date: 1920 Residence place: Weavers, Calhoun, Alabama.

1022   Ancestry.com, 1910 United States Federal Census (Online publication - Provo, UT, USA: Ancestry.com Operations Inc, 2006. Original data - Thirteenth Census of the United States, 1910 (NARA microfilm publication T624, 1,178 rolls). Records of the Bureau of the Census, Record Group 29. National Archives, Washington), Ancestry.com, http://www.Ancestry.com, Year: 1910; Census Place: Weaver, Calhoun, Alabama; Roll: ; Page: ; Enumeration District: ; Image:. Birth date: about 1908 Birth place: Alabama Residence date: 1910 Residence place: Weaver, Calhoun, Alabama.

1023   Ancestry.com, 1920 United States Federal Census (Online publication - Provo, UT, USA: Ancestry.com Operations Inc, 2010. Images reproduced by FamilySearch. Original data - Fourteenth Census of the United States, 1920. (NARA microfilm publication T625, 2076 rolls). Records of the Bureau of the Census, Record), Ancestry.com, http://www.Ancestry.com, Year: 1920; Census Place: Weavers, Calhoun, Alabama; Roll: T625_5; Page: 6A; Enumeration District: 4; Image:. Birth date: about 1907 Birth place: Alabama Residence date: 1920 Residence place: Weavers, Calhoun, Alabama.

1024   Ancestry.com, 1930 United States Federal Census (Online publication - Provo, UT, USA: Ancestry.com Operations Inc, 2002. Original data - United States of America, Bureau of the Census. Fifteenth Census of the United States, 1930. Washington, D.C.: National Archives and Records Administration, 1930. T626,), Ancestry.com, http://www.Ancestry.com, Year: 1930; Census Place: Gadsden, Etowah, Alabama; Roll: 16; Page: 17B; Enumeration District: 3; Image: 116.0. Birth date: about 1907 Birth place: Residence date: 1930 Residence place: Gadsden, Etowah, Alabama.

1025   Ancestry.com, 1910 United States Federal Census (Online publication - Provo, UT, USA: Ancestry.com Operations Inc, 2006. Original data - Thirteenth Census of the United States, 1910 (NARA microfilm publication T624, 1,178 rolls). Records of the Bureau of the Census, Record Group 29. National Archives, Washington), Ancestry.com, http://www.Ancestry.com, Year: 1910; Census Place: Weaver, Calhoun, Alabama; Roll: ; Page: ; Enumeration District: ; Image:. Birth date: about 1907 Birth place: Alabama Residence date: 1910 Residence place: Weaver, Calhoun, Alabama.

1026   Ancestry.com, Social Security Death Index (Online publication - Provo, UT, USA: Ancestry.com Operations Inc, 2010. Original data - Social Security Administration. Social Security Death Index, Master File. Social Security Administration. Original data: Social Security Administration. Social Security D), Ancestry.com, http://www.Ancestry.com, Number: 422-01-3857; Issue State: Alabama; Issue Date: Before 1951. Birth date: 13 Oct 1910 Birth place: Death date: Feb 1991 Death place:.

1027   Ancestry.com, 1920 United States Federal Census (Online publication - Provo, UT, USA: Ancestry.com Operations Inc, 2010. Images reproduced by FamilySearch. Original data - Fourteenth Census of the United States, 1920. (NARA microfilm publication T625, 2076 rolls). Records of the Bureau of the Census, Record), Ancestry.com, http://www.Ancestry.com, Year: 1920; Census Place: Weavers, Calhoun, Alabama; Roll: T625_5; Page: 6A; Enumeration

District: 4; Image:. Birth date: about 1911 Birth place: Alabama Residence date: 1920 Residence place: Weavers, Calhoun, Alabama.

1028   Ancestry.com, Social Security Death Index (Online publication - Provo, UT, USA: Ancestry.com Operations Inc, 2010. Original data - Social Security Administration. Social Security Death Index, Master File. Social Security Administration. Original data: Social Security Administration. Social Security D), Ancestry.com, http://www.Ancestry.com, Number: 419-09-0459; Issue State: Alabama; Issue Date: Before 1951. Birth date: 9 Nov 1914 Birth place: Death date: 5 Sep 1995 Death place: Anniston, Calhoun, Alabama, United States of America.

1029   Ancestry.com, 1920 United States Federal Census (Online publication - Provo, UT, USA: Ancestry.com Operations Inc, 2010. Images reproduced by FamilySearch. Original data - Fourteenth Census of the United States, 1920. (NARA microfilm publication T625, 2076 rolls). Records of the Bureau of the Census, Record), Ancestry.com, http://www.Ancestry.com, Year: 1920; Census Place: Weavers, Calhoun, Alabama; Roll: T625_5; Page: 6A; Enumeration District: 4; Image:. Birth date: about 1915 Birth place: Alabama Residence date: 1920 Residence place: Weavers, Calhoun, Alabama.

1030   Ancestry.com, 1920 United States Federal Census (Online publication - Provo, UT, USA: Ancestry.com Operations Inc, 2010. Images reproduced by FamilySearch. Original data - Fourteenth Census of the United States, 1920. (NARA microfilm publication T625, 2076 rolls). Records of the Bureau of the Census, Record), Ancestry.com, http://www.Ancestry.com, Year: 1920; Census Place: Weavers, Calhoun, Alabama; Roll: T625_5; Page: 6A; Enumeration District: 4; Image:. Birth date: about 1917 Birth place: Alabama Residence date: 1920 Residence place: Weavers, Calhoun, Alabama.

1031   Ancestry.com, 1920 United States Federal Census (Online publication - Provo, UT, USA: Ancestry.com Operations Inc, 2010. Images reproduced by FamilySearch. Original data - Fourteenth Census of the United States, 1920. (NARA microfilm publication T625, 2076 rolls). Records of the Bureau of the Census, Record), Ancestry.com, http://www.Ancestry.com, Year: 1920; Census Place: Weavers, Calhoun, Alabama; Roll: T625_5; Page: 8B; Enumeration District: 4; Image:. Birth date: about 1870 Birth place: Alabama Residence date: 1920 Residence place: Weavers, Calhoun, Alabama.

1032   Ancestry.com, 1910 United States Federal Census (Online publication - Provo, UT, USA: Ancestry.com Operations Inc, 2006. Original data - Thirteenth Census of the United States, 1910 (NARA microfilm publication T624, 1,178 rolls). Records of the Bureau of the Census, Record Group 29. National Archives, Washington), Ancestry.com, http://www.Ancestry.com, Year: 1910; Census Place: Weaver, Calhoun, Alabama; Roll: ; Page: ; Enumeration District: ; Image:. Birth date: about 1870 Birth place: Alabama Residence date: 1910 Residence place: Weaver, Calhoun, Alabama.

1033   Ancestry.com, 1900 United States Federal Census (Online publication - Provo, UT, USA: Ancestry.com Operations Inc, 2004. Original data - United States of America, Bureau of the Census. Twelfth Census of the United States, 1900. Washington, D.C.: National Archives and Records Administration, 1900. T623, 18), Ancestry.com, http://www.Ancestry.com, Year: 1900; Census Place: Weavers, Calhoun, Alabama; Roll: T623_5; Page: 3A; Enumeration District: 27. Birth date: Jul 1892 Birth place: Alabama Residence date: 1900 Residence place: Weavers, Calhoun, Alabama.

1034   Ancestry.com, 1910 United States Federal Census (Online publication - Provo, UT, USA: Ancestry.com Operations Inc, 2006. Original data - Thirteenth Census of the United States, 1910 (NARA microfilm publication T624, 1,178 rolls). Records of the Bureau of the Census, Record Group 29. National Archives, Washington), Ancestry.com, http://www.Ancestry.com, Year: 1910; Census Place: Weaver, Calhoun, Alabama; Roll: ; Page: ; Enumeration District: ; Image:. Birth date: about 1892 Birth place: Alabama Residence date: 1910 Residence place: Weaver, Calhoun, Alabama.

1035   Ancestry.com, 1910 United States Federal Census (Online publication - Provo, UT, USA: Ancestry.com Operations Inc, 2006. Original data - Thirteenth Census of the United States, 1910 (NARA microfilm publication T624, 1,178 rolls). Records of the Bureau of the Census, Record Group 29. National Archives, Washington), Ancestry.com, http://www.Ancestry.com, Year: 1910; Census Place: Weaver, Calhoun, Alabama; Roll: ; Page: ; Enumeration District: ; Image:. Birth date: about 1894 Birth place: Alabama Residence date: 1910 Residence place: Weaver, Calhoun, Alabama.

1036   Ancestry.com, 1900 United States Federal Census (Online publication - Provo, UT, USA: Ancestry.com Operations Inc, 2004. Original data - United States of America, Bureau of the Census. Twelfth Census of the United States, 1900. Washington, D.C.: National Archives and Records Administration, 1900. T623, 18), Ancestry.com, http://www.Ancestry.com, Year: 1900; Census Place: Weavers, Calhoun, Alabama; Roll: T623_5; Page: 3A; Enumeration District: 27. Birth date: Jan 1893 Birth place: Alabama Residence date: 1900 Residence place: Weavers, Calhoun, Alabama.

1037   Ancestry.com, 1900 United States Federal Census (Online publication - Provo, UT, USA: Ancestry.com Operations Inc, 2004. Original data - United States of America, Bureau of the Census. Twelfth Census of the United States, 1900. Washington, D.C.: National Archives and Records Administration, 1900. T623, 18), Ancestry.com, http://www.Ancestry.com, Year: 1900; Census Place: Weavers, Calhoun, Alabama; Roll: T623_5; Page: 3A; Enumeration District: 27. Birth date: Jan 1896 Birth place: Alabama Residence date: 1900 Residence place: Weavers, Calhoun, Alabama.

1038   Ancestry.com, 1920 United States Federal Census (Online publication - Provo, UT, USA: Ancestry.com Operations Inc, 2010. Images reproduced by FamilySearch. Original data - Fourteenth Census of the United States, 1920. (NARA microfilm publication T625, 2076 rolls). Records of the Bureau of the Census, Record), Ancestry.com, http://www.Ancestry.com, Year: 1920; Census Place: Weavers, Calhoun, Alabama; Roll: T625_5; Page: 8B; Enumeration

District: 4; Image:. Birth date: about 1901 Birth place: Alabama Residence date: 1920 Residence place: Weavers, Calhoun, Alabama.

1039   Ancestry.com, 1910 United States Federal Census (Online publication - Provo, UT, USA: Ancestry.com Operations Inc, 2006. Original data - Thirteenth Census of the United States, 1910 (NARA microfilm publication T624, 1,178 rolls). Records of the Bureau of the Census, Record Group 29. National Archives, Washington), Ancestry.com, http://www.Ancestry.com, Year: 1910; Census Place: Weaver, Calhoun, Alabama; Roll: ; Page: ; Enumeration District: ; Image:. Birth date: about 1900 Birth place: Alabama Residence date: 1910 Residence place: Weaver, Calhoun, Alabama.

1040   Ancestry.com, 1910 United States Federal Census (Online publication - Provo, UT, USA: Ancestry.com Operations Inc, 2006. Original data - Thirteenth Census of the United States, 1910 (NARA microfilm publication T624, 1,178 rolls). Records of the Bureau of the Census, Record Group 29. National Archives, Washington), Ancestry.com, http://www.Ancestry.com, Year: 1910; Census Place: Weaver, Calhoun, Alabama; Roll: ; Page: ; Enumeration District: ; Image:. Birth date: about 1903 Birth place: Alabama Residence date: 1910 Residence place: Weaver, Calhoun, Alabama.

1041   Ancestry.com, 1920 United States Federal Census (Online publication - Provo, UT, USA: Ancestry.com Operations Inc, 2010. Images reproduced by FamilySearch. Original data - Fourteenth Census of the United States, 1920. (NARA microfilm publication T625, 2076 rolls). Records of the Bureau of the Census, Record), Ancestry.com, http://www.Ancestry.com, Year: 1920; Census Place: Weavers, Calhoun, Alabama; Roll: T625_5; Page: 8B; Enumeration District: 4; Image:. Birth date: about 1903 Birth place: Alabama Residence date: 1920 Residence place: Weavers, Calhoun, Alabama.

1042   Ancestry.com, 1920 United States Federal Census (Online publication - Provo, UT, USA: Ancestry.com Operations Inc, 2010. Images reproduced by FamilySearch. Original data - Fourteenth Census of the United States, 1920. (NARA microfilm publication T625, 2076 rolls). Records of the Bureau of the Census, Record), Ancestry.com, http://www.Ancestry.com, Year: 1920; Census Place: Weavers, Calhoun, Alabama; Roll: T625_5; Page: 8B; Enumeration District: 4; Image:. Birth date: about 1908 Birth place: Alabama Residence date: 1920 Residence place: Weavers, Calhoun, Alabama.

1043   Ancestry.com, 1920 United States Federal Census (Online publication - Provo, UT, USA: Ancestry.com Operations Inc, 2010. Images reproduced by FamilySearch. Original data - Fourteenth Census of the United States, 1920. (NARA microfilm publication T625, 2076 rolls). Records of the Bureau of the Census, Record), Ancestry.com, http://www.Ancestry.com, Year: 1920; Census Place: Weavers, Calhoun, Alabama; Roll: T625_5; Page: 8B; Enumeration District: 4; Image:. Birth date: about 1911 Birth place: Alabama Residence date: 1920 Residence place: Weavers, Calhoun, Alabama.

1044   Ancestry.com, 1920 United States Federal Census (Online publication - Provo, UT, USA: Ancestry.com Operations Inc, 2010. Images reproduced by FamilySearch. Original data - Fourteenth Census of the United States, 1920. (NARA microfilm publication T625, 2076 rolls). Records of the Bureau of the Census, Record), Ancestry.com, http://www.Ancestry.com, Year: 1920; Census Place: Weavers, Calhoun, Alabama; Roll: T625_5; Page: 8B; Enumeration District: 4; Image:. Birth date: about 1914 Birth place: Alabama Residence date: 1920 Residence place: Weavers, Calhoun, Alabama.

1045   Ancestry.com, 1920 United States Federal Census (Online publication - Provo, UT, USA: Ancestry.com Operations Inc, 2010. Images reproduced by FamilySearch. Original data - Fourteenth Census of the United States, 1920. (NARA microfilm publication T625, 2076 rolls). Records of the Bureau of the Census, Record), Ancestry.com, http://www.Ancestry.com, Year: 1920; Census Place: Weavers, Calhoun, Alabama; Roll: T625_5; Page: 8B; Enumeration District: 4; Image:. Birth date: about 1918 Birth place: Alabama Residence date: 1920 Residence place: Weavers, Calhoun, Alabama.

1046   Ancestry.com, 1930 United States Federal Census (Online publication - Provo, UT, USA: Ancestry.com Operations Inc, 2002. Original data - United States of America, Bureau of the Census. Fifteenth Census of the United States, 1930. Washington, D.C.: National Archives and Records Administration, 1930. T626,), Ancestry.com, http://www.Ancestry.com, Year: 1930; Census Place: Jay Bird, Marshall, Alabama; Roll: 39; Page: 5A; Enumeration District: 8; Image: 757.0. Birth date: about 1922 Birth place: Residence date: 1930 Residence place: Jay Bird, Marshall, Alabama.

1047   Ancestry.com, 1930 United States Federal Census (Online publication - Provo, UT, USA: Ancestry.com Operations Inc, 2002. Original data - United States of America, Bureau of the Census. Fifteenth Census of the United States, 1930. Washington, D.C.: National Archives and Records Administration, 1930. T626,), Ancestry.com, http://www.Ancestry.com, Year: 1930; Census Place: Jay Bird, Marshall, Alabama; Roll: 39; Page: 5A; Enumeration District: 8; Image: 757.0. Birth date: about 1924 Birth place: Residence date: 1930 Residence place: Jay Bird, Marshall, Alabama.

1048   Ancestry.com, 1930 United States Federal Census (Online publication - Provo, UT, USA: Ancestry.com Operations Inc, 2002. Original data - United States of America, Bureau of the Census. Fifteenth Census of the United States, 1930. Washington, D.C.: National Archives and Records Administration, 1930. T626,), Ancestry.com, http://www.Ancestry.com, Year: 1930; Census Place: Jay Bird, Marshall, Alabama; Roll: 39; Page: 5A; Enumeration District: 8; Image: 757.0. Birth date: about 1926 Birth place: Residence date: 1930 Residence place: Jay Bird, Marshall, Alabama.

1049   Ancestry.com, 1930 United States Federal Census (Online publication - Provo, UT, USA: Ancestry.com Operations Inc, 2002. Original data - United States of America, Bureau of the Census. Fifteenth Census of the United States, 1930. Washington, D.C.: National Archives and Records Administration, 1930. T626,), Ancestry.com,

http://www.Ancestry.com, Year: 1930; Census Place: Jay Bird, Marshall, Alabama; Roll: 39; Page: 5A; Enumeration District: 8; Image: 757.0. Birth date: about 1928 Birth place: Residence date: 1930 Residence place: Jay Bird, Marshall, Alabama.

1050   Ancestry.com, 1930 United States Federal Census (Online publication - Provo, UT, USA: Ancestry.com Operations Inc, 2002. Original data - United States of America, Bureau of the Census. Fifteenth Census of the United States, 1930. Washington, D.C.: National Archives and Records Administration, 1930. T626,), Ancestry.com, http://www.Ancestry.com, Year: 1930; Census Place: Jay Bird, Marshall, Alabama; Roll: 39; Page: 5A; Enumeration District: 8; Image: 757.0. Birth date: about 1928 Birth place: Residence date: 1930 Residence place: Jay Bird, Marshall, Alabama.

1051   Ancestry.com, 1920 United States Federal Census (Online publication - Provo, UT, USA: Ancestry.com Operations Inc, 2010. Images reproduced by FamilySearch. Original data - Fourteenth Census of the United States, 1920. (NARA microfilm publication T625, 2076 rolls). Records of the Bureau of the Census, Record), Ancestry.com, http://www.Ancestry.com, Year: 1920; Census Place: Lincoln, Talladega, Alabama; Roll: T625_41; Page: 1A; Enumeration District: 129; Image:. Birth date: about 1892 Birth place: Alabama Residence date: 1920 Residence place: Lincoln, Talladega, Alabama.

1052   Ancestry.com, 1930 United States Federal Census (Online publication - Provo, UT, USA: Ancestry.com Operations Inc, 2002. Original data - United States of America, Bureau of the Census. Fifteenth Census of the United States, 1930. Washington, D.C.: National Archives and Records Administration, 1930. T626,), Ancestry.com, http://www.Ancestry.com, Year: 1930; Census Place: Jay Bird, Marshall, Alabama; Roll: 39; Page: 5A; Enumeration District: 8; Image: 757.0. Birth date: about 1916 Birth place: Residence date: 1930 Residence place: Jay Bird, Marshall, Alabama.

1053   Ancestry.com, 1920 United States Federal Census (Online publication - Provo, UT, USA: Ancestry.com Operations Inc, 2010. Images reproduced by FamilySearch. Original data - Fourteenth Census of the United States, 1920. (NARA microfilm publication T625, 2076 rolls). Records of the Bureau of the Census, Record), Ancestry.com, http://www.Ancestry.com, Year: 1920; Census Place: Lincoln, Talladega, Alabama; Roll: T625_41; Page: 1A; Enumeration District: 129; Image:. Birth date: about 1916 Birth place: Alabama Residence date: 1920 Residence place: Lincoln, Talladega, Alabama.

1054   Ancestry.com, 1920 United States Federal Census (Online publication - Provo, UT, USA: Ancestry.com Operations Inc, 2010. Images reproduced by FamilySearch. Original data - Fourteenth Census of the United States, 1920. (NARA microfilm publication T625, 2076 rolls). Records of the Bureau of the Census, Record), Ancestry.com, http://www.Ancestry.com, Year: 1920; Census Place: Lincoln, Talladega, Alabama; Roll: T625_41; Page: 1A; Enumeration District: 129; Image:. Birth date: about 1918 Birth place: Alabama Residence date: 1920 Residence place: Lincoln, Talladega, Alabama.

1055   Ancestry.com, 1930 United States Federal Census (Online publication - Provo, UT, USA: Ancestry.com Operations Inc, 2002. Original data - United States of America, Bureau of the Census. Fifteenth Census of the United States, 1930. Washington, D.C.: National Archives and Records Administration, 1930. T626,), Ancestry.com, http://www.Ancestry.com, Year: 1930; Census Place: Jay Bird, Marshall, Alabama; Roll: 39; Page: 5A; Enumeration District: 8; Image: 757.0. Birth date: about 1918 Birth place: Residence date: 1930 Residence place: Jay Bird, Marshall, Alabama.

1056   Ancestry.com, 1920 United States Federal Census (Online publication - Provo, UT, USA: Ancestry.com Operations Inc, 2010. Images reproduced by FamilySearch. Original data - Fourteenth Census of the United States, 1920. (NARA microfilm publication T625, 2076 rolls). Records of the Bureau of the Census, Record), Ancestry.com, http://www.Ancestry.com, Year: 1920; Census Place: Lincoln, Talladega, Alabama; Roll: T625_41; Page: 1A; Enumeration District: 129; Image:. Birth date: about 1920 Birth place: Alabama Residence date: 1920 Residence place: Lincoln, Talladega, Alabama.

1057   Ancestry.com, 1860 United States Federal Census (Online publication - Provo, UT, USA: Ancestry.com Operations, Inc., 2009. Images reproduced by FamilySearch. Original data - 1860 U.S. census, population schedule. NARA microfilm publication M653, 1,438 rolls. Washington, D.C.: National Archives and Records), Ancestry.com, http://www.Ancestry.com, Year: 1860; Census Place: , Union, Louisiana; Roll: ; Page: 533; Image: 69. Name: Chas Autry Birth: about 1850 in Louisiana Death:.

1058   Ancestry.com, Louisiana Statewide Death Index, 1900-1949 (Online publication - Provo, UT, USA: Ancestry.com Operations Inc, 2002. Original data - State of Louisiana, Secretary of State, Division of Archives, Records Management, and History. Vital Records Indices. Baton Rouge, LA, USA. Original data: State of Louisiana), Ancestry.com, http://www.Ancestry.com, Birth date: 1850 Birth place: Death date: 2 Nov 1917 Death place: Louisiana.

1059   Ancestry.com, 1900 United States Federal Census (Online publication - Provo, UT, USA: Ancestry.com Operations Inc, 2004. Original data - United States of America, Bureau of the Census. Twelfth Census of the United States, 1900. Washington, D.C.: National Archives and Records Administration, 1900. T623, 18), Ancestry.com, http://www.Ancestry.com, Year: 1900; Census Place: Police Jury Ward 6, Lincoln, Louisiana; Roll: T623_568; Page: 21A; Enumeration District: 63. Birth date: Apr 1850 Birth place: Louisiana Marriage date: 1889 Marriage place: Residence date: 1900 Residence place: Ward 7, Lincoln, Louisiana.

1060   Ancestry.com, 1910 United States Federal Census (Online publication - Provo, UT, USA: Ancestry.com Operations Inc, 2006. Original data - Thirteenth Census of the United States, 1910 (NARA microfilm publication T624, 1,178 rolls). Records of the Bureau of the Census, Record Group 29. National Archives, Washington), Ancestry.com,

http://www.Ancestry.com, Year: 1910; Census Place: Police Jury Ward 6, Lincoln, Louisiana; Roll: ; Page: ; Enumeration District: ; Image:. Birth date: 1850 Birth place: Louisiana Residence date: 1910 Residence place: Police Jury Ward 6, Lincoln, Louisiana.

1061   Ancestry.com, 1900 United States Federal Census (Online publication - Provo, UT, USA: Ancestry.com Operations Inc, 2004. Original data - United States of America, Bureau of the Census. Twelfth Census of the United States, 1900. Washington, D.C.: National Archives and Records Administration, 1900. T623, 18), Ancestry.com, http://www.Ancestry.com, Year: 1900; Census Place: Police Jury Ward 6, Lincoln, Louisiana; Roll: T623_568; Page: 14A; Enumeration District: 63. Birth date: Aug 1874 Birth place: Louisiana Marriage date: 1892 Marriage place: Residence date: 1900 Residence place: Ward 7, Lincoln, Louisiana.

1062   Ancestry.com, 1900 United States Federal Census (Online publication - Provo, UT, USA: Ancestry.com Operations Inc, 2004. Original data - United States of America, Bureau of the Census. Twelfth Census of the United States, 1900. Washington, D.C.: National Archives and Records Administration, 1900. T623, 18), Ancestry.com, http://www.Ancestry.com, Year: 1900; Census Place: Police Jury Ward 6, Lincoln, Louisiana; Roll: T623_568; Page: 21A; Enumeration District: 63. Birth date: Nov 1884 Birth place: Louisiana Residence date: 1900 Residence place: Ward 7, Lincoln, Louisiana.

1063   Ancestry.com, 1860 United States Federal Census (Online publication - Provo, UT, USA: Ancestry.com Operations, Inc., 2009. Images reproduced by FamilySearch. Original data - 1860 U.S. census, population schedule. NARA microfilm publication M653, 1,438 rolls. Washington, D.C.: National Archives and Records), Ancestry.com, http://www.Ancestry.com, Year: 1860; Census Place: , Union, Louisiana; Roll: ; Page: 533; Image: 69. Birth date: about 1848 Birth place: Alabama Residence date: 1860 Residence place: Union, Louisiana, United States.

1064   Ancestry.com, 1900 United States Federal Census (Online publication - Provo, UT, USA: Ancestry.com Operations Inc, 2004. Original data - United States of America, Bureau of the Census. Twelfth Census of the United States, 1900. Washington, D.C.: National Archives and Records Administration, 1900. T623, 18), Ancestry.com, http://www.Ancestry.com, Year: 1900; Census Place: Justice Precinct 1, Coryell, Texas; Roll: T623_1624; Page: 15A; Enumeration District: 38. Birth date: May 1847 Birth place: Alabama Marriage date: 1891 Marriage place: Residence date: 1900 Residence place: Justice Precinct 1 (West Part Excl. Gatesville City), Coryell, Texas.

1065   Ancestry.com, 1920 United States Federal Census (Online publication - Provo, UT, USA: Ancestry.com Operations Inc, 2010. Images reproduced by FamilySearch. Original data - Fourteenth Census of the United States, 1920. (NARA microfilm publication T625, 2076 rolls). Records of the Bureau of the Census, Record), Ancestry.com, http://www.Ancestry.com, Year: 1920; Census Place: Gatesville, Coryell, Texas; Roll: T625_1787; Page: 14A; Enumeration District: 54; Image:. Birth date: about 1848 Birth place: Alabama Residence date: 1920 Residence place: Gatesville, Coryell, Texas.

1066   Ancestry.com, Texas Death Index, 1903-2000 (Online publication - Provo, UT, USA: Ancestry.com Operations Inc, 2006. Original data - Texas Department of Health. Texas Death Indexes, 1903-2000. Austin, TX, USA: Texas Department of Health, State Vital Statistics Unit. Original data: Texas Department of H), Ancestry.com, http://www.Ancestry.com, Death date: 4 Mar 1922 Death place: Mclennan, Texas.

1067   Ancestry.com, 1900 United States Federal Census (Online publication - Provo, UT, USA: Ancestry.com Operations Inc, 2004. Original data - United States of America, Bureau of the Census. Twelfth Census of the United States, 1900. Washington, D.C.: National Archives and Records Administration, 1900. T623, 18), Ancestry.com, http://www.Ancestry.com, Year: 1900; Census Place: Justice Precinct 1, Coryell, Texas; Roll: T623_1624; Page: 15B; Enumeration District: 38. Birth date: Aug 1874 Birth place: Texas Residence date: 1900 Residence place: Justice Precinct 1 (West Part Excl. Gatesville City), Coryell, Texas.

1068   Ancestry.com, 1910 United States Federal Census (Online publication - Provo, UT, USA: Ancestry.com Operations Inc, 2006. Original data - Thirteenth Census of the United States, 1910 (NARA microfilm publication T624, 1,178 rolls). Records of the Bureau of the Census, Record Group 29. National Archives, Washington), Ancestry.com, http://www.Ancestry.com, Year: 1910; Census Place: Justice Precinct 1, Coryell, Texas; Roll: ; Page: ; Enumeration District: ; Image:. Birth date: about 1875 Birth place: Louisiana Residence date: 1910 Residence place: Justice Precinct 1, Coryell, Texas.

1069   Ancestry.com, 1920 United States Federal Census (Online publication - Provo, UT, USA: Ancestry.com Operations Inc, 2010. Images reproduced by FamilySearch. Original data - Fourteenth Census of the United States, 1920. (NARA microfilm publication T625, 2076 rolls). Records of the Bureau of the Census, Record), Ancestry.com, http://www.Ancestry.com, Year: 1920; Census Place: Purcell, McClain, Oklahoma; Roll: T625_1470; Page: 30A; Enumeration District: 81; Image:. Birth date: about 1873 Birth place: Louisiana Residence date: 1920 Residence place: Purcell, McClain, Oklahoma.

1070   Ancestry.com, 1930 United States Federal Census (Online publication - Provo, UT, USA: Ancestry.com Operations Inc, 2002. Original data - United States of America, Bureau of the Census. Fifteenth Census of the United States, 1930. Washington, D.C.: National Archives and Records Administration, 1930. T626,), Ancestry.com, http://www.Ancestry.com, Year: 1930; Census Place: Precinct 3, Martin, Texas; Roll: 2374; Page: 3B; Enumeration District: 6; Image: 1052.0. Birth date: about 1875 Birth place: Residence date: 1930 Residence place: Precinct 3, Martin, Texas.

1071   Ancestry.com, Texas Death Index, 1903-2000 (Online publication - Provo, UT, USA: Ancestry.com Operations Inc, 2006. Original data - Texas Department of Health. Texas Death Indexes, 1903-2000. Austin, TX, USA: Texas

Department of Health, State Vital Statistics Unit. Original data: Texas Department of H), Ancestry.com, http://www.Ancestry.com, Death date: 24 May 1968 Death place: Midland, Texas.

1072   Ancestry.com and The Church of Jesus Christ of Latter-day Saints, 1880 United States Federal Census (Online publication - Provo, UT, USA: Ancestry.com Operations Inc, 2010. 1880 U.S. Census Index provided by The Church of Jesus Christ of Latter-day Saints © Copyright 1999 Intellectual Reserve, Inc. All rights reserved. All use is subject to the limited), Ancestry.com, http://www.Ancestry.com, Year: 1880; Census Place: 4th Ward, Union, Louisiana; Roll: 473; Family History Film: 1254473; Page: 480A; Enumeration District: 88; Image: 0242. Birth date: about 1838 Birth place: Louisiana Residence date: 1880 Residence place: 4th Ward, Union, Louisiana, United States.

1073   Ancestry.com, 1900 United States Federal Census (Online publication - Provo, UT, USA: Ancestry.com Operations Inc, 2004. Original data - United States of America, Bureau of the Census. Twelfth Census of the United States, 1900. Washington, D.C.: National Archives and Records Administration, 1900. T623, 18), Ancestry.com, http://www.Ancestry.com, Year: 1900; Census Place: Police Jury Ward 4, Union, Louisiana; Roll: T623_585; Page: 15B; Enumeration District: 122. Birth date: Apr 1838 Birth place: Louisiana Marriage date: 1870 Marriage place: Residence date: 1900 Residence place: Bernice Town, Union, Louisiana.

1074   Ancestry.com, 1910 United States Federal Census (Online publication - Provo, UT, USA: Ancestry.com Operations Inc, 2006. Original data - Thirteenth Census of the United States, 1910 (NARA microfilm publication T624, 1,178 rolls). Records of the Bureau of the Census, Record Group 29. National Archives, Washington), Ancestry.com, http://www.Ancestry.com, Year: 1910; Census Place: Police Jury Ward 4, Union, Louisiana; Roll: ; Page: ; Enumeration District: ; Image:. Birth date: about 1838 Birth place: Louisiana Residence date: 1910 Residence place: Police Jury Ward 4, Union, Louisiana.

1075   Ancestry.com and The Church of Jesus Christ of Latter-day Saints, 1880 United States Federal Census (Online publication - Provo, UT, USA: Ancestry.com Operations Inc, 2010. 1880 U.S. Census Index provided by The Church of Jesus Christ of Latter-day Saints © Copyright 1999 Intellectual Reserve, Inc. All rights reserved. All use is subject to the limited), Ancestry.com, http://www.Ancestry.com, Year: 1880; Census Place: 4th Ward, Union, Louisiana; Roll: 473; Family History Film: 1254473; Page: 480A; Enumeration District: 88; Image: 0242. Birth date: about 1870 Birth place: Louisiana Residence date: 1880 Residence place: 4th Ward, Union, Louisiana, United States.

1076   Ancestry.com and The Church of Jesus Christ of Latter-day Saints, 1880 United States Federal Census (Online publication - Provo, UT, USA: Ancestry.com Operations Inc, 2010. 1880 U.S. Census Index provided by The Church of Jesus Christ of Latter-day Saints © Copyright 1999 Intellectual Reserve, Inc. All rights reserved. All use is subject to the limited), Ancestry.com, http://www.Ancestry.com, Year: 1880; Census Place: 4th Ward, Union, Louisiana; Roll: 473; Family History Film: 1254473; Page: 480A; Enumeration District: 88; Image: 0242. Birth date: about 1872 Birth place: Louisiana Residence date: 1880 Residence place: 4th Ward, Union, Louisiana, United States.

1077   Ancestry.com and The Church of Jesus Christ of Latter-day Saints, 1880 United States Federal Census (Online publication - Provo, UT, USA: Ancestry.com Operations Inc, 2010. 1880 U.S. Census Index provided by The Church of Jesus Christ of Latter-day Saints © Copyright 1999 Intellectual Reserve, Inc. All rights reserved. All use is subject to the limited), Ancestry.com, http://www.Ancestry.com, Year: 1880; Census Place: 4th Ward, Union, Louisiana; Roll: 473; Family History Film: 1254473; Page: 480A; Enumeration District: 88; Image: 0242. Birth date: about 1875 Birth place: Louisiana Residence date: 1880 Residence place: 4th Ward, Union, Louisiana, United States.

1078   Ancestry.com, 1900 United States Federal Census (Online publication - Provo, UT, USA: Ancestry.com Operations Inc, 2004. Original data - United States of America, Bureau of the Census. Twelfth Census of the United States, 1900. Washington, D.C.: National Archives and Records Administration, 1900. T623, 18), Ancestry.com, http://www.Ancestry.com, Year: 1900; Census Place: Police Jury Ward 4, Union, Louisiana; Roll: T623_585; Page: 15B; Enumeration District: 122. Birth date: Aug 1875 Birth place: Louisiana Residence date: 1900 Residence place: Bernice Town, Union, Louisiana.

1079   Ancestry.com, 1900 United States Federal Census (Online publication - Provo, UT, USA: Ancestry.com Operations Inc, 2004. Original data - United States of America, Bureau of the Census. Twelfth Census of the United States, 1900. Washington, D.C.: National Archives and Records Administration, 1900. T623, 18), Ancestry.com, http://www.Ancestry.com, Year: 1900; Census Place: Police Jury Ward 4, Union, Louisiana; Roll: T623_585; Page: 15B; Enumeration District: 122. Birth date: Oct 1878 Birth place: Louisiana Residence date: 1900 Residence place: Bernice Town, Union, Louisiana.

1080   Ancestry.com, 1900 United States Federal Census (Online publication - Provo, UT, USA: Ancestry.com Operations Inc, 2004. Original data - United States of America, Bureau of the Census. Twelfth Census of the United States, 1900. Washington, D.C.: National Archives and Records Administration, 1900. T623, 18), Ancestry.com, http://www.Ancestry.com, Year: 1900; Census Place: Police Jury Ward 8, Claiborne, Louisiana; Roll: T623_562; Page: 11A; Enumeration District: 27. Birth date: May 1853 Birth place: Louisiana Marriage date: 1869 Marriage place: Residence date: 1900 Residence place: Ward 8 (South Half), Claiborne, Louisiana.

1081   Ancestry.com, 1910 United States Federal Census (Online publication - Provo, UT, USA: Ancestry.com Operations Inc, 2006. Original data - Thirteenth Census of the United States, 1910 (NARA microfilm publication T624, 1,178 rolls). Records of the Bureau of the Census, Record Group 29. National Archives, Washington), Ancestry.com, http://www.Ancestry.com, Year: 1910; Census Place: Police Jury Ward 8, Claiborne, Louisiana; Roll: ; Page: ; Enumeration District: ; Image:. Birth date: 1852 Birth place: Louisiana Residence date: 1910 Residence place: Police Jury Ward 8, Claiborne, Louisiana.

1082   Ancestry.com and The Church of Jesus Christ of Latter-day Saints, 1880 United States Federal Census (Online publication - Provo, UT, USA: Ancestry.com Operations Inc, 2010. 1880 U.S. Census Index provided by The Church of Jesus Christ of Latter-day Saints © Copyright 1999 Intellectual Reserve, Inc. All rights reserved. All use is subject to the limited), Ancestry.com, http://www.Ancestry.com, Year: 1880; Census Place: 8th Ward, Claiborne, Louisiana; Roll: 451; Family History Film: 1254451; Page: 403A; Enumeration District: 16; Image: 0600. Birth date: about 1852 Birth place: Louisiana Residence date: 1880 Residence place: 8th Ward, Claiborne, Louisiana, United States.

1083   Ancestry.com, 1920 United States Federal Census (Online publication - Provo, UT, USA: Ancestry.com Operations Inc, 2010. Images reproduced by FamilySearch. Original data - Fourteenth Census of the United States, 1920. (NARA microfilm publication T625, 2076 rolls). Records of the Bureau of the Census, Record), Ancestry.com, http://www.Ancestry.com, Year: 1920; Census Place: Police Jury Ward 8, Claiborne, Louisiana; Roll: T625_609; Page: 11B; Enumeration District: 98; Image:. Birth date: about 1852 Birth place: Louisiana Residence date: 1920 Residence place: Police Jury Ward 8, Claiborne, Louisiana.

1084   Ancestry.com, Louisiana Statewide Death Index, 1900-1949 (Online publication - Provo, UT, USA: Ancestry.com Operations Inc, 2002. Original data - State of Louisiana, Secretary of State, Division of Archives, Records Management, and History. Vital Records Indices. Baton Rouge, LA, USA. Original data: State of Louisiana), Ancestry.com, http://www.Ancestry.com, Birth date: 1851 Birth place: Death date: 15 Jun 1920 Death place: Louisiana.

1085   Ancestry.com and The Church of Jesus Christ of Latter-day Saints, 1880 United States Federal Census (Online publication - Provo, UT, USA: Ancestry.com Operations Inc, 2010. 1880 U.S. Census Index provided by The Church of Jesus Christ of Latter-day Saints © Copyright 1999 Intellectual Reserve, Inc. All rights reserved. All use is subject to the limited), Ancestry.com, http://www.Ancestry.com, Year: 1880; Census Place: 8th Ward, Claiborne, Louisiana; Roll: 451; Family History Film: 1254451; Page: 403A; Enumeration District: 16; Image: 0600. Birth date: about 1871 Birth place: Louisiana Residence date: 1880 Residence place: 8th Ward, Claiborne, Louisiana, United States.

1086   Ancestry.com, 1920 United States Federal Census (Online publication - Provo, UT, USA: Ancestry.com Operations Inc, 2010. Images reproduced by FamilySearch. Original data - Fourteenth Census of the United States, 1920. (NARA microfilm publication T625, 2076 rolls). Records of the Bureau of the Census, Record), Ancestry.com, http://www.Ancestry.com, Year: 1920; Census Place: Police Jury Ward 4, Union, Louisiana; Roll: T625_632; Page: 17A; Enumeration District: 129; Image:. Birth date: about 1871 Birth place: Louisiana Residence date: 1920 Residence place: Police Jury Ward 4, Union, Louisiana.

1087   Ancestry.com, 1910 United States Federal Census (Online publication - Provo, UT, USA: Ancestry.com Operations Inc, 2006. Original data - Thirteenth Census of the United States, 1910 (NARA microfilm publication T624, 1,178 rolls). Records of the Bureau of the Census, Record Group 29. National Archives, Washington), Ancestry.com, http://www.Ancestry.com, Year: 1910; Census Place: Police Jury Ward 6, Lincoln, Louisiana; Roll: ; Page: ; Enumeration District: ; Image:. Birth date: 1873 Birth place: Louisiana Residence date: 1910 Residence place: Police Jury Ward 6, Lincoln, Louisiana.

1088   Ancestry.com, 1900 United States Federal Census (Online publication - Provo, UT, USA: Ancestry.com Operations Inc, 2004. Original data - United States of America, Bureau of the Census. Twelfth Census of the United States, 1900. Washington, D.C.: National Archives and Records Administration, 1900. T623, 18), Ancestry.com, http://www.Ancestry.com, Year: 1900; Census Place: Police Jury Ward 8, Claiborne, Louisiana; Roll: T623_562; Page: 11A; Enumeration District: 27. Birth date: Sep 1872 Birth place: Louisiana Residence date: 1900 Residence place: Ward 8 (South Half), Claiborne, Louisiana.

1089   Ancestry.com and The Church of Jesus Christ of Latter-day Saints, 1880 United States Federal Census (Online publication - Provo, UT, USA: Ancestry.com Operations Inc, 2010. 1880 U.S. Census Index provided by The Church of Jesus Christ of Latter-day Saints © Copyright 1999 Intellectual Reserve, Inc. All rights reserved. All use is subject to the limited), Ancestry.com, http://www.Ancestry.com, Year: 1880; Census Place: 8th Ward, Claiborne, Louisiana; Roll: 451; Family History Film: 1254451; Page: 403A; Enumeration District: 16; Image: 0600. Birth date: about 1872 Birth place: Louisiana Residence date: 1880 Residence place: 8th Ward, Claiborne, Louisiana, United States.

1090   Ancestry.com, 1910 United States Federal Census (Online publication - Provo, UT, USA: Ancestry.com Operations Inc, 2006. Original data - Thirteenth Census of the United States, 1910 (NARA microfilm publication T624, 1,178 rolls). Records of the Bureau of the Census, Record Group 29. National Archives, Washington), Ancestry.com, http://www.Ancestry.com, Year: 1910; Census Place: Police Jury Ward 8, Claiborne, Louisiana; Roll: ; Page: ; Enumeration District: ; Image:. Birth date: 1873 Birth place: Louisiana Residence date: 1910 Residence place: Police Jury Ward 8, Claiborne, Louisiana.

1091   Ancestry.com, 1900 United States Federal Census (Online publication - Provo, UT, USA: Ancestry.com Operations Inc, 2004. Original data - United States of America, Bureau of the Census. Twelfth Census of the United States, 1900. Washington, D.C.: National Archives and Records Administration, 1900. T623, 18), Ancestry.com, http://www.Ancestry.com, Year: 1900; Census Place: Police Jury Ward 8, Claiborne, Louisiana; Roll: T623_562; Page: 11A; Enumeration District: 27. Birth date: Jan 1874 Birth place: Louisiana Residence date: 1900 Residence place: Ward 8 (South Half), Claiborne, Louisiana.

1092   Ancestry.com and The Church of Jesus Christ of Latter-day Saints, 1880 United States Federal Census (Online publication - Provo, UT, USA: Ancestry.com Operations Inc, 2010. 1880 U.S. Census Index provided by The Church of Jesus Christ of Latter-day Saints © Copyright 1999 Intellectual Reserve, Inc. All rights reserved. All use is subject to the limited), Ancestry.com, http://www.Ancestry.com, Year: 1880; Census Place: 8th Ward, Claiborne, Louisiana; Roll: 451;

Family History Film: 1254451; Page: 403A; Enumeration District: 16; Image: 0600. Birth date: about 1877 Birth place: Louisiana Residence date: 1880 Residence place: 8th Ward, Claiborne, Louisiana, United States.

1093   Ancestry.com, 1900 United States Federal Census (Online publication - Provo, UT, USA: Ancestry.com Operations Inc, 2004. Original data - United States of America, Bureau of the Census. Twelfth Census of the United States, 1900. Washington, D.C.: National Archives and Records Administration, 1900. T623, 18), Ancestry.com, http://www.Ancestry.com, Year: 1900; Census Place: Police Jury Ward 8, Claiborne, Louisiana; Roll: T623_562; Page: 11A; Enumeration District: 27. Birth date: Feb 1880 Birth place: Louisiana Residence date: 1900 Residence place: Ward 8 (South Half), Claiborne, Louisiana.

1094   Ancestry.com, 1900 United States Federal Census (Online publication - Provo, UT, USA: Ancestry.com Operations Inc, 2004. Original data - United States of America, Bureau of the Census. Twelfth Census of the United States, 1900. Washington, D.C.: National Archives and Records Administration, 1900. T623, 18), Ancestry.com, http://www.Ancestry.com, Year: 1900; Census Place: Police Jury Ward 8, Claiborne, Louisiana; Roll: T623_562; Page: 11A; Enumeration District: 27. Birth date: Apr 1882 Birth place: Louisiana Residence date: 1900 Residence place: Ward 8 (South Half), Claiborne, Louisiana.

1095   Ancestry.com, 1900 United States Federal Census (Online publication - Provo, UT, USA: Ancestry.com Operations Inc, 2004. Original data - United States of America, Bureau of the Census. Twelfth Census of the United States, 1900. Washington, D.C.: National Archives and Records Administration, 1900. T623, 18), Ancestry.com, http://www.Ancestry.com, Year: 1900; Census Place: Police Jury Ward 8, Claiborne, Louisiana; Roll: T623_562; Page: 11A; Enumeration District: 27. Birth date: Sep 1884 Birth place: Louisiana Residence date: 1900 Residence place: Ward 8 (South Half), Claiborne, Louisiana.

1096   Ancestry.com, 1900 United States Federal Census (Online publication - Provo, UT, USA: Ancestry.com Operations Inc, 2004. Original data - United States of America, Bureau of the Census. Twelfth Census of the United States, 1900. Washington, D.C.: National Archives and Records Administration, 1900. T623, 18), Ancestry.com, http://www.Ancestry.com, Year: 1900; Census Place: Police Jury Ward 8, Claiborne, Louisiana; Roll: T623_562; Page: 11A; Enumeration District: 27. Birth date: Mar 1887 Birth place: Louisiana Residence date: 1900 Residence place: Ward 8 (South Half), Claiborne, Louisiana.

1097   Ancestry.com, 1910 United States Federal Census (Online publication - Provo, UT, USA: Ancestry.com Operations Inc, 2006. Original data - Thirteenth Census of the United States, 1910 (NARA microfilm publication T624, 1,178 rolls). Records of the Bureau of the Census, Record Group 29. National Archives, Washington), Ancestry.com, http://www.Ancestry.com, Year: 1910; Census Place: Police Jury Ward 8, Claiborne, Louisiana; Roll: ; Page: ; Enumeration District: ; Image:. Birth date: 1888 Birth place: Louisiana Residence date: 1910 Residence place: Police Jury Ward 8, Claiborne, Louisiana.

1098   Ancestry.com, 1900 United States Federal Census (Online publication - Provo, UT, USA: Ancestry.com Operations Inc, 2004. Original data - United States of America, Bureau of the Census. Twelfth Census of the United States, 1900. Washington, D.C.: National Archives and Records Administration, 1900. T623, 18), Ancestry.com, http://www.Ancestry.com, Year: 1900; Census Place: Police Jury Ward 8, Claiborne, Louisiana; Roll: T623_562; Page: 11A; Enumeration District: 27. Birth date: Feb 1889 Birth place: Louisiana Residence date: 1900 Residence place: Ward 8 (South Half), Claiborne, Louisiana.

1099   Ancestry.com, 1900 United States Federal Census (Online publication - Provo, UT, USA: Ancestry.com Operations Inc, 2004. Original data - United States of America, Bureau of the Census. Twelfth Census of the United States, 1900. Washington, D.C.: National Archives and Records Administration, 1900. T623, 18), Ancestry.com, http://www.Ancestry.com, Year: 1900; Census Place: Police Jury Ward 8, Claiborne, Louisiana; Roll: T623_562; Page: 11A; Enumeration District: 27. Birth date: Jun 1892 Birth place: Louisiana Residence date: 1900 Residence place: Ward 8 (South Half), Claiborne, Louisiana.

1100   Ancestry.com, 1910 United States Federal Census (Online publication - Provo, UT, USA: Ancestry.com Operations Inc, 2006. Original data - Thirteenth Census of the United States, 1910 (NARA microfilm publication T624, 1,178 rolls). Records of the Bureau of the Census, Record Group 29. National Archives, Washington), Ancestry.com, http://www.Ancestry.com, Year: 1910; Census Place: Police Jury Ward 8, Claiborne, Louisiana; Roll: ; Page: ; Enumeration District: ; Image:. Birth date: 1893 Birth place: Louisiana Residence date: 1910 Residence place: Police Jury Ward 8, Claiborne, Louisiana.

1101   Ancestry.com, 1910 United States Federal Census (Online publication - Provo, UT, USA: Ancestry.com Operations Inc, 2006. Original data - Thirteenth Census of the United States, 1910 (NARA microfilm publication T624, 1,178 rolls). Records of the Bureau of the Census, Record Group 29. National Archives, Washington), Ancestry.com, http://www.Ancestry.com, Year: 1910; Census Place: Precinct 4, Chilton, Alabama; Roll: ; Page: ; Enumeration District: ; Image:. Birth date: about 1877 Birth place: Alabama Residence date: 1910 Residence place: Precinct 4, Chilton, Alabama.

1102   Ancestry.com, 1910 United States Federal Census (Online publication - Provo, UT, USA: Ancestry.com Operations Inc, 2006. Original data - Thirteenth Census of the United States, 1910 (NARA microfilm publication T624, 1,178 rolls). Records of the Bureau of the Census, Record Group 29. National Archives, Washington), Ancestry.com, http://www.Ancestry.com, Year: 1910; Census Place: Precinct 4, Chilton, Alabama; Roll: ; Page: ; Enumeration District: ; Image:. Birth date: about 1889 Birth place: Alabama Residence date: 1910 Residence place: Precinct 4, Chilton, Alabama.

1103   Ancestry.com, 1910 United States Federal Census (Online publication - Provo, UT, USA: Ancestry.com Operations Inc, 2006. Original data - Thirteenth Census of the United States, 1910 (NARA microfilm publication T624, 1,178 rolls). Records of the Bureau of the Census, Record Group 29. National Archives, Washington), Ancestry.com, http://www.Ancestry.com, Year: 1910; Census Place: Precinct 4, Chilton, Alabama; Roll: ; Page: ; Enumeration District: ; Image:. Birth date: about 1892 Birth place: Alabama Residence date: 1910 Residence place: Precinct 4, Chilton, Alabama.

1104   Ancestry.com, 1910 United States Federal Census (Online publication - Provo, UT, USA: Ancestry.com Operations Inc, 2006. Original data - Thirteenth Census of the United States, 1910 (NARA microfilm publication T624, 1,178 rolls). Records of the Bureau of the Census, Record Group 29. National Archives, Washington), Ancestry.com, http://www.Ancestry.com, Year: 1910; Census Place: Precinct 4, Chilton, Alabama; Roll: ; Page: ; Enumeration District: ; Image:. Birth date: about 1894 Birth place: Alabama Residence date: 1910 Residence place: Precinct 4, Chilton, Alabama.

1105   Ancestry.com, 1910 United States Federal Census (Online publication - Provo, UT, USA: Ancestry.com Operations Inc, 2006. Original data - Thirteenth Census of the United States, 1910 (NARA microfilm publication T624, 1,178 rolls). Records of the Bureau of the Census, Record Group 29. National Archives, Washington), Ancestry.com, http://www.Ancestry.com, Year: 1910; Census Place: Precinct 4, Chilton, Alabama; Roll: ; Page: ; Enumeration District: ; Image:. Birth date: about 1906 Birth place: Alabama Residence date: 1910 Residence place: Precinct 4, Chilton, Alabama.

1106   National Cemetery Administration, U.S. Veterans Gravesites, ca.1775-2006 (Online publication - Provo, UT, USA: Ancestry.com Operations Inc, 2006. Original data - National Cemetery Administration. Nationwide Gravesite Locator. Original data: National Cemetery Administration. Nationwide Gravesite Locator), Ancestry.com, http://www.Ancestry.com, Death date: 06/14/1928 Death place: TN.

1107   Ancestry.com, 1930 United States Federal Census (Online publication - Provo, UT, USA: Ancestry.com Operations Inc, 2002. Original data - United States of America, Bureau of the Census. Fifteenth Census of the United States, 1930. Washington, D.C.: National Archives and Records Administration, 1930. T626,), Ancestry.com, http://www.Ancestry.com, Year: 1930; Census Place: Beat 2, Tippah, Mississippi; Roll: 1167; Page: 22B; Enumeration District: 6; Image: 397.0. Birth date: about 1897 Birth place: Residence date: 1930 Residence place: Beat 2, Tippah, Mississippi.

1108   Ancestry.com, Social Security Death Index (Online publication - Provo, UT, USA: Ancestry.com Operations Inc, 2010. Original data - Social Security Administration. Social Security Death Index, Master File. Social Security Administration. Original data: Social Security Administration. Social Security D), Ancestry.com, http://www.Ancestry.com, Number: 412-09-2596; Issue State: Tennessee; Issue Date: Before 1951. Birth date: 16 Dec 1895 Birth place: Death date: Apr 1981 Death place: Memphis, Shelby, Tennessee, United States of America.

1109   Ancestry.com, 1920 United States Federal Census (Online publication - Provo, UT, USA: Ancestry.com Operations Inc, 2010. Images reproduced by FamilySearch. Original data - Fourteenth Census of the United States, 1920. (NARA microfilm publication T625, 2076 rolls). Records of the Bureau of the Census, Record), Ancestry.com, http://www.Ancestry.com, Year: 1920; Census Place: Ripley, Tippah, Mississippi; Roll: T625_896; Page: 4B; Enumeration District: 104; Image:. Birth date: about 1897 Birth place: Mississippi Residence date: 1920 Residence place: Ripley, Tippah, Mississippi.

1110   Ancestry.com, Social Security Death Index (Online publication - Provo, UT, USA: Ancestry.com Operations Inc, 2010. Original data - Social Security Administration. Social Security Death Index, Master File. Social Security Administration. Original data: Social Security Administration. Social Security D), Ancestry.com, http://www.Ancestry.com, Number: 412-03-4999; Issue State: Tennessee; Issue Date: Before 1951. Birth date: 18 Feb 1898 Birth place: Death date: Jan 1973 Death place: Memphis, Shelby, Tennessee, United States of America.

1111   Ancestry.com, 1900 United States Federal Census (Online publication - Provo, UT, USA: Ancestry.com Operations Inc, 2004. Original data - United States of America, Bureau of the Census. Twelfth Census of the United States, 1900. Washington, D.C.: National Archives and Records Administration, 1900. T623, 18), Ancestry.com, http://www.Ancestry.com, Year: 1900; Census Place: Orizaba, Tippah, Mississippi; Roll: T623_829; Page: 7B; Enumeration District: 108. Birth date: Feb 1897 Birth place: Mississippi Residence date: 1900 Residence place: Orizaba, Tippah, Mississippi.

1112   Ancestry.com, 1920 United States Federal Census (Online publication - Provo, UT, USA: Ancestry.com Operations Inc, 2010. Images reproduced by FamilySearch. Original data - Fourteenth Census of the United States, 1920. (NARA microfilm publication T625, 2076 rolls). Records of the Bureau of the Census, Record), Ancestry.com, http://www.Ancestry.com, Year: 1920; Census Place: Memphis Ward 18, Shelby, Tennessee; Roll: T625_1764; Page: 5B; Enumeration District: 167; Image:. Birth date: about 1898 Birth place: Mississippi Residence date: 1920 Residence place: Memphis Ward 18, Shelby, Tennessee.

1113   Ancestry.com, World War I Draft Registration Cards, 1917-1918 (Online publication - Provo, UT, USA: Ancestry.com Operations Inc, 2005. Original data - United States, Selective Service System. World War I Selective Service System Draft Registration Cards, 1917-1918. Washington, D.C.: National Archives and Records Administration), Ancestry.com, http://www.Ancestry.com, Registration Location: Shelby County, Tennessee; Roll: 1877497; Draft Board: 2. Birth date: 18 Feb 1898 Birth place: Residence date: Residence place: Memphis, Shelby, Tennessee.

1114   Ancestry.com, 1900 United States Federal Census (Online publication - Provo, UT, USA: Ancestry.com Operations Inc, 2004. Original data - United States of America, Bureau of the Census. Twelfth Census of the United

States, 1900. Washington, D.C.: National Archives and Records Administration, 1900. T623, 18), Ancestry.com, http://www.Ancestry.com, Year: 1900; Census Place: Orizaba, Tippah, Mississippi; Roll: T623_829; Page: 5B; Enumeration District: 108. Birth date: Aug 1863 Birth place: Mississippi Marriage date: 1889 Marriage place: Residence date: 1900 Residence place: Orizaba, Tippah, Mississippi.

1115   Ancestry.com, 1920 United States Federal Census (Online publication - Provo, UT, USA: Ancestry.com Operations Inc, 2010. Images reproduced by FamilySearch. Original data - Fourteenth Census of the United States, 1920. (NARA microfilm publication T625, 2076 rolls). Records of the Bureau of the Census, Record), Ancestry.com, http://www.Ancestry.com, Year: 1920; Census Place: Halls, Lauderdale, Tennessee; Roll: T625_1751; Page: 14B; Enumeration District: 105; Image:. Birth date: about 1865 Birth place: Mississippi Residence date: 1920 Residence place: Halls, Lauderdale, Tennessee.

1116   Ancestry.com, 1900 United States Federal Census (Online publication - Provo, UT, USA: Ancestry.com Operations Inc, 2004. Original data - United States of America, Bureau of the Census. Twelfth Census of the United States, 1900. Washington, D.C.: National Archives and Records Administration, 1900. T623, 18), Ancestry.com, http://www.Ancestry.com, Year: 1900; Census Place: Orizaba, Tippah, Mississippi; Roll: T623_829; Page: 5B; Enumeration District: 108. Birth date: Dec 1889 Birth place: Mississippi Residence date: 1900 Residence place: Orizaba, Tippah, Mississippi.

1117   Ancestry.com, 1910 United States Federal Census (Online publication - Provo, UT, USA: Ancestry.com Operations Inc, 2006. Original data - Thirteenth Census of the United States, 1910 (NARA microfilm publication T624, 1,178 rolls). Records of the Bureau of the Census, Record Group 29. National Archives, Washington), Ancestry.com, http://www.Ancestry.com, Year: 1910; Census Place: Beat 3, Tippah, Mississippi; Roll: ; Page: ; Enumeration District: ; Image:. Birth date: about 1890 Birth place: Mississippi Residence date: 1910 Residence place: Beat 3, Tippah, Mississippi.

1118   Ancestry.com, 1900 United States Federal Census (Online publication - Provo, UT, USA: Ancestry.com Operations Inc, 2004. Original data - United States of America, Bureau of the Census. Twelfth Census of the United States, 1900. Washington, D.C.: National Archives and Records Administration, 1900. T623, 18), Ancestry.com, http://www.Ancestry.com, Year: 1900; Census Place: Orizaba, Tippah, Mississippi; Roll: T623_829; Page: 5B; Enumeration District: 108. Birth date: Feb 1891 Birth place: Mississippi Residence date: 1900 Residence place: Orizaba, Tippah, Mississippi.

1119   Ancestry.com, 1910 United States Federal Census (Online publication - Provo, UT, USA: Ancestry.com Operations Inc, 2006. Original data - Thirteenth Census of the United States, 1910 (NARA microfilm publication T624, 1,178 rolls). Records of the Bureau of the Census, Record Group 29. National Archives, Washington), Ancestry.com, http://www.Ancestry.com, Year: 1910; Census Place: Beat 3, Tippah, Mississippi; Roll: ; Page: ; Enumeration District: ; Image:. Birth date: about 1892 Birth place: Mississippi Residence date: 1910 Residence place: Beat 3, Tippah, Mississippi.

1120   Ancestry.com, 1900 United States Federal Census (Online publication - Provo, UT, USA: Ancestry.com Operations Inc, 2004. Original data - United States of America, Bureau of the Census. Twelfth Census of the United States, 1900. Washington, D.C.: National Archives and Records Administration, 1900. T623, 18), Ancestry.com, http://www.Ancestry.com, Year: 1900; Census Place: Orizaba, Tippah, Mississippi; Roll: T623_829; Page: 5B; Enumeration District: 108. Birth date: Mar 1894 Birth place: Mississippi Residence date: 1900 Residence place: Orizaba, Tippah, Mississippi.

1121   Ancestry.com, 1910 United States Federal Census (Online publication - Provo, UT, USA: Ancestry.com Operations Inc, 2006. Original data - Thirteenth Census of the United States, 1910 (NARA microfilm publication T624, 1,178 rolls). Records of the Bureau of the Census, Record Group 29. National Archives, Washington), Ancestry.com, http://www.Ancestry.com, Year: 1910; Census Place: Beat 3, Tippah, Mississippi; Roll: ; Page: ; Enumeration District: ; Image:. Birth date: about 1895 Birth place: Mississippi Residence date: 1910 Residence place: Beat 3, Tippah, Mississippi.

1122   Ancestry.com, 1910 United States Federal Census (Online publication - Provo, UT, USA: Ancestry.com Operations Inc, 2006. Original data - Thirteenth Census of the United States, 1910 (NARA microfilm publication T624, 1,178 rolls). Records of the Bureau of the Census, Record Group 29. National Archives, Washington), Ancestry.com, http://www.Ancestry.com, Year: 1910; Census Place: Beat 3, Tippah, Mississippi; Roll: ; Page: ; Enumeration District: ; Image:. Birth date: about 1898 Birth place: Mississippi Residence date: 1910 Residence place: Beat 3, Tippah, Mississippi.

1123   Ancestry.com, 1900 United States Federal Census (Online publication - Provo, UT, USA: Ancestry.com Operations Inc, 2004. Original data - United States of America, Bureau of the Census. Twelfth Census of the United States, 1900. Washington, D.C.: National Archives and Records Administration, 1900. T623, 18), Ancestry.com, http://www.Ancestry.com, Year: 1900; Census Place: Orizaba, Tippah, Mississippi; Roll: T623_829; Page: 5B; Enumeration District: 108. Birth date: Dec 1897 Birth place: Mississippi Residence date: 1900 Residence place: Orizaba, Tippah, Mississippi.

1124   Ancestry.com, 1900 United States Federal Census (Online publication - Provo, UT, USA: Ancestry.com Operations Inc, 2004. Original data - United States of America, Bureau of the Census. Twelfth Census of the United States, 1900. Washington, D.C.: National Archives and Records Administration, 1900. T623, 18), Ancestry.com, http://www.Ancestry.com, Year: 1900; Census Place: Orizaba, Tippah, Mississippi; Roll: T623_829; Page: 5B;

Enumeration District: 108. Birth date: Feb 1900 Birth place: Mississippi Residence date: 1900 Residence place: Orizaba, Tippah, Mississippi.

1125   Ancestry.com, 1910 United States Federal Census (Online publication - Provo, UT, USA: Ancestry.com Operations Inc, 2006. Original data - Thirteenth Census of the United States, 1910 (NARA microfilm publication T624, 1,178 rolls). Records of the Bureau of the Census, Record Group 29. National Archives, Washington), Ancestry.com, http://www.Ancestry.com, Year: 1910; Census Place: Beat 3, Tippah, Mississippi; Roll: ; Page: ; Enumeration District: ; Image:. Birth date: about 1900 Birth place: Mississippi Residence date: 1910 Residence place: Beat 3, Tippah, Mississippi.

1126   Ancestry.com, Social Security Death Index (Online publication - Provo, UT, USA: Ancestry.com Operations Inc, 2010. Original data - Social Security Administration. Social Security Death Index, Master File. Social Security Administration. Original data: Social Security Administration. Social Security D), Ancestry.com, http://www.Ancestry.com, Number: 425-10-6920; Issue State: Mississippi; Issue Date: Before 1951. Birth date: 5 Dec 1908 Birth place: Death date: Feb 1954 Death place:.

1127   Ancestry.com, 1920 United States Federal Census (Online publication - Provo, UT, USA: Ancestry.com Operations Inc, 2010. Images reproduced by FamilySearch. Original data - Fourteenth Census of the United States, 1920. (NARA microfilm publication T625, 2076 rolls). Records of the Bureau of the Census, Record), Ancestry.com, http://www.Ancestry.com, Year: 1920; Census Place: Halls, Lauderdale, Tennessee; Roll: T625_1751; Page: 14B; Enumeration District: 105; Image:. Birth date: about 1905 Birth place: Mississippi Residence date: 1920 Residence place: Halls, Lauderdale, Tennessee.

1128   Ancestry.com, 1920 United States Federal Census (Online publication - Provo, UT, USA: Ancestry.com Operations Inc, 2010. Images reproduced by FamilySearch. Original data - Fourteenth Census of the United States, 1920. (NARA microfilm publication T625, 2076 rolls). Records of the Bureau of the Census, Record), Ancestry.com, http://www.Ancestry.com, Year: 1920; Census Place: Halls, Lauderdale, Tennessee; Roll: T625_1751; Page: 14B; Enumeration District: 105; Image:. Birth date: about 1908 Birth place: Mississippi Residence date: 1920 Residence place: Halls, Lauderdale, Tennessee.

1129   Ancestry.com, 1910 United States Federal Census (Online publication - Provo, UT, USA: Ancestry.com Operations Inc, 2006. Original data - Thirteenth Census of the United States, 1910 (NARA microfilm publication T624, 1,178 rolls). Records of the Bureau of the Census, Record Group 29. National Archives, Washington), Ancestry.com, http://www.Ancestry.com, Year: 1910; Census Place: Beat 3, Tippah, Mississippi; Roll: ; Page: ; Enumeration District: ; Image:. Birth date: about 1908 Birth place: Mississippi Residence date: 1910 Residence place: Beat 3, Tippah, Mississippi.

1130   Ancestry.com, 1910 United States Federal Census (Online publication - Provo, UT, USA: Ancestry.com Operations Inc, 2006. Original data - Thirteenth Census of the United States, 1910 (NARA microfilm publication T624, 1,178 rolls). Records of the Bureau of the Census, Record Group 29. National Archives, Washington), Ancestry.com, http://www.Ancestry.com, Year: 1910; Census Place: Beat 3, Tippah, Mississippi; Roll: ; Page: ; Enumeration District: ; Image:. Birth date: about 1910 Birth place: Mississippi Residence date: 1910 Residence place: Beat 3, Tippah, Mississippi.

1131   Ancestry.com, 1920 United States Federal Census (Online publication - Provo, UT, USA: Ancestry.com Operations Inc, 2010. Images reproduced by FamilySearch. Original data - Fourteenth Census of the United States, 1920. (NARA microfilm publication T625, 2076 rolls). Records of the Bureau of the Census, Record), Ancestry.com, http://www.Ancestry.com, Year: 1920; Census Place: Halls, Lauderdale, Tennessee; Roll: T625_1751; Page: 14B; Enumeration District: 105; Image:. Birth date: about 1911 Birth place: Mississippi Residence date: 1920 Residence place: Halls, Lauderdale, Tennessee.

1132   Ancestry.com, 1900 United States Federal Census (Online publication - Provo, UT, USA: Ancestry.com Operations Inc, 2004. Original data - United States of America, Bureau of the Census. Twelfth Census of the United States, 1900. Washington, D.C.: National Archives and Records Administration, 1900. T623, 18), Ancestry.com, http://www.Ancestry.com, Year: 1900; Census Place: Clay, Dunklin, Missouri; Roll: T623_853; Page: B; Enumeration District: 40. Birth date: Dec 1860 Birth place: Missouri Marriage date: 1876 Marriage place: Residence date: 1900 Residence place: Clay, Dunklin, Missouri.

1133   Ancestry.com, 1900 United States Federal Census (Online publication - Provo, UT, USA: Ancestry.com Operations Inc, 2004. Original data - United States of America, Bureau of the Census. Twelfth Census of the United States, 1900. Washington, D.C.: National Archives and Records Administration, 1900. T623, 18), Ancestry.com, http://www.Ancestry.com, Year: 1900; Census Place: Clay, Dunklin, Missouri; Roll: T623_853; Page: B; Enumeration District: 40. Birth date: Dec 1881 Birth place: Missouri Residence date: 1900 Residence place: Clay, Dunklin, Missouri.

1134   Ancestry.com, 1900 United States Federal Census (Online publication - Provo, UT, USA: Ancestry.com Operations Inc, 2004. Original data - United States of America, Bureau of the Census. Twelfth Census of the United States, 1900. Washington, D.C.: National Archives and Records Administration, 1900. T623, 18), Ancestry.com, http://www.Ancestry.com, Year: 1900; Census Place: Clay, Dunklin, Missouri; Roll: T623_853; Page: B; Enumeration District: 40. Birth date: Aug 1890 Birth place: Missouri Residence date: 1900 Residence place: Clay, Dunklin, Missouri.

1135   Ancestry.com, 1900 United States Federal Census (Online publication - Provo, UT, USA: Ancestry.com Operations Inc, 2004. Original data - United States of America, Bureau of the Census. Twelfth Census of the United States, 1900. Washington, D.C.: National Archives and Records Administration, 1900. T623, 18), Ancestry.com,

http://www.Ancestry.com, Year: 1900; Census Place: Clay, Dunklin, Missouri; Roll: T623_853; Page: B; Enumeration District: 40. Birth date: May 1894 Birth place: Missouri Residence date: 1900 Residence place: Clay, Dunklin, Missouri.

1136   Ancestry.com and The Church of Jesus Christ of Latter-day Saints, 1880 United States Federal Census (Online publication - Provo, UT, USA: Ancestry.com Operations Inc, 2010. 1880 U.S. Census Index provided by The Church of Jesus Christ of Latter-day Saints © Copyright 1999 Intellectual Reserve, Inc. All rights reserved. All use is subject to the limited), Ancestry.com, http://www.Ancestry.com, Year: 1880; Census Place: Precinct 6, Hopkins, Texas; Roll: 1311; Family History Film: 1255311; Page: 212B; Enumeration District: 61; Image:. Birth date: about 1859 Birth place: Texas Residence date: 1880 Residence place: Precinct 6, Hopkins, Texas, United States.

1137   Ancestry.com, 1930 United States Federal Census (Online publication - Provo, UT, USA: Ancestry.com Operations Inc, 2002. Original data - United States of America, Bureau of the Census. Fifteenth Census of the United States, 1930. Washington, D.C.: National Archives and Records Administration, 1930. T626,), Ancestry.com, http://www.Ancestry.com, Year: 1930; Census Place: Precinct 6, Hopkins, Texas; Roll: 2358; Page: 11A; Enumeration District: 23; Image: 506.0. Birth date: about 1858 Birth place: Texas Residence date: 1930 Residence place: Precinct 6, Hopkins, Texas.

1138   Ancestry.com, 1920 United States Federal Census (Online publication - Provo, UT, USA: Ancestry.com Operations Inc, 2010. Images reproduced by FamilySearch. Original data - Fourteenth Census of the United States, 1920. (NARA microfilm publication T625, 2076 rolls). Records of the Bureau of the Census, Record), Ancestry.com, http://www.Ancestry.com, Year: 1920; Census Place: Justice Precinct 6, Hopkins, Texas; Roll: T625_1817; Page: 3A; Enumeration District: 79; Image:. Birth date: about 1858 Birth place: Texas Residence date: 1920 Residence place: Justice Precinct 6, Hopkins, Texas.

1139   Ancestry.com, 1900 United States Federal Census (Online publication - Provo, UT, USA: Ancestry.com Operations Inc, 2004. Original data - United States of America, Bureau of the Census. Twelfth Census of the United States, 1900. Washington, D.C.: National Archives and Records Administration, 1900. T623, 18), Ancestry.com, http://www.Ancestry.com, Year: 1900; Census Place: Justice Precinct 6, Hopkins, Texas; Roll: T623_1646; Page: 3A; Enumeration District: 57. Birth date: May 1880 Birth place: Texas Residence date: 1900 Residence place: Justice Precinct 6, Hopkins, Texas.

1140   Ancestry.com, 1900 United States Federal Census (Online publication - Provo, UT, USA: Ancestry.com Operations Inc, 2004. Original data - United States of America, Bureau of the Census. Twelfth Census of the United States, 1900. Washington, D.C.: National Archives and Records Administration, 1900. T623, 18), Ancestry.com, http://www.Ancestry.com, Year: 1900; Census Place: Justice Precinct 6, Hopkins, Texas; Roll: T623_1646; Page: 3A; Enumeration District: 57. Birth date: Sep 1881 Birth place: Texas Residence date: 1900 Residence place: Justice Precinct 6, Hopkins, Texas.

1141   Ancestry.com, 1900 United States Federal Census (Online publication - Provo, UT, USA: Ancestry.com Operations Inc, 2004. Original data - United States of America, Bureau of the Census. Twelfth Census of the United States, 1900. Washington, D.C.: National Archives and Records Administration, 1900. T623, 18), Ancestry.com, http://www.Ancestry.com, Year: 1900; Census Place: Justice Precinct 6, Hopkins, Texas; Roll: T623_1646; Page: 3A; Enumeration District: 57. Birth date: Feb 1884 Birth place: Texas Residence date: 1900 Residence place: Justice Precinct 6, Hopkins, Texas.

1142   Ancestry.com, 1900 United States Federal Census (Online publication - Provo, UT, USA: Ancestry.com Operations Inc, 2004. Original data - United States of America, Bureau of the Census. Twelfth Census of the United States, 1900. Washington, D.C.: National Archives and Records Administration, 1900. T623, 18), Ancestry.com, http://www.Ancestry.com, Year: 1900; Census Place: Justice Precinct 6, Hopkins, Texas; Roll: T623_1646; Page: 3A; Enumeration District: 57. Birth date: Sep 1886 Birth place: Texas Residence date: 1900 Residence place: Justice Precinct 6, Hopkins, Texas.

1143   Ancestry.com, 1900 United States Federal Census (Online publication - Provo, UT, USA: Ancestry.com Operations Inc, 2004. Original data - United States of America, Bureau of the Census. Twelfth Census of the United States, 1900. Washington, D.C.: National Archives and Records Administration, 1900. T623, 18), Ancestry.com, http://www.Ancestry.com, Year: 1900; Census Place: Justice Precinct 6, Hopkins, Texas; Roll: T623_1646; Page: 3A; Enumeration District: 57. Birth date: Dec 1891 Birth place: Texas Residence date: 1900 Residence place: Justice Precinct 6, Hopkins, Texas.

1144   Ancestry.com, 1900 United States Federal Census (Online publication - Provo, UT, USA: Ancestry.com Operations Inc, 2004. Original data - United States of America, Bureau of the Census. Twelfth Census of the United States, 1900. Washington, D.C.: National Archives and Records Administration, 1900. T623, 18), Ancestry.com, http://www.Ancestry.com, Year: 1900; Census Place: Justice Precinct 6, Hopkins, Texas; Roll: T623_1646; Page: 3A; Enumeration District: 57. Birth date: Sep 1896 Birth place: Texas Residence date: 1900 Residence place: Justice Precinct 6, Hopkins, Texas.

1145   Ancestry.com, 1920 United States Federal Census (Online publication - Provo, UT, USA: Ancestry.com Operations Inc, 2010. Images reproduced by FamilySearch. Original data - Fourteenth Census of the United States, 1920. (NARA microfilm publication T625, 2076 rolls). Records of the Bureau of the Census, Record), Ancestry.com, http://www.Ancestry.com, Year: 1920; Census Place: Justice Precinct 6, Hopkins, Texas; Roll: T625_1817; Page: 3B; Enumeration District: 79; Image:. Birth date: about 1897 Birth place: Texas Residence date: 1920 Residence place: Justice Precinct 6, Hopkins, Texas.

1146   Ancestry.com, 1910 United States Federal Census (Online publication - Provo, UT, USA: Ancestry.com Operations Inc, 2006. Original data - Thirteenth Census of the United States, 1910 (NARA microfilm publication T624, 1,178 rolls). Records of the Bureau of the Census, Record Group 29. National Archives, Washington), Ancestry.com, http://www.Ancestry.com, Year: 1910; Census Place: Cox, Etowah, Alabama; Roll: ; Page: ; Enumeration District: ; Image:. Birth date: about 1885 Birth place: Alabama Residence date: 1910 Residence place: Cox, Etowah, Alabama.

1147   Ancestry.com, 1930 United States Federal Census (Online publication - Provo, UT, USA: Ancestry.com Operations Inc, 2002. Original data - United States of America, Bureau of the Census. Fifteenth Census of the United States, 1930. Washington, D.C.: National Archives and Records Administration, 1930. T626,), Ancestry.com, http://www.Ancestry.com, Year: 1930; Census Place: Cox, Etowah, Alabama; Roll: 16; Page: 2B; Enumeration District: 23; Image: 724.0. Birth date: about 1885 Birth place: Residence date: 1930 Residence place: Cox, Etowah, Alabama.

1148   Ancestry.com, 1910 United States Federal Census (Online publication - Provo, UT, USA: Ancestry.com Operations Inc, 2006. Original data - Thirteenth Census of the United States, 1910 (NARA microfilm publication T624, 1,178 rolls). Records of the Bureau of the Census, Record Group 29. National Archives, Washington), Ancestry.com, http://www.Ancestry.com, Year: 1910; Census Place: Cox, Etowah, Alabama; Roll: ; Page: ; Enumeration District: ; Image:. Birth date: about 1906 Birth place: Alabama Residence date: 1910 Residence place: Cox, Etowah, Alabama.

1149   Ancestry.com, 1910 United States Federal Census (Online publication - Provo, UT, USA: Ancestry.com Operations Inc, 2006. Original data - Thirteenth Census of the United States, 1910 (NARA microfilm publication T624, 1,178 rolls). Records of the Bureau of the Census, Record Group 29. National Archives, Washington), Ancestry.com, http://www.Ancestry.com, Year: 1910; Census Place: Cox, Etowah, Alabama; Roll: ; Page: ; Enumeration District: ; Image:. Birth date: about 1908 Birth place: Alabama Residence date: 1910 Residence place: Cox, Etowah, Alabama.

1150   Ancestry.com, 1930 United States Federal Census (Online publication - Provo, UT, USA: Ancestry.com Operations Inc, 2002. Original data - United States of America, Bureau of the Census. Fifteenth Census of the United States, 1930. Washington, D.C.: National Archives and Records Administration, 1930. T626,), Ancestry.com, http://www.Ancestry.com, Year: 1930; Census Place: Cox, Etowah, Alabama; Roll: 16; Page: 2B; Enumeration District: 23; Image: 724.0. Birth date: about 1911 Birth place: Residence date: 1930 Residence place: Cox, Etowah, Alabama.

1151   Ancestry.com, 1930 United States Federal Census (Online publication - Provo, UT, USA: Ancestry.com Operations Inc, 2002. Original data - United States of America, Bureau of the Census. Fifteenth Census of the United States, 1930. Washington, D.C.: National Archives and Records Administration, 1930. T626,), Ancestry.com, http://www.Ancestry.com, Year: 1930; Census Place: Cox, Etowah, Alabama; Roll: 16; Page: 2B; Enumeration District: 23; Image: 724.0. Birth date: about 1916 Birth place: Residence date: 1930 Residence place: Cox, Etowah, Alabama.

1152   Ancestry.com, 1930 United States Federal Census (Online publication - Provo, UT, USA: Ancestry.com Operations Inc, 2002. Original data - United States of America, Bureau of the Census. Fifteenth Census of the United States, 1930. Washington, D.C.: National Archives and Records Administration, 1930. T626,), Ancestry.com, http://www.Ancestry.com, Year: 1930; Census Place: Cox, Etowah, Alabama; Roll: 16; Page: 2B; Enumeration District: 23; Image: 724.0. Birth date: about 1919 Birth place: Residence date: 1930 Residence place: Cox, Etowah, Alabama.

1153   Ancestry.com, 1920 United States Federal Census (Online publication - Provo, UT, USA: Ancestry.com Operations Inc, 2010. Images reproduced by FamilySearch. Original data - Fourteenth Census of the United States, 1920. (NARA microfilm publication T625, 2076 rolls). Records of the Bureau of the Census, Record), Ancestry.com, http://www.Ancestry.com, Year: 1920; Census Place: Greens Schoolhouse, Calhoun, Alabama; Roll: T625_5; Page: 1A; Enumeration District: 10; Image:. Birth date: about 1882 Birth place: Georgia Residence date: 1920 Residence place: Greens Schoolhouse, Calhoun, Alabama.

1154   Ancestry.com, 1910 United States Federal Census (Online publication - Provo, UT, USA: Ancestry.com Operations Inc, 2006. Original data - Thirteenth Census of the United States, 1910 (NARA microfilm publication T624, 1,178 rolls). Records of the Bureau of the Census, Record Group 29. National Archives, Washington), Ancestry.com, http://www.Ancestry.com, Year: 1910; Census Place: Greens Schoolhouse, Calhoun, Alabama; Roll: ; Page: ; Enumeration District: ; Image:. Birth date: about 1885 Birth place: Georgia Residence date: 1910 Residence place: Greens Schoolhouse, Calhoun, Alabama.

1155   Ancestry.com, 1920 United States Federal Census (Online publication - Provo, UT, USA: Ancestry.com Operations Inc, 2010. Images reproduced by FamilySearch. Original data - Fourteenth Census of the United States, 1920. (NARA microfilm publication T625, 2076 rolls). Records of the Bureau of the Census, Record), Ancestry.com, http://www.Ancestry.com, Year: 1920; Census Place: Greens Schoolhouse, Calhoun, Alabama; Roll: T625_5; Page: 1A; Enumeration District: 10; Image:. Birth date: about 1905 Birth place: Alabama Residence date: 1920 Residence place: Greens Schoolhouse, Calhoun, Alabama.

1156   Ancestry.com, Social Security Death Index (Online publication - Provo, UT, USA: Ancestry.com Operations Inc, 2010. Original data - Social Security Administration. Social Security Death Index, Master File. Social Security Administration. Original data: Social Security Administration. Social Security D), Ancestry.com, http://www.Ancestry.com, Number: 422-10-4708; Issue State: Alabama; Issue Date: Before 1951. Birth date: 2 Sep 1904 Birth place: Death date: Dec 1979 Death place: Gadsden, Etowah, Alabama, United States of America.

1157   Ancestry.com, 1910 United States Federal Census (Online publication - Provo, UT, USA: Ancestry.com Operations Inc, 2006. Original data - Thirteenth Census of the United States, 1910 (NARA microfilm publication T624, 1,178 rolls). Records of the Bureau of the Census, Record Group 29. National Archives, Washington), Ancestry.com, http://www.Ancestry.com, Year: 1910; Census Place: Greens Schoolhouse, Calhoun, Alabama; Roll: ; Page: ;

Enumeration District: ; Image:. Birth date: about 1905 Birth place: Alabama Residence date: 1910 Residence place: Greens Schoolhouse, Calhoun, Alabama.

1158   Ancestry.com, 1920 United States Federal Census (Online publication - Provo, UT, USA: Ancestry.com Operations Inc, 2010. Images reproduced by FamilySearch. Original data - Fourteenth Census of the United States, 1920. (NARA microfilm publication T625, 2076 rolls). Records of the Bureau of the Census, Record), Ancestry.com, http://www.Ancestry.com, Year: 1920; Census Place: Greens Schoolhouse, Calhoun, Alabama; Roll: T625_5; Page: 1A; Enumeration District: 10; Image:. Birth date: about 1915 Birth place: Alabama Residence date: 1920 Residence place: Greens Schoolhouse, Calhoun, Alabama.

1159   Ancestry.com, 1920 United States Federal Census (Online publication - Provo, UT, USA: Ancestry.com Operations Inc, 2010. Images reproduced by FamilySearch. Original data - Fourteenth Census of the United States, 1920. (NARA microfilm publication T625, 2076 rolls). Records of the Bureau of the Census, Record), Ancestry.com, http://www.Ancestry.com, Year: 1920; Census Place: Greens Schoolhouse, Calhoun, Alabama; Roll: T625_5; Page: 1A; Enumeration District: 10; Image:. Birth date: about 1910 Birth place: Alabama Residence date: 1920 Residence place: Greens Schoolhouse, Calhoun, Alabama.

1160   Ancestry.com, 1910 United States Federal Census (Online publication - Provo, UT, USA: Ancestry.com Operations Inc, 2006. Original data - Thirteenth Census of the United States, 1910 (NARA microfilm publication T624, 1,178 rolls). Records of the Bureau of the Census, Record Group 29. National Archives, Washington), Ancestry.com, http://www.Ancestry.com, Year: 1910; Census Place: Greens Schoolhouse, Calhoun, Alabama; Roll: ; Page: ; Enumeration District: ; Image:. Birth date: about 1909 Birth place: Alabama Residence date: 1910 Residence place: Greens Schoolhouse, Calhoun, Alabama.

1161   Ancestry.com, Social Security Death Index (Online publication - Provo, UT, USA: Ancestry.com Operations Inc, 2010. Original data - Social Security Administration. Social Security Death Index, Master File. Social Security Administration. Original data: Social Security Administration. Social Security D), Ancestry.com, http://www.Ancestry.com, Number: 423-18-2334; Issue State: Alabama; Issue Date: Before 1951. Birth date: 17 Mar 1909 Birth place: Death date: Dec 1980 Death place: Gadsden, Etowah, Alabama, United States of America.

1162   Ancestry.com, 1920 United States Federal Census (Online publication - Provo, UT, USA: Ancestry.com Operations Inc, 2010. Images reproduced by FamilySearch. Original data - Fourteenth Census of the United States, 1920. (NARA microfilm publication T625, 2076 rolls). Records of the Bureau of the Census, Record), Ancestry.com, http://www.Ancestry.com, Year: 1920; Census Place: Greens Schoolhouse, Calhoun, Alabama; Roll: T625_5; Page: 1A; Enumeration District: 10; Image:. Birth date: about 1912 Birth place: Alabama Residence date: 1920 Residence place: Greens Schoolhouse, Calhoun, Alabama.

1163   Ancestry.com, 1920 United States Federal Census (Online publication - Provo, UT, USA: Ancestry.com Operations Inc, 2010. Images reproduced by FamilySearch. Original data - Fourteenth Census of the United States, 1920. (NARA microfilm publication T625, 2076 rolls). Records of the Bureau of the Census, Record), Ancestry.com, http://www.Ancestry.com, Year: 1920; Census Place: Greens Schoolhouse, Calhoun, Alabama; Roll: T625_5; Page: 1A; Enumeration District: 10; Image:. Birth date: about 1917 Birth place: Alabama Residence date: 1920 Residence place: Greens Schoolhouse, Calhoun, Alabama.

1164   Ancestry.com, 1930 United States Federal Census (Online publication - Provo, UT, USA: Ancestry.com Operations Inc, 2002. Original data - United States of America, Bureau of the Census. Fifteenth Census of the United States, 1930. Washington, D.C.: National Archives and Records Administration, 1930. T626,), Ancestry.com, http://www.Ancestry.com, Year: 1930; Census Place: Greens Schoolhouse, Calhoun, Alabama; Roll: 5; Page: 1A; Enumeration District: 11; Image: 242.0. Birth date: about 1917 Birth place: Residence date: 1930 Residence place: Greens Schoolhouse, Calhoun, Alabama.

1165   Ancestry.com, 1920 United States Federal Census (Online publication - Provo, UT, USA: Ancestry.com Operations Inc, 2010. Images reproduced by FamilySearch. Original data - Fourteenth Census of the United States, 1920. (NARA microfilm publication T625, 2076 rolls). Records of the Bureau of the Census, Record), Ancestry.com, http://www.Ancestry.com, Year: 1920; Census Place: Greens Schoolhouse, Calhoun, Alabama; Roll: T625_5; Page: 1A; Enumeration District: 10; Image:. Birth date: about 1920 Birth place: Alabama Residence date: 1920 Residence place: Greens Schoolhouse, Calhoun, Alabama.

1166   Ancestry.com, 1920 United States Federal Census (Online publication - Provo, UT, USA: Ancestry.com Operations Inc, 2010. Images reproduced by FamilySearch. Original data - Fourteenth Census of the United States, 1920. (NARA microfilm publication T625, 2076 rolls). Records of the Bureau of the Census, Record), Ancestry.com, http://www.Ancestry.com, Year: 1920; Census Place: Corinth, DeKalb, Alabama; Roll: T625_12; Page: 18A; Enumeration District: 86; Image:. Birth date: about 1848 Birth place: Georgia Residence date: 1920 Residence place: Corinth, DeKalb, Alabama.

1167   Ancestry.com, 1910 United States Federal Census (Online publication - Provo, UT, USA: Ancestry.com Operations Inc, 2006. Original data - Thirteenth Census of the United States, 1910 (NARA microfilm publication T624, 1,178 rolls). Records of the Bureau of the Census, Record Group 29. National Archives, Washington), Ancestry.com, http://www.Ancestry.com, Year: 1910; Census Place: Corinth, DeKalb, Alabama; Roll: ; Page: ; Enumeration District: ; Image:. Birth date: about 1845 Birth place: Georgia Residence date: 1910 Residence place: Corinth, DeKalb, Alabama.

1168   Ancestry.com, 1850 United States Federal Census (Online publication - Provo, UT, USA: Ancestry.com Operations, Inc., 2009. Images reproduced by FamilySearch. Original data - Seventh Census of the United States, 1850; (National Archives Microfilm Publication M432, 1009 rolls); Records of the Bureau of the), Ancestry.com,

215

http://www.Ancestry.com, Year: 1850; Census Place: District 2, Habersham, Georgia; Roll: M432_72; Page: 244A; Image:. Birth date: about 1847 Birth place: Georgia Residence date: 1850 Residence place: District 2, Habersham, Georgia.

1169   Ancestry.com, 1860 United States Federal Census (Online publication - Provo, UT, USA: Ancestry.com Operations, Inc., 2009. Images reproduced by FamilySearch. Original data - 1860 U.S. census, population schedule. NARA microfilm publication M653, 1,438 rolls. Washington, D.C.: National Archives and Records), Ancestry.com, http://www.Ancestry.com, Year: 1860; Census Place: , Habersham, Georgia; Roll: ; Page: 833; Image: 383. Birth date: about 1846 Birth place: Georgia Residence date: 1860 Residence place: Habersham, Georgia, United States.

1170   Ancestry.com, 1900 United States Federal Census (Online publication - Provo, UT, USA: Ancestry.com Operations Inc, 2004. Original data - United States of America, Bureau of the Census. Twelfth Census of the United States, 1900. Washington, D.C.: National Archives and Records Administration, 1900. T623, 18), Ancestry.com, http://www.Ancestry.com, Year: 1900; Census Place: Van Buren, Dekalb, Alabama; Roll: T623_14; Page: 6B; Enumeration District: 66. Birth date: Feb 1847 Birth place: Georgia Marriage date: 1890 Marriage place: Residence date: 1900 Residence place: Van Buren, Dekalb, Alabama.

1171   Ancestry.com, Alabama Deaths, 1908-59 (Online publication - Provo, UT, USA: Ancestry.com Operations Inc, 2000. Original data - State of Alabama. Index of Vital Records for Alabama: Deaths, 1908-1959. Montgomery, AL, USA: State of Alabama Center for Health Statistics, Record Services Division. Original), Ancestry.com, http://www.Ancestry.com, Death date: 17 Feb 1922 Death place: Dekalb.

1172   Ancestry.com, 1900 United States Federal Census (Online publication - Provo, UT, USA: Ancestry.com Operations Inc, 2004. Original data - United States of America, Bureau of the Census. Twelfth Census of the United States, 1900. Washington, D.C.: National Archives and Records Administration, 1900. T623, 18), Ancestry.com, http://www.Ancestry.com, Year: 1900; Census Place: Van Buren, Dekalb, Alabama; Roll: T623_14; Page: 6B; Enumeration District: 66. Birth date: Nov 1880 Birth place: Alabama Residence date: 1900 Residence place: Van Buren, Dekalb, Alabama.

1173   Ancestry.com, Alabama Deaths, 1908-59 (Online publication - Provo, UT, USA: Ancestry.com Operations Inc, 2000. Original data - State of Alabama. Index of Vital Records for Alabama: Deaths, 1908-1959. Montgomery, AL, USA: State of Alabama Center for Health Statistics, Record Services Division. Original), Ancestry.com, http://www.Ancestry.com, Death date: 30 Apr 1914 Death place: Dekalb.

1174   Ancestry.com, 1910 United States Federal Census (Online publication - Provo, UT, USA: Ancestry.com Operations Inc, 2006. Original data - Thirteenth Census of the United States, 1910 (NARA microfilm publication T624, 1,178 rolls). Records of the Bureau of the Census, Record Group 29. National Archives, Washington), Ancestry.com, http://www.Ancestry.com, Year: 1910; Census Place: Corinth, DeKalb, Alabama; Roll: ; Page: ; Enumeration District: ; Image:. Birth date: about 1888 Birth place: Alabama Residence date: 1910 Residence place: Corinth, DeKalb, Alabama.

1175   Ancestry.com, 1900 United States Federal Census (Online publication - Provo, UT, USA: Ancestry.com Operations Inc, 2004. Original data - United States of America, Bureau of the Census. Twelfth Census of the United States, 1900. Washington, D.C.: National Archives and Records Administration, 1900. T623, 18), Ancestry.com, http://www.Ancestry.com, Year: 1900; Census Place: Van Buren, Dekalb, Alabama; Roll: T623_14; Page: 6B; Enumeration District: 66. Birth date: Apr 1892 Birth place: Alabama Residence date: 1900 Residence place: Van Buren, Dekalb, Alabama.

1176   Ancestry.com, 1910 United States Federal Census (Online publication - Provo, UT, USA: Ancestry.com Operations Inc, 2006. Original data - Thirteenth Census of the United States, 1910 (NARA microfilm publication T624, 1,178 rolls). Records of the Bureau of the Census, Record Group 29. National Archives, Washington), Ancestry.com, http://www.Ancestry.com, Year: 1910; Census Place: Corinth, DeKalb, Alabama; Roll: ; Page: ; Enumeration District: ; Image:. Birth date: about 1897 Birth place: Alabama Residence date: 1910 Residence place: Corinth, DeKalb, Alabama.

1177   Ancestry.com, 1900 United States Federal Census (Online publication - Provo, UT, USA: Ancestry.com Operations Inc, 2004. Original data - United States of America, Bureau of the Census. Twelfth Census of the United States, 1900. Washington, D.C.: National Archives and Records Administration, 1900. T623, 18), Ancestry.com, http://www.Ancestry.com, Year: 1900; Census Place: Van Buren, Dekalb, Alabama; Roll: T623_14; Page: 6B; Enumeration District: 66. Birth date: Jun 1895 Birth place: Alabama Residence date: 1900 Residence place: Van Buren, Dekalb, Alabama.

1178   Ancestry.com, 1920 United States Federal Census (Online publication - Provo, UT, USA: Ancestry.com Operations Inc, 2010. Images reproduced by FamilySearch. Original data - Fourteenth Census of the United States, 1920. (NARA microfilm publication T625, 2076 rolls). Records of the Bureau of the Census, Record), Ancestry.com, http://www.Ancestry.com, Year: 1920; Census Place: Section, Jackson, Alabama; Roll: T625_19; Page: 8A; Enumeration District: 47; Image:. Birth date: about 1897 Birth place: Alabama Residence date: 1920 Residence place: Section, Jackson, Alabama.

1179   Ancestry.com, 1930 United States Federal Census (Online publication - Provo, UT, USA: Ancestry.com Operations Inc, 2002. Original data - United States of America, Bureau of the Census. Fifteenth Census of the United States, 1930. Washington, D.C.: National Archives and Records Administration, 1930. T626,), Ancestry.com, http://www.Ancestry.com, Year: 1930; Census Place: Wrights, Marshall, Alabama; Roll: 40; Page: 11B; Enumeration District: 27; Image: 81.0. Birth date: about 1896 Birth place: Residence date: 1930 Residence place: Wrights, Marshall, Alabama.

1180   Ancestry.com, Social Security Death Index (Online publication - Provo, UT, USA: Ancestry.com Operations Inc, 2010. Original data - Social Security Administration. Social Security Death Index, Master File. Social Security Administration. Original data: Social Security Administration. Social Security D), Ancestry.com, http://www.Ancestry.com, Number: 420-86-1075; Issue State: Alabama; Issue Date: 1973. Birth date: 15 Jun 1896 Birth place: Death date: Jan 1985 Death place: Collinsville, Dekalb, Alabama, United States of America.

1181   Ancestry.com, DeKalb County, Alabama Marriage Index, 1836-1916 (Online publication - Provo, UT, USA: The Generations Network, Inc., 2006. Original data - Duff, Dorothy Smith. DeKalb County, Alabama Marriage Index, 1836-1916. Baltimore, MD, USA: Genealogical Publishing Co., 2003. Original data: Duff, Dorothy Smith. DeKalb), Ancestry.com, http://www.Ancestry.com.

1182   Ancestry.com, DeKalb County, Alabama Marriage Index, 1836-1916 (Online publication - Provo, UT, USA: The Generations Network, Inc., 2006. Original data - Duff, Dorothy Smith. DeKalb County, Alabama Marriage Index, 1836-1916. Baltimore, MD, USA: Genealogical Publishing Co., 2003. Original data: Duff, Dorothy Smith. DeKalb), Ancestry.com, http://www.Ancestry.com, Marriage record.

1183   Ancestry.com, 1920 United States Federal Census (Online publication - Provo, UT, USA: Ancestry.com Operations Inc, 2010. Images reproduced by FamilySearch. Original data - Fourteenth Census of the United States, 1920. (NARA microfilm publication T625, 2076 rolls). Records of the Bureau of the Census, Record), Ancestry.com, http://www.Ancestry.com, Year: 1920; Census Place: Corinth, DeKalb, Alabama; Roll: T625_12; Page: 18A; Enumeration District: 86; Image:. Birth date: about 1899 Birth place: Alabama Residence date: 1920 Residence place: Corinth, DeKalb, Alabama.

1184   Ancestry.com, 1910 United States Federal Census (Online publication - Provo, UT, USA: Ancestry.com Operations Inc, 2006. Original data - Thirteenth Census of the United States, 1910 (NARA microfilm publication T624, 1,178 rolls). Records of the Bureau of the Census, Record Group 29. National Archives, Washington), Ancestry.com, http://www.Ancestry.com, Year: 1910; Census Place: Corinth, DeKalb, Alabama; Roll: ; Page: ; Enumeration District: ; Image:. Birth date: about 1899 Birth place: Alabama Residence date: 1910 Residence place: Corinth, DeKalb, Alabama.

1185   Ancestry.com, 1930 United States Federal Census (Online publication - Provo, UT, USA: Ancestry.com Operations Inc, 2002. Original data - United States of America, Bureau of the Census. Fifteenth Census of the United States, 1930. Washington, D.C.: National Archives and Records Administration, 1930. T626,), Ancestry.com, http://www.Ancestry.com, Year: 1930; Census Place: Corinth, Dekalb, Alabama; Roll: 12; Page: 16A; Enumeration District: 33; Image: 1027.0. Birth date: about 1899 Birth place: Alabama Residence date: 1930 Residence place: Corinth, Dekalb, Alabama.

1186   Ancestry.com, World War I Draft Registration Cards, 1917-1918 (Online publication - Provo, UT, USA: Ancestry.com Operations Inc, 2005. Original data - United States, Selective Service System. World War I Selective Service System Draft Registration Cards, 1917-1918. Washington, D.C.: National Archives and Records Administration), Ancestry.com, http://www.Ancestry.com, Registration Location: Dekalb County, Alabama; Roll: 1509379; Draft Board: 0. Birth date: 14 Jul 1898 Birth place: Residence date: Residence place: Dekalb, Alabama.

1187   Banks, Ray, comp., WWI Civilian Draft Registrations (Online publication - Provo, UT, USA: Ancestry.com Operations Inc, 2000.), Ancestry.com, http://www.Ancestry.com, Birth date: 4 Jul 1898 Birth place: Residence date: Residence place: Dekalb.

1188   Ancestry.com, Social Security Death Index (Online publication - Provo, UT, USA: Ancestry.com Operations Inc, 2010. Original data - Social Security Administration. Social Security Death Index, Master File. Social Security Administration. Original data: Social Security Administration. Social Security D), Ancestry.com, http://www.Ancestry.com, Number: 423-18-3462; Issue State: Alabama; Issue Date: Before 1951. Birth date: 4 Jul 1898 Birth place: Death date: Feb 1978 Death place: Fyffe, Dekalb, Alabama, United States of America.

1189   Ancestry.com, 1900 United States Federal Census (Online publication - Provo, UT, USA: Ancestry.com Operations Inc, 2004. Original data - United States of America, Bureau of the Census. Twelfth Census of the United States, 1900. Washington, D.C.: National Archives and Records Administration, 1900. T623, 18), Ancestry.com, http://www.Ancestry.com, Year: 1900; Census Place: Van Buren, Dekalb, Alabama; Roll: T623_14; Page: 6B; Enumeration District: 66. Birth date: Jul 1898 Birth place: Alabama Residence date: 1900 Residence place: Van Buren, Dekalb, Alabama.

1190   Ancestry.com and The Church of Jesus Christ of Latter-day Saints, 1880 United States Federal Census (Online publication - Provo, UT, USA: Ancestry.com Operations Inc, 2010. 1880 U.S. Census Index provided by The Church of Jesus Christ of Latter-day Saints © Copyright 1999 Intellectual Reserve, Inc. All rights reserved. All use is subject to the limited), Ancestry.com, http://www.Ancestry.com, Year: 1880; Census Place: Hokes Bluff and Turkey Town, Etowah, Alabama; Roll: 13; Family History Film: 1254013; Page: 323B; Enumeration District: 66; Image: 0154. Birth date: about 1852 Birth place: Georgia Residence date: 1880 Residence place: Hokes Bluff and Turkey Town, Etowah, Alabama, United States.

1191   Ancestry.com, 1870 United States Federal Census (Online publication - Provo, UT, USA: Ancestry.com Operations, Inc., 2009. Images reproduced by FamilySearch. Original data - 1870 U.S. census, population schedules. NARA microfilm publication M593, 1,761 rolls. Washington, D.C.: National Archives and Record), Ancestry.com, http://www.Ancestry.com, Year: 1870; Census Place: Township 12 Range 7, Etowah, Alabama; Roll: M593_; Page: ; Image:. Birth date: about 1850 Birth place: Georgia Residence date: 1870 Residence place: Township 12 Range 7, Etowah, Alabama, United States.

217

1192   Ancestry.com, 1860 United States Federal Census (Online publication - Provo, UT, USA: Ancestry.com Operations, Inc., 2009. Images reproduced by FamilySearch. Original data - 1860 U.S. census, population schedule. NARA microfilm publication M653, 1,438 rolls. Washington, D.C.: National Archives and Records), Ancestry.com, http://www.Ancestry.com, Year: 1860; Census Place: Division 1, Cherokee, Alabama; Roll: ; Page: 265; Image: 271. Birth date: about 1849 Birth place: Alabama Residence date: 1860 Residence place: Division 1, Cherokee, Alabama, United States.

1193   Ancestry.com, Alabama Deaths, 1908-59 (Online publication - Provo, UT, USA: Ancestry.com Operations Inc, 2000. Original data - State of Alabama. Index of Vital Records for Alabama: Deaths, 1908-1959. Montgomery, AL, USA: State of Alabama Center for Health Statistics, Record Services Division. Original), Ancestry.com, http://www.Ancestry.com, Death date: 15 Jul 1945 Death place: Etowah.

1194   Ancestry.com, 1930 United States Federal Census (Online publication - Provo, UT, USA: Ancestry.com Operations Inc, 2002. Original data - United States of America, Bureau of the Census. Fifteenth Census of the United States, 1930. Washington, D.C.: National Archives and Records Administration, 1930. T626,), Ancestry.com, http://www.Ancestry.com, Year: 1930; Census Place: Hokes Bluff, Etowah, Alabama; Roll: 16; Page: 8B; Enumeration District: 16; Image: 608.0. Birth date: about 1877 Birth place: Alabama Residence date: 1930 Residence place: Hokes Bluff, Etowah, Alabama.

1195   Ancestry.com, World War I Draft Registration Cards, 1917-1918 (Online publication - Provo, UT, USA: Ancestry.com Operations Inc, 2005. Original data - United States, Selective Service System. World War I Selective Service System Draft Registration Cards, 1917-1918. Washington, D.C.: National Archives and Records Administration), Ancestry.com, http://www.Ancestry.com, Registration Location: Etowah County, Alabama; Roll: 1509384; Draft Board: 0. Birth date: 14 Oct 1876 Birth place: Residence date: Residence place: Etowah, Alabama.

1196   Ancestry.com, 1900 United States Federal Census (Online publication - Provo, UT, USA: Ancestry.com Operations Inc, 2004. Original data - United States of America, Bureau of the Census. Twelfth Census of the United States, 1900. Washington, D.C.: National Archives and Records Administration, 1900. T623, 18), Ancestry.com, http://www.Ancestry.com, Year: 1900; Census Place: Hokes Bluff, Etowah, Alabama; Roll: T623_15; Page: 9B; Enumeration District: 151. Birth date: Oct 1876 Birth place: Alabama Marriage date: 1898 Marriage place: Residence date: 1900 Residence place: Hokes Bluff, Etowah, Alabama.

1197   Ancestry.com, 1920 United States Federal Census (Online publication - Provo, UT, USA: Ancestry.com Operations Inc, 2010. Images reproduced by FamilySearch. Original data - Fourteenth Census of the United States, 1920. (NARA microfilm publication T625, 2076 rolls). Records of the Bureau of the Census, Record), Ancestry.com, http://www.Ancestry.com, Year: 1920; Census Place: Hokes Bluff, Etowah, Alabama; Roll: T625_15; Page: 8B; Enumeration District: 99; Image:. Birth date: about 1877 Birth place: Alabama Residence date: 1920 Residence place: Hokes Bluff, Etowah, Alabama.

1198   Ancestry.com and The Church of Jesus Christ of Latter-day Saints, 1880 United States Federal Census (Online publication - Provo, UT, USA: Ancestry.com Operations Inc, 2010. 1880 U.S. Census Index provided by The Church of Jesus Christ of Latter-day Saints © Copyright 1999 Intellectual Reserve, Inc. All rights reserved. All use is subject to the limited), Ancestry.com, http://www.Ancestry.com, Year: 1880; Census Place: Hokes Bluff and Turkey Town, Etowah, Alabama; Roll: 13; Family History Film: 1254013; Page: 323B; Enumeration District: 66; Image: 0154. Birth date: about 1876 Birth place: Alabama Residence date: 1880 Residence place: Hokes Bluff and Turkey Town, Etowah, Alabama, United States.

1199   Ancestry.com, Alabama Marriage Collection, 1800-1969 (Online publication - Provo, UT, USA: Ancestry.com Operations Inc, 2006. Original data - Alabama Center for Health Statistics. Alabama Marriage Index, 1936-1969. Alabama Center for Health Statistics, Montgomery, Alabama. Dodd, Jordan R., et. al. Early America), Ancestry.com, http://www.Ancestry.com, Marriage date: 2 Jan 1898 Marriage place: Etowah, Alabama.

1200   Dodd, Jordan R., comp., Alabama Marriages, 1809-1920 (Selected Counties) (Online publication - Provo, UT, USA: The Generations Network, Inc., 1999. Original data - Early American Marriages: Alabama, 1800 to 1920. Original data: Early American Marriages: Alabama, 1800 to 1920), Ancestry.com, http://www.Ancestry.com, Marriage date: 02 Jan 1898 Marriage place: Etowah.

1201   Ancestry.com, Alabama Marriage Collection, 1800-1969 (Online publication - Provo, UT, USA: Ancestry.com Operations Inc, 2006. Original data - Alabama Center for Health Statistics. Alabama Marriage Index, 1936-1969. Alabama Center for Health Statistics, Montgomery, Alabama. Dodd, Jordan R., et. al. Early America), Ancestry.com, http://www.Ancestry.com, Marriage date: 2 Jan 1898 Marriage place: Etowah, Alabama.

1202   Ancestry.com and The Church of Jesus Christ of Latter-day Saints, 1880 United States Federal Census (Online publication - Provo, UT, USA: Ancestry.com Operations Inc, 2010. 1880 U.S. Census Index provided by The Church of Jesus Christ of Latter-day Saints © Copyright 1999 Intellectual Reserve, Inc. All rights reserved. All use is subject to the limited), Ancestry.com, http://www.Ancestry.com, Year: 1880; Census Place: Hokes Bluff and Turkey Town, Etowah, Alabama; Roll: 13; Family History Film: 1254013; Page: 323B; Enumeration District: 66; Image: 0154. Birth date: about 1879 Birth place: Alabama Residence date: 1880 Residence place: Hokes Bluff and Turkey Town, Etowah, Alabama, United States.

1203   Ancestry.com, 1930 United States Federal Census (Online publication - Provo, UT, USA: Ancestry.com Operations Inc, 2002. Original data - United States of America, Bureau of the Census. Fifteenth Census of the United States, 1930. Washington, D.C.: National Archives and Records Administration, 1930. T626,), Ancestry.com, http://www.Ancestry.com, Year: 1930; Census Place: Gadsden, Etowah, Alabama; Roll: 16; Page: 19B; Enumeration

District: 9; Image: 416.0. Birth date: about 1880 Birth place: Alabama Residence date: 1930 Residence place: Gadsden, Etowah, Alabama.

1204   Ancestry.com, 1920 United States Federal Census (Online publication - Provo, UT, USA: Ancestry.com Operations Inc, 2010. Images reproduced by FamilySearch. Original data - Fourteenth Census of the United States, 1920. (NARA microfilm publication T625, 2076 rolls). Records of the Bureau of the Census, Record), Ancestry.com, http://www.Ancestry.com, Year: 1920; Census Place: Hokes Bluff, Etowah, Alabama; Roll: T625_15; Page: 8B; Enumeration District: 99; Image:. Birth date: about 1880 Birth place: Alabama Residence date: 1920 Residence place: Hokes Bluff, Etowah, Alabama.

1205   Ancestry.com, 1910 United States Federal Census (Online publication - Provo, UT, USA: Ancestry.com Operations Inc, 2006. Original data - Thirteenth Census of the United States, 1910 (NARA microfilm publication T624, 1,178 rolls). Records of the Bureau of the Census, Record Group 29. National Archives, Washington), Ancestry.com, http://www.Ancestry.com, Year: 1910; Census Place: Hokes Bluff, Etowah, Alabama; Roll: ; Page: ; Enumeration District: ; Image:. Birth date: about 1880 Birth place: Alabama Residence date: 1910 Residence place: Hokes Bluff, Etowah, Alabama.

1206   Ancestry.com, World War I Draft Registration Cards, 1917-1918 (Online publication - Provo, UT, USA: Ancestry.com Operations Inc, 2005. Original data - United States, Selective Service System. World War I Selective Service System Draft Registration Cards, 1917-1918. Washington, D.C.: National Archives and Records Administration), Ancestry.com, http://www.Ancestry.com, Registration Location: Etowah County, Alabama; Roll: 1509384; Draft Board: 0. Birth date: 27 Dec 1879 Birth place: Residence date: Residence place: Etowah, Alabama.

1207   Ancestry.com, Alabama Deaths, 1908-59 (Online publication - Provo, UT, USA: Ancestry.com Operations Inc, 2000. Original data - State of Alabama. Index of Vital Records for Alabama: Deaths, 1908-1959. Montgomery, AL, USA: State of Alabama Center for Health Statistics, Record Services Division. Original), Ancestry.com, http://www.Ancestry.com, Death date: 12 Apr 1941 Death place: Etowah.

1208   Ancestry.com, 1920 United States Federal Census (Online publication - Provo, UT, USA: Ancestry.com Operations Inc, 2010. Images reproduced by FamilySearch. Original data - Fourteenth Census of the United States, 1920. (NARA microfilm publication T625, 2076 rolls). Records of the Bureau of the Census, Record), Ancestry.com, http://www.Ancestry.com, Year: 1920; Census Place: Hokes Bluff, Etowah, Alabama; Roll: T625_15; Page: 2A; Enumeration District: 99; Image:. Birth date: about 1884 Birth place: Alabama Residence date: 1920 Residence place: Hokes Bluff, Etowah, Alabama.

1209   Ancestry.com, 1910 United States Federal Census (Online publication - Provo, UT, USA: Ancestry.com Operations Inc, 2006. Original data - Thirteenth Census of the United States, 1910 (NARA microfilm publication T624, 1,178 rolls). Records of the Bureau of the Census, Record Group 29. National Archives, Washington), Ancestry.com, http://www.Ancestry.com, Year: 1910; Census Place: Hokes Bluff, Etowah, Alabama; Roll: ; Page: ; Enumeration District: ; Image:. Birth date: about 1883 Birth place: Alabama Residence date: 1910 Residence place: Hokes Bluff, Etowah, Alabama.

1210   Ancestry.com, 1930 United States Federal Census (Online publication - Provo, UT, USA: Ancestry.com Operations Inc, 2002. Original data - United States of America, Bureau of the Census. Fifteenth Census of the United States, 1930. Washington, D.C.: National Archives and Records Administration, 1930. T626,), Ancestry.com, http://www.Ancestry.com, Year: 1930; Census Place: Hokes Bluff, Etowah, Alabama; Roll: 16; Page: 9A; Enumeration District: 16; Image: 609.0. Birth date: about 1885 Birth place: Residence date: 1930 Residence place: Hokes Bluff, Etowah, Alabama.

1211   Ancestry.com, Alabama Marriage Collection, 1800-1969 (Online publication - Provo, UT, USA: Ancestry.com Operations Inc, 2006. Original data - Alabama Center for Health Statistics. Alabama Marriage Index, 1936-1969. Alabama Center for Health Statistics, Montgomery, Alabama. Dodd, Jordan R., et. al. Early America), Ancestry.com, http://www.Ancestry.com, Marriage date: 1 Jan 1899 Marriage place: Etowah, Alabama.

1212   Dodd, Jordan R., comp., Alabama Marriages, 1809-1920 (Selected Counties) (Online publication - Provo, UT, USA: The Generations Network, Inc., 1999. Original data - Early American Marriages: Alabama, 1800 to 1920. Original data: Early American Marriages: Alabama, 1800 to 1920), Ancestry.com, http://www.Ancestry.com, Marriage date: 01 Jan 1899 Marriage place: Etowah.

1213   Ancestry.com, 1900 United States Federal Census (Online publication - Provo, UT, USA: Ancestry.com Operations Inc, 2004. Original data - United States of America, Bureau of the Census. Twelfth Census of the United States, 1900. Washington, D.C.: National Archives and Records Administration, 1900. T623, 18), Ancestry.com, http://www.Ancestry.com, Year: 1900; Census Place: Hokes Bluff, Etowah, Alabama; Roll: T623_15; Page: 5B; Enumeration District: 151. Birth date: Aug 1880 Birth place: Alabama Marriage date: 1898 Marriage place: Residence date: 1900 Residence place: Hokes Bluff, Etowah, Alabama.

1214   Ancestry.com, Alabama Marriage Collection, 1800-1969 (Online publication - Provo, UT, USA: Ancestry.com Operations Inc, 2006. Original data - Alabama Center for Health Statistics. Alabama Marriage Index, 1936-1969. Alabama Center for Health Statistics, Montgomery, Alabama. Dodd, Jordan R., et. al. Early America), Ancestry.com, http://www.Ancestry.com, Marriage date: 1 Jan 1899 Marriage place: Etowah, Alabama.

1215   Ancestry.com, 1930 United States Federal Census (Online publication - Provo, UT, USA: Ancestry.com Operations Inc, 2002. Original data - United States of America, Bureau of the Census. Fifteenth Census of the United States, 1930. Washington, D.C.: National Archives and Records Administration, 1930. T626,), Ancestry.com,

http://www.Ancestry.com, Year: 1930; Census Place: Keysburg, Etowah, Alabama; Roll: 16; Page: 4A; Enumeration District: 43; Image: 1021.0. Birth date: about 1883 Birth place: Residence date: 1930 Residence place: Keysburg, Etowah, Alabama.

1216   Ancestry.com, 1910 United States Federal Census (Online publication - Provo, UT, USA: Ancestry.com Operations Inc, 2006. Original data - Thirteenth Census of the United States, 1910 (NARA microfilm publication T624, 1,178 rolls). Records of the Bureau of the Census, Record Group 29. National Archives, Washington), Ancestry.com, http://www.Ancestry.com, Year: 1910; Census Place: Hokes Bluff, Etowah, Alabama; Roll: ; Page: ; Enumeration District: ; Image:. Birth date: about 1883 Birth place: Alabama Residence date: 1910 Residence place: Hokes Bluff, Etowah, Alabama.

1217   Ancestry.com, 1920 United States Federal Census (Online publication - Provo, UT, USA: Ancestry.com Operations Inc, 2010. Images reproduced by FamilySearch. Original data - Fourteenth Census of the United States, 1920. (NARA microfilm publication T625, 2076 rolls). Records of the Bureau of the Census, Record), Ancestry.com, http://www.Ancestry.com, Year: 1920; Census Place: Anniston Ward 6, Calhoun, Alabama; Roll: T625_5; Page: 5A; Enumeration District: 158; Image:. Birth date: about 1884 Birth place: Alabama Residence date: 1920 Residence place: Anniston Ward 6, Calhoun, Alabama.

1218   Ancestry.com, 1900 United States Federal Census (Online publication - Provo, UT, USA: Ancestry.com Operations Inc, 2004. Original data - United States of America, Bureau of the Census. Twelfth Census of the United States, 1900. Washington, D.C.: National Archives and Records Administration, 1900. T623, 18), Ancestry.com, http://www.Ancestry.com, Year: 1900; Census Place: Hokes Bluff, Etowah, Alabama; Roll: T623_15; Page: 9B; Enumeration District: 151. Birth date: Jul 1882 Birth place: Alabama Marriage date: 1899 Marriage place: Residence date: 1900 Residence place: Hokes Bluff, Etowah, Alabama.

1219   Ancestry.com, 1900 United States Federal Census (Online publication - Provo, UT, USA: Ancestry.com Operations Inc, 2004. Original data - United States of America, Bureau of the Census. Twelfth Census of the United States, 1900. Washington, D.C.: National Archives and Records Administration, 1900. T623, 18), Ancestry.com, http://www.Ancestry.com, Year: 1900; Census Place: Hokes Bluff, Etowah, Alabama; Roll: T623_15; Page: 9B; Enumeration District: 151. Birth date: Aug 1876 Birth place: Alabama Marriage date: 1899 Marriage place: Residence date: 1900 Residence place: Hokes Bluff, Etowah, Alabama.

1220   Ancestry.com, Alabama Deaths, 1908-59 (Online publication - Provo, UT, USA: Ancestry.com Operations Inc, 2000. Original data - State of Alabama. Index of Vital Records for Alabama: Deaths, 1908-1959. Montgomery, AL, USA: State of Alabama Center for Health Statistics, Record Services Division. Original), Ancestry.com, http://www.Ancestry.com, Death date: 08 Mar 1959 Death place: Jefferson.

1221   Ancestry.com, 1900 United States Federal Census (Online publication - Provo, UT, USA: Ancestry.com Operations Inc, 2004. Original data - United States of America, Bureau of the Census. Twelfth Census of the United States, 1900. Washington, D.C.: National Archives and Records Administration, 1900. T623, 18), Ancestry.com, http://www.Ancestry.com, Year: 1900; Census Place: Hokes Bluff, Etowah, Alabama; Roll: T623_15; Page: 9B; Enumeration District: 151. Birth date: Jun 1889 Birth place: Alabama Residence date: 1900 Residence place: Hokes Bluff, Etowah, Alabama.

1222   Ancestry.com, 1920 United States Federal Census (Online publication - Provo, UT, USA: Ancestry.com Operations Inc, 2010. Images reproduced by FamilySearch. Original data - Fourteenth Census of the United States, 1920. (NARA microfilm publication T625, 2076 rolls). Records of the Bureau of the Census, Record), Ancestry.com, http://www.Ancestry.com, Year: 1920; Census Place: Hokes Bluff, Etowah, Alabama; Roll: T625_15; Page: 2A; Enumeration District: 99; Image:. Birth date: about 1890 Birth place: Alabama Residence date: 1920 Residence place: Hokes Bluff, Etowah, Alabama.

1223   Ancestry.com, 1930 United States Federal Census (Online publication - Provo, UT, USA: Ancestry.com Operations Inc, 2002. Original data - United States of America, Bureau of the Census. Fifteenth Census of the United States, 1930. Washington, D.C.: National Archives and Records Administration, 1930. T626,), Ancestry.com, http://www.Ancestry.com, Year: 1930; Census Place: Hokes Bluff, Etowah, Alabama; Roll: 16; Page: 9A; Enumeration District: 16; Image: 609.0. Birth date: about 1890 Birth place: Residence date: 1930 Residence place: Hokes Bluff, Etowah, Alabama.

1224   Ancestry.com, 1910 United States Federal Census (Online publication - Provo, UT, USA: Ancestry.com Operations Inc, 2006. Original data - Thirteenth Census of the United States, 1910 (NARA microfilm publication T624, 1,178 rolls). Records of the Bureau of the Census, Record Group 29. National Archives, Washington), Ancestry.com, http://www.Ancestry.com, Year: 1910; Census Place: Hokes Bluff, Etowah, Alabama; Roll: ; Page: ; Enumeration District: ; Image:. Birth date: about 1889 Birth place: Alabama Residence date: 1910 Residence place: Hokes Bluff, Etowah, Alabama.

1225   Ancestry.com and The Church of Jesus Christ of Latter-day Saints, 1880 United States Federal Census (Online publication - Provo, UT, USA: Ancestry.com Operations Inc, 2010. 1880 U.S. Census Index provided by The Church of Jesus Christ of Latter-day Saints © Copyright 1999 Intellectual Reserve, Inc. All rights reserved. All use is subject to the limited), Ancestry.com, http://www.Ancestry.com, Year: 1880; Census Place: Greenwood, Etowah, Alabama; Roll: 13; Family History Film: 1254013; Page: 405A; Enumeration District: 72; Image: 0317. Birth date: about 1853 Birth place: Alabama Residence date: 1880 Residence place: Greenwood, Etowah, Alabama, United States.

1226   Ancestry.com and The Church of Jesus Christ of Latter-day Saints, 1880 United States Federal Census (Online publication - Provo, UT, USA: Ancestry.com Operations Inc, 2010. 1880 U.S. Census Index provided by The Church of

Jesus Christ of Latter-day Saints © Copyright 1999 Intellectual Reserve, Inc. All rights reserved. All use is subject to the limited), Ancestry.com, http://www.Ancestry.com, Year: 1880; Census Place: Greenwood, Etowah, Alabama; Roll: 13; Family History Film: 1254013; Page: 405A; Enumeration District: 72; Image: 0317. Birth date: about 1874 Birth place: Alabama Residence date: 1880 Residence place: Greenwood, Etowah, Alabama, United States.

1227   Ancestry.com and The Church of Jesus Christ of Latter-day Saints, 1880 United States Federal Census (Online publication - Provo, UT, USA: Ancestry.com Operations Inc, 2010. 1880 U.S. Census Index provided by The Church of Jesus Christ of Latter-day Saints © Copyright 1999 Intellectual Reserve, Inc. All rights reserved. All use is subject to the limited), Ancestry.com, http://www.Ancestry.com, Year: 1880; Census Place: Greenwood, Etowah, Alabama; Roll: 13; Family History Film: 1254013; Page: 405A; Enumeration District: 72; Image: 0317. Birth date: about 1874 Birth place: Alabama Residence date: 1880 Residence place: Greenwood, Etowah, Alabama, United States.

1228   Ancestry.com and The Church of Jesus Christ of Latter-day Saints, 1880 United States Federal Census (Online publication - Provo, UT, USA: Ancestry.com Operations Inc, 2010. 1880 U.S. Census Index provided by The Church of Jesus Christ of Latter-day Saints © Copyright 1999 Intellectual Reserve, Inc. All rights reserved. All use is subject to the limited), Ancestry.com, http://www.Ancestry.com, Year: 1880; Census Place: Greenwood, Etowah, Alabama; Roll: 13; Family History Film: 1254013; Page: 405A; Enumeration District: 72; Image: 0317. Birth date: about 1879 Birth place: Alabama Residence date: 1880 Residence place: Greenwood, Etowah, Alabama, United States.

1229   Ancestry.com, 1870 United States Federal Census (Online publication - Provo, UT, USA: Ancestry.com Operations, Inc., 2009. Images reproduced by FamilySearch. Original data - 1870 U.S. census, population schedules. NARA microfilm publication M593, 1,761 rolls. Washington, D.C.: National Archives and Record), Ancestry.com, http://www.Ancestry.com, Year: 1870; Census Place: Township 15, Calhoun, Alabama; Roll: M593_; Page: ; Image:. Birth date: about 1840 Birth place: Alabama Residence date: 1870 Residence place: Township 15, Calhoun, Alabama, United States.

1230   Ancestry.com and The Church of Jesus Christ of Latter-day Saints, 1880 United States Federal Census (Online publication - Provo, UT, USA: Ancestry.com Operations Inc, 2010. 1880 U.S. Census Index provided by The Church of Jesus Christ of Latter-day Saints © Copyright 1999 Intellectual Reserve, Inc. All rights reserved. All use is subject to the limited), Ancestry.com, http://www.Ancestry.com, Year: 1880; Census Place: Beat 2, Warren, Mississippi; Roll: 667; Family History Film: 1254667; Page: 472B; Enumeration District: 74; Image: 0297. Birth date: about 1840 Birth place: Alabama Residence date: 1880 Residence place: Beat 2, Warren, Mississippi, United States.

1231   Ancestry.com, 1900 United States Federal Census (Online publication - Provo, UT, USA: Ancestry.com Operations Inc, 2004. Original data - United States of America, Bureau of the Census. Twelfth Census of the United States, 1900. Washington, D.C.: National Archives and Records Administration, 1900. T623, 18), Ancestry.com, http://www.Ancestry.com, Year: 1900; Census Place: Beat 2, Warren, Mississippi; Roll: T623_831; Page: 10B; Enumeration District: 126. Birth date: Mar 1841 Birth place: Alabama Marriage date: 1865 Marriage place: Residence date: 1900 Residence place: Beat 2, Warren, Mississippi.

1232   Ancestry.com and The Church of Jesus Christ of Latter-day Saints, 1880 United States Federal Census (Online publication - Provo, UT, USA: Ancestry.com Operations Inc, 2010. 1880 U.S. Census Index provided by The Church of Jesus Christ of Latter-day Saints © Copyright 1999 Intellectual Reserve, Inc. All rights reserved. All use is subject to the limited), Ancestry.com, http://www.Ancestry.com, Year: 1880; Census Place: Beat 2, Warren, Mississippi; Roll: 667; Family History Film: 1254667; Page: 472B; Enumeration District: 74; Image: 0297. Birth date: about 1865 Birth place: Alabama Residence date: 1880 Residence place: Beat 2, Warren, Mississippi, United States.

1233   Ancestry.com, 1900 United States Federal Census (Online publication - Provo, UT, USA: Ancestry.com Operations Inc, 2004. Original data - United States of America, Bureau of the Census. Twelfth Census of the United States, 1900. Washington, D.C.: National Archives and Records Administration, 1900. T623, 18), Ancestry.com, http://www.Ancestry.com, Year: 1900; Census Place: Beat 2, Warren, Mississippi; Roll: T623_831; Page: 10B; Enumeration District: 126. Birth date: Nov 1865 Birth place: Alabama Marriage date: 1894 Marriage place: Residence date: 1900 Residence place: Beat 2, Warren, Mississippi.

1234   Ancestry.com and The Church of Jesus Christ of Latter-day Saints, 1880 United States Federal Census (Online publication - Provo, UT, USA: Ancestry.com Operations Inc, 2010. 1880 U.S. Census Index provided by The Church of Jesus Christ of Latter-day Saints © Copyright 1999 Intellectual Reserve, Inc. All rights reserved. All use is subject to the limited), Ancestry.com, http://www.Ancestry.com, Year: 1880; Census Place: Beat 2, Warren, Mississippi; Roll: 667; Family History Film: 1254667; Page: 472B; Enumeration District: 74; Image: 0297. Birth date: about 1867 Birth place: Alabama Residence date: 1880 Residence place: Beat 2, Warren, Mississippi, United States.

1235   Ancestry.com and The Church of Jesus Christ of Latter-day Saints, 1880 United States Federal Census (Online publication - Provo, UT, USA: Ancestry.com Operations Inc, 2010. 1880 U.S. Census Index provided by The Church of Jesus Christ of Latter-day Saints © Copyright 1999 Intellectual Reserve, Inc. All rights reserved. All use is subject to the limited), Ancestry.com, http://www.Ancestry.com, Year: 1880; Census Place: Beat 2, Warren, Mississippi; Roll: 667; Family History Film: 1254667; Page: 472B; Enumeration District: 74; Image: 0297. Birth date: about 1869 Birth place: Alabama Residence date: 1880 Residence place: Beat 2, Warren, Mississippi, United States.

1236   Ancestry.com, 1900 United States Federal Census (Online publication - Provo, UT, USA: Ancestry.com Operations Inc, 2004. Original data - United States of America, Bureau of the Census. Twelfth Census of the United States, 1900. Washington, D.C.: National Archives and Records Administration, 1900. T623, 18), Ancestry.com, http://www.Ancestry.com, Year: 1900; Census Place: Beat 2, Warren, Mississippi; Roll: T623_831; Page: 10B;

Enumeration District: 126. Birth date: Jan 1873 Birth place: Alabama Marriage date: 1894 Marriage place: Residence date: 1900 Residence place: Beat 2, Warren, Mississippi.

1237   Ancestry.com and The Church of Jesus Christ of Latter-day Saints, 1880 United States Federal Census (Online publication - Provo, UT, USA: Ancestry.com Operations Inc, 2010. 1880 U.S. Census Index provided by The Church of Jesus Christ of Latter-day Saints © Copyright 1999 Intellectual Reserve, Inc. All rights reserved. All use is subject to the limited), Ancestry.com, http://www.Ancestry.com, Year: 1880; Census Place: Beat 2, Warren, Mississippi; Roll: 667; Family History Film: 1254667; Page: 472B; Enumeration District: 74; Image: 0297. Birth date: about 1870 Birth place: Alabama Residence date: 1880 Residence place: Beat 2, Warren, Mississippi, United States.

1238   Ancestry.com and The Church of Jesus Christ of Latter-day Saints, 1880 United States Federal Census (Online publication - Provo, UT, USA: Ancestry.com Operations Inc, 2010. 1880 U.S. Census Index provided by The Church of Jesus Christ of Latter-day Saints © Copyright 1999 Intellectual Reserve, Inc. All rights reserved. All use is subject to the limited), Ancestry.com, http://www.Ancestry.com, Year: 1880; Census Place: Beat 2, Warren, Mississippi; Roll: 667; Family History Film: 1254667; Page: 472B; Enumeration District: 74; Image: 0297. Birth date: about 1874 Birth place: Louisiana Residence date: 1880 Residence place: Beat 2, Warren, Mississippi, United States.

1239   Ancestry.com, World War I Draft Registration Cards, 1917-1918 (Online publication - Provo, UT, USA: Ancestry.com Operations Inc, 2005. Original data - United States, Selective Service System. World War I Selective Service System Draft Registration Cards, 1917-1918. Washington, D.C.: National Archives and Records Administration), Ancestry.com, http://www.Ancestry.com, Registration Location: East Baton Rouge County, Louisiana; Roll: 1684671; Draft Board: 0. Birth date: 2 Feb 1875 Birth place: Residence date: Residence place: East Baton Rouge, Louisiana.

1240   Ancestry.com, Louisiana Statewide Death Index, 1900-1949 (Online publication - Provo, UT, USA: Ancestry.com Operations Inc, 2002. Original data - State of Louisiana, Secretary of State, Division of Archives, Records Management, and History. Vital Records Indices. Baton Rouge, LA, USA. Original data: State of Louisiana), Ancestry.com, http://www.Ancestry.com, Birth date: 1875 Birth place: Death date: 27 Jun 1931 Death place: Louisiana.

1241   Ancestry.com and The Church of Jesus Christ of Latter-day Saints, 1880 United States Federal Census (Online publication - Provo, UT, USA: Ancestry.com Operations Inc, 2010. 1880 U.S. Census Index provided by The Church of Jesus Christ of Latter-day Saints © Copyright 1999 Intellectual Reserve, Inc. All rights reserved. All use is subject to the limited), Ancestry.com, http://www.Ancestry.com, Year: 1880; Census Place: Beat 2, Warren, Mississippi; Roll: 667; Family History Film: 1254667; Page: 472B; Enumeration District: 74; Image: 0297. Birth date: about 1875 Birth place: Mississippi Residence date: 1880 Residence place: Beat 2, Warren, Mississippi, United States.

1242   Ancestry.com and The Church of Jesus Christ of Latter-day Saints, 1880 United States Federal Census (Online publication - Provo, UT, USA: Ancestry.com Operations Inc, 2010. 1880 U.S. Census Index provided by The Church of Jesus Christ of Latter-day Saints © Copyright 1999 Intellectual Reserve, Inc. All rights reserved. All use is subject to the limited), Ancestry.com, http://www.Ancestry.com, Year: 1880; Census Place: Beat 2, Warren, Mississippi; Roll: 667; Family History Film: 1254667; Page: 472B; Enumeration District: 74; Image: 0297. Birth date: about 1878 Birth place: Mississippi Residence date: 1880 Residence place: Beat 2, Warren, Mississippi, United States.

1243   Ancestry.com, 1900 United States Federal Census (Online publication - Provo, UT, USA: Ancestry.com Operations Inc, 2004. Original data - United States of America, Bureau of the Census. Twelfth Census of the United States, 1900. Washington, D.C.: National Archives and Records Administration, 1900. T623, 18), Ancestry.com, http://www.Ancestry.com, Year: 1900; Census Place: Beat 2, Warren, Mississippi; Roll: T623_831; Page: 10B; Enumeration District: 126. Birth date: Nov 1883 Birth place: Mississippi Marriage date: 1894 Marriage place: Residence date: 1900 Residence place: Beat 2, Warren, Mississippi.

1244   Ancestry.com, 1900 United States Federal Census (Online publication - Provo, UT, USA: Ancestry.com Operations Inc, 2004. Original data - United States of America, Bureau of the Census. Twelfth Census of the United States, 1900. Washington, D.C.: National Archives and Records Administration, 1900. T623, 18), Ancestry.com, http://www.Ancestry.com, Year: 1900; Census Place: Beat 2, Warren, Mississippi; Roll: T623_831; Page: 10B; Enumeration District: 126. Birth date: Oct 1891 Birth place: Mississippi Residence date: 1900 Residence place: Beat 2, Warren, Mississippi.

1245   Ancestry.com, 1910 United States Federal Census (Online publication - Provo, UT, USA: Ancestry.com Operations Inc, 2006. Original data - Thirteenth Census of the United States, 1910 (NARA microfilm publication T624, 1,178 rolls). Records of the Bureau of the Census, Record Group 29. National Archives, Washington), Ancestry.com, http://www.Ancestry.com, Year: 1910; Census Place: Hokes Bluff, Etowah, Alabama; Roll: ; Page: ; Enumeration District: ; Image:. Birth date: about 1862 Birth place: Alabama Residence date: 1910 Residence place: Hokes Bluff, Etowah, Alabama.

1246   Ancestry.com, 1900 United States Federal Census (Online publication - Provo, UT, USA: Ancestry.com Operations Inc, 2004. Original data - United States of America, Bureau of the Census. Twelfth Census of the United States, 1900. Washington, D.C.: National Archives and Records Administration, 1900. T623, 18), Ancestry.com, http://www.Ancestry.com, Year: 1900; Census Place: Turkeytown, Etowah, Alabama; Roll: T623_16; Page: 4A; Enumeration District: 154. Birth date: Mar 1862 Birth place: Alabama Marriage date: 1879 Marriage place: Residence date: 1900 Residence place: Turkeytown, Etowah, Alabama.

1247   Ancestry.com, 1930 United States Federal Census (Online publication - Provo, UT, USA: Ancestry.com Operations Inc, 2002. Original data - United States of America, Bureau of the Census. Fifteenth Census of the United States, 1930. Washington, D.C.: National Archives and Records Administration, 1930. T626,), Ancestry.com, http://www.Ancestry.com, Year: 1930; Census Place: Fairview, Etowah, Alabama; Roll: 16; Page: 6A; Enumeration

District: 20; Image: 679.0. Birth date: about 1865 Birth place: Residence date: 1930 Residence place: Fairview, Etowah, Alabama.

1248   Ancestry.com, Alabama Deaths, 1908-59 (Online publication - Provo, UT, USA: Ancestry.com Operations Inc, 2000. Original data - State of Alabama. Index of Vital Records for Alabama: Deaths, 1908-1959. Montgomery, AL, USA: State of Alabama Center for Health Statistics, Record Services Division. Original), Ancestry.com, http://www.Ancestry.com, Death date: 22 May 1953 Death place: Etowah.

1249   Ancestry.com, 1900 United States Federal Census (Online publication - Provo, UT, USA: Ancestry.com Operations Inc, 2004. Original data - United States of America, Bureau of the Census. Twelfth Census of the United States, 1900. Washington, D.C.: National Archives and Records Administration, 1900. T623, 18), Ancestry.com, http://www.Ancestry.com, Year: 1900; Census Place: Turkeytown, Etowah, Alabama; Roll: T623_16; Page: 4A; Enumeration District: 154. Birth date: Jan 1880 Birth place: Alabama Residence date: 1900 Residence place: Turkeytown, Etowah, Alabama.

1250   Ancestry.com, Alabama Deaths, 1908-59 (Online publication - Provo, UT, USA: Ancestry.com Operations Inc, 2000. Original data - State of Alabama. Index of Vital Records for Alabama: Deaths, 1908-1959. Montgomery, AL, USA: State of Alabama Center for Health Statistics, Record Services Division. Original), Ancestry.com, http://www.Ancestry.com, Death date: May 1933 Death place: Etowah.

1251   Ancestry.com, 1900 United States Federal Census (Online publication - Provo, UT, USA: Ancestry.com Operations Inc, 2004. Original data - United States of America, Bureau of the Census. Twelfth Census of the United States, 1900. Washington, D.C.: National Archives and Records Administration, 1900. T623, 18), Ancestry.com, http://www.Ancestry.com, Year: 1900; Census Place: Turkeytown, Etowah, Alabama; Roll: T623_16; Page: 4A; Enumeration District: 154. Birth date: Sep 1881 Birth place: Alabama Residence date: 1900 Residence place: Turkeytown, Etowah, Alabama.

1252   Ancestry.com, World War I Draft Registration Cards, 1917-1918 (Online publication - Provo, UT, USA: Ancestry.com Operations Inc, 2005. Original data - United States, Selective Service System. World War I Selective Service System Draft Registration Cards, 1917-1918. Washington, D.C.: National Archives and Records Administration), Ancestry.com, http://www.Ancestry.com, Registration Location: Etowah County, Alabama; Roll: 1509384; Draft Board: 0. Birth date: 10 Sep 1881 Birth place: Residence date: Residence place: Etowah, Alabama.

1253   Ancestry.com, 1920 United States Federal Census (Online publication - Provo, UT, USA: Ancestry.com Operations Inc, 2010. Images reproduced by FamilySearch. Original data - Fourteenth Census of the United States, 1920. (NARA microfilm publication T625, 2076 rolls). Records of the Bureau of the Census, Record), Ancestry.com, http://www.Ancestry.com, Year: 1920; Census Place: Carlisle, Etowah, Alabama; Roll: T625_15; Page: 4B; Enumeration District: 105; Image:. Birth date: about 1882 Birth place: Alabama Residence date: 1920 Residence place: Carlisle, Etowah, Alabama.

1254   Ancestry.com, 1930 United States Federal Census (Online publication - Provo, UT, USA: Ancestry.com Operations Inc, 2002. Original data - United States of America, Bureau of the Census. Fifteenth Census of the United States, 1930. Washington, D.C.: National Archives and Records Administration, 1930. T626,), Ancestry.com, http://www.Ancestry.com, Year: 1930; Census Place: Fairview, Etowah, Alabama; Roll: 16; Page: 6B; Enumeration District: 20; Image: 680.0. Birth date: about 1883 Birth place: Alabama Residence date: 1930 Residence place: Fairview, Etowah, Alabama.

1255   Ancestry.com, 1920 United States Federal Census (Online publication - Provo, UT, USA: Ancestry.com Operations Inc, 2010. Images reproduced by FamilySearch. Original data - Fourteenth Census of the United States, 1920. (NARA microfilm publication T625, 2076 rolls). Records of the Bureau of the Census, Record), Ancestry.com, http://www.Ancestry.com, Year: 1920; Census Place: Gadsden Ward 4, Etowah, Alabama; Roll: T625_15; Page: 9A; Enumeration District: 94; Image:. Birth date: about 1884 Birth place: Alabama Residence date: 1920 Residence place: Gadsden Ward 4, Etowah, Alabama.

1256   Ancestry.com, 1900 United States Federal Census (Online publication - Provo, UT, USA: Ancestry.com Operations Inc, 2004. Original data - United States of America, Bureau of the Census. Twelfth Census of the United States, 1900. Washington, D.C.: National Archives and Records Administration, 1900. T623, 18), Ancestry.com, http://www.Ancestry.com, Year: 1900; Census Place: Turkeytown, Etowah, Alabama; Roll: T623_16; Page: 4A; Enumeration District: 154. Birth date: Nov 1884 Birth place: Alabama Residence date: 1900 Residence place: Turkeytown, Etowah, Alabama.

1257   Ancestry.com, 1930 United States Federal Census (Online publication - Provo, UT, USA: Ancestry.com Operations Inc, 2002. Original data - United States of America, Bureau of the Census. Fifteenth Census of the United States, 1930. Washington, D.C.: National Archives and Records Administration, 1930. T626,), Ancestry.com, http://www.Ancestry.com, Year: 1930; Census Place: Fairview, Etowah, Alabama; Roll: 16; Page: 6A; Enumeration District: 20; Image: 679.0. Birth date: about 1884 Birth place: Alabama Residence date: 1930 Residence place: Fairview, Etowah, Alabama.

1258   Ancestry.com, World War I Draft Registration Cards, 1917-1918 (Online publication - Provo, UT, USA: Ancestry.com Operations Inc, 2005. Original data - United States, Selective Service System. World War I Selective Service System Draft Registration Cards, 1917-1918. Washington, D.C.: National Archives and Records Administration), Ancestry.com, http://www.Ancestry.com, Registration Location: Etowah County, Alabama; Roll: 1509384; Draft Board: 0. Birth date: 12 Nov 1883 Birth place: Residence date: Residence place: Etowah, Alabama.

1259   Ancestry.com, 1910 United States Federal Census (Online publication - Provo, UT, USA: Ancestry.com Operations Inc, 2006. Original data - Thirteenth Census of the United States, 1910 (NARA microfilm publication T624, 1,178 rolls). Records of the Bureau of the Census, Record Group 29. National Archives, Washington), Ancestry.com, http://www.Ancestry.com, Year: 1910; Census Place: Gadsden, Etowah, Alabama; Roll: ; Page: ; Enumeration District: ; Image:. Birth date: about 1885 Birth place: Alabama Residence date: 1910 Residence place: Gadsden, Etowah, Alabama.

1260   Ancestry.com, Social Security Death Index (Online publication - Provo, UT, USA: Ancestry.com Operations Inc, 2010. Original data - Social Security Administration. Social Security Death Index, Master File. Social Security Administration. Original data: Social Security Administration. Social Security D), Ancestry.com, http://www.Ancestry.com, Number: 422-50-1676; Issue State: Alabama; Issue Date: 1956. Birth date: 12 Nov 1883 Birth place: Death date: Jan 1971 Death place: Gadsden, Etowah, Alabama, United States of America.

1261   Ancestry.com, 1900 United States Federal Census (Online publication - Provo, UT, USA: Ancestry.com Operations Inc, 2004. Original data - United States of America, Bureau of the Census. Twelfth Census of the United States, 1900. Washington, D.C.: National Archives and Records Administration, 1900. T623, 18), Ancestry.com, http://www.Ancestry.com, Year: 1900; Census Place: Turkeytown, Etowah, Alabama; Roll: T623_16; Page: 4A; Enumeration District: 154. Birth date: Aug 1886 Birth place: Alabama Residence date: 1900 Residence place: Turkeytown, Etowah, Alabama.

1262   Ancestry.com, 1900 United States Federal Census (Online publication - Provo, UT, USA: Ancestry.com Operations Inc, 2004. Original data - United States of America, Bureau of the Census. Twelfth Census of the United States, 1900. Washington, D.C.: National Archives and Records Administration, 1900. T623, 18), Ancestry.com, http://www.Ancestry.com, Year: 1900; Census Place: Turkeytown, Etowah, Alabama; Roll: T623_16; Page: 4A; Enumeration District: 154. Birth date: Apr 1889 Birth place: Alabama Residence date: 1900 Residence place: Turkeytown, Etowah, Alabama.

1263   Ancestry.com, 1900 United States Federal Census (Online publication - Provo, UT, USA: Ancestry.com Operations Inc, 2004. Original data - United States of America, Bureau of the Census. Twelfth Census of the United States, 1900. Washington, D.C.: National Archives and Records Administration, 1900. T623, 18), Ancestry.com, http://www.Ancestry.com, Year: 1900; Census Place: Turkeytown, Etowah, Alabama; Roll: T623_16; Page: 4A; Enumeration District: 154. Birth date: Mar 1892 Birth place: Alabama Residence date: 1900 Residence place: Turkeytown, Etowah, Alabama.

1264   Ancestry.com, 1910 United States Federal Census (Online publication - Provo, UT, USA: Ancestry.com Operations Inc, 2006. Original data - Thirteenth Census of the United States, 1910 (NARA microfilm publication T624, 1,178 rolls). Records of the Bureau of the Census, Record Group 29. National Archives, Washington), Ancestry.com, http://www.Ancestry.com, Year: 1910; Census Place: Hokes Bluff, Etowah, Alabama; Roll: ; Page: ; Enumeration District: ; Image:. Birth date: about 1895 Birth place: Alabama Residence date: 1910 Residence place: Hokes Bluff, Etowah, Alabama.

1265   Ancestry.com, 1900 United States Federal Census (Online publication - Provo, UT, USA: Ancestry.com Operations Inc, 2004. Original data - United States of America, Bureau of the Census. Twelfth Census of the United States, 1900. Washington, D.C.: National Archives and Records Administration, 1900. T623, 18), Ancestry.com, http://www.Ancestry.com, Year: 1900; Census Place: Turkeytown, Etowah, Alabama; Roll: T623_16; Page: 4A; Enumeration District: 154. Birth date: Feb 1895 Birth place: Alabama Residence date: 1900 Residence place: Turkeytown, Etowah, Alabama.

1266   Ancestry.com, 1870 United States Federal Census (Online publication - Provo, UT, USA: Ancestry.com Operations, Inc., 2009. Images reproduced by FamilySearch. Original data - 1870 U.S. census, population schedules. NARA microfilm publication M593, 1,761 rolls. Washington, D.C.: National Archives and Record), Ancestry.com, http://www.Ancestry.com, Year: 1870; Census Place: Township 9, Butler, Alabama; Roll: M593_; Page: ; Image:. Birth date: about 1864 Birth place: Alabama Residence date: 1870 Residence place: Township 9, Butler, Alabama, United States.

1267   Ancestry.com, 1910 United States Federal Census (Online publication - Provo, UT, USA: Ancestry.com Operations Inc, 2006. Original data - Thirteenth Census of the United States, 1910 (NARA microfilm publication T624, 1,178 rolls). Records of the Bureau of the Census, Record Group 29. National Archives, Washington), Ancestry.com, http://www.Ancestry.com, Year: 1910; Census Place: Hagerman, Chaves, New Mexico; Roll: ; Page: ; Enumeration District: ; Image:. Birth date: about 1866 Birth place: Alabama Residence date: 1910 Residence place: Hagerman, Chaves, New Mexico.

1268   Ancestry.com, 1930 United States Federal Census (Online publication - Provo, UT, USA: Ancestry.com Operations Inc, 2002. Original data - United States of America, Bureau of the Census. Fifteenth Census of the United States, 1930. Washington, D.C.: National Archives and Records Administration, 1930. T626,), Ancestry.com, http://www.Ancestry.com, Year: 1930; Census Place: Lake Arthur, Chaves, New Mexico; Roll: 1393; Page: 1A; Enumeration District: 17; Image: 377.0. Birth date: about 1866 Birth place: Residence date: 1930 Residence place: Lake Arthur, Chaves, New Mexico.

1269   Ancestry.com, 1920 United States Federal Census (Online publication - Provo, UT, USA: Ancestry.com Operations Inc, 2010. Images reproduced by FamilySearch. Original data - Fourteenth Census of the United States, 1920. (NARA microfilm publication T625, 2076 rolls). Records of the Bureau of the Census, Record), Ancestry.com, http://www.Ancestry.com, Year: 1920; Census Place: Dexter, Chaves, New Mexico; Roll: T625_1074; Page: 3B;

Enumeration District: 10; Image:. Birth date: about 1866 Birth place: Alabama Residence date: 1920 Residence place: Dexter, Chaves, New Mexico.

1270   Ancestry.com, 1910 United States Federal Census (Online publication - Provo, UT, USA: Ancestry.com Operations Inc, 2006. Original data - Thirteenth Census of the United States, 1910 (NARA microfilm publication T624, 1,178 rolls). Records of the Bureau of the Census, Record Group 29. National Archives, Washington), Ancestry.com, http://www.Ancestry.com, Year: 1910; Census Place: Hagerman, Chaves, New Mexico; Roll: ; Page: ; Enumeration District: ; Image:. Birth date: about 1901 Birth place: Texas Residence date: 1910 Residence place: Hagerman, Chaves, New Mexico.

1271   Ancestry.com, 1920 United States Federal Census (Online publication - Provo, UT, USA: Ancestry.com Operations Inc, 2010. Images reproduced by FamilySearch. Original data - Fourteenth Census of the United States, 1920. (NARA microfilm publication T625, 2076 rolls). Records of the Bureau of the Census, Record), Ancestry.com, http://www.Ancestry.com, Year: 1920; Census Place: Greens Schoolhouse, Calhoun, Alabama; Roll: T625_5; Page: 3B; Enumeration District: 10; Image:. Birth date: about 1896 Birth place: Georgia Residence date: 1920 Residence place: Greens Schoolhouse, Calhoun, Alabama.

1272   Ancestry.com, 1920 United States Federal Census (Online publication - Provo, UT, USA: Ancestry.com Operations Inc, 2010. Images reproduced by FamilySearch. Original data - Fourteenth Census of the United States, 1920. (NARA microfilm publication T625, 2076 rolls). Records of the Bureau of the Census, Record), Ancestry.com, http://www.Ancestry.com, Year: 1920; Census Place: Greens Schoolhouse, Calhoun, Alabama; Roll: T625_5; Page: 3B; Enumeration District: 10; Image:. Birth date: about 1911 Birth place: Alabama Residence date: 1920 Residence place: Greens Schoolhouse, Calhoun, Alabama.

1273   Ancestry.com, 1920 United States Federal Census (Online publication - Provo, UT, USA: Ancestry.com Operations Inc, 2010. Images reproduced by FamilySearch. Original data - Fourteenth Census of the United States, 1920. (NARA microfilm publication T625, 2076 rolls). Records of the Bureau of the Census, Record), Ancestry.com, http://www.Ancestry.com, Year: 1920; Census Place: Greens Schoolhouse, Calhoun, Alabama; Roll: T625_5; Page: 3B; Enumeration District: 10; Image:. Birth date: about 1913 Birth place: Alabama Residence date: 1920 Residence place: Greens Schoolhouse, Calhoun, Alabama.

1274   Ancestry.com, 1920 United States Federal Census (Online publication - Provo, UT, USA: Ancestry.com Operations Inc, 2010. Images reproduced by FamilySearch. Original data - Fourteenth Census of the United States, 1920. (NARA microfilm publication T625, 2076 rolls). Records of the Bureau of the Census, Record), Ancestry.com, http://www.Ancestry.com, Year: 1920; Census Place: Greens Schoolhouse, Calhoun, Alabama; Roll: T625_5; Page: 3B; Enumeration District: 10; Image:. Birth date: about 1916 Birth place: Alabama Residence date: 1920 Residence place: Greens Schoolhouse, Calhoun, Alabama.

1275   Ancestry.com, 1920 United States Federal Census (Online publication - Provo, UT, USA: Ancestry.com Operations Inc, 2010. Images reproduced by FamilySearch. Original data - Fourteenth Census of the United States, 1920. (NARA microfilm publication T625, 2076 rolls). Records of the Bureau of the Census, Record), Ancestry.com, http://www.Ancestry.com, Year: 1920; Census Place: Piedmont, Calhoun, Alabama; Roll: T625_5; Page: 11A; Enumeration District: 12; Image:. Birth date: about 1891 Birth place: Alabama Residence date: 1920 Residence place: Piedmont, Calhoun, Alabama.

1276   Ancestry.com, 1930 United States Federal Census (Online publication - Provo, UT, USA: Ancestry.com Operations Inc, 2002. Original data - United States of America, Bureau of the Census. Fifteenth Census of the United States, 1930. Washington, D.C.: National Archives and Records Administration, 1930. T626,), Ancestry.com, http://www.Ancestry.com, Year: 1930; Census Place: Snows, Calhoun, Alabama; Roll: 5; Page: 4A; Enumeration District: 43; Image: 534.0. Birth date: about 1888 Birth place: Residence date: 1930 Residence place: Snows, Calhoun, Alabama.

1277   Ancestry.com, 1920 United States Federal Census (Online publication - Provo, UT, USA: Ancestry.com Operations Inc, 2010. Images reproduced by FamilySearch. Original data - Fourteenth Census of the United States, 1920. (NARA microfilm publication T625, 2076 rolls). Records of the Bureau of the Census, Record), Ancestry.com, http://www.Ancestry.com, Year: 1920; Census Place: Piedmont, Calhoun, Alabama; Roll: T625_5; Page: 11A; Enumeration District: 12; Image:. Birth date: about 1913 Birth place: Alabama Residence date: 1920 Residence place: Piedmont, Calhoun, Alabama.

1278   Ancestry.com, 1930 United States Federal Census (Online publication - Provo, UT, USA: Ancestry.com Operations Inc, 2002. Original data - United States of America, Bureau of the Census. Fifteenth Census of the United States, 1930. Washington, D.C.: National Archives and Records Administration, 1930. T626,), Ancestry.com, http://www.Ancestry.com, Year: 1930; Census Place: Snows, Calhoun, Alabama; Roll: 5; Page: 4A; Enumeration District: 43; Image: 534.0. Birth date: about 1913 Birth place: Residence date: 1930 Residence place: Snows, Calhoun, Alabama.

1279   Ancestry.com, 1920 United States Federal Census (Online publication - Provo, UT, USA: Ancestry.com Operations Inc, 2010. Images reproduced by FamilySearch. Original data - Fourteenth Census of the United States, 1920. (NARA microfilm publication T625, 2076 rolls). Records of the Bureau of the Census, Record), Ancestry.com, http://www.Ancestry.com, Year: 1920; Census Place: Piedmont, Calhoun, Alabama; Roll: T625_5; Page: 11A; Enumeration District: 12; Image:. Birth date: about 1916 Birth place: Alabama Residence date: 1920 Residence place: Piedmont, Calhoun, Alabama.

1280   Ancestry.com, 1930 United States Federal Census (Online publication - Provo, UT, USA: Ancestry.com Operations Inc, 2002. Original data - United States of America, Bureau of the Census. Fifteenth Census of the United States, 1930. Washington, D.C.: National Archives and Records Administration, 1930. T626,), Ancestry.com,

http://www.Ancestry.com, Year: 1930; Census Place: Snows, Calhoun, Alabama; Roll: 5; Page: 4A; Enumeration District: 43; Image: 534.0. Birth date: about 1916 Birth place: Residence date: 1930 Residence place: Snows, Calhoun, Alabama.

1281 Ancestry.com, 1920 United States Federal Census (Online publication - Provo, UT, USA: Ancestry.com Operations Inc, 2010. Images reproduced by FamilySearch. Original data - Fourteenth Census of the United States, 1920. (NARA microfilm publication T625, 2076 rolls). Records of the Bureau of the Census, Record), Ancestry.com, http://www.Ancestry.com, Year: 1920; Census Place: Piedmont, Calhoun, Alabama; Roll: T625_5; Page: 11A; Enumeration District: 12; Image:. Birth date: about 1918 Birth place: Alabama Residence date: 1920 Residence place: Piedmont, Calhoun, Alabama.

1282 Ancestry.com, 1930 United States Federal Census (Online publication - Provo, UT, USA: Ancestry.com Operations Inc, 2002. Original data - United States of America, Bureau of the Census. Fifteenth Census of the United States, 1930. Washington, D.C.: National Archives and Records Administration, 1930. T626,), Ancestry.com, http://www.Ancestry.com, Year: 1930; Census Place: Snows, Calhoun, Alabama; Roll: 5; Page: 4A; Enumeration District: 43; Image: 534.0. Birth date: about 1918 Birth place: Residence date: 1930 Residence place: Snows, Calhoun, Alabama.

1283 Ancestry.com, 1930 United States Federal Census (Online publication - Provo, UT, USA: Ancestry.com Operations Inc, 2002. Original data - United States of America, Bureau of the Census. Fifteenth Census of the United States, 1930. Washington, D.C.: National Archives and Records Administration, 1930. T626,), Ancestry.com, http://www.Ancestry.com, Year: 1930; Census Place: Snows, Calhoun, Alabama; Roll: 5; Page: 4A; Enumeration District: 43; Image: 534.0. Birth date: about 1920 Birth place: Residence date: 1930 Residence place: Snows, Calhoun, Alabama.

1284 Ancestry.com, 1930 United States Federal Census (Online publication - Provo, UT, USA: Ancestry.com Operations Inc, 2002. Original data - United States of America, Bureau of the Census. Fifteenth Census of the United States, 1930. Washington, D.C.: National Archives and Records Administration, 1930. T626,), Ancestry.com, http://www.Ancestry.com, Year: 1930; Census Place: Snows, Calhoun, Alabama; Roll: 5; Page: 4A; Enumeration District: 43; Image: 534.0. Birth date: about 1925 Birth place: Residence date: 1930 Residence place: Snows, Calhoun, Alabama.

1285 Ancestry.com, 1930 United States Federal Census (Online publication - Provo, UT, USA: Ancestry.com Operations Inc, 2002. Original data - United States of America, Bureau of the Census. Fifteenth Census of the United States, 1930. Washington, D.C.: National Archives and Records Administration, 1930. T626,), Ancestry.com, http://www.Ancestry.com, Year: 1930; Census Place: Snows, Calhoun, Alabama; Roll: 5; Page: 4A; Enumeration District: 43; Image: 534.0. Birth date: about 1928 Birth place: Residence date: 1930 Residence place: Snows, Calhoun, Alabama.

1286 Ancestry.com, 1920 United States Federal Census (Online publication - Provo, UT, USA: Ancestry.com Operations Inc, 2010. Images reproduced by FamilySearch. Original data - Fourteenth Census of the United States, 1920. (NARA microfilm publication T625, 2076 rolls). Records of the Bureau of the Census, Record), Ancestry.com, http://www.Ancestry.com, Year: 1920; Census Place: Jacksonville, Calhoun, Alabama; Roll: T625_5; Page: 22A; Enumeration District: 2; Image:. Birth date: about 1914 Birth place: Alabama Residence date: 1920 Residence place: Jacksonville, Calhoun, Alabama.

1287 Ancestry.com, 1930 United States Federal Census (Online publication - Provo, UT, USA: Ancestry.com Operations Inc, 2002. Original data - United States of America, Bureau of the Census. Fifteenth Census of the United States, 1930. Washington, D.C.: National Archives and Records Administration, 1930. T626,), Ancestry.com, http://www.Ancestry.com, Year: 1930; Census Place: Chattanooga, Hamilton, Tennessee; Roll: 2252; Page: 24A; Enumeration District: 47; Image: 163.0. Birth date: about 1914 Birth place: Residence date: 1930 Residence place: Chattanooga, Hamilton, Tennessee.

1288 Ancestry.com, Social Security Death Index (Online publication - Provo, UT, USA: Ancestry.com Operations Inc, 2010. Original data - Social Security Administration. Social Security Death Index, Master File. Social Security Administration. Original data: Social Security Administration. Social Security D), Ancestry.com, http://www.Ancestry.com, Number: 253-07-9867; Issue State: Georgia; Issue Date: Before 1951. Birth date: 28 Aug 1913 Birth place: Death date: Mar 1980 Death place: Anniston, Calhoun, Alabama, United States of America.

1289 Ancestry.com, 1920 United States Federal Census (Online publication - Provo, UT, USA: Ancestry.com Operations Inc, 2010. Images reproduced by FamilySearch. Original data - Fourteenth Census of the United States, 1920. (NARA microfilm publication T625, 2076 rolls). Records of the Bureau of the Census, Record), Ancestry.com, http://www.Ancestry.com, Year: 1920; Census Place: Jacksonville, Calhoun, Alabama; Roll: T625_5; Page: 22A; Enumeration District: 2; Image:. Birth date: about 1915 Birth place: Alabama Residence date: 1920 Residence place: Jacksonville, Calhoun, Alabama.

1290 Ancestry.com, 1930 United States Federal Census (Online publication - Provo, UT, USA: Ancestry.com Operations Inc, 2002. Original data - United States of America, Bureau of the Census. Fifteenth Census of the United States, 1930. Washington, D.C.: National Archives and Records Administration, 1930. T626,), Ancestry.com, http://www.Ancestry.com, Year: 1930; Census Place: Chattanooga, Hamilton, Tennessee; Roll: 2252; Page: 24A; Enumeration District: 47; Image: 163.0. Birth date: about 1915 Birth place: Residence date: 1930 Residence place: Chattanooga, Hamilton, Tennessee.

1291 Ancestry.com, 1920 United States Federal Census (Online publication - Provo, UT, USA: Ancestry.com Operations Inc, 2010. Images reproduced by FamilySearch. Original data - Fourteenth Census of the United States, 1920. (NARA microfilm publication T625, 2076 rolls). Records of the Bureau of the Census, Record), Ancestry.com, http://www.Ancestry.com, Year: 1920; Census Place: Henryetta Ward 1, Okmulgee, Oklahoma; Roll: T625_1476; Page: 5B; Enumeration District: 115; Image:. Birth date: about 1897 Birth place: Texas Residence date: 1920 Residence place: Henryetta Ward 1, Okmulgee, Oklahoma.

1292   Ancestry.com, 1930 United States Federal Census (Online publication - Provo, UT, USA: Ancestry.com Operations Inc, 2002. Original data - United States of America, Bureau of the Census. Fifteenth Census of the United States, 1930. Washington, D.C.: National Archives and Records Administration, 1930. T626,), Ancestry.com, http://www.Ancestry.com, Year: 1930; Census Place: Henryetta, Okmulgee, Oklahoma; Roll: 1921; Page: 18A; Enumeration District: 17; Image: 1054.0. Birth date: about 1897 Birth place: Residence date: 1930 Residence place: Henryetta, Okmulgee, Oklahoma.

1293   Ancestry.com, 1920 United States Federal Census (Online publication - Provo, UT, USA: Ancestry.com Operations Inc, 2010. Images reproduced by FamilySearch. Original data - Fourteenth Census of the United States, 1920. (NARA microfilm publication T625, 2076 rolls). Records of the Bureau of the Census, Record), Ancestry.com, http://www.Ancestry.com, Year: 1920; Census Place: Henryetta Ward 1, Okmulgee, Oklahoma; Roll: T625_1476; Page: 5B; Enumeration District: 115; Image:. Birth date: about 1917 Birth place: Oklahoma Residence date: 1920 Residence place: Henryetta Ward 1, Okmulgee, Oklahoma.

1294   Ancestry.com, 1930 United States Federal Census (Online publication - Provo, UT, USA: Ancestry.com Operations Inc, 2002. Original data - United States of America, Bureau of the Census. Fifteenth Census of the United States, 1930. Washington, D.C.: National Archives and Records Administration, 1930. T626,), Ancestry.com, http://www.Ancestry.com, Year: 1930; Census Place: Henryetta, Okmulgee, Oklahoma; Roll: 1921; Page: 18A; Enumeration District: 17; Image: 1054.0. Birth date: about 1917 Birth place: Residence date: 1930 Residence place: Henryetta, Okmulgee, Oklahoma.

1295   Ancestry.com, 1930 United States Federal Census (Online publication - Provo, UT, USA: Ancestry.com Operations Inc, 2002. Original data - United States of America, Bureau of the Census. Fifteenth Census of the United States, 1930. Washington, D.C.: National Archives and Records Administration, 1930. T626,), Ancestry.com, http://www.Ancestry.com, Year: 1930; Census Place: Henryetta, Okmulgee, Oklahoma; Roll: 1921; Page: 18A; Enumeration District: 17; Image: 1054.0. Birth date: about 1922 Birth place: Residence date: 1930 Residence place: Henryetta, Okmulgee, Oklahoma.

1296   Ancestry.com, 1920 United States Federal Census (Online publication - Provo, UT, USA: Ancestry.com Operations Inc, 2010. Images reproduced by FamilySearch. Original data - Fourteenth Census of the United States, 1920. (NARA microfilm publication T625, 2076 rolls). Records of the Bureau of the Census, Record), Ancestry.com, http://www.Ancestry.com, Year: 1920; Census Place: Henryetta Ward 1, Okmulgee, Oklahoma; Roll: T625_1476; Page: 5A; Enumeration District: 115; Image:. Birth date: about 1895 Birth place: Texas Residence date: 1920 Residence place: Henryetta Ward 1, Okmulgee, Oklahoma.

1297   Ancestry.com, 1930 United States Federal Census (Online publication - Provo, UT, USA: Ancestry.com Operations Inc, 2002. Original data - United States of America, Bureau of the Census. Fifteenth Census of the United States, 1930. Washington, D.C.: National Archives and Records Administration, 1930. T626,), Ancestry.com, http://www.Ancestry.com, Year: 1930; Census Place: Hobbs, Lea, New Mexico; Roll: 1395; Page: 2B; Enumeration District: 18; Image: 1029.0. Birth date: about 1895 Birth place: Texas Residence date: 1930 Residence place: Hobbs, Lea, New Mexico.

1298   Ancestry.com, 1930 United States Federal Census (Online publication - Provo, UT, USA: Ancestry.com Operations Inc, 2002. Original data - United States of America, Bureau of the Census. Fifteenth Census of the United States, 1930. Washington, D.C.: National Archives and Records Administration, 1930. T626,), Ancestry.com, http://www.Ancestry.com, Year: 1930; Census Place: Hobbs, Lea, New Mexico; Roll: 1395; Page: 2B; Enumeration District: 18; Image: 1029.0. Birth date: about 1923 Birth place: Residence date: 1930 Residence place: Hobbs, Lea, New Mexico.

1299   Ancestry.com, 1930 United States Federal Census (Online publication - Provo, UT, USA: Ancestry.com Operations Inc, 2002. Original data - United States of America, Bureau of the Census. Fifteenth Census of the United States, 1930. Washington, D.C.: National Archives and Records Administration, 1930. T626,), Ancestry.com, http://www.Ancestry.com, Year: 1930; Census Place: Hobbs, Lea, New Mexico; Roll: 1395; Page: 2B; Enumeration District: 18; Image: 1029.0. Birth date: about 1925 Birth place: Residence date: 1930 Residence place: Hobbs, Lea, New Mexico.

1300   Ancestry.com, 1930 United States Federal Census (Online publication - Provo, UT, USA: Ancestry.com Operations Inc, 2002. Original data - United States of America, Bureau of the Census. Fifteenth Census of the United States, 1930. Washington, D.C.: National Archives and Records Administration, 1930. T626,), Ancestry.com, http://www.Ancestry.com, Year: 1930; Census Place: Hobbs, Lea, New Mexico; Roll: 1395; Page: 2B; Enumeration District: 18; Image: 1029.0. Birth date: about 1927 Birth place: Residence date: 1930 Residence place: Hobbs, Lea, New Mexico.

1301   Ancestry.com, 1930 United States Federal Census (Online publication - Provo, UT, USA: Ancestry.com Operations Inc, 2002. Original data - United States of America, Bureau of the Census. Fifteenth Census of the United States, 1930. Washington, D.C.: National Archives and Records Administration, 1930. T626,), Ancestry.com, http://www.Ancestry.com, Year: 1930; Census Place: Borger, Hutchinson, Texas; Roll: 2360; Page: 1B; Enumeration District: 3; Image: 576.0. Birth date: about 1902 Birth place: Residence date: 1930 Residence place: Borger, Hutchinson, Texas.

1302   Ancestry.com, 1920 United States Federal Census (Online publication - Provo, UT, USA: Ancestry.com Operations Inc, 2010. Images reproduced by FamilySearch. Original data - Fourteenth Census of the United States, 1920. (NARA microfilm publication T625, 2076 rolls). Records of the Bureau of the Census, Record), Ancestry.com,

http://www.Ancestry.com, Year: 1920; Census Place: Henryetta Ward 1, Okmulgee, Oklahoma; Roll: T625_1476; Page: 4B; Enumeration District: 115; Image:. Birth date: about 1903 Birth place: Oklahoma Residence date: 1920 Residence place: Henryetta Ward 1, Okmulgee, Oklahoma.

1303   Ancestry.com, 1930 United States Federal Census (Online publication - Provo, UT, USA: Ancestry.com Operations Inc, 2002. Original data - United States of America, Bureau of the Census. Fifteenth Census of the United States, 1930. Washington, D.C.: National Archives and Records Administration, 1930. T626,), Ancestry.com, http://www.Ancestry.com, Year: 1930; Census Place: Borger, Hutchinson, Texas; Roll: 2360; Page: 1B; Enumeration District: 3; Image: 576.0. Birth date: about 1921 Birth place: Residence date: 1930 Residence place: Borger, Hutchinson, Texas.

1304   Ancestry.com, 1930 United States Federal Census (Online publication - Provo, UT, USA: Ancestry.com Operations Inc, 2002. Original data - United States of America, Bureau of the Census. Fifteenth Census of the United States, 1930. Washington, D.C.: National Archives and Records Administration, 1930. T626,), Ancestry.com, http://www.Ancestry.com, Year: 1930; Census Place: Borger, Hutchinson, Texas; Roll: 2360; Page: 1B; Enumeration District: 3; Image: 576.0. Birth date: about 1927 Birth place: Residence date: 1930 Residence place: Borger, Hutchinson, Texas.

1305   Ancestry.com, 1900 United States Federal Census (Online publication - Provo, UT, USA: Ancestry.com Operations Inc, 2004. Original data - United States of America, Bureau of the Census. Twelfth Census of the United States, 1900. Washington, D.C.: National Archives and Records Administration, 1900. T623, 18), Ancestry.com, http://www.Ancestry.com, Year: 1900; Census Place: Wicker, Clay, Alabama; Roll: T623_9; Page: 11A; Enumeration District: 113. Birth date: Dec 1879 Birth place: Alabama Residence date: 1900 Residence place: Wicker, Clay, Alabama.

1306   Ancestry.com, 1920 United States Federal Census (Online publication - Provo, UT, USA: Ancestry.com Operations Inc, 2010. Images reproduced by FamilySearch. Original data - Fourteenth Census of the United States, 1920. (NARA microfilm publication T625, 2076 rolls). Records of the Bureau of the Census, Record), Ancestry.com, http://www.Ancestry.com, Year: 1920; Census Place: Renfroe, Talladega, Alabama; Roll: T625_41; Page: 9A; Enumeration District: 141; Image:. Birth date: about 1880 Birth place: Alabama Residence date: 1920 Residence place: Renfroe, Talladega, Alabama.

1307   Ancestry.com, 1900 United States Federal Census (Online publication - Provo, UT, USA: Ancestry.com Operations Inc, 2004. Original data - United States of America, Bureau of the Census. Twelfth Census of the United States, 1900. Washington, D.C.: National Archives and Records Administration, 1900. T623, 18), Ancestry.com, http://www.Ancestry.com, Year: 1900; Census Place: Cast, Talladega, Alabama; Roll: T623_40; Page: 10B; Enumeration District: 92. Birth date: Dec 1880 Birth place: Alabama Marriage date: 1895 Marriage place: Residence date: 1900 Residence place: Cast, Talladega, Alabama.

1308   Ancestry.com, 1930 United States Federal Census (Online publication - Provo, UT, USA: Ancestry.com Operations Inc, 2002. Original data - United States of America, Bureau of the Census. Fifteenth Census of the United States, 1930. Washington, D.C.: National Archives and Records Administration, 1930. T626,), Ancestry.com, http://www.Ancestry.com, Year: 1930; Census Place: Renfroe, Talladega, Alabama; Roll: 49; Page: 6A; Enumeration District: 18; Image: 993.0. Birth date: about 1880 Birth place: Residence date: 1930 Residence place: Renfroe, Talladega, Alabama.

1309   Ancestry.com, World War I Draft Registration Cards, 1917-1918 (Online publication - Provo, UT, USA: Ancestry.com Operations Inc, 2005. Original data - United States, Selective Service System. World War I Selective Service System Draft Registration Cards, 1917-1918. Washington, D.C.: National Archives and Records Administration), Ancestry.com, http://www.Ancestry.com, Registration Location: Covington County, Alabama; Roll: 1509374; Draft Board: 0. Birth date: 6 Feb 1896 Birth place: Residence date: Residence place: Covington, Alabama.

1310   Ancestry.com, 1900 United States Federal Census (Online publication - Provo, UT, USA: Ancestry.com Operations Inc, 2004. Original data - United States of America, Bureau of the Census. Twelfth Census of the United States, 1900. Washington, D.C.: National Archives and Records Administration, 1900. T623, 18), Ancestry.com, http://www.Ancestry.com, Year: 1900; Census Place: Cast, Talladega, Alabama; Roll: T623_40; Page: 10B; Enumeration District: 92. Birth date: Oct 1896 Birth place: Alabama Residence date: 1900 Residence place: Cast, Talladega, Alabama.

1311   Ancestry.com, 1930 United States Federal Census (Online publication - Provo, UT, USA: Ancestry.com Operations Inc, 2002. Original data - United States of America, Bureau of the Census. Fifteenth Census of the United States, 1930. Washington, D.C.: National Archives and Records Administration, 1930. T626,), Ancestry.com, http://www.Ancestry.com, Year: 1930; Census Place: Renfroe, Talladega, Alabama; Roll: 49; Page: 6B; Enumeration District: 18; Image: 994.0. Birth date: about 1899 Birth place: Alabama Residence date: 1930 Residence place: Renfroe, Talladega, Alabama.

1312   Ancestry.com, 1900 United States Federal Census (Online publication - Provo, UT, USA: Ancestry.com Operations Inc, 2004. Original data - United States of America, Bureau of the Census. Twelfth Census of the United States, 1900. Washington, D.C.: National Archives and Records Administration, 1900. T623, 18), Ancestry.com, http://www.Ancestry.com, Year: 1900; Census Place: Cast, Talladega, Alabama; Roll: T623_40; Page: 10B; Enumeration District: 92. Birth date: Jul 1898 Birth place: Alabama Residence date: 1900 Residence place: Cast, Talladega, Alabama.

1313   Ancestry.com, Social Security Death Index (Online publication - Provo, UT, USA: Ancestry.com Operations Inc, 2010. Original data - Social Security Administration. Social Security Death Index, Master File. Social Security Administration. Original data: Social Security Administration. Social Security D), Ancestry.com, http://www.Ancestry.com,

Number: 417-07-7016; Issue State: Alabama; Issue Date: Before 1951. Birth date: 31 Jul 1898 Birth place: Death date: Oct 1972 Death place: Talladega, Talladega, Alabama, United States of America.

1314   Ancestry.com, World War I Draft Registration Cards, 1917-1918 (Online publication - Provo, UT, USA: Ancestry.com Operations Inc, 2005. Original data - United States, Selective Service System. World War I Selective Service System Draft Registration Cards, 1917-1918. Washington, D.C.: National Archives and Records Administration), Ancestry.com, http://www.Ancestry.com, Registration Location: Talladega County, Alabama; Roll: 1509440; Draft Board: 0. Birth date: 31 Jul 1898 Birth place: Residence date: Residence place: Talladega, Alabama.

1315   Ancestry.com, 1920 United States Federal Census (Online publication - Provo, UT, USA: Ancestry.com Operations Inc, 2010. Images reproduced by FamilySearch. Original data - Fourteenth Census of the United States, 1920. (NARA microfilm publication T625, 2076 rolls). Records of the Bureau of the Census, Record), Ancestry.com, http://www.Ancestry.com, Year: 1920; Census Place: Renfroe, Talladega, Alabama; Roll: T625_41; Page: 9A; Enumeration District: 141; Image:. Birth date: about 1899 Birth place: Alabama Residence date: 1920 Residence place: Renfroe, Talladega, Alabama.

1316   Ancestry.com, 1930 United States Federal Census (Online publication - Provo, UT, USA: Ancestry.com Operations Inc, 2002. Original data - United States of America, Bureau of the Census. Fifteenth Census of the United States, 1930. Washington, D.C.: National Archives and Records Administration, 1930. T626,), Ancestry.com, http://www.Ancestry.com, Year: 1930; Census Place: Pell City, St Clair, Alabama; Roll: 48; Page: 1A; Enumeration District: 20; Image: 294.0. Birth date: about 1901 Birth place: Alabama Residence date: 1930 Residence place: Pell City, St Clair, Alabama.

1317   Ancestry.com, 1920 United States Federal Census (Online publication - Provo, UT, USA: Ancestry.com Operations Inc, 2010. Images reproduced by FamilySearch. Original data - Fourteenth Census of the United States, 1920. (NARA microfilm publication T625, 2076 rolls). Records of the Bureau of the Census, Record), Ancestry.com, http://www.Ancestry.com, Year: 1920; Census Place: Renfroe, Talladega, Alabama; Roll: T625_41; Page: 9A; Enumeration District: 141; Image:. Birth date: about 1901 Birth place: Alabama Residence date: 1920 Residence place: Renfroe, Talladega, Alabama.

1318   Ancestry.com, Social Security Death Index (Online publication - Provo, UT, USA: Ancestry.com Operations Inc, 2010. Original data - Social Security Administration. Social Security Death Index, Master File. Social Security Administration. Original data: Social Security Administration. Social Security D), Ancestry.com, http://www.Ancestry.com, Number: 417-07-1434; Issue State: Alabama; Issue Date: Before 1951. Birth date: 13 Aug 1900 Birth place: Death date: 11 May 1992 Death place: Panama City, Bay, Florida, United States of America.

1319   Ancestry.com, World War I Draft Registration Cards, 1917-1918 (Online publication - Provo, UT, USA: Ancestry.com Operations Inc, 2005. Original data - United States, Selective Service System. World War I Selective Service System Draft Registration Cards, 1917-1918. Washington, D.C.: National Archives and Records Administration), Ancestry.com, http://www.Ancestry.com, Registration Location: Talladega County, Alabama; Roll: 1509440; Draft Board: 0. Birth date: 13 Aug 1900 Birth place: Residence date: Residence place: Talladega, Alabama.

1320   Ancestry.com, Florida Death Index, 1877-1998 (Online publication - Provo, UT, USA: Ancestry.com Operations Inc, 2004. Original data - State of Florida. Florida Death Index, 1877-1998. Florida: Florida Department of Health, Office of Vital Records, 1998. Original data: State of Florida. Florida Death Ind), Ancestry.com, http://www.Ancestry.com, Birth date: 13 Aug 1900 Birth place: Death date: 11 May 1992 Death place: Florida, United States.

1321   Ancestry.com, Social Security Death Index (Online publication - Provo, UT, USA: Ancestry.com Operations Inc, 2010. Original data - Social Security Administration. Social Security Death Index, Master File. Social Security Administration. Original data: Social Security Administration. Social Security D), Ancestry.com, http://www.Ancestry.com, Number: 423-07-1060; Issue State: Alabama; Issue Date: Before 1951. Birth date: 15 Feb 1903 Birth place: Death date: Sep 1982 Death place: Talladega, Talladega, Alabama, United States of America.

1322   Ancestry.com, 1920 United States Federal Census (Online publication - Provo, UT, USA: Ancestry.com Operations Inc, 2010. Images reproduced by FamilySearch. Original data - Fourteenth Census of the United States, 1920. (NARA microfilm publication T625, 2076 rolls). Records of the Bureau of the Census, Record), Ancestry.com, http://www.Ancestry.com, Year: 1920; Census Place: Renfroe, Talladega, Alabama; Roll: T625_41; Page: 9A; Enumeration District: 141; Image:. Birth date: about 1904 Birth place: Alabama Residence date: 1920 Residence place: Renfroe, Talladega, Alabama.

1323   Ancestry.com, 1930 United States Federal Census (Online publication - Provo, UT, USA: Ancestry.com Operations Inc, 2002. Original data - United States of America, Bureau of the Census. Fifteenth Census of the United States, 1930. Washington, D.C.: National Archives and Records Administration, 1930. T626,), Ancestry.com, http://www.Ancestry.com, Year: 1930; Census Place: Renfroe, Talladega, Alabama; Roll: 49; Page: 6A; Enumeration District: 18; Image: 993.0. Birth date: about 1904 Birth place: Residence date: 1930 Residence place: Renfroe, Talladega, Alabama.

1324   Ancestry.com, 1920 United States Federal Census (Online publication - Provo, UT, USA: Ancestry.com Operations Inc, 2010. Images reproduced by FamilySearch. Original data - Fourteenth Census of the United States, 1920. (NARA microfilm publication T625, 2076 rolls). Records of the Bureau of the Census, Record), Ancestry.com, http://www.Ancestry.com, Year: 1920; Census Place: Renfroe, Talladega, Alabama; Roll: T625_41; Page: 9A; Enumeration District: 141; Image:. Birth date: about 1907 Birth place: Alabama Residence date: 1920 Residence place: Renfroe, Talladega, Alabama.

1325   Ancestry.com, 1930 United States Federal Census (Online publication - Provo, UT, USA: Ancestry.com Operations Inc, 2002. Original data - United States of America, Bureau of the Census. Fifteenth Census of the United States, 1930. Washington, D.C.: National Archives and Records Administration, 1930. T626,), Ancestry.com, http://www.Ancestry.com, Year: 1930; Census Place: Renfroe, Talladega, Alabama; Roll: 49; Page: 8A; Enumeration District: 18; Image: 997.0. Birth date: about 1907 Birth place: Residence date: 1930 Residence place: Renfroe, Talladega, Alabama.

1326   Ancestry.com, 1920 United States Federal Census (Online publication - Provo, UT, USA: Ancestry.com Operations Inc, 2010. Images reproduced by FamilySearch. Original data - Fourteenth Census of the United States, 1920. (NARA microfilm publication T625, 2076 rolls). Records of the Bureau of the Census, Record), Ancestry.com, http://www.Ancestry.com, Year: 1920; Census Place: Renfroe, Talladega, Alabama; Roll: T625_41; Page: 9A; Enumeration District: 141; Image:. Birth date: about 1909 Birth place: Alabama Residence date: 1920 Residence place: Renfroe, Talladega, Alabama.

1327   Ancestry.com, 1930 United States Federal Census (Online publication - Provo, UT, USA: Ancestry.com Operations Inc, 2002. Original data - United States of America, Bureau of the Census. Fifteenth Census of the United States, 1930. Washington, D.C.: National Archives and Records Administration, 1930. T626,), Ancestry.com, http://www.Ancestry.com, Year: 1930; Census Place: Renfroe, Talladega, Alabama; Roll: 49; Page: 6A; Enumeration District: 18; Image: 993.0. Birth date: about 1909 Birth place: Residence date: 1930 Residence place: Renfroe, Talladega, Alabama.

1328   Ancestry.com, Social Security Death Index (Online publication - Provo, UT, USA: Ancestry.com Operations Inc, 2010. Original data - Social Security Administration. Social Security Death Index, Master File. Social Security Administration. Original data: Social Security Administration. Social Security D), Ancestry.com, http://www.Ancestry.com, Number: 420-10-6669; Issue State: Alabama; Issue Date: Before 1951. Birth date: 28 Oct 1908 Birth place: Death date: Nov 1975 Death place: Talladega, Talladega, Alabama, United States of America.

1329   Ancestry.com, 1920 United States Federal Census (Online publication - Provo, UT, USA: Ancestry.com Operations Inc, 2010. Images reproduced by FamilySearch. Original data - Fourteenth Census of the United States, 1920. (NARA microfilm publication T625, 2076 rolls). Records of the Bureau of the Census, Record), Ancestry.com, http://www.Ancestry.com, Year: 1920; Census Place: Renfroe, Talladega, Alabama; Roll: T625_41; Page: 9A; Enumeration District: 141; Image:. Birth date: about 1911 Birth place: Alabama Residence date: 1920 Residence place: Renfroe, Talladega, Alabama.

1330   Ancestry.com, 1930 United States Federal Census (Online publication - Provo, UT, USA: Ancestry.com Operations Inc, 2002. Original data - United States of America, Bureau of the Census. Fifteenth Census of the United States, 1930. Washington, D.C.: National Archives and Records Administration, 1930. T626,), Ancestry.com, http://www.Ancestry.com, Year: 1930; Census Place: Renfroe, Talladega, Alabama; Roll: 49; Page: 6A; Enumeration District: 18; Image: 993.0. Birth date: about 1911 Birth place: Residence date: 1930 Residence place: Renfroe, Talladega, Alabama.

1331   Ancestry.com, 1920 United States Federal Census (Online publication - Provo, UT, USA: Ancestry.com Operations Inc, 2010. Images reproduced by FamilySearch. Original data - Fourteenth Census of the United States, 1920. (NARA microfilm publication T625, 2076 rolls). Records of the Bureau of the Census, Record), Ancestry.com, http://www.Ancestry.com, Year: 1920; Census Place: Renfroe, Talladega, Alabama; Roll: T625_41; Page: 9A; Enumeration District: 141; Image:. Birth date: about 1914 Birth place: Alabama Residence date: 1920 Residence place: Renfroe, Talladega, Alabama.

1332   Ancestry.com, 1930 United States Federal Census (Online publication - Provo, UT, USA: Ancestry.com Operations Inc, 2002. Original data - United States of America, Bureau of the Census. Fifteenth Census of the United States, 1930. Washington, D.C.: National Archives and Records Administration, 1930. T626,), Ancestry.com, http://www.Ancestry.com, Year: 1930; Census Place: Renfroe, Talladega, Alabama; Roll: 49; Page: 6A; Enumeration District: 18; Image: 993.0. Birth date: about 1913 Birth place: Residence date: 1930 Residence place: Renfroe, Talladega, Alabama.

1333   Ancestry.com, Social Security Death Index (Online publication - Provo, UT, USA: Ancestry.com Operations Inc, 2010. Original data - Social Security Administration. Social Security Death Index, Master File. Social Security Administration. Original data: Social Security Administration. Social Security D), Ancestry.com, http://www.Ancestry.com, Number: 424-09-5051; Issue State: Alabama; Issue Date: Before 1951. Birth date: 12 Oct 1916 Birth place: Death date: 21 Jan 1998 Death place: Talladega, Talladega, Alabama, United States of America.

1334   Ancestry.com, 1920 United States Federal Census (Online publication - Provo, UT, USA: Ancestry.com Operations Inc, 2010. Images reproduced by FamilySearch. Original data - Fourteenth Census of the United States, 1920. (NARA microfilm publication T625, 2076 rolls). Records of the Bureau of the Census, Record), Ancestry.com, http://www.Ancestry.com, Year: 1920; Census Place: Renfroe, Talladega, Alabama; Roll: T625_41; Page: 9A; Enumeration District: 141; Image:. Birth date: about 1917 Birth place: Alabama Residence date: 1920 Residence place: Renfroe, Talladega, Alabama.

1335   Ancestry.com, 1930 United States Federal Census (Online publication - Provo, UT, USA: Ancestry.com Operations Inc, 2002. Original data - United States of America, Bureau of the Census. Fifteenth Census of the United States, 1930. Washington, D.C.: National Archives and Records Administration, 1930. T626,), Ancestry.com, http://www.Ancestry.com, Year: 1930; Census Place: Renfroe, Talladega, Alabama; Roll: 49; Page: 6A; Enumeration

District: 18; Image: 993.0. Birth date: about 1917 Birth place: Residence date: 1930 Residence place: Renfroe, Talladega, Alabama.

1336   Ancestry.com, 1920 United States Federal Census (Online publication - Provo, UT, USA: Ancestry.com Operations Inc, 2010. Images reproduced by FamilySearch. Original data - Fourteenth Census of the United States, 1920. (NARA microfilm publication T625, 2076 rolls). Records of the Bureau of the Census, Record), Ancestry.com, http://www.Ancestry.com, Year: 1920; Census Place: Renfroe, Talladega, Alabama; Roll: T625_41; Page: 9A; Enumeration District: 141; Image:. Birth date: about 1919 Birth place: Alabama Residence date: 1920 Residence place: Renfroe, Talladega, Alabama.

1337   Ancestry.com, 1930 United States Federal Census (Online publication - Provo, UT, USA: Ancestry.com Operations Inc, 2002. Original data - United States of America, Bureau of the Census. Fifteenth Census of the United States, 1930. Washington, D.C.: National Archives and Records Administration, 1930. T626,), Ancestry.com, http://www.Ancestry.com, Year: 1930; Census Place: Renfroe, Talladega, Alabama; Roll: 49; Page: 6A; Enumeration District: 18; Image: 993.0. Birth date: about 1919 Birth place: Residence date: 1930 Residence place: Renfroe, Talladega, Alabama.

1338   Ancestry.com, 1930 United States Federal Census (Online publication - Provo, UT, USA: Ancestry.com Operations Inc, 2002. Original data - United States of America, Bureau of the Census. Fifteenth Census of the United States, 1930. Washington, D.C.: National Archives and Records Administration, 1930. T626,), Ancestry.com, http://www.Ancestry.com, Year: 1930; Census Place: Renfroe, Talladega, Alabama; Roll: 49; Page: 6A; Enumeration District: 18; Image: 993.0. Birth date: about 1922 Birth place: Residence date: 1930 Residence place: Renfroe, Talladega, Alabama.

1339   Ancestry.com, 1930 United States Federal Census (Online publication - Provo, UT, USA: Ancestry.com Operations Inc, 2002. Original data - United States of America, Bureau of the Census. Fifteenth Census of the United States, 1930. Washington, D.C.: National Archives and Records Administration, 1930. T626,), Ancestry.com, http://www.Ancestry.com, Year: 1930; Census Place: Talladega, Talladega, Alabama; Roll: 49; Page: 1B; Enumeration District: 13; Image: 803.0. Birth date: about 1886 Birth place: Residence date: 1930 Residence place: Talladega, Talladega, Alabama.

1340   Ancestry.com, 1930 United States Federal Census (Online publication - Provo, UT, USA: Ancestry.com Operations Inc, 2002. Original data - United States of America, Bureau of the Census. Fifteenth Census of the United States, 1930. Washington, D.C.: National Archives and Records Administration, 1930. T626,), Ancestry.com, http://www.Ancestry.com, Year: 1930; Census Place: Talladega, Talladega, Alabama; Roll: 49; Page: 1B; Enumeration District: 13; Image: 803.0. Birth date: about 1909 Birth place: Residence date: 1930 Residence place: Talladega, Talladega, Alabama.

1341   Ancestry.com, 1930 United States Federal Census (Online publication - Provo, UT, USA: Ancestry.com Operations Inc, 2002. Original data - United States of America, Bureau of the Census. Fifteenth Census of the United States, 1930. Washington, D.C.: National Archives and Records Administration, 1930. T626,), Ancestry.com, http://www.Ancestry.com, Year: 1930; Census Place: Talladega, Talladega, Alabama; Roll: 49; Page: 1B; Enumeration District: 13; Image: 803.0. Birth date: about 1915 Birth place: Residence date: 1930 Residence place: Talladega, Talladega, Alabama.

1342   Ancestry.com, 1930 United States Federal Census (Online publication - Provo, UT, USA: Ancestry.com Operations Inc, 2002. Original data - United States of America, Bureau of the Census. Fifteenth Census of the United States, 1930. Washington, D.C.: National Archives and Records Administration, 1930. T626,), Ancestry.com, http://www.Ancestry.com, Year: 1930; Census Place: Talladega, Talladega, Alabama; Roll: 49; Page: 1B; Enumeration District: 13; Image: 803.0. Birth date: about 1916 Birth place: Residence date: 1930 Residence place: Talladega, Talladega, Alabama.

1343   Ancestry.com, 1930 United States Federal Census (Online publication - Provo, UT, USA: Ancestry.com Operations Inc, 2002. Original data - United States of America, Bureau of the Census. Fifteenth Census of the United States, 1930. Washington, D.C.: National Archives and Records Administration, 1930. T626,), Ancestry.com, http://www.Ancestry.com, Year: 1930; Census Place: Talladega, Talladega, Alabama; Roll: 49; Page: 1B; Enumeration District: 13; Image: 803.0. Birth date: about 1918 Birth place: Residence date: 1930 Residence place: Talladega, Talladega, Alabama.

1344   Ancestry.com, 1930 United States Federal Census (Online publication - Provo, UT, USA: Ancestry.com Operations Inc, 2002. Original data - United States of America, Bureau of the Census. Fifteenth Census of the United States, 1930. Washington, D.C.: National Archives and Records Administration, 1930. T626,), Ancestry.com, http://www.Ancestry.com, Year: 1930; Census Place: Talladega, Talladega, Alabama; Roll: 49; Page: 1B; Enumeration District: 13; Image: 803.0. Birth date: about 1926 Birth place: Residence date: 1930 Residence place: Talladega, Talladega, Alabama.

1345   Ancestry.com, 1930 United States Federal Census (Online publication - Provo, UT, USA: Ancestry.com Operations Inc, 2002. Original data - United States of America, Bureau of the Census. Fifteenth Census of the United States, 1930. Washington, D.C.: National Archives and Records Administration, 1930. T626,), Ancestry.com, http://www.Ancestry.com, Year: 1930; Census Place: Talladega, Talladega, Alabama; Roll: 49; Page: 1B; Enumeration District: 13; Image: 803.0. Birth date: about 1926 Birth place: Residence date: 1930 Residence place: Talladega, Talladega, Alabama.

1346   Ancestry.com, 1930 United States Federal Census (Online publication - Provo, UT, USA: Ancestry.com Operations Inc, 2002. Original data - United States of America, Bureau of the Census. Fifteenth Census of the United States, 1930. Washington, D.C.: National Archives and Records Administration, 1930. T626,), Ancestry.com, http://www.Ancestry.com, Year: 1930; Census Place: Anniston, Calhoun, Alabama; Roll: 5; Page: 10B; Enumeration District: 24; Image: 654.0. Birth date: about 1925 Birth place: Residence date: 1930 Residence place: Anniston, Calhoun, Alabama.

1347   Ancestry.com, 1930 United States Federal Census (Online publication - Provo, UT, USA: Ancestry.com Operations Inc, 2002. Original data - United States of America, Bureau of the Census. Fifteenth Census of the United States, 1930. Washington, D.C.: National Archives and Records Administration, 1930. T626,), Ancestry.com, http://www.Ancestry.com, Year: 1930; Census Place: Anniston, Calhoun, Alabama; Roll: 5; Page: 10B; Enumeration District: 24; Image: 654.0. Birth date: about 1928 Birth place: Residence date: 1930 Residence place: Anniston, Calhoun, Alabama.

1348   Ancestry.com, 1920 United States Federal Census (Online publication - Provo, UT, USA: Ancestry.com Operations Inc, 2010. Images reproduced by FamilySearch. Original data - Fourteenth Census of the United States, 1920. (NARA microfilm publication T625, 2076 rolls). Records of the Bureau of the Census, Record), Ancestry.com, http://www.Ancestry.com, Year: 1920; Census Place: Anniston Ward 2, Calhoun, Alabama; Roll: T625_5; Page: 18A; Enumeration District: 23; Image:. Birth date: about 1892 Birth place: Georgia Residence date: 1920 Residence place: Anniston Ward 2, Calhoun, Alabama.

1349   Ancestry.com, 1930 United States Federal Census (Online publication - Provo, UT, USA: Ancestry.com Operations Inc, 2002. Original data - United States of America, Bureau of the Census. Fifteenth Census of the United States, 1930. Washington, D.C.: National Archives and Records Administration, 1930. T626,), Ancestry.com, http://www.Ancestry.com, Year: 1930; Census Place: Anniston, Calhoun, Alabama; Roll: 5; Page: 10B; Enumeration District: 24; Image: 654.0. Birth date: about 1890 Birth place: Residence date: 1930 Residence place: Anniston, Calhoun, Alabama.

1350   Ancestry.com, 1900 United States Federal Census (Online publication - Provo, UT, USA: Ancestry.com Operations Inc, 2004. Original data - United States of America, Bureau of the Census. Twelfth Census of the United States, 1900. Washington, D.C.: National Archives and Records Administration, 1900. T623, 18), Ancestry.com, http://www.Ancestry.com, Year: 1900; Census Place: Keysburg, Etowah, Alabama; Roll: T623_15; Page: 2A; Enumeration District: 150. Birth date: Feb 1890 Birth place: Georgia Residence date: 1900 Residence place: Precincts 3, 25 Kansas, Keysburg, Etowah, Alabama.

1351   Ancestry.com, Alabama Deaths, 1908-59 (Online publication - Provo, UT, USA: Ancestry.com Operations Inc, 2000. Original data - State of Alabama. Index of Vital Records for Alabama: Deaths, 1908-1959. Montgomery, AL, USA: State of Alabama Center for Health Statistics, Record Services Division. Original), Ancestry.com, http://www.Ancestry.com, Death date: 02 Mar 1946 Death place: Calhoun.

1352   Ancestry.com, 1920 United States Federal Census (Online publication - Provo, UT, USA: Ancestry.com Operations Inc, 2010. Images reproduced by FamilySearch. Original data - Fourteenth Census of the United States, 1920. (NARA microfilm publication T625, 2076 rolls). Records of the Bureau of the Census, Record), Ancestry.com, http://www.Ancestry.com, Year: 1920; Census Place: Anniston Ward 2, Calhoun, Alabama; Roll: T625_5; Page: 18A; Enumeration District: 23; Image:. Birth date: about 1904 Birth place: Alabama Residence date: 1920 Residence place: Anniston Ward 2, Calhoun, Alabama.

1353   Ancestry.com, 1920 United States Federal Census (Online publication - Provo, UT, USA: Ancestry.com Operations Inc, 2010. Images reproduced by FamilySearch. Original data - Fourteenth Census of the United States, 1920. (NARA microfilm publication T625, 2076 rolls). Records of the Bureau of the Census, Record), Ancestry.com, http://www.Ancestry.com, Year: 1920; Census Place: Anniston Ward 2, Calhoun, Alabama; Roll: T625_5; Page: 18A; Enumeration District: 23; Image:. Birth date: about 1906 Birth place: Alabama Residence date: 1920 Residence place: Anniston Ward 2, Calhoun, Alabama.

1354   Ancestry.com, 1910 United States Federal Census (Online publication - Provo, UT, USA: Ancestry.com Operations Inc, 2006. Original data - Thirteenth Census of the United States, 1910 (NARA microfilm publication T624, 1,178 rolls). Records of the Bureau of the Census, Record Group 29. National Archives, Washington), Ancestry.com, http://www.Ancestry.com, Year: 1910; Census Place: Anniston Ward 1, Calhoun, Alabama; Roll: ; Page: ; Enumeration District: ; Image:. Birth date: about 1907 Birth place: Alabama Residence date: 1910 Residence place: Anniston Ward 1, Calhoun, Alabama.

1355   Ancestry.com, 1920 United States Federal Census (Online publication - Provo, UT, USA: Ancestry.com Operations Inc, 2010. Images reproduced by FamilySearch. Original data - Fourteenth Census of the United States, 1920. (NARA microfilm publication T625, 2076 rolls). Records of the Bureau of the Census, Record), Ancestry.com, http://www.Ancestry.com, Year: 1920; Census Place: Anniston Ward 2, Calhoun, Alabama; Roll: T625_5; Page: 18A; Enumeration District: 23; Image:. Birth date: about 1908 Birth place: Alabama Residence date: 1920 Residence place: Anniston Ward 2, Calhoun, Alabama.

1356   Ancestry.com, 1920 United States Federal Census (Online publication - Provo, UT, USA: Ancestry.com Operations Inc, 2010. Images reproduced by FamilySearch. Original data - Fourteenth Census of the United States, 1920. (NARA microfilm publication T625, 2076 rolls). Records of the Bureau of the Census, Record), Ancestry.com, http://www.Ancestry.com, Year: 1920; Census Place: Anniston Ward 2, Calhoun, Alabama; Roll: T625_5; Page: 18A;

Enumeration District: 23; Image:. Birth date: about 1911 Birth place: Alabama Residence date: 1920 Residence place: Anniston Ward 2, Calhoun, Alabama.

1357   Ancestry.com, 1930 United States Federal Census (Online publication - Provo, UT, USA: Ancestry.com Operations Inc, 2002. Original data - United States of America, Bureau of the Census. Fifteenth Census of the United States, 1930. Washington, D.C.: National Archives and Records Administration, 1930. T626,), Ancestry.com, http://www.Ancestry.com, Year: 1930; Census Place: Anniston, Calhoun, Alabama; Roll: 5; Page: 10B; Enumeration District: 24; Image: 654.0. Birth date: about 1910 Birth place: Residence date: 1930 Residence place: Anniston, Calhoun, Alabama.

1358   Ancestry.com, 1920 United States Federal Census (Online publication - Provo, UT, USA: Ancestry.com Operations Inc, 2010. Images reproduced by FamilySearch. Original data - Fourteenth Census of the United States, 1920. (NARA microfilm publication T625, 2076 rolls). Records of the Bureau of the Census, Record), Ancestry.com, http://www.Ancestry.com, Year: 1920; Census Place: Anniston Ward 2, Calhoun, Alabama; Roll: T625_5; Page: 18A; Enumeration District: 23; Image:. Birth date: about 1911 Birth place: Alabama Residence date: 1920 Residence place: Anniston Ward 2, Calhoun, Alabama.

1359   Ancestry.com, 1910 United States Federal Census (Online publication - Provo, UT, USA: Ancestry.com Operations Inc, 2006. Original data - Thirteenth Census of the United States, 1910 (NARA microfilm publication T624, 1,178 rolls). Records of the Bureau of the Census, Record Group 29. National Archives, Washington), Ancestry.com, http://www.Ancestry.com, Year: 1910; Census Place: Anniston Ward 1, Calhoun, Alabama; Roll: ; Page: ; Enumeration District: ; Image:. Birth date: about 1910 Birth place: Alabama Residence date: 1910 Residence place: Anniston Ward 1, Calhoun, Alabama.

1360   Ancestry.com, 1920 United States Federal Census (Online publication - Provo, UT, USA: Ancestry.com Operations Inc, 2010. Images reproduced by FamilySearch. Original data - Fourteenth Census of the United States, 1920. (NARA microfilm publication T625, 2076 rolls). Records of the Bureau of the Census, Record), Ancestry.com, http://www.Ancestry.com, Year: 1920; Census Place: Anniston Ward 2, Calhoun, Alabama; Roll: T625_5; Page: 18A; Enumeration District: 23; Image:. Birth date: about 1913 Birth place: Alabama Residence date: 1920 Residence place: Anniston Ward 2, Calhoun, Alabama.

1361   Ancestry.com, 1920 United States Federal Census (Online publication - Provo, UT, USA: Ancestry.com Operations Inc, 2010. Images reproduced by FamilySearch. Original data - Fourteenth Census of the United States, 1920. (NARA microfilm publication T625, 2076 rolls). Records of the Bureau of the Census, Record), Ancestry.com, http://www.Ancestry.com, Year: 1920; Census Place: Anniston Ward 2, Calhoun, Alabama; Roll: T625_5; Page: 18A; Enumeration District: 23; Image:. Birth date: about 1915 Birth place: Alabama Residence date: 1920 Residence place: Anniston Ward 2, Calhoun, Alabama.

1362   Ancestry.com, 1930 United States Federal Census (Online publication - Provo, UT, USA: Ancestry.com Operations Inc, 2002. Original data - United States of America, Bureau of the Census. Fifteenth Census of the United States, 1930. Washington, D.C.: National Archives and Records Administration, 1930. T626,), Ancestry.com, http://www.Ancestry.com, Year: 1930; Census Place: Anniston, Calhoun, Alabama; Roll: 5; Page: 10B; Enumeration District: 24; Image: 654.0. Birth date: about 1920 Birth place: Residence date: 1930 Residence place: Anniston, Calhoun, Alabama.

1363   Ancestry.com, 1930 United States Federal Census (Online publication - Provo, UT, USA: Ancestry.com Operations Inc, 2002. Original data - United States of America, Bureau of the Census. Fifteenth Census of the United States, 1930. Washington, D.C.: National Archives and Records Administration, 1930. T626,), Ancestry.com, http://www.Ancestry.com, Year: 1930; Census Place: Anniston, Calhoun, Alabama; Roll: 5; Page: 10B; Enumeration District: 24; Image: 654.0. Birth date: about 1922 Birth place: Residence date: 1930 Residence place: Anniston, Calhoun, Alabama.

1364   Ancestry.com, 1930 United States Federal Census (Online publication - Provo, UT, USA: Ancestry.com Operations Inc, 2002. Original data - United States of America, Bureau of the Census. Fifteenth Census of the United States, 1930. Washington, D.C.: National Archives and Records Administration, 1930. T626,), Ancestry.com, http://www.Ancestry.com, Year: 1930; Census Place: Anniston, Calhoun, Alabama; Roll: 5; Page: 10B; Enumeration District: 24; Image: 654.0. Birth date: about 1924 Birth place: Residence date: 1930 Residence place: Anniston, Calhoun, Alabama.

1365   Ancestry.com, 1910 United States Federal Census (Online publication - Provo, UT, USA: Ancestry.com Operations Inc, 2006. Original data - Thirteenth Census of the United States, 1910 (NARA microfilm publication T624, 1,178 rolls). Records of the Bureau of the Census, Record Group 29. National Archives, Washington), Ancestry.com, http://www.Ancestry.com, Year: 1910; Census Place: Anniston Ward 1, Calhoun, Alabama; Roll: ; Page: ; Enumeration District: ; Image:. Birth date: about 1880 Birth place: Alabama Residence date: 1910 Residence place: Anniston Ward 1, Calhoun, Alabama.

1366   Ancestry.com, 1910 United States Federal Census (Online publication - Provo, UT, USA: Ancestry.com Operations Inc, 2006. Original data - Thirteenth Census of the United States, 1910 (NARA microfilm publication T624, 1,178 rolls). Records of the Bureau of the Census, Record Group 29. National Archives, Washington), Ancestry.com, http://www.Ancestry.com, Year: 1910; Census Place: Anniston Ward 1, Calhoun, Alabama; Roll: ; Page: ; Enumeration District: ; Image:. Birth date: about 1902 Birth place: Alabama Residence date: 1910 Residence place: Anniston Ward 1, Calhoun, Alabama.

1367   Ancestry.com, 1910 United States Federal Census (Online publication - Provo, UT, USA: Ancestry.com Operations Inc, 2006. Original data - Thirteenth Census of the United States, 1910 (NARA microfilm publication T624, 1,178 rolls). Records of the Bureau of the Census, Record Group 29. National Archives, Washington), Ancestry.com, http://www.Ancestry.com, Year: 1910; Census Place: Anniston Ward 1, Calhoun, Alabama; Roll: ; Page: ; Enumeration District: ; Image:. Birth date: about 1910 Birth place: Alabama Residence date: 1910 Residence place: Anniston Ward 1, Calhoun, Alabama.

1368   Ancestry.com, 1910 United States Federal Census (Online publication - Provo, UT, USA: Ancestry.com Operations Inc, 2006. Original data - Thirteenth Census of the United States, 1910 (NARA microfilm publication T624, 1,178 rolls). Records of the Bureau of the Census, Record Group 29. National Archives, Washington), Ancestry.com, http://www.Ancestry.com, Year: 1910; Census Place: Precinct 9, Mobile, Alabama; Roll: ; Page: ; Enumeration District: ; Image:. Birth date: about 1885 Birth place: Alabama Residence date: 1910 Residence place: Precinct 9, Mobile, Alabama.

1369   Ancestry.com, 1910 United States Federal Census (Online publication - Provo, UT, USA: Ancestry.com Operations Inc, 2006. Original data - Thirteenth Census of the United States, 1910 (NARA microfilm publication T624, 1,178 rolls). Records of the Bureau of the Census, Record Group 29. National Archives, Washington), Ancestry.com, http://www.Ancestry.com, Year: 1910; Census Place: Precinct 9, Mobile, Alabama; Roll: ; Page: ; Enumeration District: ; Image:. Birth date: about 1905 Birth place: Alabama Residence date: 1910 Residence place: Precinct 9, Mobile, Alabama.

1370   Ancestry.com, 1910 United States Federal Census (Online publication - Provo, UT, USA: Ancestry.com Operations Inc, 2006. Original data - Thirteenth Census of the United States, 1910 (NARA microfilm publication T624, 1,178 rolls). Records of the Bureau of the Census, Record Group 29. National Archives, Washington), Ancestry.com, http://www.Ancestry.com, Year: 1910; Census Place: Precinct 9, Mobile, Alabama; Roll: ; Page: ; Enumeration District: ; Image:. Birth date: about 1909 Birth place: Alabama Residence date: 1910 Residence place: Precinct 9, Mobile, Alabama.

1371   Ancestry.com, 1900 United States Federal Census (Online publication - Provo, UT, USA: Ancestry.com Operations Inc, 2004. Original data - United States of America, Bureau of the Census. Twelfth Census of the United States, 1900. Washington, D.C.: National Archives and Records Administration, 1900. T623, 18), Ancestry.com, http://www.Ancestry.com, Year: 1900; Census Place: Auburn, Montgomery, Virginia; Roll: T623_1718; Page: 6B; Enumeration District: 64. Birth date: Aug 1893 Birth place: Virginia Residence date: 1900 Residence place: Auburn District, Montgomery, Virginia.

1372   Ancestry.com, 1920 United States Federal Census (Online publication - Provo, UT, USA: Ancestry.com Operations Inc, 2010. Images reproduced by FamilySearch. Original data - Fourteenth Census of the United States, 1920. (NARA microfilm publication T625, 2076 rolls). Records of the Bureau of the Census, Record), Ancestry.com, http://www.Ancestry.com, Year: 1920; Census Place: Radford, Radford (Independent City), Virginia; Roll: T625_1908; Page: 18A; Enumeration District: 18; Image:. Birth date: about 1894 Birth place: Virginia Residence date: 1920 Residence place: Radford, Radford (Independent City), Virginia.

1373   Ancestry.com, Florida Death Index, 1877-1998 (Online publication - Provo, UT, USA: Ancestry.com Operations Inc, 2004. Original data - State of Florida. Florida Death Index, 1877-1998. Florida: Florida Department of Health, Office of Vital Records, 1998. Original data: State of Florida. Florida Death Ind), Ancestry.com, http://www.Ancestry.com, Birth date: 22 Aug 1893 Birth place: Death date: 6 Jun 1974 Death place: Pinellas, Florida, United States.

1374   Ancestry.com, Social Security Death Index (Online publication - Provo, UT, USA: Ancestry.com Operations Inc, 2010. Original data - Social Security Administration. Social Security Death Index, Master File. Social Security Administration. Original data: Social Security Administration. Social Security D), Ancestry.com, http://www.Ancestry.com, Number: 174-03-3922; Issue State: Pennsylvania; Issue Date: Before 1951. Birth date: 22 Aug 1893 Birth place: Death date: Jun 1974 Death place: Plant City, Hillsborough, Florida, United States of America.

1375   Ancestry.com, World War I Draft Registration Cards, 1917-1918 (Online publication - Provo, UT, USA: Ancestry.com Operations Inc, 2005. Original data - United States, Selective Service System. World War I Selective Service System Draft Registration Cards, 1917-1918. Washington, D.C.: National Archives and Records Administration), Ancestry.com, http://www.Ancestry.com, Registration Location: Hamilton County, Ohio; Roll: 1819891; Draft Board: 10. Birth date: 22 Aug 1893 Birth place: Virginia; United States of America Residence date: Residence place: Cincinnati, Hamilton, Ohio.

1376   Ancestry.com, 1910 United States Federal Census (Online publication - Provo, UT, USA: Ancestry.com Operations Inc, 2006. Original data - Thirteenth Census of the United States, 1910 (NARA microfilm publication T624, 1,178 rolls). Records of the Bureau of the Census, Record Group 29. National Archives, Washington), Ancestry.com, http://www.Ancestry.com, Year: 1910; Census Place: Radford West Ward, Radford (Independent City), Virginia; Roll: ; Page: ; Enumeration District: ; Image:. Birth date: about 1893 Birth place: Virginia Residence date: 1910 Residence place: Radford West Ward, Radford (Independent City), Virginia.

1377   Ancestry.com, 1930 United States Federal Census (Online publication - Provo, UT, USA: Ancestry.com Operations Inc, 2002. Original data - United States of America, Bureau of the Census. Fifteenth Census of the United States, 1930. Washington, D.C.: National Archives and Records Administration, 1930. T626,), Ancestry.com, http://www.Ancestry.com, Year: 1930; Census Place: Anniston, Calhoun, Alabama; Roll: 5; Page: 2B; Enumeration District: 23; Image: 612.0. Birth date: about 1891 Birth place: Residence date: 1930 Residence place: Anniston, Calhoun, Alabama.

1378   Ancestry.com, 1920 United States Federal Census (Online publication - Provo, UT, USA: Ancestry.com Operations Inc, 2010. Images reproduced by FamilySearch. Original data - Fourteenth Census of the United States, 1920. (NARA microfilm publication T625, 2076 rolls). Records of the Bureau of the Census, Record), Ancestry.com,

http://www.Ancestry.com, Year: 1920; Census Place: La Grange, Troup, Georgia; Roll: T625_281; Page: 2A; Enumeration District: 137; Image:. Birth date: about 1892 Birth place: Georgia Residence date: 1920 Residence place: La Grange, Troup, Georgia.

1379   Ancestry.com, Alabama Deaths, 1908-59 (Online publication - Provo, UT, USA: Ancestry.com Operations Inc, 2000. Original data - State of Alabama. Index of Vital Records for Alabama: Deaths, 1908-1959. Montgomery, AL, USA: State of Alabama Center for Health Statistics, Record Services Division. Original), Ancestry.com, http://www.Ancestry.com, Death date: 01 Feb 1942 Death place: Calhoun.

1380   Ancestry.com, 1900 United States Federal Census (Online publication - Provo, UT, USA: Ancestry.com Operations Inc, 2004. Original data - United States of America, Bureau of the Census. Twelfth Census of the United States, 1900. Washington, D.C.: National Archives and Records Administration, 1900. T623, 18), Ancestry.com, http://www.Ancestry.com, Year: 1900; Census Place: Franklin, Heard, Georgia; Roll: T623_204; Page: 6A; Enumeration District: 75. Birth date: Mar 1891 Birth place: Georgia Residence date: 1900 Residence place: Franklin, Heard, Georgia.

1381   Ancestry.com, New Orleans Passenger Lists, 1820-1945 (Online publication - Provo, UT, USA: Ancestry.com Operations, Inc., 2006. Original data - Passenger Lists of Vessels Arriving at New Orleans, Louisiana, 1820-1902. Microfilm publication M259. 93 rolls. Record Group 36.Passenger Lists of Vessels Arriving at), Ancestry.com, http://www.Ancestry.com, Birth date: about 1915 Birth place: Alabama, Anniston Arrival date: 11 Jul 1945Arrival place: New Orleans, Louisiana Departure date: Departure place: Buenos Aires, Argentina.

1382   Ancestry.com, 1930 United States Federal Census (Online publication - Provo, UT, USA: Ancestry.com Operations Inc, 2002. Original data - United States of America, Bureau of the Census. Fifteenth Census of the United States, 1930. Washington, D.C.: National Archives and Records Administration, 1930. T626,), Ancestry.com, http://www.Ancestry.com, Year: 1930; Census Place: Anniston, Calhoun, Alabama; Roll: 5; Page: 2B; Enumeration District: 23; Image: 612.0. Birth date: about 1915 Birth place: Residence date: 1930 Residence place: Anniston, Calhoun, Alabama.

1383   Ancestry.com, Social Security Death Index (Online publication - Provo, UT, USA: Ancestry.com Operations Inc, 2010. Original data - Social Security Administration. Social Security Death Index, Master File. Social Security Administration. Original data: Social Security Administration. Social Security D), Ancestry.com, http://www.Ancestry.com, Number: 267-82-8754; Issue State: Florida; Issue Date: 1963. Birth date: 22 Oct 1914 Birth place: Death date: Jun 1978 Death place: Panama City, Bay, Florida, United States of America.

1384   Ancestry.com, Florida State Census, 1867-1945 (Online publication - Provo, UT, USA: Ancestry.com Operations Inc, 2008. Original data - Schedules of the Florida State Census of 1885; (National Archives Microfilm Publication M845, 13 Rolls); Records of the Bureau of the Census, Record Group 29; National A), Ancestry.com, http://www.Ancestry.com, Birth date: about 1915 Birth place: Alabama Residence date: 1945Residence place: Bay, Florida.

1385   Ancestry.com, U.S. Public Records Index, Volume 2 (Online publication - Provo, UT, USA: Ancestry.com Operations, Inc., 2010. Original data - Voter Registration Lists, Public Record Filings, Historical Residential Records, and Other Household Database Listings. Original data: Voter Registration Lists, Public), Ancestry.com, http://www.Ancestry.com, Birth date: 22 Oct 1914 Birth place: Residence date: 1935-1993Residence place: Panama City, FL.

1386   Ancestry.com, 1920 United States Federal Census (Online publication - Provo, UT, USA: Ancestry.com Operations Inc, 2010. Images reproduced by FamilySearch. Original data - Fourteenth Census of the United States, 1920. (NARA microfilm publication T625, 2076 rolls). Records of the Bureau of the Census, Record), Ancestry.com, http://www.Ancestry.com, Year: 1920; Census Place: La Grange, Troup, Georgia; Roll: T625_281; Page: 2A; Enumeration District: 137; Image:. Birth date: about 1917 Birth place: Alabama Residence date: 1920 Residence place: La Grange, Troup, Georgia.

1387   Ancestry.com, Florida Death Index, 1877-1998 (Online publication - Provo, UT, USA: Ancestry.com Operations Inc, 2004. Original data - State of Florida. Florida Death Index, 1877-1998. Florida: Florida Department of Health, Office of Vital Records, 1998. Original data: State of Florida. Florida Death Ind), Ancestry.com, http://www.Ancestry.com, Birth date: 22 Oct 1914 Birth place: Death date: 26 Jun 1978 Death place: Bay, Florida, United States.

1388   Ancestry.com, World War I Draft Registration Cards, 1917-1918 (Online publication - Provo, UT, USA: Ancestry.com Operations Inc, 2005. Original data - United States, Selective Service System. World War I Selective Service System Draft Registration Cards, 1917-1918. Washington, D.C.: National Archives and Records Administration), Ancestry.com, http://www.Ancestry.com, Occupation included on card.

1389   Ancestry.com, Social Security Death Index (Online publication - Provo, UT, USA: Ancestry.com Operations Inc, 2010. Original data - Social Security Administration. Social Security Death Index, Master File. Social Security Administration. Original data: Social Security Administration. Social Security D), Ancestry.com, http://www.Ancestry.com, Number: 455-42-9401; Issue State: Texas; Issue Date: Before 1951. Birth date: 11 Aug 1893 Birth place: Death date: Dec 1973 Death place: Tatum, Rusk, Texas, United States of America.

1390   Ancestry.com, 1930 United States Federal Census (Online publication - Provo, UT, USA: Ancestry.com Operations Inc, 2002. Original data - United States of America, Bureau of the Census. Fifteenth Census of the United States, 1930. Washington, D.C.: National Archives and Records Administration, 1930. T626,), Ancestry.com, http://www.Ancestry.com, Year: 1930; Census Place: Jonesboro, Craighead, Arkansas; Roll: 70; Page: 11A; Enumeration

District: 16; Image: 619.0. Birth date: about 1891 Birth place: Residence date: 1930 Residence place: Jonesboro, Craighead, Arkansas.

1391   Ancestry.com, 1920 United States Federal Census (Online publication - Provo, UT, USA: Ancestry.com Operations Inc, 2010. Images reproduced by FamilySearch. Original data - Fourteenth Census of the United States, 1920. (NARA microfilm publication T625, 2076 rolls). Records of the Bureau of the Census, Record), Ancestry.com, http://www.Ancestry.com, Year: 1920; Census Place: Justice Precinct 1, Tarrant, Texas; Roll: T625_1848; Page: 41A; Enumeration District: 87; Image:. Birth date: about 1893 Birth place: Alabama Residence date: 1920 Residence place: Justice Precinct 1, Tarrant, Texas.

1392   Ancestry.com, 1920 United States Federal Census (Online publication - Provo, UT, USA: Ancestry.com Operations Inc, 2010. Images reproduced by FamilySearch. Original data - Fourteenth Census of the United States, 1920. (NARA microfilm publication T625, 2076 rolls). Records of the Bureau of the Census, Record), Ancestry.com, http://www.Ancestry.com, Year: 1920; Census Place: Justice Precinct 1, Tarrant, Texas; Roll: T625_1848; Page: 41A; Enumeration District: 87; Image:. Birth date: about 1913 Birth place: Alabama Residence date: 1920 Residence place: Justice Precinct 1, Tarrant, Texas.

1393   Ancestry.com, 1930 United States Federal Census (Online publication - Provo, UT, USA: Ancestry.com Operations Inc, 2002. Original data - United States of America, Bureau of the Census. Fifteenth Census of the United States, 1930. Washington, D.C.: National Archives and Records Administration, 1930. T626,), Ancestry.com, http://www.Ancestry.com, Year: 1930; Census Place: Jonesboro, Craighead, Arkansas; Roll: 70; Page: 11A; Enumeration District: 16; Image: 619.0. Birth date: about 1913 Birth place: Residence date: 1930 Residence place: Jonesboro, Craighead, Arkansas.

1394   Ancestry.com, 1930 United States Federal Census (Online publication - Provo, UT, USA: Ancestry.com Operations Inc, 2002. Original data - United States of America, Bureau of the Census. Fifteenth Census of the United States, 1930. Washington, D.C.: National Archives and Records Administration, 1930. T626,), Ancestry.com, http://www.Ancestry.com, Year: 1930; Census Place: Jonesboro, Craighead, Arkansas; Roll: 70; Page: 11A; Enumeration District: 16; Image: 619.0. Birth date: about 1916 Birth place: Residence date: 1930 Residence place: Jonesboro, Craighead, Arkansas.

1395   Ancestry.com, 1920 United States Federal Census (Online publication - Provo, UT, USA: Ancestry.com Operations Inc, 2010. Images reproduced by FamilySearch. Original data - Fourteenth Census of the United States, 1920. (NARA microfilm publication T625, 2076 rolls). Records of the Bureau of the Census, Record), Ancestry.com, http://www.Ancestry.com, Year: 1920; Census Place: Justice Precinct 1, Tarrant, Texas; Roll: T625_1848; Page: 41A; Enumeration District: 87; Image:. Birth date: about 1916 Birth place: Alabama Residence date: 1920 Residence place: Justice Precinct 1, Tarrant, Texas.

1396   Ancestry.com, 1930 United States Federal Census (Online publication - Provo, UT, USA: Ancestry.com Operations Inc, 2002. Original data - United States of America, Bureau of the Census. Fifteenth Census of the United States, 1930. Washington, D.C.: National Archives and Records Administration, 1930. T626,), Ancestry.com, http://www.Ancestry.com, Year: 1930; Census Place: Jonesboro, Craighead, Arkansas; Roll: 70; Page: 11A; Enumeration District: 16; Image: 619.0. Birth date: about 1923 Birth place: Residence date: 1930 Residence place: Jonesboro, Craighead, Arkansas.

1397   Ancestry.com, 1920 United States Federal Census (Online publication - Provo, UT, USA: Ancestry.com Operations Inc, 2010. Images reproduced by FamilySearch. Original data - Fourteenth Census of the United States, 1920. (NARA microfilm publication T625, 2076 rolls). Records of the Bureau of the Census, Record), Ancestry.com, http://www.Ancestry.com, Year: 1920; Census Place: Redland, Hempstead, Arkansas; Roll: T625_64; Page: 6A; Enumeration District: 105; Image:. Birth date: about 1879 Birth place: Arkansas Residence date: 1920 Residence place: Redland, Hempstead, Arkansas.

1398   Ancestry.com, 1920 United States Federal Census (Online publication - Provo, UT, USA: Ancestry.com Operations Inc, 2010. Images reproduced by FamilySearch. Original data - Fourteenth Census of the United States, 1920. (NARA microfilm publication T625, 2076 rolls). Records of the Bureau of the Census, Record), Ancestry.com, http://www.Ancestry.com, Year: 1920; Census Place: Redland, Hempstead, Arkansas; Roll: T625_64; Page: 6A; Enumeration District: 105; Image:. Birth date: about 1913 Birth place: Arkansas Residence date: 1920 Residence place: Redland, Hempstead, Arkansas.

1399   Ancestry.com, 1920 United States Federal Census (Online publication - Provo, UT, USA: Ancestry.com Operations Inc, 2010. Images reproduced by FamilySearch. Original data - Fourteenth Census of the United States, 1920. (NARA microfilm publication T625, 2076 rolls). Records of the Bureau of the Census, Record), Ancestry.com, http://www.Ancestry.com, Year: 1920; Census Place: Redland, Hempstead, Arkansas; Roll: T625_64; Page: 6A; Enumeration District: 105; Image:. Birth date: about 1915 Birth place: Arkansas Residence date: 1920 Residence place: Redland, Hempstead, Arkansas.

1400   Ancestry.com, 1920 United States Federal Census (Online publication - Provo, UT, USA: Ancestry.com Operations Inc, 2010. Images reproduced by FamilySearch. Original data - Fourteenth Census of the United States, 1920. (NARA microfilm publication T625, 2076 rolls). Records of the Bureau of the Census, Record), Ancestry.com, http://www.Ancestry.com, Year: 1920; Census Place: Redland, Hempstead, Arkansas; Roll: T625_64; Page: 16A; Enumeration District: 105; Image:. Birth date: about 1908 Birth place: Arkansas Residence date: 1920 Residence place: Redland, Hempstead, Arkansas.

1401   Ancestry.com, 1930 United States Federal Census (Online publication - Provo, UT, USA: Ancestry.com Operations Inc, 2002. Original data - United States of America, Bureau of the Census. Fifteenth Census of the United States, 1930. Washington, D.C.: National Archives and Records Administration, 1930. T626,), Ancestry.com, http://www.Ancestry.com, Year: 1930; Census Place: Saline, Pike, Arkansas; Roll: 88; Page: 7A; Enumeration District: 14; Image: 475.0. Birth date: about 1908 Birth place: Residence date: 1930 Residence place: Saline, Pike, Arkansas.

1402   Ancestry.com, Social Security Death Index (Online publication - Provo, UT, USA: Ancestry.com Operations Inc, 2010. Original data - Social Security Administration. Social Security Death Index, Master File. Social Security Administration. Original data: Social Security Administration. Social Security D), Ancestry.com, http://www.Ancestry.com, Number: 453-52-1791; Issue State: Texas; Issue Date: Before 1951. Birth date: 10 Aug 1908 Birth place: Death date: 14 Jun 1988 Death place: Prescott, Nevada, Arkansas, United States of America.

1403   Ancestry.com, 1910 United States Federal Census (Online publication - Provo, UT, USA: Ancestry.com Operations Inc, 2006. Original data - Thirteenth Census of the United States, 1910 (NARA microfilm publication T624, 1,178 rolls). Records of the Bureau of the Census, Record Group 29. National Archives, Washington), Ancestry.com, http://www.Ancestry.com, Year: 1910; Census Place: Missouri, Pike, Arkansas; Roll: ; Page: ; Enumeration District: ; Image:. Birth date: about 1904 Birth place: Arkansas Residence date: 1910 Residence place: Missouri, Pike, Arkansas.

1404   Ancestry.com, Social Security Death Index (Online publication - Provo, UT, USA: Ancestry.com Operations Inc, 2010. Original data - Social Security Administration. Social Security Death Index, Master File. Social Security Administration. Original data: Social Security Administration. Social Security D), Ancestry.com, http://www.Ancestry.com, Number: 431-32-9720; Issue State: Arkansas; Issue Date: Before 1951. Birth date: 4 Mar 1928 Birth place: Death date: Jan 1976 Death place:.

1405   Ancestry.com, Selected U.S. Headstone Photos (Online publication - Provo, UT, USA: Ancestry.com Operations Inc, 2005. Original data - Photos provided by Allen Wheatley, teafor2.com. Original data: Photos provided by Allen Wheatley, teafor2.com.), Ancestry.com, http://www.Ancestry.com, Birth date: 1928 Birth place: Death date: 1976 Death place:.

1406   Ancestry.com, Texas Death Index, 1903-2000 (Online publication - Provo, UT, USA: Ancestry.com Operations Inc, 2006. Original data - Texas Department of Health. Texas Death Indexes, 1903-2000. Austin, TX, USA: Texas Department of Health, State Vital Statistics Unit. Original data: Texas Department of H), Ancestry.com, http://www.Ancestry.com, Death date: 14 Jan 1976 Death place: Harris, Texas.

1407   National Archives and Records Administration, U.S. World War II Army Enlistment Records, 1938-1946 (Online publication - Provo, UT, USA: Ancestry.com Operations Inc, 2005. Original data - Electronic Army Serial Number Merged File, 1938-1946 [Archival Database]; World War II Army Enlistment Records; Records of the National Archives and Records Administration), Ancestry.com, http://www.Ancestry.com, Birth date: 1928 Birth place: Residence date: Residence place: Arkansas.

1408   Ancestry.com, 1930 United States Federal Census (Online publication - Provo, UT, USA: Ancestry.com Operations Inc, 2002. Original data - United States of America, Bureau of the Census. Fifteenth Census of the United States, 1930. Washington, D.C.: National Archives and Records Administration, 1930. T626,), Ancestry.com, http://www.Ancestry.com, Year: 1930; Census Place: Saline, Pike, Arkansas; Roll: 88; Page: 7A; Enumeration District: 14; Image: 475.0. Birth date: about 1927 Birth place: Residence date: 1930 Residence place: Saline, Pike, Arkansas.

1409   Ancestry.com, Social Security Death Index (Online publication - Provo, UT, USA: Ancestry.com Operations Inc, 2010. Original data - Social Security Administration. Social Security Death Index, Master File. Social Security Administration. Original data: Social Security Administration. Social Security D), Ancestry.com, http://www.Ancestry.com, Number: 430-48-0782; Issue State: Arkansas; Issue Date: Before 1951. Birth date: 14 Dec 1931 Birth place: Death date: 15 Mar 1997 Death place: Crosby, Harris, Texas, United States of America.

1410   Ancestry.com, Texas Death Index, 1903-2000 (Online publication - Provo, UT, USA: Ancestry.com Operations Inc, 2006. Original data - Texas Department of Health. Texas Death Indexes, 1903-2000. Austin, TX, USA: Texas Department of Health, State Vital Statistics Unit. Original data: Texas Department of H), Ancestry.com, http://www.Ancestry.com, Death date: 21 Mar 1997 Death place: Harris, Texas.

1411   National Cemetery Administration, U.S. Veterans Gravesites, ca.1775-2006 (Online publication - Provo, UT, USA: Ancestry.com Operations Inc, 2006. Original data - National Cemetery Administration. Nationwide Gravesite Locator. Original data: National Cemetery Administration. Nationwide Gravesite Locator), Ancestry.com, http://www.Ancestry.com, Birth date: 12/14/1931 Birth place: Death date: 03/21/1997 Death place: TX.

1412   Ancestry.com, 1920 United States Federal Census (Online publication - Provo, UT, USA: Ancestry.com Operations Inc, 2010. Images reproduced by FamilySearch. Original data - Fourteenth Census of the United States, 1920. (NARA microfilm publication T625, 2076 rolls). Records of the Bureau of the Census, Record), Ancestry.com, http://www.Ancestry.com, Year: 1920; Census Place: Greens Schoolhouse, Calhoun, Alabama; Roll: T625_5; Page: 6B; Enumeration District: 10; Image:. Birth date: about 1908 Birth place: Alabama Residence date: 1920 Residence place: Greens Schoolhouse, Calhoun, Alabama.

1413   Ancestry.com, 1910 United States Federal Census (Online publication - Provo, UT, USA: Ancestry.com Operations Inc, 2006. Original data - Thirteenth Census of the United States, 1910 (NARA microfilm publication T624, 1,178 rolls). Records of the Bureau of the Census, Record Group 29. National Archives, Washington), Ancestry.com, http://www.Ancestry.com, Year: 1910; Census Place: Ballplay, Etowah, Alabama; Roll: ; Page: ; Enumeration District: ; Image:. Birth date: 1909 Birth place: Alabama Residence date: 1910 Residence place: Ballplay, Etowah, Alabama.

1414   Ancestry.com, 1920 United States Federal Census (Online publication - Provo, UT, USA: Ancestry.com Operations Inc, 2010. Images reproduced by FamilySearch. Original data - Fourteenth Census of the United States, 1920. (NARA microfilm publication T625, 2076 rolls). Records of the Bureau of the Census, Record), Ancestry.com, http://www.Ancestry.com, Year: 1920; Census Place: Greens Schoolhouse, Calhoun, Alabama; Roll: T625_5; Page: 6B; Enumeration District: 10; Image:. Birth date: about 1910 Birth place: Alabama Residence date: 1920 Residence place: Greens Schoolhouse, Calhoun, Alabama.

1415   Ancestry.com, 1920 United States Federal Census (Online publication - Provo, UT, USA: Ancestry.com Operations Inc, 2010. Images reproduced by FamilySearch. Original data - Fourteenth Census of the United States, 1920. (NARA microfilm publication T625, 2076 rolls). Records of the Bureau of the Census, Record), Ancestry.com, http://www.Ancestry.com, Year: 1920; Census Place: Greens Schoolhouse, Calhoun, Alabama; Roll: T625_5; Page: 6B; Enumeration District: 10; Image:. Birth date: about 1912 Birth place: Alabama Residence date: 1920 Residence place: Greens Schoolhouse, Calhoun, Alabama.

1416   Ancestry.com, 1920 United States Federal Census (Online publication - Provo, UT, USA: Ancestry.com Operations Inc, 2010. Images reproduced by FamilySearch. Original data - Fourteenth Census of the United States, 1920. (NARA microfilm publication T625, 2076 rolls). Records of the Bureau of the Census, Record), Ancestry.com, http://www.Ancestry.com, Year: 1920; Census Place: Greens Schoolhouse, Calhoun, Alabama; Roll: T625_5; Page: 6B; Enumeration District: 10; Image:. Birth date: about 1914 Birth place: Alabama Residence date: 1920 Residence place: Greens Schoolhouse, Calhoun, Alabama.

1417   Ancestry.com, 1930 United States Federal Census (Online publication - Provo, UT, USA: Ancestry.com Operations Inc, 2002. Original data - United States of America, Bureau of the Census. Fifteenth Census of the United States, 1930. Washington, D.C.: National Archives and Records Administration, 1930. T626,), Ancestry.com, http://www.Ancestry.com, Year: 1930; Census Place: Greens Schoolhouse, Calhoun, Alabama; Roll: 5; Page: 5B; Enumeration District: 11; Image: 251.0. Birth date: about 1913 Birth place: Residence date: 1930 Residence place: Greens Schoolhouse, Calhoun, Alabama.

1418   Ancestry.com, 1920 United States Federal Census (Online publication - Provo, UT, USA: Ancestry.com Operations Inc, 2010. Images reproduced by FamilySearch. Original data - Fourteenth Census of the United States, 1920. (NARA microfilm publication T625, 2076 rolls). Records of the Bureau of the Census, Record), Ancestry.com, http://www.Ancestry.com, Year: 1920; Census Place: Greens Schoolhouse, Calhoun, Alabama; Roll: T625_5; Page: 6B; Enumeration District: 10; Image:. Birth date: about 1915 Birth place: Alabama Residence date: 1920 Residence place: Greens Schoolhouse, Calhoun, Alabama.

1419   Ancestry.com, 1930 United States Federal Census (Online publication - Provo, UT, USA: Ancestry.com Operations Inc, 2002. Original data - United States of America, Bureau of the Census. Fifteenth Census of the United States, 1930. Washington, D.C.: National Archives and Records Administration, 1930. T626,), Ancestry.com, http://www.Ancestry.com, Year: 1930; Census Place: Greens Schoolhouse, Calhoun, Alabama; Roll: 5; Page: 5B; Enumeration District: 11; Image: 251.0. Birth date: about 1911 Birth place: Residence date: 1930 Residence place: Greens Schoolhouse, Calhoun, Alabama.

1420   Ancestry.com, 1920 United States Federal Census (Online publication - Provo, UT, USA: Ancestry.com Operations Inc, 2010. Images reproduced by FamilySearch. Original data - Fourteenth Census of the United States, 1920. (NARA microfilm publication T625, 2076 rolls). Records of the Bureau of the Census, Record), Ancestry.com, http://www.Ancestry.com, Year: 1920; Census Place: Greens Schoolhouse, Calhoun, Alabama; Roll: T625_5; Page: 6B; Enumeration District: 10; Image:. Birth date: about 1917 Birth place: Alabama Residence date: 1920 Residence place: Greens Schoolhouse, Calhoun, Alabama.

1421   Ancestry.com, 1930 United States Federal Census (Online publication - Provo, UT, USA: Ancestry.com Operations Inc, 2002. Original data - United States of America, Bureau of the Census. Fifteenth Census of the United States, 1930. Washington, D.C.: National Archives and Records Administration, 1930. T626,), Ancestry.com, http://www.Ancestry.com, Year: 1930; Census Place: Greens Schoolhouse, Calhoun, Alabama; Roll: 5; Page: 5B; Enumeration District: 11; Image: 251.0. Birth date: about 1918 Birth place: Residence date: 1930 Residence place: Greens Schoolhouse, Calhoun, Alabama.

1422   Ancestry.com, 1920 United States Federal Census (Online publication - Provo, UT, USA: Ancestry.com Operations Inc, 2010. Images reproduced by FamilySearch. Original data - Fourteenth Census of the United States, 1920. (NARA microfilm publication T625, 2076 rolls). Records of the Bureau of the Census, Record), Ancestry.com, http://www.Ancestry.com, Year: 1920; Census Place: Greens Schoolhouse, Calhoun, Alabama; Roll: T625_5; Page: 6B; Enumeration District: 10; Image:. Birth date: about 1919 Birth place: Alabama Residence date: 1920 Residence place: Greens Schoolhouse, Calhoun, Alabama.

1423   Ancestry.com, 1930 United States Federal Census (Online publication - Provo, UT, USA: Ancestry.com Operations Inc, 2002. Original data - United States of America, Bureau of the Census. Fifteenth Census of the United States, 1930. Washington, D.C.: National Archives and Records Administration, 1930. T626,), Ancestry.com, http://www.Ancestry.com, Year: 1930; Census Place: Greens Schoolhouse, Calhoun, Alabama; Roll: 5; Page: 5B; Enumeration District: 11; Image: 251.0. Birth date: about 1919 Birth place: Residence date: 1930 Residence place: Greens Schoolhouse, Calhoun, Alabama.

1424   Ancestry.com, 1930 United States Federal Census (Online publication - Provo, UT, USA: Ancestry.com Operations Inc, 2002. Original data - United States of America, Bureau of the Census. Fifteenth Census of the United States, 1930. Washington, D.C.: National Archives and Records Administration, 1930. T626,), Ancestry.com,

http://www.Ancestry.com, Year: 1930; Census Place: Greens Schoolhouse, Calhoun, Alabama; Roll: 5; Page: 5B; Enumeration District: 11; Image: 251.0. Birth date: about 1922 Birth place: Residence date: 1930 Residence place: Greens Schoolhouse, Calhoun, Alabama.

1425   Ancestry.com, 1930 United States Federal Census (Online publication - Provo, UT, USA: Ancestry.com Operations Inc, 2002. Original data - United States of America, Bureau of the Census. Fifteenth Census of the United States, 1930. Washington, D.C.: National Archives and Records Administration, 1930. T626,), Ancestry.com, http://www.Ancestry.com, Year: 1930; Census Place: Greens Schoolhouse, Calhoun, Alabama; Roll: 5; Page: 5B; Enumeration District: 11; Image: 251.0. Birth date: about 1924 Birth place: Residence date: 1930 Residence place: Greens Schoolhouse, Calhoun, Alabama.

1426   Ancestry.com, 1930 United States Federal Census (Online publication - Provo, UT, USA: Ancestry.com Operations Inc, 2002. Original data - United States of America, Bureau of the Census. Fifteenth Census of the United States, 1930. Washington, D.C.: National Archives and Records Administration, 1930. T626,), Ancestry.com, http://www.Ancestry.com, Year: 1930; Census Place: Greens Schoolhouse, Calhoun, Alabama; Roll: 5; Page: 5B; Enumeration District: 11; Image: 251.0. Birth date: about 1925 Birth place: Residence date: 1930 Residence place: Greens Schoolhouse, Calhoun, Alabama.

1427   Ancestry.com, 1930 United States Federal Census (Online publication - Provo, UT, USA: Ancestry.com Operations Inc, 2002. Original data - United States of America, Bureau of the Census. Fifteenth Census of the United States, 1930. Washington, D.C.: National Archives and Records Administration, 1930. T626,), Ancestry.com, http://www.Ancestry.com, Year: 1930; Census Place: Anniston, Calhoun, Alabama; Roll: 5; Page: 8B; Enumeration District: 37; Image: 1096.0. Birth date: about 1906 Birth place: Residence date: 1930 Residence place: Anniston, Calhoun, Alabama.

1428   Ancestry.com, 1930 United States Federal Census (Online publication - Provo, UT, USA: Ancestry.com Operations Inc, 2002. Original data - United States of America, Bureau of the Census. Fifteenth Census of the United States, 1930. Washington, D.C.: National Archives and Records Administration, 1930. T626,), Ancestry.com, http://www.Ancestry.com, Year: 1930; Census Place: Anniston, Calhoun, Alabama; Roll: 5; Page: 8B; Enumeration District: 37; Image: 1096.0. Birth date: about 1910 Birth place: Residence date: 1930 Residence place: Anniston, Calhoun, Alabama.

1429   Ancestry.com, 1930 United States Federal Census (Online publication - Provo, UT, USA: Ancestry.com Operations Inc, 2002. Original data - United States of America, Bureau of the Census. Fifteenth Census of the United States, 1930. Washington, D.C.: National Archives and Records Administration, 1930. T626,), Ancestry.com, http://www.Ancestry.com, Year: 1930; Census Place: Anniston, Calhoun, Alabama; Roll: 5; Page: 8B; Enumeration District: 37; Image: 1096.0. Birth date: about 1917 Birth place: Residence date: 1930 Residence place: Anniston, Calhoun, Alabama.

1430   Ancestry.com, 1920 United States Federal Census (Online publication - Provo, UT, USA: Ancestry.com Operations Inc, 2010. Images reproduced by FamilySearch. Original data - Fourteenth Census of the United States, 1920. (NARA microfilm publication T625, 2076 rolls). Records of the Bureau of the Census, Record), Ancestry.com, http://www.Ancestry.com, Year: 1920; Census Place: Greens Schoolhouse, Calhoun, Alabama; Roll: T625_5; Page: 7B; Enumeration District: 10; Image:. Birth date: about 1886 Birth place: Alabama Residence date: 1920 Residence place: Greens Schoolhouse, Calhoun, Alabama.

1431   Ancestry.com, 1920 United States Federal Census (Online publication - Provo, UT, USA: Ancestry.com Operations Inc, 2010. Images reproduced by FamilySearch. Original data - Fourteenth Census of the United States, 1920. (NARA microfilm publication T625, 2076 rolls). Records of the Bureau of the Census, Record), Ancestry.com, http://www.Ancestry.com, Year: 1920; Census Place: Greens Schoolhouse, Calhoun, Alabama; Roll: T625_5; Page: 7B; Enumeration District: 10; Image:. Birth date: about 1904 Birth place: Alabama Residence date: 1920 Residence place: Greens Schoolhouse, Calhoun, Alabama.

1432   Ancestry.com, 1920 United States Federal Census (Online publication - Provo, UT, USA: Ancestry.com Operations Inc, 2010. Images reproduced by FamilySearch. Original data - Fourteenth Census of the United States, 1920. (NARA microfilm publication T625, 2076 rolls). Records of the Bureau of the Census, Record), Ancestry.com, http://www.Ancestry.com, Year: 1920; Census Place: Greens Schoolhouse, Calhoun, Alabama; Roll: T625_5; Page: 7B; Enumeration District: 10; Image:. Birth date: about 1910 Birth place: Alabama Residence date: 1920 Residence place: Greens Schoolhouse, Calhoun, Alabama.

1433   Ancestry.com, 1920 United States Federal Census (Online publication - Provo, UT, USA: Ancestry.com Operations Inc, 2010. Images reproduced by FamilySearch. Original data - Fourteenth Census of the United States, 1920. (NARA microfilm publication T625, 2076 rolls). Records of the Bureau of the Census, Record), Ancestry.com, http://www.Ancestry.com, Year: 1920; Census Place: Greens Schoolhouse, Calhoun, Alabama; Roll: T625_5; Page: 8A; Enumeration District: 10; Image:. Birth date: about 1912 Birth place: Alabama Residence date: 1920 Residence place: Greens Schoolhouse, Calhoun, Alabama.

1434   Ancestry.com, 1930 United States Federal Census (Online publication - Provo, UT, USA: Ancestry.com Operations Inc, 2002. Original data - United States of America, Bureau of the Census. Fifteenth Census of the United States, 1930. Washington, D.C.: National Archives and Records Administration, 1930. T626,), Ancestry.com, http://www.Ancestry.com, Year: 1930; Census Place: Anniston, Calhoun, Alabama; Roll: 5; Page: 8B; Enumeration District: 37; Image: 1096.0. Birth date: about 1911 Birth place: Residence date: 1930 Residence place: Anniston, Calhoun, Alabama.

1435   Ancestry.com, 1920 United States Federal Census (Online publication - Provo, UT, USA: Ancestry.com Operations Inc, 2010. Images reproduced by FamilySearch. Original data - Fourteenth Census of the United States, 1920. (NARA microfilm publication T625, 2076 rolls). Records of the Bureau of the Census, Record), Ancestry.com, http://www.Ancestry.com, Year: 1920; Census Place: Greens Schoolhouse, Calhoun, Alabama; Roll: T625_5; Page: 8A; Enumeration District: 10; Image:. Birth date: about 1920 Birth place: Alabama Residence date: 1920 Residence place: Greens Schoolhouse, Calhoun, Alabama.

1436   Ancestry.com and The Church of Jesus Christ of Latter-day Saints, 1880 United States Federal Census (Online publication - Provo, UT, USA: Ancestry.com Operations Inc, 2010. 1880 U.S. Census Index provided by The Church of Jesus Christ of Latter-day Saints © Copyright 1999 Intellectual Reserve, Inc. All rights reserved. All use is subject to the limited), Ancestry.com, http://www.Ancestry.com, Year: 1880; Census Place: Peaks Hill, Calhoun, Alabama; Roll: 4; Family History Film: 1254004; Page: 614C; Enumeration District: 9; Image: 0787. Birth date: about 1870 Birth place: Alabama Residence date: 1880 Residence place: Peaks Hill, Calhoun, Alabama, United States.

1437   Ancestry.com, 1920 United States Federal Census (Online publication - Provo, UT, USA: Ancestry.com Operations Inc, 2010. Images reproduced by FamilySearch. Original data - Fourteenth Census of the United States, 1920. (NARA microfilm publication T625, 2076 rolls). Records of the Bureau of the Census, Record), Ancestry.com, http://www.Ancestry.com, Year: 1920; Census Place: Gum Spring, Etowah, Alabama; Roll: T625_15; Page: 4B; Enumeration District: 110; Image:. Birth date: about 1872 Birth place: Alabama Residence date: 1920 Residence place: Gum Spring, Etowah, Alabama.

1438   Ancestry.com, 1910 United States Federal Census (Online publication - Provo, UT, USA: Ancestry.com Operations Inc, 2006. Original data - Thirteenth Census of the United States, 1910 (NARA microfilm publication T624, 1,178 rolls). Records of the Bureau of the Census, Record Group 29. National Archives, Washington), Ancestry.com, http://www.Ancestry.com, Year: 1910; Census Place: De Armanville, Calhoun, Alabama; Roll: ; Page: ; Enumeration District: ; Image:. Birth date: about 1872 Birth place: Alabama Residence date: 1910 Residence place: De Armanville, Calhoun, Alabama.

1439   Ancestry.com, 1900 United States Federal Census (Online publication - Provo, UT, USA: Ancestry.com Operations Inc, 2004. Original data - United States of America, Bureau of the Census. Twelfth Census of the United States, 1900. Washington, D.C.: National Archives and Records Administration, 1900. T623, 18), Ancestry.com, http://www.Ancestry.com, Year: 1900; Census Place: Allen, Calhoun, Alabama; Roll: T623_5; Page: 3B; Enumeration District: 32. Birth date: Jun 1892 Birth place: Alabama Residence date: 1900 Residence place: Precinct 8 Green's Schoolhouse, Calhoun, Alabama.

1440   Ancestry.com, 1900 United States Federal Census (Online publication - Provo, UT, USA: Ancestry.com Operations Inc, 2004. Original data - United States of America, Bureau of the Census. Twelfth Census of the United States, 1900. Washington, D.C.: National Archives and Records Administration, 1900. T623, 18), Ancestry.com, http://www.Ancestry.com, Year: 1900; Census Place: Allen, Calhoun, Alabama; Roll: T623_5; Page: 3B; Enumeration District: 32. Birth date: Aug 1895 Birth place: Alabama Residence date: 1900 Residence place: Precinct 8 Green's Schoolhouse, Calhoun, Alabama.

1441   Ancestry.com, 1900 United States Federal Census (Online publication - Provo, UT, USA: Ancestry.com Operations Inc, 2004. Original data - United States of America, Bureau of the Census. Twelfth Census of the United States, 1900. Washington, D.C.: National Archives and Records Administration, 1900. T623, 18), Ancestry.com, http://www.Ancestry.com, Year: 1900; Census Place: Allen, Calhoun, Alabama; Roll: T623_5; Page: 3B; Enumeration District: 32. Birth date: Sep 1897 Birth place: Alabama Residence date: 1900 Residence place: Precinct 8 Green's Schoolhouse, Calhoun, Alabama.

1442   Ancestry.com, 1900 United States Federal Census (Online publication - Provo, UT, USA: Ancestry.com Operations Inc, 2004. Original data - United States of America, Bureau of the Census. Twelfth Census of the United States, 1900. Washington, D.C.: National Archives and Records Administration, 1900. T623, 18), Ancestry.com, http://www.Ancestry.com, Year: 1900; Census Place: Allen, Calhoun, Alabama; Roll: T623_5; Page: 3B; Enumeration District: 32. Birth date: Nov 1898 Birth place: Alabama Residence date: 1900 Residence place: Precinct 8 Green's Schoolhouse, Calhoun, Alabama.

1443   Ancestry.com, 1920 United States Federal Census (Online publication - Provo, UT, USA: Ancestry.com Operations Inc, 2010. Images reproduced by FamilySearch. Original data - Fourteenth Census of the United States, 1920. (NARA microfilm publication T625, 2076 rolls). Records of the Bureau of the Census, Record), Ancestry.com, http://www.Ancestry.com, Year: 1920; Census Place: Gum Spring, Etowah, Alabama; Roll: T625_15; Page: 4B; Enumeration District: 110; Image:. Birth date: about 1907 Birth place: Alabama Residence date: 1920 Residence place: Gum Spring, Etowah, Alabama.

1444   Ancestry.com, 1920 United States Federal Census (Online publication - Provo, UT, USA: Ancestry.com Operations Inc, 2010. Images reproduced by FamilySearch. Original data - Fourteenth Census of the United States, 1920. (NARA microfilm publication T625, 2076 rolls). Records of the Bureau of the Census, Record), Ancestry.com, http://www.Ancestry.com, Year: 1920; Census Place: Gum Spring, Etowah, Alabama; Roll: T625_15; Page: 4B; Enumeration District: 110; Image:. Birth date: about 1909 Birth place: Alabama Residence date: 1920 Residence place: Gum Spring, Etowah, Alabama.

1445   Ancestry.com, 1920 United States Federal Census (Online publication - Provo, UT, USA: Ancestry.com Operations Inc, 2010. Images reproduced by FamilySearch. Original data - Fourteenth Census of the United States, 1920. (NARA microfilm publication T625, 2076 rolls). Records of the Bureau of the Census, Record), Ancestry.com,

http://www.Ancestry.com, Year: 1920; Census Place: Gum Spring, Etowah, Alabama; Roll: T625_15; Page: 4B; Enumeration District: 110; Image:. Birth date: about 1912 Birth place: Alabama Residence date: 1920 Residence place: Gum Spring, Etowah, Alabama.

1446   Ancestry.com, Social Security Death Index (Online publication - Provo, UT, USA: Ancestry.com Operations Inc, 2010. Original data - Social Security Administration. Social Security Death Index, Master File. Social Security Administration. Original data: Social Security Administration. Social Security D), Ancestry.com, http://www.Ancestry.com, Number: 417-66-8806; Issue State: Alabama; Issue Date: 1964. Birth date: 2 Apr 1914 Birth place: Death date: 11 Mar 1998 Death place: Gadsden, Etowah, Alabama, United States of America.

1447   Ancestry.com, 1910 United States Federal Census (Online publication - Provo, UT, USA: Ancestry.com Operations Inc, 2006. Original data - Thirteenth Census of the United States, 1910 (NARA microfilm publication T624, 1,178 rolls). Records of the Bureau of the Census, Record Group 29. National Archives, Washington), Ancestry.com, http://www.Ancestry.com, Year: 1910; Census Place: Greens Schoolhouse, Calhoun, Alabama; Roll: ; Page: ; Enumeration District: ; Image:. Birth date: about 1882 Birth place: Alabama Residence date: 1910 Residence place: Greens Schoolhouse, Calhoun, Alabama.

1448   Ancestry.com, 1910 United States Federal Census (Online publication - Provo, UT, USA: Ancestry.com Operations Inc, 2006. Original data - Thirteenth Census of the United States, 1910 (NARA microfilm publication T624, 1,178 rolls). Records of the Bureau of the Census, Record Group 29. National Archives, Washington), Ancestry.com, http://www.Ancestry.com, Year: 1910; Census Place: Greens Schoolhouse, Calhoun, Alabama; Roll: ; Page: ; Enumeration District: ; Image:. Birth date: about 1904 Birth place: Alabama Residence date: 1910 Residence place: Greens Schoolhouse, Calhoun, Alabama.

1449   Ancestry.com, 1910 United States Federal Census (Online publication - Provo, UT, USA: Ancestry.com Operations Inc, 2006. Original data - Thirteenth Census of the United States, 1910 (NARA microfilm publication T624, 1,178 rolls). Records of the Bureau of the Census, Record Group 29. National Archives, Washington), Ancestry.com, http://www.Ancestry.com, Year: 1910; Census Place: Greens Schoolhouse, Calhoun, Alabama; Roll: ; Page: ; Enumeration District: ; Image:. Birth date: about 1905 Birth place: Alabama Residence date: 1910 Residence place: Greens Schoolhouse, Calhoun, Alabama.

1450   Ancestry.com, 1910 United States Federal Census (Online publication - Provo, UT, USA: Ancestry.com Operations Inc, 2006. Original data - Thirteenth Census of the United States, 1910 (NARA microfilm publication T624, 1,178 rolls). Records of the Bureau of the Census, Record Group 29. National Archives, Washington), Ancestry.com, http://www.Ancestry.com, Year: 1910; Census Place: Greens Schoolhouse, Calhoun, Alabama; Roll: ; Page: ; Enumeration District: ; Image:. Birth date: about 1909 Birth place: Alabama Residence date: 1910 Residence place: Greens Schoolhouse, Calhoun, Alabama.

1451   Ancestry.com, 1910 United States Federal Census (Online publication - Provo, UT, USA: Ancestry.com Operations Inc, 2006. Original data - Thirteenth Census of the United States, 1910 (NARA microfilm publication T624, 1,178 rolls). Records of the Bureau of the Census, Record Group 29. National Archives, Washington), Ancestry.com, http://www.Ancestry.com, Year: 1910; Census Place: Greens Schoolhouse, Calhoun, Alabama; Roll: ; Page: ; Enumeration District: ; Image:. Birth date: about 1875 Birth place: Alabama Residence date: 1910 Residence place: Greens Schoolhouse, Calhoun, Alabama.

1452   Ancestry.com, 1900 United States Federal Census (Online publication - Provo, UT, USA: Ancestry.com Operations Inc, 2004. Original data - United States of America, Bureau of the Census. Twelfth Census of the United States, 1900. Washington, D.C.: National Archives and Records Administration, 1900. T623, 18), Ancestry.com, http://www.Ancestry.com, Year: 1900; Census Place: Allen, Calhoun, Alabama; Roll: T623_5; Page: 3B; Enumeration District: 32. Birth date: Mar 1898 Birth place: Alabama Residence date: 1900 Residence place: Precinct 8 Green's Schoolhouse, Calhoun, Alabama.

1453   Ancestry.com, 1910 United States Federal Census (Online publication - Provo, UT, USA: Ancestry.com Operations Inc, 2006. Original data - Thirteenth Census of the United States, 1910 (NARA microfilm publication T624, 1,178 rolls). Records of the Bureau of the Census, Record Group 29. National Archives, Washington), Ancestry.com, http://www.Ancestry.com, Year: 1860; Census Place: Philadelphia Ward 3, Philadelphia, Pennsylvania; Roll: ; Page: 471; Image: 477. Birth date: about 1898 Birth place: Alabama Residence date: 1910 Residence place: Greens Schoolhouse, Calhoun, Alabama.

1454   Ancestry.com, 1900 United States Federal Census (Online publication - Provo, UT, USA: Ancestry.com Operations Inc, 2004. Original data - United States of America, Bureau of the Census. Twelfth Census of the United States, 1900. Washington, D.C.: National Archives and Records Administration, 1900. T623, 18), Ancestry.com, http://www.Ancestry.com, Year: 1900; Census Place: Allen, Calhoun, Alabama; Roll: T623_5; Page: 3B; Enumeration District: 32. Birth date: Jul 1899 Birth place: Alabama Residence date: 1900 Residence place: Precinct 8 Green's Schoolhouse, Calhoun, Alabama.

1455   Ancestry.com, 1910 United States Federal Census (Online publication - Provo, UT, USA: Ancestry.com Operations Inc, 2006. Original data - Thirteenth Census of the United States, 1910 (NARA microfilm publication T624, 1,178 rolls). Records of the Bureau of the Census, Record Group 29. National Archives, Washington), Ancestry.com, http://www.Ancestry.com, Year: 1910; Census Place: Greens Schoolhouse, Calhoun, Alabama; Roll: ; Page: ; Enumeration District: ; Image:. Birth date: about 1899 Birth place: Alabama Residence date: 1910 Residence place: Greens Schoolhouse, Calhoun, Alabama.

1456   Ancestry.com, 1910 United States Federal Census (Online publication - Provo, UT, USA: Ancestry.com Operations Inc, 2006. Original data - Thirteenth Census of the United States, 1910 (NARA microfilm publication T624, 1,178 rolls). Records of the Bureau of the Census, Record Group 29. National Archives, Washington), Ancestry.com, http://www.Ancestry.com, Year: 1910; Census Place: Greens Schoolhouse, Calhoun, Alabama; Roll: ; Page: ; Enumeration District: ; Image:. Birth date: about 1901 Birth place: Alabama Residence date: 1910 Residence place: Greens Schoolhouse, Calhoun, Alabama.

1457   Ancestry.com, 1910 United States Federal Census (Online publication - Provo, UT, USA: Ancestry.com Operations Inc, 2006. Original data - Thirteenth Census of the United States, 1910 (NARA microfilm publication T624, 1,178 rolls). Records of the Bureau of the Census, Record Group 29. National Archives, Washington), Ancestry.com, http://www.Ancestry.com, Year: 1910; Census Place: Greens Schoolhouse, Calhoun, Alabama; Roll: ; Page: ; Enumeration District: ; Image:. Birth date: about 1903 Birth place: Alabama Residence date: 1910 Residence place: Greens Schoolhouse, Calhoun, Alabama.

1458   Ancestry.com, 1910 United States Federal Census (Online publication - Provo, UT, USA: Ancestry.com Operations Inc, 2006. Original data - Thirteenth Census of the United States, 1910 (NARA microfilm publication T624, 1,178 rolls). Records of the Bureau of the Census, Record Group 29. National Archives, Washington), Ancestry.com, http://www.Ancestry.com, Year: 1910; Census Place: Greens Schoolhouse, Calhoun, Alabama; Roll: ; Page: ; Enumeration District: ; Image:. Birth date: about 1905 Birth place: Alabama Residence date: 1910 Residence place: Greens Schoolhouse, Calhoun, Alabama.

1459   Ancestry.com, 1910 United States Federal Census (Online publication - Provo, UT, USA: Ancestry.com Operations Inc, 2006. Original data - Thirteenth Census of the United States, 1910 (NARA microfilm publication T624, 1,178 rolls). Records of the Bureau of the Census, Record Group 29. National Archives, Washington), Ancestry.com, http://www.Ancestry.com, Year: 1910; Census Place: Greens Schoolhouse, Calhoun, Alabama; Roll: ; Page: ; Enumeration District: ; Image:. Birth date: about 1908 Birth place: Alabama Residence date: 1910 Residence place: Greens Schoolhouse, Calhoun, Alabama.

1460   Ancestry.com, 1910 United States Federal Census (Online publication - Provo, UT, USA: Ancestry.com Operations Inc, 2006. Original data - Thirteenth Census of the United States, 1910 (NARA microfilm publication T624, 1,178 rolls). Records of the Bureau of the Census, Record Group 29. National Archives, Washington), Ancestry.com, http://www.Ancestry.com, Year: 1910; Census Place: Greens Schoolhouse, Calhoun, Alabama; Roll: ; Page: ; Enumeration District: ; Image:. Birth date: about 1910 Birth place: Alabama Residence date: 1910 Residence place: Greens Schoolhouse, Calhoun, Alabama.

1461   Ancestry.com, 1920 United States Federal Census (Online publication - Provo, UT, USA: Ancestry.com Operations Inc, 2010. Images reproduced by FamilySearch. Original data - Fourteenth Census of the United States, 1920. (NARA microfilm publication T625, 2076 rolls). Records of the Bureau of the Census, Record), Ancestry.com, http://www.Ancestry.com, Year: 1920; Census Place: Oxford, Calhoun, Alabama; Roll: T625_5; Page: 10A; Enumeration District: 16; Image:. Birth date: about 1903 Birth place: Alabama Residence date: 1920 Residence place: Oxford, Calhoun, Alabama.

1462   Ancestry.com, 1910 United States Federal Census (Online publication - Provo, UT, USA: Ancestry.com Operations Inc, 2006. Original data - Thirteenth Census of the United States, 1910 (NARA microfilm publication T624, 1,178 rolls). Records of the Bureau of the Census, Record Group 29. National Archives, Washington), Ancestry.com, http://www.Ancestry.com, Year: 1910; Census Place: Greens Schoolhouse, Calhoun, Alabama; Roll: ; Page: ; Enumeration District: ; Image:. Birth date: about 1903 Birth place: Alabama Residence date: 1910 Residence place: Greens Schoolhouse, Calhoun, Alabama.

1463   Ancestry.com, 1930 United States Federal Census (Online publication - Provo, UT, USA: Ancestry.com Operations Inc, 2002. Original data - United States of America, Bureau of the Census. Fifteenth Census of the United States, 1930. Washington, D.C.: National Archives and Records Administration, 1930. T626,), Ancestry.com, http://www.Ancestry.com, Year: 1930; Census Place: Oxford, Calhoun, Alabama; Roll: 5; Page: 5A; Enumeration District: 20; Image: 484.0. Birth date: about 1902 Birth place: Alabama Residence date: 1930 Residence place: Oxford, Calhoun, Alabama.

1464   Ancestry.com, 1910 United States Federal Census (Online publication - Provo, UT, USA: Ancestry.com Operations Inc, 2006. Original data - Thirteenth Census of the United States, 1910 (NARA microfilm publication T624, 1,178 rolls). Records of the Bureau of the Census, Record Group 29. National Archives, Washington), Ancestry.com, http://www.Ancestry.com, Year: 1910; Census Place: Greens Schoolhouse, Calhoun, Alabama; Roll: ; Page: ; Enumeration District: ; Image:. Birth date: about 1904 Birth place: Alabama Residence date: 1910 Residence place: Greens Schoolhouse, Calhoun, Alabama.

1465   Ancestry.com, Social Security Death Index (Online publication - Provo, UT, USA: Ancestry.com Operations Inc, 2010. Original data - Social Security Administration. Social Security Death Index, Master File. Social Security Administration. Original data: Social Security Administration. Social Security D), Ancestry.com, http://www.Ancestry.com, Number: 417-30-3266; Issue State: Alabama; Issue Date: Before 1951. Birth date: 23 Jan 1904 Birth place: Death date: Jan 1984 Death place: Alexandria, Calhoun, Alabama, United States of America.

1466   Ancestry.com, 1930 United States Federal Census (Online publication - Provo, UT, USA: Ancestry.com Operations Inc, 2002. Original data - United States of America, Bureau of the Census. Fifteenth Census of the United States, 1930. Washington, D.C.: National Archives and Records Administration, 1930. T626,), Ancestry.com,

http://www.Ancestry.com, Year: 1930; Census Place: Oxford, Calhoun, Alabama; Roll: 5; Page: 17B; Enumeration District: 20; Image: 509.0. Birth date: about 1905 Birth place: Residence date: 1930 Residence place: Oxford, Calhoun, Alabama.

1467   Ancestry.com, 1920 United States Federal Census (Online publication - Provo, UT, USA: Ancestry.com Operations Inc, 2010. Images reproduced by FamilySearch. Original data - Fourteenth Census of the United States, 1920. (NARA microfilm publication T625, 2076 rolls). Records of the Bureau of the Census, Record), Ancestry.com, http://www.Ancestry.com, Year: 1920; Census Place: Oxford, Calhoun, Alabama; Roll: T625_5; Page: 10A; Enumeration District: 16; Image:. Birth date: about 1904 Birth place: Alabama Residence date: 1920 Residence place: Oxford, Calhoun, Alabama.

1468   Ancestry.com, 1910 United States Federal Census (Online publication - Provo, UT, USA: Ancestry.com Operations Inc, 2006. Original data - Thirteenth Census of the United States, 1910 (NARA microfilm publication T624, 1,178 rolls). Records of the Bureau of the Census, Record Group 29. National Archives, Washington), Ancestry.com, http://www.Ancestry.com, Year: 1910; Census Place: Greens Schoolhouse, Calhoun, Alabama; Roll: ; Page: ; Enumeration District: ; Image:. Birth date: about 1906 Birth place: Alabama Residence date: 1910 Residence place: Greens Schoolhouse, Calhoun, Alabama.

1469   Ancestry.com, 1920 United States Federal Census (Online publication - Provo, UT, USA: Ancestry.com Operations Inc, 2010. Images reproduced by FamilySearch. Original data - Fourteenth Census of the United States, 1920. (NARA microfilm publication T625, 2076 rolls). Records of the Bureau of the Census, Record), Ancestry.com, http://www.Ancestry.com, Year: 1920; Census Place: Oxford, Calhoun, Alabama; Roll: T625_5; Page: 10A; Enumeration District: 16; Image:. Birth date: about 1912 Birth place: Alabama Residence date: 1920 Residence place: Oxford, Calhoun, Alabama.

1470   Ancestry.com, 1920 United States Federal Census (Online publication - Provo, UT, USA: Ancestry.com Operations Inc, 2010. Images reproduced by FamilySearch. Original data - Fourteenth Census of the United States, 1920. (NARA microfilm publication T625, 2076 rolls). Records of the Bureau of the Census, Record), Ancestry.com, http://www.Ancestry.com, Year: 1920; Census Place: Oxford, Calhoun, Alabama; Roll: T625_5; Page: 10A; Enumeration District: 16; Image:. Birth date: about 1915 Birth place: Alabama Residence date: 1920 Residence place: Oxford, Calhoun, Alabama.

1471   Ancestry.com, Social Security Death Index (Online publication - Provo, UT, USA: Ancestry.com Operations Inc, 2010. Original data - Social Security Administration. Social Security Death Index, Master File. Social Security Administration. Original data: Social Security Administration. Social Security D), Ancestry.com, http://www.Ancestry.com, Number: 059-18-2393; Issue State: New York; Issue Date: Before 1951. Birth date: 13 Sep 1914 Birth place: Death date: 16 Jun 1990 Death place: Oswego, Oswego, New York, United States of America.

1472   Ancestry.com, 1920 United States Federal Census (Online publication - Provo, UT, USA: Ancestry.com Operations Inc, 2010. Images reproduced by FamilySearch. Original data - Fourteenth Census of the United States, 1920. (NARA microfilm publication T625, 2076 rolls). Records of the Bureau of the Census, Record), Ancestry.com, http://www.Ancestry.com, Year: 1920; Census Place: Ball Play, Etowah, Alabama; Roll: T625_15; Page: 3B; Enumeration District: 100; Image:. Birth date: about 1898 Birth place: Alabama Residence date: 1920 Residence place: Ball Play, Etowah, Alabama.

1473   Ancestry.com, 1920 United States Federal Census (Online publication - Provo, UT, USA: Ancestry.com Operations Inc, 2010. Images reproduced by FamilySearch. Original data - Fourteenth Census of the United States, 1920. (NARA microfilm publication T625, 2076 rolls). Records of the Bureau of the Census, Record), Ancestry.com, http://www.Ancestry.com, Year: 1920; Census Place: Ball Play, Etowah, Alabama; Roll: T625_15; Page: 3B; Enumeration District: 100; Image:. Birth date: about 1917 Birth place: Alabama Residence date: 1920 Residence place: Ball Play, Etowah, Alabama.

1474   Ancestry.com, 1920 United States Federal Census (Online publication - Provo, UT, USA: Ancestry.com Operations Inc, 2010. Images reproduced by FamilySearch. Original data - Fourteenth Census of the United States, 1920. (NARA microfilm publication T625, 2076 rolls). Records of the Bureau of the Census, Record), Ancestry.com, http://www.Ancestry.com, Year: 1920; Census Place: Ball Play, Etowah, Alabama; Roll: T625_15; Page: 3B; Enumeration District: 100; Image:. Birth date: about 1919 Birth place: Alabama Residence date: 1920 Residence place: Ball Play, Etowah, Alabama.

1475   Ancestry.com, 1930 United States Federal Census (Online publication - Provo, UT, USA: Ancestry.com Operations Inc, 2002. Original data - United States of America, Bureau of the Census. Fifteenth Census of the United States, 1930. Washington, D.C.: National Archives and Records Administration, 1930. T626,), Ancestry.com, http://www.Ancestry.com, Year: 1930; Census Place: Greens Schoolhouse, Calhoun, Alabama; Roll: 5; Page: 4B; Enumeration District: 11; Image: 249.0. Birth date: about 1899 Birth place: Residence date: 1930 Residence place: Greens Schoolhouse, Calhoun, Alabama.

1476   Ancestry.com, 1920 United States Federal Census (Online publication - Provo, UT, USA: Ancestry.com Operations Inc, 2010. Images reproduced by FamilySearch. Original data - Fourteenth Census of the United States, 1920. (NARA microfilm publication T625, 2076 rolls). Records of the Bureau of the Census, Record), Ancestry.com, http://www.Ancestry.com, Year: 1920; Census Place: Greens Schoolhouse, Calhoun, Alabama; Roll: T625_5; Page: 4B; Enumeration District: 10; Image:. Birth date: about 1899 Birth place: North Carolina Residence date: 1920 Residence place: Greens Schoolhouse, Calhoun, Alabama.

1477   Ancestry.com, 1920 United States Federal Census (Online publication - Provo, UT, USA: Ancestry.com Operations Inc, 2010. Images reproduced by FamilySearch. Original data - Fourteenth Census of the United States, 1920.

(NARA microfilm publication T625, 2076 rolls). Records of the Bureau of the Census, Record), Ancestry.com, http://www.Ancestry.com, Year: 1920; Census Place: Greens Schoolhouse, Calhoun, Alabama; Roll: T625_5; Page: 4B; Enumeration District: 10; Image:. Birth date: about 1919 Birth place: Alabama Residence date: 1920 Residence place: Greens Schoolhouse, Calhoun, Alabama.

1478   Ancestry.com, 1930 United States Federal Census (Online publication - Provo, UT, USA: Ancestry.com Operations Inc, 2002. Original data - United States of America, Bureau of the Census. Fifteenth Census of the United States, 1930. Washington, D.C.: National Archives and Records Administration, 1930. T626,), Ancestry.com, http://www.Ancestry.com, Year: 1930; Census Place: Greens Schoolhouse, Calhoun, Alabama; Roll: 5; Page: 4B; Enumeration District: 11; Image: 249.0. Birth date: about 1919 Birth place: Residence date: 1930 Residence place: Greens Schoolhouse, Calhoun, Alabama.

1479   Ancestry.com, 1930 United States Federal Census (Online publication - Provo, UT, USA: Ancestry.com Operations Inc, 2002. Original data - United States of America, Bureau of the Census. Fifteenth Census of the United States, 1930. Washington, D.C.: National Archives and Records Administration, 1930. T626,), Ancestry.com, http://www.Ancestry.com, Year: 1930; Census Place: Greens Schoolhouse, Calhoun, Alabama; Roll: 5; Page: 4B; Enumeration District: 11; Image: 249.0. Birth date: about 1920 Birth place: Residence date: 1930 Residence place: Greens Schoolhouse, Calhoun, Alabama.

1480   Ancestry.com, 1930 United States Federal Census (Online publication - Provo, UT, USA: Ancestry.com Operations Inc, 2002. Original data - United States of America, Bureau of the Census. Fifteenth Census of the United States, 1930. Washington, D.C.: National Archives and Records Administration, 1930. T626,), Ancestry.com, http://www.Ancestry.com, Year: 1930; Census Place: Greens Schoolhouse, Calhoun, Alabama; Roll: 5; Page: 4B; Enumeration District: 11; Image: 249.0. Birth date: about 1922 Birth place: Residence date: 1930 Residence place: Greens Schoolhouse, Calhoun, Alabama.

1481   Ancestry.com, 1930 United States Federal Census (Online publication - Provo, UT, USA: Ancestry.com Operations Inc, 2002. Original data - United States of America, Bureau of the Census. Fifteenth Census of the United States, 1930. Washington, D.C.: National Archives and Records Administration, 1930. T626,), Ancestry.com, http://www.Ancestry.com, Year: 1930; Census Place: Greens Schoolhouse, Calhoun, Alabama; Roll: 5; Page: 4B; Enumeration District: 11; Image: 249.0. Birth date: about 1924 Birth place: Residence date: 1930 Residence place: Greens Schoolhouse, Calhoun, Alabama.

1482   Ancestry.com, 1930 United States Federal Census (Online publication - Provo, UT, USA: Ancestry.com Operations Inc, 2002. Original data - United States of America, Bureau of the Census. Fifteenth Census of the United States, 1930. Washington, D.C.: National Archives and Records Administration, 1930. T626,), Ancestry.com, http://www.Ancestry.com, Year: 1930; Census Place: Greens Schoolhouse, Calhoun, Alabama; Roll: 5; Page: 4B; Enumeration District: 11; Image: 249.0. Birth date: about 1928 Birth place: Residence date: 1930 Residence place: Greens Schoolhouse, Calhoun, Alabama.

1483   Ancestry.com, 1900 United States Federal Census (Online publication - Provo, UT, USA: Ancestry.com Operations Inc, 2004. Original data - United States of America, Bureau of the Census. Twelfth Census of the United States, 1900. Washington, D.C.: National Archives and Records Administration, 1900. T623, 18), Ancestry.com, http://www.Ancestry.com, Year: 1900; Census Place: Oxford, Calhoun, Alabama; Roll: T623_5; Page: 10B; Enumeration District: 37. Birth date: Dec 1874 Birth place: Alabama Marriage date: 1899 Marriage place: Residence date: 1900 Residence place: Precinct 13 (Excl. Hobson & Oxford Towns), Calhoun, Alabama.

1484   Ancestry.com, 1910 United States Federal Census (Online publication - Provo, UT, USA: Ancestry.com Operations Inc, 2006. Original data - Thirteenth Census of the United States, 1910 (NARA microfilm publication T624, 1,178 rolls). Records of the Bureau of the Census, Record Group 29. National Archives, Washington), Ancestry.com, http://www.Ancestry.com, Year: 1910; Census Place: Oxford, Calhoun, Alabama; Roll: ; Page: ; Enumeration District: ; Image:. Birth date: 1871 Birth place: Alabama Residence date: 1910 Residence place: Oxford, Calhoun, Alabama.

1485   Ancestry.com, 1920 United States Federal Census (Online publication - Provo, UT, USA: Ancestry.com Operations Inc, 2010. Images reproduced by FamilySearch. Original data - Fourteenth Census of the United States, 1920. (NARA microfilm publication T625, 2076 rolls). Records of the Bureau of the Census, Record), Ancestry.com, http://www.Ancestry.com, Year: 1920; Census Place: Oxford, Calhoun, Alabama; Roll: T625_5; Page: 7B; Enumeration District: 16; Image:. Birth date: about 1872 Birth place: Alabama Residence date: 1920 Residence place: Oxford, Calhoun, Alabama.

1486   Ancestry.com, Alabama Deaths, 1908-59 (Online publication - Provo, UT, USA: Ancestry.com Operations Inc, 2000. Original data - State of Alabama. Index of Vital Records for Alabama: Deaths, 1908-1959. Montgomery, AL, USA: State of Alabama Center for Health Statistics, Record Services Division. Original), Ancestry.com, http://www.Ancestry.com, Death date: 21 Jun 1951 Death place: Calhoun.

1487   Ancestry.com, 1900 United States Federal Census (Online publication - Provo, UT, USA: Ancestry.com Operations Inc, 2004. Original data - United States of America, Bureau of the Census. Twelfth Census of the United States, 1900. Washington, D.C.: National Archives and Records Administration, 1900. T623, 18), Ancestry.com, http://www.Ancestry.com, Year: 1900; Census Place: Oxford, Calhoun, Alabama; Roll: T623_5; Page: 10B; Enumeration District: 37. Birth date: Oct 1899 Birth place: Alabama Residence date: 1900 Residence place: Precinct 13 (Excl. Hobson & Oxford Towns), Calhoun, Alabama.

1488   Ancestry.com, 1910 United States Federal Census (Online publication - Provo, UT, USA: Ancestry.com Operations Inc, 2006. Original data - Thirteenth Census of the United States, 1910 (NARA microfilm publication T624,

1,178 rolls). Records of the Bureau of the Census, Record Group 29. National Archives, Washington), Ancestry.com, http://www.Ancestry.com, Year: 1910; Census Place: Oxford, Calhoun, Alabama; Roll: ; Page: ; Enumeration District: ; Image:. Birth date: 1900 Birth place: Alabama Residence date: 1910 Residence place: Oxford, Calhoun, Alabama.

1489   Ancestry.com, 1910 United States Federal Census (Online publication - Provo, UT, USA: Ancestry.com Operations Inc, 2006. Original data - Thirteenth Census of the United States, 1910 (NARA microfilm publication T624, 1,178 rolls). Records of the Bureau of the Census, Record Group 29. National Archives, Washington), Ancestry.com, http://www.Ancestry.com, Year: 1910; Census Place: Oxford, Calhoun, Alabama; Roll: ; Page: ; Enumeration District: ; Image:. Birth date: about 1883 Birth place: Georgia Residence date: 1910 Residence place: Oxford, Calhoun, Alabama.

1490   Ancestry.com, 1920 United States Federal Census (Online publication - Provo, UT, USA: Ancestry.com Operations Inc, 2010. Images reproduced by FamilySearch. Original data - Fourteenth Census of the United States, 1920. (NARA microfilm publication T625, 2076 rolls). Records of the Bureau of the Census, Record), Ancestry.com, http://www.Ancestry.com, Year: 1920; Census Place: Oxford, Calhoun, Alabama; Roll: T625_5; Page: 10B; Enumeration District: 16; Image:. Birth date: about 1883 Birth place: Georgia Residence date: 1920 Residence place: Oxford, Calhoun, Alabama.

1491   Ancestry.com, 1910 United States Federal Census (Online publication - Provo, UT, USA: Ancestry.com Operations Inc, 2006. Original data - Thirteenth Census of the United States, 1910 (NARA microfilm publication T624, 1,178 rolls). Records of the Bureau of the Census, Record Group 29. National Archives, Washington), Ancestry.com, http://www.Ancestry.com, Year: 1910; Census Place: Oxford, Calhoun, Alabama; Roll: ; Page: ; Enumeration District: ; Image:. Birth date: about 1902 Birth place: Alabama Residence date: 1910 Residence place: Oxford, Calhoun, Alabama.

1492   Ancestry.com, 1910 United States Federal Census (Online publication - Provo, UT, USA: Ancestry.com Operations Inc, 2006. Original data - Thirteenth Census of the United States, 1910 (NARA microfilm publication T624, 1,178 rolls). Records of the Bureau of the Census, Record Group 29. National Archives, Washington), Ancestry.com, http://www.Ancestry.com, Year: 1910; Census Place: Oxford, Calhoun, Alabama; Roll: ; Page: ; Enumeration District: ; Image:. Birth date: about 1903 Birth place: Alabama Residence date: 1910 Residence place: Oxford, Calhoun, Alabama.

1493   Ancestry.com, 1920 United States Federal Census (Online publication - Provo, UT, USA: Ancestry.com Operations Inc, 2010. Images reproduced by FamilySearch. Original data - Fourteenth Census of the United States, 1920. (NARA microfilm publication T625, 2076 rolls). Records of the Bureau of the Census, Record), Ancestry.com, http://www.Ancestry.com, Year: 1920; Census Place: Oxford, Calhoun, Alabama; Roll: T625_5; Page: 10B; Enumeration District: 16; Image:. Birth date: about 1903 Birth place: Alabama Residence date: 1920 Residence place: Oxford, Calhoun, Alabama.

1494   Ancestry.com, 1920 United States Federal Census (Online publication - Provo, UT, USA: Ancestry.com Operations Inc, 2010. Images reproduced by FamilySearch. Original data - Fourteenth Census of the United States, 1920. (NARA microfilm publication T625, 2076 rolls). Records of the Bureau of the Census, Record), Ancestry.com, http://www.Ancestry.com, Year: 1920; Census Place: Oxford, Calhoun, Alabama; Roll: T625_5; Page: 10B; Enumeration District: 16; Image:. Birth date: about 1905 Birth place: Alabama Residence date: 1920 Residence place: Oxford, Calhoun, Alabama.

1495   Ancestry.com, 1910 United States Federal Census (Online publication - Provo, UT, USA: Ancestry.com Operations Inc, 2006. Original data - Thirteenth Census of the United States, 1910 (NARA microfilm publication T624, 1,178 rolls). Records of the Bureau of the Census, Record Group 29. National Archives, Washington), Ancestry.com, http://www.Ancestry.com, Year: 1910; Census Place: Oxford, Calhoun, Alabama; Roll: ; Page: ; Enumeration District: ; Image:. Birth date: about 1906 Birth place: Alabama Residence date: 1910 Residence place: Oxford, Calhoun, Alabama.

1496   Ancestry.com, 1910 United States Federal Census (Online publication - Provo, UT, USA: Ancestry.com Operations Inc, 2006. Original data - Thirteenth Census of the United States, 1910 (NARA microfilm publication T624, 1,178 rolls). Records of the Bureau of the Census, Record Group 29. National Archives, Washington), Ancestry.com, http://www.Ancestry.com, Year: 1910; Census Place: Oxford, Calhoun, Alabama; Roll: ; Page: ; Enumeration District: ; Image:. Birth date: about 1909 Birth place: Alabama Residence date: 1910 Residence place: Oxford, Calhoun, Alabama.

1497   Ancestry.com, 1920 United States Federal Census (Online publication - Provo, UT, USA: Ancestry.com Operations Inc, 2010. Images reproduced by FamilySearch. Original data - Fourteenth Census of the United States, 1920. (NARA microfilm publication T625, 2076 rolls). Records of the Bureau of the Census, Record), Ancestry.com, http://www.Ancestry.com, Year: 1920; Census Place: Oxford, Calhoun, Alabama; Roll: T625_5; Page: 10B; Enumeration District: 16; Image:. Birth date: about 1909 Birth place: Alabama Residence date: 1920 Residence place: Oxford, Calhoun, Alabama.

1498   Ancestry.com, 1930 United States Federal Census (Online publication - Provo, UT, USA: Ancestry.com Operations Inc, 2002. Original data - United States of America, Bureau of the Census. Fifteenth Census of the United States, 1930. Washington, D.C.: National Archives and Records Administration, 1930. T626,), Ancestry.com, http://www.Ancestry.com, Year: 1930; Census Place: Oxford, Calhoun, Alabama; Roll: 5; Page: 1B; Enumeration District: 20; Image: 477.0. Birth date: about 1909 Birth place: Residence date: 1930 Residence place: Oxford, Calhoun, Alabama.

1499   Ancestry.com, 1920 United States Federal Census (Online publication - Provo, UT, USA: Ancestry.com Operations Inc, 2010. Images reproduced by FamilySearch. Original data - Fourteenth Census of the United States, 1920. (NARA microfilm publication T625, 2076 rolls). Records of the Bureau of the Census, Record), Ancestry.com, http://www.Ancestry.com, Year: 1920; Census Place: Oxford, Calhoun, Alabama; Roll: T625_5; Page: 10B; Enumeration District: 16; Image:. Birth date: about 1915 Birth place: Alabama Residence date: 1920 Residence place: Oxford, Calhoun, Alabama.

1500   Ancestry.com, 1920 United States Federal Census (Online publication - Provo, UT, USA: Ancestry.com Operations Inc, 2010. Images reproduced by FamilySearch. Original data - Fourteenth Census of the United States, 1920. (NARA microfilm publication T625, 2076 rolls). Records of the Bureau of the Census, Record), Ancestry.com, http://www.Ancestry.com, Year: 1920; Census Place: Oxford, Calhoun, Alabama; Roll: T625_5; Page: 10B; Enumeration District: 16; Image:. Birth date: about 1917 Birth place: Alabama Residence date: 1920 Residence place: Oxford, Calhoun, Alabama.

1501   Ancestry.com, 1930 United States Federal Census (Online publication - Provo, UT, USA: Ancestry.com Operations Inc, 2002. Original data - United States of America, Bureau of the Census. Fifteenth Census of the United States, 1930. Washington, D.C.: National Archives and Records Administration, 1930. T626,), Ancestry.com, http://www.Ancestry.com, Year: 1930; Census Place: Oxford, Calhoun, Alabama; Roll: 5; Page: 1B; Enumeration District: 20; Image: 477.0. Birth date: about 1917 Birth place: Residence date: 1930 Residence place: Oxford, Calhoun, Alabama.

1502   Ancestry.com, 1920 United States Federal Census (Online publication - Provo, UT, USA: Ancestry.com Operations Inc, 2010. Images reproduced by FamilySearch. Original data - Fourteenth Census of the United States, 1920. (NARA microfilm publication T625, 2076 rolls). Records of the Bureau of the Census, Record), Ancestry.com, http://www.Ancestry.com, Year: 1920; Census Place: Oxford, Calhoun, Alabama; Roll: T625_5; Page: 10B; Enumeration District: 16; Image:. Birth date: about 1920 Birth place: Alabama Residence date: 1920 Residence place: Oxford, Calhoun, Alabama.

1503   Ancestry.com, 1930 United States Federal Census (Online publication - Provo, UT, USA: Ancestry.com Operations Inc, 2002. Original data - United States of America, Bureau of the Census. Fifteenth Census of the United States, 1930. Washington, D.C.: National Archives and Records Administration, 1930. T626,), Ancestry.com, http://www.Ancestry.com, Year: 1930; Census Place: Oxford, Calhoun, Alabama; Roll: 5; Page: 1B; Enumeration District: 20; Image: 477.0. Birth date: about 1920 Birth place: Residence date: 1930 Residence place: Oxford, Calhoun, Alabama.

1504   Ancestry.com, 1930 United States Federal Census (Online publication - Provo, UT, USA: Ancestry.com Operations Inc, 2002. Original data - United States of America, Bureau of the Census. Fifteenth Census of the United States, 1930. Washington, D.C.: National Archives and Records Administration, 1930. T626,), Ancestry.com, http://www.Ancestry.com, Year: 1930; Census Place: Oxford, Calhoun, Alabama; Roll: 5; Page: 3A; Enumeration District: 20; Image: 480.0. Birth date: about 1899 Birth place: Alabama Residence date: 1930 Residence place: Oxford, Calhoun, Alabama.

1505   Ancestry.com, 1910 United States Federal Census (Online publication - Provo, UT, USA: Ancestry.com Operations Inc, 2006. Original data - Thirteenth Census of the United States, 1910 (NARA microfilm publication T624, 1,178 rolls). Records of the Bureau of the Census, Record Group 29. National Archives, Washington), Ancestry.com, http://www.Ancestry.com, Year: 1910; Census Place: Weaver, Calhoun, Alabama; Roll: ; Page: ; Enumeration District: ; Image:. Birth date: about 1875 Birth place: Alabama Residence date: 1910 Residence place: Weaver, Calhoun, Alabama.

1506   Ancestry.com, 1920 United States Federal Census (Online publication - Provo, UT, USA: Ancestry.com Operations Inc, 2010. Images reproduced by FamilySearch. Original data - Fourteenth Census of the United States, 1920. (NARA microfilm publication T625, 2076 rolls). Records of the Bureau of the Census, Record), Ancestry.com, http://www.Ancestry.com, Year: 1920; Census Place: Weavers, Calhoun, Alabama; Roll: T625_5; Page: 10B; Enumeration District: 4; Image:. Birth date: about 1876 Birth place: Alabama Residence date: 1920 Residence place: Weavers, Calhoun, Alabama.

1507   Ancestry.com, 1910 United States Federal Census (Online publication - Provo, UT, USA: Ancestry.com Operations Inc, 2006. Original data - Thirteenth Census of the United States, 1910 (NARA microfilm publication T624, 1,178 rolls). Records of the Bureau of the Census, Record Group 29. National Archives, Washington), Ancestry.com, http://www.Ancestry.com, Year: 1910; Census Place: Weaver, Calhoun, Alabama; Roll: ; Page: ; Enumeration District: ; Image:. Birth date: about 1900 Birth place: Alabama Residence date: 1910 Residence place: Weaver, Calhoun, Alabama.

1508   Ancestry.com, 1920 United States Federal Census (Online publication - Provo, UT, USA: Ancestry.com Operations Inc, 2010. Images reproduced by FamilySearch. Original data - Fourteenth Census of the United States, 1920. (NARA microfilm publication T625, 2076 rolls). Records of the Bureau of the Census, Record), Ancestry.com, http://www.Ancestry.com, Year: 1920; Census Place: Weavers, Calhoun, Alabama; Roll: T625_5; Page: 10B; Enumeration District: 4; Image:. Birth date: about 1901 Birth place: Alabama Residence date: 1920 Residence place: Weavers, Calhoun, Alabama.

1509   Ancestry.com, 1900 United States Federal Census (Online publication - Provo, UT, USA: Ancestry.com Operations Inc, 2004. Original data - United States of America, Bureau of the Census. Twelfth Census of the United States, 1900. Washington, D.C.: National Archives and Records Administration, 1900. T623, 18), Ancestry.com, http://www.Ancestry.com, Year: 1900; Census Place: Weavers, Calhoun, Alabama; Roll: T623_5; Page: 4B; Enumeration District: 27. Birth date: Feb 1900 Birth place: Alabama Residence date: 1900 Residence place: Weavers, Calhoun, Alabama.

1510   Ancestry.com, 1910 United States Federal Census (Online publication - Provo, UT, USA: Ancestry.com Operations Inc, 2006. Original data - Thirteenth Census of the United States, 1910 (NARA microfilm publication T624, 1,178 rolls). Records of the Bureau of the Census, Record Group 29. National Archives, Washington), Ancestry.com, http://www.Ancestry.com, Year: 1910; Census Place: Weaver, Calhoun, Alabama; Roll: ; Page: ; Enumeration District: ; Image:. Birth date: about 1902 Birth place: Alabama Residence date: 1910 Residence place: Weaver, Calhoun, Alabama.

1511   Ancestry.com, 1910 United States Federal Census (Online publication - Provo, UT, USA: Ancestry.com Operations Inc, 2006. Original data - Thirteenth Census of the United States, 1910 (NARA microfilm publication T624,

246

1,178 rolls). Records of the Bureau of the Census, Record Group 29. National Archives, Washington), Ancestry.com, http://www.Ancestry.com, Year: 1910; Census Place: Weaver, Calhoun, Alabama; Roll: ; Page: ; Enumeration District: ; Image:. Birth date: about 1904 Birth place: Alabama Residence date: 1910 Residence place: Weaver, Calhoun, Alabama.

1512   Ancestry.com, 1920 United States Federal Census (Online publication - Provo, UT, USA: Ancestry.com Operations Inc, 2010. Images reproduced by FamilySearch. Original data - Fourteenth Census of the United States, 1920. (NARA microfilm publication T625, 2076 rolls). Records of the Bureau of the Census, Record), Ancestry.com, http://www.Ancestry.com, Year: 1920; Census Place: Weavers, Calhoun, Alabama; Roll: T625_5; Page: 10B; Enumeration District: 4; Image:. Birth date: about 1905 Birth place: Alabama Residence date: 1920 Residence place: Weavers, Calhoun, Alabama.

1513   Ancestry.com, 1910 United States Federal Census (Online publication - Provo, UT, USA: Ancestry.com Operations Inc, 2006. Original data - Thirteenth Census of the United States, 1910 (NARA microfilm publication T624, 1,178 rolls). Records of the Bureau of the Census, Record Group 29. National Archives, Washington), Ancestry.com, http://www.Ancestry.com, Year: 1910; Census Place: Weaver, Calhoun, Alabama; Roll: ; Page: ; Enumeration District: ; Image:. Birth date: about 1907 Birth place: Alabama Residence date: 1910 Residence place: Weaver, Calhoun, Alabama.

1514   Ancestry.com, 1920 United States Federal Census (Online publication - Provo, UT, USA: Ancestry.com Operations Inc, 2010. Images reproduced by FamilySearch. Original data - Fourteenth Census of the United States, 1920. (NARA microfilm publication T625, 2076 rolls). Records of the Bureau of the Census, Record), Ancestry.com, http://www.Ancestry.com, Year: 1920; Census Place: Weavers, Calhoun, Alabama; Roll: T625_5; Page: 10B; Enumeration District: 4; Image:. Birth date: about 1907 Birth place: Alabama Residence date: 1920 Residence place: Weavers, Calhoun, Alabama.

1515   Ancestry.com, 1930 United States Federal Census (Online publication - Provo, UT, USA: Ancestry.com Operations Inc, 2002. Original data - United States of America, Bureau of the Census. Fifteenth Census of the United States, 1930. Washington, D.C.: National Archives and Records Administration, 1930. T626,), Ancestry.com, http://www.Ancestry.com, Year: 1930; Census Place: Weavers, Calhoun, Alabama; Roll: 5; Page: 4A; Enumeration District: 5; Image: 128.0. Birth date: about 1911 Birth place: Residence date: 1930 Residence place: Weavers, Calhoun, Alabama.

1516   Ancestry.com, 1920 United States Federal Census (Online publication - Provo, UT, USA: Ancestry.com Operations Inc, 2010. Images reproduced by FamilySearch. Original data - Fourteenth Census of the United States, 1920. (NARA microfilm publication T625, 2076 rolls). Records of the Bureau of the Census, Record), Ancestry.com, http://www.Ancestry.com, Year: 1920; Census Place: Weavers, Calhoun, Alabama; Roll: T625_5; Page: 10B; Enumeration District: 4; Image:. Birth date: about 1910 Birth place: Alabama Residence date: 1920 Residence place: Weavers, Calhoun, Alabama.

1517   Ancestry.com, 1910 United States Federal Census (Online publication - Provo, UT, USA: Ancestry.com Operations Inc, 2006. Original data - Thirteenth Census of the United States, 1910 (NARA microfilm publication T624, 1,178 rolls). Records of the Bureau of the Census, Record Group 29. National Archives, Washington), Ancestry.com, http://www.Ancestry.com, Year: 1910; Census Place: Weaver, Calhoun, Alabama; Roll: ; Page: ; Enumeration District: ; Image:. Birth date: about 1910 Birth place: Alabama Residence date: 1910 Residence place: Weaver, Calhoun, Alabama.

1518   Ancestry.com, 1930 United States Federal Census (Online publication - Provo, UT, USA: Ancestry.com Operations Inc, 2002. Original data - United States of America, Bureau of the Census. Fifteenth Census of the United States, 1930. Washington, D.C.: National Archives and Records Administration, 1930. T626,), Ancestry.com, http://www.Ancestry.com, Year: 1930; Census Place: Weavers, Calhoun, Alabama; Roll: 5; Page: 4A; Enumeration District: 5; Image: 128.0. Birth date: about 1913 Birth place: Residence date: 1930 Residence place: Weavers, Calhoun, Alabama.

1519   Ancestry.com, 1920 United States Federal Census (Online publication - Provo, UT, USA: Ancestry.com Operations Inc, 2010. Images reproduced by FamilySearch. Original data - Fourteenth Census of the United States, 1920. (NARA microfilm publication T625, 2076 rolls). Records of the Bureau of the Census, Record), Ancestry.com, http://www.Ancestry.com, Year: 1920; Census Place: Weavers, Calhoun, Alabama; Roll: T625_5; Page: 10B; Enumeration District: 4; Image:. Birth date: about 1913 Birth place: Alabama Residence date: 1920 Residence place: Weavers, Calhoun, Alabama.

1520   Ancestry.com, 1930 United States Federal Census (Online publication - Provo, UT, USA: Ancestry.com Operations Inc, 2002. Original data - United States of America, Bureau of the Census. Fifteenth Census of the United States, 1930. Washington, D.C.: National Archives and Records Administration, 1930. T626,), Ancestry.com, http://www.Ancestry.com, Year: 1930; Census Place: Weavers, Calhoun, Alabama; Roll: 5; Page: 4A; Enumeration District: 5; Image: 128.0. Birth date: about 1920 Birth place: Residence date: 1930 Residence place: Weavers, Calhoun, Alabama.

1521   Ancestry.com, 1910 United States Federal Census (Online publication - Provo, UT, USA: Ancestry.com Operations Inc, 2006. Original data - Thirteenth Census of the United States, 1910 (NARA microfilm publication T624, 1,178 rolls). Records of the Bureau of the Census, Record Group 29. National Archives, Washington), Ancestry.com, http://www.Ancestry.com, Year: 1910; Census Place: Weaver, Calhoun, Alabama; Roll: ; Page: ; Enumeration District: ; Image:. Birth date: about 1879 Birth place: Alabama Residence date: 1910 Residence place: Weaver, Calhoun, Alabama.

1522   Ancestry.com, 1910 United States Federal Census (Online publication - Provo, UT, USA: Ancestry.com Operations Inc, 2006. Original data - Thirteenth Census of the United States, 1910 (NARA microfilm publication T624, 1,178 rolls). Records of the Bureau of the Census, Record Group 29. National Archives, Washington), Ancestry.com,

http://www.Ancestry.com, Year: 1910; Census Place: Weaver, Calhoun, Alabama; Roll: ; Page: ; Enumeration District: ; Image:. Birth date: about 1906 Birth place: Alabama Residence date: 1910 Residence place: Weaver, Calhoun, Alabama.

1523   Ancestry.com, 1910 United States Federal Census (Online publication - Provo, UT, USA: Ancestry.com Operations Inc, 2006. Original data - Thirteenth Census of the United States, 1910 (NARA microfilm publication T624, 1,178 rolls). Records of the Bureau of the Census, Record Group 29. National Archives, Washington), Ancestry.com, http://www.Ancestry.com, Year: 1910; Census Place: Weaver, Calhoun, Alabama; Roll: ; Page: ; Enumeration District: ; Image:. Birth date: about 1907 Birth place: Alabama Residence date: 1910 Residence place: Weaver, Calhoun, Alabama.

1524   Ancestry.com, 1910 United States Federal Census (Online publication - Provo, UT, USA: Ancestry.com Operations Inc, 2006. Original data - Thirteenth Census of the United States, 1910 (NARA microfilm publication T624, 1,178 rolls). Records of the Bureau of the Census, Record Group 29. National Archives, Washington), Ancestry.com, http://www.Ancestry.com, Year: 1910; Census Place: Weaver, Calhoun, Alabama; Roll: ; Page: ; Enumeration District: ; Image:. Birth date: about 1908 Birth place: Alabama Residence date: 1910 Residence place: Weaver, Calhoun, Alabama.

1525   Ancestry.com, 1910 United States Federal Census (Online publication - Provo, UT, USA: Ancestry.com Operations Inc, 2006. Original data - Thirteenth Census of the United States, 1910 (NARA microfilm publication T624, 1,178 rolls). Records of the Bureau of the Census, Record Group 29. National Archives, Washington), Ancestry.com, http://www.Ancestry.com, Year: 1910; Census Place: Weaver, Calhoun, Alabama; Roll: ; Page: ; Enumeration District: ; Image:. Birth date: about 1909 Birth place: Alabama Residence date: 1910 Residence place: Weaver, Calhoun, Alabama.

1526   Ancestry.com, Georgia Deaths, 1919-98 (Online publication - Provo, UT, USA: Ancestry.com Operations Inc, 2001. Original data - State of Georgia. Indexes of Vital Records for Georgia: Deaths, 1919-1998. Georgia, USA: Georgia Health Department, Office of Vital Records, 1998. Original data: State of), Ancestry.com, http://www.Ancestry.com, Certificate number: 11068. Birth date: about 1887 Birth place: Death date: 21 May 1956 Death place: Floyd, Georgia Residence date: Residence place: Floyd.

1527   Ancestry.com, 1910 United States Federal Census (Online publication - Provo, UT, USA: Ancestry.com Operations Inc, 2006. Original data - Thirteenth Census of the United States, 1910 (NARA microfilm publication T624, 1,178 rolls). Records of the Bureau of the Census, Record Group 29. National Archives, Washington), Ancestry.com, http://www.Ancestry.com, Year: 1910; Census Place: Jacksonville, Calhoun, Alabama; Roll: ; Page: ; Enumeration District: ; Image:. Birth date: about 1887 Birth place: Georgia Residence date: 1910 Residence place: Jacksonville, Calhoun, Alabama.

1528   Ancestry.com, 1930 United States Federal Census (Online publication - Provo, UT, USA: Ancestry.com Operations Inc, 2002. Original data - United States of America, Bureau of the Census. Fifteenth Census of the United States, 1930. Washington, D.C.: National Archives and Records Administration, 1930. T626,), Ancestry.com, http://www.Ancestry.com, Year: 1930; Census Place: Rome, Floyd, Georgia; Roll: 356; Page: 2A; Enumeration District: 21; Image: 594.0. Birth date: about 1889 Birth place: Residence date: 1930 Residence place: Rome, Floyd, Georgia.

1529   Ancestry.com, 1920 United States Federal Census (Online publication - Provo, UT, USA: Ancestry.com Operations Inc, 2010. Images reproduced by FamilySearch. Original data - Fourteenth Census of the United States, 1920. (NARA microfilm publication T625, 2076 rolls). Records of the Bureau of the Census, Record), Ancestry.com, http://www.Ancestry.com, Year: 1920; Census Place: Menlo, Chattooga, Georgia; Roll: T625_242; Page: 3B; Enumeration District: 34; Image:. Birth date: about 1888 Birth place: Georgia Residence date: 1920 Residence place: Menlo, Chattooga, Georgia.

1530   Ancestry.com, 1930 United States Federal Census (Online publication - Provo, UT, USA: Ancestry.com Operations Inc, 2002. Original data - United States of America, Bureau of the Census. Fifteenth Census of the United States, 1930. Washington, D.C.: National Archives and Records Administration, 1930. T626,), Ancestry.com, http://www.Ancestry.com, Year: 1930; Census Place: Rome, Floyd, Georgia; Roll: 356; Page: 2A; Enumeration District: 21; Image: 594.0. Birth date: about 1911 Birth place: Residence date: 1930 Residence place: Rome, Floyd, Georgia.

1531   Ancestry.com, 1910 United States Federal Census (Online publication - Provo, UT, USA: Ancestry.com Operations Inc, 2006. Original data - Thirteenth Census of the United States, 1910 (NARA microfilm publication T624, 1,178 rolls). Records of the Bureau of the Census, Record Group 29. National Archives, Washington), Ancestry.com, http://www.Ancestry.com, Year: 1910; Census Place: Jacksonville, Calhoun, Alabama; Roll: ; Page: ; Enumeration District: ; Image:. Birth date: about 1909 Birth place: Alabama Residence date: 1910 Residence place: Jacksonville, Calhoun, Alabama.

1532   Ancestry.com, 1920 United States Federal Census (Online publication - Provo, UT, USA: Ancestry.com Operations Inc, 2010. Images reproduced by FamilySearch. Original data - Fourteenth Census of the United States, 1920. (NARA microfilm publication T625, 2076 rolls). Records of the Bureau of the Census, Record), Ancestry.com, http://www.Ancestry.com, Year: 1920; Census Place: Menlo, Chattooga, Georgia; Roll: T625_242; Page: 3B; Enumeration District: 34; Image:. Birth date: about 1910 Birth place: Alabama Residence date: 1920 Residence place: Menlo, Chattooga, Georgia.

1533   Ancestry.com, Social Security Death Index (Online publication - Provo, UT, USA: Ancestry.com Operations Inc, 2010. Original data - Social Security Administration. Social Security Death Index, Master File. Social Security Administration. Original data: Social Security Administration. Social Security D), Ancestry.com, http://www.Ancestry.com, Number: 258-50-9242; Issue State: Georgia; Issue Date: 1951. Birth date: 22 Mar 1909 Birth place: Death date: 17 Oct 1993 Death place: LaGrange, Troup, Georgia, United States of America.

1534	Ancestry.com, Georgia Deaths, 1919-98 (Online publication - Provo, UT, USA: Ancestry.com Operations Inc, 2001. Original data - State of Georgia. Indexes of Vital Records for Georgia: Deaths, 1919-1998. Georgia, USA: Georgia Health Department, Office of Vital Records, 1998. Original data: State of), Ancestry.com, http://www.Ancestry.com, Certificate number: 046005. Birth date: about 1909 Birth place: Death date: 17 Oct 1993 Death place: Troup, Georgia Residence date: Residence place: Troup.

1535	Ancestry.com, 1920 United States Federal Census (Online publication - Provo, UT, USA: Ancestry.com Operations Inc, 2010. Images reproduced by FamilySearch. Original data - Fourteenth Census of the United States, 1920. (NARA microfilm publication T625, 2076 rolls). Records of the Bureau of the Census, Record), Ancestry.com, http://www.Ancestry.com, Year: 1920; Census Place: Menlo, Chattooga, Georgia; Roll: T625_242; Page: 3B; Enumeration District: 34; Image:. Birth date: about 1912 Birth place: Alabama Residence date: 1920 Residence place: Menlo, Chattooga, Georgia.

1536	Ancestry.com, 1930 United States Federal Census (Online publication - Provo, UT, USA: Ancestry.com Operations Inc, 2002. Original data - United States of America, Bureau of the Census. Fifteenth Census of the United States, 1930. Washington, D.C.: National Archives and Records Administration, 1930. T626,), Ancestry.com, http://www.Ancestry.com, Year: 1930; Census Place: Rome, Floyd, Georgia; Roll: 356; Page: 2A; Enumeration District: 21; Image: 594.0. Birth date: about 1913 Birth place: Residence date: 1930 Residence place: Rome, Floyd, Georgia.

1537	Ancestry.com, 1920 United States Federal Census (Online publication - Provo, UT, USA: Ancestry.com Operations Inc, 2010. Images reproduced by FamilySearch. Original data - Fourteenth Census of the United States, 1920. (NARA microfilm publication T625, 2076 rolls). Records of the Bureau of the Census, Record), Ancestry.com, http://www.Ancestry.com, Year: 1920; Census Place: Menlo, Chattooga, Georgia; Roll: T625_242; Page: 3B; Enumeration District: 34; Image:. Birth date: about 1914 Birth place: Alabama Residence date: 1920 Residence place: Menlo, Chattooga, Georgia.

1538	Ancestry.com, 1930 United States Federal Census (Online publication - Provo, UT, USA: Ancestry.com Operations Inc, 2002. Original data - United States of America, Bureau of the Census. Fifteenth Census of the United States, 1930. Washington, D.C.: National Archives and Records Administration, 1930. T626,), Ancestry.com, http://www.Ancestry.com, Year: 1930; Census Place: Rome, Floyd, Georgia; Roll: 356; Page: 2A; Enumeration District: 21; Image: 594.0. Birth date: about 1915 Birth place: Residence date: 1930 Residence place: Rome, Floyd, Georgia.

1539	Ancestry.com, 1920 United States Federal Census (Online publication - Provo, UT, USA: Ancestry.com Operations Inc, 2010. Images reproduced by FamilySearch. Original data - Fourteenth Census of the United States, 1920. (NARA microfilm publication T625, 2076 rolls). Records of the Bureau of the Census, Record), Ancestry.com, http://www.Ancestry.com, Year: 1920; Census Place: Menlo, Chattooga, Georgia; Roll: T625_242; Page: 3B; Enumeration District: 34; Image:. Birth date: about 1916 Birth place: Texas Residence date: 1920 Residence place: Menlo, Chattooga, Georgia.

1540	Ancestry.com, 1930 United States Federal Census (Online publication - Provo, UT, USA: Ancestry.com Operations Inc, 2002. Original data - United States of America, Bureau of the Census. Fifteenth Census of the United States, 1930. Washington, D.C.: National Archives and Records Administration, 1930. T626,), Ancestry.com, http://www.Ancestry.com, Year: 1930; Census Place: Rome, Floyd, Georgia; Roll: 356; Page: 2A; Enumeration District: 21; Image: 594.0. Birth date: about 1916 Birth place: Residence date: 1930 Residence place: Rome, Floyd, Georgia.

1541	Ancestry.com, 1920 United States Federal Census (Online publication - Provo, UT, USA: Ancestry.com Operations Inc, 2010. Images reproduced by FamilySearch. Original data - Fourteenth Census of the United States, 1920. (NARA microfilm publication T625, 2076 rolls). Records of the Bureau of the Census, Record), Ancestry.com, http://www.Ancestry.com, Year: 1920; Census Place: Menlo, Chattooga, Georgia; Roll: T625_242; Page: 3B; Enumeration District: 34; Image:. Birth date: about 1918 Birth place: Georgia Residence date: 1920 Residence place: Menlo, Chattooga, Georgia.

1542	Ancestry.com, 1930 United States Federal Census (Online publication - Provo, UT, USA: Ancestry.com Operations Inc, 2002. Original data - United States of America, Bureau of the Census. Fifteenth Census of the United States, 1930. Washington, D.C.: National Archives and Records Administration, 1930. T626,), Ancestry.com, http://www.Ancestry.com, Year: 1930; Census Place: Rome, Floyd, Georgia; Roll: 356; Page: 2A; Enumeration District: 21; Image: 594.0. Birth date: about 1918 Birth place: Residence date: 1930 Residence place: Rome, Floyd, Georgia.

1543	Ancestry.com, 1930 United States Federal Census (Online publication - Provo, UT, USA: Ancestry.com Operations Inc, 2002. Original data - United States of America, Bureau of the Census. Fifteenth Census of the United States, 1930. Washington, D.C.: National Archives and Records Administration, 1930. T626,), Ancestry.com, http://www.Ancestry.com, Year: 1930; Census Place: Rome, Floyd, Georgia; Roll: 356; Page: 2A; Enumeration District: 21; Image: 594.0. Birth date: about 1921 Birth place: Residence date: 1930 Residence place: Rome, Floyd, Georgia.

1544	Ancestry.com, 1930 United States Federal Census (Online publication - Provo, UT, USA: Ancestry.com Operations Inc, 2002. Original data - United States of America, Bureau of the Census. Fifteenth Census of the United States, 1930. Washington, D.C.: National Archives and Records Administration, 1930. T626,), Ancestry.com, http://www.Ancestry.com, Year: 1930; Census Place: Rome, Floyd, Georgia; Roll: 356; Page: 2A; Enumeration District: 21; Image: 594.0. Birth date: about 1923 Birth place: Residence date: 1930 Residence place: Rome, Floyd, Georgia.

1545	Ancestry.com, 1900 United States Federal Census (Online publication - Provo, UT, USA: Ancestry.com Operations Inc, 2004. Original data - United States of America, Bureau of the Census. Twelfth Census of the United States, 1900. Washington, D.C.: National Archives and Records Administration, 1900. T623, 18), Ancestry.com, http://www.Ancestry.com, Year: 1900; Census Place: Polkville, Calhoun, Alabama; Roll: T623_5; Page: 5A; Enumeration

249

District: 29. Birth date: Jun 1875 Birth place: Alabama Marriage date: 1896 Marriage place: Residence date: 1900 Residence place: Polkville, Calhoun, Alabama.

1546   Ancestry.com, 1910 United States Federal Census (Online publication - Provo, UT, USA: Ancestry.com Operations Inc, 2006. Original data - Thirteenth Census of the United States, 1910 (NARA microfilm publication T624, 1,178 rolls). Records of the Bureau of the Census, Record Group 29. National Archives, Washington), Ancestry.com, http://www.Ancestry.com, Year: 1910; Census Place: Polkville, Calhoun, Alabama; Roll: ; Page: ; Enumeration District: ; Image:. Birth date: about 1876 Birth place: Alabama Residence date: 1910 Residence place: Polkville, Calhoun, Alabama.

1547   Ancestry.com, 1920 United States Federal Census (Online publication - Provo, UT, USA: Ancestry.com Operations Inc, 2010. Images reproduced by FamilySearch. Original data - Fourteenth Census of the United States, 1920. (NARA microfilm publication T625, 2076 rolls). Records of the Bureau of the Census, Record), Ancestry.com, http://www.Ancestry.com, Year: 1920; Census Place: Polkville, Calhoun, Alabama; Roll: T625_5; Page: 2A; Enumeration District: 7; Image:. Birth date: about 1898 Birth place: Alabama Residence date: 1920 Residence place: Polkville, Calhoun, Alabama.

1548   Ancestry.com, 1900 United States Federal Census (Online publication - Provo, UT, USA: Ancestry.com Operations Inc, 2004. Original data - United States of America, Bureau of the Census. Twelfth Census of the United States, 1900. Washington, D.C.: National Archives and Records Administration, 1900. T623, 18), Ancestry.com, http://www.Ancestry.com, Year: 1900; Census Place: Polkville, Calhoun, Alabama; Roll: T623_5; Page: 5A; Enumeration District: 29. Birth date: Mar 1897 Birth place: Alabama Residence date: 1900 Residence place: Polkville, Calhoun, Alabama.

1549   Ancestry.com, 1910 United States Federal Census (Online publication - Provo, UT, USA: Ancestry.com Operations Inc, 2006. Original data - Thirteenth Census of the United States, 1910 (NARA microfilm publication T624, 1,178 rolls). Records of the Bureau of the Census, Record Group 29. National Archives, Washington), Ancestry.com, http://www.Ancestry.com, Year: 1910; Census Place: Polkville, Calhoun, Alabama; Roll: ; Page: ; Enumeration District: ; Image:. Birth date: about 1897 Birth place: Alabama Residence date: 1910 Residence place: Polkville, Calhoun, Alabama.

1550   Ancestry.com, 1900 United States Federal Census (Online publication - Provo, UT, USA: Ancestry.com Operations Inc, 2004. Original data - United States of America, Bureau of the Census. Twelfth Census of the United States, 1900. Washington, D.C.: National Archives and Records Administration, 1900. T623, 18), Ancestry.com, http://www.Ancestry.com, Year: 1900; Census Place: Polkville, Calhoun, Alabama; Roll: T623_5; Page: 5A; Enumeration District: 29. Birth date: May 1898 Birth place: Alabama Residence date: 1900 Residence place: Polkville, Calhoun, Alabama.

1551   Ancestry.com, 1910 United States Federal Census (Online publication - Provo, UT, USA: Ancestry.com Operations Inc, 2006. Original data - Thirteenth Census of the United States, 1910 (NARA microfilm publication T624, 1,178 rolls). Records of the Bureau of the Census, Record Group 29. National Archives, Washington), Ancestry.com, http://www.Ancestry.com, Year: 1910; Census Place: Polkville, Calhoun, Alabama; Roll: ; Page: ; Enumeration District: ; Image:. Birth date: about 1899 Birth place: Alabama Residence date: 1910 Residence place: Polkville, Calhoun, Alabama.

1552   Ancestry.com, 1900 United States Federal Census (Online publication - Provo, UT, USA: Ancestry.com Operations Inc, 2004. Original data - United States of America, Bureau of the Census. Twelfth Census of the United States, 1900. Washington, D.C.: National Archives and Records Administration, 1900. T623, 18), Ancestry.com, http://www.Ancestry.com, Year: 1900; Census Place: Polkville, Calhoun, Alabama; Roll: T623_5; Page: 5A; Enumeration District: 29. Birth date: Oct 1899 Birth place: Alabama Residence date: 1900 Residence place: Polkville, Calhoun, Alabama.

1553   Ancestry.com, 1910 United States Federal Census (Online publication - Provo, UT, USA: Ancestry.com Operations Inc, 2006. Original data - Thirteenth Census of the United States, 1910 (NARA microfilm publication T624, 1,178 rolls). Records of the Bureau of the Census, Record Group 29. National Archives, Washington), Ancestry.com, http://www.Ancestry.com, Year: 1910; Census Place: Polkville, Calhoun, Alabama; Roll: ; Page: ; Enumeration District: ; Image:. Birth date: about 1901 Birth place: Alabama Residence date: 1910 Residence place: Polkville, Calhoun, Alabama.

1554   Ancestry.com, 1910 United States Federal Census (Online publication - Provo, UT, USA: Ancestry.com Operations Inc, 2006. Original data - Thirteenth Census of the United States, 1910 (NARA microfilm publication T624, 1,178 rolls). Records of the Bureau of the Census, Record Group 29. National Archives, Washington), Ancestry.com, http://www.Ancestry.com, Year: 1910; Census Place: Polkville, Calhoun, Alabama; Roll: ; Page: ; Enumeration District: ; Image:. Birth date: about 1902 Birth place: Alabama Residence date: 1910 Residence place: Polkville, Calhoun, Alabama.

1555   Ancestry.com, 1910 United States Federal Census (Online publication - Provo, UT, USA: Ancestry.com Operations Inc, 2006. Original data - Thirteenth Census of the United States, 1910 (NARA microfilm publication T624, 1,178 rolls). Records of the Bureau of the Census, Record Group 29. National Archives, Washington), Ancestry.com, http://www.Ancestry.com, Year: 1910; Census Place: Polkville, Calhoun, Alabama; Roll: ; Page: ; Enumeration District: ; Image:. Birth date: about 1904 Birth place: Alabama Residence date: 1910 Residence place: Polkville, Calhoun, Alabama.

1556   Ancestry.com, 1910 United States Federal Census (Online publication - Provo, UT, USA: Ancestry.com Operations Inc, 2006. Original data - Thirteenth Census of the United States, 1910 (NARA microfilm publication T624, 1,178 rolls). Records of the Bureau of the Census, Record Group 29. National Archives, Washington), Ancestry.com, http://www.Ancestry.com, Year: 1910; Census Place: Polkville, Calhoun, Alabama; Roll: ; Page: ; Enumeration District: ; Image:. Birth date: about 1906 Birth place: Alabama Residence date: 1910 Residence place: Polkville, Calhoun, Alabama.

1557   Ancestry.com, 1910 United States Federal Census (Online publication - Provo, UT, USA: Ancestry.com Operations Inc, 2006. Original data - Thirteenth Census of the United States, 1910 (NARA microfilm publication T624, 1,178 rolls). Records of the Bureau of the Census, Record Group 29. National Archives, Washington), Ancestry.com, http://www.Ancestry.com, Year: 1910; Census Place: Polkville, Calhoun, Alabama; Roll: ; Page: ; Enumeration District: ; Image:. Birth date: about 1908 Birth place: Alabama Residence date: 1910 Residence place: Polkville, Calhoun, Alabama.

1558   Ancestry.com, 1920 United States Federal Census (Online publication - Provo, UT, USA: Ancestry.com Operations Inc, 2010. Images reproduced by FamilySearch. Original data - Fourteenth Census of the United States, 1920. (NARA microfilm publication T625, 2076 rolls). Records of the Bureau of the Census, Record), Ancestry.com, http://www.Ancestry.com, Year: 1920; Census Place: Polkville, Calhoun, Alabama; Roll: T625_5; Page: 2A; Enumeration District: 7; Image:. Birth date: about 1910 Birth place: Alabama Residence date: 1920 Residence place: Polkville, Calhoun, Alabama.

1559   Ancestry.com, 1930 United States Federal Census (Online publication - Provo, UT, USA: Ancestry.com Operations Inc, 2002. Original data - United States of America, Bureau of the Census. Fifteenth Census of the United States, 1930. Washington, D.C.: National Archives and Records Administration, 1930. T626,), Ancestry.com, http://www.Ancestry.com, Year: 1930; Census Place: Polkville, Calhoun, Alabama; Roll: 5; Page: 1B; Enumeration District: 8; Image: 199.0. Birth date: about 1911 Birth place: Residence date: 1930 Residence place: Polkville, Calhoun, Alabama.

1560   Ancestry.com, 1920 United States Federal Census (Online publication - Provo, UT, USA: Ancestry.com Operations Inc, 2010. Images reproduced by FamilySearch. Original data - Fourteenth Census of the United States, 1920. (NARA microfilm publication T625, 2076 rolls). Records of the Bureau of the Census, Record), Ancestry.com, http://www.Ancestry.com, Year: 1920; Census Place: Polkville, Calhoun, Alabama; Roll: T625_5; Page: 1B; Enumeration District: 7; Image:. Birth date: about 1889 Birth place: Alabama Residence date: 1920 Residence place: Polkville, Calhoun, Alabama.

1561   Ancestry.com, 1920 United States Federal Census (Online publication - Provo, UT, USA: Ancestry.com Operations Inc, 2010. Images reproduced by FamilySearch. Original data - Fourteenth Census of the United States, 1920. (NARA microfilm publication T625, 2076 rolls). Records of the Bureau of the Census, Record), Ancestry.com, http://www.Ancestry.com, Year: 1920; Census Place: Polkville, Calhoun, Alabama; Roll: T625_5; Page: 1B; Enumeration District: 7; Image:. Birth date: about 1912 Birth place: Alabama Residence date: 1920 Residence place: Polkville, Calhoun, Alabama.

1562   Ancestry.com, 1920 United States Federal Census (Online publication - Provo, UT, USA: Ancestry.com Operations Inc, 2010. Images reproduced by FamilySearch. Original data - Fourteenth Census of the United States, 1920. (NARA microfilm publication T625, 2076 rolls). Records of the Bureau of the Census, Record), Ancestry.com, http://www.Ancestry.com, Year: 1920; Census Place: Polkville, Calhoun, Alabama; Roll: T625_5; Page: 1B; Enumeration District: 7; Image:. Birth date: about 1913 Birth place: Alabama Residence date: 1920 Residence place: Polkville, Calhoun, Alabama.

1563   Ancestry.com, 1920 United States Federal Census (Online publication - Provo, UT, USA: Ancestry.com Operations Inc, 2010. Images reproduced by FamilySearch. Original data - Fourteenth Census of the United States, 1920. (NARA microfilm publication T625, 2076 rolls). Records of the Bureau of the Census, Record), Ancestry.com, http://www.Anccstry.com, Year: 1920; Census Place: Polkville, Calhoun, Alabama; Roll: T625_5; Page: 1B; Enumeration District: 7; Image:. Birth date: about 1915 Birth place: Alabama Residence date: 1920 Residence place: Polkville, Calhoun, Alabama.

1564   Ancestry.com, 1930 United States Federal Census (Online publication - Provo, UT, USA: Ancestry.com Operations Inc, 2002. Original data - United States of America, Bureau of the Census. Fifteenth Census of the United States, 1930. Washington, D.C.: National Archives and Records Administration, 1930. T626,), Ancestry.com, http://www.Ancestry.com, Year: 1930; Census Place: Turkey Creek, Stone, Arkansas; Roll: 95; Page: 1A; Enumeration District: 25; Image: 1179.0. Birth date: about 1910 Birth place: Arkansas Residence date: 1930 Residence place: Turkey Creek, Stone, Arkansas.

1565   Ancestry.com, 1930 United States Federal Census (Online publication - Provo, UT, USA: Ancestry.com Operations Inc, 2002. Original data - United States of America, Bureau of the Census. Fifteenth Census of the United States, 1930. Washington, D.C.: National Archives and Records Administration, 1930. T626,), Ancestry.com, http://www.Ancestry.com, Year: 1930; Census Place: Turkey Creek, Stone, Arkansas; Roll: 95; Page: 1A; Enumeration District: 25; Image: 1179.0. Birth date: about 1929 Birth place: Residence date: 1930 Residence place: Turkey Creek, Stone, Arkansas.

1566   Ancestry.com, 1930 United States Federal Census (Online publication - Provo, UT, USA: Ancestry.com Operations Inc, 2002. Original data - United States of America, Bureau of the Census. Fifteenth Census of the United States, 1930. Washington, D.C.: National Archives and Records Administration, 1930. T626,), Ancestry.com, http://www.Ancestry.com, Year: 1930; Census Place: Albertville, Marshall, Alabama; Roll: 39; Page: 1A; Enumeration District: 7; Image: 725.0. Birth date: about 1893 Birth place: Residence date: 1930 Residence place: Albertville, Marshall, Alabama.

1567   Ancestry.com, 1910 United States Federal Census (Online publication - Provo, UT, USA: Ancestry.com Operations Inc, 2006. Original data - Thirteenth Census of the United States, 1910 (NARA microfilm publication T624, 1,178 rolls). Records of the Bureau of the Census, Record Group 29. National Archives, Washington), Ancestry.com, http://www.Ancestry.com, Year: 1910; Census Place: Friendship, Marshall, Alabama; Roll: ; Page: ; Enumeration District: ;

Image:. Birth date: about 1893 Birth place: Alabama Residence date: 1910 Residence place: Friendship, Marshall, Alabama.

1568   Ancestry.com, 1920 United States Federal Census (Online publication - Provo, UT, USA: Ancestry.com Operations Inc, 2010. Images reproduced by FamilySearch. Original data - Fourteenth Census of the United States, 1920. (NARA microfilm publication T625, 2076 rolls). Records of the Bureau of the Census, Record), Ancestry.com, http://www.Ancestry.com, Year: 1920; Census Place: Albertville, Marshall, Alabama; Roll: T625_28; Page: 17A; Enumeration District: 122; Image:. Birth date: about 1894 Birth place: Alabama Residence date: 1920 Residence place: Albertville, Marshall, Alabama.

1569   Ancestry.com, 1900 United States Federal Census (Online publication - Provo, UT, USA: Ancestry.com Operations Inc, 2004. Original data - United States of America, Bureau of the Census. Twelfth Census of the United States, 1900. Washington, D.C.: National Archives and Records Administration, 1900. T623, 18), Ancestry.com, http://www.Ancestry.com, Year: 1900; Census Place: Friendship, Marshall, Alabama; Roll: T623_30; Page: 17B; Enumeration District: 92. Birth date: Jan 1893 Birth place: Alabama Residence date: 1900 Residence place: Friendship, Marshall, Alabama.

1570   Ancestry.com, Alabama Deaths, 1908-59 (Online publication - Provo, UT, USA: Ancestry.com Operations Inc, 2000. Original data - State of Alabama. Index of Vital Records for Alabama: Deaths, 1908-1959. Montgomery, AL, USA: State of Alabama Center for Health Statistics, Record Services Division. Original), Ancestry.com, http://www.Ancestry.com, Death date: 16 Jul 1954 Death place: Marshall.

1571   Ancestry.com, 1920 United States Federal Census (Online publication - Provo, UT, USA: Ancestry.com Operations Inc, 2010. Images reproduced by FamilySearch. Original data - Fourteenth Census of the United States, 1920. (NARA microfilm publication T625, 2076 rolls). Records of the Bureau of the Census, Record), Ancestry.com, http://www.Ancestry.com, Year: 1920; Census Place: Albertville, Marshall, Alabama; Roll: T625_28; Page: 17A; Enumeration District: 122; Image:. Birth date: about 1914 Birth place: Alabama Residence date: 1920 Residence place: Albertville, Marshall, Alabama.

1572   Ancestry.com, Social Security Death Index (Online publication - Provo, UT, USA: Ancestry.com Operations Inc, 2010. Original data - Social Security Administration. Social Security Death Index, Master File. Social Security Administration. Original data: Social Security Administration. Social Security D), Ancestry.com, http://www.Ancestry.com, Number: 420-01-7827; Issue State: Alabama; Issue Date: Before 1951. Birth date: 8 Jan 1914 Birth place: Death date: 21 Mar 1988 Death place: Lynchburg, Lynchburg City, Virginia, United States of America.

1573   Ancestry.com, 1920 United States Federal Census (Online publication - Provo, UT, USA: Ancestry.com Operations Inc, 2010. Images reproduced by FamilySearch. Original data - Fourteenth Census of the United States, 1920. (NARA microfilm publication T625, 2076 rolls). Records of the Bureau of the Census, Record), Ancestry.com, http://www.Ancestry.com, Year: 1920; Census Place: Albertville, Marshall, Alabama; Roll: T625_28; Page: 17A; Enumeration District: 122; Image:. Birth date: about 1916 Birth place: Alabama Residence date: 1920 Residence place: Albertville, Marshall, Alabama.

1574   Ancestry.com, Social Security Death Index (Online publication - Provo, UT, USA: Ancestry.com Operations Inc, 2010. Original data - Social Security Administration. Social Security Death Index, Master File. Social Security Administration. Original data: Social Security Administration. Social Security D), Ancestry.com, http://www.Ancestry.com, Number: 424-05-3052; Issue State: Alabama; Issue Date: Before 1951. Birth date: 23 Sep 1915 Birth place: Death date: 5 Mar 1994 Death place: Albertville, Marshall, Alabama, United States of America.

1575   Ancestry.com, 1920 United States Federal Census (Online publication - Provo, UT, USA: Ancestry.com Operations Inc, 2010. Images reproduced by FamilySearch. Original data - Fourteenth Census of the United States, 1920. (NARA microfilm publication T625, 2076 rolls). Records of the Bureau of the Census, Record), Ancestry.com, http://www.Ancestry.com, Year: 1920; Census Place: Albertville, Marshall, Alabama; Roll: T625_28; Page: 17A; Enumeration District: 122; Image:. Birth date: about 1919 Birth place: Alabama Residence date: 1920 Residence place: Albertville, Marshall, Alabama.

1576   Ancestry.com, 1930 United States Federal Census (Online publication - Provo, UT, USA: Ancestry.com Operations Inc, 2002. Original data - United States of America, Bureau of the Census. Fifteenth Census of the United States, 1930. Washington, D.C.: National Archives and Records Administration, 1930. T626,), Ancestry.com, http://www.Ancestry.com, Year: 1930; Census Place: Albertville, Marshall, Alabama; Roll: 39; Page: 1A; Enumeration District: 7; Image: 725.0. Birth date: about 1921 Birth place: Residence date: 1930 Residence place: Albertville, Marshall, Alabama.

1577   Ancestry.com, 1930 United States Federal Census (Online publication - Provo, UT, USA: Ancestry.com Operations Inc, 2002. Original data - United States of America, Bureau of the Census. Fifteenth Census of the United States, 1930. Washington, D.C.: National Archives and Records Administration, 1930. T626,), Ancestry.com, http://www.Ancestry.com, Year: 1930; Census Place: Albertville, Marshall, Alabama; Roll: 39; Page: 1A; Enumeration District: 7; Image: 725.0. Birth date: about 1924 Birth place: Residence date: 1930 Residence place: Albertville, Marshall, Alabama.

1578   Ancestry.com, Social Security Death Index (Online publication - Provo, UT, USA: Ancestry.com Operations Inc, 2010. Original data - Social Security Administration. Social Security Death Index, Master File. Social Security Administration. Original data: Social Security Administration. Social Security D), Ancestry.com, http://www.Ancestry.com, Number: 421-14-5803; Issue State: Alabama; Issue Date: Before 1951. Birth date: 14 Sep 1923 Birth place: Death date: Nov 1990 Death place:.

1579   Ancestry.com, 1930 United States Federal Census (Online publication - Provo, UT, USA: Ancestry.com Operations Inc, 2002. Original data - United States of America, Bureau of the Census. Fifteenth Census of the United States, 1930. Washington, D.C.: National Archives and Records Administration, 1930. T626,), Ancestry.com, http://www.Ancestry.com, Year: 1930; Census Place: Albertville, Marshall, Alabama; Roll: 39; Page: 1A; Enumeration District: 7; Image: 725.0. Birth date: about 1926 Birth place: Residence date: 1930 Residence place: Albertville, Marshall, Alabama.

1580   Ancestry.com, 1930 United States Federal Census (Online publication - Provo, UT, USA: Ancestry.com Operations Inc, 2002. Original data - United States of America, Bureau of the Census. Fifteenth Census of the United States, 1930. Washington, D.C.: National Archives and Records Administration, 1930. T626,), Ancestry.com, http://www.Ancestry.com, Year: 1930; Census Place: Albertville, Marshall, Alabama; Roll: 39; Page: 1A; Enumeration District: 7; Image: 725.0. Birth date: about 1928 Birth place: Residence date: 1930 Residence place: Albertville, Marshall, Alabama.

1581   Ancestry.com, 1920 United States Federal Census (Online publication - Provo, UT, USA: Ancestry.com Operations Inc, 2010. Images reproduced by FamilySearch. Original data - Fourteenth Census of the United States, 1920. (NARA microfilm publication T625, 2076 rolls). Records of the Bureau of the Census, Record), Ancestry.com, http://www.Ancestry.com, Year: 1920; Census Place: Albertville, Marshall, Alabama; Roll: T625_28; Page: 9A; Enumeration District: 122; Image:. Birth date: about 1894 Birth place: Alabama Residence date: 1920 Residence place: Albertville, Marshall, Alabama.

1582   Ancestry.com, 1920 United States Federal Census (Online publication - Provo, UT, USA: Ancestry.com Operations Inc, 2010. Images reproduced by FamilySearch. Original data - Fourteenth Census of the United States, 1920. (NARA microfilm publication T625, 2076 rolls). Records of the Bureau of the Census, Record), Ancestry.com, http://www.Ancestry.com, Year: 1920; Census Place: Albertville, Marshall, Alabama; Roll: T625_28; Page: 9A; Enumeration District: 122; Image:. Birth date: about 1916 Birth place: Alabama Residence date: 1920 Residence place: Albertville, Marshall, Alabama.

1583   Ancestry.com, 1920 United States Federal Census (Online publication - Provo, UT, USA: Ancestry.com Operations Inc, 2010. Images reproduced by FamilySearch. Original data - Fourteenth Census of the United States, 1920. (NARA microfilm publication T625, 2076 rolls). Records of the Bureau of the Census, Record), Ancestry.com, http://www.Ancestry.com, Year: 1920; Census Place: Albertville, Marshall, Alabama; Roll: T625_28; Page: 9A; Enumeration District: 122; Image:. Birth date: about 1919 Birth place: Alabama Residence date: 1920 Residence place: Albertville, Marshall, Alabama.

1584   Ancestry.com, 1920 United States Federal Census (Online publication - Provo, UT, USA: Ancestry.com Operations Inc, 2010. Images reproduced by FamilySearch. Original data - Fourteenth Census of the United States, 1920. (NARA microfilm publication T625, 2076 rolls). Records of the Bureau of the Census, Record), Ancestry.com, http://www.Ancestry.com, Year: 1920; Census Place: Crumley, DeKalb, Alabama; Roll: T625_12; Page: 5B; Enumeration District: 84; Image:. Birth date: about 1895 Birth place: Alabama Residence date: 1920 Residence place: Crumley, DeKalb, Alabama.

1585   Ancestry.com, 1910 United States Federal Census (Online publication - Provo, UT, USA: Ancestry.com Operations Inc, 2006. Original data - Thirteenth Census of the United States, 1910 (NARA microfilm publication T624, 1,178 rolls). Records of the Bureau of the Census, Record Group 29. National Archives, Washington), Ancestry.com, http://www.Ancestry.com, Year: 1910; Census Place: White Plains, Calhoun, Alabama; Roll: ; Page: ; Enumeration District: ; Image:. Birth date: about 1894 Birth place: Alabama Residence date: 1910 Residence place: White Plains, Calhoun, Alabama.

1586   Ancestry.com, 1930 United States Federal Census (Online publication - Provo, UT, USA: Ancestry.com Operations Inc, 2002. Original data - United States of America, Bureau of the Census. Fifteenth Census of the United States, 1930. Washington, D.C.: National Archives and Records Administration, 1930. T626,), Ancestry.com, http://www.Ancestry.com, Year: 1930; Census Place: Burns Cross Roads, Calhoun, Alabama; Roll: 5; Page: 18A; Enumeration District: 7; Image: 190.0. Birth date: about 1895 Birth place: Alabama Residence date: 1930 Residence place: Burns Cross Roads, Calhoun, Alabama.

1587   Ancestry.com, Alabama Deaths, 1908-59 (Online publication - Provo, UT, USA: Ancestry.com Operations Inc, 2000. Original data - State of Alabama. Index of Vital Records for Alabama: Deaths, 1908-1959. Montgomery, AL, USA: State of Alabama Center for Health Statistics, Record Services Division. Original), Ancestry.com, http://www.Ancestry.com, Death date: 10 May 1956 Death place: Calhoun.

1588   Ancestry.com, World War I Draft Registration Cards, 1917-1918 (Online publication - Provo, UT, USA: Ancestry.com Operations Inc, 2005. Original data - United States, Selective Service System. World War I Selective Service System Draft Registration Cards, 1917-1918. Washington, D.C.: National Archives and Records Administration), Ancestry.com, http://www.Ancestry.com, Registration Location: Calhoun County, Alabama; Roll: 1509364; Draft Board: 0. Birth date: 21 Jan 1895 Birth place: Residence date: Residence place: Calhoun, Alabama.

1589   Ancestry.com, Social Security Death Index (Online publication - Provo, UT, USA: Ancestry.com Operations Inc, 2010. Original data - Social Security Administration. Social Security Death Index, Master File. Social Security Administration. Original data: Social Security Administration. Social Security D), Ancestry.com, http://www.Ancestry.com, Number: 418-16-8485; Issue State: Alabama; Issue Date: Before 1951. Birth date: 1 Jun 1916 Birth place: Death date: 28 Sep 2002 Death place: Leavenworth, Leavenworth, Kansas, United States of America.

253

1590   Ancestry.com, 1920 United States Federal Census (Online publication - Provo, UT, USA: Ancestry.com Operations Inc, 2010. Images reproduced by FamilySearch. Original data - Fourteenth Census of the United States, 1920. (NARA microfilm publication T625, 2076 rolls). Records of the Bureau of the Census, Record), Ancestry.com, http://www.Ancestry.com, Year: 1920; Census Place: Crumley, DeKalb, Alabama; Roll: T625_12; Page: 5B; Enumeration District: 84; Image:. Birth date: about 1916 Birth place: Alabama Residence date: 1920 Residence place: Crumley, DeKalb, Alabama.

1591   Ancestry.com, 1930 United States Federal Census (Online publication - Provo, UT, USA: Ancestry.com Operations Inc, 2002. Original data - United States of America, Bureau of the Census. Fifteenth Census of the United States, 1930. Washington, D.C.: National Archives and Records Administration, 1930. T626,), Ancestry.com, http://www.Ancestry.com, Year: 1930; Census Place: Burns Cross Roads, Calhoun, Alabama; Roll: 5; Page: 18A; Enumeration District: 7; Image: 190.0. Birth date: about 1918 Birth place: Residence date: 1930 Residence place: Burns Cross Roads, Calhoun, Alabama.

1592   Ancestry.com, Alabama Divorce Index, 1950-1959 (Online publication - Provo, UT, USA: Ancestry.com Operations Inc, 2006. Original data - Alabama Center for Health Statistics. Alabama Divorce Index, 1950-1959. Montgomery, AL, USA: Alabama Center for Health Statistics. Original data: Alabama Center for Health), Ancestry.com, http://www.Ancestry.com, Divorce date: Jul 1954Divorce place: Calhoun, Alabama.

1593   Ancestry.com, 1920 United States Federal Census (Online publication - Provo, UT, USA: Ancestry.com Operations Inc, 2010. Images reproduced by FamilySearch. Original data - Fourteenth Census of the United States, 1920. (NARA microfilm publication T625, 2076 rolls). Records of the Bureau of the Census, Record), Ancestry.com, http://www.Ancestry.com, Year: 1920; Census Place: Crumley, DeKalb, Alabama; Roll: T625_12; Page: 5B; Enumeration District: 84; Image:.

1594   Ancestry.com, 1930 United States Federal Census (Online publication - Provo, UT, USA: Ancestry.com Operations Inc, 2002. Original data - United States of America, Bureau of the Census. Fifteenth Census of the United States, 1930. Washington, D.C.: National Archives and Records Administration, 1930. T626,), Ancestry.com, http://www.Ancestry.com, Year: 1930; Census Place: Burns Cross Roads, Calhoun, Alabama; Roll: 5; Page: 18A; Enumeration District: 7; Image: 190.0.

1595   Ancestry.com, 1920 United States Federal Census (Online publication - Provo, UT, USA: Ancestry.com Operations Inc, 2010. Images reproduced by FamilySearch. Original data - Fourteenth Census of the United States, 1920. (NARA microfilm publication T625, 2076 rolls). Records of the Bureau of the Census, Record), Ancestry.com, http://www.Ancestry.com, Year: 1920; Census Place: Crumley, DeKalb, Alabama; Roll: T625_12; Page: 5B; Enumeration District: 84; Image:. Birth date: about 1918 Birth place: Alabama Residence date: 1920 Residence place: Crumley, DeKalb, Alabama.

1596   Ancestry.com, 1930 United States Federal Census (Online publication - Provo, UT, USA: Ancestry.com Operations Inc, 2002. Original data - United States of America, Bureau of the Census. Fifteenth Census of the United States, 1930. Washington, D.C.: National Archives and Records Administration, 1930. T626,), Ancestry.com, http://www.Ancestry.com, Year: 1930; Census Place: Burns Cross Roads, Calhoun, Alabama; Roll: 5; Page: 18A; Enumeration District: 7; Image: 190.0. Birth date: about 1920 Birth place: Residence date: 1930 Residence place: Burns Cross Roads, Calhoun, Alabama.

1597   Ancestry.com, Social Security Death Index (Online publication - Provo, UT, USA: Ancestry.com Operations Inc, 2010. Original data - Social Security Administration. Social Security Death Index, Master File. Social Security Administration. Original data: Social Security Administration. Social Security D), Ancestry.com, http://www.Ancestry.com, Number: 424-56-8976; Issue State: Alabama; Issue Date: 1960. Birth date: 17 Sep 1921 Birth place: Death date: 3 Sep 1993 Death place: Heflin, Cleburne, Alabama, United States of America.

1598   Ancestry.com, 1930 United States Federal Census (Online publication - Provo, UT, USA: Ancestry.com Operations Inc, 2002. Original data - United States of America, Bureau of the Census. Fifteenth Census of the United States, 1930. Washington, D.C.: National Archives and Records Administration, 1930. T626,), Ancestry.com, http://www.Ancestry.com, Year: 1930; Census Place: Burns Cross Roads, Calhoun, Alabama; Roll: 5; Page: 18A; Enumeration District: 7; Image: 190.0. Birth date: about 1923 Birth place: Residence date: 1930 Residence place: Burns Cross Roads, Calhoun, Alabama.

1599   Ancestry.com, 1930 United States Federal Census (Online publication - Provo, UT, USA: Ancestry.com Operations Inc, 2002. Original data - United States of America, Bureau of the Census. Fifteenth Census of the United States, 1930. Washington, D.C.: National Archives and Records Administration, 1930. T626,), Ancestry.com, http://www.Ancestry.com, Year: 1930; Census Place: Burns Cross Roads, Calhoun, Alabama; Roll: 5; Page: 18A; Enumeration District: 7; Image: 190.0. Birth date: about 1925 Birth place: Residence date: 1930 Residence place: Burns Cross Roads, Calhoun, Alabama.

1600   Ancestry.com, Social Security Death Index (Online publication - Provo, UT, USA: Ancestry.com Operations Inc, 2010. Original data - Social Security Administration. Social Security Death Index, Master File. Social Security Administration. Original data: Social Security Administration. Social Security D), Ancestry.com, http://www.Ancestry.com, Number: 418-20-8153; Issue State: Alabama; Issue Date: Before 1951. Birth date: 29 Mar 1926 Birth place: Death date: 17 Oct 1995 Death place: Piedmont, Calhoun, Alabama, United States of America.

1601   Ancestry.com, 1930 United States Federal Census (Online publication - Provo, UT, USA: Ancestry.com Operations Inc, 2002. Original data - United States of America, Bureau of the Census. Fifteenth Census of the United States, 1930. Washington, D.C.: National Archives and Records Administration, 1930. T626,), Ancestry.com,

http://www.Ancestry.com, Year: 1930; Census Place: Burns Cross Roads, Calhoun, Alabama; Roll: 5; Page: 18A; Enumeration District: 7; Image: 190.0. Birth date: about 1926 Birth place: Residence date: 1930 Residence place: Burns Cross Roads, Calhoun, Alabama.

1602   Ancestry.com, Alabama Deaths, 1908-59 (Online publication - Provo, UT, USA: Ancestry.com Operations Inc, 2000. Original data - State of Alabama. Index of Vital Records for Alabama: Deaths, 1908-1959. Montgomery, AL, USA: State of Alabama Center for Health Statistics, Record Services Division. Original), Ancestry.com, http://www.Ancestry.com, Death date: Feb 1932 Death place: Calhoun.

1603   Ancestry.com, Alabama Deaths, 1908-59 (Online publication - Provo, UT, USA: Ancestry.com Operations Inc, 2000. Original data - State of Alabama. Index of Vital Records for Alabama: Deaths, 1908-1959. Montgomery, AL, USA: State of Alabama Center for Health Statistics, Record Services Division. Original), Ancestry.com, http://www.Ancestry.com, Death date: 12 Aug 1941 Death place: Calhoun.

1604   Ancestry.com, World War I Draft Registration Cards, 1917-1918 (Online publication - Provo, UT, USA: Ancestry.com Operations Inc, 2005. Original data - United States, Selective Service System. World War I Selective Service System Draft Registration Cards, 1917-1918. Washington, D.C.: National Archives and Records Administration), Ancestry.com, http://www.Ancestry.com, Registration Location: Calhoun County, Alabama; Roll: 1509364; Draft Board: 0. Birth date: 11 Jan 1889 Birth place: Residence date: Residence place: Calhoun, Alabama.

1605   Ancestry.com, 1900 United States Federal Census (Online publication - Provo, UT, USA: Ancestry.com Operations Inc, 2004. Original data - United States of America, Bureau of the Census. Twelfth Census of the United States, 1900. Washington, D.C.: National Archives and Records Administration, 1900. T623, 18), Ancestry.com, http://www.Ancestry.com, Year: 1900; Census Place: Alexandria, Calhoun, Alabama; Roll: T623_5; Page: 20B; Enumeration District: 26. Birth date: Jan 1889 Birth place: Alabama Residence date: 1900 Residence place: Alexandria, Calhoun, Alabama.

1606   Ancestry.com, Anniston Star (Anniston, Alabama) (Online publication - Provo, UT, USA: Ancestry.com Operations Inc, 2007. Original data - Anniston Star. Anniston, Alabama, United States Of America. Database created from microfilm copies of the newspaper. Original data: Anniston Star. Anniston, Alabama, Unit), Ancestry.com, http://www.Ancestry.com.

1607   Ancestry.com, Alabama Marriage Collection, 1800-1969 (Online publication - Provo, UT, USA: Ancestry.com Operations Inc, 2006. Original data - Alabama Center for Health Statistics. Alabama Marriage Index, 1936-1969. Alabama Center for Health Statistics, Montgomery, Alabama. Dodd, Jordan R., et. al. Early America), Ancestry.com, http://www.Ancestry.com, Marriage date: Jun 1962 Marriage place: Calhoun, Alabama.

1608   Ancestry.com, 1930 United States Federal Census (Online publication - Provo, UT, USA: Ancestry.com Operations Inc, 2002. Original data - United States of America, Bureau of the Census. Fifteenth Census of the United States, 1930. Washington, D.C.: National Archives and Records Administration, 1930. T626,), Ancestry.com, http://www.Ancestry.com, Year: 1930; Census Place: Gadsden, Etowah, Alabama; Roll: 16; Page: 17B; Enumeration District: 3; Image: 116.0. Birth date: about 1904 Birth place: Alabama Residence date: 1930 Residence place: Gadsden, Etowah, Alabama.

1609   Ancestry.com, Social Security Death Index (Online publication - Provo, UT, USA: Ancestry.com Operations Inc, 2010. Original data - Social Security Administration. Social Security Death Index, Master File. Social Security Administration. Original data: Social Security Administration. Social Security D), Ancestry.com, http://www.Ancestry.com, Number: 419-12-1238; Issue State: Alabama; Issue Date: Before 1951. Birth date: 21 Mar 1904 Birth place: Death date: May 1981 Death place: Gadsden, Etowah, Alabama, United States of America.

1610   Ancestry.com, 1920 United States Federal Census (Online publication - Provo, UT, USA: Ancestry.com Operations Inc, 2010. Images reproduced by FamilySearch. Original data - Fourteenth Census of the United States, 1920. (NARA microfilm publication T625, 2076 rolls). Records of the Bureau of the Census, Record), Ancestry.com, http://www.Ancestry.com, Year: 1920; Census Place: Fosters Mill, Floyd, Georgia; Roll: T625_257; Page: 3A; Enumeration District: 67; Image:. Birth date: about 1904 Birth place: Alabama Residence date: 1920 Residence place: Fosters Mill, Floyd, Georgia.

1611   Ancestry.com, 1910 United States Federal Census (Online publication - Provo, UT, USA: Ancestry.com Operations Inc, 2006. Original data - Thirteenth Census of the United States, 1910 (NARA microfilm publication T624, 1,178 rolls). Records of the Bureau of the Census, Record Group 29. National Archives, Washington), Ancestry.com, http://www.Ancestry.com, Year: 1910; Census Place: Anniston Ward 3, Calhoun, Alabama; Roll: ; Page: ; Enumeration District: ; Image:. Birth date: about 1904 Birth place: Alabama Residence date: 1910 Residence place: Anniston Ward 3, Calhoun, Alabama.

1612   Ancestry.com, 1930 United States Federal Census (Online publication - Provo, UT, USA: Ancestry.com Operations Inc, 2002. Original data - United States of America, Bureau of the Census. Fifteenth Census of the United States, 1930. Washington, D.C.: National Archives and Records Administration, 1930. T626,), Ancestry.com, http://www.Ancestry.com, Year: 1930; Census Place: Gadsden, Etowah, Alabama; Roll: 16; Page: 17B; Enumeration District: 3; Image: 116.0. Birth date: about 1925 Birth place: Residence date: 1930 Residence place: Gadsden, Etowah, Alabama.

1613   Ancestry.com, 1930 United States Federal Census (Online publication - Provo, UT, USA: Ancestry.com Operations Inc, 2002. Original data - United States of America, Bureau of the Census. Fifteenth Census of the United States, 1930. Washington, D.C.: National Archives and Records Administration, 1930. T626,), Ancestry.com,

255

http://www.Ancestry.com, Year: 1930; Census Place: Gadsden, Etowah, Alabama; Roll: 16; Page: 17B; Enumeration District: 3; Image: 116.0. Birth date: about 1927 Birth place: Residence date: 1930 Residence place: Gadsden, Etowah, Alabama.

1614   Ancestry.com, Alabama Marriage Collection, 1800-1969 (Online publication - Provo, UT, USA: Ancestry.com Operations Inc, 2006. Original data - Alabama Center for Health Statistics. Alabama Marriage Index, 1936-1969. Alabama Center for Health Statistics, Montgomery, Alabama. Dodd, Jordan R., et. al. Early America), Ancestry.com, http://www.Ancestry.com, Marriage date: 21 Jun 1953 Marriage place: Etowah, Alabama.

1615   Ancestry.com, Social Security Death Index (Online publication - Provo, UT, USA: Ancestry.com Operations Inc, 2010. Original data - Social Security Administration. Social Security Death Index, Master File. Social Security Administration. Original data: Social Security Administration. Social Security D), Ancestry.com, http://www.Ancestry.com, Number: 264-30-4829; Issue State: Florida; Issue Date: Before 1951. Birth date: 13 Nov 1927 Birth place: Death date: 4 Feb 1998 Death place: Gadsden, Etowah, Alabama, United States of America.

1616   Ancestry.com, 1930 United States Federal Census (Online publication - Provo, UT, USA: Ancestry.com Operations Inc, 2002. Original data - United States of America, Bureau of the Census. Fifteenth Census of the United States, 1930. Washington, D.C.: National Archives and Records Administration, 1930. T626,), Ancestry.com, http://www.Ancestry.com, Year: 1930; Census Place: Gadsden, Etowah, Alabama; Roll: 16; Page: 17B; Enumeration District: 3; Image: 116.0. Birth date: about 1930 Birth place: Residence date: 1930 Residence place: Gadsden, Etowah, Alabama.

1617   Ancestry.com, 1920 United States Federal Census (Online publication - Provo, UT, USA: Ancestry.com Operations Inc, 2010. Images reproduced by FamilySearch. Original data - Fourteenth Census of the United States, 1920. (NARA microfilm publication T625, 2076 rolls). Records of the Bureau of the Census, Record), Ancestry.com, http://www.Ancestry.com, Year: 1920; Census Place: Coldwater, Calhoun, Alabama; Roll: T625_5; Page: 14A; Enumeration District: 6; Image:. Birth date: about 1907 Birth place: Alabama Residence date: 1920 Residence place: Coldwater, Calhoun, Alabama.

1618   Ancestry.com, Social Security Death Index (Online publication - Provo, UT, USA: Ancestry.com Operations Inc, 2010. Original data - Social Security Administration. Social Security Death Index, Master File. Social Security Administration. Original data: Social Security Administration. Social Security D), Ancestry.com, http://www.Ancestry.com, Number: 422-01-0228; Issue State: Alabama; Issue Date: Before 1951. Birth date: 12 Nov 1906 Birth place: Death date: May 1983 Death place: Anniston, Calhoun, Alabama, United States of America.

1619   Ancestry.com, 1900 United States Federal Census (Online publication - Provo, UT, USA: Ancestry.com Operations Inc, 2004. Original data - United States of America, Bureau of the Census. Twelfth Census of the United States, 1900. Washington, D.C.: National Archives and Records Administration, 1900. T623, 18), Ancestry.com, http://www.Ancestry.com, Year: 1900; Census Place: Police Jury Ward 6, Lincoln, Louisiana; Roll: T623_568; Page: 14A; Enumeration District: 63. Birth date: Jun 1876 Birth place: Georgia Marriage date: 1892 Marriage place: Residence date: 1900 Residence place: Ward 7, Lincoln, Louisiana.

1620   Ancestry.com, 1900 United States Federal Census (Online publication - Provo, UT, USA: Ancestry.com Operations Inc, 2004. Original data - United States of America, Bureau of the Census. Twelfth Census of the United States, 1900. Washington, D.C.: National Archives and Records Administration, 1900. T623, 18), Ancestry.com, http://www.Ancestry.com, Year: 1900; Census Place: Police Jury Ward 6, Lincoln, Louisiana; Roll: T623_568; Page: 14A; Enumeration District: 63. Birth date: Apr 1899 Birth place: Louisiana Residence date: 1900 Residence place: Ward 7, Lincoln, Louisiana.

1621   Ancestry.com, 1900 United States Federal Census (Online publication - Provo, UT, USA: Ancestry.com Operations Inc, 2004. Original data - United States of America, Bureau of the Census. Twelfth Census of the United States, 1900. Washington, D.C.: National Archives and Records Administration, 1900. T623, 18), Ancestry.com, http://www.Ancestry.com, Year: 1900; Census Place: Justice Precinct 1, Coryell, Texas; Roll: T623_1624; Page: 15B; Enumeration District: 38. Birth date: May 1897 Birth place: Texas Residence date: 1900 Residence place: Justice Precinct 1 (West Part Excl. Gatesville City), Coryell, Texas.

1622   Ancestry.com, 1920 United States Federal Census (Online publication - Provo, UT, USA: Ancestry.com Operations Inc, 2010. Images reproduced by FamilySearch. Original data - Fourteenth Census of the United States, 1920. (NARA microfilm publication T625, 2076 rolls). Records of the Bureau of the Census, Record), Ancestry.com, http://www.Ancestry.com, Year: 1920; Census Place: Purcell, McClain, Oklahoma; Roll: T625_1470; Page: 30A; Enumeration District: 81; Image:. Birth date: about 1899 Birth place: Texas Residence date: 1920 Residence place: Purcell, McClain, Oklahoma.

1623   Ancestry.com, 1900 United States Federal Census (Online publication - Provo, UT, USA: Ancestry.com Operations Inc, 2004. Original data - United States of America, Bureau of the Census. Twelfth Census of the United States, 1900. Washington, D.C.: National Archives and Records Administration, 1900. T623, 18), Ancestry.com, http://www.Ancestry.com, Year: 1900; Census Place: Justice Precinct 1, Coryell, Texas; Roll: T623_1624; Page: 16B; Enumeration District: 38. Birth date: Jun 1869 Birth place: TexasMarriage date: 1893 Marriage place: Residence date: 1900 Residence place: Justice Precinct 1 (West Part Excl. Gatesville City), Coryell, Texas.

1624   Ancestry.com, 1910 United States Federal Census (Online publication - Provo, UT, USA: Ancestry.com Operations Inc, 2006. Original data - Thirteenth Census of the United States, 1910 (NARA microfilm publication T624, 1,178 rolls). Records of the Bureau of the Census, Record Group 29. National Archives, Washington), Ancestry.com, http://www.Ancestry.com, Year: 1910; Census Place: Justice Precinct 1, Coryell, Texas; Roll: ; Page: ; Enumeration

256

District: ; Image:. Birth date: 1871 Birth place: Texas Residence date: 1910 Residence place: Justice Precinct 1, Coryell, Texas.

1625   Ancestry.com, 1920 United States Federal Census (Online publication - Provo, UT, USA: Ancestry.com Operations Inc, 2010. Images reproduced by FamilySearch. Original data - Fourteenth Census of the United States, 1920. (NARA microfilm publication T625, 2076 rolls). Records of the Bureau of the Census, Record), Ancestry.com, http://www.Ancestry.com, Year: 1920; Census Place: Purcell, McClain, Oklahoma; Roll: T625_1470; Page: 30A; Enumeration District: 81; Image:. Birth date: about 1869 Birth place: Texas Residence date: 1920 Residence place: Purcell, McClain, Oklahoma.

1626   Ancestry.com, 1930 United States Federal Census (Online publication - Provo, UT, USA: Ancestry.com Operations Inc, 2002. Original data - United States of America, Bureau of the Census. Fifteenth Census of the United States, 1930. Washington, D.C.: National Archives and Records Administration, 1930. T626,), Ancestry.com, http://www.Ancestry.com, Year: 1930; Census Place: Precinct 3, Martin, Texas; Roll: 2374; Page: 3B; Enumeration District: 6; Image: 1052.0. Birth date: about 1870 Birth place: Texas Residence date: 1930 Residence place: Precinct 3, Martin, Texas.

1627   Ancestry.com, 1920 United States Federal Census (Online publication - Provo, UT, USA: Ancestry.com Operations Inc, 2010. Images reproduced by FamilySearch. Original data - Fourteenth Census of the United States, 1920. (NARA microfilm publication T625, 2076 rolls). Records of the Bureau of the Census, Record), Ancestry.com, http://www.Ancestry.com, Year: 1920; Census Place: Purcell, McClain, Oklahoma; Roll: T625_1470; Page: 30A; Enumeration District: 81; Image:. Birth date: about 1902 Birth place: Texas Residence date: 1920 Residence place: Purcell, McClain, Oklahoma.

1628   Ancestry.com, 1910 United States Federal Census (Online publication - Provo, UT, USA: Ancestry.com Operations Inc, 2006. Original data - Thirteenth Census of the United States, 1910 (NARA microfilm publication T624, 1,178 rolls). Records of the Bureau of the Census, Record Group 29. National Archives, Washington), Ancestry.com, http://www.Ancestry.com, Year: 1910; Census Place: Justice Precinct 1, Coryell, Texas; Roll: ; Page: ; Enumeration District: ; Image:. Birth date: 1906 Birth place: Texas Residence date: 1910 Residence place: Justice Precinct 1, Coryell, Texas.

1629   Ancestry.com, 1920 United States Federal Census (Online publication - Provo, UT, USA: Ancestry.com Operations Inc, 2010. Images reproduced by FamilySearch. Original data - Fourteenth Census of the United States, 1920. (NARA microfilm publication T625, 2076 rolls). Records of the Bureau of the Census, Record), Ancestry.com, http://www.Ancestry.com, Year: 1920; Census Place: Purcell, McClain, Oklahoma; Roll: T625_1470; Page: 30A; Enumeration District: 81; Image:. Birth date: about 1906 Birth place: Texas Residence date: 1920 Residence place: Purcell, McClain, Oklahoma.

1630   Ancestry.com, 1920 United States Federal Census (Online publication - Provo, UT, USA: Ancestry.com Operations Inc, 2010. Images reproduced by FamilySearch. Original data - Fourteenth Census of the United States, 1920. (NARA microfilm publication T625, 2076 rolls). Records of the Bureau of the Census, Record), Ancestry.com, http://www.Ancestry.com, Year: 1920; Census Place: Purcell, McClain, Oklahoma; Roll: T625_1470; Page: 30A; Enumeration District: 81; Image:. Birth date: about 1907 Birth place: Texas Residence date: 1920 Residence place: Purcell, McClain, Oklahoma.

1631   Ancestry.com, California Death Index, 1940-1997 (Online publication - Provo, UT, USA: Ancestry.com Operations Inc, 2000. Original data - State of California. California Death Index, 1940-1997. Sacramento, CA, USA: State of California Department of Health Services, Center for Health Statistics. Original data), Ancestry.com, http://www.Ancestry.com, Birth date: 17 Oct 1908 Birth place: Texas Death date: 3 Mar 1981 Death place: Los Angeles, California.

1632   Ancestry.com, 1920 United States Federal Census (Online publication - Provo, UT, USA: Ancestry.com Operations Inc, 2010. Images reproduced by FamilySearch. Original data - Fourteenth Census of the United States, 1920. (NARA microfilm publication T625, 2076 rolls). Records of the Bureau of the Census, Record), Ancestry.com, http://www.Ancestry.com, Year: 1920; Census Place: Purcell, McClain, Oklahoma; Roll: T625_1470; Page: 30A; Enumeration District: 81; Image:. Birth date: about 1908 Birth place: Texas Residence date: 1920 Residence place: Purcell, McClain, Oklahoma.

1633   Ancestry.com, U.S. Public Records Index, Volume 1 (Online publication - Provo, UT, USA: Ancestry.com Operations, Inc., 2010. Original data - Voter Registration Lists, Public Record Filings, Historical Residential Records, and Other Household Database Listings. Original data: Voter Registration Lists, Public), Ancestry.com, http://www.Ancestry.com, Birth date: 22 Sep 1910 Birth place: Residence date: 1986Residence place: Midland, TX.

1634   Ancestry.com, Social Security Death Index (Online publication - Provo, UT, USA: Ancestry.com Operations Inc, 2010. Original data - Social Security Administration. Social Security Death Index, Master File. Social Security Administration. Original data: Social Security Administration. Social Security D), Ancestry.com, http://www.Ancestry.com, Number: 457-26-7922; Issue State: Texas; Issue Date: Before 1951. Birth date: 22 Sep 1910 Birth place: Death date: 11 Jan 1989 Death place: Midland, Midland, Texas, United States of America.

1635   Ancestry.com, 1920 United States Federal Census (Online publication - Provo, UT, USA: Ancestry.com Operations Inc, 2010. Images reproduced by FamilySearch. Original data - Fourteenth Census of the United States, 1920. (NARA microfilm publication T625, 2076 rolls). Records of the Bureau of the Census, Record), Ancestry.com, http://www.Ancestry.com, Year: 1920; Census Place: Purcell, McClain, Oklahoma; Roll: T625_1470; Page: 30A;

Enumeration District: 81; Image:. Birth date: about 1910 Birth place: Texas Residence date: 1920 Residence place: Purcell, McClain, Oklahoma.

1636   Ancestry.com, Texas Death Index, 1903-2000 (Online publication - Provo, UT, USA: Ancestry.com Operations Inc, 2006. Original data - Texas Department of Health. Texas Death Indexes, 1903-2000. Austin, TX, USA: Texas Department of Health, State Vital Statistics Unit. Original data: Texas Department of H), Ancestry.com, http://www.Ancestry.com, Death date: 11 Jan 1989 Death place: Midland, Texas.

1637   Ancestry.com, 1920 United States Federal Census (Online publication - Provo, UT, USA: Ancestry.com Operations Inc, 2010. Images reproduced by FamilySearch. Original data - Fourteenth Census of the United States, 1920. (NARA microfilm publication T625, 2076 rolls). Records of the Bureau of the Census, Record), Ancestry.com, http://www.Ancestry.com, Year: 1920; Census Place: Purcell, McClain, Oklahoma; Roll: T625_1470; Page: 30A; Enumeration District: 81; Image:. Birth date: about 1912 Birth place: Texas Residence date: 1920 Residence place: Purcell, McClain, Oklahoma.

1638   Ancestry.com, Social Security Death Index (Online publication - Provo, UT, USA: Ancestry.com Operations Inc, 2010. Original data - Social Security Administration. Social Security Death Index, Master File. Social Security Administration. Original data: Social Security Administration. Social Security D), Ancestry.com, http://www.Ancestry.com, Number: 452-05-0297; Issue State: Texas; Issue Date: Before 1951. Birth date: 9 Jan 1912 Birth place: Death date: Dec 1974 Death place: Maurice, Vermilion, Louisiana, United States of America.

1639   Ancestry.com, 1930 United States Federal Census (Online publication - Provo, UT, USA: Ancestry.com Operations Inc, 2002. Original data - United States of America, Bureau of the Census. Fifteenth Census of the United States, 1930. Washington, D.C.: National Archives and Records Administration, 1930. T626,), Ancestry.com, http://www.Ancestry.com, Year: 1930; Census Place: Precinct 3, Martin, Texas; Roll: 2374; Page: 3B; Enumeration District: 6; Image: 1052.0. Birth date: about 1912 Birth place: Residence date: 1930 Residence place: Precinct 3, Martin, Texas.

1640   Ancestry.com, 1920 United States Federal Census (Online publication - Provo, UT, USA: Ancestry.com Operations Inc, 2010. Images reproduced by FamilySearch. Original data - Fourteenth Census of the United States, 1920. (NARA microfilm publication T625, 2076 rolls). Records of the Bureau of the Census, Record), Ancestry.com, http://www.Ancestry.com, Year: 1920; Census Place: Purcell, McClain, Oklahoma; Roll: T625_1470; Page: 30A; Enumeration District: 81; Image:. Birth date: about 1914 Birth place: Texas Residence date: 1920 Residence place: Purcell, McClain, Oklahoma.

1641   Ancestry.com, 1920 United States Federal Census (Online publication - Provo, UT, USA: Ancestry.com Operations Inc, 2010. Images reproduced by FamilySearch. Original data - Fourteenth Census of the United States, 1920. (NARA microfilm publication T625, 2076 rolls). Records of the Bureau of the Census, Record), Ancestry.com, http://www.Ancestry.com, Year: 1920; Census Place: Police Jury Ward 4, Union, Louisiana; Roll: T625_632; Page: 17A; Enumeration District: 129; Image:. Birth date: about 1914 Birth place: Louisiana Residence date: 1920 Residence place: Police Jury Ward 4, Union, Louisiana.

1642   Ancestry.com, 1910 United States Federal Census (Online publication - Provo, UT, USA: Ancestry.com Operations Inc, 2006. Original data - Thirteenth Census of the United States, 1910 (NARA microfilm publication T624, 1,178 rolls). Records of the Bureau of the Census, Record Group 29. National Archives, Washington), Ancestry.com, http://www.Ancestry.com, Year: 1910; Census Place: Police Jury Ward 6, Lincoln, Louisiana; Roll: ; Page: ; Enumeration District: ; Image:. Birth date: 1878 Birth place: Louisiana Residence date: 1910 Residence place: Police Jury Ward 6, Lincoln, Louisiana.

1643   Ancestry.com, 1910 United States Federal Census (Online publication - Provo, UT, USA: Ancestry.com Operations Inc, 2006. Original data - Thirteenth Census of the United States, 1910 (NARA microfilm publication T624, 1,178 rolls). Records of the Bureau of the Census, Record Group 29. National Archives, Washington), Ancestry.com, http://www.Ancestry.com, Year: 1910; Census Place: Police Jury Ward 6, Lincoln, Louisiana; Roll: ; Page: ; Enumeration District: ; Image:. Birth date: 1896 Birth place: Louisiana Residence date: 1910 Residence place: Police Jury Ward 6, Lincoln, Louisiana.

1644   Ancestry.com, 1910 United States Federal Census (Online publication - Provo, UT, USA: Ancestry.com Operations Inc, 2006. Original data - Thirteenth Census of the United States, 1910 (NARA microfilm publication T624, 1,178 rolls). Records of the Bureau of the Census, Record Group 29. National Archives, Washington), Ancestry.com, http://www.Ancestry.com, Year: 1910; Census Place: Police Jury Ward 6, Lincoln, Louisiana; Roll: ; Page: ; Enumeration District: ; Image:. Birth date: 1897 Birth place: Louisiana Residence date: 1910 Residence place: Police Jury Ward 6, Lincoln, Louisiana.

1645   Ancestry.com, 1910 United States Federal Census (Online publication - Provo, UT, USA: Ancestry.com Operations Inc, 2006. Original data - Thirteenth Census of the United States, 1910 (NARA microfilm publication T624, 1,178 rolls). Records of the Bureau of the Census, Record Group 29. National Archives, Washington), Ancestry.com, http://www.Ancestry.com, Year: 1910; Census Place: Police Jury Ward 6, Lincoln, Louisiana; Roll: ; Page: ; Enumeration District: ; Image:. Birth date: 1906 Birth place: Louisiana Residence date: 1910 Residence place: Police Jury Ward 6, Lincoln, Louisiana.

1646   Ancestry.com, 1920 United States Federal Census (Online publication - Provo, UT, USA: Ancestry.com Operations Inc, 2010. Images reproduced by FamilySearch. Original data - Fourteenth Census of the United States, 1920. (NARA microfilm publication T625, 2076 rolls). Records of the Bureau of the Census, Record), Ancestry.com, http://www.Ancestry.com, Year: 1920; Census Place: Police Jury Ward 4, Union, Louisiana; Roll: T625_632; Page: 17A;

Enumeration District: 129; Image:. Birth date: about 1906 Birth place: Louisiana Residence date: 1920 Residence place: Police Jury Ward 4, Union, Louisiana.

1647 Ancestry.com, 1900 United States Federal Census (Online publication - Provo, UT, USA: Ancestry.com Operations Inc, 2004. Original data - United States of America, Bureau of the Census. Twelfth Census of the United States, 1900. Washington, D.C.: National Archives and Records Administration, 1900. T623, 18), Ancestry.com, http://www.Ancestry.com, Year: 1900; Census Place: Civil District 1, Hickman, Tennessee; Roll: T623_1579; Page: 3B; Enumeration District: 38. Birth date: Jul 1896 Birth place: Tennessee Residence date: 1900 Residence place: Civil District 1, Hickman, Tennessee.

1648 Ancestry.com, 1920 United States Federal Census (Online publication - Provo, UT, USA: Ancestry.com Operations Inc, 2010. Images reproduced by FamilySearch. Original data - Fourteenth Census of the United States, 1920. (NARA microfilm publication T625, 2076 rolls). Records of the Bureau of the Census, Record), Ancestry.com, http://www.Ancestry.com, Year: 1920; Census Place: Memphis Ward 18, Shelby, Tennessee; Roll: T625_1764; Page: 5B; Enumeration District: 167; Image:. Birth date: about 1897 Birth place: Tennessee Residence date: 1920 Residence place: Memphis Ward 18, Shelby, Tennessee.

1649 Ancestry.com, Social Security Death Index (Online publication - Provo, UT, USA: Ancestry.com Operations Inc, 2010. Original data - Social Security Administration. Social Security Death Index, Master File. Social Security Administration. Original data: Social Security Administration. Social Security D), Ancestry.com, http://www.Ancestry.com, Number: 412-09-4838; Issue State: Tennessee; Issue Date: Before 1951. Birth date: 29 Jul 1896 Birth place: Death date: 1 Sep 1988 Death place: Memphis, Shelby, Tennessee, United States of America.

1650 Ancestry.com, 1920 United States Federal Census (Online publication - Provo, UT, USA: Ancestry.com Operations Inc, 2010. Images reproduced by FamilySearch. Original data - Fourteenth Census of the United States, 1920. (NARA microfilm publication T625, 2076 rolls). Records of the Bureau of the Census, Record), Ancestry.com, http://www.Ancestry.com, Year: 1920; Census Place: Memphis Ward 18, Shelby, Tennessee; Roll: T625_1764; Page: 5B; Enumeration District: 167; Image:. Birth date: about 1920 Birth place: Tennessee Residence date: 1920 Residence place: Memphis Ward 18, Shelby, Tennessee.

1651 Ancestry.com, Social Security Death Index (Online publication - Provo, UT, USA: Ancestry.com Operations Inc, 2010. Original data - Social Security Administration. Social Security Death Index, Master File. Social Security Administration. Original data: Social Security Administration. Social Security D), Ancestry.com, http://www.Ancestry.com, Number: 415-01-4249; Issue State: Tennessee; Issue Date: Before 1951. Birth date: 10 Jun 1892 Birth place: Death date: Jun 1982 Death place: Buckholts, Milam, Texas, United States of America.

1652 Ancestry.com, Texas Death Index, 1903-2000 (Online publication - Provo, UT, USA: Ancestry.com Operations Inc, 2006. Original data - Texas Department of Health. Texas Death Indexes, 1903-2000. Austin, TX, USA: Texas Department of Health, State Vital Statistics Unit. Original data: Texas Department of H), Ancestry.com, http://www.Ancestry.com, Death date: 10 Jun 1982 Death place: Milam, Texas.

1653 Ancestry.com, 1920 United States Federal Census (Online publication - Provo, UT, USA: Ancestry.com Operations Inc, 2010. Images reproduced by FamilySearch. Original data - Fourteenth Census of the United States, 1920. (NARA microfilm publication T625, 2076 rolls). Records of the Bureau of the Census, Record), Ancestry.com, http://www.Ancestry.com, Year: 1920; Census Place: Ripley, Tippah, Mississippi; Roll: T625_896; Page: 4B; Enumeration District: 104; Image:. Birth date: about 1893 Birth place: Mississippi Residence date: 1920 Residence place: Ripley, Tippah, Mississippi.

1654 Ancestry.com, 1930 United States Federal Census (Online publication - Provo, UT, USA: Ancestry.com Operations Inc, 2002. Original data - United States of America, Bureau of the Census. Fifteenth Census of the United States, 1930. Washington, D.C.: National Archives and Records Administration, 1930. T626,), Ancestry.com, http://www.Ancestry.com, Year: 1930; Census Place: Beat 2, Tippah, Mississippi; Roll: 1167; Page: 22B; Enumeration District: 6; Image: 397.0. Birth date: about 1893 Birth place: Mississippi Residence date: 1930 Residence place: Beat 2, Tippah, Mississippi.

1655 Ancestry.com, World War I Draft Registration Cards, 1917-1918 (Online publication - Provo, UT, USA: Ancestry.com Operations Inc, 2005. Original data - United States, Selective Service System. World War I Selective Service System Draft Registration Cards, 1917-1918. Washington, D.C.: National Archives and Records Administration), Ancestry.com, http://www.Ancestry.com, Registration Location: Tippah County, Mississippi; Roll: 1683988; Draft Board: 0. Birth date: 10 Jun 1892 Birth place: Residence date: Residence place: Tippah, Mississippi.

1656 Banks, Ray, comp., WWI Civilian Draft Registrations (Online publication - Provo, UT, USA: Ancestry.com Operations Inc, 2000.), Ancestry.com, http://www.Ancestry.com, Birth date: 10 Jun 1892 Birth place: Ripley MSResidence date: Residence place: Tippah.

1657 Ancestry.com, 1900 United States Federal Census (Online publication - Provo, UT, USA: Ancestry.com Operations Inc, 2004. Original data - United States of America, Bureau of the Census. Twelfth Census of the United States, 1900. Washington, D.C.: National Archives and Records Administration, 1900. T623, 18), Ancestry.com, http://www.Ancestry.com, Year: 1900; Census Place: Ripley, Tippah, Mississippi; Roll: T623_829; Page: 9A; Enumeration District: 105. Birth date: Jun 1890 Birth place: Mississippi Residence date: 1900 Residence place: Ripley, Tippah, Mississippi.

1658 Ancestry.com, 1930 United States Federal Census (Online publication - Provo, UT, USA: Ancestry.com Operations Inc, 2002. Original data - United States of America, Bureau of the Census. Fifteenth Census of the United

States, 1930. Washington, D.C.: National Archives and Records Administration, 1930. T626,), Ancestry.com, http://www.Ancestry.com, Year: 1930; Census Place: Beat 2, Tippah, Mississippi; Roll: 1167; Page: 22B; Enumeration District: 6; Image: 397.0. Birth date: about 1914 Birth place: Residence date: 1930 Residence place: Beat 2, Tippah, Mississippi.

1659   Ancestry.com, 1920 United States Federal Census (Online publication - Provo, UT, USA: Ancestry.com Operations Inc, 2010. Images reproduced by FamilySearch. Original data - Fourteenth Census of the United States, 1920. (NARA microfilm publication T625, 2076 rolls). Records of the Bureau of the Census, Record), Ancestry.com, http://www.Ancestry.com, Year: 1920; Census Place: Ripley, Tippah, Mississippi; Roll: T625_896; Page: 4B; Enumeration District: 104; Image:. Birth date: about 1914 Birth place: Mississippi Residence date: 1920 Residence place: Ripley, Tippah, Mississippi.

1660   Ancestry.com, 1930 United States Federal Census (Online publication - Provo, UT, USA: Ancestry.com Operations Inc, 2002. Original data - United States of America, Bureau of the Census. Fifteenth Census of the United States, 1930. Washington, D.C.: National Archives and Records Administration, 1930. T626,), Ancestry.com, http://www.Ancestry.com, Year: 1930; Census Place: Beat 2, Tippah, Mississippi; Roll: 1167; Page: 22B; Enumeration District: 6; Image: 397.0. Birth date: about 1916 Birth place: Residence date: 1930 Residence place: Beat 2, Tippah, Mississippi.

1661   Ancestry.com, 1920 United States Federal Census (Online publication - Provo, UT, USA: Ancestry.com Operations Inc, 2010. Images reproduced by FamilySearch. Original data - Fourteenth Census of the United States, 1920. (NARA microfilm publication T625, 2076 rolls). Records of the Bureau of the Census, Record), Ancestry.com, http://www.Ancestry.com, Year: 1920; Census Place: Ripley, Tippah, Mississippi; Roll: T625_896; Page: 4B; Enumeration District: 104; Image:. Birth date: about 1917 Birth place: Mississippi Residence date: 1920 Residence place: Ripley, Tippah, Mississippi.

1662   Ancestry.com, 1930 United States Federal Census (Online publication - Provo, UT, USA: Ancestry.com Operations Inc, 2002. Original data - United States of America, Bureau of the Census. Fifteenth Census of the United States, 1930. Washington, D.C.: National Archives and Records Administration, 1930. T626,), Ancestry.com, http://www.Ancestry.com, Year: 1930; Census Place: Beat 2, Tippah, Mississippi; Roll: 1167; Page: 22B; Enumeration District: 6; Image: 397.0. Birth date: about 1922 Birth place: Residence date: 1930 Residence place: Beat 2, Tippah, Mississippi.

1663   Ancestry.com, 1930 United States Federal Census (Online publication - Provo, UT, USA: Ancestry.com Operations Inc, 2002. Original data - United States of America, Bureau of the Census. Fifteenth Census of the United States, 1930. Washington, D.C.: National Archives and Records Administration, 1930. T626,), Ancestry.com, http://www.Ancestry.com, Year: 1930; Census Place: Beat 2, Tippah, Mississippi; Roll: 1167; Page: 23A; Enumeration District: 6; Image: 398.0. Birth date: about 1927 Birth place: Residence date: 1930 Residence place: Beat 2, Tippah, Mississippi.

1664   Ancestry.com, Social Security Death Index (Online publication - Provo, UT, USA: Ancestry.com Operations Inc, 2010. Original data - Social Security Administration. Social Security Death Index, Master File. Social Security Administration. Original data: Social Security Administration. Social Security D), Ancestry.com, http://www.Ancestry.com, Number: 411-30-7875; Issue State: Tennessee; Issue Date: Before 1951. Birth date: 6 May 1927 Birth place: Death date: 3 Nov 2008 Death place: Millington, Shelby, Tennessee.

1665   Ancestry.com, World War I Draft Registration Cards, 1917-1918 (Online publication - Provo, UT, USA: Ancestry.com Operations Inc, 2005. Original data - United States, Selective Service System. World War I Selective Service System Draft Registration Cards, 1917-1918. Washington, D.C.: National Archives and Records Administration), Ancestry.com, http://www.Ancestry.com, Registration Location: Tippah County, Mississippi; Roll: 1683988; Draft Board: 0. Birth date: 13 Jun 1891 Birth place: Residence date: Residence place: Tippah, Mississippi.

1666   Banks, Ray, comp., WWI Civilian Draft Registrations (Online publication - Provo, UT, USA: Ancestry.com Operations Inc, 2000.), Ancestry.com, http://www.Ancestry.com, Birth date: 13 Jun 1891 Birth place: Groham (Graham) MS Residence date: Residence place: Tippah.

1667   Ancestry.com, Social Security Death Index (Online publication - Provo, UT, USA: Ancestry.com Operations Inc, 2010. Original data - Social Security Administration. Social Security Death Index, Master File. Social Security Administration. Original data: Social Security Administration. Social Security D), Ancestry.com, http://www.Ancestry.com, Number: 428-34-0939; Issue State: Mississippi; Issue Date: Before 1951. Birth date: 14 Jan 1926 Birth place: Death date: 6 Oct 1996 Death place: Flint, Genesee, Michigan, United States of America.

1668   Ancestry.com, 1920 United States Federal Census (Online publication - Provo, UT, USA: Ancestry.com Operations Inc, 2010. Images reproduced by FamilySearch. Original data - Fourteenth Census of the United States, 1920. (NARA microfilm publication T625, 2076 rolls). Records of the Bureau of the Census, Record), Ancestry.com, http://www.Ancestry.com, Year: 1920; Census Place: Section, Jackson, Alabama; Roll: T625_19; Page: 8A; Enumeration District: 47; Image:. Birth date: about 1892 Birth place: Alabama Residence date: 1920 Residence place: Section, Jackson, Alabama.

1669   Ancestry.com, 1930 United States Federal Census (Online publication - Provo, UT, USA: Ancestry.com Operations Inc, 2002. Original data - United States of America, Bureau of the Census. Fifteenth Census of the United States, 1930. Washington, D.C.: National Archives and Records Administration, 1930. T626,), Ancestry.com, http://www.Ancestry.com, Year: 1930; Census Place: Wrights, Marshall, Alabama; Roll: 40; Page: 11B; Enumeration

District: 27; Image: 81.0. Birth date: about 1914 Birth place: Residence date: 1930 Residence place: Wrights, Marshall, Alabama.

1670   Ancestry.com, 1920 United States Federal Census (Online publication - Provo, UT, USA: Ancestry.com Operations Inc, 2010. Images reproduced by FamilySearch. Original data - Fourteenth Census of the United States, 1920. (NARA microfilm publication T625, 2076 rolls). Records of the Bureau of the Census, Record), Ancestry.com, http://www.Ancestry.com, Year: 1920; Census Place: Section, Jackson, Alabama; Roll: T625_19; Page: 8A; Enumeration District: 47; Image:. Birth date: about 1915 Birth place: Alabama Residence date: 1920 Residence place: Section, Jackson, Alabama.

1671   Ancestry.com, 1920 United States Federal Census (Online publication - Provo, UT, USA: Ancestry.com Operations Inc, 2010. Images reproduced by FamilySearch. Original data - Fourteenth Census of the United States, 1920. (NARA microfilm publication T625, 2076 rolls). Records of the Bureau of the Census, Record), Ancestry.com, http://www.Ancestry.com, Year: 1920; Census Place: Section, Jackson, Alabama; Roll: T625_19; Page: 8A; Enumeration District: 47; Image:. Birth date: about 1917 Birth place: Alabama Residence date: 1920 Residence place: Section, Jackson, Alabama.

1672   Ancestry.com, 1920 United States Federal Census (Online publication - Provo, UT, USA: Ancestry.com Operations Inc, 2010. Images reproduced by FamilySearch. Original data - Fourteenth Census of the United States, 1920. (NARA microfilm publication T625, 2076 rolls). Records of the Bureau of the Census, Record), Ancestry.com, http://www.Ancestry.com, Year: 1920; Census Place: Section, Jackson, Alabama; Roll: T625_19; Page: 8A; Enumeration District: 47; Image:. Birth date: about 1919 Birth place: Alabama Residence date: 1920 Residence place: Section, Jackson, Alabama.

1673   Ancestry.com, 1930 United States Federal Census (Online publication - Provo, UT, USA: Ancestry.com Operations Inc, 2002. Original data - United States of America, Bureau of the Census. Fifteenth Census of the United States, 1930. Washington, D.C.: National Archives and Records Administration, 1930. T626,), Ancestry.com, http://www.Ancestry.com, Year: 1930; Census Place: Wrights, Marshall, Alabama; Roll: 40; Page: 11B; Enumeration District: 27; Image: 81.0. Birth date: about 1922 Birth place: Residence date: 1930 Residence place: Wrights, Marshall, Alabama.

1674   Ancestry.com, 1930 United States Federal Census (Online publication - Provo, UT, USA: Ancestry.com Operations Inc, 2002. Original data - United States of America, Bureau of the Census. Fifteenth Census of the United States, 1930. Washington, D.C.: National Archives and Records Administration, 1930. T626,), Ancestry.com, http://www.Ancestry.com, Year: 1930; Census Place: Wrights, Marshall, Alabama; Roll: 40; Page: 11B; Enumeration District: 27; Image: 81.0. Birth date: about 1923 Birth place: Residence date: 1930 Residence place: Wrights, Marshall, Alabama.

1675   Ancestry.com, 1930 United States Federal Census (Online publication - Provo, UT, USA: Ancestry.com Operations Inc, 2002. Original data - United States of America, Bureau of the Census. Fifteenth Census of the United States, 1930. Washington, D.C.: National Archives and Records Administration, 1930. T626,), Ancestry.com, http://www.Ancestry.com, Year: 1930; Census Place: Wrights, Marshall, Alabama; Roll: 40; Page: 11B; Enumeration District: 27; Image: 81.0. Birth date: about 1926 Birth place: Residence date: 1930 Residence place: Wrights, Marshall, Alabama.

1676   Ancestry.com, 1930 United States Federal Census (Online publication - Provo, UT, USA: Ancestry.com Operations Inc, 2002. Original data - United States of America, Bureau of the Census. Fifteenth Census of the United States, 1930. Washington, D.C.: National Archives and Records Administration, 1930. T626,), Ancestry.com, http://www.Ancestry.com, Year: 1930; Census Place: Wrights, Marshall, Alabama; Roll: 40; Page: 11B; Enumeration District: 27; Image: 81.0. Birth date: about 1929 Birth place: Residence date: 1930 Residence place: Wrights, Marshall, Alabama.

1677   Ancestry.com, 1930 United States Federal Census (Online publication - Provo, UT, USA: Ancestry.com Operations Inc, 2002. Original data - United States of America, Bureau of the Census. Fifteenth Census of the United States, 1930. Washington, D.C.: National Archives and Records Administration, 1930. T626,), Ancestry.com, http://www.Ancestry.com, Year: 1930; Census Place: Corinth, Dekalb, Alabama; Roll: 12; Page: 16A; Enumeration District: 33; Image: 1027.0. Birth date: about 1904 Birth place: Residence date: 1930 Residence place: Corinth, Dekalb, Alabama.

1678   Ancestry.com, 1930 United States Federal Census (Online publication - Provo, UT, USA: Ancestry.com Operations Inc, 2002. Original data - United States of America, Bureau of the Census. Fifteenth Census of the United States, 1930. Washington, D.C.: National Archives and Records Administration, 1930. T626,), Ancestry.com, http://www.Ancestry.com, Year: 1930; Census Place: Corinth, Dekalb, Alabama; Roll: 12; Page: 16A; Enumeration District: 33; Image: 1027.0. Birth date: about 1923 Birth place: Residence date: 1930 Residence place: Corinth, Dekalb, Alabama.

1679   Ancestry.com, Alabama Marriage Collection, 1800-1969 (Online publication - Provo, UT, USA: Ancestry.com Operations Inc, 2006. Original data - Alabama Center for Health Statistics. Alabama Marriage Index, 1936-1969. Alabama Center for Health Statistics, Montgomery, Alabama. Dodd, Jordan R., et. al. Early America), Ancestry.com, http://www.Ancestry.com, Marriage date: Dec 1939 Marriage place: DeKalb, Alabama.

1680   Ancestry.com, 1930 United States Federal Census (Online publication - Provo, UT, USA: Ancestry.com Operations Inc, 2002. Original data - United States of America, Bureau of the Census. Fifteenth Census of the United States, 1930. Washington, D.C.: National Archives and Records Administration, 1930. T626,), Ancestry.com,

http://www.Ancestry.com, Year: 1930; Census Place: Corinth, Dekalb, Alabama; Roll: 12; Page: 16A; Enumeration District: 33; Image: 1027.0. Birth date: about 1926 Birth place: Residence date: 1930 Residence place: Corinth, Dekalb, Alabama.

1681   Ancestry.com, 1930 United States Federal Census (Online publication - Provo, UT, USA: Ancestry.com Operations Inc, 2002. Original data - United States of America, Bureau of the Census. Fifteenth Census of the United States, 1930. Washington, D.C.: National Archives and Records Administration, 1930. T626,), Ancestry.com, http://www.Ancestry.com, Year: 1930; Census Place: Corinth, Dekalb, Alabama; Roll: 12; Page: 16A; Enumeration District: 33; Image: 1027.0. Birth date: about 1929 Birth place: Residence date: 1930 Residence place: Corinth, Dekalb, Alabama.

1682   Ancestry.com, Alabama Marriage Collection, 1800-1969 (Online publication - Provo, UT, USA: Ancestry.com Operations Inc, 2006. Original data - Alabama Center for Health Statistics. Alabama Marriage Index, 1936-1969. Alabama Center for Health Statistics, Montgomery, Alabama. Dodd, Jordan R., et. al. Early America), Ancestry.com, http://www.Ancestry.com, Marriage date: 29 Jul 1945 Marriage place: DeKalb, Alabama.

1683   Ancestry.com, 1930 United States Federal Census (Online publication - Provo, UT, USA: Ancestry.com Operations Inc, 2002. Original data - United States of America, Bureau of the Census. Fifteenth Census of the United States, 1930. Washington, D.C.: National Archives and Records Administration, 1930. T626,), Ancestry.com, http://www.Ancestry.com, Year: 1930; Census Place: Gadsden, Etowah, Alabama; Roll: 16; Page: 19B; Enumeration District: 9; Image: 416.0. Birth date: about 1882 Birth place: Residence date: 1930 Residence place: Gadsden, Etowah, Alabama.

1684   Ancestry.com, 1920 United States Federal Census (Online publication - Provo, UT, USA: Ancestry.com Operations Inc, 2010. Images reproduced by FamilySearch. Original data - Fourteenth Census of the United States, 1920. (NARA microfilm publication T625, 2076 rolls). Records of the Bureau of the Census, Record), Ancestry.com, http://www.Ancestry.com, Year: 1920; Census Place: Hokes Bluff, Etowah, Alabama; Roll: T625_15; Page: 8B; Enumeration District: 99; Image:. Birth date: about 1882 Birth place: Alabama Residence date: 1920 Residence place: Hokes Bluff, Etowah, Alabama.

1685   Ancestry.com, 1910 United States Federal Census (Online publication - Provo, UT, USA: Ancestry.com Operations Inc, 2006. Original data - Thirteenth Census of the United States, 1910 (NARA microfilm publication T624, 1,178 rolls). Records of the Bureau of the Census, Record Group 29. National Archives, Washington), Ancestry.com, http://www.Ancestry.com, Year: 1910; Census Place: Hokes Bluff, Etowah, Alabama; Roll: ; Page: ; Enumeration District: ; Image:. Birth date: about 1887 Birth place: Alabama Residence date: 1910 Residence place: Hokes Bluff, Etowah, Alabama.

1686   Ancestry.com, 1900 United States Federal Census (Online publication - Provo, UT, USA: Ancestry.com Operations Inc, 2004. Original data - United States of America, Bureau of the Census. Twelfth Census of the United States, 1900. Washington, D.C.: National Archives and Records Administration, 1900. T623, 18), Ancestry.com, http://www.Ancestry.com, Year: 1900; Census Place: Reaves, Etowah, Alabama; Roll: T623_16; Page: 8B; Enumeration District: 152. Birth date: Oct 1881 Birth place: Alabama Residence date: 1900 Residence place: Precinct 5, 19 Ball Play, Reaves, Etowah, Alabama.

1687   Ancestry.com, Alabama Deaths, 1908-59 (Online publication - Provo, UT, USA: Ancestry.com Operations Inc, 2000. Original data - State of Alabama. Index of Vital Records for Alabama: Deaths, 1908-1959. Montgomery, AL, USA: State of Alabama Center for Health Statistics, Record Services Division. Original), Ancestry.com, http://www.Ancestry.com, Death date: 09 Jan 1957 Death place: Etowah.

1688   Ancestry.com, Anniston Star (Anniston, Alabama) (Online publication - Provo, UT, USA: Ancestry.com Operations Inc, 2007. Original data - Anniston Star. Anniston, Alabama, United States Of America. Database created from microfilm copies of the newspaper. Original data: Anniston Star. Anniston, Alabama, Unit), Ancestry.com, http://www.Ancestry.com.

1689   Ancestry.com, 1920 United States Federal Census (Online publication - Provo, UT, USA: Ancestry.com Operations Inc, 2010. Images reproduced by FamilySearch. Original data - Fourteenth Census of the United States, 1920. (NARA microfilm publication T625, 2076 rolls). Records of the Bureau of the Census, Record), Ancestry.com, http://www.Ancestry.com, Year: 1920; Census Place: Hokes Bluff, Etowah, Alabama; Roll: T625_15; Page: 8B; Enumeration District: 99; Image:. Birth date: about 1903 Birth place: Alabama Residence date: 1920 Residence place: Hokes Bluff, Etowah, Alabama.

1690   Ancestry.com, 1910 United States Federal Census (Online publication - Provo, UT, USA: Ancestry.com Operations Inc, 2006. Original data - Thirteenth Census of the United States, 1910 (NARA microfilm publication T624, 1,178 rolls). Records of the Bureau of the Census, Record Group 29. National Archives, Washington), Ancestry.com, http://www.Ancestry.com, Year: 1910; Census Place: Hokes Bluff, Etowah, Alabama; Roll: ; Page: ; Enumeration District: ; Image:. Birth date: about 1902 Birth place: Alabama Residence date: 1910 Residence place: Hokes Bluff, Etowah, Alabama.

1691   Ancestry.com, 1930 United States Federal Census (Online publication - Provo, UT, USA: Ancestry.com Operations Inc, 2002. Original data - United States of America, Bureau of the Census. Fifteenth Census of the United States, 1930. Washington, D.C.: National Archives and Records Administration, 1930. T626,), Ancestry.com, http://www.Ancestry.com, Year: 1930; Census Place: Gadsden, Etowah, Alabama; Roll: 16; Page: 19B; Enumeration District: 60; Image: 334.0. Birth date: about 1901 Birth place: Alabama Residence date: 1930 Residence place: Gadsden, Etowah, Alabama.

1692   Ancestry.com, Anniston Star (Anniston, Alabama) (Online publication - Provo, UT, USA: Ancestry.com Operations Inc, 2007. Original data - Anniston Star. Anniston, Alabama, United States Of America. Database created from microfilm copies of the newspaper. Original data: Anniston Star. Anniston, Alabama, Unit), Ancestry.com, http://www.Ancestry.com, Obituary.

1693   Ancestry.com, 1920 United States Federal Census (Online publication - Provo, UT, USA: Ancestry.com Operations Inc, 2010. Images reproduced by FamilySearch. Original data - Fourteenth Census of the United States, 1920. (NARA microfilm publication T625, 2076 rolls). Records of the Bureau of the Census, Record), Ancestry.com, http://www.Ancestry.com, Year: 1920; Census Place: Hokes Bluff, Etowah, Alabama; Roll: T625_15; Page: 8B; Enumeration District: 99; Image:. Birth date: about 1906 Birth place: Alabama Residence date: 1920 Residence place: Hokes Bluff, Etowah, Alabama.

1694   Ancestry.com, 1910 United States Federal Census (Online publication - Provo, UT, USA: Ancestry.com Operations Inc, 2006. Original data - Thirteenth Census of the United States, 1910 (NARA microfilm publication T624, 1,178 rolls). Records of the Bureau of the Census, Record Group 29. National Archives, Washington), Ancestry.com, http://www.Ancestry.com, Year: 1910; Census Place: Hokes Bluff, Etowah, Alabama; Roll: ; Page: ; Enumeration District: ; Image:. Birth date: about 1906 Birth place: Alabama Residence date: 1910 Residence place: Hokes Bluff, Etowah, Alabama.

1695   Ancestry.com, Social Security Death Index (Online publication - Provo, UT, USA: Ancestry.com Operations Inc, 2010. Original data - Social Security Administration. Social Security Death Index, Master File. Social Security Administration. Original data: Social Security Administration. Social Security D), Ancestry.com, http://www.Ancestry.com, Number: 423-22-0756; Issue State: Alabama; Issue Date: Before 1951. Birth date: 10 Jul 1905 Birth place: Death date: 29 Mar 1998 Death place: Douglasville, Douglas, Georgia, United States of America.

1696   Ancestry.com, Georgia Deaths, 1919-98 (Online publication - Provo, UT, USA: Ancestry.com Operations Inc, 2001. Original data - State of Georgia. Indexes of Vital Records for Georgia: Deaths, 1919-1998. Georgia, USA: Georgia Health Department, Office of Vital Records, 1998. Original data: State of), Ancestry.com, http://www.Ancestry.com, Certificate number: 015118. Birth date: about 1906 Birth place: Death date: 29 Mar 1998 Death place: Douglas, Georgia Residence date: Residence place: Douglas.

1697   Ancestry.com, 1930 United States Federal Census (Online publication - Provo, UT, USA: Ancestry.com Operations Inc, 2002. Original data - United States of America, Bureau of the Census. Fifteenth Census of the United States, 1930. Washington, D.C.: National Archives and Records Administration, 1930. T626,), Ancestry.com, http://www.Ancestry.com, Year: 1930; Census Place: Gadsden, Etowah, Alabama; Roll: 16; Page: 25B; Enumeration District: 9; Image: 428.0. Birth date: about 1906 Birth place: Residence date: 1930 Residence place: Gadsden, Etowah, Alabama.

1698   Ancestry.com, 1930 United States Federal Census (Online publication - Provo, UT, USA: Ancestry.com Operations Inc, 2002. Original data - United States of America, Bureau of the Census. Fifteenth Census of the United States, 1930. Washington, D.C.: National Archives and Records Administration, 1930. T626,), Ancestry.com, http://www.Ancestry.com, Year: 1930; Census Place: Gadsden, Etowah, Alabama; Roll: 16; Page: 16A; Enumeration District: 8; Image: 373.0. Birth date: about 1908 Birth place: Alabama Residence date: 1930 Residence place: Gadsden, Etowah, Alabama.

1699   Ancestry.com, 1920 United States Federal Census (Online publication - Provo, UT, USA: Ancestry.com Operations Inc, 2010. Images reproduced by FamilySearch. Original data - Fourteenth Census of the United States, 1920. (NARA microfilm publication T625, 2076 rolls). Records of the Bureau of the Census, Record), Ancestry.com, http://www.Ancestry.com, Year: 1920; Census Place: Hokes Bluff, Etowah, Alabama; Roll: T625_15; Page: 8B; Enumeration District: 99; Image:. Birth date: about 1908 Birth place: Alabama Residence date: 1920 Residence place: Hokes Bluff, Etowah, Alabama.

1700   Ancestry.com, 1910 United States Federal Census (Online publication - Provo, UT, USA: Ancestry.com Operations Inc, 2006. Original data - Thirteenth Census of the United States, 1910 (NARA microfilm publication T624, 1,178 rolls). Records of the Bureau of the Census, Record Group 29. National Archives, Washington), Ancestry.com, http://www.Ancestry.com, Year: 1910; Census Place: Hokes Bluff, Etowah, Alabama; Roll: ; Page: ; Enumeration District: ; Image:. Birth date: about 1908 Birth place: Alabama Residence date: 1910 Residence place: Hokes Bluff, Etowah, Alabama.

1701   Ancestry.com, Social Security Death Index (Online publication - Provo, UT, USA: Ancestry.com Operations Inc, 2010. Original data - Social Security Administration. Social Security Death Index, Master File. Social Security Administration. Original data: Social Security Administration. Social Security D), Ancestry.com, http://www.Ancestry.com, Number: 419-09-2103; Issue State: Alabama; Issue Date: Before 1951. Birth date: 7 Dec 1907 Birth place: Death date: Sep 1960 Death place:.

1702   Ancestry.com, U.S. Public Records Index, Volume 1 (Online publication - Provo, UT, USA: Ancestry.com Operations, Inc., 2010. Original data - Voter Registration Lists, Public Record Filings, Historical Residential Records, and Other Household Database Listings. Original data: Voter Registration Lists, Public), Ancestry.com, http://www.Ancestry.com, Birth date: 1 May 1915 Birth place: Residence date: 1987 Residence place: Birmingham, AL.

1703   Ancestry.com, Alabama Marriage Collection, 1800-1969 (Online publication - Provo, UT, USA: Ancestry.com Operations Inc, 2006. Original data - Alabama Center for Health Statistics. Alabama Marriage Index, 1936-1969. Alabama Center for Health Statistics, Montgomery, Alabama. Dodd, Jordan R., et. al. Early America), Ancestry.com, http://www.Ancestry.com, Marriage date: 15 Apr 1944 Marriage place: Jefferson, Alabama.

1704   Ancestry.com, 1930 United States Federal Census (Online publication - Provo, UT, USA: Ancestry.com Operations Inc, 2002. Original data - United States of America, Bureau of the Census. Fifteenth Census of the United States, 1930. Washington, D.C.: National Archives and Records Administration, 1930. T626,), Ancestry.com, http://www.Ancestry.com, Year: 1930; Census Place: Gadsden, Etowah, Alabama; Roll: 16; Page: 19B; Enumeration District: 9; Image: 416.0. Birth date: about 1915 Birth place: Residence date: 1930 Residence place: Gadsden, Etowah, Alabama.

1705   Ancestry.com, 1920 United States Federal Census (Online publication - Provo, UT, USA: Ancestry.com Operations Inc, 2010. Images reproduced by FamilySearch. Original data - Fourteenth Census of the United States, 1920. (NARA microfilm publication T625, 2076 rolls). Records of the Bureau of the Census, Record), Ancestry.com, http://www.Ancestry.com, Year: 1920; Census Place: Hokes Bluff, Etowah, Alabama; Roll: T625_15; Page: 8B; Enumeration District: 99; Image:. Birth date: about 1916 Birth place: Alabama Residence date: 1920 Residence place: Hokes Bluff, Etowah, Alabama.

1706   Ancestry.com, Alabama Marriage Collection, 1800-1969 (Online publication - Provo, UT, USA: Ancestry.com Operations Inc, 2006. Original data - Alabama Center for Health Statistics. Alabama Marriage Index, 1936-1969. Alabama Center for Health Statistics, Montgomery, Alabama. Dodd, Jordan R., et. al. Early America), Ancestry.com, http://www.Ancestry.com, Date of marriage.

1707   Ancestry.com, Social Security Death Index (Online publication - Provo, UT, USA: Ancestry.com Operations Inc, 2010. Original data - Social Security Administration. Social Security Death Index, Master File. Social Security Administration. Original data: Social Security Administration. Social Security D), Ancestry.com, http://www.Ancestry.com, Number: 416-56-1590; Issue State: Alabama; Issue Date: 1959. Birth date: 6 Aug 1914 Birth place: Death date: 31 Aug 1992 Death place: Fairfield, Jefferson, Alabama, United States of America.

1708   Ancestry.com, Social Security Death Index (Online publication - Provo, UT, USA: Ancestry.com Operations Inc, 2010. Original data - Social Security Administration. Social Security Death Index, Master File. Social Security Administration. Original data: Social Security Administration. Social Security D), Ancestry.com, http://www.Ancestry.com, Number: 418-20-2475; Issue State: Alabama; Issue Date: Before 1951. Birth date: 8 Dec 1924 Birth place: Death date: Sep 1973 Death place: Birmingham, Jefferson, Alabama, United States of America.

1709   Ancestry.com, 1930 United States Federal Census (Online publication - Provo, UT, USA: Ancestry.com Operations Inc, 2002. Original data - United States of America, Bureau of the Census. Fifteenth Census of the United States, 1930. Washington, D.C.: National Archives and Records Administration, 1930. T626,), Ancestry.com, http://www.Ancestry.com, Year: 1930; Census Place: Gadsden, Etowah, Alabama; Roll: 16; Page: 19B; Enumeration District: 9; Image: 416.0. Birth date: about 1925 Birth place: Residence date: 1930 Residence place: Gadsden, Etowah, Alabama.

1710   Ancestry.com, 1900 United States Federal Census (Online publication - Provo, UT, USA: Ancestry.com Operations Inc, 2004. Original data - United States of America, Bureau of the Census. Twelfth Census of the United States, 1900. Washington, D.C.: National Archives and Records Administration, 1900. T623, 18), Ancestry.com, http://www.Ancestry.com, Year: 1900; Census Place: Hokes Bluff, Etowah, Alabama; Roll: T623_15; Page: 9B; Enumeration District: 151. Birth date: Feb 1879 Birth place: Alabama Marriage date: 1898 Marriage place: Residence date: 1900 Residence place: Hokes Bluff, Etowah, Alabama.

1711   Ancestry.com, 1920 United States Federal Census (Online publication - Provo, UT, USA: Ancestry.com Operations Inc, 2010. Images reproduced by FamilySearch. Original data - Fourteenth Census of the United States, 1920. (NARA microfilm publication T625, 2076 rolls). Records of the Bureau of the Census, Record), Ancestry.com, http://www.Ancestry.com, Year: 1920; Census Place: Hokes Bluff, Etowah, Alabama; Roll: T625_15; Page: 8B; Enumeration District: 99; Image:. Birth date: about 1880 Birth place: Alabama Residence date: 1920 Residence place: Hokes Bluff, Etowah, Alabama.

1712   Ancestry.com, Alabama Deaths, 1908-59 (Online publication - Provo, UT, USA: Ancestry.com Operations Inc, 2000. Original data - State of Alabama. Index of Vital Records for Alabama: Deaths, 1908-1959. Montgomery, AL, USA: State of Alabama Center for Health Statistics, Record Services Division. Original), Ancestry.com, http://www.Ancestry.com, Death date: 18 Feb 1951 Death place: Etowah.

1713   Ancestry.com, 1900 United States Federal Census (Online publication - Provo, UT, USA: Ancestry.com Operations Inc, 2004. Original data - United States of America, Bureau of the Census. Twelfth Census of the United States, 1900. Washington, D.C.: National Archives and Records Administration, 1900. T623, 18), Ancestry.com, http://www.Ancestry.com, Year: 1900; Census Place: Hokes Bluff, Etowah, Alabama; Roll: T623_15; Page: 9B; Enumeration District: 151. Birth date: Jul 1899 Birth place: Alabama Residence date: 1900 Residence place: Hokes Bluff, Etowah, Alabama.

1714   Ancestry.com, Alabama Deaths, 1908-59 (Online publication - Provo, UT, USA: Ancestry.com Operations Inc, 2000. Original data - State of Alabama. Index of Vital Records for Alabama: Deaths, 1908-1959. Montgomery, AL, USA: State of Alabama Center for Health Statistics, Record Services Division. Original), Ancestry.com, http://www.Ancestry.com, Death date: 30 Jun 1918 Death place: Etowah.

1715   Ancestry.com, 1920 United States Federal Census (Online publication - Provo, UT, USA: Ancestry.com Operations Inc, 2010. Images reproduced by FamilySearch. Original data - Fourteenth Census of the United States, 1920. (NARA microfilm publication T625, 2076 rolls). Records of the Bureau of the Census, Record), Ancestry.com, http://www.Ancestry.com, Year: 1920; Census Place: Hokes Bluff, Etowah, Alabama; Roll: T625_15; Page: 8B;

Enumeration District: 99; Image:. Birth date: about 1903 Birth place: Alabama Residence date: 1920 Residence place: Hokes Bluff, Etowah, Alabama.

1716   Ancestry.com, Social Security Death Index (Online publication - Provo, UT, USA: Ancestry.com Operations Inc, 2010. Original data - Social Security Administration. Social Security Death Index, Master File. Social Security Administration. Original data: Social Security Administration. Social Security D), Ancestry.com, http://www.Ancestry.com, Number: 420-30-7154; Issue State: Alabama; Issue Date: Before 1951. Birth date: 14 Feb 1902 Birth place: Death date: Apr 1974 Death place: Gadsden, Etowah, Alabama, United States of America.

1717   Ancestry.com, 1930 United States Federal Census (Online publication - Provo, UT, USA: Ancestry.com Operations Inc, 2002. Original data - United States of America, Bureau of the Census. Fifteenth Census of the United States, 1930. Washington, D.C.: National Archives and Records Administration, 1930. T626,), Ancestry.com, http://www.Ancestry.com, Year: 1930; Census Place: Hokes Bluff, Etowah, Alabama; Roll: 16; Page: 8B; Enumeration District: 16; Image: 608.0. Birth date: about 1902 Birth place: Alabama Residence date: 1930 Residence place: Hokes Bluff, Etowah, Alabama.

1718   Ancestry.com, Social Security Death Index (Online publication - Provo, UT, USA: Ancestry.com Operations Inc, 2010. Original data - Social Security Administration. Social Security Death Index, Master File. Social Security Administration. Original data: Social Security Administration. Social Security D), Ancestry.com, http://www.Ancestry.com, Number: 422-50-0994; Issue State: Alabama; Issue Date: 1956. Birth date: 1 Mar 1905 Birth place: Death date: Feb 1982 Death place: Gadsden, Etowah, Alabama, United States of America.

1719   Ancestry.com, 1920 United States Federal Census (Online publication - Provo, UT, USA: Ancestry.com Operations Inc, 2010. Images reproduced by FamilySearch. Original data - Fourteenth Census of the United States, 1920. (NARA microfilm publication T625, 2076 rolls). Records of the Bureau of the Census, Record), Ancestry.com, http://www.Ancestry.com, Year: 1920; Census Place: Hokes Bluff, Etowah, Alabama; Roll: T625_15; Page: 8B; Enumeration District: 99; Image:. Birth date: about 1906 Birth place: Alabama Residence date: 1920 Residence place: Hokes Bluff, Etowah, Alabama.

1720   Ancestry.com, 1930 United States Federal Census (Online publication - Provo, UT, USA: Ancestry.com Operations Inc, 2002. Original data - United States of America, Bureau of the Census. Fifteenth Census of the United States, 1930. Washington, D.C.: National Archives and Records Administration, 1930. T626,), Ancestry.com, http://www.Ancestry.com, Year: 1930; Census Place: Hokes Bluff, Etowah, Alabama; Roll: 16; Page: 8B; Enumeration District: 16; Image: 608.0. Birth date: about 1905 Birth place: Residence date: 1930 Residence place: Hokes Bluff, Etowah, Alabama.

1721   Ancestry.com, 1920 United States Federal Census (Online publication - Provo, UT, USA: Ancestry.com Operations Inc, 2010. Images reproduced by FamilySearch. Original data - Fourteenth Census of the United States, 1920. (NARA microfilm publication T625, 2076 rolls). Records of the Bureau of the Census, Record), Ancestry.com, http://www.Ancestry.com, Year: 1920; Census Place: Hokes Bluff, Etowah, Alabama; Roll: T625_15; Page: 8B; Enumeration District: 99; Image:. Birth date: about 1908 Birth place: Alabama Residence date: 1920 Residence place: Hokes Bluff, Etowah, Alabama.

1722   Ancestry.com, 1930 United States Federal Census (Online publication - Provo, UT, USA: Ancestry.com Operations Inc, 2002. Original data - United States of America, Bureau of the Census. Fifteenth Census of the United States, 1930. Washington, D.C.: National Archives and Records Administration, 1930. T626,), Ancestry.com, http://www.Ancestry.com, Year: 1930; Census Place: Hokes Bluff, Etowah, Alabama; Roll: 16; Page: 8B; Enumeration District: 16; Image: 608.0. Birth date: about 1908 Birth place: Residence date: 1930 Residence place: Hokes Bluff, Etowah, Alabama.

1723   Ancestry.com, Social Security Death Index (Online publication - Provo, UT, USA: Ancestry.com Operations Inc, 2010. Original data - Social Security Administration. Social Security Death Index, Master File. Social Security Administration. Original data: Social Security Administration. Social Security D), Ancestry.com, http://www.Ancestry.com, Number: 416-14-3139; Issue State: Alabama; Issue Date: Before 1951. Birth date: 5 Nov 1907 Birth place: Death date: Nov 1983 Death place: Gadsden, Etowah, Alabama, United States of America.

1724   Ancestry.com, 1920 United States Federal Census (Online publication - Provo, UT, USA: Ancestry.com Operations Inc, 2010. Images reproduced by FamilySearch. Original data - Fourteenth Census of the United States, 1920. (NARA microfilm publication T625, 2076 rolls). Records of the Bureau of the Census, Record), Ancestry.com, http://www.Ancestry.com, Year: 1920; Census Place: Hokes Bluff, Etowah, Alabama; Roll: T625_15; Page: 8B; Enumeration District: 99; Image:. Birth date: about 1913 Birth place: Alabama Residence date: 1920 Residence place: Hokes Bluff, Etowah, Alabama.

1725   Ancestry.com, 1930 United States Federal Census (Online publication - Provo, UT, USA: Ancestry.com Operations Inc, 2002. Original data - United States of America, Bureau of the Census. Fifteenth Census of the United States, 1930. Washington, D.C.: National Archives and Records Administration, 1930. T626,), Ancestry.com, http://www.Ancestry.com, Year: 1930; Census Place: Hokes Bluff, Etowah, Alabama; Roll: 16; Page: 8B; Enumeration District: 16; Image: 608.0. Birth date: about 1913 Birth place: Residence date: 1930 Residence place: Hokes Bluff, Etowah, Alabama.

1726   National Cemetery Administration, U.S. Veterans Gravesites, ca.1775-2006 (Online publication - Provo, UT, USA: Ancestry.com Operations Inc, 2006. Original data - National Cemetery Administration. Nationwide Gravesite Locator. Original data: National Cemetery Administration. Nationwide Gravesite Locator), Ancestry.com, http://www.Ancestry.com, Birth date: 05/10/1912 Birth place: Death date: 02/28/2004 Death place: AL.

1727   Ancestry.com, U.S. Public Records Index, Volume 1 (Online publication - Provo, UT, USA: Ancestry.com Operations, Inc., 2010. Original data - Voter Registration Lists, Public Record Filings, Historical Residential Records, and Other Household Database Listings. Original data: Voter Registration Lists, Public), Ancestry.com, http://www.Ancestry.com, Birth date: 10 May 1912 Birth place: Residence date: 1992Residence place: Gadsden, AL.

1728   National Archives and Records Administration, U.S. World War II Army Enlistment Records, 1938-1946 (Online publication - Provo, UT, USA: Ancestry.com Operations Inc, 2005. Original data - Electronic Army Serial Number Merged File, 1938-1946 [Archival Database]; World War II Army Enlistment Records; Records of the National Archives and Records Administration), Ancestry.com, http://www.Ancestry.com, Birth date: 1912 Birth place: Residence date: Residence place: Alabama.

1729   Ancestry.com, Alabama Marriage Collection, 1800-1969 (Online publication - Provo, UT, USA: Ancestry.com Operations Inc, 2006. Original data - Alabama Center for Health Statistics. Alabama Marriage Index, 1936-1969. Alabama Center for Health Statistics, Montgomery, Alabama. Dodd, Jordan R., et. al. Early America), Ancestry.com, http://www.Ancestry.com, Marriage information from Parish Records.

1730   Ancestry.com, Social Security Death Index (Online publication - Provo, UT, USA: Ancestry.com Operations Inc, 2010. Original data - Social Security Administration. Social Security Death Index, Master File. Social Security Administration. Original data: Social Security Administration. Social Security D), Ancestry.com, http://www.Ancestry.com, Number: 419-20-9010; Issue State: Alabama; Issue Date: Before 1951. Birth date: 18 Dec 1914 Birth place: Death date: 21 May 1991 Death place: Gadsden, Etowah, Alabama, United States of America.

1731   Ancestry.com, 1920 United States Federal Census (Online publication - Provo, UT, USA: Ancestry.com Operations Inc, 2010. Images reproduced by FamilySearch. Original data - Fourteenth Census of the United States, 1920. (NARA microfilm publication T625, 2076 rolls). Records of the Bureau of the Census, Record), Ancestry.com, http://www.Ancestry.com, Year: 1920; Census Place: Hokes Bluff, Etowah, Alabama; Roll: T625_15; Page: 8B; Enumeration District: 99; Image:. Birth date: about 1915 Birth place: Alabama Residence date: 1920 Residence place: Hokes Bluff, Etowah, Alabama.

1732   Ancestry.com, 1930 United States Federal Census (Online publication - Provo, UT, USA: Ancestry.com Operations Inc, 2002. Original data - United States of America, Bureau of the Census. Fifteenth Census of the United States, 1930. Washington, D.C.: National Archives and Records Administration, 1930. T626,), Ancestry.com, http://www.Ancestry.com, Year: 1930; Census Place: Hokes Bluff, Etowah, Alabama; Roll: 16; Page: 8B; Enumeration District: 16; Image: 608.0. Birth date: about 1916 Birth place: Residence date: 1930 Residence place: Hokes Bluff, Etowah, Alabama.

1733   Ancestry.com, U.S. Public Records Index, Volume 2 (Online publication - Provo, UT, USA: Ancestry.com Operations, Inc., 2010. Original data - Voter Registration Lists, Public Record Filings, Historical Residential Records, and Other Household Database Listings. Original data: Voter Registration Lists, Public), Ancestry.com, http://www.Ancestry.com, Residence date: 1935-1993Residence place: Gadsden, AL.

1734   Ancestry.com, 1920 United States Federal Census (Online publication - Provo, UT, USA: Ancestry.com Operations Inc, 2010. Images reproduced by FamilySearch. Original data - Fourteenth Census of the United States, 1920. (NARA microfilm publication T625, 2076 rolls). Records of the Bureau of the Census, Record), Ancestry.com, http://www.Ancestry.com, Year: 1920; Census Place: Hokes Bluff, Etowah, Alabama; Roll: T625_15; Page: 8B; Enumeration District: 99; Image:. Birth date: about 1919 Birth place: Alabama Residence date: 1920 Residence place: Hokes Bluff, Etowah, Alabama.

1735   Ancestry.com, 1930 United States Federal Census (Online publication - Provo, UT, USA: Ancestry.com Operations Inc, 2002. Original data - United States of America, Bureau of the Census. Fifteenth Census of the United States, 1930. Washington, D.C.: National Archives and Records Administration, 1930. T626,), Ancestry.com, http://www.Ancestry.com, Year: 1930; Census Place: Hokes Bluff, Etowah, Alabama; Roll: 16; Page: 8B; Enumeration District: 16; Image: 608.0. Birth date: about 1919 Birth place: Residence date: 1930 Residence place: Hokes Bluff, Etowah, Alabama.

1736   National Archives and Records Administration, U.S. World War II Army Enlistment Records, 1938-1946 (Online publication - Provo, UT, USA: Ancestry.com Operations Inc, 2005. Original data - Electronic Army Serial Number Merged File, 1938-1946 [Archival Database]; World War II Army Enlistment Records; Records of the National Archives and Records Administration), Ancestry.com, http://www.Ancestry.com, Birth date: 1918 Birth place: Residence date: Residence place: Alabama.

1737   National Cemetery Administration, U.S. Veterans Gravesites, ca.1775-2006 (Online publication - Provo, UT, USA: Ancestry.com Operations Inc, 2006. Original data - National Cemetery Administration. Nationwide Gravesite Locator. Original data: National Cemetery Administration. Nationwide Gravesite Locator), Ancestry.com, http://www.Ancestry.com, Birth date: 12/04/1918 Birth place: Death date: 01/27/1953 Death place: AL.

1738   Ancestry.com, Alabama Deaths, 1908-59 (Online publication - Provo, UT, USA: Ancestry.com Operations Inc, 2000. Original data - State of Alabama. Index of Vital Records for Alabama: Deaths, 1908-1959. Montgomery, AL, USA: State of Alabama Center for Health Statistics, Record Services Division. Original), Ancestry.com, http://www.Ancestry.com, Death date: 27 Jan 1953 Death place: Etowah.

1739   Ancestry.com, Alabama Marriage Collection, 1800-1969 (Online publication - Provo, UT, USA: Ancestry.com Operations Inc, 2006. Original data - Alabama Center for Health Statistics. Alabama Marriage Index, 1936-1969. Alabama

Center for Health Statistics, Montgomery, Alabama. Dodd, Jordan R., et. al. Early America), Ancestry.com, http://www.Ancestry.com, Marriage date: 13 Jul 1942 Marriage place: Etowah, Alabama.

1740   Ancestry.com, 1930 United States Federal Census (Online publication - Provo, UT, USA: Ancestry.com Operations Inc, 2002. Original data - United States of America, Bureau of the Census. Fifteenth Census of the United States, 1930. Washington, D.C.: National Archives and Records Administration, 1930. T626,), Ancestry.com, http://www.Ancestry.com, Year: 1930; Census Place: Keysburg, Etowah, Alabama; Roll: 16; Page: 4A; Enumeration District: 43; Image: 1021.0. Birth date: about 1874 Birth place: Georgia Residence date: 1930 Residence place: Keysburg, Etowah, Alabama.

1741   Ancestry.com, 1910 United States Federal Census (Online publication - Provo, UT, USA: Ancestry.com Operations Inc, 2006. Original data - Thirteenth Census of the United States, 1910 (NARA microfilm publication T624, 1,178 rolls). Records of the Bureau of the Census, Record Group 29. National Archives, Washington), Ancestry.com, http://www.Ancestry.com, Year: 1910; Census Place: Hokes Bluff, Etowah, Alabama; Roll: ; Page: ; Enumeration District: ; Image:. Birth date: about 1876 Birth place: Georgia Residence date: 1910 Residence place: Hokes Bluff, Etowah, Alabama.

1742   Ancestry.com, 1920 United States Federal Census (Online publication - Provo, UT, USA: Ancestry.com Operations Inc, 2010. Images reproduced by FamilySearch. Original data - Fourteenth Census of the United States, 1920. (NARA microfilm publication T625, 2076 rolls). Records of the Bureau of the Census, Record), Ancestry.com, http://www.Ancestry.com, Year: 1920; Census Place: Anniston Ward 6, Calhoun, Alabama; Roll: T625_5; Page: 5A; Enumeration District: 158; Image:. Birth date: about 1876 Birth place: Georgia Residence date: 1920 Residence place: Anniston Ward 6, Calhoun, Alabama.

1743   Ancestry.com, World War I Draft Registration Cards, 1917-1918 (Online publication - Provo, UT, USA: Ancestry.com Operations Inc, 2005. Original data - United States, Selective Service System. World War I Selective Service System Draft Registration Cards, 1917-1918. Washington, D.C.: National Archives and Records Administration), Ancestry.com, http://www.Ancestry.com, Registration Location: Calhoun County, Alabama; Roll: 1509363; Draft Board: 0. Birth date: 30 Aug 1876 Birth place: Residence date: Residence place: Calhoun, Alabama.

1744   Ancestry.com, Alabama Deaths, 1908-59 (Online publication - Provo, UT, USA: Ancestry.com Operations Inc, 2000. Original data - State of Alabama. Index of Vital Records for Alabama: Deaths, 1908-1959. Montgomery, AL, USA: State of Alabama Center for Health Statistics, Record Services Division. Original), Ancestry.com, http://www.Ancestry.com, Death date: 27 Apr 1942 Death place: Limestone.

1745   Ancestry.com, 1910 United States Federal Census (Online publication - Provo, UT, USA: Ancestry.com Operations Inc, 2006. Original data - Thirteenth Census of the United States, 1910 (NARA microfilm publication T624, 1,178 rolls). Records of the Bureau of the Census, Record Group 29. National Archives, Washington), Ancestry.com, http://www.Ancestry.com, Year: 1910; Census Place: Hokes Bluff, Etowah, Alabama; Roll: ; Page: ; Enumeration District: ; Image:. Birth date: about 1902 Birth place: Alabama Residence date: 1910 Residence place: Hokes Bluff, Etowah, Alabama.

1746   Ancestry.com, 1920 United States Federal Census (Online publication - Provo, UT, USA: Ancestry.com Operations Inc, 2010. Images reproduced by FamilySearch. Original data - Fourteenth Census of the United States, 1920. (NARA microfilm publication T625, 2076 rolls). Records of the Bureau of the Census, Record), Ancestry.com, http://www.Ancestry.com, Year: 1920; Census Place: Anniston Ward 6, Calhoun, Alabama; Roll: T625_5; Page: 5A; Enumeration District: 158; Image:. Birth date: about 1901 Birth place: Alabama Residence date: 1920 Residence place: Anniston Ward 6, Calhoun, Alabama.

1747   Ancestry.com, Alabama Marriage Collection, 1800-1969 (Online publication - Provo, UT, USA: Ancestry.com Operations Inc, 2006. Original data - Alabama Center for Health Statistics. Alabama Marriage Index, 1936-1969. Alabama Center for Health Statistics, Montgomery, Alabama. Dodd, Jordan R., et. al. Early America), Ancestry.com, http://www.Ancestry.com, Marriage date: 30 Mar 1945 Marriage place: Etowah, Alabama.

1748   Ancestry.com, Alabama Marriage Collection, 1800-1969 (Online publication - Provo, UT, USA: Ancestry.com Operations Inc, 2006. Original data - Alabama Center for Health Statistics. Alabama Marriage Index, 1936-1969. Alabama Center for Health Statistics, Montgomery, Alabama. Dodd, Jordan R., et. al. Early America), Ancestry.com, http://www.Ancestry.com, Marriage date: 30 Mar 1945 Marriage place: Etowah, Alabama.

1749   National Archives and Records Administration, U.S. World War II Army Enlistment Records, 1938-1946 (Online publication - Provo, UT, USA: Ancestry.com Operations Inc, 2005. Original data - Electronic Army Serial Number Merged File, 1938-1946 [Archival Database]; World War II Army Enlistment Records; Records of the National Archives and Records Administration), Ancestry.com, http://www.Ancestry.com, Birth date: 1903 Birth place: Residence date: Residence place: Alabama.

1750   Ancestry.com, 1910 United States Federal Census (Online publication - Provo, UT, USA: Ancestry.com Operations Inc, 2006. Original data - Thirteenth Census of the United States, 1910 (NARA microfilm publication T624, 1,178 rolls). Records of the Bureau of the Census, Record Group 29. National Archives, Washington), Ancestry.com, http://www.Ancestry.com, Year: 1910; Census Place: Hokes Bluff, Etowah, Alabama; Roll: ; Page: ; Enumeration District: ; Image:. Birth date: about 1904 Birth place: Alabama Residence date: 1910 Residence place: Hokes Bluff, Etowah, Alabama.

1751   Ancestry.com, 1920 United States Federal Census (Online publication - Provo, UT, USA: Ancestry.com Operations Inc, 2010. Images reproduced by FamilySearch. Original data - Fourteenth Census of the United States, 1920.

(NARA microfilm publication T625, 2076 rolls). Records of the Bureau of the Census, Record), Ancestry.com, http://www.Ancestry.com, Year: 1920; Census Place: Anniston Ward 6, Calhoun, Alabama; Roll: T625_5; Page: 5A; Enumeration District: 158; Image:. Birth date: about 1904 Birth place: Alabama Residence date: 1920 Residence place: Anniston Ward 6, Calhoun, Alabama.

1752   Ancestry.com, 1930 United States Federal Census (Online publication - Provo, UT, USA: Ancestry.com Operations Inc, 2002. Original data - United States of America, Bureau of the Census. Fifteenth Census of the United States, 1930. Washington, D.C.: National Archives and Records Administration, 1930. T626,), Ancestry.com, http://www.Ancestry.com, Year: 1930; Census Place: Anniston, Calhoun, Alabama; Roll: 5; Page: 9B; Enumeration District: 50; Image: 1030.0. Birth date: about 1904 Birth place: Alabama Residence date: 1930 Residence place: Anniston, Calhoun, Alabama.

1753   Ancestry.com, Social Security Death Index (Online publication - Provo, UT, USA: Ancestry.com Operations Inc, 2010. Original data - Social Security Administration. Social Security Death Index, Master File. Social Security Administration. Original data: Social Security Administration. Social Security D), Ancestry.com, http://www.Ancestry.com, Number: 416-07-9429; Issue State: Alabama; Issue Date: Before 1951. Birth date: 15 Oct 1903 Birth place: Death date: Jan 1971 Death place:.

1754   Ancestry.com, 1910 United States Federal Census (Online publication - Provo, UT, USA: Ancestry.com Operations Inc, 2006. Original data - Thirteenth Census of the United States, 1910 (NARA microfilm publication T624, 1,178 rolls). Records of the Bureau of the Census, Record Group 29. National Archives, Washington), Ancestry.com, http://www.Ancestry.com, Year: 1910; Census Place: Hokes Bluff, Etowah, Alabama; Roll: ; Page: ; Enumeration District: ; Image:. Birth date: about 1906 Birth place: Alabama Residence date: 1910 Residence place: Hokes Bluff, Etowah, Alabama.

1755   Ancestry.com, 1920 United States Federal Census (Online publication - Provo, UT, USA: Ancestry.com Operations Inc, 2010. Images reproduced by FamilySearch. Original data - Fourteenth Census of the United States, 1920. (NARA microfilm publication T625, 2076 rolls). Records of the Bureau of the Census, Record), Ancestry.com, http://www.Ancestry.com, Year: 1920; Census Place: Anniston Ward 6, Calhoun, Alabama; Roll: T625_5; Page: 5A; Enumeration District: 158; Image:. Birth date: about 1906 Birth place: Alabama Residence date: 1920 Residence place: Anniston Ward 6, Calhoun, Alabama.

1756   Ancestry.com, 1910 United States Federal Census (Online publication - Provo, UT, USA: Ancestry.com Operations Inc, 2006. Original data - Thirteenth Census of the United States, 1910 (NARA microfilm publication T624, 1,178 rolls). Records of the Bureau of the Census, Record Group 29. National Archives, Washington), Ancestry.com, http://www.Ancestry.com, Year: 1910; Census Place: Hokes Bluff, Etowah, Alabama; Roll: ; Page: ; Enumeration District: ; Image:. Birth date: about 1908 Birth place: Alabama Residence date: 1910 Residence place: Hokes Bluff, Etowah, Alabama.

1757   Ancestry.com, 1920 United States Federal Census (Online publication - Provo, UT, USA: Ancestry.com Operations Inc, 2010. Images reproduced by FamilySearch. Original data - Fourteenth Census of the United States, 1920. (NARA microfilm publication T625, 2076 rolls). Records of the Bureau of the Census, Record), Ancestry.com, http://www.Ancestry.com, Year: 1920; Census Place: Anniston Ward 6, Calhoun, Alabama; Roll: T625_5; Page: 5A; Enumeration District: 158; Image:. Birth date: about 1911 Birth place: Alabama Residence date: 1920 Residence place: Anniston Ward 6, Calhoun, Alabama.

1758   Ancestry.com, 1930 United States Federal Census (Online publication - Provo, UT, USA: Ancestry.com Operations Inc, 2002. Original data - United States of America, Bureau of the Census. Fifteenth Census of the United States, 1930. Washington, D.C.: National Archives and Records Administration, 1930. T626,), Ancestry.com, http://www.Ancestry.com, Year: 1930; Census Place: Hokes Bluff, Etowah, Alabama; Roll: 16; Page: 9A; Enumeration District: 16; Image: 609.0. Birth date: about 1909 Birth place: Alabama Residence date: 1930 Residence place: Hokes Bluff, Etowah, Alabama.

1759   Ancestry.com, Social Security Death Index (Online publication - Provo, UT, USA: Ancestry.com Operations Inc, 2010. Original data - Social Security Administration. Social Security Death Index, Master File. Social Security Administration. Original data: Social Security Administration. Social Security D), Ancestry.com, http://www.Ancestry.com, Number: 421-07-6507; Issue State: Alabama; Issue Date: Before 1951. Birth date: 21 May 1908 Birth place: Death date: Jan 1976 Death place: Gadsden, Etowah, Alabama, United States of America.

1760   National Archives and Records Administration, U.S. World War II Army Enlistment Records, 1938-1946 (Online publication - Provo, UT, USA: Ancestry.com Operations Inc, 2005. Original data - Electronic Army Serial Number Merged File, 1938-1946 [Archival Database]; World War II Army Enlistment Records; Records of the National Archives and Records Administration), Ancestry.com, http://www.Ancestry.com, Birth date: 1908 Birth place: Residence date: Residence place: Alabama.

1761   Ancestry.com, 1920 United States Federal Census (Online publication - Provo, UT, USA: Ancestry.com Operations Inc, 2010. Images reproduced by FamilySearch. Original data - Fourteenth Census of the United States, 1920. (NARA microfilm publication T625, 2076 rolls). Records of the Bureau of the Census, Record), Ancestry.com, http://www.Ancestry.com, Year: 1920; Census Place: Anniston Ward 6, Calhoun, Alabama; Roll: T625_5; Page: 5A; Enumeration District: 158; Image:. Birth date: about 1912 Birth place: Alabama Residence date: 1920 Residence place: Anniston Ward 6, Calhoun, Alabama.

1762   Ancestry.com, 1930 United States Federal Census (Online publication - Provo, UT, USA: Ancestry.com Operations Inc, 2002. Original data - United States of America, Bureau of the Census. Fifteenth Census of the United

States, 1930. Washington, D.C.: National Archives and Records Administration, 1930. T626,), Ancestry.com, http://www.Ancestry.com, Year: 1930; Census Place: Keysburg, Etowah, Alabama; Roll: 16; Page: 4A; Enumeration District: 43; Image: 1021.0. Birth date: about 1911 Birth place: Residence date: 1930 Residence place: Keysburg, Etowah, Alabama.

1763   Ancestry.com, Alabama Marriage Collection, 1800-1969 (Online publication - Provo, UT, USA: Ancestry.com Operations Inc, 2006. Original data - Alabama Center for Health Statistics. Alabama Marriage Index, 1936-1969. Alabama Center for Health Statistics, Montgomery, Alabama. Dodd, Jordan R., et. al. Early America), Ancestry.com, http://www.Ancestry.com, Marriage date: 2 Aug 1940 Marriage place: Calhoun, Alabama.

1764   Ancestry.com, Social Security Death Index (Online publication - Provo, UT, USA: Ancestry.com Operations Inc, 2010. Original data - Social Security Administration. Social Security Death Index, Master File. Social Security Administration. Original data: Social Security Administration. Social Security D), Ancestry.com, http://www.Ancestry.com, Number: 419-05-3365; Issue State: Alabama; Issue Date: Before 1951. Birth date: 20 Feb 1911 Birth place: Death date: Mar 1980 Death place: Huntsville, Madison, Alabama, United States of America.

1765   Ancestry.com, Anniston Star (Anniston, Alabama) (Online publication - Provo, UT, USA: Ancestry.com Operations Inc, 2007. Original data - Anniston Star. Anniston, Alabama, United States Of America. Database created from microfilm copies of the newspaper. Original data: Anniston Star. Anniston, Alabama, Unit), Ancestry.com, http://www.Ancestry.com.

1766   Ancestry.com, Tennessee State Marriages, 1780-2002 (Online publication - Provo, UT, USA: Ancestry.com Operations Inc, 2008. Original data - Tennessee State Marriages, 1780-2002. Nashville, TN, USA: Tennessee State Library and Archives. Microfilm. Original data: Tennessee State Marriages, 1780-2002. Nashville,), Ancestry.com, http://www.Ancestry.com, Marriage date: 30 Mar 1966 Marriage place: Tipton Residence date: Residence place: Tennessee.

1767   Ancestry.com, 1930 United States Federal Census (Online publication - Provo, UT, USA: Ancestry.com Operations Inc, 2002. Original data - United States of America, Bureau of the Census. Fifteenth Census of the United States, 1930. Washington, D.C.: National Archives and Records Administration, 1930. T626,), Ancestry.com, http://www.Ancestry.com, Year: 1930; Census Place: Keysburg, Etowah, Alabama; Roll: 16; Page: 4A; Enumeration District: 43; Image: 1021.0. Birth date: about 1922 Birth place: Residence date: 1930 Residence place: Keysburg, Etowah, Alabama.

1768   Ancestry.com, U.S. Public Records Index, Volume 1 (Online publication - Provo, UT, USA: Ancestry.com Operations, Inc., 2010. Original data - Voter Registration Lists, Public Record Filings, Historical Residential Records, and Other Household Database Listings. Original data: Voter Registration Lists, Public), Ancestry.com, http://www.Ancestry.com, Birth date: 28 Jul 1921 Birth place: Residence date: 1993Residence place: Memphis, TN.

1769   Ancestry.com, North Carolina Marriage Collection, 1741-2004 (Online publication - Provo, UT, USA: Ancestry.com Operations Inc, 2007. Original data - Dodd, Jordan, Liahona Research, comp. (P. O. Box 740, Orem, Utah 84059) from county marriage records on microfilm located at the Family History Library in Salt Lake City,), Ancestry.com, http://www.Ancestry.com, Data Source: North Carolina State Archives. Birth date: about 1921 Birth place: Marriage date: 2 Nov 1957 Marriage place: High Point.

1770   Ancestry.com, Social Security Death Index (Online publication - Provo, UT, USA. Ancestry.com Operations Inc, 2010. Original data - Social Security Administration. Social Security Death Index, Master File. Social Security Administration. Original data: Social Security Administration. Social Security D), Ancestry.com, http://www.Ancestry.com, Number: 423-10-6392; Issue State: Alabama; Issue Date: Before 1951. Birth date: 28 Jul 1921 Birth place: Death date: 3 Jun 1995 Death place: Memphis, Shelby, Tennessee, United States of America.

1771   Ancestry.com, Alabama Deaths, 1908-59 (Online publication - Provo, UT, USA: Ancestry.com Operations Inc, 2000. Original data - State of Alabama. Index of Vital Records for Alabama: Deaths, 1908-1959. Montgomery, AL, USA: State of Alabama Center for Health Statistics, Record Services Division. Original), Ancestry.com, http://www.Ancestry.com, Death date: Jun 1930 Death place: Etowah.

1772   Ancestry.com, 1930 United States Federal Census (Online publication - Provo, UT, USA: Ancestry.com Operations Inc, 2002. Original data - United States of America, Bureau of the Census. Fifteenth Census of the United States, 1930. Washington, D.C.: National Archives and Records Administration, 1930. T626,), Ancestry.com, http://www.Ancestry.com, Year: 1930; Census Place: Keysburg, Etowah, Alabama; Roll: 16; Page: 4A; Enumeration District: 43; Image: 1021.0. Birth date: about 1925 Birth place: Residence date: 1930 Residence place: Keysburg, Etowah, Alabama.

1773   Ancestry.com, Alabama Deaths, 1908-59 (Online publication - Provo, UT, USA: Ancestry.com Operations Inc, 2000. Original data - State of Alabama. Index of Vital Records for Alabama: Deaths, 1908-1959. Montgomery, AL, USA: State of Alabama Center for Health Statistics, Record Services Division. Original), Ancestry.com, http://www.Ancestry.com, Death date: 30 Dec 1957 Death place: Etowah.

1774   Ancestry.com, 1910 United States Federal Census (Online publication - Provo, UT, USA: Ancestry.com Operations Inc, 2006. Original data - Thirteenth Census of the United States, 1910 (NARA microfilm publication T624, 1,178 rolls). Records of the Bureau of the Census, Record Group 29. National Archives, Washington), Ancestry.com, http://www.Ancestry.com, Year: 1910; Census Place: Hokes Bluff, Etowah, Alabama; Roll: ; Page: ; Enumeration District: ; Image:. Birth date: about 1872 Birth place: Alabama Residence date: 1910 Residence place: Hokes Bluff, Etowah, Alabama.

269

1775   Ancestry.com, 1920 United States Federal Census (Online publication - Provo, UT, USA: Ancestry.com Operations Inc, 2010. Images reproduced by FamilySearch. Original data - Fourteenth Census of the United States, 1920. (NARA microfilm publication T625, 2076 rolls). Records of the Bureau of the Census, Record), Ancestry.com, http://www.Ancestry.com, Year: 1920; Census Place: Hokes Bluff, Etowah, Alabama; Roll: T625_15; Page: 2A; Enumeration District: 99; Image:. Birth date: about 1877 Birth place: Alabama Residence date: 1920 Residence place: Hokes Bluff, Etowah, Alabama.

1776   Ancestry.com and The Church of Jesus Christ of Latter-day Saints, 1880 United States Federal Census (Online publication - Provo, UT, USA: Ancestry.com Operations Inc, 2010. 1880 U.S. Census Index provided by The Church of Jesus Christ of Latter-day Saints © Copyright 1999 Intellectual Reserve, Inc. All rights reserved. All use is subject to the limited), Ancestry.com, http://www.Ancestry.com, Year: 1880; Census Place: Bells Mill, Cleburne, Alabama; Roll: 8; Family History Film: 1254008; Page: 203A; Enumeration District: 45; Image:. Birth date: about 1875 Birth place: Alabama Residence date: 1880 Residence place: Bells Mill, Cleburne, Alabama, United States.

1777   Ancestry.com, 1930 United States Federal Census (Online publication - Provo, UT, USA: Ancestry.com Operations Inc, 2002. Original data - United States of America, Bureau of the Census. Fifteenth Census of the United States, 1930. Washington, D.C.: National Archives and Records Administration, 1930. T626,), Ancestry.com, http://www.Ancestry.com, Year: 1930; Census Place: Hokes Bluff, Etowah, Alabama; Roll: 16; Page: 9A; Enumeration District: 16; Image: 609.0. Birth date: about 1879 Birth place: Alabama Residence date: 1930 Residence place: Hokes Bluff, Etowah, Alabama.

1778   Ancestry.com and The Church of Jesus Christ of Latter-day Saints, 1880 United States Federal Census (Online publication - Provo, UT, USA: Ancestry.com Operations Inc, 2010. 1880 U.S. Census Index provided by The Church of Jesus Christ of Latter-day Saints © Copyright 1999 Intellectual Reserve, Inc. All rights reserved. All use is subject to the limited), Ancestry.com, http://www.Ancestry.com, Year: 1880; Census Place: Turkey Town, Etowah, Alabama; Roll: 13; Family History Film: 1254013; Page: 322D; Enumeration District: 66; Image: 0152. Birth date: about 1879 Birth place: Alabama Residence date: 1880 Residence place: Turkey Town, Etowah, Alabama, United States.

1779   Ancestry.com, U.S. Public Records Index, Volume 2 (Online publication - Provo, UT, USA: Ancestry.com Operations, Inc., 2010. Original data - Voter Registration Lists, Public Record Filings, Historical Residential Records, and Other Household Database Listings. Original data: Voter Registration Lists, Public), Ancestry.com, http://www.Ancestry.com, Residence date: 1935-1993Residence place: Gadsden, AL.

1780   Ancestry.com, 1920 United States Federal Census (Online publication - Provo, UT, USA: Ancestry.com Operations Inc, 2010. Images reproduced by FamilySearch. Original data - Fourteenth Census of the United States, 1920. (NARA microfilm publication T625, 2076 rolls). Records of the Bureau of the Census, Record), Ancestry.com, http://www.Ancestry.com, Year: 1920; Census Place: Hokes Bluff, Etowah, Alabama; Roll: T625_15; Page: 2A; Enumeration District: 99; Image:. Birth date: about 1900 Birth place: Alabama Residence date: 1920 Residence place: Hokes Bluff, Etowah, Alabama.

1781   Ancestry.com, 1910 United States Federal Census (Online publication - Provo, UT, USA: Ancestry.com Operations Inc, 2006. Original data - Thirteenth Census of the United States, 1910 (NARA microfilm publication T624, 1,178 rolls). Records of the Bureau of the Census, Record Group 29. National Archives, Washington), Ancestry.com, http://www.Ancestry.com, Year: 1910; Census Place: Hokes Bluff, Etowah, Alabama; Roll: ; Page: ; Enumeration District: ; Image:. Birth date: about 1900 Birth place: Alabama Residence date: 1910 Residence place: Hokes Bluff, Etowah, Alabama.

1782   Ancestry.com, 1930 United States Federal Census (Online publication - Provo, UT, USA: Ancestry.com Operations Inc, 2002. Original data - United States of America, Bureau of the Census. Fifteenth Census of the United States, 1930. Washington, D.C.: National Archives and Records Administration, 1930. T626,), Ancestry.com, http://www.Ancestry.com, Year: 1930; Census Place: Hokes Bluff, Etowah, Alabama; Roll: 16; Page: 9A; Enumeration District: 16; Image: 609.0. Birth date: about 1901 Birth place: Residence date: 1930 Residence place: Hokes Bluff, Etowah, Alabama.

1783   Ancestry.com, Social Security Death Index (Online publication - Provo, UT, USA: Ancestry.com Operations Inc, 2010. Original data - Social Security Administration. Social Security Death Index, Master File. Social Security Administration. Original data: Social Security Administration. Social Security D), Ancestry.com, http://www.Ancestry.com, Number: 419-44-8690; Issue State: Alabama; Issue Date: 1951-1952. Birth date: 19 Oct 1899 Birth place: Death date: Jun 1974 Death place: Gadsden, Etowah, Alabama, United States of America.

1784   Ancestry.com, 1900 United States Federal Census (Online publication - Provo, UT, USA: Ancestry.com Operations Inc, 2004. Original data - United States of America, Bureau of the Census. Twelfth Census of the United States, 1900. Washington, D.C.: National Archives and Records Administration, 1900. T623, 18), Ancestry.com, http://www.Ancestry.com, Year: 1900; Census Place: Hokes Bluff, Etowah, Alabama; Roll: T623_15; Page: 5B; Enumeration District: 151. Birth date: Oct 1899 Birth place: Alabama Residence date: 1900 Residence place: Hokes Bluff, Etowah, Alabama.

1785   Ancestry.com, 1920 United States Federal Census (Online publication - Provo, UT, USA: Ancestry.com Operations Inc, 2010. Images reproduced by FamilySearch. Original data - Fourteenth Census of the United States, 1920. (NARA microfilm publication T625, 2076 rolls). Records of the Bureau of the Census, Record), Ancestry.com, http://www.Ancestry.com, Year: 1920; Census Place: Hokes Bluff, Etowah, Alabama; Roll: T625_15; Page: 2A; Enumeration District: 99; Image:. Birth date: about 1903 Birth place: Alabama Residence date: 1920 Residence place: Hokes Bluff, Etowah, Alabama.

1786   Ancestry.com, Social Security Death Index (Online publication - Provo, UT, USA: Ancestry.com Operations Inc, 2010. Original data - Social Security Administration. Social Security Death Index, Master File. Social Security Administration. Original data: Social Security Administration. Social Security D), Ancestry.com, http://www.Ancestry.com, Number: 421-40-0394; Issue State: Alabama; Issue Date: Before 1951. Birth date: 2 Jun 1902 Birth place: Death date: Dec 1971 Death place: Gadsden, Etowah, Alabama, United States of America.

1787   Ancestry.com, 1910 United States Federal Census (Online publication - Provo, UT, USA: Ancestry.com Operations Inc, 2006. Original data - Thirteenth Census of the United States, 1910 (NARA microfilm publication T624, 1,178 rolls). Records of the Bureau of the Census, Record Group 29. National Archives, Washington), Ancestry.com, http://www.Ancestry.com, Year: 1910; Census Place: Hokes Bluff, Etowah, Alabama; Roll: ; Page: ; Enumeration District: ; Image:. Birth date: about 1903 Birth place: Alabama Residence date: 1910 Residence place: Hokes Bluff, Etowah, Alabama.

1788   Ancestry.com, 1930 United States Federal Census (Online publication - Provo, UT, USA: Ancestry.com Operations Inc, 2002. Original data - United States of America, Bureau of the Census. Fifteenth Census of the United States, 1930. Washington, D.C.: National Archives and Records Administration, 1930. T626,), Ancestry.com, http://www.Ancestry.com, Year: 1930; Census Place: Hokes Bluff, Etowah, Alabama; Roll: 16; Page: 9A; Enumeration District: 16; Image: 609.0. Birth date: about 1903 Birth place: Alabama Residence date: 1930 Residence place: Hokes Bluff, Etowah, Alabama.

1789   Ancestry.com, 1920 United States Federal Census (Online publication - Provo, UT, USA: Ancestry.com Operations Inc, 2010. Images reproduced by FamilySearch. Original data - Fourteenth Census of the United States, 1920. (NARA microfilm publication T625, 2076 rolls). Records of the Bureau of the Census, Record), Ancestry.com, http://www.Ancestry.com, Year: 1920; Census Place: Hokes Bluff, Etowah, Alabama; Roll: T625_15; Page: 2A; Enumeration District: 99; Image:. Birth date: about 1909 Birth place: Alabama Residence date: 1920 Residence place: Hokes Bluff, Etowah, Alabama.

1790   Ancestry.com, 1930 United States Federal Census (Online publication - Provo, UT, USA: Ancestry.com Operations Inc, 2002. Original data - United States of America, Bureau of the Census. Fifteenth Census of the United States, 1930. Washington, D.C.: National Archives and Records Administration, 1930. T626,), Ancestry.com, http://www.Ancestry.com, Year: 1930; Census Place: Hokes Bluff, Etowah, Alabama; Roll: 16; Page: 7B; Enumeration District: 16; Image: 606.0. Birth date: about 1908 Birth place: Residence date: 1930 Residence place: Hokes Bluff, Etowah, Alabama.

1791   Ancestry.com, Social Security Death Index (Online publication - Provo, UT, USA: Ancestry.com Operations Inc, 2010. Original data - Social Security Administration. Social Security Death Index, Master File. Social Security Administration. Original data: Social Security Administration. Social Security D), Ancestry.com, http://www.Ancestry.com, Number: 423-70-5670; Issue State: Alabama; Issue Date: 1966. Birth date: 20 Sep 1908 Birth place: Death date: 19 Feb 1990 Death place: Gadsden, Etowah, Alabama, United States of America.

1792   Ancestry.com, 1930 United States Federal Census (Online publication - Provo, UT, USA: Ancestry.com Operations Inc, 2002. Original data - United States of America, Bureau of the Census. Fifteenth Census of the United States, 1930. Washington, D.C.: National Archives and Records Administration, 1930. T626,), Ancestry.com, http://www.Ancestry.com, Year: 1930; Census Place: Hokes Bluff, Etowah, Alabama; Roll: 16; Page: 9A; Enumeration District: 16; Image: 609.0. Birth date: about 1916 Birth place: Residence date: 1930 Residence place: Hokes Bluff, Etowah, Alabama.

1793   Ancestry.com, 1920 United States Federal Census (Online publication - Provo, UT, USA: Ancestry.com Operations Inc, 2010. Images reproduced by FamilySearch. Original data - Fourteenth Census of the United States, 1920. (NARA microfilm publication T625, 2076 rolls). Records of the Bureau of the Census, Record), Ancestry.com, http://www.Ancestry.com, Year: 1920; Census Place: Hokes Bluff, Etowah, Alabama; Roll: T625_15; Page: 2A; Enumeration District: 99; Image:. Birth date: about 1916 Birth place: Alabama Residence date: 1920 Residence place: Hokes Bluff, Etowah, Alabama.

1794   Ancestry.com, 1920 United States Federal Census (Online publication - Provo, UT, USA: Ancestry.com Operations Inc, 2010. Images reproduced by FamilySearch. Original data - Fourteenth Census of the United States, 1920. (NARA microfilm publication T625, 2076 rolls). Records of the Bureau of the Census, Record), Ancestry.com, http://www.Ancestry.com, Year: 1920; Census Place: Hokes Bluff, Etowah, Alabama; Roll: T625_15; Page: 2A; Enumeration District: 99; Image:. Birth date: about 1919 Birth place: Alabama Residence date: 1920 Residence place: Hokes Bluff, Etowah, Alabama.

1795   Ancestry.com, 1930 United States Federal Census (Online publication - Provo, UT, USA: Ancestry.com Operations Inc, 2002. Original data - United States of America, Bureau of the Census. Fifteenth Census of the United States, 1930. Washington, D.C.: National Archives and Records Administration, 1930. T626,), Ancestry.com, http://www.Ancestry.com, Year: 1930; Census Place: Hokes Bluff, Etowah, Alabama; Roll: 16; Page: 9A; Enumeration District: 16; Image: 609.0. Birth date: about 1918 Birth place: Residence date: 1930 Residence place: Hokes Bluff, Etowah, Alabama.

1796   Ancestry.com, Social Security Death Index (Online publication - Provo, UT, USA: Ancestry.com Operations Inc, 2010. Original data - Social Security Administration. Social Security Death Index, Master File. Social Security Administration. Original data: Social Security Administration. Social Security D), Ancestry.com, http://www.Ancestry.com, Number: 422-18-5599; Issue State: Alabama; Issue Date: Before 1951. Birth date: 28 Sep 1918 Birth place: Death date: 30 May 2003 Death place: Gadsden, Etowah, Alabama, United States of America.

1797   Ancestry.com, U.S. Public Records Index, Volume 1 (Online publication - Provo, UT, USA: Ancestry.com Operations, Inc., 2010. Original data - Voter Registration Lists, Public Record Filings, Historical Residential Records, and Other Household Database Listings. Original data: Voter Registration Lists, Public), Ancestry.com, http://www.Ancestry.com, Birth date: 28 Sep 1918 Birth place: Residence date: 1977Residence place: Gadsden, AL.

1798   Ancestry.com, Social Security Death Index (Online publication - Provo, UT, USA: Ancestry.com Operations Inc, 2010. Original data - Social Security Administration. Social Security Death Index, Master File. Social Security Administration. Original data: Social Security Administration. Social Security D), Ancestry.com, http://www.Ancestry.com, Number: 420-16-2803; Issue State: Alabama; Issue Date: Before 1951. Birth date: 16 Aug 1922 Birth place: Death date: 6 Feb 1992 Death place:.

1799   Ancestry.com, 1930 United States Federal Census (Online publication - Provo, UT, USA: Ancestry.com Operations Inc, 2002. Original data - United States of America, Bureau of the Census. Fifteenth Census of the United States, 1930. Washington, D.C.: National Archives and Records Administration, 1930. T626,), Ancestry.com, http://www.Ancestry.com, Year: 1930; Census Place: Hokes Bluff, Etowah, Alabama; Roll: 16; Page: 9A; Enumeration District: 16; Image: 609.0. Birth date: about 1923 Birth place: Residence date: 1930 Residence place: Hokes Bluff, Etowah, Alabama.

1800   National Archives and Records Administration, U.S. World War II Army Enlistment Records, 1938-1946 (Online publication - Provo, UT, USA: Ancestry.com Operations Inc, 2005. Original data - Electronic Army Serial Number Merged File, 1938-1946 [Archival Database]; World War II Army Enlistment Records; Records of the National Archives and Records Administration), Ancestry.com, http://www.Ancestry.com, Birth date: 1922 Birth place: Residence date: Residence place: Alabama.

1801   Ancestry.com, U.S. Public Records Index, Volume 2 (Online publication - Provo, UT, USA: Ancestry.com Operations, Inc., 2010. Original data - Voter Registration Lists, Public Record Filings, Historical Residential Records, and Other Household Database Listings. Original data: Voter Registration Lists, Public), Ancestry.com, http://www.Ancestry.com, Residence date: 1935-1993Residence place: Gadsden, AL.

1802   Ancestry.com, U.S. Public Records Index, Volume 1 (Online publication - Provo, UT, USA: Ancestry.com Operations, Inc., 2010. Original data - Voter Registration Lists, Public Record Filings, Historical Residential Records, and Other Household Database Listings. Original data: Voter Registration Lists, Public), Ancestry.com, http://www.Ancestry.com, Residence date: 1981Residence place: Gadsden, AL.

1803   Ancestry.com, Alabama Marriage Collection, 1800-1969 (Online publication - Provo, UT, USA: Ancestry.com Operations Inc, 2006. Original data - Alabama Center for Health Statistics. Alabama Marriage Index, 1936-1969. Alabama Center for Health Statistics, Montgomery, Alabama. Dodd, Jordan R., et. al. Early America), Ancestry.com, http://www.Ancestry.com, Marriage date: 26 Mar 1942 Marriage place: Etowah, Alabama.

1804   Ancestry.com, World War I Draft Registration Cards, 1917-1918 (Online publication - Provo, UT, USA: Ancestry.com Operations Inc, 2005. Original data - United States, Selective Service System. World War I Selective Service System Draft Registration Cards, 1917-1918. Washington, D.C.: National Archives and Records Administration), Ancestry.com, http://www.Ancestry.com, Registration Location: Etowah County, Alabama; Roll: 1509384; Draft Board: 0. Birth date: 28 Aug 1885 Birth place: Residence date: Residence place: Etowah, Alabama.

1805   Ancestry.com, 1920 United States Federal Census (Online publication - Provo, UT, USA: Ancestry.com Operations Inc, 2010. Images reproduced by FamilySearch. Original data - Fourteenth Census of the United States, 1920. (NARA microfilm publication T625, 2076 rolls). Records of the Bureau of the Census, Record), Ancestry.com, http://www.Ancestry.com, Year: 1920; Census Place: Hokes Bluff, Etowah, Alabama; Roll: T625_15; Page: 2A; Enumeration District: 99; Image:. Birth date: about 1886 Birth place: Alabama Residence date: 1920 Residence place: Hokes Bluff, Etowah, Alabama.

1806   Ancestry.com, 1930 United States Federal Census (Online publication - Provo, UT, USA: Ancestry.com Operations Inc, 2002. Original data - United States of America, Bureau of the Census. Fifteenth Census of the United States, 1930. Washington, D.C.: National Archives and Records Administration, 1930. T626,), Ancestry.com, http://www.Ancestry.com, Year: 1930; Census Place: Hokes Bluff, Etowah, Alabama; Roll: 16; Page: 9A; Enumeration District: 16; Image: 609.0. Birth date: about 1886 Birth place: Alabama Residence date: 1930 Residence place: Hokes Bluff, Etowah, Alabama.

1807   Ancestry.com, 1910 United States Federal Census (Online publication - Provo, UT, USA: Ancestry.com Operations Inc, 2006. Original data - Thirteenth Census of the United States, 1910 (NARA microfilm publication T624, 1,178 rolls). Records of the Bureau of the Census, Record Group 29. National Archives, Washington), Ancestry.com, http://www.Ancestry.com, Year: 1910; Census Place: Hokes Bluff, Etowah, Alabama; Roll: ; Page: ; Enumeration District: ; Image:. Birth date: about 1886 Birth place: Alabama Residence date: 1910 Residence place: Hokes Bluff, Etowah, Alabama.

1808   Ancestry.com, 1900 United States Federal Census (Online publication - Provo, UT, USA: Ancestry.com Operations Inc, 2004. Original data - United States of America, Bureau of the Census. Twelfth Census of the United States, 1900. Washington, D.C.: National Archives and Records Administration, 1900. T623, 18), Ancestry.com, http://www.Ancestry.com, Year: 1900; Census Place: Hokes Bluff, Etowah, Alabama; Roll: T623_15; Page: 6B; Enumeration District: 151. Birth date: Jul 1886 Birth place: Alabama Residence date: 1900 Residence place: Hokes Bluff, Etowah, Alabama.

1809   Ancestry.com, Alabama Deaths, 1908-59 (Online publication - Provo, UT, USA: Ancestry.com Operations Inc, 2000. Original data - State of Alabama. Index of Vital Records for Alabama: Deaths, 1908-1959. Montgomery, AL, USA: State of Alabama Center for Health Statistics, Record Services Division. Original), Ancestry.com, http://www.Ancestry.com, Death date: 05 Jun 1954 Death place: Etowah.

1810   Ancestry.com, Alabama Marriage Collection, 1800-1969 (Online publication - Provo, UT, USA: Ancestry.com Operations Inc, 2006. Original data - Alabama Center for Health Statistics. Alabama Marriage Index, 1936-1969. Alabama Center for Health Statistics, Montgomery, Alabama. Dodd, Jordan R., et. al. Early America), Ancestry.com, http://www.Ancestry.com, Marriage date: Dec 1939 Marriage place: Etowah, Alabama.

1811   Ancestry.com, 1920 United States Federal Census (Online publication - Provo, UT, USA: Ancestry.com Operations Inc, 2010. Images reproduced by FamilySearch. Original data - Fourteenth Census of the United States, 1920. (NARA microfilm publication T625, 2076 rolls). Records of the Bureau of the Census, Record), Ancestry.com, http://www.Ancestry.com, Year: 1920; Census Place: Hokes Bluff, Etowah, Alabama; Roll: T625_15; Page: 2A; Enumeration District: 99; Image:. Birth date: about 1911 Birth place: Alabama Residence date: 1920 Residence place: Hokes Bluff, Etowah, Alabama.

1812   Ancestry.com, 1930 United States Federal Census (Online publication - Provo, UT, USA: Ancestry.com Operations Inc, 2002. Original data - United States of America, Bureau of the Census. Fifteenth Census of the United States, 1930. Washington, D.C.: National Archives and Records Administration, 1930. T626,), Ancestry.com, http://www.Ancestry.com, Year: 1930; Census Place: Hokes Bluff, Etowah, Alabama; Roll: 16; Page: 9A; Enumeration District: 16; Image: 609.0. Birth date: about 1911 Birth place: Residence date: 1930 Residence place: Hokes Bluff, Etowah, Alabama.

1813   Ancestry.com, Social Security Death Index (Online publication - Provo, UT, USA: Ancestry.com Operations Inc, 2010. Original data - Social Security Administration. Social Security Death Index, Master File. Social Security Administration. Original data: Social Security Administration. Social Security D), Ancestry.com, http://www.Ancestry.com, Number: 421-28-4956; Issue State: Alabama; Issue Date: Before 1951. Birth date: 3 Aug 1910 Birth place: Death date: Jul 1978 Death place: Gadsden, Etowah, Alabama, United States of America.

1814   Ancestry.com, Alabama Deaths, 1908-59 (Online publication - Provo, UT, USA: Ancestry.com Operations Inc, 2000. Original data - State of Alabama. Index of Vital Records for Alabama: Deaths, 1908-1959. Montgomery, AL, USA: State of Alabama Center for Health Statistics, Record Services Division. Original), Ancestry.com, http://www.Ancestry.com, Death date: 18 Apr 1920 Death place: Etowah.

1815   Ancestry.com, 1910 United States Federal Census (Online publication - Provo, UT, USA: Ancestry.com Operations Inc, 2006. Original data - Thirteenth Census of the United States, 1910 (NARA microfilm publication T624, 1,178 rolls). Records of the Bureau of the Census, Record Group 29. National Archives, Washington), Ancestry.com, http://www.Ancestry.com, Year: 1910; Census Place: Gadsden, Etowah, Alabama; Roll: ; Page: ; Enumeration District: ; Image:. Birth date: about 1885 Birth place: Alabama Residence date: 1910 Residence place: Gadsden, Etowah, Alabama.

1816   Ancestry.com, 1920 United States Federal Census (Online publication - Provo, UT, USA: Ancestry.com Operations Inc, 2010. Images reproduced by FamilySearch. Original data - Fourteenth Census of the United States, 1920. (NARA microfilm publication T625, 2076 rolls). Records of the Bureau of the Census, Record), Ancestry.com, http://www.Ancestry.com, Year: 1920; Census Place: Gadsden Ward 4, Etowah, Alabama; Roll: T625_15; Page: 9A; Enumeration District: 94; Image:. Birth date: about 1911 Birth place: Alabama Residence date: 1920 Residence place: Gadsden Ward 4, Etowah, Alabama.

1817   Ancestry.com, Alabama Marriage Collection, 1800-1969 (Online publication - Provo, UT, USA: Ancestry.com Operations Inc, 2006. Original data - Alabama Center for Health Statistics. Alabama Marriage Index, 1936-1969. Alabama Center for Health Statistics, Montgomery, Alabama. Dodd, Jordan R., et. al. Early America), Ancestry.com, http://www.Ancestry.com, Marriage date: 28 Sep 1940 Marriage place: Calhoun, Alabama.

1818   Ancestry.com, 1920 United States Federal Census (Online publication - Provo, UT, USA: Ancestry.com Operations Inc, 2010. Images reproduced by FamilySearch. Original data - Fourteenth Census of the United States, 1920. (NARA microfilm publication T625, 2076 rolls). Records of the Bureau of the Census, Record), Ancestry.com, http://www.Ancestry.com, Year: 1920; Census Place: Gadsden Ward 4, Etowah, Alabama; Roll: T625_15; Page: 9A; Enumeration District: 94; Image:. Birth date: about 1914 Birth place: Alabama Residence date: 1920 Residence place: Gadsden Ward 4, Etowah, Alabama.

1819   Ancestry.com, 1930 United States Federal Census (Online publication - Provo, UT, USA: Ancestry.com Operations Inc, 2002. Original data - United States of America, Bureau of the Census. Fifteenth Census of the United States, 1930. Washington, D.C.: National Archives and Records Administration, 1930. T626,), Ancestry.com, http://www.Ancestry.com, Year: 1930; Census Place: Fairview, Etowah, Alabama; Roll: 16; Page: 6A; Enumeration District: 20; Image: 679.0. Birth date: about 1913 Birth place: Residence date: 1930 Residence place: Fairview, Etowah, Alabama.

1820   Ancestry.com, 1930 United States Federal Census (Online publication - Provo, UT, USA: Ancestry.com Operations Inc, 2002. Original data - United States of America, Bureau of the Census. Fifteenth Census of the United States, 1930. Washington, D.C.: National Archives and Records Administration, 1930. T626,), Ancestry.com, http://www.Ancestry.com, Year: 1930; Census Place: Fairview, Etowah, Alabama; Roll: 16; Page: 6B; Enumeration District: 20; Image: 680.0. Birth date: about 1888 Birth place: Residence date: 1930 Residence place: Fairview, Etowah, Alabama.

1821   Ancestry.com, 1920 United States Federal Census (Online publication - Provo, UT, USA: Ancestry.com Operations Inc, 2010. Images reproduced by FamilySearch. Original data - Fourteenth Census of the United States, 1920. (NARA microfilm publication T625, 2076 rolls). Records of the Bureau of the Census, Record), Ancestry.com, http://www.Ancestry.com, Year: 1920; Census Place: Carlisle, Etowah, Alabama; Roll: T625_15; Page: 4B; Enumeration District: 105; Image:. Birth date: about 1887 Birth place: Alabama Residence date: 1920 Residence place: Carlisle, Etowah, Alabama.

1822   Ancestry.com, 1930 United States Federal Census (Online publication - Provo, UT, USA: Ancestry.com Operations Inc, 2002. Original data - United States of America, Bureau of the Census. Fifteenth Census of the United States, 1930. Washington, D.C.: National Archives and Records Administration, 1930. T626,), Ancestry.com, http://www.Ancestry.com, Year: 1930; Census Place: Fairview, Etowah, Alabama; Roll: 16; Page: 6B; Enumeration District: 20; Image: 680.0. Birth date: about 1906 Birth place: Residence date: 1930 Residence place: Fairview, Etowah, Alabama.

1823   Ancestry.com, 1920 United States Federal Census (Online publication - Provo, UT, USA: Ancestry.com Operations Inc, 2010. Images reproduced by FamilySearch. Original data - Fourteenth Census of the United States, 1920. (NARA microfilm publication T625, 2076 rolls). Records of the Bureau of the Census, Record), Ancestry.com, http://www.Ancestry.com, Year: 1920; Census Place: Carlisle, Etowah, Alabama; Roll: T625_15; Page: 4B; Enumeration District: 105; Image:. Birth date: about 1906 Birth place: Alabama Residence date: 1920 Residence place: Carlisle, Etowah, Alabama.

1824   Ancestry.com, 1930 United States Federal Census (Online publication - Provo, UT, USA: Ancestry.com Operations Inc, 2002. Original data - United States of America, Bureau of the Census. Fifteenth Census of the United States, 1930. Washington, D.C.: National Archives and Records Administration, 1930. T626,), Ancestry.com, http://www.Ancestry.com, Year: 1930; Census Place: Fairview, Etowah, Alabama; Roll: 16; Page: 6B; Enumeration District: 20; Image: 680.0. Birth date: about 1910 Birth place: Residence date: 1930 Residence place: Fairview, Etowah, Alabama.

1825   Ancestry.com, 1920 United States Federal Census (Online publication - Provo, UT, USA: Ancestry.com Operations Inc, 2010. Images reproduced by FamilySearch. Original data - Fourteenth Census of the United States, 1920. (NARA microfilm publication T625, 2076 rolls). Records of the Bureau of the Census, Record), Ancestry.com, http://www.Ancestry.com, Year: 1920; Census Place: Carlisle, Etowah, Alabama; Roll: T625_15; Page: 4B; Enumeration District: 105; Image:. Birth date: about 1910 Birth place: Alabama Residence date: 1920 Residence place: Carlisle, Etowah, Alabama.

1826   Ancestry.com, 1920 United States Federal Census (Online publication - Provo, UT, USA: Ancestry.com Operations Inc, 2010. Images reproduced by FamilySearch. Original data - Fourteenth Census of the United States, 1920. (NARA microfilm publication T625, 2076 rolls). Records of the Bureau of the Census, Record), Ancestry.com, http://www.Ancestry.com, Year: 1920; Census Place: Carlisle, Etowah, Alabama; Roll: T625_15; Page: 4B; Enumeration District: 105; Image:. Birth date: about 1917 Birth place: Alabama Residence date: 1920 Residence place: Carlisle, Etowah, Alabama.

1827   Ancestry.com, 1930 United States Federal Census (Online publication - Provo, UT, USA: Ancestry.com Operations Inc, 2002. Original data - United States of America, Bureau of the Census. Fifteenth Census of the United States, 1930. Washington, D.C.: National Archives and Records Administration, 1930. T626,), Ancestry.com, http://www.Ancestry.com, Year: 1930; Census Place: Fairview, Etowah, Alabama; Roll: 16; Page: 6B; Enumeration District: 20; Image: 680.0. Birth date: about 1916 Birth place: Residence date: 1930 Residence place: Fairview, Etowah, Alabama.

1828   Ancestry.com, 1930 United States Federal Census (Online publication - Provo, UT, USA: Ancestry.com Operations Inc, 2002. Original data - United States of America, Bureau of the Census. Fifteenth Census of the United States, 1930. Washington, D.C.: National Archives and Records Administration, 1930. T626,), Ancestry.com, http://www.Ancestry.com, Year: 1930; Census Place: Fairview, Etowah, Alabama; Roll: 16; Page: 6B; Enumeration District: 20; Image: 680.0. Birth date: about 1922 Birth place: Residence date: 1930 Residence place: Fairview, Etowah, Alabama.

1829   Ancestry.com, 1930 United States Federal Census (Online publication - Provo, UT, USA: Ancestry.com Operations Inc, 2002. Original data - United States of America, Bureau of the Census. Fifteenth Census of the United States, 1930. Washington, D.C.: National Archives and Records Administration, 1930. T626,), Ancestry.com, http://www.Ancestry.com, Year: 1930; Census Place: Fairview, Etowah, Alabama; Roll: 16; Page: 6B; Enumeration District: 20; Image: 680.0. Birth date: about 1926 Birth place: Residence date: 1930 Residence place: Fairview, Etowah, Alabama.

1830   Ancestry.com, 1930 United States Federal Census (Online publication - Provo, UT, USA: Ancestry.com Operations Inc, 2002. Original data - United States of America, Bureau of the Census. Fifteenth Census of the United States, 1930. Washington, D.C.: National Archives and Records Administration, 1930. T626,), Ancestry.com, http://www.Ancestry.com, Year: 1930; Census Place: Renfroe, Talladega, Alabama; Roll: 49; Page: 6B; Enumeration District: 18; Image: 994.0. Birth date: about 1899 Birth place: Residence date: 1930 Residence place: Renfroe, Talladega, Alabama.

1831   Ancestry.com, 1920 United States Federal Census (Online publication - Provo, UT, USA: Ancestry.com Operations Inc, 2010. Images reproduced by FamilySearch. Original data - Fourteenth Census of the United States, 1920. (NARA microfilm publication T625, 2076 rolls). Records of the Bureau of the Census, Record), Ancestry.com,

http://www.Ancestry.com, Year: 1920; Census Place: Renfroe, Talladega, Alabama; Roll: T625_41; Page: 9A; Enumeration District: 141; Image:. Birth date: about 1899 Birth place: Alabama Residence date: 1920 Residence place: Renfroe, Talladega, Alabama.

1832   Ancestry.com, 1920 United States Federal Census (Online publication - Provo, UT, USA: Ancestry.com Operations Inc, 2010. Images reproduced by FamilySearch. Original data - Fourteenth Census of the United States, 1920. (NARA microfilm publication T625, 2076 rolls). Records of the Bureau of the Census, Record), Ancestry.com, http://www.Ancestry.com, Year: 1920; Census Place: Renfroe, Talladega, Alabama; Roll: T625_41; Page: 9A; Enumeration District: 141; Image:. Birth date: about 1920 Birth place: Alabama Residence date: 1920 Residence place: Renfroe, Talladega, Alabama.

1833   Ancestry.com, 1930 United States Federal Census (Online publication - Provo, UT, USA: Ancestry.com Operations Inc, 2002. Original data - United States of America, Bureau of the Census. Fifteenth Census of the United States, 1930. Washington, D.C.: National Archives and Records Administration, 1930. T626,), Ancestry.com, http://www.Ancestry.com, Year: 1930; Census Place: Renfroe, Talladega, Alabama; Roll: 49; Page: 6B; Enumeration District: 18; Image: 994.0. Birth date: about 1919 Birth place: Residence date: 1930 Residence place: Renfroe, Talladega, Alabama.

1834   Ancestry.com, 1930 United States Federal Census (Online publication - Provo, UT, USA: Ancestry.com Operations Inc, 2002. Original data - United States of America, Bureau of the Census. Fifteenth Census of the United States, 1930. Washington, D.C.: National Archives and Records Administration, 1930. T626,), Ancestry.com, http://www.Ancestry.com, Year: 1930; Census Place: Renfroe, Talladega, Alabama; Roll: 49; Page: 6B; Enumeration District: 18; Image: 994.0. Birth date: about 1922 Birth place: Residence date: 1930 Residence place: Renfroe, Talladega, Alabama.

1835   Ancestry.com, 1930 United States Federal Census (Online publication - Provo, UT, USA: Ancestry.com Operations Inc, 2002. Original data - United States of America, Bureau of the Census. Fifteenth Census of the United States, 1930. Washington, D.C.: National Archives and Records Administration, 1930. T626,), Ancestry.com, http://www.Ancestry.com, Year: 1930; Census Place: Renfroe, Talladega, Alabama; Roll: 49; Page: 6B; Enumeration District: 18; Image: 994.0. Birth date: about 1925 Birth place: Residence date: 1930 Residence place: Renfroe, Talladega, Alabama.

1836   Ancestry.com, 1930 United States Federal Census (Online publication - Provo, UT, USA: Ancestry.com Operations Inc, 2002. Original data - United States of America, Bureau of the Census. Fifteenth Census of the United States, 1930. Washington, D.C.: National Archives and Records Administration, 1930. T626,), Ancestry.com, http://www.Ancestry.com, Year: 1930; Census Place: Renfroe, Talladega, Alabama; Roll: 49; Page: 6B; Enumeration District: 18; Image: 994.0. Birth date: about 1928 Birth place: Residence date: 1930 Residence place: Renfroe, Talladega, Alabama.

1837   Ancestry.com, 1930 United States Federal Census (Online publication - Provo, UT, USA: Ancestry.com Operations Inc, 2002. Original data - United States of America, Bureau of the Census. Fifteenth Census of the United States, 1930. Washington, D.C.: National Archives and Records Administration, 1930. T626,), Ancestry.com, http://www.Ancestry.com, Year: 1930; Census Place: Pell City, St Clair, Alabama; Roll: 48; Page: 1A; Enumeration District: 20; Image: 294.0. Birth date: about 1909 Birth place: Residence date: 1930 Residence place: Pell City, St Clair, Alabama.

1838   Ancestry.com, 1930 United States Federal Census (Online publication - Provo, UT, USA: Ancestry.com Operations Inc, 2002. Original data - United States of America, Bureau of the Census. Fifteenth Census of the United States, 1930. Washington, D.C.: National Archives and Records Administration, 1930. T626,), Ancestry.com, http://www.Ancestry.com, Year: 1930; Census Place: Pell City, St Clair, Alabama; Roll: 48; Page: 1A; Enumeration District: 20; Image: 294.0. Birth date: about 1927 Birth place: Residence date: 1930 Residence place: Pell City, St Clair, Alabama.

1839   Ancestry.com, Alabama Marriage Collection, 1800-1969 (Online publication - Provo, UT, USA: Ancestry.com Operations Inc, 2006. Original data - Alabama Center for Health Statistics. Alabama Marriage Index, 1936-1969. Alabama Center for Health Statistics, Montgomery, Alabama. Dodd, Jordan R., et. al. Early America), Ancestry.com, http://www.Ancestry.com, Marriage date: Jun 1964 Marriage place: Etowah, Alabama.

1840   Ancestry.com, Alabama Marriage Collection, 1800-1969 (Online publication - Provo, UT, USA: Ancestry.com Operations Inc, 2006. Original data - Alabama Center for Health Statistics. Alabama Marriage Index, 1936-1969. Alabama Center for Health Statistics, Montgomery, Alabama. Dodd, Jordan R., et. al. Early America), Ancestry.com, http://www.Ancestry.com, Marriage date: Dec 1969 Marriage place: Etowah, Alabama.

1841   Ancestry.com, Alabama Marriage Collection, 1800-1969 (Online publication - Provo, UT, USA: Ancestry.com Operations Inc, 2006. Original data - Alabama Center for Health Statistics. Alabama Marriage Index, 1936-1969. Alabama Center for Health Statistics, Montgomery, Alabama. Dodd, Jordan R., et. al. Early America), Ancestry.com, http://www.Ancestry.com, Marriage date: Dec 1969 Marriage place: Etowah, Alabama.

1842   Ancestry.com, 1930 United States Federal Census (Online publication - Provo, UT, USA: Ancestry.com Operations Inc, 2002. Original data - United States of America, Bureau of the Census. Fifteenth Census of the United States, 1930. Washington, D.C.: National Archives and Records Administration, 1930. T626,), Ancestry.com, http://www.Ancestry.com, Year: 1930; Census Place: Oxford, Calhoun, Alabama; Roll: 5; Page: 17B; Enumeration District: 20; Image: 509.0. Birth date: about 1905 Birth place: Alabama Residence date: 1930 Residence place: Oxford, Calhoun, Alabama.

1843   Ancestry.com, 1930 United States Federal Census (Online publication - Provo, UT, USA: Ancestry.com Operations Inc, 2002. Original data - United States of America, Bureau of the Census. Fifteenth Census of the United States, 1930. Washington, D.C.: National Archives and Records Administration, 1930. T626,), Ancestry.com, http://www.Ancestry.com, Year: 1930; Census Place: Oxford, Calhoun, Alabama; Roll: 5; Page: 17B; Enumeration District: 20; Image: 509.0. Birth date: about 1925 Birth place: Residence date: 1930 Residence place: Oxford, Calhoun, Alabama.

1844   Ancestry.com, 1930 United States Federal Census (Online publication - Provo, UT, USA: Ancestry.com Operations Inc, 2002. Original data - United States of America, Bureau of the Census. Fifteenth Census of the United States, 1930. Washington, D.C.: National Archives and Records Administration, 1930. T626,), Ancestry.com, http://www.Ancestry.com, Year: 1930; Census Place: Oxford, Calhoun, Alabama; Roll: 5; Page: 17B; Enumeration District: 20; Image: 509.0. Birth date: about 1928 Birth place: Residence date: 1930 Residence place: Oxford, Calhoun, Alabama.

1845   Ancestry.com, 1930 United States Federal Census (Online publication - Provo, UT, USA: Ancestry.com Operations Inc, 2002. Original data - United States of America, Bureau of the Census. Fifteenth Census of the United States, 1930. Washington, D.C.: National Archives and Records Administration, 1930. T626,), Ancestry.com, http://www.Ancestry.com, Year: 1930; Census Place: Oxford, Calhoun, Alabama; Roll: 5; Page: 5A; Enumeration District: 20; Image: 484.0. Birth date: about 1906 Birth place: Residence date: 1930 Residence place: Oxford, Calhoun, Alabama.

1846   Ancestry.com, 1930 United States Federal Census (Online publication - Provo, UT, USA: Ancestry.com Operations Inc, 2002. Original data - United States of America, Bureau of the Census. Fifteenth Census of the United States, 1930. Washington, D.C.: National Archives and Records Administration, 1930. T626,), Ancestry.com, http://www.Ancestry.com, Year: 1930; Census Place: Oxford, Calhoun, Alabama; Roll: 5; Page: 5A; Enumeration District: 20; Image: 484.0. Birth date: about 1928 Birth place: Residence date: 1930 Residence place: Oxford, Calhoun, Alabama.

1847   Ancestry.com, 1930 United States Federal Census (Online publication - Provo, UT, USA: Ancestry.com Operations Inc, 2002. Original data - United States of America, Bureau of the Census. Fifteenth Census of the United States, 1930. Washington, D.C.: National Archives and Records Administration, 1930. T626,), Ancestry.com, http://www.Ancestry.com, Year: 1930; Census Place: Gadsden, Etowah, Alabama; Roll: 16; Page: 19B; Enumeration District: 60; Image: 334.0. Birth date: about 1903 Birth place: Residence date: 1930 Residence place: Gadsden, Etowah, Alabama.

1848   Ancestry.com, Social Security Death Index (Online publication - Provo, UT, USA: Ancestry.com Operations Inc, 2010. Original data - Social Security Administration. Social Security Death Index, Master File. Social Security Administration. Original data: Social Security Administration. Social Security D), Ancestry.com, http://www.Ancestry.com, Number: 423-07-8299; Issue State: Alabama; Issue Date: Before 1951. Birth date: 2 Aug 1903 Birth place: Death date: Dec 1982 Death place: Gadsden, Etowah, Alabama, United States of America.

1849   Ancestry.com, 1930 United States Federal Census (Online publication - Provo, UT, USA: Ancestry.com Operations Inc, 2002. Original data - United States of America, Bureau of the Census. Fifteenth Census of the United States, 1930. Washington, D.C.: National Archives and Records Administration, 1930. T626,), Ancestry.com, http://www.Ancestry.com, Year: 1930; Census Place: Gadsden, Etowah, Alabama; Roll: 16; Page: 19B; Enumeration District: 60; Image: 334.0. Birth date: about 1927 Birth place: Residence date: 1930 Residence place: Gadsden, Etowah, Alabama.

1850   Ancestry.com, Alabama Marriage Collection, 1800-1969 (Online publication - Provo, UT, USA: Ancestry.com Operations Inc, 2006. Original data - Alabama Center for Health Statistics. Alabama Marriage Index, 1936-1969. Alabama Center for Health Statistics, Montgomery, Alabama. Dodd, Jordan R., et. al. Early America), Ancestry.com, http://www.Ancestry.com, Marriage date: 28 Aug 1948 Marriage place: Etowah, Alabama.

1851   Ancestry.com, U.S. Public Records Index, Volume 2 (Online publication - Provo, UT, USA: Ancestry.com Operations, Inc., 2010. Original data - Voter Registration Lists, Public Record Filings, Historical Residential Records, and Other Household Database Listings. Original data: Voter Registration Lists, Public), Ancestry.com, http://www.Ancestry.com, Residence date: 1935-1993Residence place: Anniston, AL.

1852   Ancestry.com, U.S. Public Records Index, Volume 1 (Online publication - Provo, UT, USA: Ancestry.com Operations, Inc., 2010. Original data - Voter Registration Lists, Public Record Filings, Historical Residential Records, and Other Household Database Listings. Original data: Voter Registration Lists, Public), Ancestry.com, http://www.Ancestry.com, Residence date: 1980 Residence place: Anniston, AL.

1853   Ancestry.com, U.S. Public Records Index, Volume 1 (Online publication - Provo, UT, USA: Ancestry.com Operations, Inc., 2010. Original data - Voter Registration Lists, Public Record Filings, Historical Residential Records, and Other Household Database Listings. Original data: Voter Registration Lists, Public), Ancestry.com, http://www.Ancestry.com, Residence date: 1989Residence place: Anniston, AL.

1854   Ancestry.com, U.S. Phone and Address Directories, 1993-2002 (Online publication - Provo, UT, USA: Ancestry.com Operations Inc, 2005. Original data - 1993-2002 White Pages. Little Rock, AR, USA: Acxiom Corporation. Original data: 1993-2002 White Pages. Little Rock, AR, USA: Acxiom Corporation.), Ancestry.com, http://www.Ancestry.com, Residence date: 1993 1994 1995 1996 1997Residence place: Anniston, Alabama.

1855   Ancestry.com, U.S. Phone and Address Directories, 1993-2002 (Online publication - Provo, UT, USA: Ancestry.com Operations Inc, 2005. Original data - 1993-2002 White Pages. Little Rock, AR, USA: Acxiom Corporation. Original data: 1993-2002 White Pages. Little Rock, AR, USA: Acxiom Corporation.), Ancestry.com, http://www.Ancestry.com, Residence date: 1998 1999 2000 2001 2002Residence place: Anniston, Alabama.

1856   Ancestry.com, Anniston Star (Anniston, Alabama) (Online publication - Provo, UT, USA: Ancestry.com Operations Inc, 2007. Original data - Anniston Star. Anniston, Alabama, United States Of America. Database created from microfilm copies of the newspaper. Original data: Anniston Star. Anniston, Alabama, Unit), Ancestry.com, http://www.Ancestry.com.

1857   Ancestry.com, U.S. Public Records Index, Volume 1 (Online publication - Provo, UT, USA: Ancestry.com Operations, Inc., 2010. Original data - Voter Registration Lists, Public Record Filings, Historical Residential Records, and Other Household Database Listings. Original data: Voter Registration Lists, Public), Ancestry.com, http://www.Ancestry.com, Birth date: 1929 Birth place: Residence date: 1994Residence place: Gadsden, AL.

1858   Ancestry.com, 1930 United States Federal Census (Online publication - Provo, UT, USA: Ancestry.com Operations Inc, 2002. Original data - United States of America, Bureau of the Census. Fifteenth Census of the United States, 1930. Washington, D.C.: National Archives and Records Administration, 1930. T626,), Ancestry.com, http://www.Ancestry.com, Year: 1930; Census Place: Gadsden, Etowah, Alabama; Roll: 16; Page: 19B; Enumeration District: 60; Image: 334.0. Birth date: about 1929 Birth place: Residence date: 1930 Residence place: Gadsden, Etowah, Alabama.

1859   Ancestry.com, Alabama Marriage Collection, 1800-1969 (Online publication - Provo, UT, USA: Ancestry.com Operations Inc, 2006. Original data - Alabama Center for Health Statistics. Alabama Marriage Index, 1936-1969. Alabama Center for Health Statistics, Montgomery, Alabama. Dodd, Jordan R., et. al. Early America), Ancestry.com, http://www.Ancestry.com, Marriage date: 14 Jun 1952 Marriage place: Etowah, Alabama.

1860   Ancestry.com, Alabama Marriage Collection, 1800-1969 (Online publication - Provo, UT, USA: Ancestry.com Operations Inc, 2006. Original data - Alabama Center for Health Statistics. Alabama Marriage Index, 1936-1969. Alabama Center for Health Statistics, Montgomery, Alabama. Dodd, Jordan R., et. al. Early America), Ancestry.com, http://www.Ancestry.com, Marriage date: 14 Jun 1952 Marriage place: Etowah, Alabama.

1861   Ancestry.com, 1920 United States Federal Census (Online publication - Provo, UT, USA: Ancestry.com Operations Inc, 2010. Images reproduced by FamilySearch. Original data - Fourteenth Census of the United States, 1920. (NARA microfilm publication T625, 2076 rolls). Records of the Bureau of the Census, Record), Ancestry.com, http://www.Ancestry.com, Year: 1920; Census Place: Gadsden Ward 3, Etowah, Alabama; Roll: T625_15; Page: 6B; Enumeration District: 93; Image:. Birth date: about 1909 Birth place: Tennessee Residence date: 1920 Residence place: Gadsden Ward 3, Etowah, Alabama.

1862   Ancestry.com, 1910 United States Federal Census (Online publication - Provo, UT, USA: Ancestry.com Operations Inc, 2006. Original data - Thirteenth Census of the United States, 1910 (NARA microfilm publication T624, 1,178 rolls). Records of the Bureau of the Census, Record Group 29. National Archives, Washington), Ancestry.com, http://www.Ancestry.com, Year: 1910; Census Place: Civil District 24, Lincoln, Tennessee; Roll: ; Page: ; Enumeration District: ; Image:. Birth date: about 1908 Birth place: Tennessee Residence date: 1910 Residence place: Civil District 24, Lincoln, Tennessee.

1863   Ancestry.com, Social Security Death Index (Online publication - Provo, UT, USA: Ancestry.com Operations Inc, 2010. Original data - Social Security Administration. Social Security Death Index, Master File. Social Security Administration. Original data: Social Security Administration. Social Security D), Ancestry.com, http://www.Ancestry.com, Number: 418-36-5506; Issue State: Alabama; Issue Date: Before 1951. Birth date: 23 Jul 1908 Birth place: Death date: Jan 1970 Death place: Gadsden, Etowah, Alabama, United States of America.

1864   Ancestry.com, 1930 United States Federal Census (Online publication - Provo, UT, USA: Ancestry.com Operations Inc, 2002. Original data - United States of America, Bureau of the Census. Fifteenth Census of the United States, 1930. Washington, D.C.: National Archives and Records Administration, 1930. T626,), Ancestry.com, http://www.Ancestry.com, Year: 1930; Census Place: Gadsden, Etowah, Alabama; Roll: 16; Page: 16A; Enumeration District: 8; Image: 373.0. Birth date: about 1909 Birth place: Residence date: 1930 Residence place: Gadsden, Etowah, Alabama.

1865   Ancestry.com, Alabama Marriage Collection, 1800-1969 (Online publication - Provo, UT, USA: Ancestry.com Operations Inc, 2006. Original data - Alabama Center for Health Statistics. Alabama Marriage Index, 1936-1969. Alabama Center for Health Statistics, Montgomery, Alabama. Dodd, Jordan R., et. al. Early America), Ancestry.com, http://www.Ancestry.com, Marriage date: 2 Jun 1951 Marriage place: Etowah, Alabama.

1866   Ancestry.com, Alabama Marriage Collection, 1800-1969 (Online publication - Provo, UT, USA: Ancestry.com Operations Inc, 2006. Original data - Alabama Center for Health Statistics. Alabama Marriage Index, 1936-1969. Alabama Center for Health Statistics, Montgomery, Alabama. Dodd, Jordan R., et. al. Early America), Ancestry.com, http://www.Ancestry.com, Marriage date: 2 Jun 1951 Marriage place: Etowah, Alabama.

1867   Ancestry.com, U.S. Public Records Index, Volume 1 (Online publication - Provo, UT, USA: Ancestry.com Operations, Inc., 2010. Original data - Voter Registration Lists, Public Record Filings, Historical Residential Records, and Other Household Database Listings. Original data: Voter Registration Lists, Public), Ancestry.com, http://www.Ancestry.com, Birth date: 1935 Birth place: Residence date: 1992Residence place: Gadsden, AL.

1868   Ancestry.com, U.S. Phone and Address Directories, 1993-2002 (Online publication - Provo, UT, USA: Ancestry.com Operations Inc, 2005. Original data - 1993-2002 White Pages. Little Rock, AR, USA: Acxiom Corporation. Original data: 1993-2002 White Pages. Little Rock, AR, USA: Acxiom Corporation.), Ancestry.com, http://www.Ancestry.com, Residence date: 1995 1996 1997Residence place: Gadsden, Alabama.

1869   Ancestry.com, U.S. Phone and Address Directories, 1993-2002 (Online publication - Provo, UT, USA: Ancestry.com Operations Inc, 2005. Original data - 1993-2002 White Pages. Little Rock, AR, USA: Acxiom Corporation. Original data: 1993-2002 White Pages. Little Rock, AR, USA: Acxiom Corporation.), Ancestry.com, http://www.Ancestry.com, Residence date: 1998 1999 2000 2002Residence place: Gadsden, Alabama.

1870   Ancestry.com, Alabama Marriage Collection, 1800-1969 (Online publication - Provo, UT, USA: Ancestry.com Operations Inc, 2006. Original data - Alabama Center for Health Statistics. Alabama Marriage Index, 1936-1969. Alabama Center for Health Statistics, Montgomery, Alabama. Dodd, Jordan R., et. al. Early America), Ancestry.com, http://www.Ancestry.com, Marriage date: May 1954 Marriage place: Etowah, Alabama.

1871   Ancestry.com, Alabama Marriage Collection, 1800-1969 (Online publication - Provo, UT, USA: Ancestry.com Operations Inc, 2006. Original data - Alabama Center for Health Statistics. Alabama Marriage Index, 1936-1969. Alabama Center for Health Statistics, Montgomery, Alabama. Dodd, Jordan R., et. al. Early America), Ancestry.com, http://www.Ancestry.com, Marriage date: May 1954 Marriage place: Etowah, Alabama.

1872   Ancestry.com, U.S. Public Records Index, Volume 1 (Online publication - Provo, UT, USA: Ancestry.com Operations, Inc., 2010. Original data - Voter Registration Lists, Public Record Filings, Historical Residential Records, and Other Household Database Listings. Original data: Voter Registration Lists, Public), Ancestry.com, http://www.Ancestry.com, Birth date: 1936 Birth place: Residence date: 1989Residence place: Birmingham, AL.

1873   Ancestry.com, U.S. Public Records Index, Volume 1 (Online publication - Provo, UT, USA: Ancestry.com Operations, Inc., 2010. Original data - Voter Registration Lists, Public Record Filings, Historical Residential Records, and Other Household Database Listings. Original data: Voter Registration Lists, Public), Ancestry.com, http://www.Ancestry.com, Birth date: 1936 Birth place: Residence date: 1970 Residence place: Birmingham, AL.

1874   Ancestry.com, U.S. Phone and Address Directories, 1993-2002 (Online publication - Provo, UT, USA: Ancestry.com Operations Inc, 2005. Original data - 1993-2002 White Pages. Little Rock, AR, USA: Acxiom Corporation. Original data: 1993-2002 White Pages. Little Rock, AR, USA: Acxiom Corporation.), Ancestry.com, http://www.Ancestry.com, Residence date: 1995 1996 1997 1998 1999Residence place: Birmingham, Alabama.

1875   Ancestry.com, Alabama Marriage Collection, 1800-1969 (Online publication - Provo, UT, USA: Ancestry.com Operations Inc, 2006. Original data - Alabama Center for Health Statistics. Alabama Marriage Index, 1936-1969. Alabama Center for Health Statistics, Montgomery, Alabama. Dodd, Jordan R., et. al. Early America), Ancestry.com, http://www.Ancestry.com, Marriage date: Jun 1958 Marriage place: Etowah, Alabama.

1876   Ancestry.com, Alabama Marriage Collection, 1800-1969 (Online publication - Provo, UT, USA: Ancestry.com Operations Inc, 2006. Original data - Alabama Center for Health Statistics. Alabama Marriage Index, 1936-1969. Alabama Center for Health Statistics, Montgomery, Alabama. Dodd, Jordan R., et. al. Early America), Ancestry.com, http://www.Ancestry.com, Date of Marriage.

1877   Ancestry.com, U.S. Public Records Index, Volume 1 (Online publication - Provo, UT, USA: Ancestry.com Operations, Inc., 2010. Original data - Voter Registration Lists, Public Record Filings, Historical Residential Records, and Other Household Database Listings. Original data: Voter Registration Lists, Public), Ancestry.com, http://www.Ancestry.com, Birth date: 1939 Birth place: Residence date: 1985Residence place: Hokes Bluff, AL.

1878   Ancestry.com, Alabama Marriage Collection, 1800-1969 (Online publication - Provo, UT, USA: Ancestry.com Operations Inc, 2006. Original data - Alabama Center for Health Statistics. Alabama Marriage Index, 1936-1969. Alabama Center for Health Statistics, Montgomery, Alabama. Dodd, Jordan R., et. al. Early America), Ancestry.com, http://www.Ancestry.com, Marriage date: Jun 1958 Marriage place: Etowah, Alabama.

1879   Ancestry.com, Anniston Star (Anniston, Alabama) (Online publication - Provo, UT, USA: Ancestry.com Operations Inc, 2007. Original data - Anniston Star. Anniston, Alabama, United States Of America. Database created from microfilm copies of the newspaper. Original data: Anniston Star. Anniston, Alabama, Unit), Ancestry.com, http://www.Ancestry.com, Name and Residence referenced in Obituary for Floyd Reeves.

1880   Ancestry.com, 1920 United States Federal Census (Online publication - Provo, UT, USA: Ancestry.com Operations Inc, 2010. Images reproduced by FamilySearch. Original data - Fourteenth Census of the United States, 1920. (NARA microfilm publication T625, 2076 rolls). Records of the Bureau of the Census, Record), Ancestry.com, http://www.Ancestry.com, Year: 1920; Census Place: Gadsden Ward 3, Etowah, Alabama; Roll: T625_15; Page: 49A; Enumeration District: 93; Image:. Birth date: about 1904 Birth place: Alabama Residence date: 1920 Residence place: Gadsden Ward 3, Etowah, Alabama.

1881   Ancestry.com, 1930 United States Federal Census (Online publication - Provo, UT, USA: Ancestry.com Operations Inc, 2002. Original data - United States of America, Bureau of the Census. Fifteenth Census of the United States, 1930. Washington, D.C.: National Archives and Records Administration, 1930. T626,), Ancestry.com, http://www.Ancestry.com, Year: 1930; Census Place: Gadsden, Etowah, Alabama; Roll: 16; Page: 25B; Enumeration District: 9; Image: 428.0. Birth date: about 1904 Birth place: Alabama Residence date: 1930 Residence place: Gadsden, Etowah, Alabama.

1882   Ancestry.com, Social Security Death Index (Online publication - Provo, UT, USA: Ancestry.com Operations Inc, 2010. Original data - Social Security Administration. Social Security Death Index, Master File. Social Security Administration. Original data: Social Security Administration. Social Security D), Ancestry.com, http://www.Ancestry.com, Number: 419-05-0373; Issue State: Alabama; Issue Date: Before 1951. Birth date: 1 Jan 1904 Birth place: Death date: Oct 1984 Death place: Decatur, Dekalb, Georgia, United States of America.

1883   Ancestry.com, Georgia Deaths, 1919-98 (Online publication - Provo, UT, USA: Ancestry.com Operations Inc, 2001. Original data - State of Georgia. Indexes of Vital Records for Georgia: Deaths, 1919-1998. Georgia, USA: Georgia Health Department, Office of Vital Records, 1998. Original data: State of), Ancestry.com, http://www.Ancestry.com, Certificate number: 035331. Birth date: about 1904 Birth place: Death date: 13 Oct 1984 Death place: Dekalb, Georgia Residence date: Residence place: Dekalb.

1884   Ancestry.com, 1910 United States Federal Census (Online publication - Provo, UT, USA: Ancestry.com Operations Inc, 2006. Original data - Thirteenth Census of the United States, 1910 (NARA microfilm publication T624, 1,178 rolls). Records of the Bureau of the Census, Record Group 29. National Archives, Washington), Ancestry.com, http://www.Ancestry.com, Year: 1910; Census Place: Gadsden, Etowah, Alabama; Roll: ; Page: ; Enumeration District: ; Image:. Birth date: about 1904 Birth place: Alabama Residence date: 1910 Residence place: Gadsden, Etowah, Alabama.

1885   Ancestry.com, 1930 United States Federal Census (Online publication - Provo, UT, USA: Ancestry.com Operations Inc, 2002. Original data - United States of America, Bureau of the Census. Fifteenth Census of the United States, 1930. Washington, D.C.: National Archives and Records Administration, 1930. T626,), Ancestry.com, http://www.Ancestry.com, Year: 1930; Census Place: Birmingham, Jefferson, Alabama; Roll: 28; Page: 11A; Enumeration District: 77; Image: 160.0. Birth date: about 1908 Birth place: Residence date: 1930 Residence place: Birmingham, Jefferson, Alabama.

1886   Ancestry.com, 1920 United States Federal Census (Online publication - Provo, UT, USA: Ancestry.com Operations Inc, 2010. Images reproduced by FamilySearch. Original data - Fourteenth Census of the United States, 1920. (NARA microfilm publication T625, 2076 rolls). Records of the Bureau of the Census, Record), Ancestry.com, http://www.Ancestry.com, Year: 1920; Census Place: Birmingham, Jefferson, Alabama; Roll: T625_25; Page: 4A; Enumeration District: 98; Image:. Birth date: about 1908 Birth place: Alabama Residence date: 1920 Residence place: Birmingham, Jefferson, Alabama.

1887   Ancestry.com, Social Security Death Index (Online publication - Provo, UT, USA: Ancestry.com Operations Inc, 2010. Original data - Social Security Administration. Social Security Death Index, Master File. Social Security Administration. Original data: Social Security Administration. Social Security D), Ancestry.com, http://www.Ancestry.com, Number: 401-10-3336; Issue State: Kentucky; Issue Date: Before 1951. Birth date: 22 Oct 1907 Birth place: Death date: 25 Jan 1994 Death place: Birmingham, Jefferson, Alabama, United States of America.

1888   Ancestry.com, Alabama Marriage Collection, 1800-1969 (Online publication - Provo, UT, USA: Ancestry.com Operations Inc, 2006. Original data - Alabama Center for Health Statistics. Alabama Marriage Index, 1936-1969. Alabama Center for Health Statistics, Montgomery, Alabama. Dodd, Jordan R., et. al. Early America), Ancestry.com, http://www.Ancestry.com, Marriage date: 15 Apr 1944 Marriage place: Jefferson, Alabama.

1889   Ancestry.com, U.S. Phone and Address Directories, 1993-2002 (Online publication - Provo, UT, USA: Ancestry.com Operations Inc, 2005. Original data - 1993-2002 White Pages. Little Rock, AR, USA: Acxiom Corporation. Original data: 1993-2002 White Pages. Little Rock, AR, USA: Acxiom Corporation.), Ancestry.com, http://www.Ancestry.com, Residence date: 1993 1994 1995 1996 1997Residence place: Birmingham, Alabama.

1890   Ancestry.com, 1930 United States Federal Census (Online publication - Provo, UT, USA: Ancestry.com Operations Inc, 2002. Original data - United States of America, Bureau of the Census. Fifteenth Census of the United States, 1930. Washington, D.C.: National Archives and Records Administration, 1930. T626,), Ancestry.com, http://www.Ancestry.com, Year: 1930; Census Place: Birmingham, Jefferson, Alabama; Roll: 25; Page: 3B; Enumeration District: 43; Image: 1063.0. Birth date: about 1910 Birth place: Residence date: 1930 Residence place: Birmingham, Jefferson, Alabama.

1891   Ancestry.com, 1920 United States Federal Census (Online publication - Provo, UT, USA: Ancestry.com Operations Inc, 2010. Images reproduced by FamilySearch. Original data - Fourteenth Census of the United States, 1920. (NARA microfilm publication T625, 2076 rolls). Records of the Bureau of the Census, Record), Ancestry.com, http://www.Ancestry.com, Year: 1920; Census Place: Birmingham, Jefferson, Alabama; Roll: T625_23; Page: 4A; Enumeration District: 32; Image:. Birth date: about 1910 Birth place: Alabama Residence date: 1920 Residence place: Birmingham, Jefferson, Alabama.

1892   Ancestry.com, 1910 United States Federal Census (Online publication - Provo, UT, USA: Ancestry.com Operations Inc, 2006. Original data - Thirteenth Census of the United States, 1910 (NARA microfilm publication T624, 1,178 rolls). Records of the Bureau of the Census, Record Group 29. National Archives, Washington), Ancestry.com, http://www.Ancestry.com, Year: 1910; Census Place: Birmingham Ward 10, Jefferson, Alabama; Roll: ; Page: ; Enumeration District: ; Image:. Birth date: about 1909 Birth place: Alabama Residence date: 1910 Residence place: Birmingham Ward 10, Jefferson, Alabama.

1893   Ancestry.com, Social Security Death Index (Online publication - Provo, UT, USA: Ancestry.com Operations Inc, 2010. Original data - Social Security Administration. Social Security Death Index, Master File. Social Security Administration. Original data: Social Security Administration. Social Security D), Ancestry.com, http://www.Ancestry.com, Number: 428-10-9025; Issue State: Mississippi; Issue Date: Before 1951. Birth date: 10 Sep 1909 Birth place: Death date: 11 Jun 1997 Death place: Birmingham, Jefferson, Alabama, United States of America.

1894   Ancestry.com, U.S. Public Records Index, Volume 2 (Online publication - Provo, UT, USA: Ancestry.com Operations, Inc., 2010. Original data - Voter Registration Lists, Public Record Filings, Historical Residential Records, and Other Household Database Listings. Original data: Voter Registration Lists, Public), Ancestry.com, http://www.Ancestry.com, Birth date: 10 Sep 1909 Birth place: Residence date: 1935-1993 Residence place: Manchester, TN.

1895   Ancestry.com, Alabama Marriage Collection, 1800-1969 (Online publication - Provo, UT, USA: Ancestry.com Operations Inc, 2006. Original data - Alabama Center for Health Statistics. Alabama Marriage Index, 1936-1969. Alabama Center for Health Statistics, Montgomery, Alabama. Dodd, Jordan R., et. al. Early America), Ancestry.com, http://www.Ancestry.com, Marriage date: 15 Jan 1944 Marriage place: Jefferson, Alabama.

1896   Ancestry.com, 1930 United States Federal Census (Online publication - Provo, UT, USA: Ancestry.com Operations Inc, 2002. Original data - United States of America, Bureau of the Census. Fifteenth Census of the United States, 1930. Washington, D.C.: National Archives and Records Administration, 1930. T626,), Ancestry.com, http://www.Ancestry.com, Year: 1930; Census Place: Hokes Bluff, Etowah, Alabama; Roll: 16; Page: 8B; Enumeration District: 16; Image: 608.0. Birth date: about 1909 Birth place: Residence date: 1930 Residence place: Hokes Bluff, Etowah, Alabama.

1897   Ancestry.com, Social Security Death Index (Online publication - Provo, UT, USA: Ancestry.com Operations Inc, 2010. Original data - Social Security Administration. Social Security Death Index, Master File. Social Security Administration. Original data: Social Security Administration. Social Security D), Ancestry.com, http://www.Ancestry.com, Number: 424-78-9746; Issue State: Alabama; Issue Date: 1970. Birth date: 15 Oct 1908 Birth place: Death date: 16 Jun 2000 Death place: Gadsden, Etowah, Alabama, United States of America.

1898   Ancestry.com, 1910 United States Federal Census (Online publication - Provo, UT, USA: Ancestry.com Operations Inc, 2006. Original data - Thirteenth Census of the United States, 1910 (NARA microfilm publication T624, 1,178 rolls). Records of the Bureau of the Census, Record Group 29. National Archives, Washington), Ancestry.com, http://www.Ancestry.com, Year: 1910; Census Place: Hokes Bluff, Etowah, Alabama; Roll: ; Page: ; Enumeration District: ; Image:. Birth date: about 1908 Birth place: Alabama Residence date: 1910 Residence place: Hokes Bluff, Etowah, Alabama.

1899   Ancestry.com, 1920 United States Federal Census (Online publication - Provo, UT, USA: Ancestry.com Operations Inc, 2010. Images reproduced by FamilySearch. Original data - Fourteenth Census of the United States, 1920. (NARA microfilm publication T625, 2076 rolls). Records of the Bureau of the Census, Record), Ancestry.com, http://www.Ancestry.com, Year: 1920; Census Place: Hokes Bluff, Etowah, Alabama; Roll: T625_15; Page: 8B; Enumeration District: 99; Image:. Birth date: about 1909 Birth place: Alabama Residence date: 1920 Residence place: Hokes Bluff, Etowah, Alabama.

1900   Ancestry.com, 1930 United States Federal Census (Online publication - Provo, UT, USA: Ancestry.com Operations Inc, 2002. Original data - United States of America, Bureau of the Census. Fifteenth Census of the United States, 1930. Washington, D.C.: National Archives and Records Administration, 1930. T626,), Ancestry.com, http://www.Ancestry.com, Year: 1930; Census Place: Hokes Bluff, Etowah, Alabama; Roll: 16; Page: 8B; Enumeration District: 16; Image: 608.0. Birth date: about 1929 Birth place: Residence date: 1930 Residence place: Hokes Bluff, Etowah, Alabama.

1901   Ancestry.com, U.S. Public Records Index, Volume 1 (Online publication - Provo, UT, USA: Ancestry.com Operations, Inc., 2010. Original data - Voter Registration Lists, Public Record Filings, Historical Residential Records, and Other Household Database Listings. Original data: Voter Registration Lists, Public), Ancestry.com, http://www.Ancestry.com, Birth date: 1929 Birth place: Residence date: 1995Residence place: Gadsden, AL.

1902   Ancestry.com, Alabama Marriage Collection, 1800-1969 (Online publication - Provo, UT, USA: Ancestry.com Operations Inc, 2006. Original data - Alabama Center for Health Statistics. Alabama Marriage Index, 1936-1969. Alabama Center for Health Statistics, Montgomery, Alabama. Dodd, Jordan R., et. al. Early America), Ancestry.com, http://www.Ancestry.com, Marriage date: 28 Feb 1948 Marriage place: Etowah, Alabama.

1903   Ancestry.com, Alabama Marriage Collection, 1800-1969 (Online publication - Provo, UT, USA: Ancestry.com Operations Inc, 2006. Original data - Alabama Center for Health Statistics. Alabama Marriage Index, 1936-1969. Alabama Center for Health Statistics, Montgomery, Alabama. Dodd, Jordan R., et. al. Early America), Ancestry.com, http://www.Ancestry.com, Marriage date: 28 Feb 1948 Marriage place: Etowah, Alabama.

1904   Ancestry.com, 1930 United States Federal Census (Online publication - Provo, UT, USA: Ancestry.com Operations Inc, 2002. Original data - United States of America, Bureau of the Census. Fifteenth Census of the United States, 1930. Washington, D.C.: National Archives and Records Administration, 1930. T626,), Ancestry.com, http://www.Ancestry.com, Year: 1930; Census Place: Hokes Bluff, Etowah, Alabama; Roll: 16; Page: 8A; Enumeration District: 16; Image: 607.0. Birth date: about 1924 Birth place: Residence date: 1930 Residence place: Hokes Bluff, Etowah, Alabama.

1905   Ancestry.com, U.S. Phone and Address Directories, 1993-2002 (Online publication - Provo, UT, USA: Ancestry.com Operations Inc, 2005. Original data - 1993-2002 White Pages. Little Rock, AR, USA: Acxiom Corporation. Original data: 1993-2002 White Pages. Little Rock, AR, USA: Acxiom Corporation.), Ancestry.com, http://www.Ancestry.com, Residence date: 1999 2000 2001 2002Residence place: Leicester, North Carolina.

1906   Ancestry.com, Alabama Marriage Collection, 1800-1969 (Online publication - Provo, UT, USA: Ancestry.com Operations Inc, 2006. Original data - Alabama Center for Health Statistics. Alabama Marriage Index, 1936-1969. Alabama Center for Health Statistics, Montgomery, Alabama. Dodd, Jordan R., et. al. Early America), Ancestry.com, http://www.Ancestry.com, Marriage date: Apr 1963 Marriage place: Etowah, Alabama.

1907   Ancestry.com, U.S. Public Records Index, Volume 1 (Online publication - Provo, UT, USA: Ancestry.com Operations, Inc., 2010. Original data - Voter Registration Lists, Public Record Filings, Historical Residential Records, and

Other Household Database Listings. Original data: Voter Registration Lists, Public), Ancestry.com, http://www.Ancestry.com, Birth date: 1942 Birth place: Residence date: 1993Residence place: Gadsden, AL.

1908   Ancestry.com, Alabama Marriage Collection, 1800-1969 (Online publication - Provo, UT, USA: Ancestry.com Operations Inc, 2006. Original data - Alabama Center for Health Statistics. Alabama Marriage Index, 1936-1969. Alabama Center for Health Statistics, Montgomery, Alabama. Dodd, Jordan R., et. al. Early America), Ancestry.com, http://www.Ancestry.com, Marriage date: Apr 1963 Marriage place: Etowah, Alabama.

1909   Ancestry.com, Social Security Death Index (Online publication - Provo, UT, USA: Ancestry.com Operations Inc, 2010. Original data - Social Security Administration. Social Security Death Index, Master File. Social Security Administration. Original data: Social Security Administration. Social Security D), Ancestry.com, http://www.Ancestry.com, Number: 421-94-1748; Issue State: Alabama; Issue Date: 1975. Birth date: 18 Oct 1916 Birth place: Death date: Apr 1987 Death place: Gadsden, Etowah, Alabama, United States of America.

1910   Ancestry.com, 1920 United States Federal Census (Online publication - Provo, UT, USA: Ancestry.com Operations Inc, 2010. Images reproduced by FamilySearch. Original data - Fourteenth Census of the United States, 1920. (NARA microfilm publication T625, 2076 rolls). Records of the Bureau of the Census, Record), Ancestry.com, http://www.Ancestry.com, Year: 1920; Census Place: Gadsden Ward 3, Etowah, Alabama; Roll: T625_15; Page: 60B; Enumeration District: 93; Image:. Birth date: about 1917 Birth place: Alabama Residence date: 1920 Residence place: Gadsden Ward 3, Etowah, Alabama.

1911   Ancestry.com, U.S. Public Records Index, Volume 1 (Online publication - Provo, UT, USA: Ancestry.com Operations, Inc., 2010. Original data - Voter Registration Lists, Public Record Filings, Historical Residential Records, and Other Household Database Listings. Original data: Voter Registration Lists, Public), Ancestry.com, http://www.Ancestry.com, Birth date: 1936 Birth place: Residence date: 1993Residence place: Gadsden, AL.

1912   Ancestry.com, Alabama Marriage Collection, 1800-1969 (Online publication - Provo, UT, USA: Ancestry.com Operations Inc, 2006. Original data - Alabama Center for Health Statistics. Alabama Marriage Index, 1936-1969. Alabama Center for Health Statistics, Montgomery, Alabama. Dodd, Jordan R., et. al. Early America), Ancestry.com, http://www.Ancestry.com, Marriage date: Jul 1953 Marriage place: Etowah, Alabama.

1913   Ancestry.com, U.S. Public Records Index, Volume 1 (Online publication - Provo, UT, USA: Ancestry.com Operations, Inc., 2010. Original data - Voter Registration Lists, Public Record Filings, Historical Residential Records, and Other Household Database Listings. Original data: Voter Registration Lists, Public), Ancestry.com, http://www.Ancestry.com, Birth date: 1937 Birth place: Residence date: 1993 Residence place: Gadsden, AL.

1914   Ancestry.com, Alabama Marriage Collection, 1800-1969 (Online publication - Provo, UT, USA: Ancestry.com Operations Inc, 2006. Original data - Alabama Center for Health Statistics. Alabama Marriage Index, 1936-1969. Alabama Center for Health Statistics, Montgomery, Alabama. Dodd, Jordan R., et. al. Early America), Ancestry.com, http://www.Ancestry.com, Marriage date: Feb 1954 Marriage place: Etowah, Alabama.

1915   Ancestry.com, Alabama Divorce Index, 1950-1959 (Online publication - Provo, UT, USA: Ancestry.com Operations Inc, 2006. Original data - Alabama Center for Health Statistics. Alabama Divorce Index, 1950-1959. Montgomery, AL, USA: Alabama Center for Health Statistics. Original data: Alabama Center for Health), Ancestry.com, http://www.Ancestry.com, Divorce date: Oct 1955 Divorce place: Etowah, Alabama.

1916   Ancestry.com, Alabama Divorce Index, 1950-1959 (Online publication - Provo, UT, USA: Ancestry.com Operations Inc, 2006. Original data - Alabama Center for Health Statistics. Alabama Divorce Index, 1950-1959. Montgomery, AL, USA: Alabama Center for Health Statistics. Original data: Alabama Center for Health), Ancestry.com, http://www.Ancestry.com, Divorce date: Jan 1958 Divorce place: Etowah, Alabama.

1917   Ancestry.com, Alabama Marriage Collection, 1800-1969 (Online publication - Provo, UT, USA: Ancestry.com Operations Inc, 2006. Original data - Alabama Center for Health Statistics. Alabama Marriage Index, 1936-1969. Alabama Center for Health Statistics, Montgomery, Alabama. Dodd, Jordan R., et. al. Early America), Ancestry.com, http://www.Ancestry.com, Marriage Date for Otis Lawson.

1918   Ancestry.com, Alabama Marriage Collection, 1800-1969 (Online publication - Provo, UT, USA: Ancestry.com Operations Inc, 2006. Original data - Alabama Center for Health Statistics. Alabama Marriage Index, 1936-1969. Alabama Center for Health Statistics, Montgomery, Alabama. Dodd, Jordan R., et. al. Early America), Ancestry.com, http://www.Ancestry.com, Marriage date: Dec 1960 Marriage place: Etowah, Alabama.

1919   Ancestry.com, Alabama Marriage Collection, 1800-1969 (Online publication - Provo, UT, USA: Ancestry.com Operations Inc, 2006. Original data - Alabama Center for Health Statistics. Alabama Marriage Index, 1936-1969. Alabama Center for Health Statistics, Montgomery, Alabama. Dodd, Jordan R., et. al. Early America), Ancestry.com, http://www.Ancestry.com, Marriage date: Jun 1962 Marriage place: Etowah, Alabama.

1920   Ancestry.com, Alabama Marriage Collection, 1800-1969 (Online publication - Provo, UT, USA: Ancestry.com Operations Inc, 2006. Original data - Alabama Center for Health Statistics. Alabama Marriage Index, 1936-1969. Alabama Center for Health Statistics, Montgomery, Alabama. Dodd, Jordan R., et. al. Early America), Ancestry.com, http://www.Ancestry.com, Marriage date: Jun 1962 Marriage place: Etowah, Alabama.

1921   Ancestry.com, Alabama Deaths, 1908-59 (Online publication - Provo, UT, USA: Ancestry.com Operations Inc, 2000. Original data - State of Alabama. Index of Vital Records for Alabama: Deaths, 1908-1959. Montgomery, AL, USA: State of Alabama Center for Health Statistics, Record Services Division. Original), Ancestry.com, http://www.Ancestry.com, Death date: 11 Jul 1957 Death place: Etowah.

1922   Ancestry.com, Alabama Marriage Collection, 1800-1969 (Online publication - Provo, UT, USA: Ancestry.com Operations Inc, 2006. Original data - Alabama Center for Health Statistics. Alabama Marriage Index, 1936-1969. Alabama Center for Health Statistics, Montgomery, Alabama. Dodd, Jordan R., et. al. Early America), Ancestry.com, http://www.Ancestry.com, Marriage date: 26 Jun 1943 Marriage place: Etowah, Alabama.

1923   Ancestry.com, 1930 United States Federal Census (Online publication - Provo, UT, USA: Ancestry.com Operations Inc, 2002. Original data - United States of America, Bureau of the Census. Fifteenth Census of the United States, 1930. Washington, D.C.: National Archives and Records Administration, 1930. T626,), Ancestry.com, http://www.Ancestry.com, Year: 1930; Census Place: Gadsden, Etowah, Alabama; Roll: 16; Page: 7B; Enumeration District: 3; Image: 96.0. Birth date: about 1924 Birth place: Residence date: 1930 Residence place: Gadsden, Etowah, Alabama.

1924   Ancestry.com, U.S. Public Records Index, Volume 1 (Online publication - Provo, UT, USA: Ancestry.com Operations, Inc., 2010. Original data - Voter Registration Lists, Public Record Filings, Historical Residential Records, and Other Household Database Listings. Original data: Voter Registration Lists, Public), Ancestry.com, http://www.Ancestry.com, Birth date: 1950 Birth place: Residence date: 1995Residence place: Athens, GA.

1925   Ancestry.com, U.S. Public Records Index, Volume 1 (Online publication - Provo, UT, USA: Ancestry.com Operations, Inc., 2010. Original data - Voter Registration Lists, Public Record Filings, Historical Residential Records, and Other Household Database Listings. Original data: Voter Registration Lists, Public), Ancestry.com, http://www.Ancestry.com, Birth date: 1957 Birth place: Residence date: 1987Residence place: Rome, GA.

1926   National Archives and Records Administration, U.S. World War II Army Enlistment Records, 1938-1946 (Online publication - Provo, UT, USA: Ancestry.com Operations Inc, 2005. Original data - Electronic Army Serial Number Merged File, 1938-1946 [Archival Database]; World War II Army Enlistment Records; Records of the National Archives and Records Administration), Ancestry.com, http://www.Ancestry.com, Pre-enlistment occupation listed on source.

1927   Ancestry.com, 1930 United States Federal Census (Online publication - Provo, UT, USA: Ancestry.com Operations Inc, 2002. Original data - United States of America, Bureau of the Census. Fifteenth Census of the United States, 1930. Washington, D.C.: National Archives and Records Administration, 1930. T626,), Ancestry.com, http://www.Ancestry.com, Year: 1930; Census Place: Anniston, Calhoun, Alabama; Roll: 5; Page: 9B; Enumeration District: 50; Image: 1030.0. Birth date: about 1905 Birth place: Residence date: 1930 Residence place: Anniston, Calhoun, Alabama.

1928   Ancestry.com, 1920 United States Federal Census (Online publication - Provo, UT, USA: Ancestry.com Operations Inc, 2010. Images reproduced by FamilySearch. Original data - Fourteenth Census of the United States, 1920. (NARA microfilm publication T625, 2076 rolls). Records of the Bureau of the Census, Record), Ancestry.com, http://www.Ancestry.com, Year: 1920; Census Place: Anniston Ward 6, Calhoun, Alabama; Roll: T625_5; Page: 13B; Enumeration District: 157; Image:. Birth date: about 1905 Birth place: Alabama Residence date: 1920 Residence place: Anniston Ward 6, Calhoun, Alabama.

1929   Ancestry.com, Alabama Marriage Collection, 1800-1969 (Online publication - Provo, UT, USA: Ancestry.com Operations Inc, 2006. Original data - Alabama Center for Health Statistics. Alabama Marriage Index, 1936-1969. Alabama Center for Health Statistics, Montgomery, Alabama. Dodd, Jordan R., et. al. Early America), Ancestry.com, http://www.Ancestry.com, Marriage date: 2 May 1952 Marriage place: Calhoun, Alabama.

1930   Ancestry.com, Social Security Death Index (Online publication - Provo, UT, USA: Ancestry.com Operations Inc, 2010. Original data - Social Security Administration. Social Security Death Index, Master File. Social Security Administration. Original data: Social Security Administration. Social Security D), Ancestry.com, http://www.Ancestry.com, Number: 423-07-1973; Issue State: Alabama; Issue Date: Before 1951. Birth date: 12 Jan 1923 Birth place: Death date: 6 Nov 2010 Death place: Pasadena, Harris, Texas, United States of America.

1931   Ancestry.com, U.S. Public Records Index, Volume 1 (Online publication - Provo, UT, USA: Ancestry.com Operations, Inc., 2010. Original data - Voter Registration Lists, Public Record Filings, Historical Residential Records, and Other Household Database Listings. Original data: Voter Registration Lists, Public), Ancestry.com, http://www.Ancestry.com, Birth date: 1923 Birth place: Residence date: 1992 Residence place: Pasadena, TX.

1932   Ancestry.com, 1930 United States Federal Census (Online publication - Provo, UT, USA: Ancestry.com Operations Inc, 2002. Original data - United States of America, Bureau of the Census. Fifteenth Census of the United States, 1930. Washington, D.C.: National Archives and Records Administration, 1930. T626,), Ancestry.com, http://www.Ancestry.com, Year: 1930; Census Place: Anniston, Calhoun, Alabama; Roll: 5; Page: 9B; Enumeration District: 50; Image: 1030.0. Birth date: about 1923 Birth place: Residence date: 1930 Residence place: Anniston, Calhoun, Alabama.

1933   Ancestry.com, Anniston Star (Anniston, Alabama) (Online publication - Provo, UT, USA: Ancestry.com Operations Inc, 2007. Original data - Anniston Star. Anniston, Alabama, United States Of America. Database created from microfilm copies of the newspaper. Original data: Anniston Star. Anniston, Alabama, Unit), Ancestry.com, http://www.Ancestry.com.

1934   Ancestry.com, Anniston Star (Anniston, Alabama) (Online publication - Provo, UT, USA: Ancestry.com Operations Inc, 2007. Original data - Anniston Star. Anniston, Alabama, United States Of America. Database created from microfilm copies of the newspaper. Original data: Anniston Star. Anniston, Alabama, Unit), Ancestry.com, http://www.Ancestry.com.

282

1935   Ancestry.com, Anniston Star (Anniston, Alabama) (Online publication - Provo, UT, USA: Ancestry.com Operations Inc, 2007. Original data - Anniston Star. Anniston, Alabama, United States Of America. Database created from microfilm copies of the newspaper. Original data: Anniston Star. Anniston, Alabama, Unit), Ancestry.com, http://www.Ancestry.com.

1936   Ancestry.com, Alabama Marriage Collection, 1800-1969 (Online publication - Provo, UT, USA: Ancestry.com Operations Inc, 2006. Original data - Alabama Center for Health Statistics. Alabama Marriage Index, 1936-1969. Alabama Center for Health Statistics, Montgomery, Alabama. Dodd, Jordan R., et. al. Early America), Ancestry.com, http://www.Ancestry.com, Marriage date: 2 May 1952 Marriage place: Calhoun, Alabama.

1937   Ancestry.com, 1930 United States Federal Census (Online publication - Provo, UT, USA: Ancestry.com Operations Inc, 2002. Original data - United States of America, Bureau of the Census. Fifteenth Census of the United States, 1930. Washington, D.C.: National Archives and Records Administration, 1930. T626,), Ancestry.com, http://www.Ancestry.com, Year: 1930; Census Place: Anniston, Calhoun, Alabama; Roll: 5; Page: 9B; Enumeration District: 50; Image: 1030.0. Birth date: about 1925 Birth place: Residence date: 1930 Residence place: Anniston, Calhoun, Alabama.

1938   Ancestry.com, Social Security Death Index (Online publication - Provo, UT, USA: Ancestry.com Operations Inc, 2010. Original data - Social Security Administration. Social Security Death Index, Master File. Social Security Administration. Original data: Social Security Administration. Social Security D), Ancestry.com, http://www.Ancestry.com, Number: 422-20-2536; Issue State: Alabama; Issue Date: Before 1951. Birth date: 20 Jun 1925 Birth place: Death date: 31 Jan 2003 Death place: Fayetteville, Cumberland, North Carolina, United States of America.

1939   Ancestry.com, North Carolina Death Collection, 1908-2004 (Online publication - Provo, UT, USA: Ancestry.com Operations, Inc., 2007. Original data - North Carolina State Center for Health Statistics. North Caroline Deaths, 1997-2004. North Carolina State Center for Health Statistics, Raleigh, North Carolina), Ancestry.com, http://www.Ancestry.com, Source Vendor: North Carolina State Center for Health Statistics; Certificate:. Birth date: 20 Jun 1925 Birth place: Alabama Death date: 31 Jan 2003 Death place: Fayetteville, Cumberland, North Carolina Residence date: Residence place: Fayetteville, Cumberland, North Carolina.

1940   National Cemetery Administration, U.S. Veterans Gravesites, ca.1775-2006 (Online publication - Provo, UT, USA: Ancestry.com Operations Inc, 2006. Original data - National Cemetery Administration. Nationwide Gravesite Locator. Original data: National Cemetery Administration. Nationwide Gravesite Locator), Ancestry.com, http://www.Ancestry.com, Birth date: 06/20/1925 Birth place: Death date: 01/31/2003 Death place: NC.

1941   Ancestry.com, Alabama Marriage Collection, 1800-1969 (Online publication - Provo, UT, USA: Ancestry.com Operations Inc, 2006. Original data - Alabama Center for Health Statistics. Alabama Marriage Index, 1936-1969. Alabama Center for Health Statistics, Montgomery, Alabama. Dodd, Jordan R., et. al. Early America), Ancestry.com, http://www.Ancestry.com, Marriage date: 10 Nov 1950 Marriage place: Limestone, Alabama.

1942   Ancestry.com, U.S. Public Records Index, Volume 1 (Online publication - Provo, UT, USA: Ancestry.com Operations, Inc., 2010. Original data - Voter Registration Lists, Public Record Filings, Historical Residential Records, and Other Household Database Listings. Original data: Voter Registration Lists, Public), Ancestry.com, http://www.Ancestry.com, Birth date: 1926 Birth place: Residence date: 1996 Residence place: Fayetteville, NC.

1943   Ancestry.com, U.S. Public Records Index, Volume 1 (Online publication - Provo, UT, USA: Ancestry.com Operations, Inc., 2010. Original data - Voter Registration Lists, Public Record Filings, Historical Residential Records, and Other Household Database Listings. Original data: Voter Registration Lists, Public), Ancestry.com, http://www.Ancestry.com, Residence date: 1987 Residence place: Fayetteville, NC.

1944   Ancestry.com, U.S. Phone and Address Directories, 1993-2002 (Online publication - Provo, UT, USA: Ancestry.com Operations Inc, 2005. Original data - 1993-2002 White Pages. Little Rock, AR, USA: Acxiom Corporation. Original data: 1993-2002 White Pages. Little Rock, AR, USA: Acxiom Corporation.), Ancestry.com, http://www.Ancestry.com, Residence date: 1995 1996 1997 Residence place: Fayetteville, North Carolina.

1945   Ancestry.com, U.S. Phone and Address Directories, 1993-2002 (Online publication - Provo, UT, USA: Ancestry.com Operations Inc, 2005. Original data - 1993-2002 White Pages. Little Rock, AR, USA: Acxiom Corporation. Original data: 1993-2002 White Pages. Little Rock, AR, USA: Acxiom Corporation.), Ancestry.com, http://www.Ancestry.com, Residence date: 1993 1994 Residence place: Fayetteville, North Carolina.

1946   Ancestry.com, The Alabama Courier (Athens, Alabama) (Online publication - Provo, UT, USA: Ancestry.com Operations Inc, 2003. Original data - The Alabama Courier. Athens, AL, USA. Database created from microfilm copies of the newspaper. Original data: The Alabama Courier. Athens, AL, USA. Database created from), Ancestry.com, http://www.Ancestry.com.

1947   Ancestry.com, 1930 United States Federal Census (Online publication - Provo, UT, USA: Ancestry.com Operations Inc, 2002. Original data - United States of America, Bureau of the Census. Fifteenth Census of the United States, 1930. Washington, D.C.: National Archives and Records Administration, 1930. T626,), Ancestry.com, http://www.Ancestry.com, Year: 1930; Census Place: Anniston, Calhoun, Alabama; Roll: 5; Page: 9B; Enumeration District: 50; Image: 1030.0. Birth date: about 1926 Birth place: Residence date: 1930 Residence place: Anniston, Calhoun, Alabama.

1948   Ancestry.com, Anniston Star (Anniston, Alabama) (Online publication - Provo, UT, USA: Ancestry.com Operations Inc, 2007. Original data - Anniston Star. Anniston, Alabama, United States Of America. Database created from

283

microfilm copies of the newspaper. Original data: Anniston Star. Anniston, Alabama, Unit), Ancestry.com, http://www.Ancestry.com.

1949   Ancestry.com, Anniston Star (Anniston, Alabama) (Online publication - Provo, UT, USA: Ancestry.com Operations Inc, 2007. Original data - Anniston Star. Anniston, Alabama, United States Of America. Database created from microfilm copies of the newspaper. Original data: Anniston Star. Anniston, Alabama, Unit), Ancestry.com, http://www.Ancestry.com.

1950   Ancestry.com, 1930 United States Federal Census (Online publication - Provo, UT, USA: Ancestry.com Operations Inc, 2002. Original data - United States of America, Bureau of the Census. Fifteenth Census of the United States, 1930. Washington, D.C.: National Archives and Records Administration, 1930. T626,), Ancestry.com, http://www.Ancestry.com, Year: 1930; Census Place: Anniston, Calhoun, Alabama; Roll: 5; Page: 9B; Enumeration District: 50; Image: 1030.0. Birth date: about 1929 Birth place: Residence date: 1930 Residence place: Anniston, Calhoun, Alabama.

1951   Ancestry.com, 1920 United States Federal Census (Online publication - Provo, UT, USA: Ancestry.com Operations Inc, 2010. Images reproduced by FamilySearch. Original data - Fourteenth Census of the United States, 1920. (NARA microfilm publication T625, 2076 rolls). Records of the Bureau of the Census, Record), Ancestry.com, http://www.Ancestry.com, Year: 1920; Census Place: Gadsden Ward 2, Etowah, Alabama; Roll: T625_15; Page: 20A; Enumeration District: 92; Image:. Birth date: about 1907 Birth place: Alabama Residence date: 1920 Residence place: Gadsden Ward 2, Etowah, Alabama.

1952   Ancestry.com, 1930 United States Federal Census (Online publication - Provo, UT, USA: Ancestry.com Operations Inc, 2002. Original data - United States of America, Bureau of the Census. Fifteenth Census of the United States, 1930. Washington, D.C.: National Archives and Records Administration, 1930. T626,), Ancestry.com, http://www.Ancestry.com, Year: 1930; Census Place: Hokes Bluff, Etowah, Alabama; Roll: 16; Page: 9A; Enumeration District: 16; Image: 609.0. Birth date: about 1909 Birth place: Residence date: 1930 Residence place: Hokes Bluff, Etowah, Alabama.

1953   Ancestry.com, Social Security Death Index (Online publication - Provo, UT, USA: Ancestry.com Operations Inc, 2010. Original data - Social Security Administration. Social Security Death Index, Master File. Social Security Administration. Original data: Social Security Administration. Social Security D), Ancestry.com, http://www.Ancestry.com, Number: 418-40-8718; Issue State: Alabama; Issue Date: Before 1951. Birth date: 1 Jan 1907 Birth place: Death date: 27 May 1988 Death place: Gadsden, Etowah, Alabama, United States of America.

1954   Ancestry.com, Social Security Death Index (Online publication - Provo, UT, USA: Ancestry.com Operations Inc, 2010. Original data - Social Security Administration. Social Security Death Index, Master File. Social Security Administration. Original data: Social Security Administration. Social Security D), Ancestry.com, http://www.Ancestry.com, Number: 416-46-8237; Issue State: Alabama; Issue Date: 1952-1953. Birth date: 6 Dec 1932 Birth place: Death date: Feb 1965 Death place:.

1955   Ancestry.com, Social Security Death Index (Online publication - Provo, UT, USA: Ancestry.com Operations Inc, 2010. Original data - Social Security Administration. Social Security Death Index, Master File. Social Security Administration. Original data: Social Security Administration. Social Security D), Ancestry.com, http://www.Ancestry.com, Number: 419-44-8356; Issue State: Alabama; Issue Date: 1951-1952. Birth date: 21 Sep 1935 Birth place: Death date: 24 Dec 1987 Death place: Gadsden, Etowah, Alabama, United States of America.

1956   Ancestry.com, Anniston Star (Anniston, Alabama) (Online publication - Provo, UT, USA: Ancestry.com Operations Inc, 2007. Original data - Anniston Star. Anniston, Alabama, United States Of America. Database created from microfilm copies of the newspaper. Original data: Anniston Star. Anniston, Alabama, Unit), Ancestry.com, http://www.Ancestry.com.

1957   Ancestry.com, 1930 United States Federal Census (Online publication - Provo, UT, USA: Ancestry.com Operations Inc, 2002. Original data - United States of America, Bureau of the Census. Fifteenth Census of the United States, 1930. Washington, D.C.: National Archives and Records Administration, 1930. T626,), Ancestry.com, http://www.Ancestry.com, Year: 1930; Census Place: Hokes Bluff, Etowah, Alabama; Roll: 16; Page: 7B; Enumeration District: 16; Image: 606.0. Birth date: about 1906 Birth place: Alabama Residence date: 1930 Residence place: Hokes Bluff, Etowah, Alabama.

1958   Ancestry.com, Social Security Death Index (Online publication - Provo, UT, USA: Ancestry.com Operations Inc, 2010. Original data - Social Security Administration. Social Security Death Index, Master File. Social Security Administration. Original data: Social Security Administration. Social Security D), Ancestry.com, http://www.Ancestry.com, Number: 417-18-1019; Issue State: Alabama; Issue Date: Before 1951. Birth date: 17 Jun 1905 Birth place: Death date: Jun 1987 Death place: Gadsden, Etowah, Alabama, United States of America.

1959   Ancestry.com, 1920 United States Federal Census (Online publication - Provo, UT, USA: Ancestry.com Operations Inc, 2010. Images reproduced by FamilySearch. Original data - Fourteenth Census of the United States, 1920. (NARA microfilm publication T625, 2076 rolls). Records of the Bureau of the Census, Record), Ancestry.com, http://www.Ancestry.com, Year: 1920; Census Place: Reeves, Etowah, Alabama; Roll: T625_15; Page: 10A; Enumeration District: 100; Image:. Birth date: about 1906 Birth place: Alabama Residence date: 1920 Residence place: Reeves, Etowah, Alabama.

1960   Ancestry.com, 1930 United States Federal Census (Online publication - Provo, UT, USA: Ancestry.com Operations Inc, 2002. Original data - United States of America, Bureau of the Census. Fifteenth Census of the United

States, 1930. Washington, D.C.: National Archives and Records Administration, 1930. T626,), Ancestry.com, http://www.Ancestry.com, Year: 1930; Census Place: Hokes Bluff, Etowah, Alabama; Roll: 16; Page: 7B; Enumeration District: 16; Image: 606.0. Birth date: about 1926 Birth place: Residence date: 1930 Residence place: Hokes Bluff, Etowah, Alabama.

1961   Ancestry.com, U.S. Public Records Index, Volume 1 (Online publication - Provo, UT, USA: Ancestry.com Operations, Inc., 2010. Original data - Voter Registration Lists, Public Record Filings, Historical Residential Records, and Other Household Database Listings. Original data: Voter Registration Lists, Public), Ancestry.com, http://www.Ancestry.com, Birth date: 1926 Birth place: Residence date: 1995 Residence place: Gadsden, AL.

1962   Ancestry.com, U.S. Phone and Address Directories, 1993-2002 (Online publication - Provo, UT, USA: Ancestry.com Operations Inc, 2005. Original data - 1993-2002 White Pages. Little Rock, AR, USA: Acxiom Corporation. Original data: 1993-2002 White Pages. Little Rock, AR, USA: Acxiom Corporation.), Ancestry.com, http://www.Ancestry.com, Residence date: 1994 1995 1996 1997 Residence place: Hokes Bluff, Alabama.

1963   Ancestry.com, U.S. Phone and Address Directories, 1993-2002 (Online publication - Provo, UT, USA: Ancestry.com Operations Inc, 2005. Original data - 1993-2002 White Pages. Little Rock, AR, USA: Acxiom Corporation. Original data: 1993-2002 White Pages. Little Rock, AR, USA: Acxiom Corporation.), Ancestry.com, http://www.Ancestry.com, Residence date: 1998 1999 2000 2001 2002 Residence place: Gadsden, Alabama.

1964   Ancestry.com, Alabama Marriage Collection, 1800-1969 (Online publication - Provo, UT, USA: Ancestry.com Operations Inc, 2006. Original data - Alabama Center for Health Statistics. Alabama Marriage Index, 1936-1969. Alabama Center for Health Statistics, Montgomery, Alabama. Dodd, Jordan R., et. al. Early America), Ancestry.com, http://www.Ancestry.com, Marriage date: 10 Sep 1949 Marriage place: Etowah, Alabama.

1965   Ancestry.com, Social Security Death Index (Online publication - Provo, UT, USA: Ancestry.com Operations Inc, 2010. Original data - Social Security Administration. Social Security Death Index, Master File. Social Security Administration. Original data: Social Security Administration. Social Security D), Ancestry.com, http://www.Ancestry.com, Number: 418-40-9187; Issue State: Alabama; Issue Date: Before 1951. Birth date: 20 Jun 1932 Birth place: Death date: Jun 1982 Death place:.

1966   Ancestry.com, Alabama Marriage Collection, 1800-1969 (Online publication - Provo, UT, USA: Ancestry.com Operations Inc, 2006. Original data - Alabama Center for Health Statistics. Alabama Marriage Index, 1936-1969. Alabama Center for Health Statistics, Montgomery, Alabama. Dodd, Jordan R., et. al. Early America), Ancestry.com, http://www.Ancestry.com, Marriage date: Oct 1951 Marriage place: Etowah, Alabama.

1967   Ancestry.com, U.S. Public Records Index, Volume 1 (Online publication - Provo, UT, USA: Ancestry.com Operations, Inc., 2010. Original data - Voter Registration Lists, Public Record Filings, Historical Residential Records, and Other Household Database Listings. Original data: Voter Registration Lists, Public), Ancestry.com, http://www.Ancestry.com, Birth date: 1939 Birth place: Residence date: 1994 Residence place: Hokes Bluff, AL.

1968   Ancestry.com, U.S. Public Records Index, Volume 1 (Online publication - Provo, UT, USA: Ancestry.com Operations, Inc., 2010. Original data - Voter Registration Lists, Public Record Filings, Historical Residential Records, and Other Household Database Listings. Original data: Voter Registration Lists, Public), Ancestry.com, http://www.Ancestry.com, Residence date: 1996Residence place: Hokes Bluff, AL.

1969   Ancestry.com, Alabama Marriage Collection, 1800-1969 (Online publication - Provo, UT, USA: Ancestry.com Operations Inc, 2006. Original data - Alabama Center for Health Statistics. Alabama Marriage Index, 1936-1969. Alabama Center for Health Statistics, Montgomery, Alabama. Dodd, Jordan R., et. al. Early America), Ancestry.com, http://www.Ancestry.com, Marriage date: Dec 1956 Marriage place: Etowah, Alabama.

1970   Ancestry.com, 1930 United States Federal Census (Online publication - Provo, UT, USA: Ancestry.com Operations Inc, 2002. Original data - United States of America, Bureau of the Census. Fifteenth Census of the United States, 1930. Washington, D.C.: National Archives and Records Administration, 1930. T626,), Ancestry.com, http://www.Ancestry.com, Year: 1930; Census Place: Hokes Bluff, Etowah, Alabama; Roll: 16; Page: 9A; Enumeration District: 16; Image: 609.0. Birth date: about 1906 Birth place: Residence date: 1930 Residence place: Hokes Bluff, Etowah, Alabama.

1971   Ancestry.com, Social Security Death Index (Online publication - Provo, UT, USA: Ancestry.com Operations Inc, 2010. Original data - Social Security Administration. Social Security Death Index, Master File. Social Security Administration. Original data: Social Security Administration. Social Security D), Ancestry.com, http://www.Ancestry.com, Number: 419-86-4135; Issue State: Alabama; Issue Date: 1973. Birth date: 16 Apr 1905 Birth place: Death date: 1 Dec 1988 Death place: Gadsden, Etowah, Alabama, United States of America.

1972   Ancestry.com, 1920 United States Federal Census (Online publication - Provo, UT, USA: Ancestry.com Operations Inc, 2010. Images reproduced by FamilySearch. Original data - Fourteenth Census of the United States, 1920. (NARA microfilm publication T625, 2076 rolls). Records of the Bureau of the Census, Record), Ancestry.com, http://www.Ancestry.com, Year: 1920; Census Place: Hokes Bluff, Etowah, Alabama; Roll: T625_15; Page: 3B; Enumeration District: 99; Image:. Birth date: about 1906 Birth place: Alabama Residence date: 1920 Residence place: Hokes Bluff, Etowah, Alabama.

1973   Ancestry.com, 1930 United States Federal Census (Online publication - Provo, UT, USA: Ancestry.com Operations Inc, 2002. Original data - United States of America, Bureau of the Census. Fifteenth Census of the United States, 1930. Washington, D.C.: National Archives and Records Administration, 1930. T626,), Ancestry.com,

285

http://www.Ancestry.com, Year: 1930; Census Place: Hokes Bluff, Etowah, Alabama; Roll: 16; Page: 9A; Enumeration District: 16; Image: 609.0. Birth date: about 1926 Birth place: Residence date: 1930 Residence place: Hokes Bluff, Etowah, Alabama.

1974   Ancestry.com, U.S. Public Records Index, Volume 1 (Online publication - Provo, UT, USA: Ancestry.com Operations, Inc., 2010. Original data - Voter Registration Lists, Public Record Filings, Historical Residential Records, and Other Household Database Listings. Original data: Voter Registration Lists, Public), Ancestry.com, http://www.Ancestry.com, Birth date: 1926 Birth place: Residence date: 1992 Residence place: Jacksonville, FL.

1975   Ancestry.com, U.S. Public Records Index, Volume 2 (Online publication - Provo, UT, USA: Ancestry.com Operations, Inc., 2010. Original data - Voter Registration Lists, Public Record Filings, Historical Residential Records, and Other Household Database Listings. Original data: Voter Registration Lists, Public), Ancestry.com, http://www.Ancestry.com, Birth date: 1926 Birth place: Residence date: 1935-1993 Residence place: Jacksonville, FL.

1976   Ancestry.com, 1930 United States Federal Census (Online publication - Provo, UT, USA: Ancestry.com Operations Inc, 2002. Original data - United States of America, Bureau of the Census. Fifteenth Census of the United States, 1930. Washington, D.C.: National Archives and Records Administration, 1930. T626,), Ancestry.com, http://www.Ancestry.com, Year: 1930; Census Place: Hokes Bluff, Etowah, Alabama; Roll: 16; Page: 9A; Enumeration District: 16; Image: 609.0. Birth date: about 1929 Birth place: Residence date: 1930 Residence place: Hokes Bluff, Etowah, Alabama.

1977   Ancestry.com, U.S. Public Records Index, Volume 1 (Online publication - Provo, UT, USA: Ancestry.com Operations, Inc., 2010. Original data - Voter Registration Lists, Public Record Filings, Historical Residential Records, and Other Household Database Listings. Original data: Voter Registration Lists, Public), Ancestry.com, http://www.Ancestry.com, Birth date: 1929 Birth place: Residence date: 1989 Residence place: Gadsden, AL.

1978   Ancestry.com, Alabama Marriage Collection, 1800-1969 (Online publication - Provo, UT, USA: Ancestry.com Operations Inc, 2006. Original data - Alabama Center for Health Statistics. Alabama Marriage Index, 1936-1969. Alabama Center for Health Statistics, Montgomery, Alabama. Dodd, Jordan R., et. al. Early America), Ancestry.com, http://www.Ancestry.com, Marriage date: 29 Aug 1948 Marriage place: Etowah, Alabama.

1979   Ancestry.com, Social Security Death Index (Online publication - Provo, UT, USA: Ancestry.com Operations Inc, 2010. Original data - Social Security Administration. Social Security Death Index, Master File. Social Security Administration. Original data: Social Security Administration. Social Security D), Ancestry.com, http://www.Ancestry.com, Number: 424-14-9323; Issue State: Alabama; Issue Date: Before 1951. Birth date: 12 Oct 1918 Birth place: Death date: 27 Dec 2009 Death place: Gadsden, Etowah, Alabama.

1980   Ancestry.com, U.S. Public Records Index, Volume 1 (Online publication - Provo, UT, USA: Ancestry.com Operations, Inc., 2010. Original data - Voter Registration Lists, Public Record Filings, Historical Residential Records, and Other Household Database Listings. Original data: Voter Registration Lists, Public), Ancestry.com, http://www.Ancestry.com, Birth date: 1918 Birth place: Residence date: 1992 Residence place: Gadsden, AL.

1981   Ancestry.com, 1930 United States Federal Census (Online publication - Provo, UT, USA: Ancestry.com Operations Inc, 2002. Original data - United States of America, Bureau of the Census. Fifteenth Census of the United States, 1930. Washington, D.C.: National Archives and Records Administration, 1930. T626,), Ancestry.com, http://www.Ancestry.com, Year: 1930; Census Place: Hokes Bluff, Etowah, Alabama; Roll: 16; Page: 9A; Enumeration District: 16; Image: 609.0. Birth date: about 1919 Birth place: Residence date: 1930 Residence place: Hokes Bluff, Etowah, Alabama.

1982   Ancestry.com, United States Obituary Collection (Online publication - Provo, UT, USA: Ancestry.com Operations Inc, 2006. Original data - See newspaper information provided with each entry. Original data: See newspaper information provided with each entry.), Ancestry.com, http://www.Ancestry.com, Newspaper: The Gadsden Times; Publication Date: 29 Dec 2009; Publication Place: Gadsden , AL , USA. Death date: 12/27/2009 Death place:.

1983   Ancestry.com, United States Obituary Collection (Online publication - Provo, UT, USA: Ancestry.com Operations Inc, 2006. Original data - See newspaper information provided with each entry. Original data: See newspaper information provided with each entry.), Ancestry.com, http://www.Ancestry.com, Newspaper: The Gadsden Times; Publication Date: 28 Dec 2009; Publication Place: Gadsden , AL , USA. Death date: 12/27/2009 Death place:.

1984   Ancestry.com, U.S. Public Records Index, Volume 1 (Online publication - Provo, UT, USA: Ancestry.com Operations, Inc., 2010. Original data - Voter Registration Lists, Public Record Filings, Historical Residential Records, and Other Household Database Listings. Original data: Voter Registration Lists, Public), Ancestry.com, http://www.Ancestry.com, Birth date: 1944 Birth place: Residence date: 1995 Residence place: Gadsden, AL.

1985   Ancestry.com, Alabama Marriage Collection, 1800-1969 (Online publication - Provo, UT, USA: Ancestry.com Operations Inc, 2006. Original data - Alabama Center for Health Statistics. Alabama Marriage Index, 1936-1969. Alabama Center for Health Statistics, Montgomery, Alabama. Dodd, Jordan R., et. al. Early America), Ancestry.com, http://www.Ancestry.com, Marriage date: Apr 1964 Marriage place: Etowah, Alabama.

1986   Ancestry.com, Social Security Death Index (Online publication - Provo, UT, USA: Ancestry.com Operations Inc, 2010. Original data - Social Security Administration. Social Security Death Index, Master File. Social Security Administration. Original data: Social Security Administration. Social Security D), Ancestry.com, http://www.Ancestry.com, Number: 421-01-9381; Issue State: Alabama; Issue Date: Before 1951. Birth date: 20 Jul 1914 Birth place: Death date: 28 Oct 1994 Death place: Gadsden, Etowah, Alabama, United States of America.

1987   Ancestry.com, 1930 United States Federal Census (Online publication - Provo, UT, USA: Ancestry.com Operations Inc, 2002. Original data - United States of America, Bureau of the Census. Fifteenth Census of the United States, 1930. Washington, D.C.: National Archives and Records Administration, 1930. T626,), Ancestry.com, http://www.Ancestry.com, Year: 1930; Census Place: Hokes Bluff, Etowah, Alabama; Roll: 16; Page: 1A; Enumeration District: 16; Image: 593.0. Birth date: about 1915 Birth place: Residence date: 1930 Residence place: Hokes Bluff, Etowah, Alabama.

1988   Ancestry.com, 1920 United States Federal Census (Online publication - Provo, UT, USA: Ancestry.com Operations Inc, 2010. Images reproduced by FamilySearch. Original data - Fourteenth Census of the United States, 1920. (NARA microfilm publication T625, 2076 rolls). Records of the Bureau of the Census, Record), Ancestry.com, http://www.Ancestry.com, Year: 1920; Census Place: Hokes Bluff, Etowah, Alabama; Roll: T625_15; Page: 2A; Enumeration District: 99; Image:. Birth date: about 1915 Birth place: Alabama Residence date: 1920 Residence place: Hokes Bluff, Etowah, Alabama.

1989   Ancestry.com, Social Security Death Index (Online publication - Provo, UT, USA: Ancestry.com Operations Inc, 2010. Original data - Social Security Administration. Social Security Death Index, Master File. Social Security Administration. Original data: Social Security Administration. Social Security D), Ancestry.com, http://www.Ancestry.com, Number: 419-44-8448; Issue State: Alabama; Issue Date: 1951-1952. Birth date: 23 May 1935 Birth place: Death date: Apr 1985 Death place: Gadsden, Etowah, Alabama, United States of America.

1990   Ancestry.com, Social Security Death Index (Online publication - Provo, UT, USA: Ancestry.com Operations Inc, 2010. Original data - Social Security Administration. Social Security Death Index, Master File. Social Security Administration. Original data: Social Security Administration. Social Security D), Ancestry.com, http://www.Ancestry.com, Number: 421-54-7861; Issue State: Alabama; Issue Date: 1958. Birth date: 7 Sep 1942 Birth place: Death date: Mar 1985 Death place:.

1991   Ancestry.com, Alabama Marriage Collection, 1800-1969 (Online publication - Provo, UT, USA: Ancestry.com Operations Inc, 2006. Original data - Alabama Center for Health Statistics. Alabama Marriage Index, 1936-1969. Alabama Center for Health Statistics, Montgomery, Alabama. Dodd, Jordan R., et. al. Early America), Ancestry.com, http://www.Ancestry.com, Marriage date: Jun 1963 Marriage place: Etowah, Alabama.

1992   Ancestry.com, U.S. Public Records Index, Volume 1 (Online publication - Provo, UT, USA: Ancestry.com Operations, Inc., 2010. Original data - Voter Registration Lists, Public Record Filings, Historical Residential Records, and Other Household Database Listings. Original data: Voter Registration Lists, Public), Ancestry.com, http://www.Ancestry.com, Birth date: 1920 Birth place: Residence date: 1981 Residence place: Gadsden, AL.

1993   Ancestry.com, U.S. Phone and Address Directories, 1993-2002 (Online publication - Provo, UT, USA: Ancestry.com Operations Inc, 2005. Original data - 1993-2002 White Pages. Little Rock, AR, USA: Acxiom Corporation. Original data: 1993-2002 White Pages. Little Rock, AR, USA: Acxiom Corporation.), Ancestry.com, http://www.Ancestry.com, Residence date: 1996 1997 1998 1999 2000 2001 2002 Residence place: Montgomery, Alabama.

1994   Ancestry.com, U.S. Public Records Index, Volume 1 (Online publication - Provo, UT, USA: Ancestry.com Operations, Inc., 2010. Original data - Voter Registration Lists, Public Record Filings, Historical Residential Records, and Other Household Database Listings. Original data: Voter Registration Lists, Public), Ancestry.com, http://www.Ancestry.com, Birth date: 1946 Birth place: Residence date: 1980 Residence place: Montgomery, AL.

1995   Ancestry.com, Social Security Death Index (Online publication - Provo, UT, USA: Ancestry.com Operations Inc, 2010. Original data - Social Security Administration. Social Security Death Index, Master File. Social Security Administration. Original data: Social Security Administration. Social Security D), Ancestry.com, http://www.Ancestry.com, Number: 419-09-2327; Issue State: Alabama; Issue Date: Before 1951. Birth date: 11 Sep 1910 Birth place: Death date: Aug 1977 Death place: Gadsden, Etowah, Alabama, United States of America.

1996   Ancestry.com, 1930 United States Federal Census (Online publication - Provo, UT, USA: Ancestry.com Operations Inc, 2002. Original data - United States of America, Bureau of the Census. Fifteenth Census of the United States, 1930. Washington, D.C.: National Archives and Records Administration, 1930. T626,), Ancestry.com, http://www.Ancestry.com, Year: 1930; Census Place: Hokes Bluff, Etowah, Alabama; Roll: 16; Page: 9A; Enumeration District: 16; Image: 609.0. Birth date: about 1911 Birth place: Residence date: 1930 Residence place: Hokes Bluff, Etowah, Alabama.

1997   Ancestry.com, 1920 United States Federal Census (Online publication - Provo, UT, USA: Ancestry.com Operations Inc, 2010. Images reproduced by FamilySearch. Original data - Fourteenth Census of the United States, 1920. (NARA microfilm publication T625, 2076 rolls). Records of the Bureau of the Census, Record), Ancestry.com, http://www.Ancestry.com, Year: 1920; Census Place: Hokes Bluff, Etowah, Alabama; Roll: T625_15; Page: 1B; Enumeration District: 99; Image:. Birth date: about 1911 Birth place: Alabama Residence date: 1920 Residence place: Hokes Bluff, Etowah, Alabama.

1998   Ancestry.com, U.S. Public Records Index, Volume 1 (Online publication - Provo, UT, USA: Ancestry.com Operations, Inc., 2010. Original data - Voter Registration Lists, Public Record Filings, Historical Residential Records, and Other Household Database Listings. Original data: Voter Registration Lists, Public), Ancestry.com, http://www.Ancestry.com, Birth date: 1944 Birth place: Residence date: 1986 Residence place: Gadsden, AL.

1999   Ancestry.com, Alabama Marriage Collection, 1800-1969 (Online publication - Provo, UT, USA: Ancestry.com Operations Inc, 2006. Original data - Alabama Center for Health Statistics. Alabama Marriage Index, 1936-1969. Alabama

Center for Health Statistics, Montgomery, Alabama. Dodd, Jordan R., et. al. Early America), Ancestry.com, http://www.Ancestry.com, Marriage date: Jun 1964 Marriage place: Etowah, Alabama.

2000   Ancestry.com, U.S. Public Records Index, Volume 1 (Online publication - Provo, UT, USA: Ancestry.com Operations, Inc., 2010. Original data - Voter Registration Lists, Public Record Filings, Historical Residential Records, and Other Household Database Listings. Original data: Voter Registration Lists, Public), Ancestry.com, http://www.Ancestry.com, Birth date: 1965 Birth place: Residence date: 1990 Residence place: Gadsden, AL.

2001   Ancestry.com, U.S. Public Records Index, Volume 1 (Online publication - Provo, UT, USA: Ancestry.com Operations, Inc., 2010. Original data - Voter Registration Lists, Public Record Filings, Historical Residential Records, and Other Household Database Listings. Original data: Voter Registration Lists, Public), Ancestry.com, http://www.Ancestry.com, Birth date: 1966 Birth place: Residence date: 1994Residence place: Gadsden, AL.

2002   Ancestry.com, U.S. Public Records Index, Volume 1 (Online publication - Provo, UT, USA: Ancestry.com Operations, Inc., 2010. Original data - Voter Registration Lists, Public Record Filings, Historical Residential Records, and Other Household Database Listings. Original data: Voter Registration Lists, Public), Ancestry.com, http://www.Ancestry.com, Birth date: 1973 Birth place: Residence date: 1993 Residence place: Gadsden, AL.

2003   National Archives and Records Administration, U.S. World War II Army Enlistment Records, 1938-1946 (Online publication - Provo, UT, USA: Ancestry.com Operations Inc, 2005. Original data - Electronic Army Serial Number Merged File, 1938-1946 [Archival Database]; World War II Army Enlistment Records; Records of the National Archives and Records Administration), Ancestry.com, http://www.Ancestry.com, Birth date: 1927 Birth place: Residence date: Residence place: Alabama.

2004   Ancestry.com, 1930 United States Federal Census (Online publication - Provo, UT, USA: Ancestry.com Operations Inc, 2002. Original data - United States of America, Bureau of the Census. Fifteenth Census of the United States, 1930. Washington, D.C.: National Archives and Records Administration, 1930. T626,), Ancestry.com, http://www.Ancestry.com, Year: 1930; Census Place: Gadsden, Etowah, Alabama; Roll: 16; Page: 6B; Enumeration District: 61; Image: 500.0. Birth date: about 1927 Birth place: Residence date: 1930 Residence place: Gadsden, Etowah, Alabama.

2005   Ancestry.com, U.S. Public Records Index, Volume 2 (Online publication - Provo, UT, USA: Ancestry.com Operations, Inc., 2010. Original data - Voter Registration Lists, Public Record Filings, Historical Residential Records, and Other Household Database Listings. Original data: Voter Registration Lists, Public), Ancestry.com, http://www.Ancestry.com, Residence date: 1935-1993 Residence place: Gadsden, AL.

2006   Ancestry.com, Social Security Death Index (Online publication - Provo, UT, USA: Ancestry.com Operations Inc, 2010. Original data - Social Security Administration. Social Security Death Index, Master File. Social Security Administration. Original data: Social Security Administration. Social Security D), Ancestry.com, http://www.Ancestry.com, Number: 419-26-8710; Issue State: Alabama; Issue Date: Before 1951. Birth date: 18 Feb 1927 Birth place: Death date: Sep 1974 Death place: Gadsden, Etowah, Alabama, United States of America.

2007   Ancestry.com, U.S. Phone and Address Directories, 1993-2002 (Online publication - Provo, UT, USA: Ancestry.com Operations Inc, 2005. Original data - 1993-2002 White Pages. Little Rock, AR, USA: Acxiom Corporation. Original data: 1993-2002 White Pages. Little Rock, AR, USA: Acxiom Corporation.), Ancestry.com, http://www.Ancestry.com, Residence date: 1998 1999 2000 2002 Residence place: Gadsden, Alabama.

2008   Ancestry.com, U.S. Public Records Index, Volume 1 (Online publication - Provo, UT, USA: Ancestry.com Operations, Inc., 2010. Original data - Voter Registration Lists, Public Record Filings, Historical Residential Records, and Other Household Database Listings. Original data: Voter Registration Lists, Public), Ancestry.com, http://www.Ancestry.com, Birth date: 1953 Birth place: Residence date: 1978 Residence place: Gadsden, AL.

2009   Ancestry.com, U.S. Public Records Index, Volume 1 (Online publication - Provo, UT, USA: Ancestry.com Operations, Inc., 2010. Original data - Voter Registration Lists, Public Record Filings, Historical Residential Records, and Other Household Database Listings. Original data: Voter Registration Lists, Public), Ancestry.com, http://www.Ancestry.com, Birth date: 1956 Birth place: Residence date: 1989 Residence place: Gadsden, AL.

2010   Ancestry.com, Alabama Marriage Collection, 1800-1969 (Online publication - Provo, UT, USA: Ancestry.com Operations Inc, 2006. Original data - Alabama Center for Health Statistics. Alabama Marriage Index, 1936-1969. Alabama Center for Health Statistics, Montgomery, Alabama. Dodd, Jordan R., et. al. Early America), Ancestry.com, http://www.Ancestry.com, Marriage date: 28 Aug 1948 Marriage place: Etowah, Alabama.

2011   Ancestry.com, Anniston Star (Anniston, Alabama) (Online publication - Provo, UT, USA: Ancestry.com Operations Inc, 2007. Original data - Anniston Star. Anniston, Alabama, United States Of America. Database created from microfilm copies of the newspaper. Original data: Anniston Star. Anniston, Alabama, Unit), Ancestry.com, http://www.Ancestry.com.

2012   Ancestry.com, Anniston Star (Anniston, Alabama) (Online publication - Provo, UT, USA: Ancestry.com Operations Inc, 2007. Original data - Anniston Star. Anniston, Alabama, United States Of America. Database created from microfilm copies of the newspaper. Original data: Anniston Star. Anniston, Alabama, Unit), Ancestry.com, http://www.Ancestry.com.

2013   Ancestry.com, Anniston Star (Anniston, Alabama) (Online publication - Provo, UT, USA: Ancestry.com Operations Inc, 2007. Original data - Anniston Star. Anniston, Alabama, United States Of America. Database created from microfilm copies of the newspaper. Original data: Anniston Star. Anniston, Alabama, Unit), Ancestry.com, http://www.Ancestry.com.

2014   Ancestry.com, Anniston Star (Anniston, Alabama) (Online publication - Provo, UT, USA: Ancestry.com Operations Inc, 2007. Original data - Anniston Star. Anniston, Alabama, United States Of America. Database created from microfilm copies of the newspaper. Original data: Anniston Star. Anniston, Alabama, Unit), Ancestry.com, http://www.Ancestry.com.

2015   Ancestry.com, Anniston Star (Anniston, Alabama) (Online publication - Provo, UT, USA: Ancestry.com Operations Inc, 2007. Original data - Anniston Star. Anniston, Alabama, United States Of America. Database created from microfilm copies of the newspaper. Original data: Anniston Star. Anniston, Alabama, Unit), Ancestry.com, http://www.Ancestry.com.

2016   Ancestry.com, Anniston Star (Anniston, Alabama) (Online publication - Provo, UT, USA: Ancestry.com Operations Inc, 2007. Original data - Anniston Star. Anniston, Alabama, United States Of America. Database created from microfilm copies of the newspaper. Original data: Anniston Star. Anniston, Alabama, Unit), Ancestry.com, http://www.Ancestry.com, Wedding announcement.

2017   Ancestry.com, U.S. Public Records Index, Volume 1 (Online publication - Provo, UT, USA: Ancestry.com Operations, Inc., 2010. Original data - Voter Registration Lists, Public Record Filings, Historical Residential Records, and Other Household Database Listings. Original data: Voter Registration Lists, Public), Ancestry.com, http://www.Ancestry.com, Birth date: 1930 Birth place: Residence date: 1992Residence place: Gadsden, AL.

2018   Ancestry.com, Social Security Death Index (Online publication - Provo, UT, USA: Ancestry.com Operations Inc, 2010. Original data - Social Security Administration. Social Security Death Index, Master File. Social Security Administration. Original data: Social Security Administration. Social Security D), Ancestry.com, http://www.Ancestry.com, Number: 418-32-0946; Issue State: Alabama; Issue Date: Before 1951. Birth date: 7 May 1930 Birth place: Death date: 15 Dec 1998 Death place: Gadsden, Etowah, Alabama, United States of America.

2019   Ancestry.com, U.S. Phone and Address Directories, 1993-2002 (Online publication - Provo, UT, USA: Ancestry.com Operations Inc, 2005. Original data - 1993-2002 White Pages. Little Rock, AR, USA: Acxiom Corporation. Original data: 1993-2002 White Pages. Little Rock, AR, USA: Acxiom Corporation.), Ancestry.com, http://www.Ancestry.com, Residence date: 1995 1996 1997 Residence place: Gadsden, Alabama.

2020   Ancestry.com, U.S. Phone and Address Directories, 1993-2002 (Online publication - Provo, UT, USA: Ancestry.com Operations Inc, 2005. Original data - 1993-2002 White Pages. Little Rock, AR, USA: Acxiom Corporation. Original data: 1993-2002 White Pages. Little Rock, AR, USA: Acxiom Corporation.), Ancestry.com, http://www.Ancestry.com, Residence date: 1998 1999 2000 2002 Residence place: Gadsden, Alabama.

2021   Ancestry.com, U.S. Phone and Address Directories, 1993-2002 (Online publication - Provo, UT, USA: Ancestry.com Operations Inc, 2005. Original data - 1993-2002 White Pages. Little Rock, AR, USA: Acxiom Corporation. Original data: 1993-2002 White Pages. Little Rock, AR, USA: Acxiom Corporation.), Ancestry.com, http://www.Ancestry.com, Residence date: 2001 Residence place: Rainbow City, Alabama.

2022   Ancestry.com, U.S. Public Records Index, Volume 1 (Online publication - Provo, UT, USA: Ancestry.com Operations, Inc., 2010. Original data - Voter Registration Lists, Public Record Filings, Historical Residential Records, and Other Household Database Listings. Original data: Voter Registration Lists, Public), Ancestry.com, http://www.Ancestry.com, Birth date: 1957 Birth place: Residence date: 1982 Residence place: Gadsden, AL.

2023   Ancestry.com, U.S. Public Records Index, Volume 1 (Online publication - Provo, UT, USA: Ancestry.com Operations, Inc., 2010. Original data - Voter Registration Lists, Public Record Filings, Historical Residential Records, and Other Household Database Listings. Original data: Voter Registration Lists, Public), Ancestry.com, http://www.Ancestry.com, Birth date: 1961 Birth place: Residence date: 1986 Residence place: Midland, GA.

2024   Ancestry.com, U.S. Public Records Index, Volume 1 (Online publication - Provo, UT, USA: Ancestry.com Operations, Inc., 2010. Original data - Voter Registration Lists, Public Record Filings, Historical Residential Records, and Other Household Database Listings. Original data: Voter Registration Lists, Public), Ancestry.com, http://www.Ancestry.com, Birth date: 1961 Birth place: Residence date: 1996 Residence place: Midland, GA.

2025   Ancestry.com, U.S. Public Records Index, Volume 1 (Online publication - Provo, UT, USA: Ancestry.com Operations, Inc., 2010. Original data - Voter Registration Lists, Public Record Filings, Historical Residential Records, and Other Household Database Listings. Original data: Voter Registration Lists, Public), Ancestry.com, http://www.Ancestry.com, Birth date: 1954 Birth place: Residence date: 1995 Residence place: Gadsden, AL.

2026   Ancestry.com, Social Security Death Index (Online publication - Provo, UT, USA: Ancestry.com Operations Inc, 2010. Original data - Social Security Administration. Social Security Death Index, Master File. Social Security Administration. Original data: Social Security Administration. Social Security D), Ancestry.com, http://www.Ancestry.com, Number: 424-34-8056; Issue State: Alabama; Issue Date: Before 1951. Birth date: 7 Jun 1930 Birth place: Death date: 15 Apr 1993 Death place:.

2027   Ancestry.com, U.S. Public Records Index, Volume 1 (Online publication - Provo, UT, USA: Ancestry.com Operations, Inc., 2010. Original data - Voter Registration Lists, Public Record Filings, Historical Residential Records, and Other Household Database Listings. Original data: Voter Registration Lists, Public), Ancestry.com, http://www.Ancestry.com, Birth date: 1961 Birth place: Residence date: 1995 Residence place: Birmingham, AL.

2028   Ancestry.com, U.S. Public Records Index, Volume 2 (Online publication - Provo, UT, USA: Ancestry.com Operations, Inc., 2010. Original data - Voter Registration Lists, Public Record Filings, Historical Residential Records, and Other Household Database Listings. Original data: Voter Registration Lists, Public), Ancestry.com, http://www.Ancestry.com, Birth date: 1963 Birth place: Residence date: 1935-1993 Residence place:.

2029   Ancestry.com, U.S. Phone and Address Directories, 1993-2002 (Online publication - Provo, UT, USA: Ancestry.com Operations Inc, 2005. Original data - 1993-2002 White Pages. Little Rock, AR, USA: Acxiom Corporation. Original data: 1993-2002 White Pages. Little Rock, AR, USA: Acxiom Corporation.), Ancestry.com, http://www.Ancestry.com, Residence date: 1994 Residence place: Gadsden, Alabama.

2030   Ancestry.com, U.S. Public Records Index, Volume 2 (Online publication - Provo, UT, USA: Ancestry.com Operations, Inc., 2010. Original data - Voter Registration Lists, Public Record Filings, Historical Residential Records, and Other Household Database Listings. Original data: Voter Registration Lists, Public), Ancestry.com, http://www.Ancestry.com, Residence date: 1935-1993 Residence place: Gadsden, AL.

2031   Ancestry.com, Minnesota Divorce Index, 1970-1995 (Online publication - Provo, UT, USA: The Generations Network, Inc., 2006. Original data - Minnesota Statewide Divorce Index, 1970-1995. St Paul, MN, USA: Minnesota Department of Health. Original data: Minnesota Statewide Divorce Index, 1970-1995. St Paul, MN), Ancestry.com, http://www.Ancestry.com, Birth date: about 1941 Birth place: Divorce date: 22 Oct 1970 Divorce place: Hennepin, Minnesota.

2032   Ancestry.com, U.S. Public Records Index, Volume 1 (Online publication - Provo, UT, USA: Ancestry.com Operations, Inc., 2010. Original data - Voter Registration Lists, Public Record Filings, Historical Residential Records, and Other Household Database Listings. Original data: Voter Registration Lists, Public), Ancestry.com, http://www.Ancestry.com, Birth date: 1941 Birth place: Residence date: 1990 Residence place: Gadsden, AL.

2033   Ancestry.com, Minnesota Marriage Collection, 1958-2001 (Online publication - Provo, UT, USA: Ancestry.com Operations Inc, 2007. Original data - Minnesota Department of Health. Minnesota Marriages, 1997-2001. Minnesota Department of Health, St. Paul, Minnesota, Center for Health Statistics, Office of the), Ancestry.com, http://www.Ancestry.com, Birth date: about 1941 Birth place: Marriage date: 22 Aug 1959 Marriage place: Hennepin, Minnesota.

2034   Ancestry.com, U.S. Public Records Index, Volume 1 (Online publication - Provo, UT, USA: Ancestry.com Operations, Inc., 2010. Original data - Voter Registration Lists, Public Record Filings, Historical Residential Records, and Other Household Database Listings. Original data: Voter Registration Lists, Public), Ancestry.com, http://www.Ancestry.com, Birth date: 1960 Birth place: Residence date: 1989 Residence place: Minneapolis, MN.

2035   Minnesota Department of Health, Minnesota Birth Index, 1935-2002 (Online publication - Provo, UT, USA: Ancestry.com Operations Inc, 2004. Original data - Minnesota. Minnesota Birth Index, 1935-2002. Minneapolis, MN, USA: Minnesota Department of Health. Original data: Minnesota. Minnesota Birth Index, 1935-2002. Minneapolis), Ancestry.com, http://www.Ancestry.com, Birth date: 1960 Birth place: Hennepin, Minnesota.

2036   Ancestry.com, U.S. Public Records Index, Volume 1 (Online publication - Provo, UT, USA: Ancestry.com Operations, Inc., 2010. Original data - Voter Registration Lists, Public Record Filings, Historical Residential Records, and Other Household Database Listings. Original data: Voter Registration Lists, Public), Ancestry.com, http://www.Ancestry.com, Birth date: 1960 Birth place: Residence date: 1986 Residence place: Vidalia, GA.

2037   Ancestry.com, U.S. Public Records Index, Volume 1 (Online publication - Provo, UT, USA: Ancestry.com Operations, Inc., 2010. Original data - Voter Registration Lists, Public Record Filings, Historical Residential Records, and Other Household Database Listings. Original data: Voter Registration Lists, Public), Ancestry.com, http://www.Ancestry.com, Birth date: 1961 Birth place: Residence date: 1996 Residence place: Dothan, AL.

2038   Minnesota Department of Health, Minnesota Birth Index, 1935-2002 (Online publication - Provo, UT, USA: Ancestry.com Operations Inc, 2004. Original data - Minnesota. Minnesota Birth Index, 1935-2002. Minneapolis, MN, USA: Minnesota Department of Health. Original data: Minnesota. Minnesota Birth Index, 1935-2002. Minneapolis), Ancestry.com, http://www.Ancestry.com, Birth date: 1961 Birth place: Hennepin, Minnesota.

2039   Ancestry.com, U.S. Public Records Index, Volume 1 (Online publication - Provo, UT, USA: Ancestry.com Operations, Inc., 2010. Original data - Voter Registration Lists, Public Record Filings, Historical Residential Records, and Other Household Database Listings. Original data: Voter Registration Lists, Public), Ancestry.com, http://www.Ancestry.com, Birth date: 1961 Birth place: Residence date: 1993 Residence place: Birmingham, AL.

2040   Minnesota Department of Health, Minnesota Birth Index, 1935-2002 (Online publication - Provo, UT, USA: Ancestry.com Operations Inc, 2004. Original data - Minnesota. Minnesota Birth Index, 1935-2002. Minneapolis, MN, USA: Minnesota Department of Health. Original data: Minnesota. Minnesota Birth Index, 1935-2002. Minneapolis), Ancestry.com, http://www.Ancestry.com, Birth date: 1962 Birth place: Hennepin, Minnesota.

2041   Ancestry.com, U.S. Public Records Index, Volume 1 (Online publication - Provo, UT, USA: Ancestry.com Operations, Inc., 2010. Original data - Voter Registration Lists, Public Record Filings, Historical Residential Records, and Other Household Database Listings. Original data: Voter Registration Lists, Public), Ancestry.com, http://www.Ancestry.com, Birth date: 1964 Birth place: Residence date: 1984 Residence place: Burnsville, MN.

2042   Minnesota Department of Health, Minnesota Birth Index, 1935-2002 (Online publication - Provo, UT, USA: Ancestry.com Operations Inc, 2004. Original data - Minnesota. Minnesota Birth Index, 1935-2002. Minneapolis, MN, USA:

Minnesota Department of Health. Original data: Minnesota. Minnesota Birth Index, 1935-2002. Minneapolis), Ancestry.com, http://www.Ancestry.com, Birth date: 1964 Birth place: Hennepin, Minnesota.

2043   Ancestry.com, Alabama Marriage Collection, 1800-1969 (Online publication - Provo, UT, USA: Ancestry.com Operations Inc, 2006. Original data - Alabama Center for Health Statistics. Alabama Marriage Index, 1936-1969. Alabama Center for Health Statistics, Montgomery, Alabama. Dodd, Jordan R., et. al. Early America), Ancestry.com, http://www.Ancestry.com, Marriage date: Jul 1953 Marriage place: Etowah, Alabama.

2044   Ancestry.com, U.S. Public Records Index, Volume 1 (Online publication - Provo, UT, USA: Ancestry.com Operations, Inc., 2010. Original data - Voter Registration Lists, Public Record Filings, Historical Residential Records, and Other Household Database Listings. Original data: Voter Registration Lists, Public), Ancestry.com, http://www.Ancestry.com, Birth date: 1973 Birth place: Residence date: 1995 Residence place: Gadsden, AL.

2045   Ancestry.com, U.S. Public Records Index, Volume 1 (Online publication - Provo, UT, USA: Ancestry.com Operations, Inc., 2010. Original data - Voter Registration Lists, Public Record Filings, Historical Residential Records, and Other Household Database Listings. Original data: Voter Registration Lists, Public), Ancestry.com, http://www.Ancestry.com, Birth date1963 Birth place: Residence date: 1984 Residence place: Birmingham, AL.

2046   Ancestry.com, U.S. Public Records Index, Volume 1 (Online publication - Provo, UT, USA: Ancestry.com Operations, Inc., 2010. Original data - Voter Registration Lists, Public Record Filings, Historical Residential Records, and Other Household Database Listings. Original data: Voter Registration Lists, Public), Ancestry.com, http://www.Ancestry.com, Birth date: 1963 Birth place: Residence date: 1993 Residence place: Woodstock, GA.

2047   Ancestry.com, U.S. Public Records Index, Volume 1 (Online publication - Provo, UT, USA: Ancestry.com Operations, Inc., 2010. Original data - Voter Registration Lists, Public Record Filings, Historical Residential Records, and Other Household Database Listings. Original data: Voter Registration Lists, Public), Ancestry.com, http://www.Ancestry.com, Birth date: 1963 Birth place: Residence date: 1996 Residence place: Woodstock, GA.

2048   Ancestry.com, U.S. Phone and Address Directories, 1993-2002 (Online publication - Provo, UT, USA: Ancestry.com Operations Inc, 2005. Original data - 1993-2002 White Pages. Little Rock, AR, USA: Acxiom Corporation. Original data: 1993-2002 White Pages. Little Rock, AR, USA: Acxiom Corporation.), Ancestry.com, http://www.Ancestry.com, Residence date: 2002 Residence place: Birmingham, Alabama.

2049   Ancestry.com, U.S. Public Records Index, Volume 1 (Online publication - Provo, UT, USA: Ancestry.com Operations, Inc., 2010. Original data - Voter Registration Lists, Public Record Filings, Historical Residential Records, and Other Household Database Listings. Original data: Voter Registration Lists, Public), Ancestry.com, http://www.Ancestry.com, Birth date: 1974 Birth place: Residence date: 1994 Residence place: Gadsden, AL.

2050   Ancestry.com, Alabama Marriage Collection, 1800-1969 (Online publication - Provo, UT, USA: Ancestry.com Operations Inc, 2006. Original data - Alabama Center for Health Statistics. Alabama Marriage Index, 1936-1969. Alabama Center for Health Statistics, Montgomery, Alabama. Dodd, Jordan R., et. al. Early America), Ancestry.com, http://www.Ancestry.com, Marriage date: May 1962 Marriage place: Etowah, Alabama.

2051   Ancestry.com, U.S. Public Records Index, Volume 1 (Online publication - Provo, UT, USA: Ancestry.com Operations, Inc., 2010. Original data - Voter Registration Lists, Public Record Filings, Historical Residential Records, and Other Household Database Listings. Original data: Voter Registration Lists, Public), Ancestry.com, http://www.Ancestry.com, Birth date: 1965 Birth place: Residence date: 1996 Residence place: Virginia Beach, VA.

2052   Ancestry.com, U.S. Public Records Index (Online publication - Provo, UT, USA: Ancestry.com Operations Inc, 2009. Original data - Merlin Data Publishing Corporation, comp. Historical Residential White Page, Directory Assistance and Other Household Database Listings. Merlin Data Publishing Corporation), Ancestry.com, http://www.Ancestry.com, Birth date: 1965 Birth place: Residence date: 1993 Residence place: Hampton, Virginia, USA.

2053   Ancestry.com, U.S. Public Records Index (Online publication - Provo, UT, USA: Ancestry.com Operations Inc, 2009. Original data - Merlin Data Publishing Corporation, comp. Historical Residential White Page, Directory Assistance and Other Household Database Listings. Merlin Data Publishing Corporation), Ancestry.com, http://www.Ancestry.com, Birth date: 1965 Birth place: Residence date: 1990 Residence place: Middletown, Rhode Island, USA.

2054   Ancestry.com, U.S. Public Records Index (Online publication - Provo, UT, USA: Ancestry.com Operations Inc, 2009. Original data - Merlin Data Publishing Corporation, comp. Historical Residential White Page, Directory Assistance and Other Household Database Listings. Merlin Data Publishing Corporation), Ancestry.com, http://www.Ancestry.com, Birth date: 1965 Birth place: Residence date: 1993 Residence place: Auburn, Alabama, USA.

2055   Ancestry.com, U.S. Phone and Address Directories, 1993-2002 (Online publication - Provo, UT, USA: Ancestry.com Operations Inc, 2005. Original data - 1993-2002 White Pages. Little Rock, AR, USA: Acxiom Corporation. Original data: 1993-2002 White Pages. Little Rock, AR, USA: Acxiom Corporation.), Ancestry.com, http://www.Ancestry.com, Residence date: 1993 1994 Residence place: Winter Park, Florida.

2056   Ancestry.com, U.S. Phone and Address Directories, 1993-2002 (Online publication - Provo, UT, USA: Ancestry.com Operations Inc, 2005. Original data - 1993-2002 White Pages. Little Rock, AR, USA: Acxiom Corporation. Original data: 1993-2002 White Pages. Little Rock, AR, USA: Acxiom Corporation.), Ancestry.com, http://www.Ancestry.com, Residence date: 1993 1995 1996 1997 1998 1999 2000 2001 2002 Residence place: Rome, Georgia.

2057   Ancestry.com, Alabama Marriage Collection, 1800-1969 (Online publication - Provo, UT, USA: Ancestry.com Operations Inc, 2006. Original data - Alabama Center for Health Statistics. Alabama Marriage Index, 1936-1969. Alabama Center for Health Statistics, Montgomery, Alabama. Dodd, Jordan R., et. al. Early America), Ancestry.com, http://www.Ancestry.com, Marriage date: Feb 1954 Marriage place: Etowah, Alabama.

2058   Ancestry.com, U.S. Public Records Index, Volume 2 (Online publication - Provo, UT, USA: Ancestry.com Operations, Inc., 2010. Original data - Voter Registration Lists, Public Record Filings, Historical Residential Records, and Other Household Database Listings. Original data: Voter Registration Lists, Public), Ancestry.com, http://www.Ancestry.com, Birth date: 1933 Birth place: Residence date: 1935-1993 Residence place: Rome, GA.

2059   Ancestry.com, Alabama Divorce Index, 1950-1959 (Online publication - Provo, UT, USA: Ancestry.com Operations Inc, 2006. Original data - Alabama Center for Health Statistics. Alabama Divorce Index, 1950-1959. Montgomery, AL, USA: Alabama Center for Health Statistics. Original data: Alabama Center for Health), Ancestry.com, http://www.Ancestry.com, Divorce Dates.

2060   Ancestry.com, U.S. Public Records Index, Volume 1 (Online publication - Provo, UT, USA: Ancestry.com Operations, Inc., 2010. Original data - Voter Registration Lists, Public Record Filings, Historical Residential Records, and Other Household Database Listings. Original data: Voter Registration Lists, Public), Ancestry.com, http://www.Ancestry.com, Birth date: 1935 Birth place: Residence date: 1986 Residence place: Gadsden, AL.

2061   Ancestry.com, U.S. Public Records Index, Volume 1 (Online publication - Provo, UT, USA: Ancestry.com Operations, Inc., 2010. Original data - Voter Registration Lists, Public Record Filings, Historical Residential Records, and Other Household Database Listings. Original data: Voter Registration Lists, Public), Ancestry.com, http://www.Ancestry.com, Birth date: 17 Aug 1932 Birth place: Residence date: 1993 Residence place: Gadsden, AL.

2062   Ancestry.com, U.S. Public Records Index, Volume 2 (Online publication - Provo, UT, USA: Ancestry.com Operations, Inc., 2010. Original data - Voter Registration Lists, Public Record Filings, Historical Residential Records, and Other Household Database Listings. Original data: Voter Registration Lists, Public), Ancestry.com, http://www.Ancestry.com, Residence date: 1935-1993Residence place: Gadsden, AL.

2063   Ancestry.com, Alabama Marriage Collection, 1800-1969 (Online publication - Provo, UT, USA: Ancestry.com Operations Inc, 2006. Original data - Alabama Center for Health Statistics. Alabama Marriage Index, 1936-1969. Alabama Center for Health Statistics, Montgomery, Alabama. Dodd, Jordan R., et. al. Early America), Ancestry.com, http://www.Ancestry.com, Marriage date: Oct 1951 Marriage place: Etowah, Alabama.

2064   Ancestry.com, U.S. Public Records Index, Volume 1 (Online publication - Provo, UT, USA: Ancestry.com Operations, Inc., 2010. Original data - Voter Registration Lists, Public Record Filings, Historical Residential Records, and Other Household Database Listings. Original data: Voter Registration Lists, Public), Ancestry.com, http://www.Ancestry.com, Birth date: 1961 Birth place: Residence date: 1977 Residence place: Gadsden, AL.

2065   Ancestry.com, U.S. Public Records Index, Volume 1 (Online publication - Provo, UT, USA: Ancestry.com Operations, Inc., 2010. Original data - Voter Registration Lists, Public Record Filings, Historical Residential Records, and Other Household Database Listings. Original data: Voter Registration Lists, Public), Ancestry.com, http://www.Ancestry.com, Birth date: 1930 Birth place: Residence date: 1985 Residence place: Gadsden, AL.

2066   Ancestry.com, 1930 United States Federal Census (Online publication - Provo, UT, USA: Ancestry.com Operations Inc, 2002. Original data - United States of America, Bureau of the Census. Fifteenth Census of the United States, 1930. Washington, D.C.: National Archives and Records Administration, 1930. T626,), Ancestry.com, http://www.Ancestry.com, Year: 1930; Census Place: Hokes Bluff, Etowah, Alabama; Roll: 16; Page: 1A; Enumeration District: 16; Image: 593.0. Birth date: about 1930 Birth place: Residence date: 1930 Residence place: Hokes Bluff, Etowah, Alabama.

2067   Ancestry.com, Alabama Marriage Collection, 1800-1969 (Online publication - Provo, UT, USA: Ancestry.com Operations Inc, 2006. Original data - Alabama Center for Health Statistics. Alabama Marriage Index, 1936-1969. Alabama Center for Health Statistics, Montgomery, Alabama. Dodd, Jordan R., et. al. Early America), Ancestry.com, http://www.Ancestry.com, Marriage date: 10 Sep 1949 Marriage place: Etowah, Alabama.

2068   Ancestry.com, U.S. Public Records Index, Volume 1 (Online publication - Provo, UT, USA: Ancestry.com Operations, Inc., 2010. Original data - Voter Registration Lists, Public Record Filings, Historical Residential Records, and Other Household Database Listings. Original data: Voter Registration Lists, Public), Ancestry.com, http://www.Ancestry.com, Birth date: 1958 Birth place: Residence date: 1993 Residence place: Hokes Bluff, AL.

2069   Ancestry.com, U.S. Phone and Address Directories, 1993-2002 (Online publication - Provo, UT, USA: Ancestry.com Operations Inc, 2005. Original data - 1993-2002 White Pages. Little Rock, AR, USA: Acxiom Corporation. Original data: 1993-2002 White Pages. Little Rock, AR, USA: Acxiom Corporation.), Ancestry.com, http://www.Ancestry.com, Residence date: 1994 1995 1996 1997 Residence place: Hokes Bluff, Alabama.

2070   Ancestry.com, U.S. Phone and Address Directories, 1993-2002 (Online publication - Provo, UT, USA: Ancestry.com Operations Inc, 2005. Original data - 1993-2002 White Pages. Little Rock, AR, USA: Acxiom Corporation. Original data: 1993-2002 White Pages. Little Rock, AR, USA: Acxiom Corporation.), Ancestry.com, http://www.Ancestry.com, Residence date: 1998 1999 2000 2001 2002 Residence place: Gadsden, Alabama.

2071   Ancestry.com, U.S. Public Records Index, Volume 1 (Online publication - Provo, UT, USA: Ancestry.com Operations, Inc., 2010. Original data - Voter Registration Lists, Public Record Filings, Historical Residential Records, and

Other Household Database Listings. Original data: Voter Registration Lists, Public), Ancestry.com, http://www.Ancestry.com, Birth date: 1937 Birth place: Residence date: 1993 Residence place: Gadsden, AL.

2072   Ancestry.com, U.S. Phone and Address Directories, 1993-2002 (Online publication - Provo, UT, USA: Ancestry.com Operations Inc, 2005. Original data - 1993-2002 White Pages. Little Rock, AR, USA: Acxiom Corporation. Original data: 1993-2002 White Pages. Little Rock, AR, USA: Acxiom Corporation.), Ancestry.com, http://www.Ancestry.com, Residence date: 1995 1996 1997 Residence place: Hokes Bluff, Alabama.

2073   Ancestry.com, Social Security Death Index (Online publication - Provo, UT, USA: Ancestry.com Operations Inc, 2010. Original data - Social Security Administration. Social Security Death Index, Master File. Social Security Administration. Original data: Social Security Administration. Social Security D), Ancestry.com, http://www.Ancestry.com, Number: 423-46-6610; Issue State: Alabama; Issue Date: 1953-1954. Birth date: 14 Jul 1937 Birth place: Death date: 6 Nov 2005 Death place: Gadsden, Etowah, Alabama.

2074   Ancestry.com, Alabama Marriage Collection, 1800-1969 (Online publication - Provo, UT, USA: Ancestry.com Operations Inc, 2006. Original data - Alabama Center for Health Statistics. Alabama Marriage Index, 1936-1969. Alabama Center for Health Statistics, Montgomery, Alabama. Dodd, Jordan R., et. al. Early America), Ancestry.com, http://www.Ancestry.com, Marriage date: Dec 1956 Marriage place: Etowah, Alabama.

2075   Ancestry.com, U.S. Public Records Index, Volume 1 (Online publication - Provo, UT, USA: Ancestry.com Operations, Inc., 2010. Original data - Voter Registration Lists, Public Record Filings, Historical Residential Records, and Other Household Database Listings. Original data: Voter Registration Lists, Public), Ancestry.com, http://www.Ancestry.com, Birth date: 1960 Birth place: Residence date: 1994 Residence place: Glencoe, AL.

2076   Ancestry.com, U.S. Public Records Index, Volume 1 (Online publication - Provo, UT, USA: Ancestry.com Operations, Inc., 2010. Original data - Voter Registration Lists, Public Record Filings, Historical Residential Records, and Other Household Database Listings. Original data: Voter Registration Lists, Public), Ancestry.com, http://www.Ancestry.com, Birth date: 1961 Birth place: Residence date: 1993 Residence place: Birmingham, AL.

2077   Ancestry.com, U.S. Public Records Index, Volume 1 (Online publication - Provo, UT, USA: Ancestry.com Operations, Inc., 2010. Original data - Voter Registration Lists, Public Record Filings, Historical Residential Records, and Other Household Database Listings. Original data: Voter Registration Lists, Public), Ancestry.com, http://www.Ancestry.com, Birth date: 1964 Birth place: Residence date: 1994 Residence place: Hokes Bluff, AL.

2078   Ancestry.com, U.S. Public Records Index, Volume 2 (Online publication - Provo, UT, USA: Ancestry.com Operations, Inc., 2010. Original data - Voter Registration Lists, Public Record Filings, Historical Residential Records, and Other Household Database Listings. Original data: Voter Registration Lists, Public), Ancestry.com, http://www.Ancestry.com, Birth date: 1927 Birth place: Residence date: 1935-1993 Residence place: Gadsden, AL.

2079   National Archives and Records Administration, U.S. World War II Army Enlistment Records, 1938-1946 (Online publication - Provo, UT, USA: Ancestry.com Operations Inc, 2005. Original data - Electronic Army Serial Number Merged File, 1938-1946 [Archival Database]; World War II Army Enlistment Records; Records of the National Archives and Records Administration), Ancestry.com, http://www.Ancestry.com, Birth date: 1927 Birth place: Residence date: Residence place: Alabama.

2080   Ancestry.com, U.S. Public Records Index, Volume 1 (Online publication - Provo, UT, USA: Ancestry.com Operations, Inc., 2010. Original data - Voter Registration Lists, Public Record Filings, Historical Residential Records, and Other Household Database Listings. Original data: Voter Registration Lists, Public), Ancestry.com, http://www.Ancestry.com, Birth date: 1927 Birth place: Residence date: 1977 Residence place: Gadsden, AL.

2081   Ancestry.com, Social Security Death Index (Online publication - Provo, UT, USA: Ancestry.com Operations Inc, 2010. Original data - Social Security Administration. Social Security Death Index, Master File. Social Security Administration. Original data: Social Security Administration. Social Security D), Ancestry.com, http://www.Ancestry.com, Number: 421-26-5675; Issue State: Alabama; Issue Date: Before 1951. Birth date: 4 May 1927 Birth place: Death date: 18 Dec 2006 Death place: Union City, Obion, Tennessee, United States of America.

2082   Ancestry.com, U.S. Public Records Index, Volume 2 (Online publication - Provo, UT, USA: Ancestry.com Operations, Inc., 2010. Original data - Voter Registration Lists, Public Record Filings, Historical Residential Records, and Other Household Database Listings. Original data: Voter Registration Lists, Public), Ancestry.com, http://www.Ancestry.com, Birth date: 1927 Birth place: Residence date: 1935-1993 Residence place: Gadsden, AL.

2083   Ancestry.com, Alabama Marriage Collection, 1800-1969 (Online publication - Provo, UT, USA: Ancestry.com Operations Inc, 2006. Original data - Alabama Center for Health Statistics. Alabama Marriage Index, 1936-1969. Alabama Center for Health Statistics, Montgomery, Alabama. Dodd, Jordan R., et. al. Early America), Ancestry.com, http://www.Ancestry.com, Marriage date: 29 Aug 1948 Marriage place: Etowah, Alabama.

2084   Ancestry.com, U.S. Phone and Address Directories, 1993-2002 (Online publication - Provo, UT, USA: Ancestry.com Operations Inc, 2005. Original data - 1993-2002 White Pages. Little Rock, AR, USA: Acxiom Corporation. Original data: 1993-2002 White Pages. Little Rock, AR, USA: Acxiom Corporation.), Ancestry.com, http://www.Ancestry.com, Residence date: 1994 Residence place: Gadsden, Alabama.

2085   Ancestry.com, U.S. Public Records Index, Volume 1 (Online publication - Provo, UT, USA: Ancestry.com Operations, Inc., 2010. Original data - Voter Registration Lists, Public Record Filings, Historical Residential Records, and Other Household Database Listings. Original data: Voter Registration Lists, Public), Ancestry.com, http://www.Ancestry.com, Birth date: 1950 Birth place: Residence date: 1993 Residence place: Gadsden, AL.

2086   Ancestry.com, Alabama Marriage Collection, 1800-1969 (Online publication - Provo, UT, USA: Ancestry.com Operations Inc, 2006. Original data - Alabama Center for Health Statistics. Alabama Marriage Index, 1936-1969. Alabama Center for Health Statistics, Montgomery, Alabama. Dodd, Jordan R., et. al. Early America), Ancestry.com, http://www.Ancestry.com, Marriage date: Apr 1964 Marriage place: Etowah, Alabama.

2087   Ancestry.com, U.S. Public Records Index, Volume 1 (Online publication - Provo, UT, USA: Ancestry.com Operations, Inc., 2010. Original data - Voter Registration Lists, Public Record Filings, Historical Residential Records, and Other Household Database Listings. Original data: Voter Registration Lists, Public), Ancestry.com, http://www.Ancestry.com, Birth date: 1969 Birth place: Residence date: 1994 Residence place: Southside, AL.

2088   Ancestry.com, U.S. Public Records Index, Volume 1 (Online publication - Provo, UT, USA: Ancestry.com Operations, Inc., 2010. Original data - Voter Registration Lists, Public Record Filings, Historical Residential Records, and Other Household Database Listings. Original data: Voter Registration Lists, Public), Ancestry.com, http://www.Ancestry.com, Birth date: 1954 Birth place: Residence date: 1989 Residence place: Montgomery, AL.

2089   Ancestry.com, U.S. Phone and Address Directories, 1993-2002 (Online publication - Provo, UT, USA: Ancestry.com Operations Inc, 2005. Original data - 1993-2002 White Pages. Little Rock, AR, USA: Acxiom Corporation. Original data: 1993-2002 White Pages. Little Rock, AR, USA: Acxiom Corporation.), Ancestry.com, http://www.Ancestry.com, Residence date: 1996 1997 1998 1999 2000 2001 2002 Residence place: Montgomery, Alabama.

2090   Ancestry.com, U.S. Public Records Index, Volume 1 (Online publication - Provo, UT, USA: Ancestry.com Operations, Inc., 2010. Original data - Voter Registration Lists, Public Record Filings, Historical Residential Records, and Other Household Database Listings. Original data: Voter Registration Lists, Public), Ancestry.com, http://www.Ancestry.com, Birth date: 1955 Birth place: Residence date: 1993 Residence place: Rainbow City, AL.

2091   Ancestry.com, U.S. Public Records Index, Volume 1 (Online publication - Provo, UT, USA: Ancestry.com Operations, Inc., 2010. Original data - Voter Registration Lists, Public Record Filings, Historical Residential Records, and Other Household Database Listings. Original data: Voter Registration Lists, Public), Ancestry.com, http://www.Ancestry.com, Residence date: 1996 Residence place: Anniston, AL.

2092   Ancestry.com, U.S. Public Records Index, Volume 2 (Online publication - Provo, UT, USA: Ancestry.com Operations, Inc., 2010. Original data - Voter Registration Lists, Public Record Filings, Historical Residential Records, and Other Household Database Listings. Original data: Voter Registration Lists, Public), Ancestry.com, http://www.Ancestry.com, Birth date: 1975 Birth place: Residence date: 1935-1993 Residence place: Atlanta, GA.

2093   Ancestry.com, U.S. Public Records Index, Volume 1 (Online publication - Provo, UT, USA: Ancestry.com Operations, Inc., 2010. Original data - Voter Registration Lists, Public Record Filings, Historical Residential Records, and Other Household Database Listings. Original data: Voter Registration Lists, Public), Ancestry.com, http://www.Ancestry.com, Birth date: 1978 Birth place: Residence date: 1995 Residence place: Gadsden, AL.

2094   Ancestry.com, U.S. Public Records Index, Volume 2 (Online publication - Provo, UT, USA: Ancestry.com Operations, Inc., 2010. Original data - Voter Registration Lists, Public Record Filings, Historical Residential Records, and Other Household Database Listings. Original data: Voter Registration Lists, Public), Ancestry.com, http://www.Ancestry.com, Birth date: 1978 Birth place: Residence date: 1935-1993 Residence place: Rossville, GA.

2095   Ancestry.com, U.S. Public Records Index, Volume 1 (Online publication - Provo, UT, USA: Ancestry.com Operations, Inc., 2010. Original data - Voter Registration Lists, Public Record Filings, Historical Residential Records, and Other Household Database Listings. Original data: Voter Registration Lists, Public), Ancestry.com, http://www.Ancestry.com, Birth date: 1960 Birth place: Residence date: 1986 Residence place: Virginia Beach, VA.

2096   Ancestry.com, U.S. Public Records Index, Volume 2 (Online publication - Provo, UT, USA: Ancestry.com Operations, Inc., 2010. Original data - Voter Registration Lists, Public Record Filings, Historical Residential Records, and Other Household Database Listings. Original data: Voter Registration Lists, Public), Ancestry.com, http://www.Ancestry.com, Birth date: 1960 Birth place: Residence date: 1935-1993 Residence place: East Falmouth, MA.

2097   Ancestry.com, U.S. Public Records Index, Volume 1 (Online publication - Provo, UT, USA: Ancestry.com Operations, Inc., 2010. Original data - Voter Registration Lists, Public Record Filings, Historical Residential Records, and Other Household Database Listings. Original data: Voter Registration Lists, Public), Ancestry.com, http://www.Ancestry.com, Birth date: 1967 Birth place: Residence date: 1993 Residence place: Hazel Green, AL.

2098   Ancestry.com, U.S. Public Records Index, Volume 1 (Online publication - Provo, UT, USA: Ancestry.com Operations, Inc., 2010. Original data - Voter Registration Lists, Public Record Filings, Historical Residential Records, and Other Household Database Listings. Original data: Voter Registration Lists, Public), Ancestry.com, http://www.Ancestry.com, Birth date: 1973 Birth place: Residence date: 1993 Residence place: Ashville, AL.

2099   Ancestry.com, U.S. Public Records Index, Volume 1 (Online publication - Provo, UT, USA: Ancestry.com Operations, Inc., 2010. Original data - Voter Registration Lists, Public Record Filings, Historical Residential Records, and Other Household Database Listings. Original data: Voter Registration Lists, Public), Ancestry.com, http://www.Ancestry.com, Birth date: 1965 Birth place: Residence date: 1993 Residence place: Auburn, AL.

2100   Ancestry.com, U.S. Public Records Index, Volume 1 (Online publication - Provo, UT, USA: Ancestry.com Operations, Inc., 2010. Original data - Voter Registration Lists, Public Record Filings, Historical Residential Records, and Other Household Database Listings. Original data: Voter Registration Lists, Public), Ancestry.com, http://www.Ancestry.com, Birth date: 1965 Birth place: Residence date: 1995 Residence place: Portsmouth, RI.

2101   U.S. Public Records Index, Ancestry.com, http://www.Ancestry.com, Birth date: 1966 Birth place: Residence date: Residence place: Virginia Beach, Virginia Beach City, Virginia, USA.

2102   Ancestry.com, U.S. Phone and Address Directories, 1993-2002 (Online publication - Provo, UT, USA: Ancestry.com Operations Inc, 2005. Original data - 1993-2002 White Pages. Little Rock, AR, USA: Acxiom Corporation. Original data: 1993-2002 White Pages. Little Rock, AR, USA: Acxiom Corporation.), Ancestry.com, http://www.Ancestry.com, Residence date: 2000 2001 2002 Residence place: Virginia Beach, Virginia.

2103   Ancestry.com, U.S. Phone and Address Directories, 1993-2002 (Online publication - Provo, UT, USA: Ancestry.com Operations Inc, 2005. Original data - 1993-2002 White Pages. Little Rock, AR, USA: Acxiom Corporation. Original data: 1993-2002 White Pages. Little Rock, AR, USA: Acxiom Corporation.), Ancestry.com, http://www.Ancestry.com, Residence date: 1998 1999 Residence place: Virginia Beach, Virginia.

2104   Ancestry.com, U.S. Public Records Index, Volume 1 (Online publication - Provo, UT USA: Ancestry.com Operations, Inc., 2010. Original data - Voter Registration Lists, Public Record Filings, Historical Residential Records, and Other Household Database Listings. Original data: Voter Registration Lists, Public), Ancestry.com, http://www.Ancestry.com, Birth date: 1955 Birth place: Residence date: 1996 Residence place: Gadsden, AL.

WEBSITES OF INTEREST

Myfamily.com http://myfamily.com/group/ReevesFamily		FREE**

Ancestry.com	http://www.ancestry.com/	$$
Footnote.com	http://www.footnote.com/	$$
Archives.com	http://www.archives.com/	$$

A Reeves History: http://andstrat.tripod.com/reeves.html	FREE
Access Genealogy: http://www.accessgenealogy.com/	FREE
Alabama Civil War Camps: http://history-sites.com/~kjones/ALcamps.html	FREE
Alabama Department of Archives and History: http://www.archives.alabama.gov/	FREE
Alabama Gen Web/Etowah: http://hometownchronicles.com/al/etowah/	FREE
Alabama Maps: http://alabamamaps.ua.edu/historicalmaps/	FREE
Alabama Pioneers: http://www.alabamapioneers.com/	FREE
All Free Records: http://www.allfreerecords.com/	FREE

Blandford Forum Parish Church: http://www.bfpc.org.uk/	FREE
Cemetery Records Online: http://www.interment.net/	FREE
Church of England - Blandford Forum Parish Church: http://www.achurchnearyou.com/blandford-forum-st-peter-st-paul/	FREE
Civil War History: http://wwlowery.tripod.com/csalowery.htm	FREE
Confederate Unit Histories: http://community-2.webtv.net/pelhamscv/ConfederateUnit/	FREE
Dinwiddie County GenWeb: http://www.vagenweb.org/dinwiddie/rives-g/gr-01.htm	FREE
Family History 101: http://www.familyhistory101.com/	FREE
Family Search: http://www.familysearch.org/eng/default.asp	FREE
Find a Grave: http://www.findagrave.com/	FREE
History Hokes Bluff online at Family History Archives: http://contentdm.lib.byu.edu/cdm4/document.php?CISOROOT=/FH36&CISOPTR =30247&CISOSHOW=	FREE
Huguenots Society: http://manakin.addr.com/	FREE
Library of Virginia: http://www.lva.virginia.gov/	FREE
Life's Evolving Adventures: http://lifesevolvingadventures.com/Menu.html	FREE
National Archives: Resources for Genealogists: http://www.archives.gov/research/genealogy/start-research/nara-resources.html	FREE
Pubic Records Free Directory: http://publicrecords.onlinesearches.com/	FREE
Rootsweb: http://resources.rootsweb.ancestry.com/	FREE
USGenWeb Archives http://files.usgwarchives.net/	FREE

Ancestral Books: https://www.ancestralbooks.com/	FREE*
National Genealogical Society: http://www.ngsgenealogy.org/cs/home	FREE*
Random Acts of Genealogical Kindness: http://www.raogk.org/	FREE*
Virginia Historical Society: http://www.vahistorical.org/index.htm	FREE*

PRINCIPAL MEMBERS OF EACH GENERATION

Generation 1

1.   Robert Ryves

Generation 2

2.   John Ryves

Generation 3

3.   Richard Ryves

Generation 4

4.   Timothy Ryves

Generation 5

5.   William Ryves

Generation 6

6.   John Rives

Generation 7

7.   Richard Rives

Generation 8

8.   William Rives

Generation 9

9.   William Rives

Generation 10

10.   Eli Rives

12.   Nathan Reaves

28.   Edmond Reaves

Generation 11

11.   William Rives

13.   Susan Jane Reaves

29.   William Emery Reaves

121.   Nancy Reaves

133.   Ransom Columbus Reaves

145.   Emory G. Reaves

146.   Richmond Reaves

150.   Nathan Reaves

Generation 12

14.   Elizabeth Anna Farrar

19.   John Thomas Farrar

21.   Susan Jane Farrar

27.   Winfield Scott Farrar

30.   Elizabeth Reaves

31.   William McGuire Reaves

54.   Carter Hill Reaves

82.   Caroline Temple Reaves

87.   John Harrison Reaves

88.   Emory G. Reaves

91.   Sarah Ann Marinda Reaves

102.   David R. Reaves

104.   James Washington Reaves

105.   Ira Jackson Reaves

122.   William Moncrief

123.   Caleb Jackson Moncrief

131.   Mary Missouri Moncrief

134.   John Anderson Reaves

140.   Edmond Young Reaves

141.   Cassinda Ann Reaves

144.   Henry Green Reaves

147.   Benjamin W. Reaves

149.   Francis M. Reaves

151.   Rebecca Reeves

153. Nancy Ann Reaves

154. John S. Reeves

255. Betsy Green Reeves

256. Sarah A. Reeves

Generation 13

15. Samantha Alice McCollum

20. Frank Joel Farrar

22. Alice Parker

26. Lela Parker

32. Pollyann Reaves

33. Elizabeth Marinda Reaves

38. William Patrick Reaves

47. James Ashley Reaves

48. Andrew Jackson Reaves

53. John Silvanous Reaves

55. Narcissa Reaves

58. James Martin Reaves

73. Belzona Reaves

75. Alice Louisa Reaves

77. William Carey Reaves

78. George M. D. Reaves

83. John G. Kay

84. Sarah D. Henley

85. Tabitha C. Henley

86. James Carter Henley

89. George W. Reaves

90. Thomas Edward Reaves

92. David Jackson McCullars

97. Mary E. McCullars

100. Samuel M. McCullars

101. Josie F. McCullars

103. Mary Ann Reaves

106. Bunyon Rubin Britton Reaves

110. Ellen Marcilea Elizabeth Reaves

111. Sarah Malissa Caroline Reaves

112. William David Reaves

118. Amy Kentucky Reaves

119. John Perry Osburne Reaves

120. Cynthia Bitty Lugene Reaves

124. Mary Jane Moncrief

126. Georgia Ann Moncrief

128. John M. Moncrief

129. Henry Alexander Moncrief

132. Mariah Louise Grant

135. Dorothy Reaves

138. John Anderson Reaves Jr

142. Elijah Baker

143. Texas Lucy Baker

148. James Franklin Reeves

152. Sarah Irene Young

155. Irena D. Reeves

158. William Clemens Reeves

249. John H. Reeves

250. Lucinda Jane Reeves

251. Nathan C. Reeves

254. James H. Reeves

Generation 14

16. Winfield Frank Batey

17. Shelby Alloway

18. Lela Ruth Batey

23. Vernie Leroy Smith

24. Gertrude Vashti Smith

25. James Harrison Smith

34. William Monroe Henley

37.	Porter Wallace Henley	107.	Mary Etta Reaves
39.	Sylvester Reaves	108.	Claude Fredrick Reaves
40.	Margie Belle Reaves	109.	Lela Mae Reaves
41.	William Monroe Reaves	113.	Maggie Lee Reaves
42.	Lula Merendia Reaves	115.	Luna Emma Reaves
43.	Minnie Mae Reaves	116.	Sallie Irene Reaves
44.	Ida Lee Reaves	117.	Wilma Lee Reaves
45.	Josie Elva Reaves	125.	James Robert Autrey
46.	Richard Patrick Reaves	127.	Mary Lucinda Autrey
49.	Sydney Jackson Reaves	130.	Thomas James Moncrief
50.	Andrew Walter Reaves	136.	John Mark Reaves
51.	Margaret Elizabeth (Lizzie) Reaves	137.	Melba Marie Reaves
		156.	Carrie G. Absher
52.	Otha Lee Reaves	157.	Joseph Himond Absher
56.	Collie Peyton Ledbetter	159.	Luther Reeves
57.	James Wesley Ledbetter	191.	Euclid Reeves
59.	Barbara Mary Ann Reaves	217.	Riller Reeves
66.	Robert Joseph Reaves	220.	Liller Reeves
67.	Frances Elizabeth Reaves	247.	Claudie Reeves
68.	Walter Thomas Reaves	252.	Marion Frank Reeves
71.	Samuel George Reaves	253.	Arthur Columbus Reeves

Generation 15

72.	Levi Hilton Reaves	35.	Arthur Finis Henley
74.	Malvin L. Couch	36.	Winford Carl Henley
76.	Lucy Dempsey	60.	Edna Couch
79.	Huston R. Reaves	69.	Rona Mae Reaves
80.	Rufus Alexander Reaves	70.	Samuel Lee Roy Reaves
81.	Alma Irene Reaves	114.	Joseph Lark Williamson
93.	Della McCullars	160.	Floyd Leon Reeves
94.	Minnie Sara Amelia McCullars	168.	Crate Funis Reeves
95.	Monroe Jackson McCullars	182.	Neva Reeves
96.	Mollie McCullars	190.	May Reeves
98.	William Marion Doss	192.	Doyle Reeves
99.	Monroe Jackson Doss		

193. Hoyt Reeves

194. H. K. Reeves

196. Troy Reeves

211. Cresful Reeves

218. Clarence Eugene Lumpkin

219. Judson Clemens (J.C.) Lumpkin

221. Jewel McMahan

229. Slaught M. McMahan

232. Doyce McMahan

236. Lola Matril McMahan

244. Curtis Udell McMahan

248. Verna McMahan

Generation 16

61. Debra Ann Reeves

63. Gary Wendell Reeves

161. Malline Louise Reeves

164. Maurice Leon Reeves

169. Jerry Lamar Reeves

170. Marilyn Yvonne Reeves

174. Martha Evenette Reeves

180. Sherry Frances Reeves

183. Bobby Leland Barnes

Luther Boyce Barnes

187. Brenda Barnes

195. Terry Gene Reeves

197. Troy Reeves Jr

202. Haralson Kerr (Cootie) Reeves

205. Boyd McMurtrey (Mac) Reeves

208. Glenda Janice Reeves

212. Peggy Maria (Peree) Reeves

213. William Patrick (Pat) Reeves

216. Cresful (Corky) Reeves Jr

222. Donnie Marbut

226. Ennis Marbut

227. Leva Wylene Marbut

230. Edwina McMahan

233. Royce McMahan

237. Murrell Brack Shields

240. Billy Mack Shields

245. Elizabeth Ann McMahan

246. C. Wayne McMahan

Generation 17

62. Crystal Nicole (Nikki) Jones

64. Gary Scott Reeves

Steven Mark Reeves

65. Wendy Carol Reeves

162. Leon Ellis (Skipper) Watford

163. Arthur Joseph (Art) Watford II

165. Cathy Marilyn Reeves

171. Jennifer Lynn Gentry

172. Alan Gentry

175. Kerry Lee Johnson

177. Karla Eve Johnson

178. James Spearman (Jim or Jet) Johnson Jr

179. Kyle Reeves Johnson

181. Mark Craig Cardwell

Lynda Lee Cardwell

184. James David Barnes

185. Andrea Jo (Jo-Jo) Barnes

186. Gena Lynn Barnes

188. Kevin Leon Huff

189. Kristina Huff

Troy Reeves III

Jena Louise Reeves

198. Kim Renèe Reeves

199. Jacqueline Anne Couillard

200. Jill Annette Couillard

201. Jennifer Marie Couillard

204. Haralson Kerr (Chip) Reeves Jr

203. Traci Lynn Reeves

206. Jason Mack Reeves

207. Jana Elizabeth Reeves

Martha Charlene Reeves

209. Reeves Alan Daves

210. Susan Yvonne Daves

214. Abby Lane Reeves

215. Katie Pauline Reeves

223. Terry Marbut

228. Todd Landon McGinnis

231. John Slaught Kangelos

234. Kelli McMahan

235. Sharron McMahan

238. Jeffrey Brack Shields

239. Jason Lamar Shields

241. Scott Shields

242. Steve Shields

257. Christopher Alan McGinnis

258. Tim McGinnis

260. Jay Anthony Shields

261. Jana Matril Shields

Generation 18

166. Kyle Cameron Roberts

167. Bianca Melissa Roberts

173. Erin Gentry

176. Eric Lee Johnson

224. Sierra Marbut

225. Shayanna Marbut

243. Tyler Shields

259. Timothy Adam McGinnis

262. Sherri Evonne Blevins

INDEX

309

315

About the Author

Reeves Alan Daves is a professional naval officer and amateur genealogist. He spends his spare time researching and writing about his family's history. This is his first book, combining writing with his genealogy hobby. He is a member of the Virginia Historical Society.

Alan is a graduate of Auburn University and a native of Hokes Bluff, Alabama – the seat of the William Clemens Reeves family. He is the great-great grandson of William Clemens Reeves, the 5th great grandson of Edmond Reaves, and the 14th great grandson of Robert Ryves.

Alan lives in Virginia with his family.

www.ingramcontent.com/pod-product-compliance
Lightning Source LLC
Chambersburg PA
CBHW081144270326
41930CB00014B/3032